To the Pathfinders, Larry and Sarah, with appreciation.

Kevin

TOM TILL
COLORADO
IMAGES FROM ABOVE

PHOTOGRAPHY BY TOM TILL

WESTCLIFFE PUBLISHERS, INC.   ENGLEWOOD, CO

CONTENTS

Preface   9
Landscapes from the Air   12
Patterns of the Land   28
Color   42
Courses of Water   56
Microcosms from Above   72
High Rendezvous   86
Moments in Time   98
Technical Information   112

International Standard Book Number:
ISBN: 0-942394-45-3
Library of Congress Catalogue Card Number:
86-051596
Copyright, Photographs and Text: Tom Till,
1987
Designer: Gerald Miller Simpson/Denver
Typographer: Dianne J. Borneman
Printer: Dai Nippon Printing Company Ltd.
Tokyo, Japan
Publisher: Westcliffe Publishers, Inc.
2650 South Zuni Street
Englewood, CO 80110

*First frontispiece: Spring greens the Great Plains
with geometric patterns, near Greeley*

*Second frontispiece: Column spires of The Castles,
West Elk Wilderness*

*Third frontispiece: Morning sun slowly vanquishes
a spring storm, Elk Mountains*

*Title page: Rock pinnacles of The Palisades, near
Gateway*

*Right: Sinuous forms at sunset, Great Sand Dunes
National Monument*

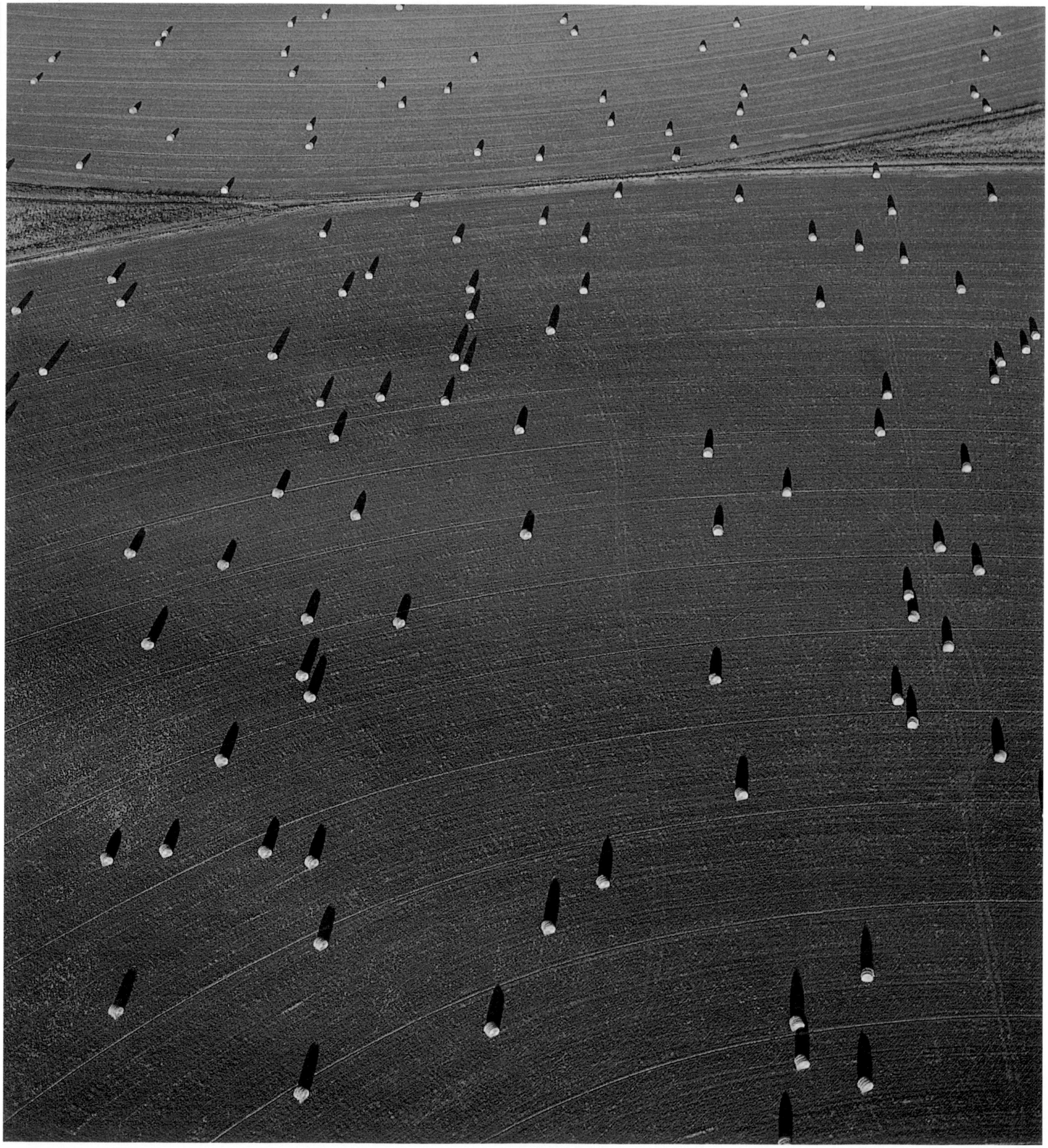

8

PREFACE

The seed for this book celebrating Colorado's beauty from the air was planted a few days after I took a quick spin above the Great Sand Dunes. Within months, I took on the job of photographing the state's mountains, plains, and plateaus from a light plane.

Many of my misconceptions about the project began to vanish with my first flights. I had tried some Colorado mountain photography before and found it unsatisfying. The flying itself was fun, but my results were poor. Much of the mountain aerial photography I'd seen had a sameness to it, with very little variety in color and composition. My first flights over the Elk and Gore ranges—where pilots took me in close to photograph granite peak faces and trees covered with a week of snow—encouraged me that I would be able to produce a portfolio that would be more than

*H*ay bales
punctuate the
landscape, near
Iliff

just scenery. Every succeeding flight encouraged me more.

Still, I was afraid that the moody landscapes I seek with a 4x5 camera on the ground would be elusive or even impossible from the air. Fog, snow, and rain, which I prize highly below, would limit my flying to the sameness of sunny days. Fortunately I was wrong here too. Summer flights across the San Luis Valley rewarded me with rainbows floating over tendrils of fog; a Rocky Mountain National Park flight allowed me to witness summer mists climbing the Continental Divide.

One of my smallest worries was whether I would be able to find pilots with whom I could work well. From the start, the pilots I flew with were able and cooperative. Many seemed just as awed by the beauty they were seeing as I was. The achievement of photographer William Garnett, who flies his own plane, was driven home to me on several occasions when the pilot was struggling and concentrating to do his job, while I was struggling and concentrating to do mine. One person doing both seems a Herculean task to me now.

An understated "Right Stuff" attitude is a big part of these mountain flyers' characters. "I'm not sure we're going to make it through that notch," one calmly mentioned on a winter mountain flight, while another confided, "We almost got boxed in back there," as we spun out of a glacial cirque. As bad as these incidents sound, I never really felt I was in any danger. Although I was often nervous, my fears disappeared as soon as I went to work.

With a few exceptions, all photographs for this book were taken during early morning or late evening. My reaction to lighting is conditioned by my experience with a large-format camera on terra firma. The fundamental difference is that flat, cloudy lighting, highly useful on the ground, tends to produce lackluster aerials. Most of the time I was hoping for, and even chasing after, sunlight. Often I was forced to pursue light, something earth-bound photographers cannot do. If I saw an illuminated area miles away, it was a simple task to have the pilot race toward it. Especially on the plains, I was able to see areas of sunlight opening up from miles away.

Aerial photography technique is fairly simple. Fast shutter speeds are mandatory, and camera focus settings are always set on infinity. A motor drive or winder is a necessity. By the time a photographer man-

ually advances the film, the subject below will be gone. Each pass of the plane over a subject is a little different from the last, no matter how good the pilot is at retracing his turn. Flying is expensive, so I shot lots of film and bracketed exposures whenever I was up. Working at such a fast pace is exhilarating and exhausting. I usually had no time to think a composition out, instead I had to rely on instinct and luck. Since all the photos were made through open windows, I was often kept alert by the below-zero wind chill outside the cabin. The slipstream always took away my breath and once even sucked a polarizing filter off my lens somewhere far above the Roan Cliffs. I saw it glisten in the sun a few times before it crashed thousands of feet below.

When I hike or backpack in the wilderness, I dislike flying distractions, so I tried

Flying above an ocean of clouds at 15,000 feet, Capitol Peak

to plan flights over wilderness areas when I thought few people would be around, maintaining high altitude over these areas. In general, elevations ranged from barely 5,000 feet for some flights over the plains, to over 17,000 feet for some mountain flights. At that altitude, operating a camera becomes a complex and laborious task.

Some of the photos were preplanned, while others were lucky discoveries. I planned the Platte River sunset shot for a clear evening late in the year when the southwesterly flow of the river would lead into the sunset. The images of the incredible western face of Ragged Mountain in the Raggeds Wilderness were created when I accidentally visited this area while shooting autumn aspen. I got tips about other good places from friends and pilots, but a lot of the photo search came down to remaining curious about the panorama unfolding below.

Even though I was cooped up in noisy, flimsy, and cramped flying machines, the experiences I've been lucky enough to enjoy while producing the images for this book have been some of the most memorable of my life. Some, in fact, have ended up in my dreams, and even now seem dreamlike. For months I tried to arrange a flight out of Durango over the Needle and Grenadier ranges, which I knew were among the most spectacular in Colorado. On a half-dozen occasions I was stopped by bad weather, and as my deadline drew near, I became frustrated that I might never get into those mountains. Finally, though, on my last flight, on a perfect evening, pilot

Stan Steck and I flew over Vallecito Reservoir up to the big peaks. I had planned to shoot the pink front range of monoliths facing west into the sunset: Eolus, Turret, and Pigeon. We circled over Chicago Basin and finally moved in closer to the massive precipices of glowing rock and snow. Even though I had spent months flying over the mountains of Colorado, the minutes we spent circling over those unforgettable spires enraptured and amazed me.

If I've accomplished anything with this book, I would hope to give those who love Colorado even more reason to do so. If you feel a tiny part of the joy and wonder I experienced while creating these photos, I will have succeeded.

Tom Till

Landscapes from the Air

Diversity is the byword of the Colorado landscape. From the
air, each mountain range takes on a character
of its own. The color of the rock is easily distinguished from
others, and its architecture becomes recognizable and distinct.
The supposed monotony of the Great Plains is replaced
by a landscape of texture and, occasionally, whimsy. To the
west, canyons, mesas, and rock forms—all sculpted
differently by chance interactions of water and stone—create
endless variety and wonder.

*Plateau escarpment below the San Juan Mountains glows
in a dying winter sun, Big Joe Valley*

*Capitol Lake nestles below Capitol Peak, Maroon
Bells/Snowmass Wilderness*

*After a solid week of snow, Lone Cone Peak
stands frigid and icy, San Juan Mountains*

16

*W̶ater has carved standing rocks from pliable Entrada sandstone,
Colorado National Monument*

*For a panoramic view, pilot Glen Baxter gained as much altitude as
possible: at nearly 17,000 feet above the Sneffels Range, a near
infinity of ranges and peaks appears, San Juan Mountains*

18

*S*een from high above Poncha Pass,
the long, thin Sangre de Cristo
Range drops precipitously,
San Luis Valley

20

*B*ig Wall, an
intrusive
volcanic dike,
spreads out in rays,
Spanish Peaks

Hogback sandstone formations march below the Front Range, between Denver and Boulder

21

*An airplane wing served as an efficient   sunshade
for this image of backlit ridges, Elk Mountains*

*Tom Till first noticed The Grand Hogback on an airliner flight,
then returned to photograph the formation
in a light plane, near New Castle*

23

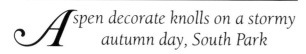

*A*spen decorate knolls on a stormy
autumn day, South Park

*P*ikes Peak
looms above
wild granite ridges,
south of Colorado
Springs

26

Shadows play across the slopes of Longs Peak, Rocky Mountain National Park

Patterns
of the Land

Many of nature's intricate patterns are familiar to us:
the detail of a fallen leaf, the abstract lines on
a human hand. These patterns are repeated on a larger scale in
Colorado's landscape. Some images undoubtedly will remind
viewers of more common structures created by nature
or by man. Are these similarities coincidence or does nature repeat
over and over again her common themes, even with man as agent?

---

*This casually tossed-off image became one of Tom Till's favorites—
he is still mystified as to why a farmer would disc such
bizarre, artistic patterns, Great Plains*

---

*R*idges of shifting sand spread like
tentacles toward Medano
Creek, Great Sand Dunes
National Monument

*R*agged Mountain comes by its name honestly—its western face is cut into unique scale-like patterns, Raggeds Wilderness

32

*S*andstone
formations atop
mesas, near
Slickrock Canyon of
the Dolores River

Unlike many of Colorado's famous canyon cliff dwellings, Far View Ruin commands an open mesa top, Mesa Verde National Park

34

*B*adlands
hummocks pick
up the morning sun
near the Utah border,
northwestern Colorado

The unconscious artistry of a Great Plains farmer, near Calhan

*E*roded desert foothills just outside Grand Junction, Book Cliff Mountains

37

*F*arm patterns,
near Cortez

*S*now patterns
shrink in
mid-summer
on a high ridge near
Maroon Bells, Elk
Range

39

*H*igh peaks of the Elk Range
crowd above Ragged Mountain
at sunset, Raggeds Wilderness

Color

The landscape's best color is reserved for the magic times
before and after sunrise and sunset. Earth's muted
tones are charged and transformed by the special light of these
moments. Seasonal color is also intrinsic to the Colorado
scene. The famous aspen golds, the Great Plains' summer
verdure, the deep blue of an alpine lake—all are facets of this
chromatic progression. In slickrock country, sandstone
adds its reds, oranges, and browns to the palette
throughout the year.

---

*Tom Till and pilot Steve Brownell spent a morning circling these
Wingate sandstone spires before deciding a narrow pass in the
rock wall was their best vantage point, near Gateway*

A foot trail negotiates a meadow, West Elk Wilderness

The Raggeds Range at sunset, westernmost edge of the Elk Mountains

M̶ount Garfield surrounded by fingers of Mancos shale, near Grand Junction

*I*solated patches
of aspen trees on
Aspen Ridge, southern
South Park

Crestone Peak backed by Crestone Needle glow in an autumn sunset, Sangre de Cristo Range

49

*F*ringe dunes
give way to the
greens of the
San Luis Valley,
Great Sand Dunes
National Monument

50

After a flight
to Grand
Junction, Tom Till
and pilots T.K.
Arnold and Glen
Lathrop
watched the moon rise,
then flew west as fast
as possible to capture
sunset, western edge
of the Uncompahgre
Plateau

*A*spen patterns,
Kebler Pass

*A*spen begin
to turn below
the front massif of
Sneffels Range near
Ouray, San Juan
Mountains

53

*F*ruit orchard takes on spring
greens near Colorado National
Monument, Grand Valley

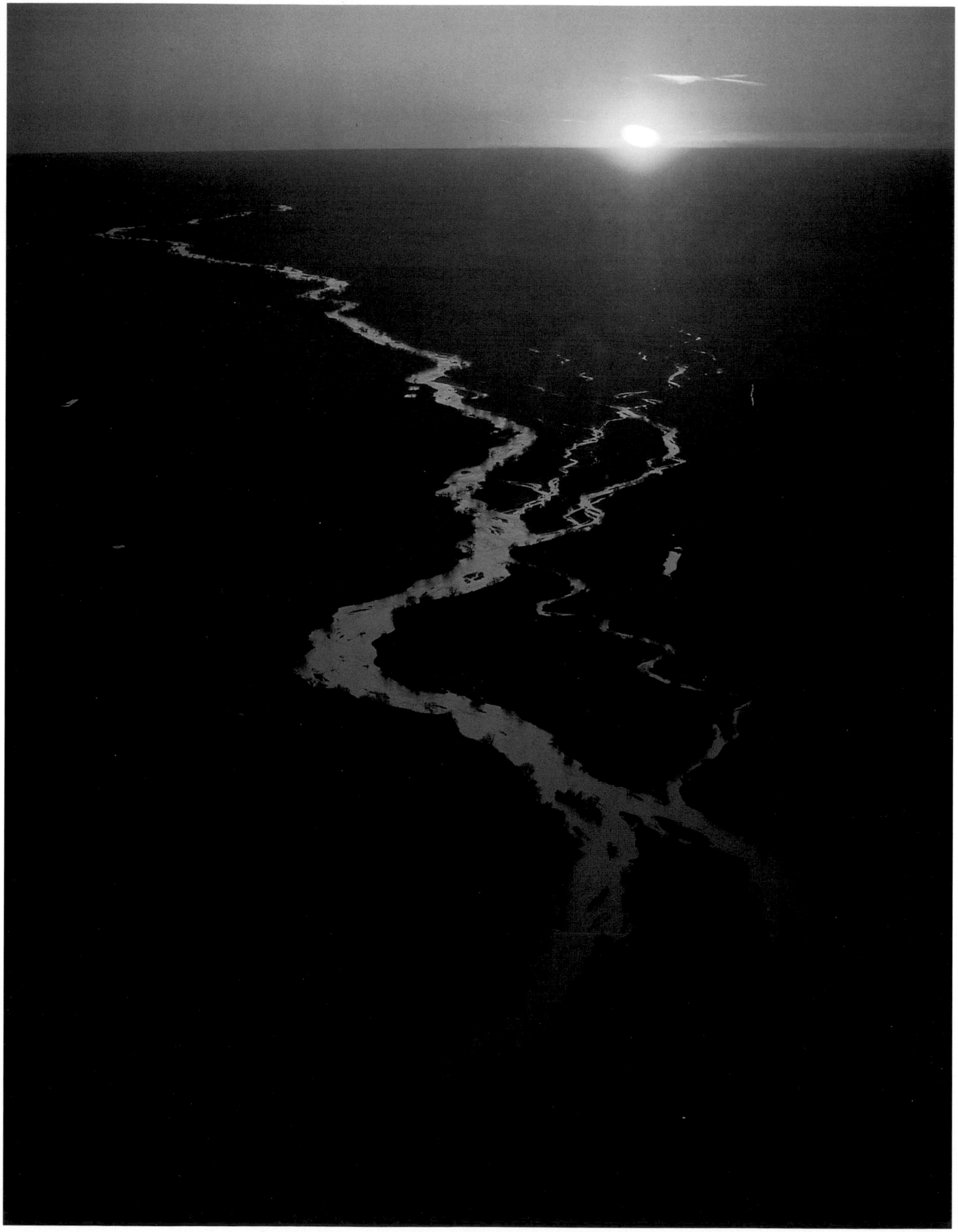

Courses of Water

The natural history of the West is the natural history of water.
Everywhere water is at work on the landscape, ultimately
destroying all in its path. Water resembles
the mythic Indian god Shiva, paradoxically the source of
both life and destruction. The great rivers,
born in the highest reaches of the mountains, play a key role
in this slow-motion catastrophe.

---

*With autumn's low flows, the Platte River leaves a Colorado
sunset to follow its braided course into Nebraska,
eastern Colorado*

58

Tomichi Creek's serpentine path, Gunnison River Valley

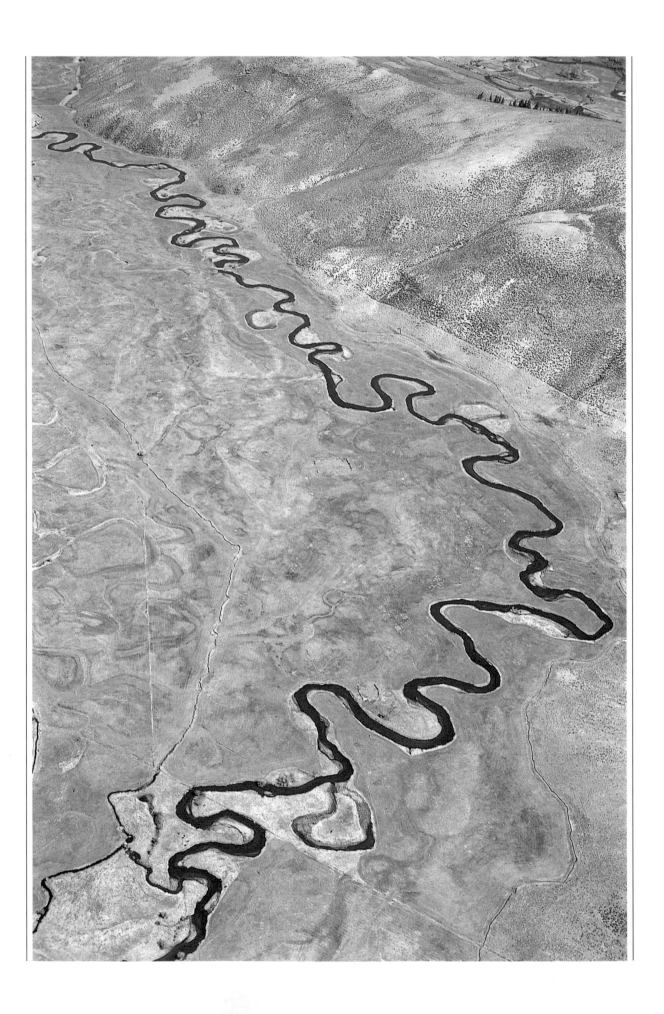

Impounded waters of the Gunnison River await their downstream plunge through Black Canyon, Cuercanti National Recreation Area

59

Exposed Entrada sandstone above Ruby Canyon channels water toward the Colorado River, Uncompahgre Plateau

60

The Colorado River leaves its mountain birthplace and begins its plateau traverse, below Glenwood Springs

62

An arroyo awaiting rain, Pawnee Buttes

63

*T*he Green River enters the Gates of Lodore, a short canyon of abrupt, rocky rapids, including Hell's Half Mile and Disaster Falls, Dinosaur National Monument

A small forest lake reflects blue sky, West Elk Wilderness

65

A rising summer sun highlights the Yampa River in a wilderness of bare Weber sandstone, Dinosaur National Monument

66

The sunlit curve of Grand Overhang's rock wall heralds the fierce waters of Warm Springs Rapid further downstream in the Yampa River Canyon, Dinosaur National Monument

67

*C*ottonwoods line the banks of a
small tributary of the Arkansas
River, near Pueblo

*B*ereft of leaves,
cottonwoods
crowd the South
Platte River, near
Sterling

*T*he deepening canyon of the Rio Grande River, near the Colorado/New Mexico border

71

Microcosms from Above

Aerial "close-ups" present relatively small pieces of the overall landscape. The desire to escape the earth carries with it the desire to see the land with new eyes and, ironically, a need to look more closely at what has been left behind. With more intimate inspection, a world of wonders hidden from the earthbound is revealed. Some elements seem comfortably familiar, others almost alien. Everything seen in microcosmic clarity is not, unfortunately, beautiful. The view too often reveals the scars of man's misuse of the land.

Tom Till and pilot Fred Schrotenboer left clear skies above the Monte Vista airport, only to find the rest of the valley, including a farmer's silo, virtually enveloped in fog, San Luis Valley

---

74

Phalange-like islands, Grand Lake

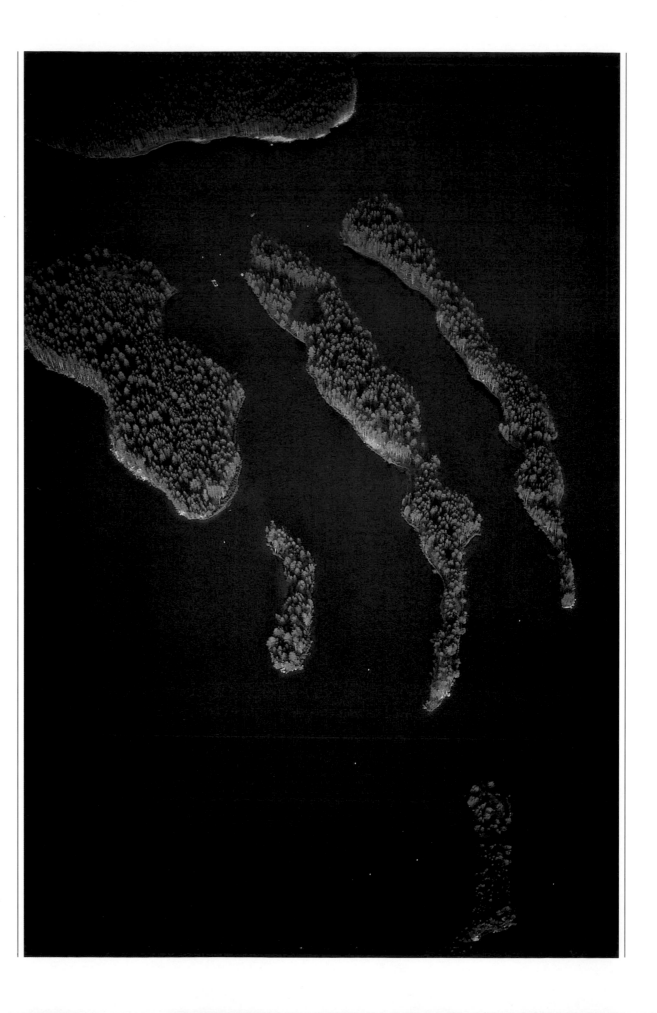

*Island in a farm
pond provides a
spring home for flocks
of waterbirds, Great
Plains*

*A*spen emblazon a ridge, near
Kebler Pass

*T*hin line of
aspen
and pines—
sometimes barely
a few trees
wide—penciled into
the barren high
plains, South Park

$\mathcal{S}$olitary
snowbank
contrasts with
the red sedimentary
rock of the Elk Range,
Maroon Bells/
Snowmass Wilderness

*S*ail-like peak
illuminated by
sunset,
Elk Range

80

*P*ilot Skip
Stanfield
introduced Tom Till
to the Castles'
mountain architecture,
West Elk
Wilderness

*T*he broad arc of a dune, Great
Sand Dunes National Monument

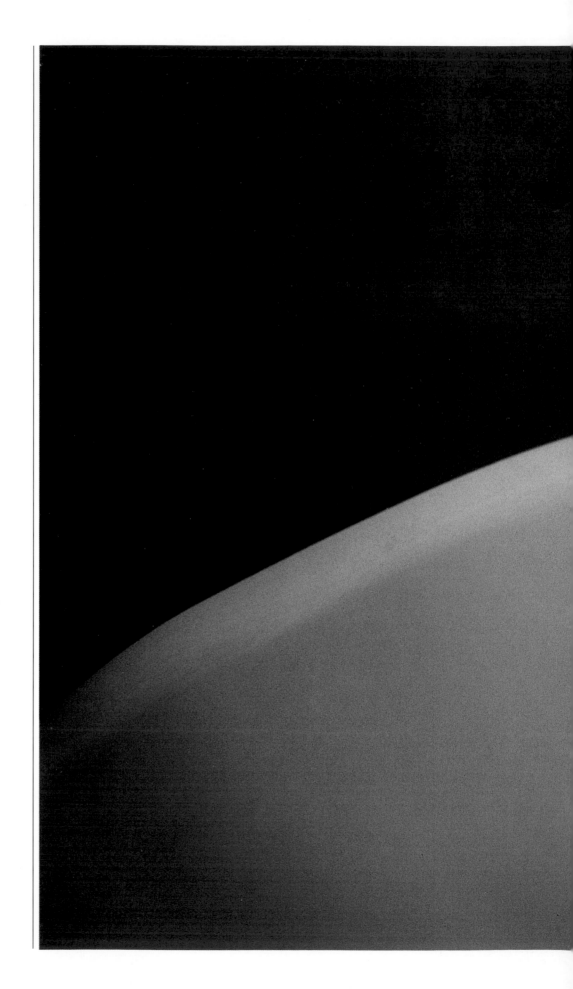

A tiny iceberg remnant floats on Capitol Lake, Maroon Bells/Snowmass Wilderness

84

ir and spruce trees pass just below the gondola on a hot air balloon flight from Steamboat Springs, Routt National Forest

85

High Rendezvous

Colorado's great wildernesses are as inspiring and spectacular
from the air as they are from below. The Gore Range impresses
with its countless tiny pinnacles and towers, while the Elk Range's
light granite and dark red sedimentary rock set up a stark
contrast. In Dinosaur National Monument, the Green and Yampa
rivers meet at Echo Park after passing through
deeply incised canyons. Perhaps most diverse of all are the
San Juan Mountains: a massive area culminating with
fourteeners in the Needles, the San Miguels, the Sneffels Range.

Ridges of the Holy Cross Range buried with a season's
heavy snow, Holy Cross Wilderness

*O*nce known as the Quartzite
Mountains, the Needles
stand sentinel above Chicago Basin,
Weminuche Wilderness

The Chalk Cliffs' quartz monzonite buttresses, Mount Princeton

*Beyond its confluence with the lighter waters of the
Yampa River, the Green River flows around massive
Steamboat Rock, Dinosaur National Monument*

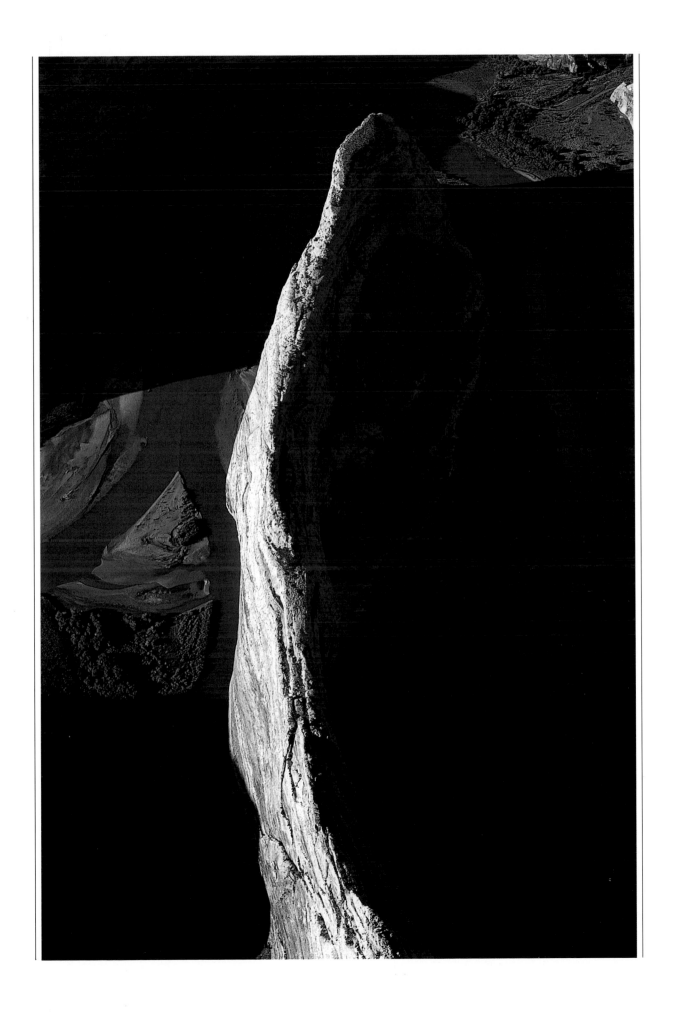

*S*carred little by mining, the Gore Range greets a winter sunset,
Gore Range/Eagles Nest Wilderness

*The Maroon Bells rise in layers of colored sedimentary rock
above a hidden Maroon Lake, Maroon
Bells/Snowmass Wilderness*

94

Rugged peaks bathe in the day's waning light, Gore Range

*The Boulder Flatirons' sandstone ridges rise before a distant
Longs Peak, west of Boulder*

*Snow clings to granite on the steep western face of
Capitol Peak, Elk Mountains*

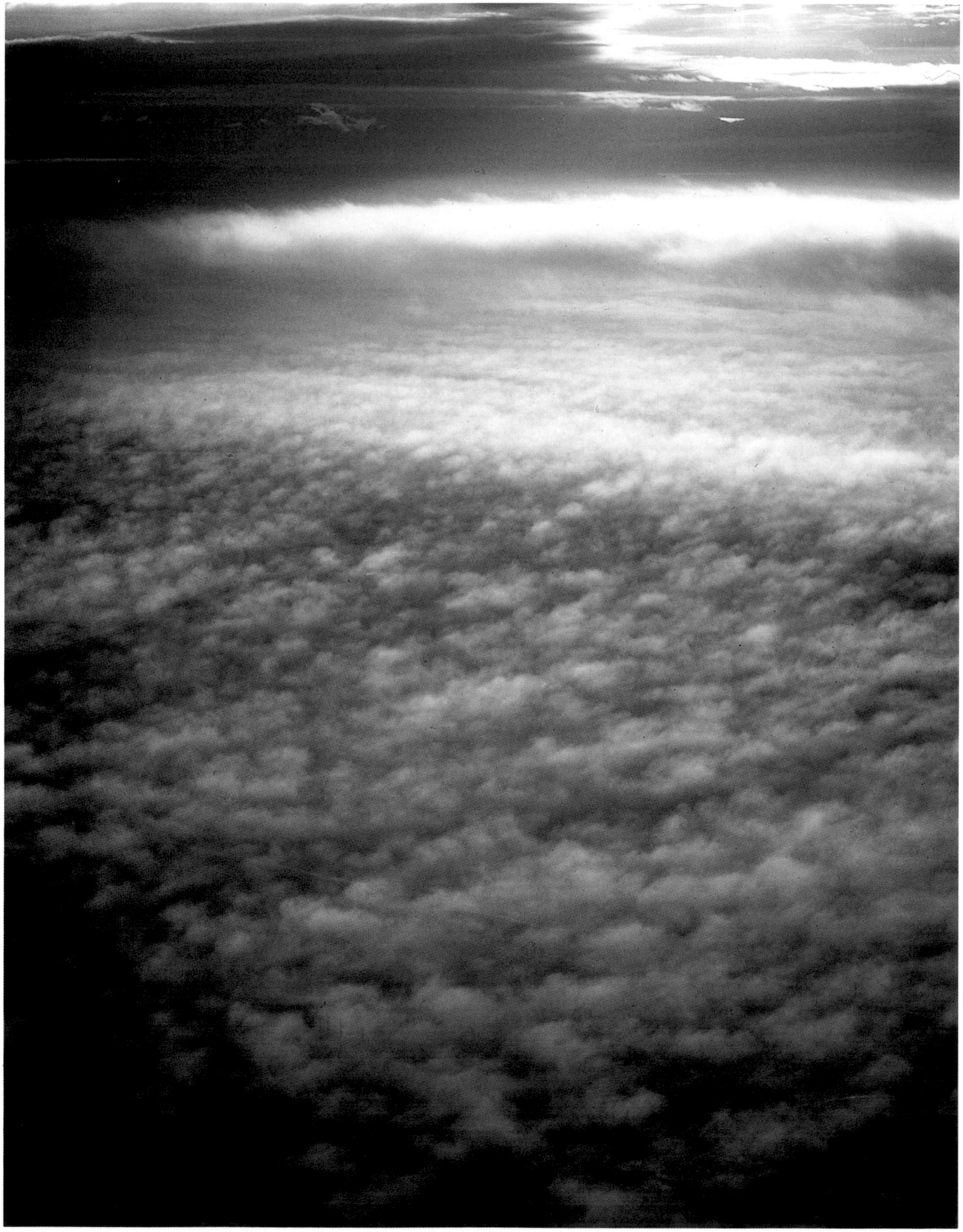

Moments
in Time

The time lapses of all the photographic exposures in this book
total considerably less than one second. The success
or failure of many of the images depended on being at the right
place at the right time, and on luck. Many times luck
involved weather and lighting conditions: fog, rain,
storm light, and sunshine. Modern photographic equipment
and materials allow fleeting moments to be captured quickly,
but in the end, what is saved is but a tiny
record of the immensity and grandeur of Colorado.

Short-lived fog after an all-night rain, San Luis Valley

*S*pring *clouds rise high above Monarch Pass, southern*
Sawatch Range

Frosted conifers dot the snowscape,
San Juan Mountains

Human-scarred Pawnee Buttes cast evening shadows,
Great Plains

Lake Granby and Monarch Lake viewed from the
Indian Peaks Wilderness, Shadow Mountain
Recreation Area

Collision of elemental forms of vapor and rock, Colorado/New Mexico border

*L*ow clouds scud above dune crests, Great Sand Dunes
National Monument

*Ebb and flow of clouds fails to crest eastern escarpment
of the Continental Divide, Rocky Mountain
National Park*

*P*eak shadows push east into South Park, northern
Sangre de Cristo Mountains

Aspen cling to a mountainside near Marble, Elk Range

*W*hile Tom Till was shooting sunrise, pilot Michael Green pointed out a rainbow that hung briefly in the sky below the San Juan Mountains, then faded above the morning mists, San Luis Valley

TECHNICAL INFORMATION

The photographs in this book were made with a series of Olympus OM-1 camera bodies and motordrives on Kodachrome 25 and 64 Professional Film. Lenses included 21mm, 24mm, 28mm, 50mm, 100mm, and 200mm focal lengths. Shutter speeds were 1/250, 1/500, and 1/1000, while aperture settings ranged from f/1.4 to f/8. A polarizing filter was used on a few of the photos; otherwise, no filtration was used. All photos were taken through the open window of a light plane or from balloons.

A balloon takes the air above the Yampa Valley, near Steamboat Springs

READER'S DIGEST

T ✶ H ✶ E

AMERICAN STORY

WHO, WHAT, WHEN, WHERE, WHY OF OUR NATION'S HERITAGE

✦ ✦ ✦

Reader's Digest

THE READER'S DIGEST ASSOCIATION, INC.
PLEASANTVILLE, NEW YORK / MONTREAL

THE AMERICAN STORY

PROJECT STAFF

Editorial

Project Editors
Suzanne E. Weiss
Nancy Shuker

Project Manager
Susan Bronson

Editor
Bryce S. Walker

Associate Editors
Audrey Peterson
Richard M. Mazurek

Art

Project Designers
Robert M. Grant
Judith Carmel

Senior Art Associate
Eleanor B. Kostyk

Art Production Associate
Antonio A. Mora

Research

Senior Editor, Research
Hildegard B. Anderson

Research Editors
Linda Ingroia
Deirdre van Dyk

Picture Research Editor
Ann Stewart

Production

Production Technology Manager
Doug Croll

Assistant Production Supervisor
Michael Gallo

Prepress Specialist
Karen Goldsmith

Prepress Manager
Garry T. Hansen

CONTRIBUTORS

Editor/Writer
Joseph L. Gardner

Research Editors
Josefa Stuart
Tony Kaye

Picture Researchers
Joan Menschenfreund
Robin Raffer

Researcher/Writers
Melinda Corey
Brett Harvey
George Ochoa
Nancy Shepherdson
Justin Smith

Consultant
Col. John R. Elting,
   U.S. Army (Retired)

Chief Writers
Joanne Barkan
Justin Cronin
Annette Foglino
Tod Olson

Writers
Neill Bogan
Tom Callahan
Rita Christopher
Jacqueline Damian
Karen Glenn
Jack El-Hai
Honey Naylor
Paula Pines

Copy Editors
Carolyn H. Lawrence
Katherine G. Ness

Indexer
Sydney Wolfe Cohen

Designer
Richard Boddy

Chief Artists
Cynthia Watts Clark
Neil Pinchin
Precision Graphics
Thomas Sperling

Artists
Academy Artworks
Howard Friedman
Andrew Newman
Doug Rugh
Robert Steimle
Roman Szolkowski

Art Production Associate
Tracey Grant

Reader's Digest Illustrated Reference Books

Editor-in-Chief
Christopher Cavanaugh

Art Director
Joan Mazzeo

Operations Manager
William J. Cassidy

Associate Editorial Director
Susan Randol

Address any comments about
THE AMERICAN STORY to
Reader's Digest, Editor-in-Chief
Illustrated Reference Books
Reader's Digest Road
Pleasantville, NY 10570

To order additional copies of
THE AMERICAN STORY call
1-800-846-2100

You can also visit us on the
World Wide Web at
www.readersdigest.com

The acknowledgments and credits that appear on pages 374–375 are hereby made a part of this copyright page.

Copyright © 2000 The Reader's Digest Association, Inc.
Copyright © 2000 The Reader's Digest Association (Canada) Ltd.
Copyright © 2000 Reader's Digest Association Far East Ltd.
Philippine Copyright 2000 Reader's Digest Association Far East Ltd.

Library of Congress Cataloging in Publication Data
The American story.
     p.   cm.
   Includes index.
   ISBN 0-89577-891-2
     1. United States—History—Chronology.   2. United States—History-
-Sources.   I. Reader's Digest Association.
E174.5 .A49 2000
973'. 02'02—dc20   96-013262

Reader's Digest and the Pegasus logo are registered trademarks of The Reader's Digest Association, Inc.

Printed in the United States of America

ABOUT THIS BOOK

There is, of course, no single American story. The pageant of our nation's past contains so many narrative strands — some running together, others branching out in a hundred surprising directions — that no one volume can include them all. Some events capture the spirit of a single place at a fleeting moment in history; others have altered the destiny of generations. This book offers a progression of the most significant and intriguing episodes from 1492 to the present. Together they combine into a unified account of the American past.

THE AMERICAN STORY contains more than 1,200 separate entries, each giving a brief, vivid account of a person, place, or occasion that has in some way shaped or enriched the overall national chronicle. It begins with the October day in 1492 when Columbus's sailors first sighted a drift of clouds above San Salvador in the Bahama Islands, thus opening the way to European settlement in the New World. It continues, year by year and decade by decade, to today's global age of blue jeans, MTV, Coca-Cola, CD-ROMs, and the Internet.

Along the way THE AMERICAN STORY visits the major historical landmarks: Thomas Jefferson writing the Declaration of Independence at a portable desk of his own invention, George Washington at Valley Forge, Abraham Lincoln proclaiming the end of slavery, John F. Kennedy facing down Nikita Khrushchev during the Cuban missile crisis. At the same time it points to little-known facts about the great and notorious. Few people know that Washington was so cash poor that he had to borrow money to get to his own inauguration. Or that Karl Marx, the father of Communism, once worked for a New York City newspaper. Or that Babe Ruth ate so many ballpark hot dogs one afternoon that he needed abdominal surgery. THE AMERICAN STORY offers hundreds of equally surprising footnotes to our national heritage.

History is shaped, for good or ill, by the deeds of individual people, and THE AMERICAN STORY highlights both the famous and the obscure. Here is young Phillis Wheatley, the 20-year-old slave who in 1773 became the nation's first published black poet. Con artist Thomas Bell, an 18th-century dropout from Harvard College whose scams outraged the Colonies from Boston to Barbados. And perky Lucille Mulhall, the rodeo-riding, bronco-busting teenager who in 1899 became the world's first cowgirl.

The many fascinating entries in THE AMERICAN STORY are divided into eight picture-filled chapters, each introduced by an opening text that swiftly sketches the political and economic background of the period. And each chapter is packed with special features — timelines, maps, informative sidebars, eyewitness reports of great events. All provide fresh insight into the impulses and events that have shaped this nation.

TABLE OF CONTENTS

EXPLORATION AND SETTLEMENT

1492 – 1599

Columbus … John Cabot and the Northwest Passage … America Is Named … Florida Is Claimed … Verrazano Lands in New York Harbor … The Lost City of Cíbola … De Soto and His Pigs … Early Fur Trade … St. Augustine … The Lost Colony of Roanoke . . . . **10 – 19**

1600 – 1650

Jamestown … Pocahontas … Powhatan … Henry Hudson … The Tobacco Trade … John Smith Maps New England … Colonists Recruit Wives … The *Mayflower* Lands … Samoset and Squanto … New World Poet … Puritans, Persecution, Providence … Harvard University … Anne Hutchinson … Log Cabins … New Amsterdam … Scalping … Triangle Slave Trade … First Woman Lawyer … Peter Stuyvesant . . . . **19 – 28**

1651 – 1763

Legal Tender … Wall Street … *The Day of Doom* … White Men on the Mississippi … William Penn … Sieur de La Salle … Leisler's Rebellion … Hawthorne's New England … The Salem Witch Trials … Raised by Indians … Blackbeard the Pirate … A Colonial Botanist … Georgia Is Founded … John Peter Zenger … Thomas Bell, Con Man … Faneuil Hall … The Indigo Industry … Franklin Gets Shocked … Lt. Col. George Washington … The French and Indian War … William Johnson … The Proclamation of 1763 . . . . . **29 – 41**

STRUGGLE FOR INDEPENDENCE

1764 – 1774

The Mason-Dixon Line … Samuel Adams's Vocation … The Stamp Act … Taverns and Revolution … George Washington, Farmer … California Missions … The Boston Massacre … Ethan Allen … The Wreck of the *Gaspée* … The Boston Tea Party … New Hampshire Patriots . . **42 – 51**

1775

Transylvania Territory … Paul Revere and Other Riders … "The Shot Heard 'Round the World" … The Minutemen … Bunker Hill … Sam Adams … Daniel Boone … Henry Knox … Ben Thompson, American Count … Black Soldiers … Yankee Doodle … The Spirit of '76 … Women in Wartime **51 – 59**

1776

Reluctant Rebels … Phillis Wheatley … The Diplomat Spy … George Mason … The Vote for Independence … *Common Sense* … The Declaration of Independence … The Liberty Bell … John Hancock … Submarine Warfare … Smallpox Epidemic . . . . **60 – 65**

1777 – 1781

Independent Vermont … The Marquis de Lafayette … Washington and the Sharpshooter … Kosciuszko … Valley Forge … General von Steuben … Chain Across the Hudson … Benjamin Franklin in Paris … George Rogers Clark … Chicago … John Paul Jones … A Morristown Winter … The Swamp Fox … Charleston Falls … Horatio Gates … Peter Francisco … Benedict Arnold … A Spaniard Aids the Americans … Admiral de Grasse … Cornwallis Surrenders . . . . **65 – 75**

1782 – 1788

The Great Seal … The Penobscot Scandal … A Revolt Is Averted … British Prison Ships … The Treaty of Paris … Noah Webster … A Territory Fights for Statehood … The Birth of Bourbon … Shays's Rebellion … The Northwest Ordinance … The Constitution: James Madison Outlines; Gouverneur Morris Drafts; The Ratification; Opposition from Patrick Henry . . . . **75 – 82**

1789

President Washington: Financial Woes; Reluctance to Take Office; The Myth of the Wooden Teeth … Vice President John Adams … Martha Washington's "Lost Days" … The Bill of Rights … Senator Maclay's Journal … Washington's Cabinet … America's First Attorney General … Samuel Slater, Industrial Capitalist … Davie Founds the University of North Carolina . . . . **82 – 87**

EARLY EXPERIMENTS IN DEMOCRACY

1790 – 1799

Early Days of the Supreme Court … U.S. Patents … Washington, D.C. … The U.S. Census … Robert Gray Sails Around the World … The Treaty of New York … Eli Whitney … John Bill Ricketts's Circus … A French Diplomat Seeks the First Asylum … The U.S. Navy … The Whiskey Rebellion … Johnny Appleseed … Russian Fur Trade in Alaska . . . . **88 – 97**

1800 – 1805

Aaron Burr Heads Tammany Hall … Washington's Biographer … The White House Is Built … Dining at the White House … Chief Justice John Marshall … The Dirty Campaign of 1800 … Thomas Jefferson Assumes the Presidency … The Second Great Awakening … The Natchez Trace … Gifts for the President … A British Architect Builds … The Louisiana Purchase … Hamilton and Burr Duel … Mercy Otis Warren Makes History . . . . **98 – 104**

1806 – 1815

The National Road … Lewis and Clark … Pike's Peak … Forced to Serve the British Navy … Fulton's Folly … Yellowstone National Park … Dolley Madison … Washington Irving … Ephraim McDowell, Surgical Pioneer … Fort Astoria … The New Madrid Earthquake … The War of 1812 … "Old Ironsides" … A Russian Outpost in America … Oliver Hazard Perry … Tecumseh … The British Burn Washington … The Star-Spangled Banner … The Battle of New Orleans . . . **105 – 114**

1816 – 1829

The Year Without Summer … The Erie Canal … Painter John Trumbull … The Missouri Compromise … Higher Education for Women … James Fenimore Cooper … The Santa Fe Trail … Sequoya … Stephen Austin Colonizes Texas … Denmark Vesey's Slave Rebellion … The Monroe Doctrine … The Great American Desert … Chewing Tobacco … Lafayette Returns to America … Pushmataha … Communal Living in New Harmony … The Eastern Pony Express … Jedediah Smith Explores California … Jackson's Inauguration . . . . **114 – 123**

THE NATION GROWS

1830 – 1835

Godey's Lady's Book … Rochester Revival … The Bowie Knife … John Quincy Adams in Congress … A Newspaper Editor Opposes Slavery … Edgar Allan Poe at West Point … Tocqueville's *Democracy in America* … Cyrus McCormick Invents the Reaper … The 1832 Cholera Epidemic … Sam Houston … Balloon Frame Houses … The End of the Mountain Men … The U.S. Pays Off the National Debt … Riverboat Gambling … The Baltimore and Ohio Railroad … The Loco Focos … Texas Rangers . . . . . **124 – 136**

1836 – 1845

The Alamo … John Deere's Steel Plow … Oberlin College … Sylvester Graham … The Trail of Tears … Pierre Jean De Smet … Actress-Abolitionist Fanny Kemble … Green-Wood Cemetery … The Aroostook War … The Origins of "OK" … Dorothea Dix … Wagon Trains to California … Charles Dickens in America … Ether … Rhode Island's Dual Governments … Manjiro, Sailor Turned Ambassador … Samuel F. B. Morse … Horace Mann and Education Reform … James K. Polk … Frederick Douglass … "Manifest Destiny" … The U.S. Naval Academy … The Birth of Baseball … Henry David Thoreau . . **136 – 148**

1846 – 1850

John Charles Frémont … The Smithsonian Institution … New Bedford Whaling … The Donner Party … The Mormon Exodus … War Correspondent George Kendall … The Mormons Find Gold … Seneca Falls … The California Gold Rush … Gold Rush by Sea … Escape from Slavery … Chewing Gum … The First Woman Doctor … California's Constitution … Juliet Brier in Death Valley … Photography Captures the Heavens … Henry Clay . . . . **148 – 156**

1851 – 1860

19th-Century Prohibition … *Moby Dick* … Karl Marx in New York … Stephen Foster … Gorrie's Ice Maker … America's Railroad Hub … Harriet Beecher Stowe … Drug Safety … George Catlin … Commodore Perry … The Crystal Palace Exhibition … Ponting's Cattle Drive … Walt Whitman's Self-Promotion … A Senate Chamber Caning … The Sewing Machine … Mardi Gras … The Dred Scott Decision … The Lincoln–Douglas Debates … The Comstock Lode … Birth of the Oil Industry … Cooper Union … The Pony Express . . . . **156 – 167**

THE CIVIL WAR AND ITS AFTERMATH

1861

Mary Boykin Chesnut … Lincoln's Inauguration … Diplomat Charles Francis Adams … The First Union Casualty … Sara Emma Edmonds, Female Soldier … West Virginia Created … Collis Huntington … The Battle of Bull Run … John Tyler and the Confederacy … Brother vs. Brother … The Civil War Death Toll … Mass-Produced Uniforms . . . . **168 – 177**

1862

Popular Songs of the Civil War ... The *Monitor* vs. the *Merrimack* ... The Confederate Draft ... The Homestead Act ... Clara Barton ... Confederate Espionage ... Antietam ... Allan Pinkerton ... Blockade Runners ... The Union Balloon Corps ... Foreign-Born Soldiers ... **178–183**

1863 – 1864

The Emancipation Proclamation ... The Press in the Civil War ... The Medal of Honor ... Gettysburg ... Home Postal Delivery ... Louisa May Alcott ... Thanksgiving Becomes a National Holiday ... The Battle of Mobile Bay ... General Sherman ... Bounty Jumpers ... A Plot to Burn New York City ... The Sand Creek Massacre **183–189**

1865

Lee vs. Grant ... Abraham Lincoln Is Assassinated ... Jefferson Davis Attempts Escape ... Robert E. Lee Regains Citizenship ... Stand Watie, the Last Confederate General ... Black Codes ... Greenbacks ... Confederate Exiles in Mexico ... Vaudeville **189–193**

1866 – 1870

The ASPCA ... Mail-Order Brides ... The Transatlantic Cable ... Queen Emma of Hawaii ... *The Black Crook* ... The First Train Robbery ... Thaddeus Stevens ... Alaska ... The Typewriter ... The Cowboy ... Prairie Fires ... Buffalo Bill Cody ... Carpetbaggers and Scalawags ... The Nation's Slaughterhouse ... President Johnson Impeached ... King Ranch ... The Adirondacks ... The Transcontinental Railroad ... The Red Stockings ... John Wesley Powell ... Black Friday ... Suffrage in the Wyoming Territory ... Thomas Edison ... The First Apartment Buildings ... Homesteaders' Frontier Schools **194–206**

1871 – 1877

The Great Chicago Fire ... The Peshtigo Fire ... P. T. Barnum ... Grand Duke Alexis ... Victoria Woodhull ... San Francisco Cable Cars ... America's First Zoo ... The Grasshopper Plagues ... Martha Summerhays, Army Wife ... The Kentucky Derby ... Dwight Moody ... The Centennial Exhibition ... The Election of 1876 ... Cartoonist Thomas Nast ... The Great Uprising ... Nicodemus, Kansas ... Chief Joseph ... Wanamaker's Department Store **207–215**

PROGRESS AND PROSPERITY

1878 – 1885

Cattlewoman Lizzie Johnson ... Gunfight at the O.K. Corral ... Woolworth's 5 and 10¢ Store ... The Vanderbilts' Great Ball ... The Brooklyn Bridge ... Standard Railway Time ... The Vanishing Buffalo ... Ida B. Wells ... Calling Cards ... *Huckleberry Finn* ... The First Skyscraper **216–224**

1886 – 1900

Coca-Cola ... Geronimo ... The Statue of Liberty ... Samuel Gompers ... America's First Female Mayor ... "Casey at the Bat" ... Hello Girls ... Oklahoma Land Rush ... The Johnstown Flood ... U.S. Weather Bureau ... The Mafia ... The Frontier Closes ... Ellis Island ... The Cathedral of St. John the Divine ... "Happy Birthday" ... The Pullman Strike ... Joshua Slocum Sails Around the World ... Gillette's Disposable Razor ... Coney Island ... Justice John Marshall Harlan ... William Jennings Bryan ... Marcus Alonzo Hanna ... Sears, Roebuck & Co ... The *Maine* ... The Spanish-American War ... Hawaii ... Cowgirl Lucille Mulhall ... Women on Campus **225–239**

1901 – 1910

McKinley Assassinated ... Theodore Roosevelt ... Annie Edson Goes over the Falls ... U. S. Steel ... The "Teddy" Bear ... Jack London ... The First World Series ... The Panama Canal ... The Wright Brothers ... The Buick Motor Company ... Filling Stations ... The San Francisco Earthquake ... America's Divorce Capital ... Upton Sinclair's *The Jungle* ... Theodore Roosevelt, Environmentalist ... Robert LaFollette's Filibuster ... Hollywood ... The FBI ... W. C. Handy ... Angel Island ... Idaho Forest Fires ... The Growth of the Railroads **239–250**

1911 – 1918

Girl Scouts ... Minimum Wage ... Modern Art ... Notre Dame Football ... Elsie De Wolfe ... The Income Tax ... The Last Passenger Pigeon ... Henry Ford ... America Enters World War I ... Jeannette Rankin ... Boys Town ... American Troops Battle the Red Army ... The Flu Epidemic ... German Foods Renamed ... The Meuse-Argonne Campaign **250–257**

BOOM, BUST, WAR, AND VICTORY

1919 – 1925

The Palmer Raids ... Women Gain the Vote ... Charles Ponzi ... Babe Ruth ... The Miss America Pageant ... The Tomb of the Unknown Soldier ... Emily Post ... White House Christmas ... Gershwin ... Johnny Weissmuller ... Little Orphan Annie ... H. L. Mencken ... Air Conditioning ... The Florida Land Boom ... The Grand Ole Opry ... Clara Bow ... *The Great Gatsby* .... **258 – 270**

1926 – 1930

Robert Goddard ... Will Rogers ... Rudolph Valentino ... Charles Lindbergh ... Movies Talk ... The Holland Tunnel ... Mickey Mouse ... The St. Valentine's Day Massacre ... The Academy Awards ... The 1929 Stock Market Crash ... Admiral Byrd ... Prohibition ... Edward Bernays ... Bobby Jones Wins Golf's Grand Slam ... Depression-Era Employment ... Sinclair Lewis .... **270 – 278**

1931 – 1939

The Bonus March ... Hattie Caraway and Huey Long ... Satchel Paige ... The Cermak Assassination ... Eleanor Roosevelt ... FDR's Bank Holiday ... Dust Bowl Blizzards ... *Life* Magazine ... John L. Lewis ... Robert Moses ... Dale Carnegie ... The *Hindenburg* ... Alcatraz ... Benny Goodman ... CBS News Radio ... The Hurricane of 1938 ... The 1939 World's Fair ... Marian Anderson ... Samuel Goldwyn ... Lou Gehrig ... Early TV ... The Neutrality Act ... FM Radio ... At the Movies .... **278 – 290**

1940 – 1942

Social Security ... Nylon ... Blood Banks ... Ernie Pyle ... Roosevelt and Churchill ... Pearl Harbor ... The Manhattan Project ... U-Boats ... GI's in Britain ... Home Front ... Wartime Rationing ... Gen. Joseph Stilwell ... The Computer ... Midway ... Eddie Rickenbacker Lost at Sea ... POW's in America ... The USO ... Cocoanut Grove Fire .... **290 – 299**

1943 – 1945

Tokyo Rose ... Women's Baseball ... D-Day Decision ... Robert Capa ... FDR's Fala ... Blue Babies ... Japanese Balloon Bombs ... Glenn Miller ... Women in Wartime ... Iwo Jima ... Truman ... The Mistranslation That Changed History ... Kilroy .... **299 – 305**

TURMOIL AND TRIUMPHS

1946 – 1955

The Baby Boom ... The Iron Curtain ... Bikini Atoll ... Las Vegas ... The New Look ... Jackie Robinson ... UFO's ... Levittowns ... Chuck Yeager ... Berlin Airlift ... The Korean War ... MASH ... Credit Cards ... Estes Kefauver ... Truman Fires MacArthur ... J. D. Salinger ... UNIVAC ... Justice Earl Warren ... Nuclear Submarines ... Polio Vaccine... *Brown v. the Board of Education* ... Elvis ... Disneyland .... **306 – 321**

1956 – 1961

The Turnpike ... The *Andrea Doria* ... The First Mall ... Joseph McCarthy ... Jimmy Hoffa ... Sputnik ... Alaska and Hawaii ... Barbie ... The St. Lawrence Seaway ... Khrushchev ... Quiz-Show Scandal ... Motown ... U-2 Spy Plane ... Wilma Rudolph ... Nixon-Kennedy Debate ... JFK ... 1961 Inauguration ... The Peace Corps ... The Bay of Pigs ... Mercury Space Program ... Desegregation .... **321 – 331**

1962 – 1969

Bob Dylan ... Princess Grace ... Rachel Carson's *Silent Spring* ... The Cuban Missile Crisis ... Martin Luther King, Jr. ... JFK Assassinated ... Betty Friedan ... The Beatles ... Civil Rights Act ... Watts ... Lady Bird Johnson ... Blackout of 1965 ... The Super Bowl ... The Chicago Convention ... The Santa Barbara Oil Spill ... Man Walks on the Moon ... Woodstock .... **332 – 340**

1970 – 1979

Earth Day ... Kent State ... Teenagers Vote ... Nixon in China ... Hughes Autobiography Hoax ... Vietnam POW's ... Agnew Resigns ... Arab Oil Embargo ... Blue Jeans ... Watergate ... Saigon Falls ... The Bicentennial ... Apple Computer ... Three Mile Island .... **340 – 347**

1980 – 2000

Commando Raid on Iran ... Mt. St. Helens Erupts ... AIDS ... Sandra Day O'Connor ... Ronald Reagan ... The *Challenger* ... The Crash of 1987 ... Operation Desert Storm ... Michael Jordan ... Jimmy Carter's New Role ... Ocean Exploration ... Cinton Faces Impeachment ... New Millenium .. **347 – 353**

A Treasury of Facts and Documents .... **354 – 373**

Credits and Acknowledgments .... **374 – 375**

Index .... **376 – 384**

EXPLORATION AND SETTLEMENT

(1492 TO 1763)

When the first Europeans set foot on the mainland of North America, there were some 6 million people living in the New World. They were descendants of the original Native Americans, who may have begun a trek from Asia through Siberia to Alaska as long ago as 40,000 B.C. These Ice Age immigrants most likely crossed the Bering Strait over a land bridge that existed when the ocean level was low. Gradually, they migrated from the frigid North to the more temperate South and West, dispersing into many tribes. Eskimos and Aleuts, who were racially different from the American Indians, arrived later by kayak or over the ice.

Of the original inhabitants, the Native Americans who settled south of the Rio Grande River developed the wealthiest, most advanced societies: the Aztec civilization in central and southern Mexico, the Maya in Central America, and the Inca in Peru. For thousands of years, North America remained more sparsely populated than its southern neighbor. Most inhabitants of North America lived in small villages or roamed as nomads, hunting, foraging, and farming with simple tools characteristic of the Iron Age. The 1908 discovery of a bison bone in a New Mexico riverbed led researchers to the oldest known human artifact in North America—a chiseled stone tool that a hunter used some 10,000 years ago.

This carved stone figure of a bearskin-clothed healer was unearthed at an Indian burial site in Ohio.

FOR THOUSANDS OF YEARS, residents of the Western and Eastern Hemispheres were unaware of each other's existence. No known contact was made until about A.D. 1000, when Norse sailors based in Greenland explored islands off the coast of Canada and perhaps ventured south along the east coast of North America. But their discoveries produced

Columbus altered his ship's log to keep his crew from becoming mutinous.

no permanent settlements of any size, and so the two worlds remained separate until 1492. In that year an Italian adventurer named Christopher Columbus set out from Spain, determined to find a new water route to the Orient by sailing west. After more than two months at sea, his three ships, the *Nina, Pinta,* and *Santa Maria,* came upon islands now known as the Bahamas in the Caribbean Sea.

Columbus made three more voyages to the Caribbean and explored Central America before he died in 1506, still convinced he had reached the Far East. But the European explorers who set out on voyages of discovery after Columbus's first trip believed otherwise. Italy's Amerigo Vespucci, Spain's Juan Ponce de León and Hernando de Soto, and others realized they had found a new world.

Central and South America, Mexico, and the West Indies offered precisely what the explorers and their financial backers in Europe wanted: riches and power. During the 1500's, the Spanish and Portuguese conquered much of the Southern Hemisphere. They either killed the Native Americans or used them as serfs to extract minerals from the earth and to work large estates. Spanish explorers, missionaries, and settlers also pushed their way north of Mexico and up the Florida peninsula and struggled with the French for control of the southeastern corner of the continent. In 1565 the Spanish founded the first permanent settlement in North America, a small outpost at St. Augustine, Florida.

SOME HALF-MILLION NATIVES lived in the piedmont and coastal areas of North America, where Europeans would first settle. Native American cultures and political structures were as rich and complex as any that Europeans would

bring. A Huron town near the Great Lakes, for example, had 100 large buildings housing an estimated 4,000 to 6,000 people. Tribes known as mound builders left huge earthworks across much of the eastern United States.

Indian tribal leaders near Jamestown lived in houses covered with matted grass or bark.

While other European nations threw themselves into the New World competition, England held back. The explorer John Cabot had claimed land in North America for the Crown in 1497, but England did not begin to make progress in colonization until more than a century later under the reign of Elizabeth I. By then, the small island nation was on its way to becoming a great maritime power, a land of bustling commerce and manufacturing, and a hotbed of strong-minded merchants.

In less than 200 years, England would dominate North America from the Atlantic Ocean to the Mississippi River. The resulting economic, social, and political impact shaped a culture unique in the New World — one that was very different, for example, from that of the Spanish colonies.

Centralized control by the Crown and the Roman Catholic Church characterized Spanish colonization. In England, on the other hand, the Crown granted charters, or patents, to individual entrepreneurs and to companies of profit-seeking stockholders. A charter entitled investors to own and develop a tract of land. For a half-century or so, those who financed a colony decided in large part how it operated. Most investors put up money expecting the settlers to reward them with minerals, furs, and other saleable items.

In addition to business entrepreneurs, religious dissidents also sought charters for colonies. British society weathered the storm of the Reformation by establishing the Church of England under government authority. But as time went on, the monarchy and the church began demanding conformity from both Roman Catholics and Protestant sects. The Puritans and Quakers hoped that, by removing themselves to the New World, they would be able to establish ideal Christian communities under their own governance.

SIR WALTER RALEIGH, a favorite of Queen Elizabeth,

made the first attempt to establish a permanent English colony in North America. Beginning in 1585, Raleigh sponsored expeditions to settle Roanoke Island, in what is now North Carolina; the colony did not survive. Then in 1607 a group chartered under the name of the London Company launched a settlement at Jamestown, Virginia. The colonists may have expected easy riches and a pleasing environment; instead, they faced assaults by Indian warriors and Spanish soldiers. In the first year, the colony was decimated by disease and starvation. But with fresh supplies, new recruits from England, and the leadership of Capt. John Smith, the beleaguered group managed to hold on, and it became the first permanent English colony in North America.

If an appetite for profit drove the Virginia Colony investors, the desire to govern their own lives inspired the Protestant dissidents. The Pilgrims — who called themselves Separatists because they wanted to break from the established church — set sail from Plymouth, England, in 1620 aboard the *Mayflower.* They founded Plymouth Colony, the second permanent English settlement, and began recruiting new settlers. By 1630 the colony numbered around 300 residents.

The Puritans, by contrast, had no intention of breaking with the church. Their program was radical reform, which they hoped to bring about by personal example.

The Mayflower Compact enabled the Pilgrims to establish their own government.

The first 17 ships of the Massachusetts Bay Company reached Boston Harbor in 1630 carrying some 1,000 devout Puritans, who busily set about creating spiritually pure communities as models. It was the first wave of a great Puritan migration to New England. In the next decade alone, some 16,000 new settlers arrived and began clearing land, building

churches, and holding town meetings. The colonists pushed out into the forest, moving south to absorb Plymouth in 1691. They built the towns of Hartford, Wethersfield, Windsor, and New Haven, which later would be grouped together as the Connecticut Colony.

Although the Puritans sought religious freedom for themselves, most of them refused to award that same liberty to others. In general, only church members could participate in the burgeoning institutions of local self-government. The quest for liberty led nonconformist Puritans to start new settlements. When the Massachusetts General Court banished Roger Williams in 1636 for his strenuous arguments in favor of the separation of church and state, he moved away to found the town of Providence. Dissident Anne Hutchinson joined him in the creation of Rhode Island.

THE QUAKERS' DESIRE to conduct a "Holy Experiment"

led to the founding of yet another colony. In 1681 William Penn received the largest tract of land ever granted by the Crown to an individual. Penn was determined to make Quaker values — religious tolerance, peace, and love of God's creation — the basis of his Pennsylvania colony. At a time when the Quakers were being persecuted in both England and the colonies, Penn's first group of settlers founded Philadelphia, the City of Brotherly Love.

The English faced formidable rivals for control of North America during the 1600's — the French, the Dutch, and the resident Native Americans. When English colonization began, the French had already established settlements from Nova Scotia to Cape Cod. A complex network of trade with native tribes tightened the French hold on the region. The Dutch, who were the leading European maritime traders at the time, gained a foothold in the mid-Atlantic region in the 1610's and 1620's, with permanent settlements radiating from New Amsterdam — east to Long Island, north to the Connecticut River valley, and south into

Competition for beaver skins set French traders against the English.

the Delaware River valley. Then in 1664 the English ousted the colony's Dutch governor, Peter Stuyvesant, and renamed its principal town New York after the brother of the English king, the duke of York.

For a time, trading partnerships allowed European settlers and Native Americans to coexist, even to cooperate. But relations invariably turned bloody when settlers moved to take permanent control of Indian lands. In 1636–1637, for example, the Puritans virtually annihilated the Pequots of Connecticut. Thirty years later, the New England colonies united to exterminate the Narragansetts, Wampanoags, and Nipmucks. In addition, the continuing rivalry between England and France for trade and territory erupted into periodic violence, both in Europe and in America. The two colonial powers battled each other in King William's War (1689-1697), Queen Anne's War (1702-1713), and King George's War (1743-1748).

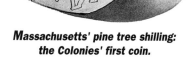

The English Crown continued to parcel out land and grant charters, authorizing colonies called New Hampshire, New York, New Jersey, Delaware, and North and South Carolina. When Georgia, the last of the 13 colonies, was established in 1733, the British possessions formed an unbroken line along the East Coast.

Massachusetts' pine tree shilling: the Colonies' first coin.

This experiment in North American colonization was a remarkable success. After tenuous beginnings, the settlements prospered. The colonists provided for their own basic needs and began to export lumber, ships, and seafood from New England; wheat, flour, beef, and pork from the middle colonies; tobacco, rice, and indigo from the South. The population grew as childhood mortality rates declined, and immigrants were attracted by the prospect of economic opportunity and personal freedom. By the 1770's more than 2 million settlers of European extraction occupied the land.

The Colonies faced dramatic labor shortages as their settlements grew in size and their commerce became more diverse. Although immigration from Scotland, Ireland, and Germany increased, there was still not enough manpower.

Towns in the North were always short of skilled artisans to man growing colonial industries. On Southern plantations, the money crops of tobacco, indigo, and rice demanded constant tending.

A slave owner advertised to sell his female servant in 1763.

Importing indentured servants, who worked for a set period without wages in return for their passage, helped relieve the shortage in the North. Another solution was to bring over slaves from the Ivory Coast in Africa.

The first slaves arrived in Virginia in 1619, and for the next half century they were given roughly the same status enjoyed by European servants. Many Africans worked their way to freedom. Then gradually the practice hardened into an institution. The first slave code in the Colonies went into effect in Virginia in the 1680's. Meanwhile, the British government reorganized the slave trade. By the early 1700's, slavery had spread throughout the Colonies, becoming the keystone of the labor system in the South. Living conditions for slaves were at best difficult, and at worst brutal.

THE COLONISTS ENJOYED A SOCIAL MOBILITY that

existed almost nowhere in Europe. In a society that was expanding in every way, almost any white male who was free and willing to work could move up. A more rigid elite of the wealthy and socially prominent developed in the 1700's; but even then, the social divisions remained small.

Besides social equality, the colonists grew accustomed also to having a say in government. England initially fostered these expectations by giving autonomy to the charter holders, who then passed it along to the colonists. As early as 1619, Virginians won the right to create an assembly that included elected "burgesses," or representatives. Eventually all the Colonies organized assemblies.

As America became more important economically, the British Parliament began to assert more control over colonial affairs. The main issue was trade. England expected to get raw materials and agricultural products from the Colonies and to use the Colonies as a market for English manufac-

tured goods. England also wanted to prevent the Colonies from competing in the European and Caribbean trades.

Starting in 1651, Parliament passed measures to restrict colonial trade and manufacturing. Since the laws limited much lucrative commerce, the colonists generally ignored them, using their local assemblies to tie the hands of the royal governors, whose job it was to enforce English law. (Most assemblies paid the governors' salaries and provided soldiers for England's many wars.) Slowly but surely, tension between the Colonies and the mother country intensified.

THE FRENCH AND INDIAN WAR (1754–63) pushed

British-Colonial relations to the breaking point. France had become England's greatest rival for dominance in Europe and for control of the fur trade, the fisheries off Newfoundland, and the territory from the Appalachian Mountains to the Mississippi River.

With the participation of the Colonies, England won the war against France and acquired vast territories: Canada, Florida, and all the land east of the Mississippi River except New Orleans. The English now dominated North America. But this new power came at a price. England needed to pay for the war, finance a standing army in the territories in order to maintain the peace, and appease the Native Americans by keeping the land-hungry colonists east of the Appalachians.

King George III and the British Parliament concluded that it was time for the unruly, overly independent colonists to obey the laws and contribute to the costs of the empire. The colonists resisted, just as they had in the past. This time, however, resistance led to revolution. 🖂

French and Indian raiders killed many of the residents of Schenectady, New York, in 1690.

A 1492
flock of birds helped guide Christopher Columbus to the New World.

When Christopher Columbus weighed anchor at Palos, Spain, in August 1492 and headed west to seek the riches of the "Indies," he was already known as a first-class navigator. "He could tell from a cloud or a single star what direction to follow," wrote one admirer. But after a month at sea, the 90 crewmen on the *Santa María,* the *Niña,* and the *Pinta* had

A frigate bird may have guided Christopher Columbus to land in the Bahamas.

their doubts. Where were they? What lay ahead? And how would they ever get back to Spain? To allay their fears, the Italian-born navigator kept a false log, shortening the mileage covered daily by his ships. But the sailors must have sensed that they had traveled more than the 2,400 nautical miles Columbus had promised them.

The Genoese explorer stuck to a westerly course, ignoring the mutinous rumblings of his men. On October 7 he spotted "a great multitude of birds" flying toward the southwest. Knowing that most of the Portuguese islands had been discovered by sailors who tracked birds in flight, he ordered his helmsman to follow them.

On October 11 crew members spotted signs of life in the water: a branch of wild roses, reeds, and a carved stick. The discovery cheered them, and their misgivings evaporated. In the predawn hours of October 12, a seaman shouted: "Tierra! Tierra! (Land! Land!)" Later that morning Columbus stepped ashore at a place he called San Salvador — most probably an island in the Bahamas — and in the name of his sponsors, King Ferdinand and Queen Isabella, claimed the land for Spain. 🚢

H 1497
e was looking for another route to Asia. Instead, John Cabot discovered a seacoast teeming with codfish.

Word of Christopher Columbus's extraordinary discovery spread across Europe like wildfire, igniting a frenzy of transatlantic exploration. Among the westbound navigators was John Cabot. A native of Genoa, Cabot had changed his name from Giovanni Caboto and moved to England. There he persuaded King Henry VII to let him sail to the "Indies," arguing that he would travel a shorter, more northerly route than the one Columbus had taken. King Henry, who earlier had refused to sponsor Columbus (thus losing the chance to be first in the New World), readily agreed to Cabot's plan.

John Cabot and other explorers of his era used this type of astrolabe to navigate.

On May 2, 1497, Cabot and an 18-man crew left Bristol, England, and headed west. They reached land on June 24, probably in Newfoundland or Nova Scotia.

By August 6 the navigator was back in England, certain that he had sailed to Asia. But while Christopher Columbus had returned with gold, Cabot brought back reports of an astonishingly rich fishing ground, fairly jumping with cod. Commercial fishermen from western Europe hurried over to "the newe founde lande" (as King Henry proclaimed it) to fill up their holds. More important than the potential profits from fish, however, Cabot's journey gave England its first claim on the North American mainland. 🚢

Exploring Hudson Bay, Martin Frobisher battled ice caps and Inuits.

T 1498
he search for a Northwest Passage to the Indies opened North America to discovery.

Hopes of finding a navigable sea route across North America — not interest in the continent itself — drew generations of explorers to the region. John Cabot, following his pioneering first attempt, tried again in 1498, but was lost at sea. His misfortune did nothing to discourage the others.

In 1535 French explorer Jacques Cartier, in search of China, sailed 1,000 miles up the St. Lawrence River instead. Englishman Francis Drake

If not for a few lies, a little self-promotion, and a mapmaker's confusion, our continent might have been called Columbia, not America.

Amerigo Vespucci was a wealthy Florentine merchant with an interest in geography — and a vivid imagination. In 1501 he sailed to Brazil; it was his first trip to the New World. Returning to Italy, he wrote up his experiences in a letter to a friend. He told in glowing colors of the region's extraordinary flora and fauna, and he bragged at length about his own navigational skills. For good measure he added a fictitious account of a visit he claimed to have made in 1497 — one year before Christopher Columbus explored the coast of Venezuela.

If Vespucci's story had been true, he would have been the first European to set foot on the mainland of South America. His letter, and a widely circulated volume by him entitled *Mundus Novus,* were welcomed by people hungry for news about the New World. His racy descriptions of native life made them

Amerigo Vespucci appears on the 1507 map that gave America its name.

both bestsellers. By contrast, the report of Columbus's Venezuelan visit appeared as a brief item in a navigation journal. The public gave it little notice.

In 1507 (a year after Columbus died) all of Vespucci's self-promotion paid off. That year, a German geographer named Martin Waldseemüller published two maps with an accompanying text. On one map Waldseemüller placed the label "America" on the New World's largest southern landmass, having concluded from Vespucci's fabricated account that "Americus Vespucius has discovered a fourth part of the world." Before long, the term "America" was used on maps to include North America, too.

Many scholars have objected to Waldseemüller's choice, calling Vespucci a fake. But Vespucci's supporters have argued that even if Columbus had reached the mainland first, Vespucci deserved to have it named after him because he was the first to recognize it as a continent in its own right, separate from both Europe and Asia. 🐚

combed the Pacific Coast in 1578 with his boat the *Golden Hind,* capturing and looting Spanish treasure ships and hunting for a western outlet to the now-fabled route; in the process, he sailed right by San Francisco Bay.

While Drake privateered, a fellow Englishman, Martin Frobisher, probed the mouth of Hudson Bay. But the discovery of fool's gold on an island there kept Frobisher tied up in a fruitless scheme to become rich.

Determined to pick up where Frobisher left off, navigator John Davis explored and mapped the area between Greenland and Canada called Baffin Bay (named after William Baffin, who explored the bay and some of its snow-covered islands). More importantly, Davis discovered an icy 750-mile channel that snaked through the Arctic islands to the west — the first leg of the true Northwest Passage. 🐚

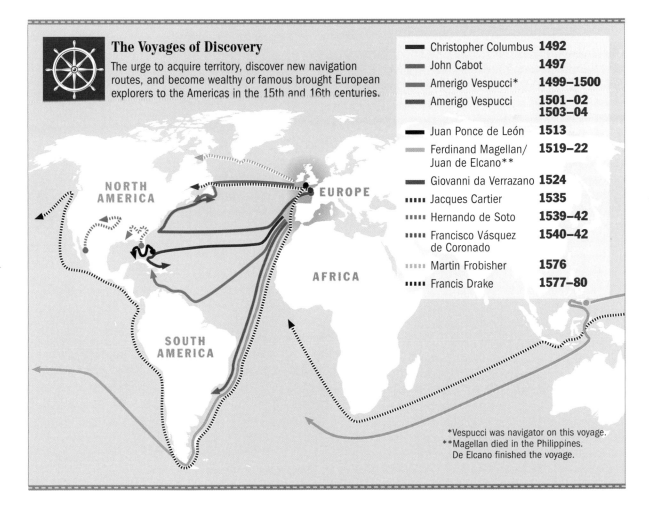

The Voyages of Discovery

The urge to acquire territory, discover new navigation routes, and become wealthy or famous brought European explorers to the Americas in the 15th and 16th centuries.

Christopher Columbus	**1492**
John Cabot	**1497**
Amerigo Vespucci*	**1499–1500**
Amerigo Vespucci	**1501–02** **1503–04**
Juan Ponce de León	**1513**
Ferdinand Magellan/ Juan de Elcano**	**1519–22**
Giovanni da Verrazano	**1524**
Jacques Cartier	**1535**
Hernando de Soto	**1539–42**
Francisco Vásquez de Coronado	**1540–42**
Martin Frobisher	**1576**
Francis Drake	**1577–80**

NORTH AMERICA

EUROPE

SOUTH AMERICA

AFRICA

*Vespucci was navigator on this voyage.
**Magellan died in the Philippines. De Elcano finished the voyage.

The New World's Native Foods

English settlers in Roanoke Island in the 16th century marveled at the efficient techniques Indians had developed for raising corn, squash, watermelons, and other crops. Other native plant foods, fowl, fish, and shellfish that for centuries had sustained Indians include:

- Black walnut
- Blueberry
- Cashew nut
- Chili pepper
- Cod
- Crab
- Cranberry
- Hickory nut
- Kidney bean
- Lima bean
- Lobster
- Maple syrup
- Peanut
- Pecan
- Persimmon
- Pumpkin
- Striped bass
- Sweet potato
- Wild rice
- Wild turkey

1513

Spanish explorer Juan Ponce de León, who tried to colonize Florida, thought it was an island.

Like many of his seafaring contemporaries, Juan Ponce de León wore many hats — soldier, politician, adventurer, navigator, and entrepreneur. In 1513, while governor of Puerto Rico, he was lured back to sea by a tale he had heard from an old Carib Indian woman. An island called Bimini, the woman told him, held unbelievable riches: gold, luscious fruit, and a spring with waters that could make an old man young again.

The gold probably meant more to Ponce de León than any vague promise of renewed vitality and youth, but as it happened he found neither one. Sailing northwest, he missed Bimini and landed instead on a large landmass blanketed in dense vegetation. Since he had just celebrated *Pascua Florida* (the Spanish name for Easter), he named the place La Florida and claimed it for the crown of Spain.

To the end of his life, Ponce de León believed that La Florida was an island. "Among my services," he later wrote to King Charles I of Spain, "I discovered at my own cost and charge the Island Florida and others in its district . . . and now I return to that island, if it please God's will, to settle it." Slave raiders and the explorer John Cabot may well have visited Florida earlier, but none of them seems to have had Ponce de León's yearning to conquer and populate it. So the explorer returned in 1521 with a group of priests and settlers. It was his final adventure. Mortally wounded in an Indian attack, he died still unaware that his "island" was the southeastern tip of the North American continent. 🛥

1524

Verrazano, master of the missed opportunity, discovered the mouth of the Hudson River 85 years before Henry Hudson — and left it unexplored.

Giovanni da Verrazano's far-reaching voyage up the coast of North America in 1524 opened European eyes to 2,000 miles of New World coastline. But what the Italian-born explorer missed is almost as remarkable as what he actually discovered.

Sailing for King Francis I of France, Verrazano was determined, he later wrote, to uncover a route to "the happy shores of Cathay" — thus joining the swarm of European sea captains who hoped to discover a Northwest Passage to the fabled lands of China and Japan.

He set out on his mission in energetic high spirits and with an unquestioning belief that God was on his side. Battered by an Atlantic hurricane, he credited his survival to "divine assistance and goodness." In 1524 he struck land in present-day North Carolina. Heading north in search of a good harbor to anchor in, the navigator glanced across a narrow of strip of land toward the open waters of Pamlico Sound; he paused long enough to decide that it was the Pacific Ocean. Then he breezed past Albemarle Sound, Chesapeake Bay, and Delaware Bay before nosing into New York Harbor. Probably the first white man to appear there, Verrazano received a warm greeting from the natives: "The people were dressed in birds' feathers of various colors, and they came toward us joyfully, uttering loud cries of wonderment and showing us the safest place to beach the boat."

Pushing deeper into the harbor in a small boat, he sighted what must have been the mouth of the Hudson River. Then, to his dismay, "a violent, unfavorable wind blew in from the sea," he recalled, "and we were forced to return to the ship, leaving the land with much regret on account of its favorable conditions and beauty." The navigator sailed as far north as Newfoundland before deciding it was time to head back across the Atlantic. On his return, Verrazano wrote a letter that contained the first known description of the North American coast. He also vividly recounted the exotic behavior and appearance of the many native tribes he encountered along the way.

Despite Verrazano's failure to find a Northwest Passage, King Francis was happy to stake a claim in the New World, and to name a sprawling stretch of coastline "New France." Verrazano, bathed in glory, sailed once again for the New World. It was his last voyage. He was slain and eaten by cannibals on the island of Guadeloupe. 🛥

The explorer Verrazano as portrayed in a 19th-century ceramic bust.

A *1539*

Spanish friar and his Moorish slave opened a path to colonization of the American Southwest.

A centuries-old story told of the Seven Cities of Cíbola, where the streets were paved with gold. So in 1539 Fray Marcos de Niza, a Spanish missionary, set out from Mexico in search of Cíbola. His guide was a Moorish slave named Esteban, a veteran of explorations in the region who spoke several Indian languages. Wearing a costume of ribbons, feathers, and bells, the flamboyant Esteban was sent ahead to reconnoiter.

To keep track of Esteban's progress, Marcos asked him to

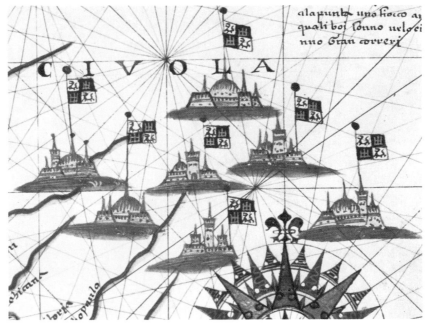

This detail from a 1578 map depicts the fabled Seven Cities of Cíbola.

send back couriers bearing wooden crosses of various sizes to convey the importance of each discovery. The crosses started arriving, each one bigger than the last, along with news of a "province of Ceuola . . . with seven great cities."

Marcos set out, tracing Esteban's northern route into what is now New Mexico. Along the way, he was met with terrible news: not only had Zuni Indians killed Esteban, but the cities of gold were only dusty adobe pueblos. Even so, the expedition was not a total failure, for it marked the beginning of the Spanish colonization of the American Southwest. ⚓

H *1539*

Hernando de Soto, in search of treasure, crossed nearly half a continent with the aid of 600 soldiers and a herd of pigs.

It was the largest land expedition yet into the untracked wilderness of North America. Explorer Hernando de Soto, veteran of conquests in Nicaragua and Peru, spent nearly a year getting ready. At his base in Cuba, he assembled a force of 600 soldiers, 213 horses, boat builders, bridge builders, and — as a hedge against starvation — 13 hardy Spanish pigs. His destination: La Florida. His goal: conquest, glory, and gold.

De Soto and his men landed near the mouth of Tampa Bay in May 1539. An advance party sent to hunt for gold came back with a discouraging report: no treasure, just "low, very wet, pondy," land "thickly covered with trees." Meanwhile, provisions began to run low, and the pig population was still too small for the expedition to start dining on pork. The hungry Spaniards survived on wild cabbage palm, watercress, and corn stolen from the local Indians.

For three years De Soto kept his huge caravan on the move, covering territory from Florida

Spanish troops led by Hernando de Soto march into a settlement of rightfully suspicious Mississippi Indians.

to North Carolina and as far west as Arkansas. Then on May 21, 1542, stalled at the swamps along the Mississippi River, De Soto died of fever. Having searched 35,000 square miles of territory, he had gained no treasure at all. He had lost half his men to disease and Indian attacks, although not to starvation — the herd of pigs had grown to more than 700.

After De Soto's death his lieutenant, Luis de Moscoso, pushed into Texas and Oklahoma. The expedition floated down the Mississippi on makeshift rafts, then made its way along the Gulf to the safety of Spanish Mexico. ⚓

17

A 1550
European fashion for sumptuous furs and tall, shiny hats helped spur colonization in North America.

It all began, by most accounts, when Jacques Cartier sailed back to France in 1536 with a load of prime American furs. The St. Lawrence River Indians were so eager to trade, the mariner reported, that they offered him the cloaks off their backs — leaving themselves "naked without anything on them." In return, Cartier handed out copper pots, steel knives, and other useful items.

By the mid 1550's a number of explorers and fishermen were making a tidy profit in the North American fur trade — which would soon become a source of almost unimaginable wealth. The French, Spanish, Dutch, English, even the Russians, all vied for a share of the profits. In the process, they helped set the pattern of New

World exploration and settlement for generations to come.

At first the traders sought ermine, lynx, otter, and similar luxury pelts used to trim the sumptuous robes of Europe's upper classes. Then attention shifted to a more humble creature — the beaver. A fashion arose for tall hats made from animal felt; and the all-around best substance for felt making, it turned out, was the soft, silky innermost hair of a beaver pelt.

Competition for beaver pelts sent backwoods adventurers trekking westward across the continent. French traders called *coureurs de bois* (runners of the forest) paddled out from Montreal into the Great Lakes and beyond. The English established trading posts along Hudson Bay and hired entire

Hardworking beavers, shown in a 1715 sketch, build a dam near Niagara Falls.

Indian tribes to do their hunting. In 1760 alone, the Hudson's Bay Company exported enough skins to make half a million beaver hats. Eventually the fur trade

declined as overtrapping depleted the beaver supply. Then in the early 1800's, men of fashion turned to a new style of headgear — the silk top hat. 🦫

S 1565
t. Augustine was the first permanent European settlement in North America.

Philip II of Spain received some disturbing news: French Huguenots, trying to escape religious persecution, had sailed to Florida and built a fort there. The mere existence of a French fort threatened the Spanish claim to the Florida coast, which had been staked by Juan Ponce de León 50 years earlier. To protect his interests in the New World, King Phillip dispatched Admiral Pedro Menéndez de Avilés, a man well seasoned in the art of combat.

With a fleet of five ships, Menéndez landed on Florida's eastern shore, just south of Fort Caroline, on September 8, 1565. Kneeling, the admiral kissed a cross, then named the sandy cape for St. Augustine. (He had first seen the land from his boat 11 days earlier on the feast day of that saint.)

In one of the earliest known views of St. Augustine, Francis Drake sails past the Florida coast in 1586. The city is in the upper left corner.

Wasting no more time, he unloaded his 600 troops and built a fort. He then ordered his two galleons, *San Pelayo* and *San Salvador*, back to Hispaniola.

France, meanwhile, had dispatched its own fleet under the command of Admiral Jean Ribaut. Ribaut arrived just in time to sight Menéndez's galleons, and he went in hot pursuit. At that very moment a hurricane blew in, scattering his ships, and the galleons escaped. On land, Menéndez marched his troops through the storm to the French base, Fort Caroline, and took its defenders by surprise. Later, he murdered the survivors of the storm-tossed French fleet, who had sought refuge on the beaches. This bloody episode ended France's hopes of colonizing Florida's coast, and the outpost of St. Augustine remained the first permanent European settlement in North America. 🦫

1590

With better weather and better luck, the Lost Colony of Roanoke might have been found.

According to the reports of a recent British expedition, the island of Roanoke was one of "the most plentifull, sweete, fruitfull and wholesome of all the world." Queen Elizabeth I was delighted to hear it. Her favorite courtier, Walter Raleigh, had been responsible for sending the expedition. Elizabeth promptly knighted him and gave him a charter to settle the new land.

Soldier, historian, and poet, Raleigh was a man of many talents who hoped to turn a profit from the New World's anticipated riches — rare oils, wine, silk, and citrus fruits. In 1585 he began the first of several attempts to settle Roanoke Island, located off the coast of present-day North Carolina. The first group of settlers returned to England after a year; the second group was killed by Indians.

Undaunted by this slow start, Raleigh sent off a third party of settlers. Led by John White, their appointed governor, 117 men, women, and children arrived in the New World with instructions to bypass Roanoke and settle at Chesapeake Bay. The captain of their ship, intent on privateering, refused to take them that far. Instead, he dropped them — at Roanoke.

Provisions at the new settlement quickly dwindled, and White was forced to return to England for more supplies. He thought the separation from his family would last just a few months, but he was detained in England for three years. After many reversals, he finally sailed back in 1590, bringing the needed supplies.

Upon his arrival, White was shocked to find the island deserted.

The only clues to the whereabouts of the settlers were the word *Croatoan* carved on a post in the stockade, and the letters *CRO* scratched into a tree trunk. This led him to hope that he might find the colonists on Croatoan Island, 20 miles to the south. White had a deeply personal reason for locating them: both his daughter and his granddaughter (Virginia Dare, the first English child to be born on the North American continent) were among the missing.

After scouring Roanoke, White and his search party headed south. Threatening weather prevented them from landing at Croatoan. In addition, the captain of the rescue vessel wanted to plunder Spanish treasure ships in the West Indies. White traveled with him to the islands, planning to spend the winter and return to Croatoan in the spring of 1591. But when White was finally able to set out, a violent storm blew the ship far off course, and he ended up in England instead.

As the years passed, White comforted himself with the thought that the colonists might be living under the protection of Manteo, a Christian tribal chief who had visited England and been given a title, Lord of Roanoke. Or perhaps the colonists had set out by small boat and had been lost at sea. Persistent tales of white men living in the wilderness led the English settlers at Jamestown to send out search parties in 1608 and 1609, more than 20 years after White's last contact with the Lost Colony. No survivors were ever found. 🛶

An Indian woman from Roanoke carries a basket and a grain pouch in this 1587 drawing by John White, an early settler.

1607

The first permanent English settlement in the New World turned out to be a breeding ground for life-threatening disease.

When the colony of Jamestown was established in May of 1607, the sponsors of the settlement, the Virginia Company of London, had instructed the colonists to do two things: search for gold and find a passage to the Orient. Instead, they found hardship, starvation, and disease.

The colonists built Jamestown at the mouth of a river they believed was a part of the long-sought passage. Not a wise choice: the site was low and marshy, and it lacked fresh water. Of the 104 original settlers, more than a third died in the first year of dysentery, typhoid, and other scourges. Similarly, attempts to grow grain were futile, touching off a period called "the starving time" — an episode so bleak that some colonists may have turned to cannibalism. 🛶

1607

Despite the romantic tales, Indian princess Pocahontas may not have saved **English settler John Smith from death.**

Capt. John Smith, whose leadership helped the Jamestown colony survive, probably met Pocahontas in 1607, when she was about 12 years old. A favorite daughter of the powerful Chief Powhatan, Pocahontas supposedly saved Smith's life. He had been taken captive and, according to his own account, "as many as could layd hands on him, dragged him to them. . . and being ready with their clubs, to beate out his brains, Pocahontas the Kings

Pocahontas wore European clothes for a 1616 portrait in England.

dearest daughter . . . got his head in her armes, and laid her owne upon his to save him from death."

Some 250 years later the story began to raise doubts among historians. Noting Smith's reputation as an adventurer with a vivid imagination, some argued that the episode never took place. It may instead have been Smith's retelling of a Spanish soldier's brush with death in 1528, when a Florida Indian chief's daughter saved the soldier from being roasted alive. Or perhaps Smith's near-execution was an initiation ceremony into the tribe.

In 1613 Pocahontas caught the eye of colonist John Rolfe. After struggling to reconcile himself with loving "one whose education hath bin rude, her manners barbarous," he married her. In 1616 Pocahontas, Rolfe, and their infant son traveled to England. There she quickly became the toast of London society. ⚓

1608

Under orders from King James I of England, Capt. John Smith and Capt. Christopher Newport crowned Chief Powhatan, leader of more than 30 tribes, emperor.

In 1608, a year after the English had settled Jamestown, the Virginia Company of London, which had the charter for Jamestown, urged King James I to bestow the title of emperor on Chief Powhatan. Making this influential chief a subject of the British Crown was a practical move. It would place the leader of some 30 Tidewater Virginia tribes under the king's power, and it would guarantee that the Indians would sell the settlers corn during the winter; otherwise, the struggling colony might not survive.

At first Powhatan refused the offer. Then he agreed to the coronation with one stipulation — it must be held in his territory. "If your King have sent me presents, I also am a King, and this is my land." Capt. Christopher Newport, a representative of the Virginia Company, and Capt. John Smith, Jamestown's leader, conducted the ceremony. When it came time to kneel in recognition of the sovereignty of King James I, Powhatan refused. After failing to persuade him, the king's emissaries pushed hard on Powhatan's shoulders to get him to stoop slightly. Then they quickly placed a copper crown on his head.

The coronation did little to foster good feelings between Indians and settlers. Powhatan refused to sell Smith all the corn he needed, and relations between the two groups remained uneasy until 1614, when Pocahontas, Powhatan's daughter, married colonist John Rolfe. ⚓

1609

Henry Hudson, an English mariner employed by a powerful Dutch trading company, was the first European to sail up the river that now bears his name.

Already seasoned by voyages into icy Arctic waters, English explorer Henry Hudson put to sea again in the spring of 1609. Sailing in the service of the Dutch East India Company, he departed from Amsterdam and headed west. His mission: to find a new passage to Asia. His small two-masted ship, the *Half Moon,* carried fewer than 20 men. Arriving in the New World, he cruised up and down the Atlantic seaboard, entering both the Delaware and Chesapeake bays — thus paving the way for later Dutch claims along the coastline.

On the morning of September 3, 1609, Hudson's ship nosed into New York Harbor. The Indians lining the shore gazed in wonder at what seemed to be an enormous house moving across the water. As it came closer, they saw what they thought were great white wings and speculated that the vessel must be bearing the Great Spirit. Hudson, decked out in a red coat with sparkling gold braid, paddled to shore in a small canoe with a few of his men. Accord-

Indians in Brooklyn give Henry Hudson a friendly greeting in this highly romanticized 19th-century rendition of the navigator's visit to New York Harbor.

"That smokie weed of Tobacco" actually saved the lives of the Jamestown settlers.

Those settlers who arrived in Virginia's Jamestown colony — a diverse group that included gentlemen adventurers and convicts

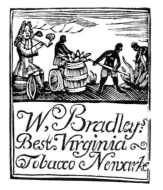

A tobacco label for the Best Virginia brand, which was popular in England.

— were ill equipped for all the hardships they faced. When they weren't fighting off Indian attacks or coping with starvation, disease, and other disasters, they were trying to eke out a living. A reliable cash crop would make the colony self-sustaining, but the harvests were too meager to provide enough food to sell abroad.

Providence came in the broad leaves of the tobacco plant. Colonist John Rolfe crossed seeds from the sweet tobacco plants of the West Indies *(Nicotiana tabacum)* with those of the hardier but bitter-tasting local plants *(Nicotiana rustica)*. The result was a milder tobacco that gave

Jamestown a product to trade in exchange for goods. In 1614, two years after development of the hybrid, Jamestown exported its first tobacco, shipping a few hundred pounds. By 1620, 40,000 pounds were sent to England, and in 10 years, 1.5 million pounds were exported annually. Tobacco growing became so profitable that virtually every square foot of available space in Jamestown was planted with the crop.

Before long, tobacco was used as legal tender. Maryland, soon after its founding in 1634, began paying debts with tobacco. Virginia followed suit. North Carolina used tobacco as money until the early 1700's.

The Puritans considered tobacco a dangerous narcotic, and King James I (for whom Jamestown was named) roundly condemned "that smokie weed of Tobacco." Courtier Sir Walter Raleigh, on the other hand, was an early devotee.

On a visit to the colony, Raleigh filled a clay Indian pipe and lit up. His servant, fearing that Raleigh was on fire, doused him with a bucket of water. Raleigh dried off, enlightened his servant, and happily continued to puff away. Back in England, he eventually fell from royal favor and in 1618 was condemned for treason. True to form, he had one final smoke on the way to the scaffold.

---

ing to tradition, he first stepped ashore in Brooklyn, at what is now Coney Island.

After mostly friendly encounters with the Indians, including profitable trading in beaver and otter skins, Hudson sailed north on the river that would eventually bear his name. He glided past the town of Peekskill and the future site of West Point. Fearing that the Indians he met near Albany might cause trouble, Hudson invited several chieftains to his cabin. He plied them with so much wine that, according to the ship's log, "they were all merrie" — an event that ushered in years of friendly cooperation and trading partnerships between the Dutch and the Indians. The *Half Moon* cruised along the Hudson River until October 4, when it again set sail for Europe.

On his first voyage to the New World, Hudson just managed to hold his disgruntled crew at bay; the next time he was not so lucky. In 1610 he set out once more for North America. In June 1611, after spending six months with the ship locked in ice, the mutinous, half-starved crew set Hudson, his son, and seven others adrift in a small boat. No trace was ever found of any of them.

IN THEIR OWN WORDS

The land is not populous, for the [Indian] men be fewe; their far greater number is of women and children. Within 60 miles of James Towne there are about some 5000 people, but of able men fit for their warres scarse 1500. . . . The people differ very much in stature, especially in language. . . . Some being very great as the Sesquesahamocks, others very little as the Wighcocomocoes: but generally tall and straight, of a comely proportion, and of a colour browne, when they are of any age, but they are borne white. Their haire is generally black; but few have any beards. The men weare halfe their heads shaven, the other halfe long. . . . They are inconstant in everie thing, but what feare constraineth them to keepe. Craftie, timerous, quicke of apprehension and very ingenuous. Some are of disposition fearefull, some bold, most cautelous, all Savage. Generally covetous of copper, beads, and such like trash. They are soone moved to anger, and so malitious, that they seldome forget an injury: they seldome steale one from another, least their conjurers should reveale it, and so they be pursued and punished. That they are thus feared is certaine, but that any can reveale their offences by conjuration I am doubtfull. Their women are care-full not to bee suspected of dishonesty without the leave of their husbands.

Capt. John Smith's account of Indians living around Jamestown, Virginia, from his book A Map of Virginia, *1612.*

1614
John Smith, who saved Jamestown from disaster, was a first-rate mapmaker who explored the northern coastline and gave New England its name.

Capt. John Smith is deservedly famous for providing the leadership that the fledgling Jamestown, Virginia, colony desperately needed. But after spending only two years there he returned to England. Then, in 1614, he crossed the Atlantic again to lead another expedition, exploring the coast from Maine to Massachusetts Bay under the auspices of a group of London merchants.

While Smith failed to find the gold and copper mines he sought, he did succeed in locating abundant fishing sites. The explorer also sent glowing — though exaggerated — accounts of the region's fertile soil and unlimited timber resources. It was Smith who named the region New England. His book entitled

Captain Smith drew a map that the Pilgrims used to navigate the New England coast.

A Description of New England, which was published in 1616, contained an accurate map of the coastal area. He became obsessed with establishing a colony there and pursued every opportunity to attract capital for new expeditions. But he never received the necessary backing.

Hearing that the Pilgrims planned to settle in the New World, Smith offered to serve as their guide and advisor. But the Pilgrims turned him down, explaining that it would be cheaper to read his books and study his map. A resentful Smith commented later on hearing of their hardships: "Their humorous ignorances caused them for more than a year to endure a wonderful deal of misery with infinite patience . . . , thinking to find things better than I advised them."

IN THEIR OWN WORDS

"Our corne did prouve well and God be praysed we had a good increase of Indian corne, and our Barly indifferent good, but our Pease not worth the gathering. . . . Our harvest being gotten in, our Governor sent foure men on fowling that so we might after a more speciall manner rejoice together, after we had gathered the fruit of our labours; they foure in one day killed as much fowle, as with little helpe beside served the Company almost a weeke, at which time amongst other Recreations, we exercised our Armes, many of the Indians coming amongst us, and among the rest their greatest King Massasoit, with some ninetie men whom for three days we entertained and feasted and they went out and killed five Deere, which they brought to the Plantation and bestowed on our Governour, and upon the Captain Miles [Standish] and others. And although it be not always so plentifull, as it was at this time with us, yet be the goodnesse of God, we are so farre from want that we often wish you partakers of our plentie."

Edward Winslow, one of the founders of the Plymouth Colony, describes the first Thanksgiving.

1619
One hundred and twenty pounds of leaf tobacco, which was legal tender in colonial Virginia, bought a wife for a lonely bachelor.

The great majority of early colonists in North America were unmarried men. Whenever the bachelors sent lists to England of badly needed supplies, the most frequently requested items were wives. Since no true gentlewoman could be expected to give up her comfortable English life for the hardships of North America, the colonists had to widen their search. One strategy (among many) was to offer freedom to convicted female felons who agreed to migrate.

In 1619 the Virginia Company launched a recruitment program for young women and the following year approximately 100 prospective wives, accompanied by chaperones, stepped ashore in Jamestown. Each colonist who succeeded in finding a bride had to reimburse the company for travel costs, which amounted to 120 pounds of tobacco leaves. Apparently, wife importing never become the booming business that the Virginia Company had anticipated: by 1642 women comprised only 10 percent of the population in the New World.

The balance between the sexes was no better in the French colonies, and in 1721 the government of Louis XV released 25 prostitutes from French prisons and sent them to Louisiana to find husbands. Meanwhile, sponsors in both France and England continued to rack their brains for other sources of brides. As a result, the first group of "casket girls" arrived in Louisiana in 1728. Poor but honest, these young recruits got their nickname from the *cassettes*, or caskets, that the French government provided for them to carry their belongings.

NOVA BRITANNIA.

OFFERING MOST

Excellent fruites by Planting in VIRGINIA.

Exciting all such as be well affected to further the same.

LONDON
Printed for SAMVEL MACHAM, and are to be sold at his Shop in Pauls Church-yard, at the Signe of the Bul-head.
1 6 0 9.

According to this early travel folder, Virginia was a paradise on earth.

1620

The first English colonists to land in New England actually held a charter entitling them to settle in Virginia.

It may have been a navigational error that took the *Mayflower* Pilgrims from England to Massachusetts instead of Virginia, or just a desire to find shelter from winter storms. Reaching Provincetown on Cape Cod on a cold day in November 1620, the travelers were only too happy for this temporary berth. Then they sailed on. On December 21 they dropped anchor at Plymouth, and an advance party stepped ashore. No one seems even to have noticed the fabled Plymouth Rock.

Of the 102 men, women, and children on board the *Mayflower,* only 35 were Pilgrims — or "saints," as they called themselves. The rest were "strangers," mostly Anglican laborers who hoped to improve their economic lot. Since the voyagers found themselves outside the jurisdiction of their original charter, which had been issued to them by the Virginia Company, they had to devise their own government. While still anchored at Provincetown, the Pilgrim leaders had drawn up the Mayflower Compact. Signed by 41 adult males, the agreement established a civil government and provided legal authority for the new colony.

Ten years later another group of religious idealists, the Puritans, settled 30 miles to the north in Massachusetts Bay. Both sects shared a deep aversion to the pomp and ceremony of the Church of England. They also had many differences. The Pilgrims were Separatists who wanted to break away entirely and worship God in their own way. The Puritans intended to bring about a strict, sober-sided reform of Anglican practices. While neither group showed much religious tolerance, the Pilgrims' zealotry never went as far as that of the Puritans, who hanged Quakers and banished dissenters.

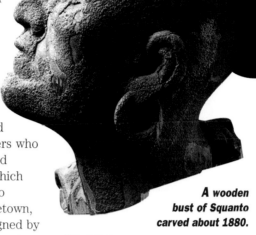

A wooden bust of Squanto carved about 1880.

1621

Two Indians, Samoset and Squanto, helped ensure the Pilgrims' survival.

The first winter had been sheer misery for the colonists in Plymouth, Massachusetts. Short of food, and ill with a flu-like virus they called the "General Sickness," almost half of them had perished. Attack by Indians was a constant worry.

So imagine their astonishment when a tall, good-looking Indian named Samoset sauntered into their camp, asked for beer, then offered his help. Once the colonists recovered their composure, they cautiously accepted his suggestion.

In time, Samoset introduced the Pilgrims to Massasoit, the powerful leader of the Wampanoags, who lived nearby on Narragansett Bay. The Pilgrims treated Massasoit to brandy and biscuits, and also gave him guns and ammunition for his ongoing war with enemy tribes. The result was an alliance between the Pilgrims and the Wampanoags that lasted half a century.

Samoset also introduced the colonists to his friend Squanto, who had lived in England for nine years and spoke fluent English. Squanto taught the colonists how to plant corn, and how to catch herring and eel — skills that proved critical to their survival.

In October 1621 Plymouth's governor, William Bradford, invited Massasoit to a harvest celebration. On that first Thanksgiving, the chief arrived with around 90 Indian retainers. For three days they feasted on venison, wild fowl, lobsters, corn, turnips, wild plums, and gooseberries — but no cranberries or pumpkin pie. Eventually, Bradford wrote *Of Plimoth Plantation,* a detailed account of this event and many others that took place during the colony's early decades.

The first Thanksgiving — pictured here by a 20th-century artist — saw both colonists and Indians celebrating the harvest.

P *1630*

Puritan writer Anne Bradstreet became America's first published poet.

When 18-year-old Anne Bradstreet arrived in New England from Britain in 1630, her heart rebelled against the prospect of life in the wilderness. Yet despite the rigors of the Massachusetts Bay Colony, she somehow found time to write.

Anne Bradstreet looks to her muse in this 1897 engraving.

Bradstreet modeled many of her early works on the Puritan belief that prose and poetry should be instructive, not frivolous. But as time went on, her voice became lyric and emotional, as in these lines to her husband:

"If ever two were one,
then surely we
If ever man were loved
by wife, then thee."

Bradstreet's poems were first published in 1650, and although she never achieved wide popularity, her poetic legacy extended well beyond her own writing. Among her direct blood descendants are authors James Russell Lowell and Oliver Wendell Holmes.

Colonial Law and Order

Although some colonial laws may seem harsh by today's standards, early settlers faced with daily survival had no choice but to make and enforce them. Later, as the colonies began to thrive, blue laws (possibly named for the blue paper on which they were printed) were passed to regulate morals. The following are just a few examples.

1642 Drunkenness in Maryland is subject to a fine of 100 pounds of tobacco.

1650 In Connecticut a father can have his teenager put to death if the boy proves "stubborn and rebellious and will not obey."

1652 In Salem, Massachusetts, laws prohibiting people from dressing beyond their means are in effect; a man is charged with wearing "excess in bootes, ribonds, gould and silver lace."

1658 The citizens of New Amsterdam, under Peter Stuyvesant, organize the first colonial police force.

1671 A Massachusetts citizen is fined for letting his married daughter visit overnight. Several communities prohibit citizens from entertaining "outsiders" unless they receive permission in advance from local authorities.

1675 Massachusetts lawmakers so strongly disapprove of long hair on men that they grant one citizen, John Gatchell, a building permit only if he will "cut...the long hair off his head into a sivil frame."

1699 Virginia's House of Burgesses passes laws making it a crime not to attend services at a house of worship on the Sabbath.

F *1635*

Freedom of religion — later a basic tenet of American democracy — was not something most early settlers could understand, or even tolerate.

A young law clerk and Puritan minister named Roger Williams, hoping to escape the oppressive doctrines of the Church of England, left London to seek refuge with his fellow believers in the Massachusetts Bay Colony. Much to his dismay, he found the local Puritans just as intolerant as the religious authorities back home. Williams thought that spiritual concerns of the church should be kept separate from the practical affairs of the state — a conviction that did not sit well with the Puritan leaders. Even worse, he criticized the common practice of simply taking land from the Indians. Buying and trading, he said, were the only proper ways to acquire land.

Williams found work as a minister in Salem, where his radical ideas soon got him into trouble. He moved on to the Plymouth colony, but he fared no better there. In 1635 the church authorities in Boston brought him to trial on charges of spreading "dyvers newe & dangerous opinions," and sentenced him to exile. Warned by friends of plans to have him shipped back to Eng-

land, he fled into the cold New England winter.

Aided by the Wampanoag Indians, whom he had earlier befriended, Williams survived the winter. Other Indians, the Narragansetts, granted him a parcel of land at the head of Narragansett Bay, in what is now Rhode Island. Here he founded Providence, a settlement dedicated to religious tolerance. It soon became a haven for Baptists, Quakers, Sephardic Jews, and other outcasts.

Williams's dangerous ideas were thus temporarily isolated. Years later they would resurface in one of the most important documents in U.S. history: the Constitution.

Friendly Wampanoag Indians offer food and lodging to Roger Williams, here shown fleeing Massachusetts with his Bible in hand.

H 1636

arvard University, the oldest institution of higher learning in the United States, had very humble beginnings.

Soon after they arrived in Boston, the Puritan founders of the Massachusetts Bay Colony resolved to establish "a schoale or colledge" for the education of future clergymen and scholars. In 1636 they set aside £400 — fully one quarter of the colony's total tax revenues. At the same time they appointed a Board of Overseers.

Two years passed. The new college still had no faculty, no students, no campus, not even a name. Then in 1638 a young Puritan minister, John Harvard, died of tuberculosis leaving the overseers 400 books and half his estate. That same year, Harvard College opened for business in a single frame farmhouse in a cow pasture near the town of Cambridge.

The first class consisted of 12 boys, most in their early teens. Their one teacher, the miserly Nathaniel Eaton, fed them a diet of corn gruel and cheap fish. Eaton was also

Harvard College by 1726 was a thriving institution in a red brick setting.

prone to fits of rage. After he attacked his assistant with a stout club, he was promptly fired, and Harvard shut down for a year.

Eventually the college grew and prospered. Students studied Latin, Greek, Hebrew, logic, mathematics, and astronomy. Seniors enrolled in additional courses in metaphysics and divinity. In keeping with the Puritan spirit, pupils were encouraged to read the Bible twice daily and warned not to "inter-meddle on other men's affairs." Nor were they to smoke tobacco without the permission of a physician or the college president. Despite these strictures, students found time for less serious pursuits. At one point so many Harvard men frequented a tavern kept by mistress Vashti Bradish that college authorities made her agree to sell no more than a penny's worth of beer to any student.

Harvard's standing as the only college in the English-speaking colonies lasted until 1693, when the College of William and Mary was established, followed by Yale in 1701. 🛥

C 1637

olonist Anne Hutchinson repeatedly criticized the Puritan establishment, causing her persecution and eventual banishment.

While still living in England, Anne Hutchinson was an avid disciple of Puritan minister John Cotton; she thought nothing of riding 30 miles on horseback to hear him preach. So when Cotton moved to the Massachusetts Bay Colony in 1632, it was no surprise that she and husband, William, soon followed. Shortly after her arrival, she began holding weekly prayer meetings in her living room. Her strong personality and piercing intellect drew people from miles around.

As a self-appointed woman preacher, Hutchinson drew the wrath of the Puritan establishment — particularly when she began criticizing some of the local clergy. She claimed she experienced direct revelations from God, and said that anyone else could, too, without help from the church. "The Holy Spirit illuminates the heart of every true believer," she maintained.

To the Puritan ministry of Massachusetts these words were pure heresy, and Gov. John Winthrop was determined to silence her. On November 3, 1637, she was brought before the General Court in Boston. Denied an attorney, she argued in her own defense. The court, shocked by this show of independence, admonished her for acting a part more suited to "a husband than a wife."

Hutchinson was found guilty and held in jail several months, then banished with her family to Aquidneck Island (now Rhode Island). When her husband died four years later, she moved south to land held by the Dutch. In 1643 she was killed by Indians near what is now New York City. John Winthrop ascribed her death to "divine judgement," but today her statue stands in front of the Massachusetts statehouse as a "monument to religious toleration." 🛥

IN THEIR OWN WORDS

❝ No scholar shall go out of his chamber without coat, gown, or cloak, and everyone everywhere shall wear modest and sober habit without strange ruffian like or newfangled fashions, without all lavish dress or excess apparel whatsoever. Nor shall any wear gold or silver or such ornaments, except to whom upon just ground the President shall permit the same; neither shall it be lawful for any to wear long hair, locks, or foretops, nor to use curling, crisping, parting, or powdering their hair. ❞

—*The dress code from the Harvard College Laws, 1655.*

1638
The log cabin, a symbol of the American pioneering spirit, originated in the forests of Scandinavia.

In early spring of 1638, a ship carrying the first Swedish immigrants to America dropped anchor at the head of Delaware Bay. Their settlement, Fort Christina, was soon swallowed up by a force of Dutch troops from New Amsterdam. But the Swedes left one enduring feature on the American landscape: the log cabin.

Using a technique developed in their own northern forests, the Swedes fitted together carefully notched logs, often without iron nails and other hardware. Chinked with clay or moss and topped with durable hardwood roofs, the resulting cabins were well suited to the region's hard winters and wet springs. One traveler, comparing various styles of New World housing, noted that the standard

For more than two centuries, sturdy cabins of hand-hewn logs provided shelter in the North American wilderness.

clapboard dwelling was so wretchedly built "that if you are not so close to the fire as almost to burn yourself, you cannot keep warm." Swedish houses, he said, were "very tight and warm."

Plentiful lumber and ease of construction made log cabins ideal for settlers as they moved westward. Proliferating across the land throughout the 18th and 19th centuries, the log cabin became a favorite national symbol of the pioneer spirit, and politicians who were associated with it — both Andrew Jackson and Abraham Lincoln were born in one — benefitted greatly from the connection. The political popularity of claiming log cabin origins persisted well into the 20th century. When Oklahoma senator Robert Kerr was campaigning for the Democratic presidential nomination in 1952, he proudly noted that he had been born in a log cabin. ⛵

1643
New York City's tradition as a multiethnic society dates back to its earliest days as the Dutch colony of New Amsterdam.

The charter to the Dutch West Indies Company was clear: people of all nationalities and religions were welcome to settle in New Amsterdam. The company patrons hoped in this way to attract enough people to make the Dutch enclave — really no more than a backwater town of several hundred citizens — a commercial center.

The strategy seemed to work. By 1643, according to French missionary Father Isaac Jogues, some 18 languages including English, Dutch, German, Turkish, Spanish, Italian, French, and various African tongues could be heard in the streets and dockyards of New Amsterdam. The island had become a multicultural haven.

Not surprisingly, New Amsterdam also became known for religious tolerance. The hubbub of alien customs and beliefs dis-

Viewed from the water, New Amsterdam was a cluster of wooden houses dominated by a church with a double-peaked roof and a windmill for grinding corn. This hand-colored engraving was made around 1655.

mayed some members of the Dutch Reformed church, to be sure. "We have here Papists, Mennonites and Lutherans . . . and many atheists and various other servants of Bäal," griped one disgruntled Dutch pastor. "Treat them quietly and leniently" or "shut your eyes" was the prompt response of the Lords Directors of the West Indies Company.

The Dutch colony expanded up the Hudson Valley and down into New Jersey and Delaware. It lasted less than 40 years. In 1664 Britain's king Charles II gave a large tract of land that included all of the New Netherlands (as the colony was called) to his brother, the duke of York.

A small English fleet sailed into New Amsterdam's harbor. When the local citizens heard

the generous surrender terms that the British were offering — the Dutch would be able to keep their property and worship freely — they gave up without a fight. By this time, New Amsterdam (renamed New York) was a bustling port city. It had a new monarch and a new name, but its reputation for tolerance would continue to attract people from all over the globe. ⛵

S *1646*
calping, a battle tradition among some Indian tribes, was practiced by colonists as well.

The goal was not slaughter, but to show that an enemy had been conquered. A Dutch writer in 1646 described how an Indian warrior would stun his victim with a blow to the head, then slice out a patch of skin with the hair attached. This gruesome trophy was then dried, decorated, and worn as a badge of honor. Sometimes the victim survived — like one Swedish woman who lost her scalp "yet lived many years thereafter, and became the mother of several children."

Yet the taking of scalps was always a murderous business. To many Native Americans the hair was the home of the soul, and a person robbed of his scalp was officially dead.

As conflicts erupted between Indians and settlers, colonial governments began offering cash bounties for enemy scalps. Massachusetts settler Hannah Dustin, captured in 1697 by Abenaki Indians, saw her baby's brains dashed out on a rock. Stealing a hatchet, she and two other captives killed 10 sleeping Abenakis, scalped them, and escaped. Presenting the scalps to the colonial authorities, Hannah and her friends received an award of 50 pounds.

At first, scalping was largely confined to tribes in the Northeast. But as settlers moved inland the practice spread. Soon both Indians and whites in the Southeast, the Great Plains, and beyond the Rockies were hunting for the morbid prizes. 🚢

The First African-Americans

In 1619 some 20 Africans, indentured as servants, arrived in Jamestown. The colonists soon realized how profitable the "traffic of menbody" could be, and as a result, until the Emancipation Proclamation in 1863, blacks were considered human chattels in many states. This did not mean, however, that the first African-Americans willingly accepted their status, as seen below.

1526 The first slaves rebel against their Spanish masters in what is now South Carolina; they escape to live with Indians in the surrounding area.

1539 A Moorish slave named Esteban leads an expedition to locate the mythical Seven Cities of Cíbola and discovers a Zuni pueblo in what is now New Mexico. The Zuni Indians, mistrusting Esteban, put him to death.

1651 Anthony Johnson, a free black who was one of the first settlers, receives a grant of 250 acres of land in Northampton County, Virginia.

1708 and 1739 Slave revolts resulting in the deaths of both blacks and whites erupt in New York and South Carolina. Despite the disastrous consequences, some slaves gain their freedom.

1746 Lucy Terry, a slave, becomes the first acknowledged black poet with her ballad "Bars Fight" about an Indian massacre. The poem is not published until 1893.

1750 Crispus Attucks escapes from slavery. In 1770 he is the first of five casualties resulting from the Boston Massacre.

1762 Samuel Fraunces, a West Indian black, establishes the Queen's Head Tavern in New York City. (It was later renamed Fraunces Tavern, which it is still called today.) The tavern becomes a stop for George Washington, who in 1783 will bid his soldiers farewell there.

An Iroquois warrior, painted and armed for battle, takes a victim's scalp.

T *1646*
he slave trade began not in the South, but in New England with the sailing of the ship *Desire*.

As the young colonies grew, the need for labor grew with them. To remedy the situation, settlers employed either Indians or indentured servants — immigrants bound by contract to work for a specific period in exchange for room, board, and passage from Europe. Then in 1641 New Englanders found a cheaper source of labor: African slaves. That year Massachusetts became the first colony to legalize slavery.

In 1646 the ship *Desire* took Pequot Indian slaves from Salem, Massachusetts, to the West Indies to trade for tobacco, cotton, and Africans. Several years after this voyage, New England shipowners began the astoundingly lucrative "triangular trade." En route from Africa, their ships would stop in the West Indies to trade slaves for sugar and molasses. They would proceed to New England, where the sugar and molasses were made into rum. The rum would then be taken to Africa, and the entire process would begin again.

Most New England ports took part in the trade, which became the source of many Yankee family fortunes. The South, too, reaped enormous profits from the slave trade. Labor-intensive crops such as rice and tobacco increased the demand for cheap labor, and falling prices made slaves affordable. By the late 1600's slavery was legal in all British colonies. To control slaves, strict codes were written denying them basic rights: blacks were forbidden to marry, to travel, to bear arms, to own property. By the early 19th century, both New England and the Middle Atlantic states abolished slavery, but in the South it remained the foundation stone of the regional economy. 🚢

He began the Sabbath at evening ... then performed family duty after supper, being longer than ordinary in exposition. After which he catechized his children and servants, and then returned to his study. The morning following, family worship being ended, he retired into his study until the bell called him away. Upon his return from meeting (where he had preached and prayed some hours), he returned again into his study (the place of his labor and prayer), unto his favorite devotion; where having a small repast carried up for his dinner, he continued until the tolling of the bell. The public service of the afternoon being over, he withdrew for a space to his pre-mentioned oratory for his sacred addresses to God, as in the forenoon, then came down, repeated the sermon in the family, prayed, after supper sang a Psalm, and toward bedtime betaking himself again to his study he closed the day with prayer. Thus he spent the Sabbath continually.

An account of how the Reverend John Cotton, a widely respected Puritan clergyman in 1650, spent his Sundays, written by a fellow minister.

1647
Margaret Brent was the first woman lawyer in colonial America.

Margaret Brent left Gloucester, England, for the colony of Maryland well prepared. The colony's proprietor, Cecilius Calvert (Lord Baltimore), had granted her more than 70 acres of land to settle. Brent quickly added to her landholdings and became well known for her business acumen. Soon she was lending money to new settlers; when some failed to repay her, she took them to court.

It was in court, collecting debts, that Brent discovered her flair for the law. In May 1647 an ailing Gov. Leonard Calvert, brother of Lord Baltimore, summoned Brent to his deathbed and in front of startled witnesses named her executor of his estate. His dying words were "take all, pay all."

She soon needed to use this authority. Calvert owed a large debt to soldiers he had hired to put down a two-year Protestant rebellion against Maryland's Catholic government. He had promised to pay the men from Calvert family estates, but as yet they had seen no money. A food shortage compounded the soldiers' misery, and a revolt seemed imminent. With Lord Baltimore out of the country, it was left to Brent to calm them.

Playing for time, she brought in an emergency shipment of corn from Virginia. Her next step was to raise more money. As executor of Calvert's will, she obtained power of attorney over Lord Baltimore's holdings; by selling some of Baltimore's cattle she was able to settle the debt, thus averting a mutiny.

Maryland's political leaders were astonished and grateful at the skillful way she kept the peace. But they were perhaps even more surprised when in

1647
Although he sometimes behaved like an inflexible tyrant, Peter Stuyvesant brought needed improvements to the struggling colony of New Netherland.

When Peter Stuyvesant arrived in New Amsterdam in 1647, the town's inhabitants stood along the shore eyeing him warily. They had good reason. Three director generals had already come and gone, each having embezzled money from the public treasury. The city was full of smugglers and black-market traders. Open privies fouled the public roads. Drinking and street brawling were practically an art form.

Stuyvesant, the son of a stern Dutch Reformed minister, wasted no time in bringing order to the city. He paved streets, made sure taverns had licenses, removed the outhouses from the roads, set up fire patrols, and founded new towns like Brooklyn (which today exists as a borough) and Flushing (now a section of the borough of Queens). In 1665 he opened trade relations with New England, and he sent an army to invade a rival Swedish trading settlement in Delaware. Two years later he set up a "burgher rights" system: eligible citizens could buy the right to trade and hold office, something denied them before.

Unfortunately, Stuyvesant's reforms carried a heavy price tag. The new director general levied stiff taxes, razed private property in order to rebuild, and laid steep penalties on anyone who disobeyed his orders. Some of his laws passed the bounds of strict common sense: a burgher could be fined if his house caught fire. When opposed, Stuyvesant often exploded into a rage, letting loose a stream of obscenities and threats that silenced even the most hardened citizens.

Stuyvesant's iron-fisted rule lasted until 1664, when the British fleet appeared in the harbor. The colony's defenses

Known derisively as Old Silver Leg, Peter Stuyvesant used a studded peg to replace a limb he had lost in battle.

January 1648, Brent made a trip to the town hall in St. Mary's City and stood up to ask for two votes in the legislature — one as a landowner and the other as Lord Baltimore's attorney. She was denied both, but the Assembly did show its gratitude by writing to Lord Baltimore: "the colony's safety at that time [was better] in her hands than in any man's [and she] deserved favor and thanks from your honour."

In 1650 Margaret Brent left Maryland and settled on a Virginia plantation that she called "Peace."

were meager at best: a primitive fort, 150 trained soldiers, and only 600 pounds of usable gunpowder. But Stuyvesant, then age 72, was determined to put up a fight. He stationed his men about the city, then hurried to the fort, climbing into the parapet to oversee the action. As two small British ships glided past, Stuyvesant raised his hand, preparing to give the signal to fire.

Wiser heads prevailed. The town's private citizens were never eager for battle, and Stuyvesant was taken gingerly by the arm and led away. The city surrendered, and Dutch rule in North America ended without a shot being fired.

Stuyvesant retired to the quiet of his *bouwerie,* or farm, outside the city. He died at age 80 and was buried in a chapel on his estate. The site is marked by another church, St. Mark's-in-the-Bouwerie, which stands to this day in New York City's Lower East Side.

A 1652
American colonists had to barter for most goods and services; then they minted their first coin — the Pine Tree shilling.

Viewing America as a source of almost limitless wealth, the British kept a close eye on the movement of currency through the colonial economy. Colonists were allowed to sell their harvests — furs, fish, and agricultural produce — only to Britain. In return, they were paid with British goods instead of cash. England wanted none of its gold or silver slipping into the coffers of French or Spanish settlers.

Foreign currency, on the other hand, did filter into British territory. French crowns, Spanish pieces-of-eight, Dutch ducats, and Portuguese *moidore* were all used by British colonists. Still, most business was done through barter, or the use of cash substitutes. Tobacco was probably the most widely accepted item, but corn, butter, beaver skins, and musket balls were all legal tender at one time or another.

By the mid-17th century North America was the world's richest source of both codfish and fur-bearing animal pelts.

Massachusetts was the first to buck the system, and in 1652 it minted the Pine Tree shilling. When Britain banned the shilling, Massachusetts substituted paper bills of credit; other colonies followed suit. The paper money remained legal tender for nearly 75 years. Then the British eliminated it as well, and the ensuing economic problems inflamed a growing colonial discontent with British rule.

W 1653
Wall Street, now the hub of American finance, began as a flimsy wooden palisade built by the citizens of New Amsterdam.

The Dutch settlers in the tiny island town of New Amsterdam lived in constant fear of attack. An economic cold war raged with England, and the fiercely ambitious New Englanders seemed poised to invade from the north. So the Dutch decided to improve their fortifications.

When bids came in from private contractors, they all seemed extravagantly high. So Gov. Peter Stuyvesant simply issued a decree: "Citizens without exception," he declared, must begin "digging a ditch from the East River to the North River [now the

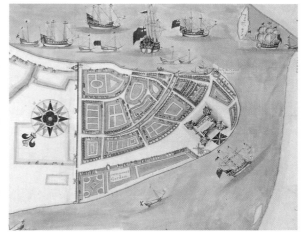

A 1664 town plan of Manhattan shows city blocks with interior yards, and a fortified wall along one side.

Hudson]." In addition, there would be a 12-foot-high wall made of sharpened wooden stakes. When the burghers of New Amsterdam complained at being made to perform forced labor, Stuyvesant responded by forbidding anyone to leave town until the work was done.

Once built, the fortification never served its intended purpose. For a decade, scavengers used it as an easy source of firewood and construction material. When the British laid claim to New Amsterdam in 1664, the city surrendered without a fight.

The wall stood until the 1690's, when the British authorities tore down the remaining timbers. The ditch was opened to traffic and called, predictably, Wall Street.

1662

One of the first bestsellers in the New World was Michael Wigglesworth's grim epic poem entitled *The Day of Doom.*

Fervently religious, and acutely aware of his own failings, the Reverend Michael Wigglesworth did not intend his grim Puritan verses to be read for pleasure. Rather, he envisioned his book-length *The Day of Doom; or, a Poetical Description of the Great and Last Judgment* (published in 1662) as an instructive text on the awesome power of God Almighty. It all but groaned aloud with vivid descriptions of the dire punishments that awaited all sinners.

To make sure readers got the point, Wigglesworth wrote *The Day of Doom* in a popular meter often used for contemporary ballads. Although the poem's cadence was familiar, its message was frightening: everyone would suffer — though God would grant children "the easiest room" in hell because of their tender years. Such harsh predictions did not stop people from buying the poem. *The Day of Doom* sold out its first edition of 1,800 copies in a year and went through at least 10 editions before 1760.

1673

The first known white men to explore the upper Mississippi River were actually searching for the Pacific Ocean. Instead they found giant catfish, trembling prairies, and a "man-destroying bird."

The ice had just melted on Lake Michigan when a trader, a priest, and five companions set out from Mackinac Island in birchbark canoes. The government of New France intended to lay claim to all of western North America, and in early 1673 this small band of explorers was being sent to look around. With luck, they might find a navigable route to the Pacific.

It is hard to imagine two more qualified leaders: Louis Jolliet, a fur trader greatly experienced in the ways of the wilderness, and Père (Father) Jacques Marquette, a Jesuit missionary who spoke six Indian languages.

The travelers paddled west across the lake and portaged their canoes across a marshy divide to the Wisconsin River, which took them west to the Mississippi. For weeks they glided down the continent's mightiest waterway, its current running fast and clear in these upper reaches. They noted the "monstrous fish" — possibly catfish or sturgeon — that "struck . . . violently against our canoes." More astonishing were two giant horned figures painted on cliffs, "on which the boldest Indian dare not gaze long" — the fearsome Piasaw, or "man-destroying bird" of Indian myth.

The explorers steered their canoes past primitive cypress groves, prehistoric mounds, and long stretches of boggy ground that one traveler described as *prairie tremblante.* When they reached the point where the still limpid Mississippi is joined by the swirling brown waters of the Missouri River, they were deeply impressed by the noise of the rapids. Drifting on, they came to the mouth of the Arkansas River.

According to reports from the local tribes, they were approaching the land of the "black gowns" who "rang bells for prayers." Since this description could only refer to Spanish priests, the explorers recognized that they were heading to the Gulf of Mexico — Spanish territory — and not the Pacific Ocean. And so they turned back.

Jolliet, in his haste to reach Quebec and report his findings, tipped over his canoe and lost all his notes. Luckily for history, Père Marquette had also kept a diary — thus providing the only surviving record of the trip.

Marquette and Jolliet traveled the Mississippi, a river at times so clear they could see "the minutest object that lies upon its bottom."

IN THEIR OWN WORDS

"I cannot but take notice of the wonderful mercy of God to me in those afflictions, in sending me a Bible. One of the Indians that came from [the] Medfield fight had brought some plunder, came to me and asked me if I would have a Bible, he had got one in his basket. I was glad of it, and asked him whether he thought the Indians would let me read? He answered, 'Yes.' So I took the Bible, and in that melancholy time, it came into my mind to read first the 28th chapter of Deuteronomy, which I did, and when I had read it my dark heart wrought on in this manner — that there was no mercy for me, that the blessings were gone, and the curses come in their room, and that I had lost my opportunity. But the Lord helped me still to go on reading til I came to chapter 30, the first seven verses, where I found, there was mercy promised again, if we would return to Him by repentance; and though we were scattered from one end of the earth to the other, yet the Lord would gather us together, and turn all those curses upon our enemies. I do not desire to forget this scripture and what comfort it was to me."

Mary Rowlandson describes an episode in her 1676 captivity by Narragansett Indians.

William Penn, an English aristocrat and a religious dissenter, established Pennsylvania as a haven of tolerance.

The son of a wealthy admiral with strong ties to the Crown, young William Penn saw the inside of several British prisons because of strong religious faith. He belonged to the outlawed Religious Society of Friends, or Quakers — a pacifist sect that believed all people were equal in the eyes of God. Fortunately for Penn, King Charles II had been a close companion of his father. After his father's death Penn was granted, in 1681, proprietorship of a 28-million-acre tract bordering present-day New Jersey and Maryland. The king named the area Pennsylvania, in honor of Penn's father.

Penn promptly set about transforming his New World property into a home for his fellow Quakers. Other religious outcasts would also be welcome, he announced. Paying his

William Penn and his fellow Quakers presenting gifts to Native Americans as part of a treaty.

first visit in the summer of 1682, he found "the land good, the air sweet and serene," and the region endowed with "provision divers and excellent." He picked a site between the Delaware and Schuylkill rivers and named it Philadelphia, the Greek term for "city of brotherly love."

Although Penn was the colony's main architect, he lived in it for only 4 of his 73 years. Shortly after arriving, he sailed back to England to petition the Crown regarding a border dispute. Returning in 1699, he served two years as governor, and was again called back to England. There, beset by financial trouble, he landed in a debtors' prison for nine months. Penn tried to sell his colony back to the Crown but died before negotiations were finalized.

Meanwhile, Pennsylvania thrived, and by 1700 the colony rivaled Virginia and Massachusetts in population and wealth. 🛥

1682

Sieur de La Salle, the first European to travel the Mississippi to the Gulf of Mexico, met a bloody end at the hands of his own men.

On April 9, 1682, Robert Cavelier, sieur de La Salle, experienced the high point of his career. On a marshy plain where the Mississippi River meets the sea, he listened to musket volleys and shouts of "Vive le Roi" from his party of 41 men. Then he raised his voice and claimed the vast territory of Louisiana, including all lands drained by the river and its many tributaries, for "the most high, mighty, invincible, and victorious Prince, Louis the Great . . . of France."

La Salle had arrived in the New World a poor man, having given up a family fortune to join the priesthood. But the call of adventure soon lured him away from holy orders. In Canada he regained his wealth, prospering in the fur trade. He built a pair of trading forts in the Great Lakes region and explored parts of Ohio and Illinois.

Indian reports of a mighty waterway flowing south to the Gulf of Mexico prompted La Salle to embark on his Mississippi venture. Spurred on by its success, he resolved to found a colony at the river's mouth.

The plan won enthusiastic support from Louis XIV, and in 1684 the explorer sailed from France with four vessels and more than 300 colonists. But by an error of navigation the ships glided past the mouth of the Mississippi, and La Salle built his colony, Fort Saint Louis, many miles to the west. The settlement did not thrive. Disease and Indian attack took a heavy toll, and in 1687 La Salle set out to get help. He soon was lost in the Louisiana wilds. His men mutinied, and he died with a bullet in his head. 🛥

"La Salle Claiming Louisiana for France, April 9, 1682" — detail from a painting by frontier artist George Catlin.

Hundreds of New York militiamen signed up to defend Jacob Leisler's republican government.

1689
Jacob Leisler commanded the first colonial uprising in New York.

Jacob Leisler, a German immigrant who built a fortune in the wine trade and married into one of New York's leading families, made an unlikely revolutionary. But during the turmoil of England's Glorious Revolution, that is exactly what he became.

When the British Parliament replaced the despised King James II with his daughter, Mary, and her husband, William of Orange, many colonists rejoiced. Massachusetts ousted its governor, who had been appointed by James II. In New York, which had long been agitating for a measure of democratic rule — and where the authorities remained loyal to the ousted king — a similar confrontation began taking shape.

It started with a rumor that Francis Nicholson, New York's lieutenant-governor, intended to burn down New York City rather than leave it to the colonists. So in the spring of 1689, Leisler and some 500 armed men, possibly spurred by this rumor, captured Fort James, the British garrison. Nicholson fled to England, and Leisler became the head of a provisional government. With the backing of farmers, artisans, and shopkeepers, he ruled for the next 20 months. In addition to collecting taxes and setting up courts, Leisler convened the colony's first representative assembly.

This experiment in democracy came to an abrupt end in January 1691 when a company of British redcoats showed up to announce the arrival of a new royal governor, Henry Sloughter. After clashing with the troops, Leisler surrendered. He was brought to trial for treason. Convicted, he and a comrade were hanged until almost dead, then cut down, decapitated, and drawn and quartered. Sympathetic bystanders, horrified at the brutality they had witnessed, carried off strands of Leisler's hair and pieces of his clothes as relics.

Four years later, in 1695, Parliament reversed his conviction, and in 1702 the New York legislature, a body born of Leisler's martyrdom, awarded his family $2,700 in reparation. 🛥

1692
As later immortalized by Nathaniel Hawthorne in *The Scarlet Letter*, New England's Puritans received harsh punishments for adultery.

In Massachusetts in the late 17th century, violators of the commandment forbidding adultery were liable to receive 40 lashes and an hour of public humiliation by being made to stand on the gallows with a chain around their neck. And like Hester Prynne, the heroine of Nathaniel Hawthorne's masterpiece, *The Scarlet Letter*, they may also have had to wear the letter A (for adultery). Offenders could count themselves lucky, however. Not long before, the Puritan fathers had adulterers put to death.

The Hawthornes were no strangers to the stern ways of Puritan justice. Nathaniel's great-great-grandfather was a judge at the Salem witch trials in 1692. This fact inspired his famous descendant to long, brooding meditations on the nature of sin and his own mortality. Legend has it that one of the condemned women placed a curse on the judge and his lineage, crying out from the gallows, "God will give you blood to drink!" A century and a half later, plagued by poverty and haunted by the ghosts of his family's past, Nathaniel would write *The House of the Seven Gables*, in which a once-powerful Salem family manages to fight off a witch's curse through the power of love. 🛥

IN THEIR OWN WORDS

> [Abigail broke into] 'a grievous fit,' some-times makeing as if she would fly stretching up her arms as high as she could and crying 'Whish, Whish, Whish' several times; Presently after she said there was Goodw. N [Nurse] and said 'Do you not see her? Why there she stands!' And then said Goodw. N offered her The Book, and she was resolved she would not take it, saying Often, 'I won't, I won't, I won't take it. I do not know what Book it is; I am sure it is none of God's Book, it is the Devil's Book, for ought I know.' After that she run to the Fire, and begun to throw Fire Brands about the house....

A description of the behavior of 12-year-old Abigail Williams during a fit in which she named Rebecca Nurse as her tormentor.

A *1692*
small colonial village was gripped by a witch-hunting hysteria that led innocent people to the gallows for "consorting with evil spirits."

It started in February, when two girls began having strange fits — growling, running wildly around the room, lapsing into trances. A medical opinion was offered by an examining physician, Dr. William Griggs. "The evil hand," he said, "is upon them."

To the Puritans, the evil hand could belong to no other than Satan himself, and the search for his demonic presence swept Salem Village (present-day Danvers), Massachusetts, into a turmoil of accusation. As a result, innocent people were put to death, hundreds were imprisoned — including a four-year-old girl who sat fettered in chains for nine months — and the town's name became a symbol of paranoia and persecution. At trials throughout the summer and fall of 1692, more than 100 suspects were charged with witchcraft. Convictions were handed down based on little substantial evidence. What set the Salem trials apart from similar cases of the period was that respected citizens were among the condemned. In all, 19 people swung from the gallows. One man was pressed slowly to death for refusing to plead either guilty or not guilty.

No one knows why the girls brought such chaos to the community of Salem, but there are some theories. Perhaps it was guilt for having indulged in divination and magic tricks with a West Indian slave. Another theory was that their fits and accusations gave the

Witches were seen as disciples of Lucifer, ruler over all manner of vices.

young women power over their elders that they did not ordinarily possess.

The girls' behavior might not have received so much attention had the village not offered fertile ground for hysteria. Along with their religion, the Puritans brought a deep-seated belief in witchcraft with them from Europe, where "witches" had been tortured, burned, and hanged for two centuries. To the Puritans, illness and death were not always the result of nature or accidents, but of supernatural influences. Such books as *Wonders of the Invisible World* by the Puritan minister Cotton Mather described witchcraft in vivid detail.

In addition, Salem, along with the rest of New England, was in a state of political and social flux. Less than a decade earlier, the Massachusetts Bay Colony had seen its charter revoked by the British Crown, and the charter had only just been reinstated. Bitter family feuds, Indian attacks, and other hazards of life in a generally hostile world added to the colonists' insecurities.

Eventually, the accusers overstepped their bounds. Soon after they charged the wife of the colony's governor, the trials were brought to an end. One judge and 12 jurors later repented, and Massachusetts made payments to the victims' survivors. A Boston merchant during the time was prophetic when he said of the witch hunt: "I am afraid that ages will not wear off that reproach and those stains which these things will leave behind upon our land." ⚓

B *1692*
efore her death on the gallows, Mary Easty pleaded not for her own life, but for the lives of other innocent victims.

The wave of paranoia sweeping Salem, Massachusetts, in 1692 caught Mary Easty in its evil tide. Accused of witchcraft, the middle-aged housewife was so calm and gentle that even her jailers spoke in her behalf. Upon re-examination Easty was found innocent and released from jail.

Her homecoming was all too brief. After Easty's release, Mercy Lewis, one of the girls who had first accused her, fell mysteriously ill. The magistrates could not ignore this occurrence, and after only three days of freedom Mary Easty was rearrested, tried, and sentenced to death. Just before her execution she sent a plea to the court: "I petition not for my own life, for I know I

A court petition of Mary Easty and her sister, Sarah Cloyce, proclaims their innocence.

must die . . . , but that, if it be possible, no more innocent blood may be shed."

On September 22 Easty, along with seven other convicted witches and one wizard, was put into a cart and hauled a mile outside

Salem to Gallows Hill. There she was hanged by the neck until dead. But the citizens of Salem at last understood that they had gone too far, and soon after Easty's death the witch trials came to an end. ⚓

1704

Raised to believe that Indians were savages, young Eunice Williams still chose to live out her life with them.

The frontier settlement of Deerfield, Massachusetts, hung precariously between two worlds. Inside its wooden stockade stood the building blocks of Puritan civilization: family, school, and church. Outside lay Indian territory, a wilderness domain that to white settlers was both savage and forbidding.

On the morning of February 29, 1704, the barrier between the two worlds shattered when a combined force of Frenchmen and Abenaki Indians stormed Deerfield's walls. It was the latest battle in Queen Anne's War, a conflict that had spread with brutal consequences from Europe to the New World.

Eunice Williams and more than 100 others were taken prisoner. Still others were not so lucky. Forty-nine villagers — including Eunice's infant sister and six-year-old brother — lay dead or dying. Eunice's mother was killed on the march to Canada. "Who can tell what sorrows pierced our souls?" her father, the Reverend John Williams, would later write.

Reverend Williams's sorrows had only just begun. When he and most of the others were ransomed, nine-year-old Eunice elected to stay behind. In time she forgot how to speak English, married an Indian, and raised a family. Worst of all, in the reverend's eyes, she converted to Catholicism. In 1729

Wielding hatchets, Abenaki Indians storm a Deerfield home.

John Williams died, having poured his sadness into a famous narrative of the Deerfield Massacre.

More than a century later, in 1837, 23 of Eunice Williams's Indian descendants emerged from the forest and spent a week in Deerfield visiting the townspeople and paying their respects at the grave of Reverend Williams.

1718

Pirates plagued colonial waters in the 18th century, often with the consent of government officials. The worst was Blackbeard.

Like many other pirates, Edward Teach, more commonly known as Blackbeard, began his career as an English privateer, sanctioned during wartime to loot the ships of enemy nations. After Queen Anne's War between the British and the French ended in 1713, Blackbeard just kept on looting.

Cultivating an image of fearsome brutality, Blackbeard terrorized colonial waters from the coast of Virginia to the Caribbean. Stories of his terrible deeds abounded. Some said he had as many as 14 "wives," each

married in a mock ceremony. According to one account, he chopped off the finger of a man who was slow to surrender a diamond ring. Once he attempted to replicate the torments of hell by locking himself and his crew in the hold of his ship with burning pots of brimstone. The last to emerge — Blackbeard, of course.

His appearance struck fear into the boldest hearts. Six feet four inches tall, 250 pounds in weight, he wore a matted waist-length beard, three braces of pistols, a cutlass, daggers, and a pair of burning cannon fuses tied to his hat. When he fought, he roared like a lion.

Edward Teach, aka Blackbeard, once shot a member of his own crew just to boost his ferocious reputation.

Instilling fear in his victims was surely a useful device for a pirate, but friends in high places also helped. It was not uncommon to see Blackbeard guide his ship, laden with plunder, into the harbor at Bath, the capital of North Carolina. He would hand over a percentage of his treasure to the governor, Charles Eden, and sell another portion to local merchants. The rest he would store in a barn belonging to his friend Tobias Knight — who just happened to be Eden's secretary.

Similar arrangements were made by other pirates in the late 17th century with the colonies of New York, Massachusetts, Pennyslvania, and Rhode Island. Politicians added to their paychecks, merchants acquired stolen goods at a steep discount, and local taverns did a brisk business while the pirates were in port.

At the same time, British colonial commerce suffered from the pirates' depredations. Blackbeard frequently patrolled the waters around Pamlico Sound in North Carolina, extracting tolls from passing mer-

Even though he had no formal education, John Bartram gained widespread celebrity as the first American botanist.

A self-taught scholar with a passionate interest in native American plants, young John Bartram purchased a 100-acre tract of bottomland along the Schuylkill River, near Philadelphia, in 1728 and began developing a model farm. One section he devoted to flowers and shrubs from different regions of the country — creating, in effect, the nation's first botanical garden.

Bartram's reputation as a collector of rare native species spread far and wide. He began corresponding with Peter Collinson, a London cloth merchant who shared his interest in American flora. Collinson regularly asked his American customers to send him plant samples, and most sent one or two. Bartram shipped crate after crate of unusual specimens. A craze for colonial gardening swept through the English aristocracy. Bartram ultimately introduced more than 100 American species to Europe, including Dutchman's pipe, ostrich fern, and many types of trees.

John Bartram's son, William, painted these watercolors of native flora: wild lime and morning glory, left; Franklinia altamaha, right.

He earned the respect of scholars and royalty. The queen of Sweden became his patron. Carolus Linneaus, the Swedish botanist who devised the first classification system for plants, called him "the greatest natural botanist in the world." Benjamin Franklin, George Washington, and hundreds of others paid visits to his Schuylkill River farm.

Bartram began devoting more time to the search for new specimens. Beginning in 1736 and for the next 30 years, he made numerous journeys into the American wilderness. Sometimes he traveled alone, sometimes with his son, William. Besides collecting plants, he brought back insects, birds, mollusks, and reptiles. In 1765 George III named Bartram, then 66, king's botanist with a yearly stipend of £50. Bartram immediately mounted an expedition to Florida, traveling up the St. Johns River from St. Augustine.

The Florida expedition was Bartram's last. He returned to his farm to take up the gentlemanly pursuits of editing his travel journal and entertaining prominent visitors. 🛳

---

chantmen. In May 1717 alone, he looted eight or nine ships. He then sailed into Charleston Harbor in South Carolina and threatened to devastate the city if he was not given a chest of medicine with which to doctor his wounded crewmen.

Blackbeard's career came abruptly to a close in November 1718. Responding to a petition from the citizens of North Carolina, who hated Blackbeard and his crimes, the governor of Virginia sent an expedition into Carolina waters. Lt. Robert Maynard, commanding the lead ship, cornered the pirate in the shallows of Oracoke Inlet. Blackbeard, swigging rum and swinging his cutlass, led his men in a charge aboard the Virginia vessel. Heavily outnumbered, he fought with savage desperation but was finally cut down.

Maynard lopped off the pirate's head and hung it as a trophy from his bowsprit. He then threw the body overboard. According to legend, the decapitated corpse swam around the ship three times before sinking. Later, the pirate's skull was fashioned into a silver-sided punch bowl. 🛳

IN THEIR OWN WORDS

"Boston, By Letters of the 17th of December last from North Carolina, we are informed, That Lieutenant Robert Maynard of His Majesty's Ship Pearl (Commanded by Capt. Gordon) being fitted out at Virginia, with two Sloops, mann'd with Fifty Men, and small Arms, but no great Guns, in quest of Capt. Teach the Pirate, called Blackbeard, who made his Escape from thence, was overtaken at North Carolina, and had ten great Guns and Twenty one Men on board his Sloop. Teach when he began the Dispute Drank Damnation to Lieutenant Maynard if he gave Quarters, Maynard replyed he would neither give nor take Quarters, whereupon he boarded the Pirate and fought it out, hand to hand, with Pistol and Sword; the Engagement was very desperate and bloody on both sides wherein Lieutenant Maynard had Thirty five of his Men killed and wounded in the Action, himself slightly wounded. Teach and most of his Men were killed, the rest carryed Prisoners to Virginia, by Lieut. Maynard, to be tryed there; who also carrys with him Teach's Head which he cut off, in order to get the Reward granted by the said Colony."

An account of the capture and death of the notorious pirate Blackbeard, in the Boston News-Letter.

1733
Georgia, last of the 13 colonies, was founded as a refuge for the deserving poor.

After visiting a friend in a London debtors' prison, James Oglethorpe, a British officer and country gentleman, became obsessed with the fate of the forgotten poor. The foul conditions in the jail appalled him. Many of the prisoners were good citizens who needed a chance to get themselves back on their feet. Why couldn't they find it in the New World's virgin land?

Oglethorpe promptly enlisted some of London's most eminent people in a plan to found a colony located just north of Spanish Florida. Enough money was soon raised to finance the first group of settlers. Oglethorpe also managed to win the support of King George II, who was mainly interested in protecting his profitable South Carolina colony from Spanish incursions.

Having obtained a royal charter for the new colony of "Georgia," Oglethorpe selected 35 families, each headed by "gentlemen of decayed circumstances." In February 1733 they landed in America. Employing a half-Indian woman named Mary Musgrove as his

James Oglethorpe introduces Indian tribal leaders to the Georgia colony's British trustees.

interpreter, Oglethorpe concluded a treaty with Chief Tomochici, the leader of the local Yamacraw Indians, that allowed the colonists to settle peacefully.

As colonial governor, Oglethorpe set about building Georgia's first city, Savannah. The plans, drawn by a man named Robert Castell — who, as it happened, would die in

debtors' prison — called for a spacious, orderly city with small, green parks. Savannah would soon boast of elegant houses, a library of more than 2,000 books, and an agricultural experiment station.

Over the next several years the colony grew and prospered. Oglethorpe sailed back to London with some of his new Indian friends, and returned with more money and another group of settlers. By 1740 more than 2,500 people had emigrated to Georgia.

Not everything Oglethorpe planned for his colony was successful. Hoping to start a silk industry, he tried breeding European silkworms on the local mulberry trees. The experiment flopped: the insects thrived only on European mulberry trees. Nor did his attempt to restrict the colony to "sober, industrious, and moral persons" have perceptible effect. Settlers flouted his prohibition on liquor and largely ignored his anti-slavery laws.

Oglethorpe's charter had a limited term of only 21 years, and in 1753 he returned to England for good. He took a seat in Parliament and served as a general in the British army. His interest in his colony never abated, however. During the Revolutionary War the 80-year-old Oglethorpe spoke out in support of the Americans — much to the consternation of his British friends. When the colonists won, he was delighted. ⚓

The Founding of the Thirteen Colonies

Between 1607 and 1732 England founded 13 permanent colonies in North America, which eventually became the United States.

Colony	Date Settled	Became Royal Colony
• Connecticut*	1635	
• Delaware*	1638	
• Georgia	1732	1752
• Maryland	1634	1632**
• Massachusetts	1620	1691
• New Hampshire	1623	1679
• New Jersey	1633	1702
• New York	1614	1685
• North Carolina	1653	1729
• Pennsylvania*	1643	
• Rhode Island	1636	1663
• South Carolina	1670	1729
• Virginia	1607	1624

*Not a royal colony   **Year charter granted by English Crown; first settlers did not arrive until 1634.

NEW HAMPSHIRE
MASSACHUSETTS
NEW YORK
PENNSYLVANIA
RHODE ISLAND
CONNECTICUT
NEW JERSEY
MARYLAND
DELAWARE
VIRGINIA
NORTH CAROLINA
SOUTH CAROLINA
GEORGIA

New England
Middle Colonies
The Chesapeake
The Lower South

1735

Until John Peter Zenger's milestone case, a publisher could be jailed for libel, even if everything he printed was true.

By all accounts William Cosby was an arrogant and contentious man. Appointed governor of New York, he arrived late to take the post — and promptly sued the acting governor, Rip Van Dam, for a part of the salary he had missed by not being there on time. When the colony's chief justice ruled for Van Dam, Cosby fired the judge.

The deposed chief justice, Lewis Morris, refused to give up so easily. Together with friends he founded an opposition party, and he bankrolled a German-born printer, John Peter Zenger, to put out a newspaper promoting his views. The *New-York Weekly Journal* appeared on November 5, 1733, proclaiming itself "a Shame and Restraint to evil ministers." Readers did not need to see Cosby's name to know which evil minister was meant. Nor did they need to be reminded of the severe libel laws in England and the colonies. Any statement disruptive to public order — whether true or not — could send its author to jail.

A year later, Zenger stood accused of "false, scandalous, malicious and seditious libels." He had repeatedly attacked the governor, and a reluctant local council had him arrested. Bail was prohibitively high, and Zenger stayed in prison for nine months awaiting trial. Meanwhile, the *Journal* continued to be published by Zenger's resourceful wife, Anna.

At Zenger's trial in 1735, the noted Philadelphia lawyer Andrew Hamilton made a forceful plea for freedom of the press. What is true, Hamilton insisted, cannot be libel, or the people would have no defense against tyranny. After 10 minutes of deliberation, the jury agreed.

Partly as a result of the Zenger case, freedom of the press became a basic principle of American democracy.

THE
New-York Weekly JOURNAL

Containing the freshest Advices, Foreign, and Domestick.

MUNDAY August 18th, 1735.

To my Subscribers and Benefactors.

Gentlemen;

I think my self in Duty bound to to make publick Acknowledgment for the many Favours received at your Hands, which I do in this Manner return you my hearty Thanks for. I very soon intend to print my Tryal at Length, that the World may see how unjust my Sufferings have been, so will only at this Time give this

John Chambers, Esq; had been appointed the Term before by the Court as my Council, in the Place of James Alexander and William Smith, who were then silenced on my Account, and to Mr. Chambers's Assistance came Andrew Hamilton, Esq; of Philadelphia Barrester at Law; when Mr Attorney offered the Information and the Proofs, Mr. Hamilton told him, he would acknowledge my Printing and Publishing the Papers in the Information, and save him the Trouble of that Proof,

Zenger's weekly Journal reports on the publisher's trial.

1735

Andrew Hamilton's plea to the jury in the Zenger case was one of the greatest orations heard in early America.

As John Peter Zenger's libel trial began, a gouty old man rose from the audience, hobbled to the bench, and announced he would be taking over Zenger's defense. His presence sent murmurs through the crowd. The man was 59-year-old Andrew Hamilton of Philadelphia, who had built a reputation as the finest lawyer in the country.

At various times a counsel to William Penn, a legislator in three colonies, and an architect of Philadelphia's Independence Hall, Hamilton possessed a broad range of skills, and he brought all his vast intellect to bear in his final address to the jury. No one can count himself free, he argued, if truth is no defense against libel: "How must a man speak or write, or what must he hear, read, or sing, or when must he laugh, so as to be secure from being taken up as a libeler?"

Hamilton defending Zenger.

Hamilton's eloquent defense of freedom was enough to convince the jury and earn the august attorney a place in history as the first person to be honored by the respectful term "Philadelphia lawyer."

1739

Expelled from Harvard, 18th-century con man Thomas Bell made a career of hoodwinking American colonists.

Harvard may well have been the cause of Tom Bell's downfall. It was there that he acquired the social polish that he would use as a confidence man. Expelled from the university in 1733 for "acts of theft . . . [and] a scandalous neglect of his college Exercises," Bell spent the next 20 years as a criminal. Changing his clothes as often as he changed his name, he robbed his way through the 13 colonies, passing himself off as a gentleman in need, often to gain the confidence — and money — of upper-class acquaintances. His exploits were not confined to the mainland, however.

In 1739 Bell arrived in Barbados posing as the son of the late governor, Bishop Burnet. Barbados society gave him its warmest welcome. His stay soured when, having robbed a Jewish man, he then sparked an anti-Semitic riot. The authorities decreed that he be whipped and pilloried.

Usually, no jail could hold him; time and again he escaped justice, sometimes by picking the locks on the cell door. Once in Boston, sentenced to death for a string of frauds, he managed to flee the executioner.

Bell was the first criminal in America to have a sense of his media value. As early as 1742, while in a prison in Rhode Island, he announced his intention to publish his memoirs. A decade later he toured the country raising subscriptions. It was to be his last scam. The record shows that Bell then disappeared from sight, never having written a word.

1742

Faneuil Hall, considered America's "Cradle of Liberty," was built as a center of commerce.

Called "the topmost merchant in all the town" by his fellow Bostonians, Peter Faneuil, descendant of a wealthy French Huguenot family, made an even larger fortune as a smuggler and slave trader. Wishing to share his good luck with the city of Boston, he offered to build a public market where citizens could buy farm produce.

At first the city fathers rejected the plan. Bostonians were accustomed to buying their groceries from door-to-door street peddlers, and many people opposed the idea of a centralized, regulated market hall. Only after the building's architect suggested adding an auditorium for public meetings did the city agree. The Georgian-style brick structure finally opened on September 10, 1742. Atop its handsome cupola perched a gilded weathervane in the shape of a giant grasshopper.

Massachusetts Magazine *printed this engraving of Faneuil Hall in 1789.*

The following year Peter Faneuil, age 43, died of "dropsy" (possibly congestive heart failure). Over the next 60 years Faneuil Hall was destroyed by fire, rebuilt, then used as a theater by the British during the siege of Boston. More important, it served as a meeting place for the patriot rebels — James Otis, Samuel Adams, and others — who laid the groundwork for American independence. It became, in Daniel Webster's words, the "Cradle of Liberty."

In the decades since, Faneuil Hall has seen many other illustrious visitors. It was the site of a dinner for the marquis de Lafayette in 1784, and in 1833 a reception was held there for President Andrew Jackson. It is now a national historical landmark. And although the original building has undergone many changes, the giant gold grasshopper still remains on its roof, showing which way the wind is blowing over Boston to this day.

New Business in the New World

Industry meant survival for settlers in the New World. Separated from the resources of their homeland, colonists were forced to produce their own goods and maintain their own services. Monarchies, private investors, and trading companies, moreover, expected to profit from the Colonies' land and natural resources. The events below identify some of the early business milestones.

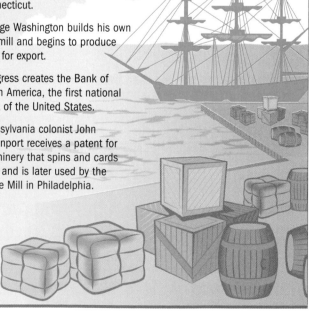

1612 John Rolfe plants the first tobacco crops, producing the first lucrative trading commodity for American colonists.

1613 Dutch fur traders set up a post on Manhattan Island.

1639 The first printing press is established in Cambridge, Massachusetts.

1640 The Massachusetts Bay Colony develops a lucrative business in cod fishing.

1644 John Winthrop, Jr., son of Massachusetts Bay Colony's first governor, builds the first productive iron furnace in the Colonies in Braintree.

1700 The first commercial rum distillery opens in Boston.

1704 The first regular newspaper, *The Boston News-Letter*, begins publication.

1712 Capt. Christopher Hussey captures the first sperm whale off Nantucket Island, expanding New England's whaling industry.

1740 Eliza Lucas plants indigo in South Carolina. The plant, which produces a blue dye, becomes the basis for an important industry for the South.

1750 Coal is mined commercially near Richmond, Virginia.

1751 Sugar, to be used in distilling rum, is grown and processed in Louisiana for the first time.

1759 The Presbyterian Ministers Fund, the first life insurance company in the Colonies, is founded in Philadelphia.

1762 Ethan Allen establishes an ironworks and blast furnace in Salisbury, Connecticut.

1770 George Washington builds his own gristmill and begins to produce flour for export.

1781 Congress creates the Bank of North America, the first national bank of the United States.

1791 Pennsylvania colonist John Davenport receives a patent for machinery that spins and cards wool and is later used by the Globe Mill in Philadelphia.

A **1744**

teenage girl, Eliza Lucas, started a new industry for South Carolina.

George Lucas, a lieutenant colonel in the British Army, was ordered in 1739 to leave his family in Charleston and go to Antigua. Hostilities had erupted between Spain and England, and the army needed him. He left the management of his estates, totaling more than 5,000 acres, in the hands of his 16-year-old daughter, Eliza.

Undaunted, Eliza rose to the occasion. Since the war with Spain had cut off the market for Carolina rice, the colony's farmers needed an alternative. She planted cotton, ginger, alfalfa, cassava, and indigo. It was the indigo, used to make dye, that was her greatest success — and her most difficult challenge.

Indigo was hard to grow, and the dye-making process was technically

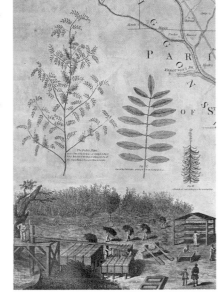

Field hands process indigo in this sketch from a 1773 South Carolina map.

complex. Frost killed her first harvest. Another was sabotaged by her dyemaker, a Caribbean islander with his own agenda. But in 1744, after years of experimentation, she succeeded in producing "17 pounds of very good Indigo." That same year she married Charles Pinckney, a local planter.

The Pinckneys gave indigo seeds to any plantation owner willing to take them, and by 1775 South Carolina farmers were exporting up to a million pounds of indigo a year. Then, during the Revolutionary War, British troops marched into Charleston and occupied the Pinckney estate. Eliza lost everything.

She moved to a plantation owned by her daughter, and in 1793 she died of breast cancer. For her services to the nation she loved, George Washington asked to serve as one of Eliza's pallbearers. ⛵

W **1752**

hile trying to electrocute a turkey, Benjamin Franklin gave himself a terrible shock.

"Two nights ago being about to kill a Turkey by the Shock from two large Glass Jarrs containing as much electrical fire as forty common Phials," he wrote to his brother John on Christmas Day, 1750, "I inadvertently took the whole thro' my own Arms and Body."

So went one of Benjamin Franklin's experiments with electricity. Known for *Poor*

Ben Franklin, wearing eyeglasses, presides over an electrical experiment requiring charged rods.

Richard's Almanack (which he began in 1732 and published until 1758), Franklin had a passion for all the sciences. But electricity was his favorite.

In 1751 he published the work that would secure his worldwide reputation, *Experiments and Observations on Electricity*. A year later he conducted his most famous experiment. By flying a kite made of cedar, silk, and wire in a thunderstorm, he proved that lightning and electricity are the same. Soon after, he installed a lightning rod on the Pennsylvania State House in Philadelphia. This time Franklin managed to avoid getting shocked. ⛵

The Practice and Perfection of Virtue

In 1728 Benjamin Franklin drew up a course for self-improvement consisting of 13 virtues to be practiced one per week for 13 weeks. Progress was to be noted carefully in a journal, with a little black dot used to represent each shortcoming. If a person repeated the course four times, a year of improved virtue could be obtained.

1. **Temperance:** Eat not to dullness; drink not to elevation.

2. **Silence:** Speak not but what may benefit others or yourself; avoid trifling conversation.

3. **Order:** Let all your things have their places; let each part of your business have its time.

4. **Resolution:** Resolve to perform what you ought; perform without fail what you resolve.

5. **Frugality:** Make no expense but to do good to others or yourself; i.e., waste nothing.

6. **Industry:** Lose no time; be always employ'd in something useful; cut off all unnecessary actions.

7. **Sincerity:** Use no hurtful deceit; think innocently and justly, and, if you speak, speak accordingly.

8. **Justice:** Wrong none by doing injuries, or omitting the benefits that are your duty.

9. **Moderation:** Avoid extremes; forbear resenting injuries so much as you think they deserve.

10. **Cleanliness:** Tolerate no uncleanliness in body, cloths, or habitation.

11. **Tranquillity:** Be not disturbed at trifles, or at accidents common or unavoidable.

12. **Chastity:** Rarely use venery but for health or offspring, never to dullness, weakness, or the injury of your own or another's peace or reputation.

13. **Humility:** Imitate Jesus and Socrates. (The original list numbered 12 virtues; Franklin added this last one after he was accused of smugness by a Quaker friend.)

1754

George Washington lost his first battle as a military commander, and his diplomatic error helped spark an international crisis.

When French soldiers began moving into the Ohio Valley — an area claimed by the British — the colonial authorities sent George Washington with 159 men to build a fort on the Ohio River. What Washington wasn't supposed to do was start a war.

A 21-year-old militia colonel, Washington was not yet ready for high command. His first mis-

Lt. Col. George Washington in his British colonial uniform.

take was to ambush a party of 32 Frenchmen, killing 10 of them. The French claimed they were on a peace mission: among the dead was a diplomat, the sieur de Jumonville.

Realizing that the French and their Indian allies would seek revenge, Washington hastily retreated to his base, Fort Necessity, at Great Meadows, Pennsylvania. Its location was a disaster. Surrounded by hills and situated in a basin, the fort was wide open to attack and susceptible to flooding. And as

luck would have it, when the French and Indians attacked on July 3, 1754, it rained. After a nine-hour siege, many of Washington's men lay dead or wounded, and the rest were waist deep in mud and blood.

Washington had no choice but to surrender. But even this did not go well. Because of an error in translation, Washington unwittingly admitted to "murdering" the diplomat Jumonville. As a result, the French could claim that the English started the French and Indian War. ⚓

1754

The French and Indian War, begun in the Ohio wilderness, sent shock waves around the globe. Before it was over, the armies of eight European powers had battled on three different continents.

Conflict between the great colonial powers erupted time and again into gunsmoke and bloodshed. For the better part of a century, starting in 1689, Britain tangled with the French, the Spanish, and

various others in a series of wars that ranged from North America to Europe, and from India to the Caribbean. So when young George Washington shot up a French encampment in the Ohio Valley in 1754 (see above), the result should have been predictable: another world war.

At stake in North America was control of the fur trade in the vast wilderness valleys of the St. Lawrence and Ohio rivers. The British struck first. Gen. Edward Braddock, leading some 1,400 regulars and 450 colonial militia, moved

French and Indian riflemen ambush Gen. Braddock and his British redcoats near Fort Duquesne.

wounding Braddock and scattering his troops. "We have been beaten, most shamefully beaten, by a handful of men," lamented one survivor, a Virginia militiaman.

The French and Indian War spread to New York and Canada, where the British suffered repeated losses. Then the tide turned. General James Wolfe took Quebec (it cost his life) and Montreal fell. The French surrendered.

Meanwhile, the bad blood between France and England had spread from North America and India into Europe. The Seven Years' War (as it was called in Europe) found England and Prussia squaring off against France and its allies — Austria, Spain, Russia, Saxony, and Sweden.

Hostilities ended in 1763. At the Treaty of Paris, France signed over virtually all of its North American empire, and most of its possessions in India, in exchange for some Caribbean sugar islands. England won Canada and all disputed

into the Ohio Valley to attack the French outpost of Fort Duquesne (present-day Pittsburgh). They never got there. A force of French troops and allied Indian warriors fell upon them in the forest, fatally

territories east of the Mississippi. Spain took Louisiana. The map was in place for the next great regional conflict — the American Revolution, in which France stepped in again to fight the British. ⚓

The Struggle for a North American Empire

The French and Indian War was the final chapter in a series of wars between the French and the British for control of the North American continent. Some significant battles are listed below.

1754 A large French expedition overpowers a Virginia detachment at the source of the Ohio River (later Fort Duquesne, now Pittsburgh) and drives them out.

1755 British general Edward Braddock mounts an attack on Fort Duquesne; he and his troops are soundly defeated.

1756 The French capture two British forts at Oswego, New York. Pennsylvania troops destroy the Delaware Indians' village of Kittanning — a major base for frontier raids — discouraging Indian participation in the war.

1758 The tide turns for the British under the newly appointed secretary of state, William Pitt. The British gain the supply depot of Fort Frontenac and capture the French fortress of Louisbourg on Cape Breton Island. Although the British are repulsed at Fort Ticonderoga, they take Fort Duquesne.

1759 The British capture Fort Ticonderoga and Fort Niagara and drive the French out of New York territory into Canada. They defeat the French at Quebec, and the city surrenders.

1760 The British march on Montreal and force the French government to surrender Canada.

1763 The Treaty of Paris is signed.

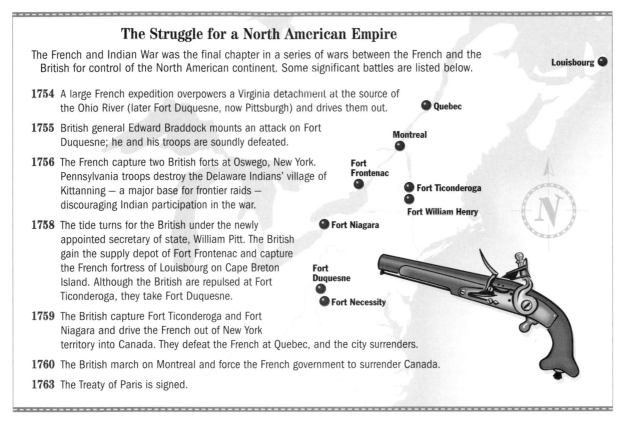

Map labels: Louisbourg, Quebec, Montreal, Fort Frontenac, Fort Ticonderoga, Fort William Henry, Fort Niagara, Fort Duquesne, Fort Necessity

---

1756

Had not fur trader William Johnson earned the lifelong trust of the Iroquois, half of North America might have remained a colony of France.

Access to the vast Northwest frontier lay in the hands of the powerful Iroquois Confederacy, an alliance of warrior tribes that dominated the region's forests from the Hudson River to Lake Erie. Both France and England sought their friendship. So when young William Johnson arrived from Ireland in 1738 to manage his uncle's lands near Schenectady, New York, he knew just what to do. He opened a trading post and made friends with the local Iroquois tribe, the Mohawks.

Johnson dressed in buckskins, learned the Mohawk language, caroused with Mohawk warriors, and took a Mohawk wife. The doors of his manor house were always open, and hundreds of Mohawks at a time would camp on his property. He was taken into the tribe and given an Iroquois name: Warraghiyagey, "He Who Does Much." His deeds became legendary. Once a Mohawk chief told Johnson of a dream in which the Irishman had given him a fancy coat. Johnson promptly gave the chief the coat off his back. Some days later, Johnson said he also had dreamt — that the chief gave him 5,000 acres of land. So the chief gave him the land.

When the French and Indian War broke out, Johnson enlisted the Iroquois on the side of the British. He led Mohawk warriors into battle against French positions, thus helping the British to seize control of the western frontier. As a reward he was made superintendent of Indian affairs in 1756, a position he held until his death eight years later. 🐚

An ornate cartouche celebrates Johnson's friendship with the Indians.

1763

The Proclamation Line, designed to restrict colonial settlement to the East Coast, contributed to the American Revolution.

After winning the French and Indian War, the English faced the problem of managing a vast North American empire. Much of it remained in turmoil. Native Americans who had been allies of the French saw no good reason to stop fighting. Chief Pontiac of the Ottawas, protesting unfair British trade practices, laid siege to Detroit for five months in 1763. Meanwhile, land-hungry settlers were pouring into the wilderness, leveling forests that had been Indian hunting grounds since time immemorial. Even Britain's Iroquois friends were angry.

Hoping to restore a measure of tranquility, Britain's king George III in 1763 issued a proclamation: beyond the crest of the Appalachian Mountains, settlement would cease. Any settlers already west of this line were "forthwith to remove themselves." With a few minor exceptions, the western lands were reserved for the Indians.

The measure was designed to be temporary, its provisions open to change as the Crown made later treaties with pacified Indian tribes. But the colonists were outraged. Not only did the Proclamation Line violate certain colonial charter rights, but it was seen as an unforgivable intrusion into colonial affairs. Settlers, fur traders, and land speculators simply ignored it. As resentments mounted, the Proclamation of 1763 became yet another grievance on the road to revolution. 🐚

STRUGGLE FOR INDEPENDENCE

(1764 TO 1789)

Britain's willingness to allow the Colonies to chart their own course ended abruptly in 1763. Although victory in the French and Indian War had expanded Britain's territorial holdings, the seven years of conflict had left the Crown deeply in debt. Naturally enough, Britain looked to its empire for help in replenishing the treasury. In addition, the Crown planned to strengthen its power over the Colonies and its newly acquired land. But policies that limited home rule conflicted with the colonists' political beliefs. And as new tax burdens affected the colonists' well-being, they began to resist these burdens. The language of republicanism, advocating the common good, equality, and independence, became a revolutionary battle cry.

PARLIAMENT WASTED NO TIME before passing laws that

hindered expansion and added to the Colonies' financial woes. The Proclamation Act of 1763, intended to pacify local Indian tribes, prohibited colonists from moving west of the Appalachians, where thousands had already settled.

In 1764 Parliament passed the Sugar Act, which taxed a variety of imported goods and became the first law passed specifically to raise money in the Colonies for the Crown. In 1765 the Stamp Act placed a tax on all printed matter, and the Quartering Act required colonists to house and feed British troops. The Townshend Acts of 1767 taxed such everyday products as tea, paper, and paint.

A 1765 law turned British troops into an occupation army in the Colonies.

The new tax measures increased the colonists' need for cash, which was already scarce. Having to pay

The imprint mandated by the hated Stamp Act.

tax bills they had not anticipated forced many colonists to take goods to market that they had produced for their own use. Evading taxes was nothing new for the colonists, but now the law allowed British officials to search the homes and shops of suspected tax dodgers.

The colonists began to put their own interests before obedience to the Crown. New England shipowners, for example, made sizable fortunes smuggling contraband goods. And in the West, despite the ban on trans-Appalachian settlement, frontier homesteaders pushed into the wilderness of Kentucky and Tennessee. They wanted land, animal skins, wealth, and adventure. Before long, such pioneers as Daniel Boone would attain the status of folk heroes.

The spontaneous defiance of individual colonists soon gave way to organized opposition to British rule. The Stamp Act Congress met in 1765 to discuss joint action against the tax. Colonists organized Committees of Correspondence to discuss their grievances.

Men whose names would become part of American history stepped forward: Patrick Henry and Thomas Jefferson in Virginia, Samuel Adams and John Adams in Massachusetts, and Benjamin Franklin in Pennsylvania. They gave passionate speeches to colonial assemblies, and they wrote newspaper articles and pamphlets, hoping to arouse feelings that would unify the 13 Colonies.

MANY COLONIAL LEADERS were influenced by the liberal

ideas of the Enlightenment and by philosophers such as John Locke, who advocated expanding individual rights and limiting the sovereignty of kings. When the colonists protested the Sugar Act or the Stamp Act, they were objecting to more than a specific law — they were rejecting the notion that Britain had the right to impose taxes on colonies that sent no elected representatives to Parliament. Taxation without rep-

ETHAN ALLEN

resentation was a form of tyranny, they claimed.

King George III, the British monarch, ruled neither wisely nor well. In his first 10 years on the throne, from 1760 to 1770, he changed ministries six times, and he stubbornly defended what he regarded as prerogatives of the empire, including his right to tax the Colonies. Thousands of loyal subjects in the Colonies turned against the Crown. Tensions mounted, along with the risk of violence.

On March 5, 1770, a gun was fired — or perhaps it discharged accidentally — as British soldiers tried to rescue a lone sentry from a group of hecklers in Boston. A melee ensued, and five civilians died. The incident, which came to be known as the Boston Massacre, shocked both the

Patriots tossed tea into the harbor from Chinese chests like this one.

Americans and the British. Two years later Rhode Island colonists set fire to the *Gaspée,* a British customs schooner that had run aground. Then in December 1773, colonists dressed as Indians staged the Boston Tea Party, dumping cargoes of tea into the harbor. Their protest was aimed at the Tea Act, which gave the British East India Company an unfair advantage over colonial merchants.

An outraged Parliament responded to the defiance in Massachusetts by passing a series of repressive measures. The Intolerable Acts, as colonists dubbed them, closed the port of Boston, forbade most town meetings, and stripped the colonial assembly of its power. Several Colonies called for a joint meeting to debate a course of action. All but Georgia agreed to attend.

Those opposed to Britain — the Patriots — were mostly farmers, artisans, and colonial legislators who believed that only the people's local representatives had the right to levy taxes. Many merchants, who had been hurt by the Crown's trade restrictions, joined their ranks. Loyalists, known as Tories, preferred to remain under British authority. Tories were often wealthy and privileged — estate holders, owners of well-established businesses who favored the status quo, and officials of the Church of England and the Crown.

THE FIRST CONTINENTAL CONGRESS came to order on September 5, 1774, at Carpenters Hall in Philadelphia. Its members adopted resolutions seeking to abolish every revenue act since 1763 and all other laws limiting their economic growth and political freedom. Most delegates wanted negotiations with the Crown, not independence. In Parliament, however, feeling ran strong against reconciliation, and in February 1775 Massachusetts was declared to be in a state of rebellion. King George endorsed additional harsh measures to punish his wayward subjects.

Meanwhile, in Massachusetts, colonists who had trained sporadically for years to fend off Indians and other attackers were stockpiling arms. On April 19, 1775, the British governor ordered soldiers to seize a rebel weapons depot in Concord. Before the troops reached the depot, they encountered armed colonists in nearby Lexington. A shot rang out. In the ensuing fight, eight colonists died. The American Revolution had begun.

At first glance, the divided colonists seemed to have no chance against the western world's most powerful empire. Besides Britain's enormous wealth and large population, its superior weapons and long tradition of military command gave it a pronounced strategic edge. But King George never

committed enough manpower, ships, or money, and his choice of military leaders was often questionable. When his soldiers managed to occupy an important center — such as Boston, Philadelphia, or Charleston — they often had to evacuate it for lack of manpower or because the troops were needed elsewhere.

The ill-advised policies of King George III helped advance the Patriots' cause.

Because the war lacked traditional fighting fronts, the conflict dragged on with an occasional decisive battle amid many inconclusive ones. One of the Patriots' strengths was being able to wage war on familiar terrain. Volunteers would

fight the British, go home to plow the fields or conduct some business, then return to the battlefield.

The colonists' final victory would have been impossible without outside help. Britain's longtime enemy, France, provided the crucial aid — money, supplies, and naval support. The struggle for freedom also attracted several European battle veterans who admired the American Revolution and were willing to bear arms to show their support. The Marquis de Lafayette, Baron von Steuben, and Tadeusz Koscuisko were among those who crossed the Atlantic to fight side by side with the Patriots. Other war heroes included John Paul Jones, the naval commander who successfully raided the British coast, and George Rogers Clark, whose military campaign in the West secured the frontier territories for the United States.

As The War Continued, it became clear that the

rebelling Colonies needed a government. Shortly after the clash at Lexington, the Second Continental Congress went into session with John Hancock as its president. This contentious but hardworking body raised an army, conducted the war, and issued paper currency. The Congress hesitated to levy taxes, however, and consequently went into debt. It was often unable to pay its soldiers, and the army's suppliers had to wait for their money.

In June 1775 the Congress named George Washington as commander in chief of the Continental Army. The Virginia native was neither a professional soldier nor a brilliant military strategist, but he possessed other traits that would prove critical. His strength of character and unshakable commitment to the cause of liberty helped to unify the beleaguered troops and keep them fighting.

When the Congress convened in 1775, the delegates and their constituents still favored reconciliation

Von Steuben taught military drills and tactics.

George Washington's bedraggled soldiers struggled through the winter at Valley Forge.

with the king. Even when the legislators met in the summer to give Congress's acts the force of law, they saw themselves as a temporary government that would disband as soon as the king shook off the influence of his ill-willed advisers. But in August, King George dispelled any such hopes. He declared the Americans in open rebellion, prohibited trade with them, and dismissed the colonists' vows of loyalty as a waffling tactic meant "only to amuse." When the colonists learned of these events, many who had been wavering turned steadfastly in favor of independence.

On July 4, 1776, the Second Continental Congress voted to

adopt a Declaration of Independence for a new nation called the United States of America. The document that Thomas Jefferson drafted listed the Americans' grievances and spelled out a philosophy of government: All people are equal and possess rights to life, liberty, and the pursuit of happiness; governments exist to protect these rights, and therefore a government's authority derives from the consent of the governed; when a government no longer protects the rights of its citizens, they must change the government or abolish it. These powerful concepts did more than inform Britain of the Americans' ideals and intentions. They served as a source of inspiration for a nation being born.

The Continental Army managed to win the war without winning many of the battles. Although the Patriots were able to score impressive victories in the battles of Trenton, Saratoga, and, finally, Yorktown in 1781, the major achievement of General Washington and his commanders was to keep the army intact long enough to wear down the British. When Britain signed a formal peace treaty in 1783, it recognized the independent United States of America. All the

lands east of the Mississippi, south of Canada, and north of Florida now belonged to the new republic.

HAVING OUTLASTED THE BRITISH and acquired a vast

territory, the Americans suddenly had to determine how to govern themselves. In 1781 the 13 states implemented the Articles of Confederation, which gave a central authority such powers as conducting foreign affairs, declaring war, raising an army, making treaties, selling public land, and printing paper money. The individual states kept all other prerogatives, including those that prompted the rebellion against Britain — the powers to tax and regulate trade.

Unfortunately, the system didn't work. The confederation did not have the authority to bring stability to the states. Monetary and trade arrangements were in disarray. The central government was unable to protect settlers in the West, and in the East a rebellion of impoverished farmers broke out in Massachusetts in 1786.

When the confederation's weaknesses became apparent, debate over government and the nature of democracy escalated. On one side were men known as Federalists, who wanted a strong central government. Mainly urban merchants, professionals, and large landowners, they were led by Alexander Hamilton and James Madison. The other side, led by Richard Henry Lee and Abraham Yates, took the name of Anti-Federalists, and included militia officers, farmers, artisans, and traders. Anti-Federalists worried that a strong central government would infringe on personal liberties. They also feared that they would become second-class citizens in the

Washington's forces used small open gunboats to attack the mighty British navy.

Federalists' proposed industrial, largely urban society.

A convention met in Philadelphia in 1787 to draft a Constitution of the United States. Rhode Island and North Carolina initially held out against it, and five states recom-

States issued their own notes to help pay for the war.

mended amendments. But the nine states needed for ratification voted in favor of it in 1787 and 1788, and the rest soon followed suit.

A product of compromise and insight, the Constitution established a government with a division of powers and a system of checks and balances. The president could appoint judges, negotiate treaties, propose legislation, and veto laws passed by Congress. The Congress ratified treaties and appropriated money, but it could also impeach a president or override a veto. The judicial branch could declare acts of the president and Congress unconstitutional.

THE CONSTITUTION failed to satisfy those delegates who

were fearful of a new tyranny, so they insisted on amending the document to protect such individual rights as the freedoms of speech, assembly, religion, and the press. The first 10 amendments were called the Bill of Rights. On the issue of slavery, the Constitution struck a compromise. The word *slavery* was omitted; but the document did protect the institution by permitting the passage of laws to require the return of fugitives, including "persons held to service" — namely slaves. By skirting the slavery question, the Constitution allowed the South to develop along lines vastly different from the North, where each state subsequently prohibited slavery. But the Founding Fathers' quandary — how a nation dedicated to the proposition that all men are created equal could hold some men and women in slavery — left unsettled a question that would ultimately be resolved by the force of arms.

With hindsight, historians can rightfully call the Constitution a work of genius — a marvel of rigid principle and flexibility that has withstood the test of time. But in 1789, when George Washington, the nation's first president, swore to uphold the Constitution, some people doubted that the rough and unruly ex-colonists would be able to govern themselves for any length of time. Both at home and abroad, many wondered whether Americans had the ability or the desire to cast aside their personal interests in order to attain the lofty goals they had set for their democracy.

1764

The Mason-Dixon Line, the famous boundary between slave and free states before the Civil War, was actually created a century earlier to settle a border dispute.

Disagreements over the boundary between Pennsylvania and Maryland began in 1681, when the English Crown granted William Penn a charter whose borders were only vaguely defined. Both colonies soon claimed the same land. Maryland's map put Philadelphia inside its territory, while Pennsylvania's map claimed Baltimore and reduced Maryland to a narrow strip. Three times during the next 80 years, agencies of the Crown tried but failed to resolve the dispute. Setting a border in the wilderness wasn't easy.

Finally two of Penn's sons, Richard and Thomas, met with Frederick Calvert, a descendant of Lord Baltimore, the founder of Maryland, and privately agreed to commission a border survey. They chose two highly recommended English astronomer-surveyors, Charles Mason and Jeremiah Dixon. From 1763 to 1767 Mason and Dixon, using the most advanced instruments available, trekked through the wilderness marking a new border and drawing it on a map. For greater accuracy, they checked their geographical position every 11.5 miles. The result was a 322-mile, L-shaped boundary line that divided Pennsylvania from Maryland, West Virginia, and Delaware.

Although Pennsylvania came out ahead from the standpoint of territorial gains, both sides declared themselves happy with the results and split the cost of the survey. It turned out to be a good investment, considering that three subsequent surveys all confirmed that Mason and Dixon had made no major mistakes.

Mason and Dixon set markers like this one along every fifth mile of the line.

1764

Sam Adams failed at every venture he tried until he led an antitax protest and discovered his true calling — political revolutionary.

The son of a prosperous Boston merchant, Samuel Adams entered the world with every advantage. He graduated from Harvard at age 18 and stayed on to earn a master's degree. Then his life seemed to hit a stone wall. He worked briefly in a counting house, but he had no head for figures. Samuel Sr., hoping to set up his son in business, gave him $1,000, but young Sam ran through the money in no time. An eight-year tenure as a tax collector ended dismally when Adams, who never bothered to keep proper accounts, came up several thousand pounds short. He was accused of dipping into the till. (The charges didn't stick.)

Sam Adams began his political career with the Caucus Club, an unlikely mix of dock workers and intellectuals who met to smoke pipes and plot political strategy. When the British Parliament passed the Sugar Act in April 1764, Adams spoke out swiftly and forcefully against taxation without representation. He became a leader in radical Boston politics. Thomas Hutchinson, the colonial lieutenant governor, called him a dangerous "incendiary." At the age of 42, Adams had discovered his calling.

When the British acted, Adams struck back. "Where there is a spark of patriotick fire, we will enkindle it," he said. He organized rival Boston street gangs into a force of 2,000 rebels — the Sons of Liberty — and

Sam Adams, known for his anti-British tirades, strikes a dignified pose after the Boston Massacre.

incited them against British troops sent to Boston to help enforce the law; he even trained his dog to snap at Redcoats. When some British soldiers, goaded into firing their guns, killed several colonists — the so-called Boston Massacre of 1770 — the incident provided Adams with still more ammunition. Then, in 1773, it was Adams who urged patriots disguised as Mohawk Indians to dump English tea into Boston harbor. "Sam Adams is in his glory," complained Hutchinson.

Brilliant of mind (though often somewhat sloppy in appearance), Adams had a natural genius for whipping up public opinion at town meetings. He was also a skillful wordsmith who wrote hundreds of articles for Boston newspapers advocating independence from Britain.

Even after he had earned a reputation as a powerful politician, he continued to dress shabbily, wearing his poverty as a badge of commitment to the people. In 1774, when Adams was chosen to attend the first Continental Congress — whose creation he had proposed — a group of friends outfitted him from head to toe and tactfully gave him some spending money. Then they proudly sent Boston's leading citizen to Philadelphia, where he helped shape discontent into a blueprint for opposition to British authority.

1765

The Stamp Act ignited a storm of opposition that drove the American colonies closer to independence.

To the British Parliament it was a fair and sensible measure — a nominal tax levy to pay for the defense of the Colonies. The Stamp Act, approved in March 1765, required that all legal and commercial papers, including newspapers, advertisements, playing cards, pamphlets, and almanacs, bear a tax stamp that cost anywhere from a halfpenny to £10.

The colonists were outraged: how could the British government dare to tax them without giving them fair representation in Parliament? Reaction was swift and tumultuous. Patrick Henry denounced the tax in the Virginia House of Burgesses, and in so doing provoked cries of "treason" from royalist members. "If this be treason, make the most of it," he shouted — much to the delight of his fellow patriots.

Henry seized the moment, proposing seven resolutions that summarized the colony's objections. Five passed, including a demand that the colonists be granted the same freedoms that the Englishmen enjoyed. Another resolution noted a long-estab-

The sorry fate of a British customs officer in the Boston Colony: tarring and feathering.

lished precedent giving colonists "the inestimable right of being governed by such laws as are derived from their own consent."

Printed copies of Henry's resolutions were sent to the other Colonies, where they ignited a firestorm of anti-British protest. "No taxation without representation" became a favorite rally cry. Mobs in Boston burned the local stamp distributor in effigy and ransacked his home; they then destroyed the lieutenant governor's residence. Similar violence erupted in New York, Delaware, and North Carolina. A radical group known as the Sons of Liberty gained members throughout the Colonies. Most significantly, as a result of the tax, colonists organized their own intercolonial assembly. Delegates from nine colonies met at the Stamp Act Congress in October 1765.

Georgia was the only colony in which any stamps were sold. Elsewhere, colonists began boycotting British imports. Parliament finally admitted its error, and six months after going into effect, the Stamp Act was repealed. It had become, as a New York broadside concluded, "the folly of England and the ruin of America."

1765

American colonists hatched plots to break with the British monarchy in their favorite meeting place — the town tavern.

As rumors circulated that the hated Stamp Act of 1765 would shortly be repealed, colonists gathered to celebrate at the Liberty Tree Tavern in Boston. More than just drinking establishments, colonial taverns were centers of community life — places to do business, collect mail, trade gossip, and talk politics.

Over well-filled pipes and tankards of ale, colonists would debate the overthrow of British rule. Fueled by strong spirits, the talk would grow heated, and as the evening wore on, the smoke-filled taverns would fairly ring with revolutionary fervor.

Taverns housed more than a few well-known patriots. Paul

Revere and his watch committee of 30 volunteers met regularly at Boston's Green Dragon Tavern. Before Patrick Henry became a revolutionary leader, he worked as a bartender in a Virginia alehouse.

Once the war began, taverns served other purposes. Many doubled as military prisons, hospitals, barracks, storage places, and military courtrooms. Gen. George Washington frequented the Fraunces Tavern in New York City. When the war ended in 1783, Washington raised his glass there in 13 toasts — one for each new state. Ten days later, he returned to the tavern to bid his loyal officers farewell.

IN THEIR OWN WORDS

I stopped one night at a tavern in Shrewsbury about forty miles from Boston, and as I was cold and wet, I sat down at a good fire in the bar-room to dry my great coat and saddle-bags, till a fire could be made in my chamber. There presently came in, one after another, half a dozen, or half a score substantial yeomen of the neighborhood, who, sitting down to the fire after lighting their pipes, began a lively conversation on politics. . . . One said, 'The people of Boston are distracted.' Another answered, 'No wonder the people of Boston are distracted. Oppression will make wise men mad.' A third said, 'What would you say if a fellow should come to your house and tell you he was come to take a list of your cattle, that Parliament might tax you for them at so much a head?' . . . After much more reasoning in this style, a fifth, who had as yet been silent, broke out: 'Well, it's high time for us to rebel; we must rebel some time or other, and we had better rebel now than at any time to come.'

A record of a 1774 conversation overheard in a tavern by John Adams.

G *1767*

eorge Washington might have led a revolution in farming practices if the Revolutionary War had not interrupted his agrarian experiments.

George Washington's instructions in 1767 for his Mount Vernon estate were emphatic — absolutely no tobacco was to be grown on any of his farms near the Potomac River. For some time he had known that growing only tobacco — a staple crop in the South — ruined the Virginia soil. Tobacco farming

also required an expensive increase in the use of slave laborers.

Eager to improve his agricultural output, Washington focused instead on raising wheat and corn. He also tried nonfood products such as hemp and flax, and he worked hard to devise better ways of producing them. Farming manuals from England were little help, he concluded, because differences in soil, weather, and other conditions limited how much he

Washington organized his laborers, managers, proprietors, and other farmworkers in a way that resembled a military chain of command.

could learn from English agricultural techniques. So he experimented on his own, planting grains in different types of soil and testing several types of fertilizers to see if he could increase the yield.

Washington could hardly wait to return to his farm in 1797, after his second term as president. He described a farmer's role as "the most pleasing occupation of my life and most congenial with my temper." The beloved military hero and leader regretted that "my absences from home have been so frequent, and so long at a time, as to have prevented me from bestowing the attention and from making the experiments which are necessary to establish facts in the Service of Agriculture."

J *1769*

ust as British colonialism slowed down on the East Coast, Spanish colonialism began to spread along the West Coast.

Fearing encroachment from Russian fur traders and other Europeans — and eager to win converts to Christianity — Spanish colonial administrators in Mexico began in 1769 to send Franciscan friars to establish missions along California's coast. Brother Junípero Serra built the first nine missions, which extended from San Diego to as far north as San Francisco. All told, the Franciscans founded 21 missions up and down the coast.

Traveling on foot and by mule, Serra and his fellow Franciscans refused to let disease, insufficient water, or difficult terrain keep them from their goal: converting Native Americans to Roman Catholicism. Although plagued by an old leg

Franciscan missionary Junípero Serra.

wound that left him lame, Serra nonetheless pursued his quest with unflagging energy. He died in 1784 at the age of 70, having trudged thousands of miles to perform baptisms and confirmations. Over the next 50 years, hundreds of missionaries baptized some 84,000 Indians in California.

The Mexicans threw off the yoke of Spanish colonialism in 1834, thus ending Franciscan mission activity. By the 1850's, California had become an attractive destination for westward-bound American settlers. The growth that eventually made California the most populous state in the nation can be credited in part to Serra and his fellow missionaries, who together with their Native American converts had constructed irrigation systems, planted vineyards, and helped tame the Pacific Coast wilderness.

Tracing Serra's Footsteps

Spanish settlement in California began with missions that served for decades as centers of agriculture, commerce, and religious and secular education for Native Americans. Franciscan Junípero Serra founded the first nine missions in the region.

	Mission	Date Established
1	San Diego	1769
2	San Carlos	1770
3	San Antonio	1771
4	San Gabriel	1771
5	San Luis Obispo	1772
6	San Francisco	1776
7	San Juan Capistrano	1776
8	Santa Clara	1777
9	San Buenaventura	1782

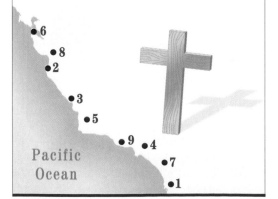

Pacific Ocean

1770

John Adams, one of America's greatest patriots, defended a British officer on trial for murder because of the notorious Boston Massacre.

It began after a night of brawling between British soldiers and colonial laborers. On March 5, 1770, a group of workmen gathered around a lone British sentry on guard duty and taunted him until he lost his temper. The sentry knocked one man over with his musket butt and in return was pelted with snowballs, ice chunks, and coal. A crowd gathered quickly, shouting, "Kill him!"

When Capt.Thomas Preston and a squad of Redcoats arrived to quell the disturbance, chimes rang out from the city's church towers, bringing more people into the streets. Despite Preston's efforts to avoid casualties, a soldier opened fire on the jeering mob. Soon five Bostonians were dead and six others lay wounded. The crowd — John Adams later called it "a motley rabble" — would not go home until the lieutenant governor, Thomas Hutchinson, appeared in person and promised that Preston and his men would go to trial for murder.

The gunsmoke had barely cleared before radical politician Sam Adams, who seized any opportunity to confront the British, went to work.

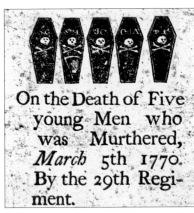

The caskets shown on this broadside bear the initials of the five men killed in the Boston Massacre.

Printed accounts of the "Horrid Massacre" began circulating within hours of the event. Paul Revere distributed an engraving, "Bloody Massacre Perpetrated in King Street, Boston," that helped transform the crowd of waterfront toughs and rabble-rousers into noble martyrs.

Not one Boston lawyer would agree to defend Preston until John Adams — Harvard-educated, a patriot, and cousin to Sam — decided to take the case. John Adams believed that denial of counsel was not worthy of a free society.

While Sam demanded an immediate trial, John won a temper-cooling delay. When a jury was chosen, John allowed at least five British sympathizers to sit on it. Presenting a skillful defense, John avoided the close cross-examination that might have revealed the role his cousin Sam may have played in helping to provoke the episode. Captain Preston was declared innocent, as were all but two soldiers, who were convicted on a lesser charge.

His fellow patriots soon forgave John Adams for defending the Britishers, and in 1774 they elected him to the First Continental Congress. He went on to serve the United States as statesman, diplomat, lawmaker, and as its second president.

1770

Ethan Allen and his Green Mountain Boys, using guerrilla tactics, tried to pressure New York into giving up territorial claims to land that eventually became Vermont.

For several years, New York and New Hampshire were embroiled in a land dispute that arose because the British Crown had inadvertently granted charters to both colonies for what is now Vermont. One resident of an area known as the New Hampshire Grants was Ethan Allen, a veteran of the French and Indian War. In 1770 the combative Allen organized a troop of raiders to persuade New York to give up its claim to the disputed territory. The hit-and-run Green Mountain Boys, led by "colonel commandant" Allen, burned down cabins, stole cattle, and destroyed fences.

Five years later, at the start of the Revolutionary War, Allen turned his energies to a military engagement in upstate New York. Linking up with Col. Benedict Arnold, in May 1775 he marched to British-held Fort Ticonderoga in hopes of capturing the fort's valuable brass cannons. Yet when Congress learned that Allen had taken Ticonderoga, there was no rejoicing. Despite recent bloodshed at Lexington and Concord, many legislators were still not ready to declare war on Britain. Later that year Allen was captured by the British while mounting an invasion of Canada. After spending nearly three years as a prisoner in England, he returned to Vermont to command the local militia and resume his feud with New York.

Waving his sword, Allen surprises the British commander at Fort Ticonderoga.

The burning of the British ship Gaspée *by Rhode Island patriots added fuel to the growing tensions between the Colonies and the British Crown.*

W 1772

hen the British ship *Gaspée* ran aground off the coast of Rhode Island, furious colonists burned it to the waterline.

To combat the widespread smuggling of goods, the British ship *Gaspée* zealously patrolled the Rhode Island coast, searching for violations of the customs law. The captain went out of his way to recover contraband, seizing almost any ship in his path. To add insult to injury, the schooner's crew developed a taste for Rhode Island mutton, pork, and chicken, and regularly raided coastal farms. Such high-handedness was not appreciated by the colonists.

Then on June 9, 1772, Rhode Islanders got a chance to vent their anger.

The *Gaspée* had run aground on a sandbar off Warwick, Rhode Island, seven miles south of Providence. The news spread quickly, and that night some 150 men rowed out to the stranded ship. They swarmed aboard and, after depositing the crew onshore, set the vessel afire.

British officials resolved to take the men to England to stand trial — further outraging the colonists, who believed that they had the same right as any other English subject to be tried by a jury of their peers. So when the commission began hearings, none of the Rhode Islanders called to testify could recall a single detail. As a result, no colonist involved in the *Gaspée* affair was ever brought to trial.

Encouraged by this remarkable display of Yankee solidarity, patriot leaders set up Committees of Correspondence throughout the Colonies to help coordinate resistance to British rule. In the months that followed, these committees would play a vital role in bringing on the American Revolution.

W 1773

ith a signal from Sam Adams, dozens of "Mohawks" turned Boston Harbor into a massive "teapot."

Francis Rotch, a prominent Boston merchant and owner of the tea ship *Dartmouth*, arrived at Boston's Old South Meeting House on December 16, 1773, looking like a condemned man. Twice Rotch had asked the colonial governor for permission to return to England with his cargo, and twice the governor had said no. If he obeyed the governor and unloaded the tea in Boston, he would suffer reprisals from angry colonists. If he disobeyed the governor and attempted to leave port without unloading, he would be charged with treason. Either way, Rotch stood to lose.

The cause of all his troubles was the Tea Act of 1773. Several years earlier, pressured by a colonial boycott of British goods, Parliament had repealed a long list of import duties — all except for the tax on tea. Then in 1773 Parliament granted a monopoly on tea sales to certain designated local merchants. To the colonists, the measure was another intol-

One of the earliest depictions of the Boston Tea Party, a 1793 engraving shows Bostonians in Indian dress dumping the cargo.

erable example of Parliamentary interference in colonial affairs.

It was near dark when a dismayed Rotch informed the gathering of patriots at the Old South Meeting House of the governor's refusal. The group's ringleader, Sam Adams, was elated; once again he could demonstrate the colonists' defiance. "This meeting can do nothing more to save the country," he announced. With that, a well-organized company of patriots disguised as Mohawk Indians descended on the harbor. They dumped 342 caskets of tea, valued at some £10,000, into the water, while thousands of Bostonians stood cheering along the shore.

In retaliation, Parliament passed severely punitive measures. The Crown ordered Boston Harbor closed, limited the self-governing powers of Massachusetts, and required the Colonies to quarter British troops — creating, in effect, an occupation army. "The die is now cast," King George wrote. "The Colonies must either submit or triumph." Little did he know how prophetic his words would be.

1774
New Hampshire Patriots took up arms four months before the battles at Lexington and Concord.

As tensions grew between the American patriots and the British during 1774, the colonials increasingly sought weapons to be used in case of trouble. One tempting munitions storehouse lay waiting at Fort William and Mary, a lightly manned British garrison at Portsmouth Harbor in New Hampshire.

In December the Patriots of Boston learned that British general Thomas Gage planned to strengthen the Portsmouth fort with additional soldiers. Once the troops were in place, it would be almost impossible for the Americans to seize the valuable munitions. To warn their New Hampshire comrades of the coming reinforcements, the Bostonians sent word by the best messenger they knew — the local silversmith Paul Revere.

Revere saddled his horse and set out on the 60-mile journey to Portsmouth. The roads lay wet and slippery from an earlier snowfall and freeze, and a piercing west wind added to his misery. By the next afternoon, when he arrived, his horse was "nearly done," an eyewitness noted. Revere quickly presented his message to the local Committee of Correspondence.

Portsmouth's citizens sprang into action. On December 14, some 400 armed Patriots boarded small boats on the Piscataqua River and splashed ashore at Fort William and Mary. They first demanded surrender, then overwhelmed a group of six British soldiers. Obviously outnumbered, the British managed to fire three cannon shots before they were forced to give in. The triumphant Americans made off with a treasure trove of booty, including 100 barrels of gunpowder and 100 small arms.

This first armed uprising of the Revolution had occurred without bloodshed. Four months later it was a different story. More than a hundred men died when the shots rang out at Lexington and Concord, launching eight long years of arduous battle. ➤

A British sentry at a wilderness fort wears a bright red coat and carries a muzzle-loading musket.

1775
The Transylvania Territory — most of present-day Kentucky — petitioned Congress to become the 14th colony.

On March 17, 1775, Richard Henderson, a land speculator, purchased from the Cherokee Indians a vast tract of Appalachian wilderness for $10,000 in guns, clothing, rum, and other sundries. Both Virginia and North Carolina claimed the area, but no matter: Henderson, as founder of the Transylvania Company, didn't mind cutting corners in order to make a profit.

Henderson enlisted the aid of wilderness scout Daniel Boone, who founded the company's first settlement, Boonesborough. The governor of North Carolina quickly branded the settlers "land pyrates" and demanded that they relinquish their holdings. But Boonesborough remained, and other towns like it soon took shape.

To protect their investment, Henderson and his partners petitioned the Continental Congress to make the Transylvania Territory America's 14th colony. But John Adams, from Massachusetts, pointed out that such a move would further strain relations with England, and the request was denied.

Meanwhile, tensions were rising among residents of Transylvania. Settlers were angry over Indian attacks, inflated land values, and overpriced goods at the company store. They petitioned to become a county of Virginia, and in December 1776 they got their wish. Less than two decades later, the region became the state of Kentucky. ➤

1775

The ride to Lexington and Concord made famous in Longfellow's poem was not the first — or even the most important — journey that Paul Revere took for the Revolution.

By the time of his celebrated midnight ride on April 18, 1775, Boston silversmith and Patriot Paul Revere was already a well-traveled town crier. Two years earlier, asked to deliver the news of the Boston Tea Party to sympathizers in New York and Philadelphia, he made the round-trip journey in just 10 days — "a much shorter time than could be expected at this Season," as one observer noted. Revere made at least four more visits to those cities, as well as shorter trips throughout New England.

An active, energetic figure in revolutionary Boston, Revere helped organize a loosely structured dissident movement and galvanize it into action. He also performed other

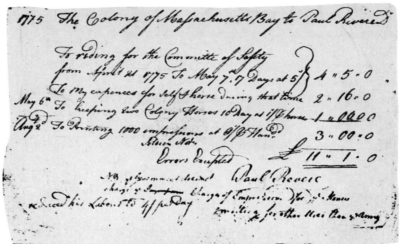

For his ride to Lexington and other patriotic services, Paul Revere handed this expense account to the Massachusetts Committee of Safety.

services, such as setting up a mill to produce gunpowder for the Continental Army, engraving plates for the printing of colonial money, and turning out pictorial engravings to be used as revolutionary propaganda. His 1770 print of the Boston Massacre helped rouse anti-British feelings in the Colonies.

His most famous ride — immortalized by Henry Wadsworth Longfellow almost a century later — began in Charlestown, across the river from Boston. Revere was waiting to relay news of expected British troop movements. At around 11 P.M. he spotted his signal — two lanterns in the belfry of Boston's Old North Church — indicating that the British would start out by boat toward Lexington and Concord. And so Revere galloped off into solitary legend.

In fact, Revere did not ride alone. Another courier, William Dawes, also went to Lexington, arriving shortly after Revere. The two were joined by a local doctor, Samuel Prescott, and all three hurried on together toward Concord. Along the way they ran into a British patrol. Dawes turned tail and fled, and Revere was held for questioning. Only Prescott galloped on to alert the Concord militia that the British were coming.

1775

Riding hell-for-leather, a determined troop of mounted couriers carried vital messages during the Revolution.

As the first casualties of war lay dead or wounded on the green at Lexington, a 23-year-old professional post rider, Israel Bissel, saddled up and headed out. In his pocket he carried a vital commission: "The bearer . . . is charged to alarm the Country quite to Connecticut. All persons are desired to furnish him with fresh horses, as they may be needed." Bissel rode from Watertown to Worcester, Massachusetts, about 33 miles, in just two hours. When he arrived, some reports say, his horse died from exhaustion. Unfazed, Bissel shouted, "To Arms! To Arms! The War has begun!" and promptly mounted a new horse. Three days later, on April 21, he arrived in New Haven with the same alarming message. He ended his circuit at Philadelphia on April 25, having ridden a total of 345 miles in six days — a long-distance record at the time — with virtually no rest.

There were others. When 27-year-old Virginia militia captain John Jouett came upon some Redcoats at a tavern in Louisa County, he learned that the British Army would shortly attempt to capture Virginia's governor, Thomas Jefferson, along with various revolutionary leaders in the Virginia legislature. He mounted his thoroughbred and rode through some 40 miles of wilderness in total darkness. Jouett arrived at Thomas Jefferson's home, Monticello, before sunrise, in plenty of time to warn him of the British attack.

Not all the midnight riders were men. In April 1777, 16-year-old Sybil Ludington from Putnam County, New York, volunteered to ride 40 miles through the dark to warn of a British advance. Ludington galloped from cabin to cabin, banging on the doors with a big stick to wake the occupants. Twenty-three-year-old Deborah Champion Gilbert of Connecticut rode more than 100 miles through enemy lines to deliver army payroll and dispatches to Gen. George Washington's headquarters in Cambridge, Massachusetts. When, covered with mud, she was stopped at the state border, one Redcoat dismissed her as "only an old woman." The next day, she was saluting Washington himself.

Teenage heroine Sybil Ludington rode through the night to warn New Yorkers of approaching Redcoats.

N *1775*
No one knows who fired "the shot heard 'round the world" — but it sparked a battle in Lexington, Massachusetts, and set off the Revolutionary War.

Alerted to the British troops' plan to commandeer a gunpowder supply at nearby Concord, some 130 militiamen had gathered on the Lexington town green in the predawn hours of April 19, 1775. Several hours passed. By the time Maj. John Pitcairn's 800 scarlet-clad troops marched in, bayonets drawn, many of the colonists had either returned home or ducked into a nearby tavern to escape the morning cold.

Major Pitcairn (right) tried in vain to prevent bloodshed.

"Lay down your arms, you rebels, and disperse!" Pitcairn repeatedly shouted. Slowly the remaining colonists began to move away. But they held on to their muskets. Suddenly, a shot rang out.

No one knows where it came from. American onlookers insisted that one of Pitcairn's soldiers had fired it. Pitcairn claimed it was a colonist, stating that he saw "a Gun in a Peasant's hand from behind a Wall" — which flashed but didn't go off — and then "found his horse wounded & also a man near him wounded." It was the only British casualty.

Ignoring Pitcairn's command to stop, the Redcoats began sending volley after volley into the crowd. "The men were so wild," a lieutenant recalled, "that they could hear no orders." Eventually the British commander brought his men under control, but the damage had been done: 8 colonists dead and 10 others wounded. Pitcairn marched his troops on to the arsenal at Concord.

Patriot leaders hurriedly circulated reports of the encounter, embellishing it with tales of British atrocities — anything to rally supporters to their cause. The American Revolution had begun.

On the Road to Independence

These dramatic events and military engagements contributed to the emergence of the United States as a nation.

- **1775** Paul Revere rides to Lexington on the night of April 18–19 to alert residents that the English are approaching.

- **1775** On June 15 the Second Continental Congress appoints George Washington of Virginia commander of the Continental Army.

- **1776** Unexpected American victories at Trenton and Princeton between December 26, 1776, to January 3, 1777, drive the overconfident British from southern New Jersey, putting them on the defensive and largely canceling earlier gains.

- **1777** In fierce battles that continue from September 19 to October 17, the Continental Army triumphs at Saratoga, New York, forcing an invading British army to surrender and at the same time gaining French support for the Patriots.

- **1779** A military victory at Vincennes, Indiana, on February 25 ensures the American claim to the Western territories.

- **1780** British major John André is arrested as a spy on September 23 for carrying plans that reveal the American defenses at West Point.

- **1781** A costly British victory at Guilford Courthouse, North Carolina, on March 15 forces the British troops, led by Gen. Charles Cornwallis, to retreat north into Virginia, where they will become an easy target at Yorktown.

- **1781** From September 28 to October 19, French and American forces lay siege to the British stronghold of Yorktown, Virginia. The British negotiate a surrender in which 8,000 troops become prisoners.

- **1783** The Treaty of Paris is signed, formally ending the American Revolution.

T *1775*
The minutemen who fought at Lexington and Concord were not the armed rabble of myth, but a well-drilled militia.

Since the early 17th century, every Massachusetts town had maintained a "training band" for its self-defense. Service was mandatory for nearly all able-bodied men, some of whom were kept on round-the-clock alert. Roxbury, for one, declared that fully a quarter of its civilian militia be ready to fight "at a minute's warning."

And so the minutemen came into being. Although they had no formal uniforms or drill manual, many were expert shots. Some had fought in the French and Indian War, and all — from age 16 to 66 — spent long hours training. By 1775 Massachusetts had some 14,000 soldiers under arms, including both minutemen and ordinary militia. So on April 19, when word went out that the British Army was on its way, the colony was ready. Men literally dropped what they were doing. Farmers left their plows in the fields, craftsmen put down their tools and grabbed their muskets and hurried to join the battle at Lexington and Concord.

1775

The famous Battle of Bunker Hill was actually fought on nearby Breed's Hill. Although the British claimed victory, they suffered twice as many casualties as did the Americans.

When American leaders learned that British troops intended to occupy Dorchester Heights, overlooking Boston Harbor, the Patriots planned a countermove: they would seize 110-foot-high Bunker Hill in nearby Charlestown. Moving in under cover of darkness, American colonel William Prescott — for reasons that have never been determined — chose Breed's Hill instead. On June 17, 1775, as Bostonians watched from rooftops and church steeples, British troops twice stormed Breed's Hill. Twice they were repulsed. By the second attack, the Americans were desperately low on ammunition. To conserve powder and shot — so the story goes — either Prescott or Gen. Israel Putnam declared: "Don't fire 'til you see the whites of their eyes." Even so, the ammunition ran out and the Americans had to retreat.

The Redcoats had won, but at a fearsome price: some 1,050 British killed or wounded. The Americans lost less than half that number — an estimated 400 to 450 men. The sad irony of the victory was not lost on the British. "Another such would have ruined us," lamented Gen. Henry Clinton.

Charlestown erupts into flame after the British capture Breed's Hill (at right).

IN THEIR OWN WORDS

"I am now set down to write to you on a subject, which fills me with inexpressible concern, and this concern is greatly aggravated and increased, when I reflect upon the uneasiness I know it will cause you. It has been determined in Congress, that the whole army raised for the defense of the American cause shall be put under my care, and that it is necessary for me to proceed immediately to Boston to take upon me the command of it.
You may believe me, my dear Patsy, when I assure you, in the most solemn manner that, so far from seeking this appointment, I have used every endeavor in my power to avoid it, not only from my unwillingness to part with you and the family, but from a consciousness of its being a trust too great for my capacity, and that I should enjoy more real happiness in one month with you at home, than I have the most distant prospect of finding abroad, if my stay were to be seven times seven years. But as it has been a kind of destiny, that has thrown me upon this service, I shall hope that my undertaking it is designed to answer some good purpose."

George Washington in a letter to his wife, written June 18, 1775, on having been unanimously elected commander in chief of the Continental Army.

1775

Samuel Adams helped mastermind the American Revolution before he mastered horseback riding.

In colonial times, most children learned to ride horses as early as children today learn to ride bicycles. But not Samuel Adams. He didn't learn to ride until he was 52 years old. Getting Adams into the saddle required an appeal to his patriotism — as well as a push from two servants.

Riding skills would certainly have come in handy in April 1775, when the British army marched into Lexington. One of its objectives was to capture Sam Adams and John Hancock, who were hiding out there. But instead of fleeing the British on horseback, the two men had to wait for Hancock's carriage.

When Sam traveled with his cousin, John Adams, from Boston to a Congressional meeting in Philadelphia in September, John

1775

AKentucky pioneer named Daniel Boone became a living legend — all thanks to a visiting schoolmaster.

The list of his accomplishments runs on and on. By his early teens Daniel Boone could shoe a horse, plow a field, fire a rifle, and skin a deer. Though he never learned to spell, he picked up enough arithmetic to become a competent land surveyor. During the French and Indian War — he had just turned 21 — Boone left the family farm at Buffalo Lick, North Carolina, to join the colonial militia. Hearing tales of a bountiful land beyond the Appalachians, he went to see for himself, first as a hunter and then as agent for a land developer. In 1775, with 30 men, he blazed the Wilderness Road across the mountains from Virginia to Kentucky, and he led the first families (including his own wife and children) along it to found the wilderness town of Boonesborough.

As the Revolutionary War swept south from New England, fighting in the back country took the form of raids by Indians — who were mostly pro-British — on American settlements.

Boonesborough was a natural target. The settlers lived behind a wooden stockade in constant fear of attack. One February day in 1778, having ventured out to gather salt, Boone and his companions were set upon by Shawnee warriors and taken prisoner. Ever cool in a crisis, Boone bargained his way into the good graces of the Shawnee chief, who adopted him into the tribe. Then, seizing a chance to escape, Boone hastened back to Boonesborough. The inevitable attack soon came — a combined assault by 450 Indian warriors and British soldiers, which the town rebuffed after a nine-day siege. The process of turning Boone into a larger-than-life frontier hero began when a traveling schoolteacher, John Filson, arrived in the region to write a book. The resulting work, *The Discovery, Settlement, and Present State of Kentucke*, contained a florid, romanticized account of Boone's exploits. Large sections were presented as being direct quotes from the frontiersman himself — though they hardly seemed typical of the speaker's normally down-to-earth style, as seen in an inscription he once carved: "D. Boon cilled a bar on this tree."

Boone's backwoods exploits won him worldwide renown.

No matter. The book was a huge success, both in America and across Europe, and its hero became world famous as a frontier archetype. In time even Boone himself, who lived to age 85, came to believe his own legend. In his later years, as Filson's book was read aloud to him, he would murmur, "Every word true. Not a lie in it."

---

was finally able to convince him that riding a horse was crucial "to the character of a statesman." So Sam dutifully mounted one of the Adams family horses, described as a "very genteel and easy little creature."

His first full day of riding may have been good for his patriotism, but it did not benefit his posterior. To ease the pain of Sam's saddle sores, John had a seamstress sew him a pair of padded drawers. Thus reinforced, Sam Adams took surprisingly well to riding. Instead of having two servants boost him into the saddle, he learned to mount a horse by himself.

By the time the pair reached Philadelphia, their servants agreed that Sam was the better rider. When members of Congress had to flee Philadelphia to avoid capture by the British Army, Sam had his cousin to thank — not only for his equestrian skills, but probably for his life.

1775

Henry Knox had never fought in a battle, but that didn't prevent him from becoming a colonel in the American Army.

Henry Knox learned about warfare in his Boston bookstore, where he pored over volumes on military strategy and engineering. His knowledge so impressed George Washington that the American commander not only commissioned Knox a colonel but also entrusted him with a crucial task: transporting British heavy artillery, captured at Fort Ticonderoga in 1775, from upstate New York to Boston. Washington considered the weapons so important to the city's defense that he warned that "no Trouble or Experience must be spared to obtain them."

Combining engineering skill and perseverance, Knox and his men transported 43 cannons and 16 mortars (some weighing as much as a ton) by boat, sled, and oxen through 200 miles of wilderness in the dead of winter. The Americans mounted the artillery in Dorchester Heights, near Boston. When the British commander learned of the patriots' entrenched armament, he withdrew from Boston without a fight.

After Washington was elected President, he appointed Knox secretary of war. Today Knox's military exploits are honored in a way unlike those of any other war hero. The government installation famous for storing gold bullion is named Fort Knox.

Knox acquired his expertise on cannons from books.

B¹⁷⁷⁵enjamin Thompson left New Hampshire for Europe, where he became one of the few American-born counts.

Benjamin Thompson, a New Hampshire resident interested in mathematics and physics, was jailed on suspicion of spying for the British in 1775. Never an advocate of colonial independence, the 22-year-old Thompson joined up to fight for the British upon his release from detention.

Soon Thompson left for England, where he developed an expertise in firearms and explosives. After the Revolution, he worked from 1784 to 1795 for the elector of Bavaria, whom he had met during his travels. Thompson distinguished himself as the chief of Bavaria's War Department, and by creating a park in Munich known as the English Garden. In appreciation, the elector made him a count. To create his title, Thompson took the name Rumford, the New Hampshire town (now called Concord) where he had taught school.

When he returned to his work as a scientist, Count von Rumford studied the kinetic basis of heat, developed an improved fireplace design, and invented a device to measure the calories given off by burning fuel.

New Hampshire–born scientist Benjamin Thompson, aka Count von Rumford.

Peter Salem, crouching at right, was one of two black soldiers honored for valor and leadership at the Battle of Bunker Hill.

D¹⁷⁷⁵espite George Washington's initial attempt to bar them, black soldiers fought in most major battles of the Revolution.

When the first shots were fired at Lexington and Concord, black and white patriots fought elbow to elbow against the British. Then in July 1775 Gen. George Washington took command of the Continental Army, and the system changed. Washington, a Virginia slave owner, banned all blacks — both slave and free — from military service.

At the end of the year, the system changed again. The royal governor of Virginia, seeking recruits, offered freedom to all slaves who agreed to fight on the British side; thousands fled the plantations to join up. When Washington learned what was happening, he quickly reversed himself. Blacks became welcome in the Continental Army.

In all, some 5,000 black soldiers and sailors enlisted on the side of the colonists. Some served in all-black units, including the Fontages Legion from Haiti, but most joined integrated regiments. Two black soldiers, Oliver Cromwell and Prince Whipple, crossed the Delaware with Washington on December 25, 1776, and the black spy Pompey helped bring victory at Stony Point, New York, in 1779. John Banks, a freeman, was one of the few blacks allowed to ride in the cavalry.

Many black slaves, anticipating that military service would end their state of bondage, assumed new names. Among the 48 black members of a Connecticut regiment were Jeffrey, Pomp, Sharp, and Cuff Liberty. By the war's end, both Britain and the United States were giving freedom to all slaves who had fought.

T¹⁷⁷⁵he British Redcoats sang "Yankee Doodle" to mock the colonial militia, yet the tune became our first national song.

Some say it came from a Dutch farm song: "Yanker dudel, dudel down." Others trace it to a Scottish dance, a Lancashire hornpipe, or a Hungarian folk ditty. But most likely "Yankee Doodle" was born in America — written perhaps, as one account has it, by a British Army doctor during the French and Indian War. The ragtag appearance of the colonial militia so tickled the doctor's sense of absurdity, it seems, that he scribbled a set of nonsense lyrics and set them to an old English nursery tune.

A broadside of "Yankee Doodle," circa 1775.

Even the most rustic colonial knew he was being turned into a figure of fun: "Yankee Doodle came to town / Riding on a pony, / Stuck a feather in his cap / And called it macaroni." A "Yankee" was a New England rube (by British standards), and "macaroni" referred to a foppish

"Taxation without representation is tyranny."
James Otis, 1761

"If *this* be treason, make the most of it!"
Patrick Henry, 1765 *(reaction to the Stamp Act at the Virginia Convention)*

"Men, you are all marksmen — don't fire 'til you see the whites of their eyes."
Gen. Israel Putnam or Col. William Prescott, 1775 *(to the colonial troops at the Battle of Bunker Hill)*

"In the name of the Great Jehovah and the Continental Congress."
Ethan Allen, 1775 *(when the British commander asked in whose name he spoke at the surrender of Saratoga)*

"I know not what course others may take, but as for me, give me liberty or give me death!"
Patrick Henry, 1775 *(at the Virginia Convention, Richmond)*

"I only regret that I have but one life to lose for my country."
Nathan Hale, 1776 *(last words to the British before being hanged as a spy)*

"These are the times that try men's souls."
Thomas Paine, 1776 *(in the tract* The Crisis*)*

"Sir, I have not yet begun to fight!"
John Paul Jones, 1779 *(in response to the captain of the British ship* Serapis *when asked if he was ready to surrender)*

style of dress adopted by young men who had traveled abroad and returned with a taste for exotic foods and fashions. In time, the song acquired as many as 199 verses, some unrepeatable in a family setting.

By the time of the Revolution, British soldiers billeted in America were taunting residents with "Yankee Doodle" every chance they got, even shouting it outside churches during services. Patriot leaders came in for special ridicule: "Yankee Doodle came to town / For to buy a firelock; / We will tar and feather him, / And so we will John Hancock."

But like so many taunts, this one backfired, and the Americans adopted "Yankee Doodle" as their anthem. After the Battle of Bunker Hill, they belted it out with patriotic pride. And during the British surrender at Yorktown in 1781, so it is said, the defeated British played a dirge called "The World Turned Upside Down." At which the Americans' fife-and-drum corps piped up with their liveliest marching tune: "It suits for peace, / it suits for fun; / And just as well for fighting!"

C 1776 ontrary to popular belief, Betsy Ross probably did not design the first American flag.

Everyone knows the story: how one spring day in 1776, shortly before America declared its independence, Gen. George Washington paid a visit to Philadelphia seamstress Betsy Ross and asked her to create a new national flag. The colonists had been using a variation of the British Union Jack, with its superimposed crosses of St. George and St. Andrew — both suggesting loyalty to the Crown. Clearly something else was needed.

Ross and Washington were no strangers. The general had visited her shop several times already and asked her to embroider the ruffles on his

Betsy Ross proudly unfurls the Stars and Stripes for George Washington (far left) and others in a fanciful 19th-century depiction entitled "The Birth of Our Nation's Flag."

shirts. Now he showed her a proposed flag design: 13 stripes of red and white, and 13 stars randomly scattered in a blue field. Supposedly, Ross suggested placing the stars in a pattern, and giving them five points rather than the six depicted in Washington's design. Then she put scissors to cloth and went to work.

Only it may not have happened that way. The story comes down through Ross's grandson, William J. Canby, who remembered hearing it as a boy and then later, in 1870, passed it on to the Philadelphia Historical Society. But several facts suggest that Canby may have remembered wrong. The name of Betsy Ross is absent from the 1776 Congressional Record, for one thing. For another, Francis Hopkinson, a congressman and a signer of the Declaration of Independence, also claimed credit for the design. Hopkinson's claim is supported by the record of a bill he sent to the Board of Admiralty for his work on the flag.

The truth about the flag's origins may never be known, but it is certain that Ross contributed to the cause. Records show that she made flags for the Pennsylvania Navy in 1777. The design for the first national flag was adopted by Congress on June 14, 1777.

1775-80
American women in the late 1770's did their best for the Revolutionary War effort.

Believing that independence was just as important for women as for men, Abigail Adams wrote to her husband, John, in March 1776, asking

Patriotic North Carolina ladies (lampooned here in a Tory cartoon) draw up a resolution to boycott British tea.

him to "remember the ladies" in the new laws being drafted by the Continental Congress. "Do not put such unlimited power in the hands of husbands. . . , " she warned, or wives "will not hold ourselves bound to obey the laws in which we have no voice of representation."

In the same proudly defiant spirit, women throughout the Colonies embraced the cause of national independence. As their men marched off to battle, they shouldered the burden at home, taking on new roles as everything from newspaper publish-

ers to morticians, from farmers to butchers to gunsmiths.

Women also raised money to buy food and clothing for the Continental Army. Esther Reed of Pennsylvania organized a volunteer group, The Association, which distributed a broadside from New England to Georgia calling for a "gift of Gratitude" to the country's soldiers. Another Philadelphia women's group distinguished itself by raising $7,500 in gold and silver.

Not all American men approved of women's entry into public life. Thomas Jefferson, for one, declared that women were "too wise to wrinkle their foreheads with politics."

But a group called the Daughters of Liberty felt otherwise. Early on, its members had protested the British tea tax and boycotted British goods. Then in 1777 they held a "coffee party" that mimicked the Boston Tea Party. Some 100 angry women stormed the warehouse of a Boston coffee merchant — presumably a Tory — who, they felt, was gouging prices. Refused keys to the storeroom, one woman grabbed the man by his neck and tossed him into a cart. The keys were soon produced, and the women helped themselves to coffee sacks as the men of Boston stood by, astonished.

1775-80
Baroness Frederica von Riedesel recorded the dangers and hardships of life on the battlefront.

Ignoring the advice of relatives and friends, Baroness Frederica von Riedesel sailed across the Atlantic in 1776 with her three small daughters. Her husband, Maj. Gen. Friederich von Riedesel, was a German soldier of fortune employed by the English, who had ordered him to America in command of the first detachment of Hessian troops. And the baroness insisted on going, too.

Over the next six years she followed her husband through victory and defeat, enduring all the perils and discomforts of life at war, and faithfully recording her experiences in her diary. "We spent the whole day in a pouring rain, ready to march at a moment's warning," went a typical entry. There were periods of eerie calm: "We passed through boundless forests and magnificent tracts of country, which, however, were abandoned by all the inhabitants, who had fled before us." And mornings of sheer terror: "Many cannon balls flew not far from me, but I had my eyes fixed upon a hill, where I distinctly saw my husband in the midst of the enemy's fire."

At Saratoga, where the British suffered their first major defeat, the baroness — her husband called her Mrs. General — helped tend wounded officers. She fumigated a cellar housing soldiers laid low by dysentery. The general begged her to escape with the children to the American side, where prisoners were known to be well treated; she refused to leave. Before the surrender, she sewed the Hessians' regimental flags into a mattress to hide them from the enemy.

As a prisoner of war, the baroness changed her mind about the Americans. High-ranking officers entertained her. Thomas Jefferson befriended her. In the spring of 1780 she gave birth to her fourth daughter — whom she gratefully christened America.

IN THEIR OWN WORDS

"... in the passage through the American camp, I observed ... that no one cast at us scornful glances. On the contrary, they all greeted me, even showing compassion seeing a mother with her little children in such a situation. When I approached the tents, a noble looking man came toward me, took the children out of the wagon, embraced and kissed them, and then with tears in his eyes helped me also to alight. He then led me to the tent of General Gates, with whom I found [our] Generals Burgoyne and Phillips, who were upon an extremely friendly footing with him. Burgoyne said to me, 'You may now dismiss all your apprehensions, for your sufferings are at an end.' "

From the Letters and Journals Relating to the War of the American Revolution and the Capture of the German Troops at Saratoga, by Baroness Frederica von Riedesel, 1800.

C 1775-83
amp followers — women who went to war to tend to their men — included everyone from courtesans to officers' wives.

The number of women following men from camp to camp during the Revolutionary War grew to such an extent that in the summer of 1777 Gen. George Washington ordered his troops to get rid of all females who were "not absolutely necessary." But Washington refrained from being too strict lest some of his best men decide to desert. Many of the camp followers were soldiers' wives, and they formed a necessary support system; they cooked meals, laundered uniforms, nursed the wounded and sick, and otherwise served to boost the

George and Martha Washington visit the troops in 1777.

morale of the men. In return, they were paid company rations. Not all the camp followers were wives, to be sure. There were also mistresses and prostitutes, some of whom engaged in the illicit selling of rum. It was these "lewd women" Washington hoped to weed out.

Women of dubious virtue notwithstanding, ladies of high rank sometimes followed their husbands onto the battlefield. George Washington's wife, Martha, joined him on several occasions. Mrs. Washington, along with other officers' wives, not only assisted her husband but wrapped bandages and calmed the nerves of regular soldiers. These women won the hearts of many for braving the hazardous conditions of life on the firing line.

W 1775-83
omen joined men in the Revolutionary War as both soldiers and spies.

Most of the women who fought for independence have remained unknown, but there are some whose names have became a part of history. At the age of 20, Deborah Sampson dressed herself in men's clothes and enlisted in the army under the name of Robert Shurtleff. Her fellow soldiers called her "blooming boy" because she didn't have a beard. In 1783 her real identity was discovered after she was taken, unconscious, to a hospital. Mustered out of service, she was later awarded a full pension by the U.S. government.

Molly Pitcher, ramrod in hand, helps fight the Redcoats at Monmouth.

Molly Pitcher was another woman who received a pension for her military service. Pitcher, whose real name was Mary Ludwig Hays, followed her husband, a gunner in the Pennsylvania artillery, into the field. One blistering hot day in June 1778, during the Battle of Monmouth in Freehold, New Jersey, she carried water from a nearby spring to ease the soldiers' thirst and to wet the sponges used to cool the cannons. "Here comes Molly with her pitcher!" the grateful soldiers shouted, and Mary got her nickname. When her husband fell from heatstroke behind his

cannon, Molly seized a ramrod, loaded up, and fired shot after shot.

Other women waged battle in a different way. When British forces occupied Augusta, Georgia, Nancy Hart provided the Patriots with intelligence by going to British camps disguised as a man who was a bit "touched." After several months some Americans loyal to the Crown caught on to her act, and six men burst into her cabin to interrogate her. By the time help arrived, Hart had killed one intruder, wounded another, and was holding a gun on the rest of them.

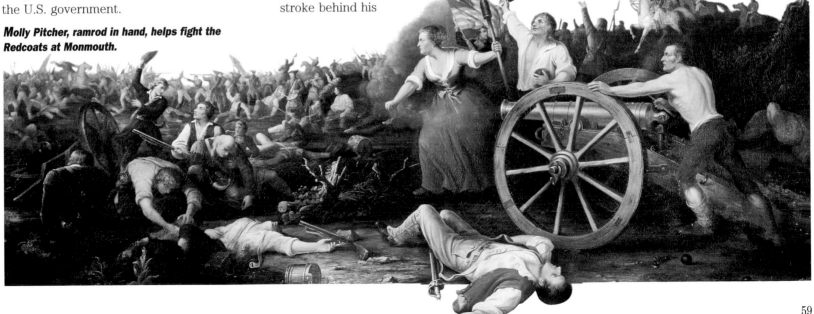

A **1776**
lthough they opposed the way the British treated them, not all the colonists were united behind the cause of American independence.

New Year's Day 1776 dawned over a troubled American landscape. In May of the previous year the Second Continental Congress, a group of 56 colonial delegates, had convened in Philadelphia to address the escalating conflict with Britain. They decided to send troops to Massachusetts, where American forces would soon lay siege to British-occupied Boston, and to make George Washington commander in chief of the Continental Army. Then in July 1775 the Congress, in deference to moderate members who continued to seek compromise rather than conflict, drew up the Olive Branch Petition. This document (which was ultimately rejected by King George III) cited a long list of grievances and petitioned for their redress. Each member of the Congress added his signature.

Even after months of armed confrontation, many colonists still had no desire to separate from the Crown. Some people feared that the Colonies lacked the military strength to win a war against Britain. Others hoped to prevent the Colonies from falling into the hands of hot-headed radicals who lacked experience in government. Still others — mostly aristocrats, wealthy merchants, lawyers, and Anglican clergymen — felt they owed the Crown a debt of grati-

The Continental Congress met at the Pennsylvania State House, now called Independence Hall.

tude for their money and position. As a result, many colonists either remained neutral or supported King George. Moderate colonial delegates continued to balk at openly defying the king. In January 1776 the Continental Congress firmly announced that it "had no design to set up as an independent nation."

Yet the thrust for independence was unstoppable. In March 1776 the British were forced to quit Boston. An American army under Benedict Arnold was camped outside Quebec. A British fleet sailed into Charleston, South Carolina, and a British army prepared to move against New York. The Revolutionary War had begun.

T **1776**
he first African-American woman to have her poems published was a slave.

At the age of only eight years, she was kidnapped in Africa and taken to the United States aboard a slave ship. A Boston tailor, John Wheatley, bought her as a servant for his wife, who treated her like a daughter. She was given an American name, Phillis Wheatley, and taught to read and write.

Phillis Wheatley turned out to be an intellectual prodigy. While still in her teens, she wrote her first poem, "To the University," a criticism of rowdy Harvard students. In 1773 she traveled to London, and her first book of poetry was published there that same year. Since the public might be skeptical about the creative abili-

ties of an African slave, the book included a foreword signed by 18 prominent men — one was John Hancock — attesting to the fact that the poems were hers.

Later Wheatley wrote a poem honoring George Washington, who was so taken with her genius that in 1776 he invited her to visit him at army headquarters: "If you should ever come to Cambridge . . . , I shall be happy to see a person so favoured by the Muses." It was her last moment of glory. No one would publish her second book of poems. She married a free black man; then in 1784, at age 31, she died while working as a servant in a boarding-house.

Phillis Wheatley, on the frontispiece of her book of poems, summons her muse.

Silas Deane, America's first official diplomat, was also its first secret agent.

In 1776 Congress sent Connecticut patriot Silas Deane to France to buy arms for the Revolutionary Army. At the same time, he was to forge an alliance with the French government.

To keep his mission secret, Deane traveled in disguise using the alias Timothy Jones. Once in France, he sent back reports written in invisible ink. One of these dispatches included information that the British were ready to use force against the rebellious colonists.

The diplomat had little difficulty obtaining arms, but his very success would lead to his downfall. Arthur Lee, another American diplomat working in France, disliked Deane intensely and accused him of financial chicanery. Lee claimed that the weapons and supplies that Deane had supposedly purchased from the French were in fact gifts, and that Deane would be reimbursed for supplies he had never paid for. Deane immediately left France for America to answer these charges, and in his haste he failed to bring back all his financial records. Because he had no proof of sales, he was unable to clear his name or recover his expenses.

After spending two years trying to exonerate himself, Deane returned to Europe. A broken and bitter man, he had lost all faith in the American cause. In letter after letter to friends back in the Colonies, he strongly urged reconciliation with England. Financially ruined and alone, Deane died while sailing to Canada in 1789.

Silas Deane's name was not cleared until after his death. In 1842 Congress paid his heirs $37,000 in restitution for the injustices against him.

IN THEIR OWN WORDS

> **Miss. Phillis: Your favour of the 26th of October did not reach my hands 'till the middle of December. Time enough, you will say, to have given an answer ere this. Granted . . . . I thank you most sincerely for your polite notice of me, in the elegant lines you enclosed; and however undeserving I may be of such encomium and panegyrick, the style and manner exhibit a striking proof of your great poetical Talents. In honour of which, and in a tribute justly due you, I would have published the Poem, had I not been apprehensive, that, while I only meant to give the World this new instance of your genius, I might have incurred the imputation of Vanity. This and nothing else, determined me not to give it place in the public prints.**
>
> **If you should ever come to Cambridge, or near Head Quarters, I shall be happy to see a person so favoured by the Muses, and to whom Nature has been so liberal and beneficient in her dispensations. I am, with great Respect, etc.**

George Washington in a letter of thanks to Phillis Wheatley dated February 28, 1776.

George Mason, the man most responsible for the Bill of Rights, refused to sign the Constitution.

George Mason, a Virginia planter, was also one of the leading legal thinkers of his day. Although he despised politics and refused to accept office, he did consent to take part in a 1776 convention called by leading Virginians to draft a state constitution.

A crotchety man with a bad case of gout, Mason arrived in Williamsburg almost two weeks after the convention began. Turning his attention to the issue of civil rights, he was horrified to discover that the committee responsible for drawing up a state bill of rights was "overcharged with useless members" who would offer "a thousand ridiculous and impracticable proposals." So Mason took it over.

Some of the rights Mason put into the bill, such as trial by jury and the writ of habeas corpus (the right to release from unlawful imprisonment), had their roots in the Magna Carta. Others, including freedom of the press and freedom of religion, were new. The Virginia document became America's first declaration of civil rights.

George Mason, a champion of civil rights, was one of the first Southerners to favor freeing the slaves.

Thomas Jefferson drew partly on Mason's ideas when drafting the Declaration of Independence. But the U.S. Constitution, adopted in Philadelphia in 1787, contained no mention of civil rights. George Mason and Patrick Henry pressed hard on the issue, even waging a campaign to keep Virginia from ratifying the document. When the Constitution was adopted anyway — without a statement on individual rights — Mason refused to sign it.

Mason's views ultimately held sway; in 1791 the first 10 Constitutional amendments, called the Bill of Rights, were ratified by the states. Mason's ideas also appeared in every state constitution, as well as in the French *Déclaration des droits de l'homme et du citoyen* of 1789. And in 1948 the United Nations general assembly voted to adopt a Universal Declaration of Human Rights.

1776
The deciding vote for American independence was cast by a mud-covered delegate from Delaware.

July 2, 1776, dawned muggy and overcast; the State House had been battered by thunderstorms the day before and was steaming hot. Inside the building, delegates prepared to vote on a motion by Richard Lee of Virginia for American independence. The atmosphere was tense: three colonies — New York, Pennsylvania, and South Carolina — had been squarely against independence. Then Pennsylvania and South Carolina changed their votes, and New York decided to abstain. It was up to Delaware to make the vote for independence unanimous. But the colony's two present delegates were on opposite sides, and the man who could break the tie — a pro-independence delegate named Caesar Rodney — was missing.

Caesar Rodney (right) arrives at the Pennsylvania State House just in time to cast his vote.

Suddenly, the door burst open and a mud-covered Rodney, who had been in Delaware and had ridden all night in a torrential downpour, strode in and cast the deciding vote: 12 delegations were for independence, and the motion carried.

With the vote assured, the time came for setting a formal declaration down on paper. Thomas Jefferson submitted a first draft, and the Continental Congress launched into a harsh critique. As its author sat in embarrassed silence, 25 percent of the document was cut. Among the passages removed was an attack on the slave trade and on King George III for encouraging it. But what remained on July 4, when the Declaration of Independence was approved, was extraordinary. One particular passage would have far-reaching results in the shaping of American democracy: "governments are instituted among men, deriving their just powers from the consent of the governed." America would not be ruled by kings and queens but by its own citizens. All the declaration needed now was to be legitimized by the signatures of the members of the Continental Congress.

1776
Thomas Paine's *Common Sense* and Thomas Jefferson's Declaration of Independence proved that the pen can be as mighty as the sword.

It was Benjamin Franklin who urged Thomas Paine, a gifted English writer, to come to America. Paine cherished freedom, and Franklin believed that his skills would prove useful in promoting the cause of independence. So Paine crossed the Atlantic to Philadelphia, where like-minded people helped him publish a slim pamphlet called *Common Sense*.

Released only a few days after the Continental Congress's decision not to break from the Crown, Paine's little book shouted what many people had only whispered: the king was a royal brute, and armed resistance was the only reasonable response. The object of the struggle was clear — total independence from Britain. Paine's reasoning was simple: "There is something very absurd in supposing a continent to be perpetually governed by an island." Such phrases touched a popular nerve and set off a debate

Patriotic New Yorkers demonstrate their feelings about the British Crown in 1776 by pulling down a statue of King George III.

so furious that the political climate quickly changed. *Common Sense* blazed through the Colonies like a bolt of lightning, selling nearly 175,000 copies — an astonishing number, considering the population of the Colonies was only about 2 million.

In response to the growing support for independence, the Continental Congress quickly reconvened. On June 7 Virginia radical Richard Henry Lee offered a resolution that "these United colonies are & of right ought to be free & independent states."

Lee's resolution was tabled until July 1 so that local assemblies in the individual colonies would have time to read it. Meanwhile, a five-man committee set about drafting a formal document. The task of composition fell to the committee's least-known member, Thomas Jefferson. The young Virginian had few enemies, came from a powerful state, and — while no orator — was a talented writer. Over the next 17 days, working at a portable writing case he had designed himself, Jefferson crafted a document that would be pivotal in arousing support: the Declaration of Independence.

W¹⁷⁷⁶**hen the delegates of the Continental Congress signed the Declaration of Independence, they knew they might also be signing their own death warrants.**

As soon as the Declaration of Independence was read in public on July 8, 1776, it caused a sensation, persuading a generally reluctant populace to embrace independence. Spread throughout the Colonies on printed broadsides, it inspired parades in Philadelphia and Baltimore, where an effigy of King George III was marched through the streets. People burned candles in the windows in the main building of the College of New Jersey (later Princeton University) for the "prosperity of the United States."

A detail from "The Declaration of Independence" by John Trumbull shows (left to right) John Adams, Roger Sherman, Robert Livingston, Thomas Jefferson, and Benjamin Franklin presenting the declaration to John Hancock (seated).

By August 2 the declaration, copied onto parchment and titled "The Unanimous Declaration of the Thirteen United States of America," was ready for signing. John Hancock went first, writing large enough for the British to read his name "without spectacles." The palsied Stephen Hopkins of Rhode Island averred "my hand trembles, but my heart does not," and others followed with bravado or gallows humor. Their dark jokes contained a serious element of truth; each man knew that he might be signing his own death warrant should the revolution fail. The plucky Delaware delegate Caesar Rodney knew he could never go to England for surgery for his cancer. Rodney

Less gentle in its show of support was a mob of New York colonists who pulled down a huge equestrian statue of the king that stood in New York's Bowling Green and enthusiastically smashed it to pieces. (The chunks were later made into bullets for Patriot guns.)

and the other 55 men who signed the declaration could only count on their faith in each other and their fellow Americans. Benjamin Franklin expressed this feeling succinctly: "We must indeed all hang together, or most assuredly we shall all hang separately."

T¹⁷⁷⁶**he Liberty Bell did not crack on the day the Declaration of Independence was approved, nor was it given its famous name until more than half a century later.**

The story that the Liberty Bell cracked when it rang out to celebrate the Declaration of Independence on July 4, 1776, is just a legend. The bell first cracked a quarter of a century earlier in 1751.

The Pennsylvania State House had ordered a 2,080-pound bell from England to call its members to Assembly and to commemorate the fiftieth anniversary of William Penn's Charter of Privileges, which gave Pennsylvanians religious freedom. It was inscribed with a Biblical verse: "Proclaim liberty throughout all the land unto all the inhabitants thereof." Unfortunately, the bell cracked the

first time it was ever tested.

Two local ironworkers melted the bell down and recast it. For many years it served the Assembly well. And it did in fact ring out to announce America's independence — but not until July 8, four days after the declaration was approved.

The second bell's famous crack did not develop until 1835 when, the story goes, it tolled for the death of Chief Justice John Marshall. It was rung the last time on Washington's Birthday in 1846, then retired from service. After traveling to expositions across the country, it now resides in its own pavilion in Philadelphia.

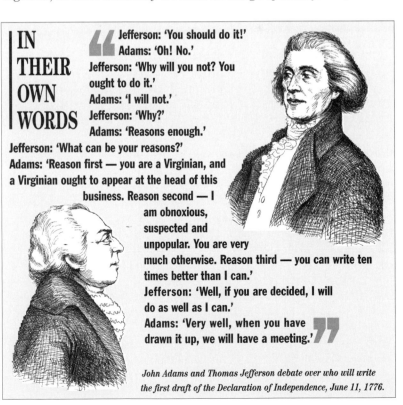

IN THEIR OWN WORDS

Jefferson: 'You should do it!'
Adams: 'Oh! No.'
Jefferson: 'Why will you not? You ought to do it.'
Adams: 'I will not.'
Jefferson: 'Why?'
Adams: 'Reasons enough.'
Jefferson: 'What can be your reasons?'
Adams: 'Reason first — you are a Virginian, and a Virginian ought to appear at the head of this business. Reason second — I am obnoxious, suspected and unpopular. You are very much otherwise. Reason third — you can write ten times better than I can.'
Jefferson: 'Well, if you are decided, I will do as well as I can.'
Adams: 'Very well, when you have drawn it up, we will have a meeting.'

John Adams and Thomas Jefferson debate over who will write the first draft of the Declaration of Independence, June 11, 1776.

1776

Nicknamed "king" by admirers, John Hancock risked his wealth and his life for American independence.

John Hancock had not always been wealthy. His father, a minister, died when John was only seven, leaving the family destitute. The boy was taken in by his uncle, a wealthy Boston merchant. When the uncle died, he left Hancock, then age 27, more than £70,000.

Now one of the richest men in America, Hancock proved to be generous and public-spirited, giving Boston its first street lamps and its first concert hall, a thousand books to Harvard, and large sums of money to people in need.

The altruistic aristocrat looked like a Tory, but in his heart he was a democrat. When England passed the Stamp Act, Hancock saw the measure as a threat to freedom, and as a newly elected Boston selectman, he wrote letters to England denouncing it. When the Stamp Act was repealed, he threw a huge party. Everyone was welcome, and Hancock rolled out a 126-gallon hogshead of wine to celebrate. Immersing himself in politics almost entirely, he was elected president of the Massachusetts Provincial Congress in 1774 and served for two terms.

As relations with England worsened, Hancock devoted his energies to promoting the radical cause. He had much to lose by speaking out, but was never afraid to do so. When the British seized one of his ships, the *Liberty*, on charges of smuggling, Hancock became a true patriot in the eyes of the people.

By the time he was elected president of the Second Continental Congress, Hancock was one of the Crown's most wanted men. The British considered him a traitor because of his support of American independence. British general Thomas Gage offered a pardon to all but two of the rebels: Samuel Adams and John Hancock. Yet while Adams frightened many delegates with his radicalism, Hancock's moderation reassured them. He was a natural politician. For two years, at no pay, he mediated between opposing factions of conservative and radical delegates, and by smoothing things over, he kept the burgeoning American government alive. Hancock was also the first, in 1776, to boldly sign the Declaration of Independence, an act of highest treason to the British Crown.

John Hancock died in 1793, a revolutionary hero. Twenty thousand people marched in his funeral procession, creating a column of humanity that stretched four abreast for half a mile. The aristocrat in Hancock would have loved the pomp, but the democratic Hancock would have appreciated the turnout of the common people even more. 🦅

John Hancock and his wife, Dorothy Quincy Hancock.

1776

The Americans initiated the first submarine warfare during the Revolutionary War.

The world had never before seen anything like the contraption that was towed into New York Harbor on the night of September 6, 1776. The 7½-foot-high wood-framed vessel bobbing in the water looked like nothing so much as two tortoise shells joined together. Indeed, it was called the *Turtle* by its inventor, David Bushnell.

A 35-year-old Yale mathematics student, Bushnell came up with the idea for a "submarine mine or torpedo" in 1772 while demonstrating that gunpowder could explode underwater. His one-man vessel was powered by a hand-cranked propeller and could remain submerged for 30 minutes at a stretch. Attached to the craft was Bushnell's "torpedo" — a container with 150 pounds of gunpowder.

The idea was simple: the operator would maneuver the submarine beneath an enemy ship and screw the torpedo to the ship's bottom. A timing device would detonate the torpedo after the submarine had retreated to a safe distance.

The weapon's first target was the *Eagle*, British admiral Richard Howe's 64-gun flagship. Unfortunately, the volunteer in the sub was unable to cut through the ship's heavy timbers to attach the torpedo. The *Turtle* returned to Manhattan, and its charge exploded harmlessly in the East River. 🦅

A cutaway view of the Turtle: The long screw at the top was designed to fasten a bomb to enemy ships.

IN THEIR OWN WORDS

" These are the times that try men's souls. The summer soldier and the sunshine patriot will, in this crisis, shrink from the service of his country; but he that stands it now deserves the love and thanks of man and woman. Tyranny, like hell, is not easily conquered; yet we have this consolation with us — that the harder the conflict, the more glorious the triumph. . . . Heaven knows how to put a proper price upon its goods; and it would be strange indeed if so celestial an article as freedom should not be highly rated. Britain, with an army to enforce her tyranny, has declared that she has a right not only to tax but 'to bind us in all cases whatsoever,' and if being bound in that manner is not slavery, then is there not such a thing as slavery upon earth. Even the expression is impious, for so unlimited a power can belong only to God. . . . Not a place upon earth might be so happy as America. . . . and I am as confident, as I am that God governs the world, that America will never be happy till she gets clear of foreign dominion. . . . For though the flame of liberty may sometimes cease to shine, the coal can never expire. *"*

Thomas Paine in the Revolutionary tract The Crisis, *published in December 1776.*

1776

George Washington took the controversial step of inoculating his army against the greatest killer of the Revolutionary War: smallpox.

Smallpox was more deadly than enemy bullets during the American Revolution. By 1776 there had already been 50 epidemics in America, and the crowded conditions of military life made armies highly vulnerable to contagion. When Benedict Arnold led American troops into Canada, more than 2,000 of his 8,000 men became ill. They suffered higher losses from disease than from battle.

As a young man, George Washington had contracted smallpox, making him immune in later life. Inoculation, he felt, was the only way to protect his army. The procedure was relatively new, and highly controversial: the live virus then used would bring on a minor case of the disease. (During an early test of 500 soldiers in New York, 4 men actually died.) Even so, Washington ordered the inoculation of all his troops encamped at Morristown, New Jersey, in the spring of 1777. Churches in Morristown were turned into inoculation centers, and soon the British Redcoats, not smallpox, would again be the principal threat to Washington's army.

A Colonial physician takes the pulse of a female patient thought to be suffering from smallpox. Curtains were used in hopes they would keep the disease from spreading — and for modesty's sake.

1777

Declaring itself independent, the republic of Vermont did not join the original 13 colonies in statehood until 8 years after the Revolution.

The region now called Vermont was an isolated, mountainous area with no colonial charter and no distinct boundaries. Both New York and New Hampshire claimed sections of it. When its residents applied to the Continental Congress for statehood, they were turned down, mostly because of objections from New York. So the region declared itself independent, and on January 15, 1777, it began life as the Republic of New Connecticut. Six months later the republic

The Great Seal of Vermont.

adopted a formal constitution and changed its name to Vermont.

For 14 years Vermont operated as an independent government with its own currency, postal system, and ambassadors.

During the Revolution it sent troops to fight with the Continental Army. But with the arrival of peace, Vermont went back to scrapping over land with New Hampshire and New York. At one point its great Revolutionary hero, Ethan Allen, leader of the Green Mountain Boys, began secretly negotiating to join Vermont to Canada. But the land disputes were eventually resolved, and on March 4, 1791, at the invitation of Congress, Vermont entered the Union as the 14th state.

1777

George Washington's youngest general was a Frenchman who helped the revolutionary cause both on and off the battlefield.

The Marquis de Lafayette was 19 years old and filled with enthusiasm for the American cause when he sailed to America and talked the Continental Congress into giving him a commission. "After the sacrifices that I have made, I have the right to demand two favors," he wrote to the Congress. "One is to serve at my own expense. The other is to begin my service as a volunteer." Soon after his arrival in the early summer of 1777, Lafayette was given the rank of major general, but without pay and without a command. The next day he received an invitation from the commander in chief of the Continental Army, George Washington.

From the moment they met on August 1, 1777, Lafayette and Washington, who was ordinarily somewhat distant and taciturn, became fast friends. As their relationship developed, the marquis (who had been orphaned when he was two) began to call the childless general "father" and to share with him such dark hours as Benedict Arnold's treason and the hardships at Valley Forge.

In the military arena, Lafayette helped Gen. John Sullivan hold back the British during a skirmish at Brandywine, Pennsylvania, when frightened Continental troops panicked and fled. Lafayette fought until the British were within 20 yards, withdrawing only after being shot in the leg. After Brandywine, Lafayette repeatedly petitioned Washington for his own command. He finally received one in December 1777 and led skirmishes at Barren Hill, Pennsylvania, and Monmouth, New Jersey.

The young Marquis de Lafayette.

Although Lafayette accomplished much on the battlefield, his biggest contributions were diplomatic. With his eagerness to aid the revolutionary cause, he became a symbol of French support to the Americans. On his trip back to France in 1779, he was welcomed as a hero, and he managed to procure additional aid from Louis XVI. In April 1780 he returned to America, taking on an army command and serving as a liaison between American troops and some newly arrived French regiments. Lafayette's final military action in America was at the Battle of Yorktown, the last big engagement of the Revolutionary War, when he skillfully handled a small force of 400 soldiers that helped trap General Cornwallis.

1777

A British sharpshooter had the chance to kill George Washington and perhaps American independence — but chivalry stayed his hand.

Maj. Patrick Ferguson was a famous marksman — he had demonstrated his ability before King George III — and the inventor of a highly regarded breech-loading rifle. In September 1777 Ferguson was on patrol with three other British soldiers near Brandywine Creek, Pennsylvania. Suddenly, two enemy officers galloped into a clearing. One was a Frenchman in a large cocked hat. The other was George Washington, out doing some

The breech-loading rifle was quick, accurate, and lethally effective.

of his own reconnaissance.

Ferguson ordered his men, still hidden among the trees, "to steal near them and fire at them." Then abruptly he changed his mind, and shouted for the riders to surrender.

The two men wheeled their horses and sped away. But for a brief moment, Ferguson had been given a clear shot at Washington. "I could have lodged half a dozen of balls in or about him," he later said, "but it was not pleasant to fire at the back of an unoffending individual who was acquitting himself very coolly of his duty, and so I let him alone."

This chivalrous act may have been fatal for Ferguson; he was killed three years later in the battle of King's Mountain in South Carolina, an event that might not have occurred if he had pulled the trigger on the American leader.

IN THEIR OWN WORDS

"I will now tell you about the country and its inhabitants. They are as agreeable as my enthusiasm had painted them. Simplicity of manners, kindness, love of country and of liberty, and a delightful equality everywhere prevail. The wealthiest man and the poorest are on a level. . . . I challenge anyone to discover the slightest difference between the manners of these two classes respectively towards each other. . . . The American women are very pretty, simple in their manners, and exhibit a neatness, which is even cultivated even more studiously than in England. What most charms me is, that all the citizens are brethren. In America, there are no poor, nor even what we call peasantry. . . ."

Excerpt of a 1777 letter from the Marquis de Lafayette, newly arrived in America, to his wife, Marie Adrienne, in France.

A¹⁷⁷⁷ lthough the quiet Tadeusz Kosciuszko helped America win its independence, he was unable to do the same for his beloved Poland.

One of the Continental Army's greatest assets was a Polish military engineer who was so modest that he refused to ask for a promotion or even for the pay that was due him. Tadeusz Kosciuszko, the son of impoverished landowners, received a superb military education in Poland and France but lacked the money to purchase a commission. Learning of the American Revolution, he traveled to the Colonies to offer his services. In 1777 he was at the Battle of Ticonderoga where, as a colonel of engineers, he urged the fortification of a nearby mountain. When British forces seized the peak, he fled with the rest of the garrison, but he managed to slow pursuers with a combination of felled trees and dammed creeks.

Tadeusz Kosciuszko as a colonial general.

Kosciuszko was next asked to help block a British advance on Saratoga. He studied the terrain, then built entrenchments and barricades on the hills. Unable to penetrate the American defenses, the British suffered their first great defeat, an event that was to be a turning point of the war.

Soon after, Kosciuszko directed the fortification of West Point on the Hudson River, employing a series of interlocking bastions. These defenses, known as the American Gibraltar, were considered impregnable. West Point became a key strategic position.

Kosciuszko returned to Poland after the war and joined the Polish Army. Hoping to free his beloved homeland from Russian tyranny, he led a massive armed insurrection against the Tzar. Defeated on the battlefield, he returned briefly to America with the idea of becoming a farmer. But soon he was back in Europe with the hope that Napoleon would help free his country. He died in Switzerland in 1817, still pursuing his country's independence.

T^{1777–78} he conditions at Valley Forge during the winter of 1777–78 were no worse than at most army camps during the Revolutionary War.

For the average soldier, and even for most officers, the winter spent at Valley Forge, Pennsylvania, was an exhausting and dispiriting experience. It was cold, and food and blankets were always in short supply. Many soldiers wore their clothes down to bare threads for lack of new ones. But for all the discomforts endured, the conditions at Valley Forge were no worse than at any other military camp in the Colonies. The winter was comparatively mild, in fact, and the huts the soldiers built for themselves gave them protection from wind and snow. Morale was not so low as to prevent the troops from learning complex drills from Prussian general Friedrich von Steuben, and by spring they had been shaped into a formidable fighting force.

The complaints preserved in diaries and letters may have been written by troops unaccustomed to the rigors of military life: "I can't endure it," griped one soldier, "— why are we sent here to starve and freeze? What sweet felicities have I left at home: A charming wife — pretty children — good beds — good food . . . — all agreeable! . . . pox on my bad luck!"

Despite such grievances, actual starvation did not occur. But hunger was a common complaint throughout the war. There were food shortages caused by government graft and mismanagement, and by American farmers who preferred to sell their crops for British gold rather than colonial scrip. In a shrewd effort to get supplies more quickly, Washington appealed to Congress with accounts of privation among his troops. His tactics worked; his tales of woe shamed Congress into reorganizing the supply department. Over a three-month period, 1 million pounds of flour and 1 million pounds of meat and fish were provided for his 10,000 troops.

By the spring of 1778, conditions in the camp were so tolerable that civilians such as painter Charles Willson Peale and even Martha Washington joined the troops at Valley Forge.

Gen. George Washington reviews his hungry, ragged troops during the march to Valley Forge.

A *1778*
colorful Prussian captain whipped the ragtag Continental Army into fighting shape at Valley Forge.

Gen. George Washington welcomed a new volunteer to the army camp at Valley Forge on February 23, 1778. Friedrich Wilhelm Ludolf Gerhard Augustin, Baron von Steuben, had distinguished himself in the crack Prussian infantry of Frederick the Great and had also served as an aide-de-camp to the king at royal headquarters. His military acumen had come to the attention of Benjamin Franklin and Silas Deane in Paris, who sent letters introducing him to Washington. In order to give von Steuben the prestige of a high rank, Franklin and Deane conspired to present him as a lieutenant general, even though he had left the Prussian army with the rank of captain. Furthermore, his claim to the title "baron" was also suspect. But in the battle for American independence, titles hardly mattered.

Witty and profane, with an impressive bearing, the ornately uniformed von Steuben personally transformed Washington's bedraggled, undisciplined soldiers into a well-trained army. His accomplishments bordered on the miraculous, considering that he spoke broken English and little French, sometimes sprinkling his commands with a few colorful German oaths. Using translators, he prepared a manual of drills and personally instructed every squad.

In 1784 von Steuben retired, and two years later he became an American citizen. A lifelong bachelor, he moved in the highest circles of New York society, spending his winters in Manhattan and his summers in upstate New York. He died of a stroke in 1794.

Baron von Steuben instructs a squad of Revolutionary troops in the basics of Prussian rifle drill.

G *1778*
George Washington's "watch chain" stretched across the Hudson River between 1778 and 1783 to prevent the British from gaining control of the waterway.

Throughout the Revolution, the Hudson River was a waterway of vital strategic importance, used by the Americans to transport arms and provisions to troops camped as far north as Albany. Should the British gain control of it, the upriver encampments would be badly imperiled. To prevent British ships from sailing upstream, Washington's soldiers carried out a feat of engineering that was both simple and effective.

Under the direction of artillery officer Thomas Machin, the Americans forged an iron chain nearly a third of a mile long and buoyed up by logs. West Point was selected as the installation site because there the river narrowed and the winds and currents were deemed favorable. In the spring of 1778, the giant chain was winched across the river and secured to large rock cribs on either side. Dubbed General Washington's Watch Chain by the Americans, and the Yankee Pumpkin Vine by the British, the 750-link chain was taken up each autumn and set down again in the spring. Then in 1783 it was put away for good. As it happened, the chain was never tested; no enemy vessels sailed that far up the Hudson.

American army engineers hung a 1,700-foot iron chain across the Hudson River at West Point.

IN THEIR OWN WORDS

"The Links are about 12 inches wide and 18 inches long, the Bars about 2 inches square. It is buoyed up by very large Logs about 16 feet long, pointed at the ends to lessen their opposition to the Force of the Current at flood and ebb Tide. The Logs are placed at short distance from each other, the Chain carried over them and made fast by Staples. There are also a number of Anchors dropped at proper distances, with cables made fast to the Chain to give it greater stability."

Dr. James Thacher, an army surgeon at West Point, describing the Hudson River chain.

1778

Benjamin Franklin, a public relations genius, persuaded the French to support the American Revolution.

Traveling to Paris in 1776 as representatives of the Continental Congress, Silas Deane, Arthur Lee, and Benjamin Franklin sought to obtain official French assistance for the independence of the American colonies. With the intent of weakening its British rival, France had already supplied covert aid. But French officials hesitated to openly endorse the American cause, for if England triumphed, the consequences for France would be calamitous. The French foreign minister, Charles Gravier, count de Vergennes, wanted assurance of an American victory. That came with the surrender of British general John Burgoyne at Saratoga on October 17, 1777.

In the meantime, Franklin employed his diplomatic skills in courting the French public. Wearing a marten-fur cap and plain Quaker clothes, he played the quintessential

Franklin in his trademark spectacles and fur hat, as caught by Revolutionary War artist John Trumbull.

American "rustic." The French were captivated. Franklin became so popular that his portrait was copied onto everything from snuffboxes to commodes.

His efforts paid off. The French government eventually agreed to two treaties: one of alliance, and the other of amity and commerce. The first pledged France to maintain the freedom, independence, and sovereignty of the United States; it also provided for military aid. The second called for mutual protection of ships and convoys, as well as the establishment of consulates in the two countries.

Congress ratified the treaties on May 4, 1778. The signing of the agreements was celebrated with prayers of thanksgiving, parades, and fireworks. "I look at the past condition of America," wrote Patrick Henry to Virginia statesman Richard Henry Lee, "as a dreadful precipice from which we have escaped by means of the generous French." Support from France — more than $8 million, as well as a fleet of warships anchored off the American coast — gave the Colonies the strength needed to persevere in the fight for freedom.

1779

Making his small army appear more than five times larger than it was, Col. George Rogers Clark captured a vital British stronghold and secured the Northwest Territory.

Col. George Rogers Clark was growing increasingly alarmed. Reports had filtered in from the west that Shawnee and Delaware Indians were massacring western colonists. Behind these raids was British commander Col. Henry Hamilton, who craftily exploited long-standing antagonisms that had developed between American settlers and the local tribes. Hamilton's willingness to pay the Indians for American scalps had already earned him a grim moniker: Hair Buyer.

Determined to drive the British out, Clark gathered a force of 170 fellow Kentuckians and marched west. By late summer of 1778 he had seized control of a large part of the Illinois country. His next target was the fort at Vincennes, overlooking the Wabash River in present-day Indiana, where Hamilton had set up his headquarters.

Clark and his men set out in February 1779. After a cold start, an early thaw transformed the frozen landscape into a swamp. From then on, Clark's men were nearly always wet, sometimes slogging through bone-chilling, chest-high water. When they finally sighted Vincennes, across the flooded Wabash, some were too weary to go on. Undaunted, Clark gave a war whoop and waded in, giving orders that any laggards would be shot. Everyone survived the crossing.

To intimidate the enemy, Clark then marched his 170 men back and forth so quickly that they looked like a thousand. His sharpshooters skirmished for three hours with Hamilton's small combined

George Rogers Clark leads his men through icy waters to mount a surprise attack on the British at Vincennes.

force of British, French, and Indians. During a cease-fire, Clark's men captured a group returning with American scalps for Hamilton. Clark ordered four of the men tomahawked, and Hamilton quickly surrendered. With this victory, British power in the area was effectively broken, and the entire region, known as the Northwest Territory, was ultimately ceded to the new United States. Clark, who was never paid for his service, died penniless in 1818.

The Chicago River in 1789 with du Sable's cabin (inset left) on one bank and some Indian visitors on the other. Du Sable (inset right) became rich trading furs.

1779

The founder of Chicago's first permanent settlement was a black fur trader who may also have been an American spy.

Sometime in the 1770's a French-speaking black man named Jean Baptiste Pointe du Sable built a log cabin on the Chicago River near Lake Michigan and began trading in furs. He may have been the mixed-blood descendant of an old French Canadian family, as some sources say. Or he could have arrived via New Orleans from the West Indies, the son of a French sailor and an African mother. No one really knows. What is certain is that on July 4, 1779, the British commandant in Illinois arrested du Sable on charges of spying for the Americans. For the next four years he was held at a British fort.

After the war, du Sable resumed his Chicago fur-trading business. Besides bartering with the Indians for beaver, fox, and other pelts, he operated a farm and sawmill. A resourceful man with educated tastes, du Sable built himself a 40-by-22-foot log house, filled it with imported paintings and furniture (including a French cabinet with glass doors), slept on a feather bed with his Indian wife, and reared two children.

His business success helped attract other people to the region. By the 1790's white settlers were moving to Chicago in a steady stream. Du Sable himself had made a modest fortune. The records show that when he sold out in 1796, after some 20 years of profitable dealings, his possessions included a bakehouse, dairy, smokehouse, stables, two mules, 30 head of cattle, plus hogs, hens, and farm machinery. Moving on to St. Charles, Missouri, du Sable continued to trade and farm until his death in 1818.

1779

John Paul Jones had only begun to fight when he brought the Revolutionary War to England's doorstep.

For more than a year, John Paul Jones, a Scottish-born sea captain sailing under the Stars and Stripes, had been harassing British shipping in the Irish Sea — raiding seaports, picking off an occasional prize vessel. Then came the victory that made him famous.

Jones was prowling Britain's east coast in September 1779 with a small squadron. His flagship, the 40-gun *Bonhomme Richard,* was a gift from the French government. Two other ships — the French frigate *Pallas* and the American-built *Alliance* — completed his force. Toward evening on September 23 he spotted a British convoy heading in with naval stores from the Baltic.

The next few hours saw the bloodiest ship-to-ship clash in American naval history. For reasons never fully explained, both the *Alliance* and the *Pallas* stood aside, leaving Jones to confront the lead British warship: the powerful, newly built, 50-gun H.M.S. *Serapis.* Knowing that the heavier British armament could pound him into driftwood, Jones saw only one option. He would sail alongside the *Serapis,* braving her guns, and attempt to lead his men aboard.

Dusk fell. The first broadsides were fired. Jones moved in close and — partly because the *Serapis* fouled her bowsprit in the *Richard*'s rigging — was able to bind the two vessels rail-to-rail. For the next three hours, the British gunners, firing at point-blank range, blasted holes in the *Richard*'s hull. The decks sloshed with blood. The *Richard* began filling with water.

Any sensible commander would have surrendered. But when the *Serapis*'s captain, Richard Pearson, inquired, he heard Jones's now-legendary retort: "Sir, I have not yet begun to fight." Eventually Pearson himself gave in, fearing that Jones would rather sink them both than admit defeat. The battered *Richard* went down the next day.

The battle had no real impact on the war's outcome. Even so, it threw the British into a state of shock. Until then, the American Revolution had been a colonial dispute fought an entire ocean away. Now it had reached home waters.

To his English enemies John Paul Jones was a scurrilous pirate — no more, no less — as this British caricature implies.

1779-80

Frozen rivers, six-foot snowdrifts — the Continental Army never spent a worse winter than the one at Morristown.

The grim, cold months at Valley Forge have always been held up as a symbol of American courage and endurance. But conditions at Morristown, New Jersey, two years later were as terrible as any during the war.

On December 1, 1779, Gen. George Washington and his troops arrived in Morristown, a place so heavily populated with Tories that Washington called it "enemy country." But the true enemy was not so much the Tories as the bitter weather. For the first time in living memory, the Hudson River froze so solidly that sleighs, heavy carriages, and cannons could roll across it. Snow was four to six feet deep and the soldiers — freezing, unshod, and half-naked — sometimes went for days without food. Anger and starvation provoked two Connecticut regiments to mutiny, and only swift action on the part of officers prevented the trouble from spreading. "Your officers suffer as much as you do," a colonel lectured his miserable troops. "You . . . have won immortal honor to yourselves the winter past, by your perseverance, patience, and bravery, and now you are shaking it off at your heels."

A nearly empty goverment treasury could be blamed for much of the misery. In addition, the tightfisted Congress did not believe that America should bankrupt itself to support an army. Washington begged for help, and in March a congressional committee was finally

dispatched to Morristown. Observing the miserable state of the troops, the committee quickly determined that help was needed. Congress continued to procrastinate, however.

Conditions did not really improve until warmer weather arrived. Then soon after the thaw, General Lafayette brought news that 6,000 French soldiers and a French fleet were on their way to help.

1780

The British believed they had destroyed the Continental Army in the South — that is, until Swamp Fox Francis Marion materialized out of the marshes.

In one of the worst disasters of the War of Independence, more than 5,000 American troops surrendered on May 12, 1780, at Charleston, South Carolina. One who should have been there, but who wasn't, was Lt. Col. Francis Marion. He was at home nursing a broken ankle. It was the Continental Army's luckiest injury.

Shortly after the surrender at Charleston, Marion, having recovered enough to walk, assembled a force of volunteers to help retake his home state. He then began a series of lightning raids against the British. One of his first, undertaken after an all-night march, secured the release of 150 American prisoners.

"Marion's brigade," never more than a few hundred strong (and sometimes just a dozen), relied on stealth and familiarity with the Southern wilderness rather than on strength. Using tactics inspired by Indian methods of fighting, they would strike without warning. One tale relates how Marion and his men caught a British encampment so totally by surprise that one defender died still holding a hand of playing cards — he'd been shot in the middle of a game. The guerrillas chose their targets with a healthy regard for their own safety, and they would vanish into Carolina's broad coastal marshes when the odds were against them.

Although Marion never won large victories, his swift, pernicious attacks

Francis Marion welcomes a captured British officer to a humble meal of roast potatoes at his swamp encampment.

played an important role by wearing down enemy resistance. Try as they might, the British could never capture him. After Lt. Col. Banastre Tarleton trailed Marion for several days through miles of marshy wilderness, the British commander finally gave up: "Come on my boys, let's go back. . . . But as for this damned old fox, the devil himself could not catch him." The fitting name stuck, and the elusive Marion was known thereafter as the Swamp Fox.

1780

British general Sir Henry Clinton, who had reluctantly agreed to lay siege to Charleston, cost the Americans their biggest defeat in the Revolutionary War.

He could not have picked a worse time to travel. Sir Henry Clinton set sail from New York on December 26, 1779, with 8,000 troops, bound for Charleston, South Carolina. For 38 days violent storms buffeted his ships. Valuable supplies washed overboard, and nearly all the horses had to be destroyed after the heaving and pitching of the transport vessels broke their legs. Besides the weather disasters, Clinton was at odds with the fleet's unpredictable vice admiral, Marriott Arbuthnot, who commanded a large force of sailors and marines.

Landing well south of the intended spot, Clinton's troops took seven weeks to make their way up the swampy coast to positions around Charleston. In the end, their patience paid off. Creeping forward through carefully dug trenches, the Redcoats cut off the American garrison's escape routes. They took the city with few casualties, despite an artillery duel in which the defenders fired scrap metal and broken glass. Approximately 5,000 Americans surrendered on May 12, 1780, representing the largest Continental Army loss during the war. The British also captured some 5,300 muskets and 33,000 rounds of small-arms ammunition.

The siege at Charleston was one of the last important British victories.

Clinton's initial reservations about the invasion were a sign of the many problems that plagued the British. Far from their home country, they had difficulty replenishing supplies and obtaining military reinforcements. The victory at Charleston was one of the few that the British enjoyed in the final months of the war. The city was of small strategic value, and during the next 18 months the British campaign in the South began to falter. In little more than a year, with the help of the French, General Washington defeated the enemy at Yorktown, Virginia.

1780

Many officers schemed for advancement during the War for Independence, but few fell out of favor so fast as the British-born Horatio Gates.

Even as a working-class youth in England, Horatio Gates had dreamed of power and prestige. Joining the British Army, he rose to the rank of major; his career then stumbled to a halt. So he resigned his commission and came to America.

He arrived in time to go back into uniform. General Washington, knowing of Gates's administrative skills, appointed him to a staff position. But Gates had his sights on a field command — at one point lobbying Congress in person. Edging out a rival, Gen. Philip Schuyler, he was named

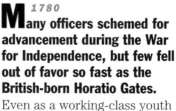

Gen. Horatio Gates reflects on his success at Saratoga, a career high point.

to lead the army in the north, with orders to stop a British offensive in upper New York.

And stop it he did. At the Battle of Saratoga in 1777, Gates's troops routed the forces of British general John Burgoyne. His friends in Congress were dazzled — even though some observers thought that credit for the victory should have gone to Maj. Benedict Arnold, who rode bravely into battle while Gates himself stayed out of the line of fire.

By then, the relationship between Gates and Washington had soured. Rumors began circulating that Gates was conspiring to take Washington's job; he was removed from the field. Then through his congressional friends he obtained the command of the army in the south.

The new post would bring his downfall. In Camden, South Carolina, on August 16, 1780, Gates's new army was trounced by a British force under Gen. Charles Cornwallis.

Some said that Gates was foolish to lead tired, hungry men into combat; others argued that no one could have done better under the circumstances. Gates fled the battlefield, covering 180 miles on horseback in three days. He later claimed that he was trying to raise troops for a counterattack.

Gates was released from the army in disgrace, but he never stopped trying. Reinstated at the war's end, he served briefly as Washington's second in command at Newburgh, New York. But whatever his qualifications as a general, few men emerged from the war with their reputations more in tatters.

Revolutionary Cloak and Dagger

These British and American spies and traitors took part in daring — and often successful — exploits during the American Revolution.

James Armistead — This black spy infiltrated the ranks of Gen. Charles Cornwallis's camp in Virginia, where he learned of British battle plans.

Benedict Arnold — An American general, Benedict Arnold plotted to sell the plans of the American defenses at West Point for £20,000 and a high rank in the British Army.

Dr. Benjamin Church — This high-living doctor, writer, and political activist gave the British advance notice of American plans at Bunker Hill. Imprisoned for nearly two years, Church was allowed to leave the Colonies in 1777.

Nathan Hale — An army captain who, disguised as a teacher, in September 1776 slipped behind British lines and was captured with incriminating documents. Since he was not in uniform, Hale was hanged without a trial.

Pompey — In 1779 this black soldier helped Gen. Anthony Wayne capture the British fort at Stony Point, New York, by tricking a British soldier into providing the password and by overpowering a lookout.

C *1780*
alled the Hercules of the Revolution, Peter Francisco killed 11 enemy soldiers in a single encounter.

By the age of 16, when Peter Francisco enlisted in the Continental Army, he was 6 feet 6 inches tall and weighed 260 pounds. The youth attracted attention in his first battle, at Brandywine, where he fought furiously and was seriously wounded. When Gen. George Washington offered Francisco an officer's rank, he turned it

Strongman Peter Francisco was renowned for battling formidable odds.

down, saying that his lack of formal education disqualified him. The general saluted Francisco's courage by presenting him with a custom-made sword.

At a time when Washington had trouble convincing some of his soldiers to reenlist, each engagement seemed to whet Francisco's appetite for more. He fought hard at Germantown and Fort Mifflin and was

wounded again in the fighting at Monmouth. His reputation as a Hercules grew after the battle at Camden, South Carolina, in August 1780, when Francisco reportedly hauled away a 1,100-pound American cannon to keep it out of British hands. In March 1781 Francisco is said to have killed at least 11 men at Guilford after he sustained a life-threatening bayonet wound. ➤

H *1780*
ad he not turned traitor, Benedict Arnold might have been revered as the greatest combat general of the Revolution.

Fearless but mercurial, Benedict Arnold was George Washington's most aggressive officer. While the rest of the army was getting organized, Arnold and Ethan Allen led bold attacks at Ticonderoga and into Canada, then prevented a British counterinvasion by building a fleet on Lake Champlain. In October 1777 Arnold helped win the Battle of Saratoga for Gen. Horatio Gates by leading charge after charge.

Arnold became bitter when the Continental Congress refused to grant him the promotion he felt he deserved. Nursing a serious leg wound sustained at Saratoga, he appealed to his friend General Washington, who appointed him military commander of Philadelphia. He gained a reputation for arrogance, and was also caught profiteering in public goods — an event that led to his court-martial. Resentful over his failure to advance in rank, angered by the court-martial — and perhaps anticipating victory by the British — Arnold decided to switch sides. Still one of Washington's favorites, he finagled command of the all-important fort at West Point, intending to turn it over to the British. (Control of West Point would give the Royal Navy access to the upper Hudson River — a significant military advantage.)

On the night of September 21, 1780, British Major John André met Arnold by the river. Arnold gave André several top-secret documents to deliver to the British, including a plan of the fortifications at West Point and minutes of a secret war council held by Washington. Disguised as a civilian, André headed back toward British headquarters in Manhattan. Along the way he was stopped by three militiamen, who found the papers hidden in his boot. When André offered the men money to let him go, they promptly turned him over to an American commander.

André was hanged as a spy, facing death so bravely that he won the affection of his captors. When Arnold heard the news of André's death, he quickly escaped to the British in Manhattan. Appointed a brigadier general in the British Army, he led raids in Virginia and Connecticut in 1780 and 1781. ➤

Maj. John André sketched this self-portrait the night before he was executed as a British spy.

1781

A Spanish officer, Bernardo de Gálvez, ended British control of West Florida and paved the way for American expansion in the Mississippi River Valley.

One of the Revolution's most remarkable unsung heroes, Bernardo de Gálvez proved himself as loyal to the American cause as any man alive. Appointed governor of Spain's Louisiana province in 1776, at just 29 years of age, Gálvez waged a two-year campaign of harassment that vexed the British at every turn. Among his tactics were seizing British ships running contraband along the Louisiana coast and funneling money —

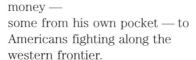

Bernardo de Gálvez battled against formidable odds to oust the British from West Florida.

some from his own pocket — to Americans fighting along the western frontier.

When Spain joined France in the war in mid-1779, Gálvez quickly took the offensive, marching his small force of Spanish regulars and Creole militiamen on Baton Rouge, Manchac, and Natchez. With additional soldiers recruited from Havana, Gálvez then turned to Mobile, in British-controlled West Florida.

At first, the enterprise seemed doomed to failure. Six ships ran aground in Mobile Bay, and Gálvez lost much of his artillery and many supplies. News of this mishap reached the British commander at Pensacola, who headed toward

Mobile with the intention of routing Gálvez. But before the Redcoats could arrive, the unstoppable Gálvez, strengthened with 600 more Havana recruits, marched on the British fort, set up his remaining cannon, and pounded the defenders into submission.

His greatest exploit was yet to come. Pensacola, the last major British fortress, was guarded by 2,500 soldiers and a murderous battery of 32-pound guns. Gálvez planned a joint attack by his own Louisiana-based troops and additional Spanish regiments arriving directly by sea from Havana. But when the Spanish admiral saw the English guns, he refused to approach.

So Gálvez decided to lead by example. On March 1, 1781, striding the deck of the small ship *Gálveztown*, he sailed through a barrage of British cannon fire into Pensacola Harbor. The reluctant admiral was shamed into following.

After a two-month siege (during which Gálvez was wounded twice), the Spanish guns found the bastion's powder magazine. A thunderous explosion breached the walls of the fort, ending British control of West Florida — and erasing all chances for the Crown to claim land west or south of the original 13 colonies.

1781

In one of the boldest strategies of the Revolutionary War, French admiral François Joseph Paul de Grasse sealed off Chesapeake Bay, blocking a British escape from Yorktown and ensuring an American victory.

Cooperation between the French Navy and American forces under George Washington proved to be a winning combination during the last days of the war. In late August of 1781, Washington learned that French admiral François Joseph Paul de Grasse had sailed to America via the West Indies, where he had enlarged his fleet, and that his flotilla of 28 ships was headed for Chesapeake Bay.

Washington quickly dispatched troops from New York to Virginia to trap the British. Meanwhile, 19 British ships under the command of Rear Adm. Thomas Graves — who knew nothing of de Grasse's plans — had set sail from New York to stiffen the forces of Gen. Charles Cornwallis, which were encamped at Yorktown, Virginia. With two fleets and two armies converging, Yorktown was set to be the final confrontation of the war.

On September 5, when the British appeared at the mouth of the bay, they discovered that the French fleet had already arrived. Graves caught de Grasse's ships as they were emerging from the bay's entrance and before they had drawn into a battle line. But the British commander, overly cautious, was slow to attack.

That pause may have cost Britain the war. In the one-day skirmish that followed — known as the Battle of the Virginia Capes — Graves's fleet was badly damaged. By the time he had made repairs, several days later, eight more French ships had arrived from Newport, Rhode Island. With his fleet outnumbered two to one, Graves hastily set sail for New York, leaving the Chesapeake to de Grasse and Cornwallis to his fate. As one naval historian put it, Graves "lost no engagement, no ships. . . . He had merely lost America."

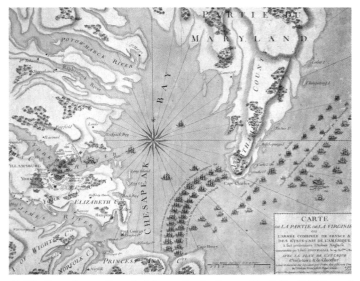

Battle lines drawn, French ships under de Grasse block the British fleet from entering Chesapeake Bay and relieving Yorktown (lower left).

1781

Exactly four years after British forces suffered a humiliating defeat at Saratoga, British general Cornwallis agreed to an unconditional surrender at Yorktown.

In the summer of 1777, Gen. John Burgoyne had marched south from Canada, leading 7,500 British troops on what was meant to be a victorious sweep down the Hudson Valley. The American fort at Ticonderoga fell quickly. But as the season wore on and reinforcements failed to arrive, Burgoyne was in trouble. Near Saratoga, New York, he found himself surrounded and outnumbered by a large American force. Twice he tried to fight his way out, and twice the Americans turned him back. On October 17 he was compelled to surrender. It was England's first major defeat of the war.

The final defeat came October 17, 1781 — four years later to the day. Gen. Charles Cornwallis, encamped at Yorktown, Virginia, with 7,200 men, lay under siege by a joint force of Americans and French. British warships sent to evacuate him had been turned back by a French fleet under de Grasse. For

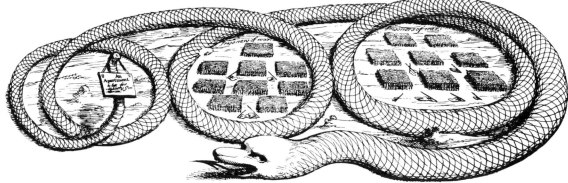

An American rattlesnake holds captive two British armies — one at Yorktown, the other at Saratoga — in a 1782 British cartoon that reflects growing disillusionment with the American war.

more than two weeks, his men had endured a punishing bombardment by enemy guns. So on the morning of October 17, Cornwallis raised the white flag of surrender.

For two days messengers crisscrossed the lines, and in the end Washington got his way: Cornwallis would surrender unconditionally. When the moment arrived to turn over his sword, Cornwallis claimed illness and sent his deputy instead. Washington, not to be slighted in his moment of triumph, waved aside the British weapon.

With the British still occupying New York City, Washington didn't believe that Cornwallis's defeat would end the fighting. But except for minor skirmishes, hostilities ceased. On the other side of the ocean, Yorktown was seen as a clear signal that the expensive and unpopular American war was no longer worth pursuing. "Oh, God, it is all over!" the British prime minister reportedly moaned when he heared the news. Two years later, the Treaty of Paris brought the war to its official conclusion.

1782

It took almost as long for the Congress to approve a design for the Great Seal of the United States as it took the Continental Army to win the Revolutionary War.

To the nation's founders, creating a national seal was a matter of great pride. The Continental Congress appointed a committee to design one just hours after signing the Declaration of Independence. But nothing the committee came up with seemed right. One proposal showed a pharaoh drowning in the Red Sea. Subsequent committees did no better. In desperation, Congress turned to its secretary, Charles Thomson.

Thomson's design, adopted on June 20, 1782, captured the spirit of the infant republic: a bald eagle clutching arrows and an olive branch, for war and peace; a constellation of 13 stars representing a new nation; and an unfinished pyramid beneath the eye of Divine Providence. The motto *E Pluribus Unum* ("out of many, one") came from the title page of an English magazine. Thomson added *Novus Ordo Seclorum* ("a new order of the ages") and *Annuit Coeptis* ("God has favored our undertakings").

Thomson's first design for the Great Seal (left) and the current version.

A **1782**

botched military operation off the coast of Maine tarnished the image of Paul Revere.

In June 1779 the British began building a fort at Penobscot Bay in Maine as a base for naval operations against American shipping. When the legislature in Massachusetts, whose territory included Maine, learned of the plan, it sent an expedition to disrupt it. Lt. Col. Paul Revere was ordered to join the expedition as chief of artillery.

Victory appeared certain. The British garrison had less than 800 men and only three warships. The Americans arrived with an armada of 19 armed vessels, 24 transports, and 3,000 sailors, marines, and state militia. But due to a series of mistakes — not to mention the timidity of Capt. Dudley Saltonstall, the U.S. naval commander — they delayed their attack. Then sails appeared on the horizon: a relief force of British men-of-war.

Saltonstall fled up the Penobscot River, where his ships ran aground. What resulted was the country's worst naval disaster up

Paul Revere put aside his work as a silversmith to take an artillery command.

until Pearl Harbor. The Americans lost 474 men to England's 70 men dead or wounded. Even worse, almost the entire American fleet, including transport ships on loan from

civilian owners, was captured or destroyed. The cost to Massachusetts for their replacement was a staggering $7 million.

Blame for the fiasco lay squarely with the commanding officers. Revere had landed his artillery in preparation for an assault on the British fort, but when the British relief force appeared, he had fled along with the others. At an initial inquiry he was charged with cowardice and other misdeeds.

Revere heatedly denied the allegations and pleaded for a full military trial to clear his name. Finally, in 1782, he got his wish: a court-martial acquitted him of all charges. Saltonstall, on the other hand, was judged incompetent and dismissed from the navy.

After the Penobscot incident, Revere returned to his silversmith shop and involved himself in civic affairs. He was a familiar figure around Boston until his death in 1818, at age 83, easily identified by his quaint attire — clothing that dated back to the era of the Revolutionary War.

Resplendent astride his snow-white battle charger, General Washington is the very image of a patriotic hero. Two centuries later Congress would make him America's first six-star general.

G **1783**

George Washington's failing eyesight may have averted a possible mutiny by his unpaid soldiers.

Although the Continental Army won the battle of Yorktown in 1781, many officers and recruits grew resentful as the war wound down. They were annoyed because Congress had not yet provided their salaries, food and clothing allowances, and bonuses.

Seizing upon the discontent, the power-hungry Gen. Horatio Gates saw an opportunity to promote his own ambitions. By 1783 veiled threats had begun to circulate: if the lawmakers didn't pay up, there might be a mutiny, or worse, and Gates himself might step in as head of the army. To head off such a possibility, General Washington called a meeting on March 15 at army headquarters in Newburgh, New York. The dissidents would have a chance to air their grievances. With tactful deference, Washington named Gates as the meeting's chairman.

Washington knew perfectly well that he had to control the discourse himself. Normally a hesitant speaker, he now pulled out all the stops. He appealed to patriotism and honor, then finally to personal sympathy. Attempting to read from a Congressional dispatch, he paused, fumbled in his vest, and extracted a pair of shiny new eyeglasses. "Gentlemen, you must pardon me," he said. "I have grown gray in your service and now find myself growing blind."

More than one officer wiped away a tear. "There was something so natural, so unaffected in this appeal," said one observer, "as rendered it superior to the most studied oratory. It forced its way to the heart." All talk of mutiny quickly evaporated.

A floating jail for prisoners of war, the Jersey was notorious for its wretched conditions. Thousands of American prisoners died there of disease or starvation.

1783
More American soldiers may have died on prison ships than on battlefields.

Neither England nor America was prepared to deal with the huge number of prisoners taken during the Revolutionary War. Early in the conflict, jails were crammed with POW's from both sides. Churches, warehouses, and other buildings were converted into military jails.

When space ran out on land, the British began to use ships as prisons. Over the course of several years, more than a dozen nearly derelict vessels were anchored in the mud flats of Wallabout Bay in Brooklyn to hold captured American soldiers. The most notorious of these was the *Jersey*, nicknamed Hell Afloat. Conditions aboard every one of the floating prisons were uniformly atrocious, however.

Patriot soldiers were considered common criminals rather than POW's, and some had to endure beatings and other brutalities from their guards. The poorly clothed captives froze in the winter and suffocated in the summer heat; sanitation was virtually nonexistent. Food rations were barely adequate to prevent starvation. Rancid pork and moldy, weevil-infested biscuits were standard fare. Deprived of fresh vegetables, many prisoners suffered from scurvy. Worse yet, diseases such as dysentery, smallpox, typhoid, and yellow fever ravaged the prison population.

On the *Jersey*, mornings began with the sentry call, "Rebels, turn out your dead." And with what little strength they had, the living brought the dead up on deck to be taken ashore for burial. It was not unusual for 10 or 11 prisoners to die in a day.

By the end of the war, in 1783, an estimated 11,000 American prisoners had died on the prison ships in Wallabout Bay, considerably more than the estimated 7,200 American soldiers killed in combat.

1783
Defying Congress, Benjamin Franklin negotiated American independence with Britain without any French representatives on hand.

Six months after its defeat at Yorktown, Britain sent peace feelers both to its former colony and to France. All sides were exhausted and eager to negotiate a truce. Complicating the new nation's diplomatic maneuvers, however, was its debt to the French for the military and economic aid that had kept it afloat during the hostilities. Congress, knowing that additional loans would be needed in the future, agreed that France must be included in the peace negotiations.

The talks began in Paris in 1782. Benjamin Franklin was already in the city, and Congress dispatched John Jay and John Adams to assist him. But Jay and Adams had their own agenda. Suspecting that France wanted to limit the borders of the new nation, they urged Franklin to deal only with the British. Franklin reluctantly agreed.

Though suffering severe pain from a gout attack and a kidney stone, Franklin, age 75, managed to win his most important goal: independence for the United States. Its borders would extend from Maine to Florida, west to the Mississippi River, and north to the lower half of the Great Lakes. The treaty allowed fishing rights in Canadian coastal waters, a provision that was crucial to the economy of New England. On September 3, 1783, the Peace of Paris was signed.

From left: Jay, Adams, Franklin, and two other diplomats negotiate peace. The painting was left unfinished because the British envoys refused to sit for their portraits.

1783

As America was celebrating peace with Great Britain, Noah Webster was fomenting his own revolt by changing the spelling and usage of the king's English.

The ink was barely dry on the Treaty of Paris, which officially ended the War of Independence, when Noah Webster took up a new argument for independence. "Our honor requires us to have a system of our own in language as well as government," declared Webster, a teacher who disliked having to use the English textbooks that were available. In 1783 he published *The American Spelling Book,* which was emphatically American in content and sensibility. It was followed by a grammar in 1784 and a reader in 1785. The trilogy, *A Grammatical Institute of the English Language,* sold more copies in Webster's lifetime than any other book except the Bible.

In 1806 Webster published his first dictionary, which contained some 5,000 words that had not previously appeared in any lexicon. "There is nothing which, in my opinion, so debases the genius and character of my countrymen," he said, "as the implicit confidence they place in English authors and their unhesitating submission to their *opinions,* their *decision,* and their *frowns.*"

Webster's 1783 book taught millions to read and spell.

Webster's belief that language should embrace new words — the basic concept of modern lexicography — appalled the British. One traditionalist argued that English had "words enough already." But Webster was unmoved. Determined to promote a national vocabulary and usage, in 1828 he published his masterpiece, *An American Dictionary of the English Language.* Although the volume sold few copies at first, today it is prized as the first major American dictionary.

John Sevier helped found the short-lived state of Franklin.

1784

Irked by what they thought was rude treatment by distant legislators, settlers on the far edge of North Carolina set up their own state.

Frontier families had begun moving to the region as early as 1769, settling into a mountainous no-man's-land in what is now northeastern Tennessee. They formed a government, the Watauga Association, named after a river back in Virginia. With the onset of the Revolution, fearing Indian attack, they applied to become a part of nearby North Carolina.

No sooner had the North Carolina legislature voted to adopt the area than it regretted its decision. The Wataugans were a difficult lot (some were wanted outlaws) who required protection but refused to pay taxes. Carolinians called them "off-scourings of the earth." So after much debate, the legislature agreed in 1784 to cede the region to the federal government. Then later that year the legislators had second thoughts and demanded it back again.

Rebuffed and insulted, the Wataugans decided to stay independent. Drawing up a constitution, they declared themselves to be the state of Franklin, after Benjamin Franklin. John Sevier, a local judge and land speculator, was elected governor.

From the very first, Franklin was torn by friction between residents loyal to North Carolina and their independence-minded peers. For several years North Carolina regained control, and Sevier was thrown briefly into prison. Then in 1796 all North Carolina territory west of the Appalachians, including the territory of Franklin, was formed into the new state of Tennessee. The state's first governor: John Sevier.

IN THEIR OWN WORDS

"Wasteland, unhealthy climate, poor people, ragged clothing — such is approximately the general idea of this continent in Europe. But oh how far from the truth is this! The land requires too little work to remain uncultivated. The robustness of the men and the fine color of the women attest to the healthiness of the climate. Not only the abundance, but also the luxury in which people live belies their reputed poverty. And the pleasure which everyone who is introduced to their society experiences is incontestable evidence of their gracious manner of living. The [American] peasant does not know what misery is; he eats meat four times a day and drinks tea twice a day. . . . The quantity of all kinds of lumber, fish, oil, blubber, material for soap, flour, and salt meat will, before long, bring to this continent enough money to enable it to be recognized as a wealthy country."

Francesco Dal Verme, writing about his journey to the United States in 1783.

S *1785*
ettlers in the Kentucky wilderness named a huge area Bourbon County, in honor of the ruling house of France. Years later the region produced a distinctly American whiskey fit for kings and moonshine drinkers alike.

When settlers in what is now Kentucky's bluegrass region learned how important the French government's support had been during the American Revolution, they proposed to name their new county Bourbon, after the royal family of France. The unofficial expression of gratitude became a permanent feature in 1785 when a legislator of French ancestry, James Garrard, helped steer a bill through the Virginia Assembly creating Bourbon County. (The region was then part of Virginia.)

When the Francophile county — already famous for its rye whiskey — found itself with a surplus of corn, distillers decided to add corn to their mash. Among the first to do so was a Baptist minister, Elijah Craig, who began distilling the liquor sometime between 1791 and

The first distillery, built in 1786, was nearly as important to Kentucky as home and church.

1798. Legend has it that the whiskey acquired its characteristic color and taste when Craig stored it in barrels charred by fire. Its smooth flavor caught on immediately, and during the 19th century, its name changed from corn spirits to mountain dew, corn, corn whiskey, and Bourbon County whiskey, until it finally became just plain "bourbon."

Daniel Shays, standing at the top of the stairs, rallies Massachusetts farmers in an antitax protest that threatened the sovereignty of the federal government.

A *1786*
short-lived revolt against the heavy tax burden in Massachusetts found former rebel Sam Adams calling for the perpetrators to be hanged.

Many farmers and tradesmen suffered financial setbacks during and after the Revolutionary War, but none as badly as those in Massachusetts. Other states provided relief to citizens who were financially drained, but Massachusetts legislators refused to help. Instead, to pay off state debts accrued during the war, they made matters worse by levying high taxes. Debtors either had their possessions auctioned off or were thrown into prison.

Repeated attempts by farmers to seek relief from the tax load had almost no effect. On August 29, 1786, some 800 farmers staged a protest at a state court. Four weeks later, their leaders organized a shutdown of the supreme court in Springfield, and the local militia was called out. As tempers flared, Daniel Shays, a hero of the Revolutionary War, offered to negotiate a settlement. Like many of his peers, Shays had fallen on hard times; to raise cash, he had been forced to sell a sword given to him by General Lafayette.

Despite Shays's offer, the Massachusetts legislature passed no tax reforms, and by January 1787 the farmers had suffered enough. Arming themselves, they called on Shays to lead them. After a failed attempt to take the federal arsenal in Springfield, and a few minor skirmishes, the state militia defeated the insurgents at Petersham.

Shays's Rebellion was over in a month, but it had long-lasting consequences. The threat to the state's authority raised nationwide fears of civil unrest and fueled the movement for a new constitution that would grant stronger powers to the federal government. Ironically, Sam Adams and others who had instigated the American Revolution were alarmed by the uprising. Adams even urged that the leaders be hanged. (They were eventually pardoned.) Thomas Jefferson, on the other hand, took an easier view: "A little rebellion now and then is a good thing; the tree of liberty must be refreshed from time to time with the blood of patriots and tyrants."

1787
The Northwest Ordinance, passed in 1787, set the rules by which future states entered the Union.

At the Revolution's end the young United States found itself with a restless population looking westward. The defeat of Britain had placed some 200 million acres in the hands of the states. Soon thousands of settlers were streaming past the Appalachians in wagon trains and flatboats, staking a claim to every piece of land in sight.

In July 1787, while delegates were crafting a new Constitution in Philadelphia, the Congress of the Confederation (the nation's acting government, formed in 1781) met to decide the fate of the vast new lands in western America. On July 13 Congress passed the Northwest Ordinance, allowing each territory to be admitted as a state on an equal basis with the original 13 when its population reached 60,000. The ordinance provided that new states would be "at liberty to form a permanent constitution and State government . . . in conformity to the principles contained in these [six] articles." Slavery was prohibited, and the writ of habeas corpus and trial by jury were guaranteed. (The antislavery provision would be overtaken in later decades by the course of events.)

The future states of Ohio, Indiana, Illinois, Michigan, and Wisconsin were soon the sites of a new land boom. The number of white settlers in these territories soared from a few thousand to 120,000 people by 1790. Within the next decade some 700,000 whites were living west of the Appalachians in an area that extended as far south as Alabama and Mississippi.

The ordinance proved fatal to another resident group, however. To Native Americans, the law's text had promised liberty, property rights, and "the utmost good faith." But as conflicts over land developed into all-out war, the Northwest Ordinance turned into an eviction notice for the region's original inhabitants: untold thousands would soon be displaced from their ancestral hunting grounds.

George Washington and Benjamin Franklin (seated, with cane) witness the signing of the Constitution.

The Northwest Ordinance

Before passage of the Northwest Ordinance in 1787, the following states held colonial claims in the Northwest Territory. Dates indicate when claims were ceded to the Continental Congress.

State	Date Claim Ceded	Claim Became
• New York	1780	Ohio
• Virginia	1784	Ohio Kentucky
• Massachusetts	1785	Wisconsin Indiana Illinois Michigan Ohio
• Connecticut	1786, 1800*	Ohio (Western Reserve)
• South Carolina	1787	Alabama Georgia Mississippi
• North Carolina	1789	Tennessee
• Georgia	1802	Alabama Mississippi

*Connecticut held multiple claims.

▮ Area ceded to the Continental Congress

1787
Quiet of voice and small in stature, James Madison came to dominate the Constitutional Convention by the sheer force of his intellect.

James Madison stood approximately 5½ feet tall and weighed just 100 pounds. One contemporary praised him for his "remarkable sweet temper." At the Constitutional Convention of 1787, however, Madison won a reputation that belied his appearance. His intellect shone through his quiet demeanor. In preparing for the convention, he had pored over texts on ancient and contemporary confederacies. He also drew on his 13 years of experience in American politics. Every day at the convention, he took copious notes and transcribed them by candlelight at night.

Madison's main contribution to the convention, the Virginia Plan, formed the backbone of the final document and eventually earned him the title Father of the Constitution. The plan called for a "national executive," a national judiciary, and a bicameral legislature, with the balance of power distributed evenly among the three branches. Madison insisted that the government's authority should be derived from the people, and that in one of the legislative houses members should be elected by popular vote.

Madison went on to become a two-term president, but the crowning achievement of his life was the Constitution. He rose to speak more than 200 times in Philadelphia, where his temperate disposition often gave way to heated enthusiasm. He allegedly became so involved in debate that he enlisted a friend to tug on his coattails whenever he got too excited. Apologizing once for letting Madison storm through a particularly rousing speech, the friend said, "I would rather have laid a finger on the lightning."

G *1787*
ouverneur Morris, who originally had hoped for reconciliation with the British Crown, ended up becoming one of the drafters of the U.S. Constitution.

A year before America's quarrel with England erupted into violence on the village green at Lexington, Massachussetts, Gouverneur Morris thought his countrymen were headed for disaster. "If the disputes with Britain continue," wrote the young lawyer in 1774, "we shall be under the worst of all possible dominions — the domination of a riotous mob."

Morris's distaste for revolution was hardly surprising. Born on the 2,000-acre farm of one of New York's prominent families, he exuded sophistication and conservatism. Luxury, he once wrote, was not "such a bad thing as people believed."

Once the Revolution had begun, however, Morris proved to be the most devoted of patriots. Still in his mid-twenties, he chaired several committees in the Continental Congress, and in debate he pleaded eloquently for its supremacy over the states.

The aristocratic Gouverneur Morris favored a strong central government.

After independence was won, Morris brought his fervent nationalism to the Constitutional Convention, but his conservative politics often ran afoul of the democratic atmosphere in Philadelphia. Rising to speak more frequently than any other delegate, he called for life terms for senators and the president and a suffrage restricted to the freeholders. But when the Convention opposed his motions, Morris gracefully gave in.

It was this high-minded adaptability, no doubt, as well as his facility with a pen, that won Morris the job of drafting the final constitutional document. On Monday, September 10, 1787, the Committee of Style and Arrangement, which included Morris, received a sheaf of notes from the Convention. By Wednesday the draft was ready. Among other changes, Morris stamped his own nationalism on the constitution. The Convention's preamble had read, "We the undersigned delegates of the States of New Hampshire, Massachusetts. . . ." Morris substituted simply, "We the People of the United States. . . ."

A *1788*
fter one of the most contentious political debates in American history, the U.S. Constitution became the "supreme law of the land."

On September 17, 1787, the Constitutional Convention closed on a sour note; after sitting through four months of conflict and compromise, 16 of the 55 delegates refused to sign the Constitution, vowing to fight its adoption in the state conventions that would be held to ratify it.

What followed was one of the hottest debates in American history. Taking pseudonyms like "Brutus," the "Plain Dealer," or "Landholder," writers filled the local newspapers with arguments both for and against the Constitution. In New York a series of articles later published as *The Federalist* defended the document with unparalleled eloquence. The men who wrote the articles — James Madison, Alexander Hamilton, and John Jay — were among the greatest political thinkers in America. Without a strong central government, they argued, the United States was sure to drift into anarchy.

The members of a determined opposition, calling themselves Anti-Federalists, insisted that all the work of the eight-year Revolution would be sacrificed to the ambitions of a powerful few. In Pennsylvania one Anti-Federalist wrote that the Constitution was "a scheme of the wealthy and ambitious, who . . . think they have the right to lord it over their fellow creatures." The Constitution with its emphasis on federal governance, the Anti-Federalists claimed, would destroy the sovereignty of the states.

Most important, the document failed to include a Bill of Rights.

Still, state by state, the Federalists triumphed. Delaware ratified the Constitution first, then Pennsylvania, then other states, until New Hampshire, on June 21, 1788, offered the ninth official "yea" that provided the two-thirds majority required for adoption. Shortly thereafter, Virginia and New York gave their approval. North Carolina waited for the passage of the Bill of Rights, and Rhode Island finally relented on May 29, 1790. The world's first modern democracy at last had a framework for government.

A 1788 cartoon shows New Hampshire as the "ninth and sufficient pillar" needed to ratify the Constitution.

1788

Patrick Henry, whose bold words "Give me liberty, or give me death" helped fire the Revolution, argued vehemently against the Constitution.
History remembers Patrick Henry as an ardent patriot and a gifted orator. Thomas Jefferson considered him "the idol of his country beyond any man who ever lived." But the same man who helped turn the tide of American sentiment toward revolution also opposed the Constitution.

An eloquent speaker, Henry dazzled the First Continental Congress with a speech urging resistance against the British. At the second Virginia convention in 1775, he urged the arming and training of a militia, and again spoke vehemently about the need for revolt: "Is life so dear, or peace so sweet, as to be purchased at the price of chains and slavery?" he asked. "I know not what course others may take; but as for me, give me liberty or give me death!" A year later he was elected Virginia's first governor under its new Constitution.

After the Revolution, Henry took up a new battle — against the U.S. Constitution. He became one of the leaders of the Anti-Federalists, a group that distrusted a strong central government and opposed the Constitution on the grounds that it offered no

Refusing to bow to the British, Patrick Henry instead offered an uncompromising challenge.

guarantee of state or individual rights. At the Virginia Convention of 1788, he called on his powers as orator once again to describe the shortcomings of the document and the tyranny that would result if it were accepted. "The Constitution is said to have beautiful features; but when I come to examine these features, Sir, they appear to me horribly frightful. Among other deformities, it has an awful squinting — it squints toward monarchy." Despite Henry's opposition, on June 25, 1788, Virginia's Federalists eked out a narrow victory, due in part to their promise to support amendments that later became the Bill of Rights.

What may never be understood is why Patrick Henry, the staunch Anti-Federalist, then switched camps and began siding with the Federalists. Just as the popularity of the Washington administration began to wane, Henry became a vocal supporter of centralized government; he was even offered several government posts, including secretary of state and chief justice of the Supreme Court. Although he declined both jobs, he did agree to run for the Virginia House of Delegates, to which he was elected. He died on June 6, 1799, just before his first appearance in the Assembly as a Federalist.

George Washington's Guide to Good Manners

George Washington always had a keen sense of propriety and dignity. He probably wrote these rules when he was 15.

- Sleep not when others Speak, Sit not when others stand, Speak not when you Should hold your Peace.

- If you Cough, Sneeze, Sigh or Yawn, do it not Loud but Privately; and Speak not in your Yawning, but put Your handkercheif or Hand before your face and turn aside.

- Do not Puff up the Cheeks; loll not out the tongue.

- Think before you Speak; pronounce not imperfectly.

- Shew not yourself glad at the Misfortune of another though he were your enemy.

- In visiting the Sick, do not Presently play the Physicion if you be not Knowing therein.

- Wherein you reprove Another be unblameable yourself; for example is more prevalent than Precepts.

- Drink not nor talk with your mouth full neither Gaze about you while you are Drinking.

- Labour to keep alive in your Breast that Little Spark of Celestial fire Called Conscience.

(This image has been colorized for The American Story.*)*

1789

The first president of the United States did not have enough cash to pay the travel costs to his own inauguration.
George Washington had many things on his mind when he was elected president in 1789. It is clear that one of them was money — not just the country's deficits, but his own empty pockets.

As commander in chief of the Continental Army, Washington had declined a salary. Congress, itself short of cash, reimbursed his numerous expenses with promissory notes. Washington had also lost a large amount of money by allowing his debtors to pay him in Continental currency, which was worth only a fraction of the British pound sterling with which he should have been paid. With Washing-

ton away at war, his plantation lost money, and the cost of entertaining the many people who descended upon Mount Vernon further added to his debts. Refusing to skimp, Washington often went beyond the limit of his cash resources.

Although the government would pay his living and entertainment expenses while he was president, Washington nonetheless wanted to clear his debts. When he heard the news of his election, he attempted to borrow more than £1,000 to settle his accounts before leaving Virginia, but his credit was found wanting. In the end he turned to a wealthy citizen for a loan of £500 and was later forced to borrow another £100 to finance the journey to his inauguration in New York City.

G *1789*
eorge Washington faced his presidency with great reluctance.
After the Revolutionary War was won, the weary commander of the Continental Army resigned his commission, wishing to spend his last years as a gentleman farmer. The people of the United States had other ideas, however. On February 4, 1789, all 69 members of the Electoral College chose George Washington to be the nation's first leader under the new Constitution.

Washington himself had significant doubts, and he set out for the temporary capital of New York "with more anxious and painful sensations than I have words to express." He knew full well that the destiny of the nation — and of democracy itself — would be shaped by his actions. "So much is expected, so many untoward circumstances may intervene, in such a new and critical situation that I feel an insuperable diffidence in my own abilities."

The enthusiasm of the crowds en route was enormous. Choirs sang, church bells rang, and flowers were strewn before Washington's horse. Upon his arrival in New York, there were parades, and processions of ships in the harbor fired booming salutes over the roar of a wildly cheering crowd. Washington was overcome with emotion.

At sunrise on April 30, 13 guns marked the dawn of the first Inauguration Day. That afternoon, wearing a plain brown suit and his best silk stockings, Washington took the oath of office, promising to "preserve, protect, and defend the Constitution of the United States" — words repeated by every president who has succeeded him. "Long live George Washington, President of the United States!" Chancellor Robert Livingston of New York shouted after administering the oath, and crowds of people echoed his enthusiasm in the streets outside Federal Hall.

Washington delivered his inaugural address in a quiet, trembling voice, his expression "grave almost to sadness." A solitary critic remarked that he "left a rather ungainly impression," but most people were deeply moved. Said orator Fisher Ames after the inauguration: "It [Washington's speech] seemed to me an allegory in which virtue was personified, and addressing those whom she would make her votaries. Her power over the heart was never greater."

Amid much fanfare and celebration, President-elect Washington arrives in New York Harbor.

T *1789*
he legend is partly right — George Washington did indeed wear false teeth. But they were made of ivory and human teeth, not wood.
Dental care in colonial days usually meant either a visit to a barber or blacksmith — both often doubled as dentists — or else a painful session with a traveling tooth-puller. Understandably, the colonists' teeth were among the worst in the world. Even our first president had serious dental problems.

Troubled by toothaches all his adult life, George Washington was only 21 when his teeth began to fall out. Even during the Revolutionary War, he searched desperately for dental help. When he heard of Jean Pierre LeMayeur, a French dentist who practiced in New York, he summoned him to his headquarters, where LeMayeur resorted to pulling the problem teeth. (Most dentists of the period would have done the same thing.) By the time of his inauguration in 1789, Washington had only one tooth left.

Washington next turned to a New York dentist, John Greenwood, who made beeswax casts of his mouth, then fashioned dentures of ivory and human teeth (bought from the poor), which he attached with gold wire to plates of hippopotamus tusk.

The false teeth were often uncomfortable, and they made it difficult for Washington to laugh or smile. They also distorted the shape of his mouth. The dentures "bulge my lips out in such a manner as to make them appear considerably swelled," he complained to Greenwood. Even so, Washington was satisfied enough with his false choppers that he never sought another dentist for help.

1789

John Adams, the first vice president, tried to bring the trappings of royalty to the new American government.

As vice president under George Washington, John Adams had strong opinions about how elected officials should be treated. Despite America's hard-won freedom, he believed that the nation should honor its highest elected officials with designations that recalled the defeated monarchy. Taking office in 1789, he suggested that Washington be called "His Most Benign Highness." Adams also tried to initiate bowing, a practice that was rejected outright by the House of Representatives. His behavior was not surprising, since he had spent a decade in Europe exposed to royal protocol.

There was strong opposition in Congress to Adams's ideas, as well as much derision and resentment. Some took delight in referring to the overweight Adams as "His Rotundity." Benjamin Franklin even suggested "Your Superfluous Excellency." Eventually, Adams decided that the trappings of royalty had no place in a democracy.

Although sometimes pompous and overbearing, Adams was a brilliant debater who had been an early champion of independence from Britain. He had played an important role in the Continental Congress — first by helping to draft the Declaration of Independence, then by arguing for its adoption. When the war ended, he expertly handled peace negotiations with Britain. Little wonder, then, that Adams hoped to take an active part in the new government.

Instead, as vice president, Adams's only important duty was to preside over the Senate. He set a dignified tone in the Senate chamber, loudly tapping a silver pencil case whenever anyone was out of order. Occasionally he would step in to break a tie vote; or, impatient with the debate, he might interrupt to deliver his own opinion. The vice presidency, Adams decided, was the "most insignificant office that ever the invention of man contrived or his imagination conceived." Biding his time, he suffered through his term, mostly in silence, until he was elected president in 1796.

John Adams felt he "had not the smallest degree of power to do any good."

1789

Martha Washington privately called her tenure as America's original first lady the "lost days."

Throughout eight long years in the nation's capital, Martha Washington never stopped longing for her beloved home at Mount Vernon, Virginia. As wife of the young democracy's first president, she knew that the entire world was watching her. In running the presidential household, she resolved to set the highest standards of social decorum and to serve as a role model for all subsequent first ladies. She succeeded beautifully. Abigail Adams praised her "unaffected deportment, which renders her the object of veneration and respect," and she became known as an adept and lively hostess.

It was an exhausting task. On Tuesdays the president held an afternoon "levee," or reception, for foreign dignitaries and government officials; on Thursdays, a dinner; and on Fridays Mrs. Washington hosted an evening tea party, a favorite event of the president.

The Thursday dinners, in particular, were grand social events. They usually began at precisely 4:00 P.M. The always punctual first lady once informed a tardy guest that the cook "never

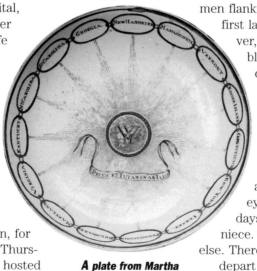

A plate from Martha Washington's tea service.

asks whether the company has come, but whether the hour has come." At table the Washingtons sat opposite each other, the men flanking the president and the women flanking the first lady. The table was lavishly set with the family silver, and the talk remained decorous. To avoid possible disputes, the hostess carefully steered the conversation away from politics and government. When dinner was over, the women withdrew and the men remained at the table. At the evening's end, Mrs. Washington would sometimes announce: "The General always retires at nine, and I usually precede him."

Martha Washington's gracious manner hid an abiding discontent at always being in the public eye; she called her tenure as first lady her "lost days." "I live a very dull life here," she wrote to her niece. "I am more like a State prisoner than anything else. There are certain bounds set for me which I must not depart from, and as I cannot do as I like, I am obstinate and stay home a great deal." When Washington left office in 1797 and the couple returned to Mount Vernon, she wrote to a friend: "I cannot tell you . . . how much I enjoy home after having been deprived of one so long."

1789

The Bill of Rights was proposed in 1789, but it was not until 150 years later that three of the original states finally ratified this precious guarantee of personal liberties.

When George Mason, a Virginia lawyer, stood in Congress and suggested adding a bill of rights to the Constitution in order to give "great quiet to the people," he provoked a storm of opposition. Alexander Hamilton, for instance, felt that "the Constitution is itself, in every rational sense, and to every useful purpose, a bill of rights." But others disagreed. Even George Washington in his inaugural address asked for amendments that demonstrated "a reverence for the characteristic rights of freemen."

James Madison elaborated on the necessity of a bill of rights in a letter to Thomas Jefferson: "Although it be generally true . . . that the danger of oppression lies in the interested majorities of the people rather than in usurped acts of Government, yet there may be occasions on which . . . a bill of rights will be a good ground for an appeal to the sense of the community." Once Congress finally decided to add a bill of rights, suggestions for Constitutional amendments poured in from various states: at one point there were 145. With the help of Congress, Madison winnowed the amendments, most of which he took from the declarations of rights of Virginia and Massachusetts, down to 12.

Ratification of the amendments was a slow state-by-state process. By now there were 14 states in the Union, and 11 affirmative votes were needed. New Jersey, on November 20, 1789, was the first state to ratify the amendments. Vermont, which was admitted to the Union in March 1791, became the tenth. On December 15 of that year Virginia became the eleventh — and decisive — state to vote for the bill. The Bill of Rights, which to this day protects our freedom of speech, press, religion, and more, had become the law of the land. During the ratification process, two of the proposed rights — one that controlled the number of congressional representatives, and another that would ban salary raises for members of Congress during their terms — were dropped as being irrelevant.

Several states took their time ratifying the measure. Not until 1939 — in a ceremonial gesture that marked the 150th anniversary of the Constitution — did Connecticut, Georgia, and Massachusetts finally cast their votes for this historic guarantee of personal freedoms.

1789

Full of wry commentary and sharp opinion, Sen. William Maclay's personal journal is the only continuous record of the proceedings of the First Constitutional Congress.

Legislative debates in the young republic took place behind closed doors, with no available public record. But the Senate's major decisions and minor skirmishes from 1789 to 1791 were fully documented in the diary of Pennsylvania senator William Maclay.

Maclay's sharp pen recorded all the quirks and foibles of the Founding Fathers at work. Here, for instance, is John Adams who, as president of the Senate, was prevented from taking an active role in the daily congressional give-and-take. He fidgeted "with a kind of eagerness or restlessness," the diarist recorded, "as if a nettle had been in his breeches." In exasperation Maclay admonished: "Adams, Adams, what a wretch art thou!"

Even an elegant dinner at the home of the Washingtons — although acknowledged by Maclay as "the best of the kind" — came in for its share of caustic comment: "It was the most solemn dinner ever I sat at," he observed, and the room was "disagreeably warm." Before the evening was officially concluded, Maclay confessed: "I took my hat and came home."

No one was safe from Maclay's close scrutiny.

America's Changing Capital

For 25 years the center of government in America moved back and forth among nine cities. In 1789 the Congress was authorized under the Constitution to choose a permanent site. Finally, after a decade of debate and a donation of land by Maryland and Virginia, the capital city of Washington, D.C., was founded.

1. **Philadelphia,** Pennsylvania	September 5, 1774, to December 12, 1776
2. **Baltimore,** Maryland	December 20, 1776, to February 27, 1777
3. **Philadelphia,** Pennsylvania	March 4, 1777, to September 18, 1777
4. **Lancaster,** Pennsylvania	September 27, 1777 (only one day)
5. **York,** Pennsylvania	September 30, 1777, to June 27, 1778
6. **Philadelphia,** Pennsylvania	July 2, 1778, to March 1, 1781
7. **Philadelphia,** Pennsylvania	March 2, 1781, to June 21, 1783
8. **Princeton,** New Jersey	June 30, 1783, to November 4, 1783
9. **Annapolis,** Maryland	November 26, 1783, to June 3, 1784
10. **Trenton,** New Jersey	November 1, 1784, to December 24, 1784
11. **New York,** New York	January 11, 1785, to August 12, 1790
12. **Philadelphia,** Pennsylvania	December 6, 1790, to May 14, 1800
13. **Washington,** D.C.	November 17, 1800, to the present

1789

As a military leader, George Washington got the job done; as the nation's first president, surrounded by carefully chosen aides, he was magnificent.

Building a stable government in the wake of a revolution, George Washington was deeply aware of the gravity of his every action. "I walk on untrodden ground," he wrote. "There is scarcely any part of my conduct which may not hereafter be drawn into precedent." One of his most important tasks was to appoint capable assistants to head the newly created executive departments. The president believed that these essential posts should be filled by men of high purpose and integrity.

Rarely has a group of supporting players been so gifted. The secretary of the treasury, Alexander Hamilton, was a brilliant lawyer who had been an aide to Washington during the war. His daunting new assignment: to develop a fiscal plan for a government with an empty treasury and heavy debt.

Thomas Jefferson, who had been an excellent minister to France, became the new secretary of state, with a long list of varied responsibilities. Jefferson was put in charge of foreign affairs, managing the Mint, taking the census, and granting copyrights and patents. Edmund Randolph of Virginia became attorney general, arguing federal cases before the Supreme Court and providing legal counsel. For secretary of war, Washington selected Henry Knox, a man who had held the position under the prior Confederation government.

Throughout his eight years in office, Washington proved to be a tireless hands-on administrator who involved himself in every aspect of government. Jefferson wrote that the president "was always in accurate possession of all facts and proceedings in every part of the Union. He formed a central point for the different branches and met himself the due responsibility for whatever was done." In this dedicated manner America's primary public servant carried out the business of running the country.

1789

President George Washington lost an attorney general — and a dear friend — under the cloud of a political scandal.

For the job of attorney general, President George Washington selected his close friend of 20 years, Edmund Randolph. In making the appointment, he noted the wisdom of having an aide with whom he shared "habits of intimacy." Washington had no way of knowing that his decision would ultimately lead to a political scandal and would rupture the bonds of friendship between the two men.

Randolph was eminently qualified for the post. In 1776, at age 23, he was the youngest member of the Virginia Constitutional Convention; he then became the state's first attorney general, and later its governor. He was a delegate to the Constitutional Congress and also the Federal Convention, where he introduced the Virginia Plan, an ambitious proposal that would have given wide-ranging powers to the federal government at the expense of the individual states.

America's first attorney general, Edmund Randolph.

After serving as attorney general for five years, Randolph took over the position of secretary of state when Thomas Jefferson resigned in 1794. It was a grueling job that required him to maintain the fragile and complex diplomatic ties that existed between the United States and the warring nations of France and Great Britain. Even someone as capable as Randolph found it difficult juggling diplomats, ambassadors, and his fellow Cabinet members — and keeping them all satisfied. He inevitably stepped on some toes and made a few enemies. In 1795 he was accused — falsely, it is believed today — of attempting to bribe the French ambassador to the United States.

A heavy-hearted Washington investigated the charges, humiliating his longtime friend in the process. Randolph resigned his post, shouting at Washington that he "could not continue in the office one second after such treatment." He later wrote a lengthy *Vindication,* indicating that he had been framed.

The friendship between the two Virginians had been irretrievably broken. Randolph went home to Virginia, where he became one of the state's most prominent lawyers. Among his important cases was the trial of Aaron Burr, whom he successfully defended against charges of treason in 1807.

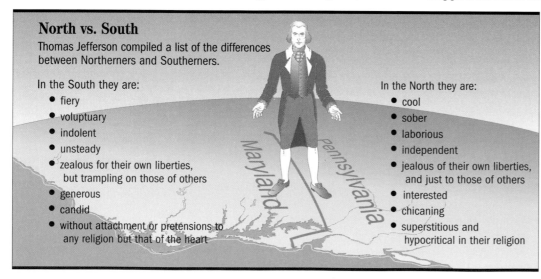

North vs. South

Thomas Jefferson compiled a list of the differences between Northerners and Southerners.

In the South they are:
- fiery
- voluptuary
- indolent
- unsteady
- zealous for their own liberties, but trampling on those of others
- generous
- candid
- without attachment or pretensions to any religion but that of the heart

In the North they are:
- cool
- sober
- laborious
- independent
- jealous of their own liberties, and just to those of others
- interested
- chicaning
- superstitious and hypocritical in their religion

Maryland

Pennsylvania

The cascading waters of Pawtucket Falls fueled Samuel Slater's textile mills — the first in America to use hydraulic-powered machines to spin yarn.

Samuel Slater slipped out of England in 1789 and became a driving force in the American Industrial Revolution.

1789

Because English law prohibited skilled textile workers from leaving the country, 21-year-old Samuel Slater sailed secretly for America in 1789 disguised as a farmer. An apprentice in a textile mill, Slater was concerned that overproduction in British mills might lead to industry layoffs, thus seriously limiting his professional future.

In America, the conversion from hand-woven fabrics to factory-made textiles was just beginning. A man with Slater's experience — he had worked with Sir Richard Arkwright's newly invented spinning frame, and was adept at both operations and management — was destined to go far. Teaming up with Providence merchant Moses Brown, Slater retooled Brown's existing machinery, showed him how to run his plant at full capacity, and explained how to manage a textile firm according to the best modern methods. The two men set up a brilliantly successful cotton mill in Pawtucket, Rhode Island; Slater has since been called New England's first industrial capitalist.

One of the lesser-known figures of colonial history, William Richardson Davie founded America's first state university to grant degrees, the University of North Carolina.

1789

William Richardson Davie was a Revolutionary War officer who was described as "one of those cool, quick men who apply master-wit to the art of war." He was also an attorney, a North Carolina delegate to the 1787 Constitutional Convention in Philadelphia, a state governor, and a peace envoy to France for President John Adams.

Despite his many roles, Davie may be best remembered for a single groundbreaking accomplishment. In December 1789 the North Carolina General Assembly passed a bill, introduced by Davie, to charter a state university. In the bill's preamble Davie wrote that "it is the indispensable duty of every Legislature to consult the happiness of a rising generation and endeavor to fit

A silhouette of the University of North Carolina in 1814.

them for an honourable discharge of the social duties of life, by paying the strictest attention to their education."

A site for the school was chosen at a major crossroads near the center of the state. Davie drew up a state law creating an endowment; he also oversaw the choice of professors and the development of a curriculum that included social science and literature as well as such traditional subjects as Latin and mathematics. Students began arriving for classes at the University of North Carolina in 1795. The first degrees were awarded in 1798, making North Carolina the only state university in the country to graduate students in the 18th century.

EARLY EXPERIMENTS IN DEMOCRACY

(1790 TO 1829)

During his two terms in office, from 1789 to 1797, President George Washington proved himself an agile leader. With his personal popularity and dignified image, he helped establish the United States as an independent nation that commanded respect both at home and abroad. He avoided entangling the young republic in conflicts between France and England, and he also managed to place the presidency above the partisan rivalry that developed between Secretary of State Thomas Jefferson and Secretary of the Treasury Alexander Hamilton. These two men quickly became the leading proponents of opposing views of republican democracy. Time and again over the next 40 years, the new nation faced controversies that echoed the terms of their dispute.

Alexander Hamilton led the Federalists. This group stood for a broad interpretation of the Constitution that would give the national government substantial powers. It envisioned a United States that was devoted to commerce and manufacturing, a nation similar to England and closely allied with it. The Federalists wanted government to actively support merchants, bankers, manufacturers, wealthy Southern planters, and others engaged in business enterprises.

THOMAS JEFFERSON led the Democratic-Republicans, who

saw the United States as a nation of small farmers and artisans. They opposed a national government that promoted commerce and manufacturing. Instead, they preferred that the government take its cues from the states. Support for Jefferson's faction came from small farmers and planters, urban laborers, and pioneers moving West.

Hamilton gave priority to putting the country on a sound financial footing. His program included paying back all war debts at full value, setting up a national currency mint, and chartering a national Bank of the United States. He favored tariffs, such as those imposed by the 1789 Tariff Act, which taxed imports in order to protect domestic producers.

Despite Jeffersonian opposition, Hamilton was able to implement the major features of his program. The most dra-

matic consequences resulted from the Whiskey Act of 1791, which taxed alcoholic beverages and stills. The law's greatest burden fell on backwoods farmers who used surplus grain to make spirits. In 1794 the farmers' protests escalated into a violent insurgency in western Pennsylvania. The upheaval, called the Whiskey Rebellion, collapsed only after President Washington led a large militia into the area. In the end, the incident affirmed the federal government's right to collect taxes, enforce its laws, and keep order.

AS THE NASCENT GOVERNMENT grappled with these

domestic issues, the pressures of international affairs mounted. The U.S. government declared neutrality in the Napoleonic Wars, which preoccupied Europe until 1815. The new nation had traded extensively with France, Spain, and the Netherlands since 1776, and with Britain since the end of

the Revolutionary War, and the United States hoped to continue these profitable trade relationships. Britain and France, however, wanted to thwart each other's commerce, so they both interfered with American shipping. Their vessels fired on and seized U.S. ships and confiscated cargo. The British boarded American ships and car-

A cartoonist shows how a war between England and France drained U.S. coffers.

ried off sailors whom they accused of being defectors from the Royal Navy — a form of kidnapping known as impressment. Interference with American shipping remained a vexing foreign policy issue for decades.

In 1796 George Washington declined a third term as president. Tired of the factional bickering that surrounded him, he warned Americans against the terrible divisiveness of politi-

cal parties. Yet an electoral system without organized parties was not to be. Jefferson, who resigned from Washington's cabinet in 1793, had already assembled his political faction into the Democratic-Republican party. Backed by this organization, Jefferson ran for president in 1796 against John Adams, the Federalist who had served as vice president for eight years. Adams narrowly defeated Jefferson, but the Democratic-Republicans were clearly a force to be reckoned with.

Nothing in the Adams administration did more to provoke the opposition of Jefferson and the Democratic-Republicans than the infamous Alien and Sedition Acts of 1798. These laws made it a crime punishable by fines and imprisonment to say or write anything that brought the president or Congress "into contempt or disrepute." They also allowed the deportation of foreigners in both peacetime and war. The legislation smacked of monarchy to Jefferson, and it provoked a public outcry.

In the 1800 presidential election, Jefferson tied for the highest number of votes with Aaron Burr, a prominent New York lawyer and former senator. Adams came in third. The election went to the House of Representatives, where 19 tie ballots were cast before Jefferson was elected president.

THE ELECTION MARKED the first peaceful transfer of power between opposing parties in American history, as well as the eclipse of the Federalist party and the rise of the Jeffersonian democrats and their Republican party. Two of Jefferson's fellow Virginians, James Madison and James Monroe, succeeded him in the White House, and all three served two terms. The Virginia dynasty and the Republican party controlled the White House for a quarter century.

The Jeffersonians may have dominated the executive and legislative branches of government, but the Federalists still wielded influence in the courts. Just before leaving office, President Adams appointed a new chief justice of the Supreme Court, the Federalist John Marshall. Serving as chief justice until his death in 1835, Marshall used the Court to define the Constitutional relationships among branches and levels of government. The crucial *Marbury* v. *Madison* decision of 1803 established the Supreme Court's power to strike down legislation it deemed unconstitutional. The *McCulloch* v. *Maryland* decision of 1819 would uphold the principle of federal sovereignty over the states.

Ironically, over the course of 25 years, the Republicans gradually adopted many Federalist policies. Jefferson and his successors tried to accommodate the tremendous transformation that the country was undergoing. As the population grew and settlement pushed inland and westward, the values of a commercial society challenged the old republican ideals. In response, the Jeffersonians adopted positions that they had once rejected, such as federal spending on public works and the military, a national bank, tariffs to protect manufacturing, federal authority over the states, and a broad interpretation of the Constitution necessary to enact these policies.

One striking example of this evolution was the Louisiana Purchase. As settlers pushed west of the Appalachian Mountains, more than 500,000 Americans came to rely on the Mississippi River to ship their goods. But in 1800 France reacquired Louisiana from Spain. American access to the Mississippi — and thus to New Orleans and the Gulf of Mexico — suddenly appeared vulnerable to the ambitious and unpredictable emperor of France, Napoleon Bonaparte. President Jefferson sent James Monroe to France in 1803 with instructions to try to buy New Orleans from Napoleon. To Monroe's great surprise,

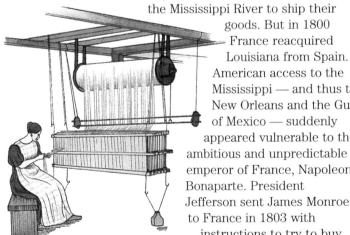

The availability of cotton looms spurred the growth of textile factories.

Napoleon offered to sell not just the city, but the entire Louisiana territory, which stretched from the mouth of the Mississippi to what is present-day Montana.

Napoleon's offer put Jefferson in an ideological bind. The Constitution did not explicitly authorize the president to buy land from other nations. Jefferson, casting about for a way to justify the purchase, decided

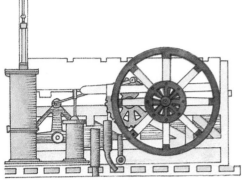

Inventor Robert Fulton's original sketch for a steamboat engine.

that the Constitution did in fact give the chief executive "implied powers" to pursue the nation's general welfare. (Ironically, Jefferson had opposed this same doctrine when the Federalists invoked it during the 1790's.)

The Louisiana Purchase changed the course of American history. It nearly doubled the size of the United States, expanded American commerce, and led to an aggressive foreign policy. Beyond that, it undermined Jefferson's own ideal of a republic of small farmers.

CRAVING MORE TERRITORY in which to trap furs, build

forts, carve out farms, and set up trading outposts, settlers were never far behind such explorers as Meriwether Lewis, William Clark, and Zebulon Pike, who set out to map the Southwest and the Great Plains. John Jacob Astor sponsored the first permanent American settlement in the Pacific Northwest, a fur-trading post named Astoria near the mouth of the Columbia River. Trailblazers climbed Pike's Peak, discovered the Great Salt Lake, and pushed southwest across the Rockies to San Diego.

To the pioneers, the West was uncharted territory, a rich new resource to be conquered and transformed. To Native Americans, the land was home: the birthplace of their children and the sacred burial ground of their ancestors. The pattern of treating — or mistreating — Indians that had been established on the East Coast during the colonial period was repeated in the West. Many Indian tribes eagerly traded with the first white settlers, then fought tenaciously when they saw their land being overrun. Some tribes prevailed in battle, but the newcomers' armies were larger and their weapons were more powerful.

With more territory to develop and commercial activity to promote, the federal and state governments began building a network of roads and canals. Americans started to travel and transport their products by steamboat and horse-drawn railroad wagon. In 1811 construction began on the National Road, which eventually carried traffic from Maryland to Illinois. Meanwhile the number of non–Native Americans was growing rapidly. Census takers counted 3.9 million people in 1790, 5.3 million in 1800, and 7.2 million in 1810.

INVENTIONS THAT CHANGED farming practices and other

commercial enterprises affected the nation's growth. Perhaps no inventor transformed so much of the landscape as Eli Whitney. His invention of the cotton gin in 1793 enabled "King Cotton" to take over the economy of the South. A single machine could remove the seeds from cotton fiber as fast as 50 human workers. Its widespread use revived the plantation system and rooted slavery more deeply than ever. Planters cleared immense tracts of land in what became Alabama, Mississippi, Louisiana, and Texas. A brisk domestic slave trade supplied laborers to these cotton fields even after a ban on importing slaves from Africa took effect in 1808.

Depleted soil reduced the demands for slave labor in the border South and Atlantic seaboard, and as a result these states sent about 25,000 slaves each year to the Deep South. Thousands of slave families were cruelly split apart. Although the Northern states gradually freed the slaves within their borders, an economic link to slavery remained, since the burgeoning textile industry in New England used the raw cotton of the slave states.

Coincidentally, Whitney had an even more direct impact on the North. A few years after inventing the cotton gin, he originated a factory system of mass production, using uniform, interchangeable parts to make guns. This innovation spurred an industrial revolution that would transform the Northeast. Across the nation, growing regions diverged signif-

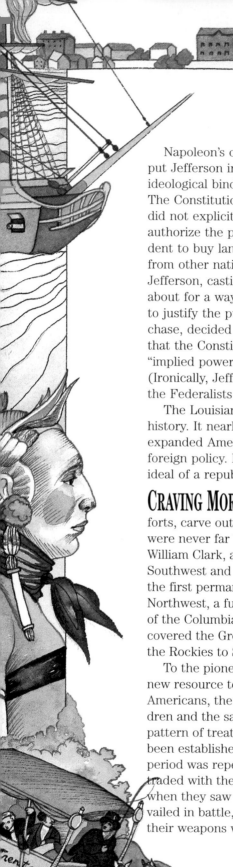

Slave labor was a major factor in cotton production.

icantly in their economic development. In the far North, New Englanders relied on shipping, commercial fishing, and manufacturing for their livelihood. Residents of the Middle Atlantic states depended on commercial farming and livestock production. In the West, small farmers and trappers held sway. Cotton planters dominated the South. These differences often translated into conflicting political demands. The Northeast supported tariffs to protect domestic manufacturing. The rural South opposed tariffs because they made imports more expensive. The West demanded lower land prices in order to attract settlers. The Northeast opposed cheap land because too much of its labor force was migrating westward.

SECTIONAL INTERESTS

such as these helped to draw the United States into a controversial war. Settlers along the frontier with Canada wanted a chance to defeat the British and to annex British territory. New England maritime interests, on the other hand, eager to return to business as usual in their trade with Britain, opposed the outbreak of hostilities. Having failed to get Britain to stop harassing American ships, a practice that had continued for a decade, President Madison felt compelled to ask Congress for a declaration of war in June 1812.

The British suffered major losses at the Battle of New Orleans.

Each side had its share of victories and defeats. To retaliate for the sacking of York (now Toronto), the British burned Washington. A peace treaty was signed in December 1814, but word of the truce was slow to circulate, and the Battle of New Orleans, a major triumph for Gen. Andrew Jackson, was fought the following month.

In the end, the Americans won neither more territory nor neutral shipping rights. The War of 1812 did, however, gain the United States recognition as a military power capable of holding its own against other, more established nations.

Soon the United States set forth its interests in the Western Hemisphere. In 1823 President Monroe declared the following principles: No new colonization or imposition of the European system of government would be permitted in this hemisphere; in return, the United States would not interfere with existing colonies or meddle in strictly internal European affairs. Other nations acquiesced to the Monroe Doctrine, which became the basis of U.S. foreign policy.

NATIONAL IDENTITY

expressed itself in education and the arts as well as politics. The first American dictionary, cookbook, and scholarly journal appeared during this period. Writers of distinctly American fiction, such as Washington Irving, Nathaniel Hawthorne, and James Fenimore Cooper, began publishing their work. The number of colleges increased from 30 in 1810 to 49 in 1830.

As they celebrated their past, many Americans saw the need for an improved future. They organized reform movements for women's rights, better education, and temperance. Voting rights were expanded. Many states dropped property qualifications for voters, although the change affected only white males. In 1828 Andrew Jackson ran for president as the first candidate of the "common man" and won.

Hovering constantly over the republic was the tortured issue of slavery. As the South steadfastly defended its way of life, moral anguish increased in the Northeast and parts of the West. Abolitionist organizations and publications multiplied. Congress avoided an explosive confrontation by balancing the entry of each new slave state with the entry of a free state.

This precarious deal threatened to collapse when a single territory, Missouri, requested status as a slave state. In the Missouri Compromise of 1820, Massachusetts agreed to give up some of its territory to create a free state called Maine. The compromise postponed the crisis, but it did not solve the problem. As Jefferson had predicted, the dispute over slavery would ring out for the United States "like a fire bell in the night." ⚒

A life-size cast-iron bullfrog touted Andrew Jackson's candidacy.

1790

The early Supreme Court justices needed to be fearless travelers as well as legal scholars.

When the U.S. Supreme Court first convened, on February 1, 1790, three of the six justices failed to appear. One was delayed a day in arriving, one was ill, and the other stayed away in protest over not having been chosen chief justice. At the Court's opening session, the justices wore the British jurists' black-and-scarlet robes, and some put on wigs, which drew a strong rebuke from Thomas Jefferson. Rules of procedure were established, and the judicial system was organized at this first meeting, but no cases were decided.

Between sessions the justices kept busy riding the circuit, which meant that they presided over cases and appeals at district courts throughout the country. Justice Joseph Story covered some 2,000 miles a year on the New England circuit. Justice James Iredell, traveling the Southern circuit, was robbed, nearly drowned trying to cross a swamp, and suffered severe injuries when his horse bolted and his carriage hit a tree. Because of the dangers and such inconveniences as long absences from home, many well-qualified jurists refused to serve on the Supreme Court.

By 1792, justices were already complaining to George Washington about circuit riding. "Some of the present Judges," a plea from the Court noted, "do not enjoy health and strength of body sufficient to enable them to undergo the toilsome journies through different climates and seasons." The dangerous job did

A makeshift courtroom for the Supreme Court.

take its toll. The death of Justice Iredell at the age of 48 was widely attributed to overwork and the rigors of travel on the circuit.

Supporters of the practice claimed that circuit riding brought the national government closer to the citizenry. Without it, wrote one 19th-century senator, "your supreme judges will be completely cloistered within the city of Washington, and their decisions, instead of emanating from enlarged and liberalized minds, will assume a severe and local character." Although the system was modified over time, mandatory circuit riding was not eliminated until 1891.

The Patent Office (right) housed models of every patented invention.

1790

With the creation of the Patent Office, the United States became the first nation ever to protect the rights of artists, writers, and inventors.

President George Washington signed the first patent law on April 10, 1790, and on May 31 he approved the nation's copyright law. The measures gave exclusive ownership to any writer, artist, or person who devised a practical invention, as well as the right to profit from his or her work.

As secretary of state, Thomas Jefferson supervised the patent registry, but because of his fear of monopoly, he was reluctant to grant patents. Of the three applications that were approved in 1790, the first went to Samuel Hopkins of Philadelphia, on July 31. Hopkins had devised a better method of making potash and pearl ash, ingredients in soap.

More than a half-century later, in 1849, Abraham Lincoln received a patent for "A Device for Buoying Vessels over Shoals." No other U.S. president has ever been granted a patent.

Curiously, Joseph Henry, a renowned 19th-century inventor of electrical devices, refused to apply for a patent, believing the patent process might stifle the free flow of ideas. The majority of the Founding Fathers had no such qualms, however. The Constitution states that "Congress shall have Power . . . To promote the Progress of Science and useful Arts by securing for limited Times to Authors and Inventors the exclusive Right to their respective Writings and Discoveries."

When British troops burned Washington, D.C., during the War of 1812, the commissioner of patents pleaded with them to spare his headquarters. As a result, the Patent Office was the only public building that remained standing. Unfortunately, many of the earliest records of the office (and the replicas of the inventions themselves) were destroyed in a fire in 1836. The requirement that inventors must submit models with their applications was discontinued in the late 19th century, when the Patent Office ran out of space to display and store the models.

1790

The selection of the site for the nation's capital ended seven years of heated debate, during which some 50 cities and towns vied to be chosen.

Both North and South wanted the honor — and the political and economic benefits — of having the nation's capital. The competition was not resolved until Alexander Hamilton, the first secretary of the treasury, devised a plan that suited both regions. The capital would be located on land ceded to the national government by Maryland and Virginia for the creation of a special federal district, rather than within an existing state.

In exchange for agreeing to this plan, the two states got the federal government to pay all their remaining Revolutionary War debts. Congress authorized the selection of a site on July 12, 1790.

President George Washington, along with Hamilton and Thomas Jefferson, chose a location along the Potomac River that was quite picturesque, not the swamp that legend has held it to be. Critics objected immediately, charging that developing the site would increase the value of property that Washington owned nearby.

Although he did stand to profit, Washington hoped that siting the capital there would enhance Virginia's status as a center

Choosing a site on the Potomac River for the U.S. capital required substantial political maneuvering.

of domestic and international commerce. He was just one of many area residents whose appreciation of the river's beauty was equaled only by the desire to have a major trade center, a passion that became known as Potomac Fever.

In 1791 Congress voted to name the new city Washington, but the president modestly referred to the capital as "Federal City." Ironically, he never got to live there; his second term of office expired in 1797, while the capital was still in Philadelphia.

New and Improved: 200 Years of Patented Progress

America has always been a land of invention and ingenuity. The following are just a few of the highlights in the history of the U.S. Patent Office.

Inventor	Invention
Eli Whitney (1794)	Cotton gin
Cyrus H. McCormick (1834)	Reaper
Samuel F. B. Morse (1840)	Telegraph
Charles Goodyear (1844)	Vulcanization of rubber
Alexander Graham Bell (1876)	Telephone
Thomas A. Edison (1880)	Electric lamp
Whitcomb J. Judson (1893)	Zipper
Henry Ford (1901)	Improved motor carriage
Orville and Wilbur Wright (1906)	Improvements in flying machines
Enrico Fermi and Leo Szilard (1955)	Neutronic reactor
Harvard University (1988)	Mouse bred for cancer research

1790

The first census of the United States provided a statistical snapshot of a country that was predominantly rural.

On August 2, 1790, circuit riders fanned out over the countryside. For 18 months they would count the nation's population in order to determine how seats would be apportioned in the House of Representatives and how direct taxes would be levied.

The first census takers counted 3,929,000 people, although the official tally probably erred on the low side. Some individuals refused to participate, and American Indians were not counted until 1860. No census was taken in the Northwest Territory, which today embraces Ohio, Indiana, Illinois, Michigan, and part of Minnesota.

Most people lived in rural areas. Of the 12 cities with more than 5,000 residents, only 4 had more than 16,000: New York, Philadelphia, Boston, and Charleston, South Carolina. Virginia was the most populous state, with 747,614 citizens; Pennsylvania was next with 434,373. The average family size was 5.7 persons. The population was 80 percent white and 20 percent black, and 90 percent of the African-Americans were slaves.

1790
Robert Gray was the first American to sail the nation's flag around the world.

A 13-gun salute greeted Robert Gray when he sailed into Boston Harbor on August 9, 1790. The festivities honored the first American to circumnavigate the globe in an American ship. A Rhode Islander who served in the Continental navy during the Revolutionary War, Gray had been hired by Massachusetts businessmen who were eager to extend the American fur trade to China. Heading the expedition was Capt. John Kendrick, who commanded the 200-ton ship *Columbia.* Gray, who was the junior captain, was at the helm of the sloop *Lady Washington.*

On Gray's second voyage, an artist sailing with the expedition depicted an Indian attack.

In September 1787 Gray and Kendrick left Boston and headed south. To reach the Northwest Coast, they circled Cape Horn, becoming the first American sea captains to round this stormy cape at the southernmost tip of South America. When they reached Hawaii, Kendrick suddenly decided that he wanted to make the Pacific island his home and he called off his trading mission. Gray, the better sailor of the two, continued to China on the *Columbia* with sea otter furs he had acquired in the Northwest, as well as sandalwood from Hawaii. After a three-year voyage of almost 49,000 miles, he finally returned to Boston with a cargo of tea.

Gray's trip opened the door to a thriving trade that developed between China and the Northwest. Just six weeks after his triumphant return, Gray again left Boston for the Northwest Coast and then China. He spent the winter of 1791–92 near Vancouver Island, British Columbia. In the spring of 1792 he ventured south, sailing into what is now Gray's Harbor, in Washington State, then on to the long-sought River of the West, or River Oregon. Gray rechristened this mighty stream the Columbia, after his ship. His discovery later helped America win a dispute with Britain over which nation could claim the Oregon Territory. ⚑

1790
An Indian chief named Alexander McGillivray drove a hard bargain in negotiating a treaty with President Washington.

The son of a wealthy Scottish trader and a Creek-French mother, Alexander McGillivray was born around 1759 near present-day Montgomery, Alabama. He spent his boyhood among the Creeks, but his father sent him at age 14 to Charleston, South Carolina, and Savannah, Georgia, where he studied the classics and English history and literature. Three years later he returned to the Creeks and began to show a leadership ability far beyond that of most 17-year-olds.

McGillivray served with the British during the Revolutionary War. Afterward, the British betrayed the Creeks by signing over much of their territory to the U.S. government. A skillful diplomat, McGillivray secured a prominent role as the leader of the Creeks. In April 1786 the Creek nation declared war on the state of Georgia, primarily because of disputed territorial claims.

Following his inauguration in 1789, President George Washington invited Chief McGillivray to New York, the nation's capital, for negotiations to end the fighting. In 1790 McGillivray traveled north with an entourage that had grown to 26 chiefs and warriors by the time it reached New York on July 21. Feelings of respect were mutual. "I am glad you have come, Colonel," said Washington. "I have long felt we had much in common."

On August 13, 1790, after several weeks of intense bargaining, the Treaty of New York was signed. It set the boundary of Creek territory farther east than the state of Georgia had wanted, gave trade concessions to the Creeks, and provided government subsidies so that some Creek youths could attend school. The treaty's guarantee of protection for the Creek homeland was never enforced, however, and westbound settlers continued to encroach on Creek land. In 1832 the Creeks were banished from their land and driven west. ⚑

A Creek chief negotiated with President Washington to obtain rights to tribal land in Georgia. At left, a typical Creek cabin.

E
1793
Eli Whitney, the inventor of the cotton gin, barely profited from the machine that revolutionized the economy of the South.

After graduating from college in 1793, Massachusetts-born Eli Whitney traveled to Savannah, Georgia, where he was a guest of Catherine Greene. Noting how well Whitney built and repaired machines, Mrs. Greene offered him a handyman's job on her plantation. One day, as planters talked of their need for a simple method of separating cotton fiber from seed, she suggested that Whitney take on that assignment. He spent about six months working on what came to be called a gin — shorthand for the word *engine*.

The machine enabled a worker to clean cotton 50 times faster than before, and production skyrocketed. Unfortunately, the gin also led to the expansion of slavery in Southern cotton-producing states, when plantation owners realized that they could get rich quickly by using unpaid laborers to operate the gins.

Before long, copies of the gin began to appear on plantations all over the South. Whitney, who had expected that he would soon become wealthy, complained that "an invention can be so valuable as to be worthless to the inventor."

Whitney's cotton gin, which separated seeds from fiber, deepened slavery's hold on the South.

Having received his patent in 1794, Whitney spent more than a decade fighting some 60 patent-infringement lawsuits, and the cost of the legal battles drained most of his profits. Not until 1798, when he developed a musket-making process that involved interchangeable parts, did Whitney's mechanical genius make him rich. 🔺

Circus entrepreneur John Bill Ricketts.

A
1793
A daredevil Scotsman is the father of the American circus.

John Bill Ricketts came to the United States from Scotland in 1792 and opened a riding academy in Philadelphia. On April 3, 1793, he dazzled the people there by presenting a circus. In the audience on April 22 was President George Washington, who marveled as Ricketts hung from his horse by one leg, swept the ground with his hat, mounted his galloping horse, and rode balanced on only one foot on the saddle. The president and the showman became good friends and riding partners; Washington even sold his favorite war horse to Ricketts.

Soon the troupe was performing up and down the East Coast from the province of Quebec to Charleston, South Carolina. With the circus growing in popularity, Ricketts decided to build covered amphitheaters in Philadelphia and New York. Spectators enjoyed not only equestrian acts, but clowns, mimes, ropewalkers, and acrobats. Ricketts's circus captivated audiences until 1799, when fires destroyed the amphitheaters. 🔺

A
1793
A French envoy who sought to overthrow the U.S. government became the first diplomat to seek political asylum in America.

Edmond Charles Genêt was the first minister to the United States from the new French republic. When Genêt landed in Charleston, South Carolina, on April 8, 1793, the French king had just been beheaded and France had declared war on England, Spain, and Holland. In violation of the U.S. Proclamation of Neutrality, Genêt distributed military commissions, hoping to raise an army to wrest Florida and Louisiana from Spain. He repeatedly breached diplomatic protocol and international law.

When he finally met George Washington in Philadelphia, Genêt disliked him and voiced hopes that he would be driven

French envoy Edmond Charles Genêt, also known as Citizen Genêt.

from office. When many insisted that France recall him, Genêt pleaded for diplomatic asylum, fearing that the bloodthirsty Jacobins would execute him upon his return. Overlooking Genêt's animosity, Washington granted his request. 🔺

1794
The U.S. Navy was founded as a result of the capture of American seamen by Barbary pirates.

For centuries, dating back to the Crusades, cutthroat pirates from the Barbary states of Morocco, Tunisia, Algeria, and Tripoli had terrorized ships on the Mediterranean Sea and the Atlantic Ocean off the coast of Africa.

As early as the 16th century, the Barbary rulers demanded that maritime nations pay tribute, or protection money, to prevent their ships from being captured and their crews enslaved. (The Barbary states relied upon captured cargo and slave ransom for their revenue.) Until the United States declared independence from the mother country, Great Britain had paid the money to protect American ships. Then from 1778 to 1783, an alliance with France gave the United States continued protection,

The entire crew of the U.S.S. Intrepid was killed in the harbor of Tripoli in 1804.

but after 1783, the new nation had to fend for itself.

In 1784 Congress earmarked $80,000 to keep Barbary pirates away: harassment was stunting the growth of commercial shipping in the Mediterranean. But no sooner did one state sign a treaty than another state would attack.

In July 1785 Algeria captured two U.S. ships and demanded more than $59,000 in ransom for 21 seamen. Later, when Algeria attacked 11 ships, enslaved 106 Americans, and demanded a ransom, Congress decided to end highway robbery on the high seas, appropriating $600,000 to build and outfit six heavily gunned frigates. The bill, passed on March 27, 1794, also provided salaries for captains, gunners, and other crew members. The nation had itself a navy. The piracy continued, however, until the 1830's. ▲

1794
To suppress the Whiskey Rebellion, George Washington commanded as many troops as he had at any time during the Revolutionary War.

The first serious challenge to the new Constitution came in 1791, when backcountry farmers rebelled against an excise tax that the financially strapped federal government had levied on distilleries. To the farmers, who used kegs of whiskey as barter, the tax was as unfair as the British Stamp Act had been. In some cases, violators of the law had to travel for several days in order to appear in federal court in Philadelphia to defend themselves.

Tax collectors and distillers who complied with the whiskey-tax law were attacked. A Kentucky revenue collector was hanged in effigy. In parts of western Pennsylvania, there was talk of seceding from the new nation. One farmer was killed and six were wounded when they accosted a tax collector in his home near Pittsburgh.

Mounting resentment eventually took the form of a march of 5,000 men toward Pittsburgh in the summer of 1794. Realizing that he had to prevent anarchy in the new republic, President George Washington called up the militia in New Jersey, Pennsylvania, Maryland, and Virginia.

Some 13,000 troops were placed under Washington's command. The commander in chief chose Gen. Henry Lee to lead the troops into battle. Secretary of the Treasury Alexander Hamilton accompanied Lee as a civilian representative of the government.

The contingent marched from Philadelphia, the nation's capital, toward a site in western Pennsylvania to quell what came to be known as the Whiskey Rebellion. But as it happened, the expected violent encounter never took place. As the troops approached, the rebels simply melted into the surrounding countryside. When several dissidents were tried for treason, two leaders of the

Preparing to quash the Whiskey Rebellion, Washington reviews the troops.

uprising — the largest armed challenge to the federal government until the Civil War — were convicted, but Washington pardoned both of them. ▲

The myth of Johnny Appleseed was based on the life of the dedicated John Chapman.

J 1798
John Chapman sowed so many apple seeds in 50 years that apple trees blossomed over some 100,000 square miles in the Ohio Valley.

The folk hero who came to be known as Johnny Appleseed was born John Chapman in 1774 in Leominster, Massachusetts. In 1798 he embarked on his life's work: planting apple orchards in the Ohio Valley. A gentle eccentric, he sometimes traveled thousands of miles yearly, his belongings limited to the clothes he wore. More often than not, he appeared barefoot in a gunnysack tunic, with a tin plate or a cardboard hat perched on his head.

Chapman slept outdoors or bartered apple seeds for clothing, food, and a night's lodging. A loner, he befriended wild animals and believed that riding a horse was a form of cruelty; as a result, he thought nothing of walking hundreds of miles to care for the trees he had planted. He spared no effort to avoid harming living things. Once, seeing mosquitoes fatally attracted to his campfire, he doused his only source of warmth in order to prevent the insects from dying.

The protector of all living creatures was devoutly religious. Chapman was a follower of Emanuel Swedenborg, and he liked to spread the gospel of the 18th-century Swedish mystic, whose devotion to nature he shared. Indians considered Chapman a gifted medicine man because of his skill in using herbs for healing.

A 1799
As the longtime director of the Russian-American Company in Alaska, Alexander Baranov claimed a vast stretch of land in the North Pacific for Russia.

Alexander Baranov, a native of Poland, was named director of operations for the Russian-American Company in 1790. Nine years later Czar Paul I granted the company exclusive fur-trading rights in Alaska and gave it authority over all the Russian settlements in the territory.

In 1799 Baranov, who was based on Kodiak Island, established Fort St. Michael and the town of New Archangel (now Sitka) on land that was inhabited by the Tlingit Indians in southeastern Alaska. Although the colonial outpost had to struggle to survive — starvation posed a frequent threat to the settlers, and the Indians repeatedly attacked the trappers and the Russian settlements along the Northwest Coast — Baranov's commercial ventures thrived.

The artist who sketched the harbor of present-day Sitka, Alaska, sailed on Russia's first around-the-world voyage, a joint venture of the Russian Navy and the Russian-American Company, headed by Alexander Baranov.

During his 19 years in Alaska, Baranov extended the Russian fur trade south to San Francisco. He even attempted negotiations with Hawaii, sending an emissary to King Kamehameha I. Baranov hoped to persuade Hawaiians to export food and other products needed in Alaska, but the plan failed when Baranov's emissary angered the king in an episode that derailed the trade baron's expansion plans.

Baranov's repeated pleas to be relieved of his duties were ignored until 1818, when the Russian czar finally allowed him to retire. Baranov's goal of maintaining a colony in the region was undone when Russia sold Alaska to the United States for $7.2 million in 1867.

1800

Tammany Hall, which became a synonym for political corruption, was founded by Revolutionary War veterans as a patriotic, nonpartisan organization.

Officially organized on May 12, 1789, and named for Tamanend, a Delaware Indian chief, the Tammany Society attracted tradesmen, artisans, professionals, and workmen. Before long, the society was known for the colorful parades it staged in New York City several times a year. Its members met monthly for drinking and story-telling in the Wigwam, a room in a local tavern that was soon called Tammany Hall.

Aaron Burr, Tammany's first boss, wasn't even a member of the club, but he was a shrewd political operator who somehow managed to seize control. Sometime around 1798 he began to exploit the society in order to advance his own political agenda.

The desire of Tammany members to uphold the democratic commitment to equality took the form of opposition to the politics of Alexander Hamilton. Burr was an outspoken foe of Hamilton, a Federalist known for his aristocratic principles. A majority of Tammany members objected to Hamilton's successful lobbying on behalf of

Burr was a talented organizer who set up a political machine that outlived him.

former Tories, whom the government forgave for their pro-British stance.

Although Tammany was officially neutral, by 1800 its members were inclined to side with the Republicans, known previously as Anti-Federalists. In the bitterly fought presidential election between Federalist John Adams, the incumbent, and Republican Thomas Jefferson, statewide elections in New York were crucial: presidential electors were chosen then by the party that controlled the state legislature.

Burr, a Republican leader, was determined to have his candidates win the statewide election and thereby decide the presidential election. His supporters, who included Tammany Hall members known as Burrites, organized and canvassed voters, did extensive fundraising, and even provided carriages to take people to the polls. New York went Republican, and Burr's reward was the vice presidential nomination.

Ironically, following the election, Burr's political career foundered. A tie in electoral votes between Jefferson and Burr allowed the House of Representatives to decide the outcome. Jefferson resented what he considered Burr's self-serving maneuvering in his failed effort to become president.

Burr's killing of Hamilton in an 1804 duel further damaged his career. But Burr's influence enabled his closest associates to take over Tammany Hall. Over the years, it evolved into what one historian has termed "the most powerful and insidious political machine in the country." Until 1934, when Mayor Fiorello La Guardia pushed through reforms, Tammany flourished as a source of influence peddling, graft, and extortion in New York City politics.

1800

The author of the first biography of George Washington — a huge best-seller in its day — never intended for the cherry tree story to be taken literally.

Mason Locke Weems may have been the most successful traveling book salesman of his day. Full of conviction and enthusiasm, the one-time Episcopal clergyman felt no qualms about leaving the ministry to sell books, because, as he explained, he was "doing God's work in a wider field."

Over time, Weems decided to turn himself into an author and began writing morality tales. One such effort was a pamphlet about the life of George Washington that he expanded into a book.

Weems's biography, *The Life and Memorable Actions of George Washington*, published about 1800, became a best-seller and went into more than 70 printings, including five in Germany. Weems never claimed that his volume was anything but biographical fiction, so he felt free to create anecdotes that emphasized Washington's virtues.

The famous tale of young George admitting to cutting down a cherry tree was not added until the fifth edition, published in 1806. Weems's book influenced generations of schoolchildren while elevating Washington to a figure of mythic proportions.

American painter Grant Wood put his imprint on the story of George Washington cutting down a cherry tree. Parson Weems is at right.

A contest to design the presidential home offered the winner $500, but only nine people vied for the prize.

1800

George Washington chose the location of the White House in 1791. Pierre Charles L'Enfant, who designed the city of Washington, wanted to use the site along the Potomac River for a presidential palace. Offended by this elitist notion, Thomas Jefferson suggested a design contest. Only nine people entered.

Jefferson, a self-taught architect, anonymously submitted a design, but it was rejected. James Hoban, an Irish-American architect, won the contest. His plan bore a striking resemblance to the duke of Leinster's palace (which later housed the Irish Parliament) in Dublin, as well as the Condé Palace in Paris.

Although the cornerstone was laid in 1792, construction was delayed repeatedly because of lack of money. Finally, Maryland and Virginia chipped in $200,000 for the project. When those funds ran out, city-owned property was auctioned off, an effort that produced little capital.

Only 6 of the 20 rooms were finished by November 1, 1800, when John and Abigail Adams moved in. The roof leaked, the main staircase was incomplete, and there wasn't enough firewood to heat the residence on chilly days. The first lady used the unfurnished East Room for drying laundry.

Supplies and paraphernalia left behind by construction workers littered the yard around the mansion. One visitor complained that "in a dark night, instead of finding your way to the house, you may, perchance, fall into a pit, or stumble over a heap of rubbish." He called the house "a disgrace to the country."

Although a Baltimore newspaper first called the building the "white house" in 1810, the name did not become official until 1902. Prior to that, it was known as the President's House or the Executive Mansion. The origin of the name itself remains uncertain. Some people claim that it was named after the house where Martha Washington was raised. Others point to the building's whitish sandstone exterior that was in stark contrast to the reddish brick of the adjacent structures.

The winning design for the White House: Washington chose the site but never lived there.

When Abigail Adams moved into the White House, she was amazed at how expensive it was to entertain guests there.

1800

In November 1800 President and Mrs. John Adams moved into the brand-new residence that had been built for the first family. The Adamses soon discovered that their food costs exceeded their food budget, especially with important visitors frequently joining them for dinner. Starting in the 1920's, federal funds have covered official presidential functions, but the first family has always paid for personal meals and parties.

Fine dining and lavish entertaining appealed more to some presidents than watching costs. Thomas Jefferson, for example, who was the second president to occupy the White House, loved to serve such foreign treats as Italian anchovies, Dutch waffles, and French wines.

Many presidents followed in Jefferson's footsteps and enjoyed the good life. During Ulysses S. Grant's era, 30 courses were often served at state dinners. The Herbert Hoovers invited guests to join them for lunch, afternoon tea, and dinner — even during the Depression. Not all presidents enjoyed playing the role of host, however. Martin Van Buren held only one public party a year, on New Year's Day, and he served neither food nor drink.

To save himself money, Warren G. Harding even invited officials to dine with him at breakfast, because a law provided government stipends for presidential business meals. William H. Taft economized on buying milk by letting cows graze on the grounds of the White House.

Calvin Coolidge asked the kitchen staff to reduce the amount of meat served at large dinners. When his term ended, Coolidge said that his greatest regret about the White House was that he never knew what happened to the leftovers.

The White House in Transition

From 1800 to the present, the president's home has been a work in progress. Here are a few of the changes our presidents have made.

1814 James Madison orders the White House to be rebuilt after the British burn it down in the War of 1812.

1824 James Monroe has the south portico added to the house.

1829–33 Andrew Jackson adds the north portico and installs running water.

1889 Benjamin Harrison has the White House wired for electricity.

1902 Theodore Roosevelt has the entire interior remodeled and wings added; the second floor is turned into living quarters and the West Wing is extended for office space.

1941–43 Franklin Delano Roosevelt approves an East Wing extension and secretly has a bomb shelter built.

1947–52 Harry S. Truman oversees a complete reconstruction, during which a balcony is added above the south portico.

1801

Chief Justice John Marshall attended law school for just six weeks; yet no man has had a greater influence on the development of American constitutional law.

John Marshall was born in 1755 in a log cabin in the Virginia wilderness. Since he had to help raise his 14 younger brothers and sisters, he had little time to pursue an education. In fact, his formal schooling lasted just two years, one spent studying with a clergyman, the other with a tutor.

After fighting in the Revolutionary War, Marshall attended a six-week lecture series on the law given by the chancellor of the College of William and Mary in 1780. Later that year he was admitted to the bar in Virginia. Extremely intelligent and an excellent debater, Marshall was a quick study and learned by practicing law.

Although Marshall was described by one of his contemporaries as inelegant in "dress, attitudes, gesture," his appearance and demeanor did not stand in the way of a career in public service. By the time President John Adams appointed his secretary of state to be the fourth chief justice of the Supreme Court in 1801, Marshall had already won election to the Virginia

Chief Justice Marshall left an indelible mark on the Court.

legislature and the U.S. House of Representatives and had served as an envoy to France.

When the chief justice took his seat on the Court in February 1801, the judiciary was the weakest branch of the government and the Constitution was still legally undefined. Over the next 34 years, Marshall made the judicial branch the final interpreter of the Constitution. He also upheld the doctrine of judicial review — the power of the courts to strike down laws and executive orders that they considered to be in conflict with the Constitution. In effect, he molded the Constitution according to his conservative Federalist philosophy of a strong central government.

Over the years several presidents named Republicans to the Court with the hope that the new justices would offset Marshall's influence. More often than not, however, Marshall's precise and eloquent use of language, mastery of logic, and judicial genius persuaded his colleagues on the bench to accept his constitutional views. By the time he died in 1835 at the age of 79, he had earned the title of the Great Chief Justice.▲

1801

The chaotic election of 1800, whose outcome was not settled until 1801, not only was one of the dirtiest presidential campaigns in history but also marked the first defeat of the party in power.

Federalist president John Adams was seeking reelection in 1800. His Republican challenger was Thomas Jefferson. In those days

candidates did not campaign; rather, their supporters did the job for them, with the help of partisan newspapers.

The campaign turned ugly and personal. Jefferson was denounced as a traitor, a revolutionary, an embezzler, and a libertine. Federalist papers predicted that the election of Jefferson would "spread the seeds of confusion, anarchy, and slavery throughout the United States." Hearing Jefferson branded an atheist, some Federalist women wondered whether they would need to hide their Bibles if he won.

Adams didn't fare much better. His adversaries accused him of wanting to become king. One rumor had Adams conspiring with King George III to marry one of Adams's sons to the king's daughter and produce a dynasty. Adams was even attacked by Alexander

Hamilton, a leading Federalist, as having "great and intrinsic defects" of character.

As electioneering heated up, Federalist newspapers reported with barely concealed delight that Jefferson had died. The same publications were slow to print a correction saying that it was actually a slave named Thomas Jefferson who had died.

The election resulted in a tie between Jefferson and his vice presidential running mate, Aaron Burr, with each receiving 73 electoral votes. (At the time, electors cast two votes in a double-balloting system: the candidate with the most votes was to become president; the other, vice president.) It fell to the Federalist House of Representatives to break the deadlock and elect the president. On February 17, 1801, after 36 ballots had been tallied over several days, Jefferson was declared the winner.

Jefferson was exaggerating when he called his victory the "Revolution of 1800." The election did, however, set an important precedent — the peaceful transfer of power between presidents of opposing parties.▲

A hand-painted flag commemorated Jefferson's election.

1801
Thomas Jefferson was the first president to take the oath of office in Washington, D.C.

On March 4, 1801, as Thomas Jefferson strolled the one block from his boardinghouse to his swearing-in ceremony in the nation's new capital, the bitterness of the presidential campaign against incumbent John Adams was still a fresh memory.

More than 1,000 people jammed into the Senate chamber for the inauguration of the first president to be sworn into office in Washington, D.C. Those who expected to hear a great oration from the author of the Declaration of Independence, however, were largely disappointed. Jefferson hated public speaking, and he delivered his address in a soft voice that few could hear beyond the first several rows. He did, however, give an advance copy of his remarks to a newspaper, which printed it in what became the first "extra" in U.S. history.

In the speech Jefferson tried to defuse the hostility that the election had aroused. "We are all Republicans — we are all Federalists," he declared, urging both parties to "unite in common efforts for the common good." He tried to calm fears about the ability of the

The Thomas Jefferson Commemorative Medal.

newly elected officials to govern and extolled the republic as "a rising nation, spread over a wide and fruitful land . . . advancing rapidly to destinies beyond the reach of mortal eye."

In addition to conciliation, Jefferson promoted informality and "republican etiquette." Every morning, for example, the White House was open to the public. Small dinners replaced the Federalists' formal receptions, and Jefferson seated his guests around a circular table, so that no one would feel more important than anyone else. 🔔

1801
In the summer of 1801, some 25,000 people attended a religious revival in Cane Ridge, Kentucky. For a week they prayed with 40 ministers at what turned into the first camp meeting in America.

Religion swept over America's frontier during the second Great Awakening at the start of the 19th century. (The first Great Awakening occurred during the mid 18th century.) It was a time when some Americans had turned away from the more established, orthodox teachings. Revivalist denominations, including Methodists, Baptists, and Presbyterians, quickly gained a following.

Preachin' Jim McGready, a Presbyterian evangelist from Pennsylvania, was a leading promoter of open-air religious meetings, or camp meetings. Beginning in the 1790's, he stomped through the backwoods, exhorting sinners to repent and be saved. In the summer of 1801, an estimated 25,000 people flocked to Cane Ridge, Kentucky, to hear McGready and others preach hellfire sermons. One minister marveled that "drunkards, profane swearers, liars, quarrelsome persons, et cetera, are remarkably reformed."

Some camp meetings lasted for five days. Overwhelmed by emotion, participants collapsed by the hundreds in the "mourners' clearing," while many others fell victim to "the jerks" — involuntary muscular contortions. Some found themselves laughing uncontrollably or barking like dogs around trees — a practice called "treeing the devil."

By 1820, some 1,000 such meetings were held annually in the United States. Frontier evangelists who spoke to the common people and questioned church dogma and authority helped set the stage for the political movement known as Jacksonian democracy. 🔔

Ministers' sermons could stir up emotional outbursts at camp meetings.

1801

The Natchez Trace, a well-used Indian trail, was for a decade the nation's most traveled land route from north to south in the Old Southwest.

A maze of trails connecting villages of the Chickasaw, Choctaw, and Natchez Indian tribes, the Natchez Trace was named by the French, who explored it when they arrived in the Old Southwest in 1699. *Trace* means "a line of footprints" in old French. The footprints extended some 500 miles from Natchez, Mississippi, to Nashville, Tennessee, and were followed over the years by explorers, trappers, and such conquerors as Hernando de Soto.

When he took office, President Thomas Jefferson decided to expand the trail into a major thoroughfare. After negotiating a treaty with the Indians in 1801, he dispatched Gen. James Wilkinson, the commander of the U.S. Army in the West, to improve and map the road. From about 1801 to 1820, the Natchez Trace was an important artery for business activity. Men from the frontier states would load cattle, furs, and other goods on flatboats, float down the Mississippi to markets in Natchez and New Orleans, and then walk or ride a horse back home. (Before steamboats came along, it was impossible to travel upriver against the heavy current.)

Traders who returned home along the trace with saddlebags full of silver sometimes fell prey to bandits and murderers. The most notorious highwayman of them all was Samuel Mason, a well-dressed

Andrew Jackson followed the Natchez Trace during the War of 1812.

Revolutionary War veteran who left placards reading "Mason of the Woods" on his dead victims.

Explorer Meriwether Lewis died of a self-inflicted gunshot wound at an inn on the trace in 1809, three years after his expedition to the Northwest. By the 1820's, steamboats had transformed the river into a two-way artery, all but ending commerce along the trace.

1802

President Thomas Jefferson set high ethical standards for accepting gifts, but not all residents of the White House followed his example.

When the congregation of John Leland, a Baptist minister from Massachusetts, sent Thomas Jefferson a 1,235-pound cheese in 1802, the president was both amazed and embarrassed. The cheese, produced by farmers who had milked some 900 cows, bore a sign that read, "The greatest cheese in America for the greatest man in America."

Knowing that the lavish gift came from poor farmers made Jefferson so uncomfortable that he insisted on paying $200 for it, a good deal more than its market value. The cheese, which measured approximately four feet in diameter and more than a foot in height, was served at the White House over a period of three years.

Some gift-givers offered presents of lasting value. President Ulysses S. Grant got a Turkish carpet and a 36-piece silver coffee set, for example, while President Dwight D. Eisenhower received an original proof of an etching by Rembrandt.

Other presidents received presents that were whimsical, rather than practical or beautiful. President James Polk was given a porcelain model of Tom

Lava rock from Mt. Vesuvius served as an inkwell for President Polk's wife.

Thumb's foot; President Abraham Lincoln, a whistle made from a pig's tail (his son Tad enjoyed playing with it); and President William McKinley, a 78-pound melon that came wrapped in an American flag.

Four-legged gifts sometimes posed major quandaries.

In January 1834, when the emperor of Morocco offered a lion and two African stud horses as gifts for the president, Congress debated for months about what to do with them. The issue was finally resolved a year later, when the Senate Agriculture Committee passed a resolution to sell the horses and let President Andrew Jackson decide what to do with the lion. Jackson sold the lion for $3,350 and donated the money to two orphanages.

A few years later President Martin Van Buren squabbled with Congress over a pair of tiger cubs that the sultan of Oman had sent. The sultan had offered the tigers when Van Buren's predecessor, Andrew Jackson, was in office, and Congress determined that the cubs belonged to the people of the United States.

Van Buren disagreed, claiming that the tigers were gifts intended for the president and therefore his. But Congress prevailed, and the tiger cubs ended up in a zoo.

1803

The country's first professional architect was an Englishman who left his mark on several American cities.

Benjamin Henry Latrobe had a promising future as an architect in his native England. After his wife died, however, he decided to cross the Atlantic and relaunch his career. Not long after arriving in Virginia in 1796, Latrobe was commissioned to design a prison in Richmond.

Two years later Latrobe moved to Philadelphia, the nation's capital. Soon he won the backing of the president of the Bank of Pennsylvania to design the bank's headquarters. This edifice, with its stately Ionic marble columns, was the first American building in the Greek Revival style, and it served as a model for the architectural movement that would change the look of the new nation.

President Thomas Jefferson appointed Latrobe to be Surveyor of Public Buildings in 1803. The architect designed the Capitol

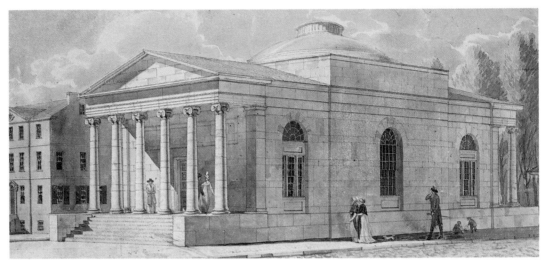

Latrobe not only designed the Bank of Pennsylvania but painted this watercolor of it.

building, only to have it burned down by the British during the War of 1812. So in 1815 he began rebuilding it. For better acoustics and lighting, he altered the House chamber from a rectangle connecting two semicircles to one large semicircle.

Commissioned by the bishop of Baltimore to construct that city's cathedral, Latrobe supervised the complex project from 1805 to 1818. His design of this magnificent structure ushered in a new era in American ecclesiastical architecture. ▲

1803

Thomas Jefferson made the first major real estate deal in American history.

President Thomas Jefferson began to worry when, in 1802, he learned that France had taken back its Louisiana Territory from the Spanish. New Orleans had become a major port in North America, and if the French decided to interfere with American shipping, the president knew he would face a diplomatic crisis. Jefferson's fears were confirmed later that year, when the French barred American ships from leaving their ocean-going cargo in New Orleans.

The president promptly asked Robert Livingston, his ambassador to France, to deliver a letter to the French emperor, Napoleon. Jefferson warned that if France intended to keep the United States out of New Orleans, "we must marry ourselves to the British fleet and nation." Such an alliance would do substantial harm to France's interests worldwide. As an alternative, Jefferson made an offer to purchase both New Orleans and the Floridas.

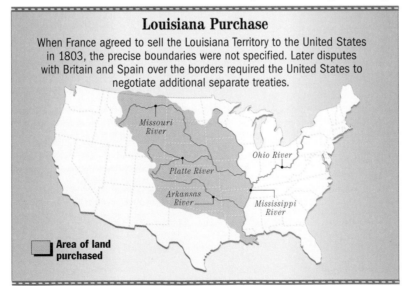

Louisiana Purchase

When France agreed to sell the Louisiana Territory to the United States in 1803, the precise boundaries were not specified. Later disputes with Britain and Spain over the borders required the United States to negotiate additional separate treaties.

Missouri River

Ohio River

Platte River

Arkansas River

Mississippi River

☐ Area of land purchased

Initially Napoleon refused to commit himself. Then he decided to concentrate on expanding in Europe, rather than in North or Central America, and so he offered to sell the entire Louisiana Territory, which stretched east from the Rocky Mountains to the Mississippi River, and south from the Canadian forests to the Gulf of Mexico.

Knowing Napoleon's tendency to change his mind at a moment's notice, American negotiators got right to work. After several days of haggling, during which France refused to specify the boundaries of the territory, both sides settled on a price of about $15 million. A treaty was signed April 30, 1803.

Although delighted with the results, Jefferson had serious misgivings — the Constitution said nothing about acquiring land. The Federalists and some Republicans in Jefferson's own party opposed the treaty, but the Senate quickly ratified it. The title was transferred in December 1803. This acquisition of 828,000 square miles gave the United States control of the Mississippi River and doubled the size of the country. ▲

1804

Despite their long-simmering feud, Alexander Hamilton hesitated before accepting the invitation for a duel with Aaron Burr.

Alexander Hamilton, a Federalist who served as the first secretary of the U.S. Treasury, and Aaron Burr, an anti-Federalist who defeated Hamilton's father-in-law for a Senate seat, had long traded insults. Hamilton had accused Burr of contemptible acts of private and public misconduct. By writing damaging letters and spreading unflattering opinions, Hamilton helped sink Burr's Senate reelection campaign in 1796. He also lobbied against Burr's candidacy when Burr ran against Thomas Jefferson for the Republican presidential nomination in 1800.

During Burr's run for the New York governorship in 1804, the war of words reached a new level, in Burr's opinion. A newspaper reported Hamilton's criticism that Burr was "a dangerous man, and one who ought not to be trusted with the reins of government." Burr demanded an explanation. When Hamilton replied evasively, Burr challenged him to a duel. Hamilton wavered before accepting — his son Philip had died three years earlier in a duel.

A doctor rushes to Hamilton, who died the day after his duel with Burr.

Since the state of New York had outlawed dueling, the event was held across the Hudson River in Weehawken, New Jersey, the same site where Philip Hamilton had died. On July 11, 1804, Hamilton and Burr faced each other at 10 paces and leveled their pistols. A well-aimed bullet struck Hamilton, lodging near his spine, and he died the next day.

Although Hamilton had made many enemies as a politician and as secretary of the treasury, a wave of mourning engulfed the nation. Flags were lowered, and newspapers published special editions with lengthy laudatory obituaries.

The fury his fellow New Yorkers directed against him astounded Burr. Knowing he would probably face murder charges, Burr left the region — although he remained vice president until his term expired in March 1805. After that Burr was involved in a scheme that encouraged secession in the Western states; he was acquitted of treason in 1807.

1805

In an era when few women were taught to write, a female playwright, poet, and political activist composed a voluminous history of the American Revolution.

It took Mercy Otis Warren more than 20 years to complete her three-volume *History of the Rise, Progress, and Termination of the American Revolution.* The prolific author of plays, poems, and letters to prominent people had enjoyed a front-row seat at some of the major debates on dissension with England. Both before and during the Revolutionary War, Samuel Adams, John Adams, and others frequently gathered at her Plymouth, Massachusetts, home.

Warren, the daughter of a politically prominent lawyer, married a man who became a Massachusetts legislator. A brother, James Otis, was a leading orator for the radicals.

In her history, published in

Warren's book cost her the friendship of an ex-president.

1805, the 77-year-old author analyzed events as a Republican, promoting the ability of the people to govern themselves and blasting the Federalists for clinging to the old ways of the mother country. John Adams received some of her most searing criticism. When the former president served as ambassador to Great Britain, from 1785 to 1788, Warren wrote, he "became so enamoured with the British constitution and the government, manners, and laws of the nation, that a partiality for monarchy appeared which was inconsistent with his former professions of republicanism."

"History is not the Province of Ladies," Adams fumed in response to the charges. The two longtime friends exchanged angry letters and then severed all contact. Finally, in 1812, two years before Warren's death, Adams reconciled with her.

IN THEIR OWN WORDS

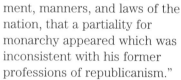

"Colonel Burr's request was, in the first instance, proposed in a form the most simple, in order that General Hamilton might give to the affair that course to which he might be induced by his temper and his knowledge of facts. Colonel Burr trusted with confidence, that, from the frankness of a soldier and the candour of a gentleman, he might expect an ingenuous declaration. That if, as he had reason to believe, General Hamilton had used expressions derogatory to his honour, he would have had the magnanimity to retract them. . . . Colonel Burr disavows all motives of predetermined hostility, a charge by which he thinks insult added to injury. He feels as a gentleman should when his honour is impeached or assailed; and, without sensations of hostility or wishes of revenge, he is determined to vindicate that honour."

William P. Van Ness, a close friend of Aaron Burr, warns of Burr's willingness to take drastic measures against Alexander Hamilton to avenge Burr's injured reputation, in a letter dated June 27, 1804.

1806
The National Road, the first federally funded highway, helped unite the East with the Western frontier.

In the country's first decades, westward travel was slow and difficult. When it rained, highways could be so muddy that horses had to fight their way through the mire; precarious bridges posed problems regardless of the weather. Roads were so deeply rutted that stagecoaches would sometimes overturn. Recognizing the importance of good transportation routes for the country's expansion and economic growth, Congress in 1806 authorized the survey and construction of the National Road, which became the first federally funded highway in the United States.

Initially, advocates of states' rights had opposed the creation of any highway that was built and maintained by the federal government. Despite their opposition, the project went ahead. Construction on what would serve for many years as the primary road west began at Cumberland, Maryland, in 1811.

Seven years later the National Road had reached the Ohio River at Wheeling, in what is now West Virginia. From there the road continued on a route that passed through Pennsylvania, Ohio, and Indiana. By 1852, after the expenditure of more than $7 million in federal funds, the project ended in Vandalia, Illinois. 🔔

Construction of a national highway, shown here in the 1820's, helped propel westward movement.

1806
Against formidable odds, Lewis and Clark led an expedition through some 6,000 miles of wilderness with the only loss of life attributed to appendicitis.

Meriwether Lewis and William Clark headed the first party of Americans to reach the Pacific Ocean by a land route. During their 30-month trek, hostile Indians, severe hunger, blizzards, and insects continually imperiled their journey.

President Thomas Jefferson had chosen Lewis, his personal secretary, to explore the new Louisiana Purchase territory. Lewis then selected Clark, a dependable administrator and army veteran, to assist him. Knowing that good planning would help ensure success, they spent the winter of 1803–04 gathering supplies and recruiting some 30 soldiers, frontiersmen,

Clark traveled with a sketch pad. Among his works: a white salmon trout (left) and a sage grouse.

and keelboat operators for the expedition.

Lewis and Clark began their journey on March 14, 1804, leaving St. Louis and heading north up the Missouri River to a Mandan camp near what is now Bismarck, North Dakota. Their one setback was the death of a soldier from a ruptured appendix. Along the way, an Indian woman named Sacagawea and her husband, a French fur trader hired as a translator, joined the group. The presence of Sacagawea — and that of her son, who was born on the journey — helped to assure Indians farther west that the expedition's mission was peaceful.

Crossing the Rockies, Lewis and Clark worried about survival. A snowstorm moved in just as they approached the mountains, and the expedition faced a shortage of pro-

visions. Perhaps the greatest challenge of all was the descent along a high plateau between the Rockies and the Cascades (an area that would become the common border of Idaho and Washington State). With their supplies of flour and corn running out, the men had to subsist on berries and even some of their own colts that they slaughtered for food. Finally, in November 1805 the party sighted the Pacific Ocean at the mouth of the Columbia River.

The trip back also had its share of dangers. After leaving Clark temporarily to explore different rivers, Lewis's group fought with Indians. Later Lewis was shot in the leg by one of his men, who mistook him for an elk (a mishap blamed on the man's poor eyesight and Lewis's buckskin outfit).

Lewis and Clark returned to St. Louis on September 23, 1806, having fulfilled most of their mission by charting the territory, observing the climate, and studying Indian life. They also reported on indigenous minerals, plants, and animals. Among the creatures discovered were prairie dogs, black-tailed deer, pronghorns, and mountain sheep. A prairie dog and four magpies were sent as gifts to President Jefferson. 🔔

1806

Overshadowed by the exploration of Lewis and Clark, Zebulon Pike made a daring expedition of his own.

At 27, Zebulon Pike was already the veteran of an army expedition to explore the headwaters of the Mississippi River when Gen. James Wilkinson sent him on an even more difficult trek. Pike was chosen to lead a group to investigate the headwaters of the Arkansas and Red rivers.

Pike left St. Louis on July 15, 1806, and headed up the Arkansas River. Four months later, near present-day Pueblo, Colorado, he noted in his journal: "In the afternoon I thought I could distinguish a mountain to our right, which appeared like a small blue cloud."

Pike detoured from his planned route, but after three

While trying to scale the mountain, Pike went two days without food.

days he realized that he could not scale the highest summit. The difficult terrain, freezing weather, and a lack of supplies kept him from climbing any higher than a spur of the mountain. He called the distant point the Great Peak; it later became known as Pikes Peak.

When Pike entered Spanish-held territory in present-day New Mexico in February 1807, Spanish troops arrested his party and detained them in Santa Fe for several months. Returning to his military career a few years later, Pike died in battle during the War of 1812. ▲

1807

Efforts to keep the British Navy from kidnapping U.S. sailors reached a low point when an American ship was fired on and three sailors were killed.

By the early 1800's, it was apparent to Great Britain that the French emperor Napoleon Bonaparte posed a serious threat. The Royal Navy needed more men to counter Napoleon's aggressive buildup of his empire, but the continuing desertion of British seamen undermined recruitment efforts. Attracted by better pay, food, and treatment, 20,000 of His Majesty's sailors jumped ship to serve on American vessels after the Revolutionary War.

The British Navy used high-handed tactics on the high seas.

As a result, the British stepped up their practice of impressment: British seamen were removed from neutral vessels and forced into service in the navy. British ships frequently stopped American vessels on the high seas to search for and seize

deserters. In addition, about 10,000 Americans were forced into Royal Navy service between 1800 and 1810. Anyone who could not prove he was a native-born U.S. citizen was fair game.

On June 22, 1807, the H.M.S. *Leopard* approached the U.S.S. *Chesapeake* off Norfolk, Virginia. Eager to find deserters, a British officer demanded that the captain of the *Chesapeake* muster his men on deck. When the American captain refused, the *Leopard* opened fire, killing three men, wounding 18, and severely damaging the *Chesapeake*. Four men — three of them Americans who had fled from British service — were abducted. Outraged, President Thomas Jefferson banned all British ships from U.S. ports. Britain's searches for deserters on U.S. ships continued, nonetheless, until after the War of 1812. ▲

IN THEIR OWN WORDS

"Arose hungry, dry, and extremely sore from the inequality of the rocks on which we had lain all night, but were amply compensated for toil by the sublimity of the prospect below. The unbounded prairie was overhung with clouds, which appeared like the ocean in a storm; wave piled on wave and foaming, whilst the sky was perfectly clear where we were. Commenced our march up the mountain and in about one hour arrived at the summit of this chain. Here we found the snow middle deep; no sign of beast or bird inhabiting this region. The thermometer, which stood at 9° above zero at the foot of the mountain, here fell to 4° below zero. The summit of the Grand Peak, which was entirely bare of vegetation and covered with snow, now appeared at the distance of fifteen or sixteen miles from us, and as high again as what we had ascended, and would have taken a whole day's march to have arrived at its base, when I believe no human being could have ascended to its pinnacle. This, with the condition of my soldiers, who had only light overalls on and no stockings . . . determined us to return."

Zebulon Pike describes his failed attempt to reach the peak that now bears his name.

1807

Fulton's Folly, as the first successful steam-powered boat was called, forever changed inland water travel in the United States.

Praise for his work as a young artist in Philadelphia had given Robert Fulton the confidence to move to London in 1786 to study with Benjamin West, an influential American émigré painter. After several years in England, however, Fulton's attention was diverted from his easel.

Studying the huge construction projects under way in Europe, the artist, who had a flair for practical inventions, started to explore mechanical and civil engineering. Fulton invented a power saw to cut canal channels and equipment to twist hemp and saw marble slabs. He also spent a decade developing an early submarine that attracted the attention of French emperor Napoleon Bonaparte. The underwater vessel had limited capabilities, however, and Fulton abandoned the project.

In France in 1802, Fulton met Robert R. Livingston, the U.S. minister to France and the first New York state chancellor (equivalent to today's governor). The inventor and the diplomat were a good match. The well-to-do and politically well-connected Livingston had already secured exclusive rights for steam-powered travel on the waterways of New York. Fulton had a vision of the

The Clermont offered passengers comfortable cabins and various amenities.

steamboat he wanted to invent as well as considerable technical expertise. With Livingston's financial backing, Fulton commissioned an English engineering firm to manufacture the engine he needed. It was two years in the making. In 1806 the inventor and his steam engine sailed for the United States.

Fulton's timing was excellent. America's primitive road system could not handle the expanding trade in farm products, cotton, tobacco, and manufactured goods. Hauling goods upstream against heavy river currents was virtually impossible. Several inventors had developed steam-powered engines before Fulton, but no one had turned the engines into profitable commercial ventures.

Within a year of his return to the United States, Fulton had built the *Clermont,* a 133-foot-long paddle wheeler whose steam, sparks, and racket earned it the nickname Fulton's Folly. On August 17, 1807, the ship proved itself a success, traveling north on the Hudson River from New York City to Albany. Soon passengers and merchants were boarding the *Clermont* for trips up and down the waterway. By the 1820's, steamships were also plying the Mississippi and Ohio rivers and other great waterways, and the churning paddles and flying sparks had become a familiar sight.

1807

Fur trapper John Colter may have been the first white man to witness the gushing geysers, sputtering volcanoes, and bubbling hot springs in Yellowstone National Park.

John Colter, a Virginian, joined the Lewis and Clark expedition in 1803; following this, he became a trapper. After spending time in an area that is now northern Wyoming, he headed west to set up a fur-trading venture with the Crow Indians.

In the winter of 1807–08, Colter traveled along the Yellowstone River, crossed to Jackson Hole, brushed by the Tetons, and traipsed along the western shore of Yellowstone

Lake. From 1808 to 1810 he lived mostly in the wilderness, trapping fur and managing to survive Indian attacks.

Before he died in 1813, Colter provided details of the Yellowstone region that appeared on a map in the journals of Lewis and Clark. The area was virtually ignored, however, until the 1863 gold rush in Montana. In response to heightened interest in that part of the West, Congress decided in 1872 to set aside 2.2 million acres in northwestern Wyoming, eastern Idaho, and southern Montana as Yellowstone National Park, which became the world's first national park.

Majestic vistas at Yellowstone National Park, as it looked in 1872.

1809
Vivacious and stylish, Dolley Madison was the first White House fashion plate.

Although she was born a Quaker, Dolley Payne Todd changed her "plain" ways when she married James Madison. New York senator Aaron Burr introduced the young widow and mother to the Virginia congressman, who was 17 years her senior. Madison was no taller than Dolley Todd and weighed less.

He was as reserved as she was outgoing. Despite these differences, the two were perfectly matched.

When Madison became secretary of state in 1801, his wife took Washington by storm. Among her many social duties was serving as White House hostess for President Thomas Jefferson, who was a widower.

Dolley Madison in her trademark turban.

In 1809 Madison was inaugurated president. As first lady — or Lady Presidentess — Dolley Madison earned a reputation as a brilliant entertainer. She was almost as well known for her elegant clothes (some of them imported from France) and her feathered turbans. In fact, her influence was so great that turbans briefly became a sensation in Europe as well as in America. Her example also led Washington ladies to take up snuff.

In 1817, after eight years in the White House, the president and Mrs. Madison retired to Montpelier, his Virginia estate. Upon her husband's death in 1836, Mrs. Madison returned to Washington to lead society once again.

Her son Payne was the one blot on her happiness. A handsome charmer, he was also a gambler. He accumulated such huge debts that in her last years she had to sell Montpelier in order to pay them off.

IN THEIR OWN WORDS

"I arrived at the Inn about dusk; and, understanding that Mrs. Madison was to have her levee or drawing room that very evening, I swore by all my gods I would be there. But how? was the question. I had got away down into Georgetown, and the persons to whom my letters of introduction were directed lived all upon Capitol Hill, about three miles off, while the President's house was exactly halfway. Here was a non-plus enough to startle any man of less enterprising spirit; but I had sworn to be there, and I determined to keep my oath. So I mounted with a stout heart to my room; resolved to put on my pease blossoms and silk stockings; gird up my loins; sally forth on my expedition; and like a vagabond knight-errant, trust to Providence for success and whole bones. . . . I emerged . . . into the blazing splendor of Mrs. Madison's drawing room. Here I was most graciously received; found a crowded collection of great and little men, of ugly old women and beautiful young ones, and in ten minutes was hand and glove with half the people in the assemblage. Mrs. Madison is a fine, portly, buxom dame, who has a smile and a pleasant word for everybody. Her sisters, Mrs. Cutts and Mrs. Washington, are like the two Merry Wives of Windsor; but as to Jemmy Madison — ah! poor Jemmy! — he is but a withered little apple-John."

Washington Irving describes one of Dolley Madison's receptions, in a letter.

1809
Washington Irving wrote the Hudson Valley tales, which were to make him famous, while living in England.

The youngest of 11 children, Washington Irving was born in New York City in 1783. His father, a merchant who had fought in the Revolutionary War, named him after his commander in chief. Irving grew up to study law, but he seldom practiced it, preferring to write essays for the *Morning Chronicle*, his brother's newspaper.

Tragedy struck Irving in 1809 when his fiancée, Matilda Hoffman, died of consumption. Although he courted other women (including Mary Shelley, the author of *Frankenstein*), he never married. Burying his grief in his work, he completed *Knickerbocker's History of New York* (1809), a humorous account that poked fun

A scene from Irving's "Rip Van Winkle."

at the ways of the early Dutch settlers.

In 1815 Irving moved to England to work in the family cutlery business. After it went bankrupt, he decided to write for a living. His most enduring work, known as *The Sketch Book* (1819–20), included the classic stories "The Legend of Sleepy Hollow" and "Rip Van Winkle." Based on European folk legends, Irving's entertaining tales of New York's Hudson Valley were the first American short stories.

After 17 years abroad, Irving returned to America in 1832. He refused offers to run for Congress, become mayor of New York City, or serve as secretary of the navy. He did, however, become minister to Spain from 1842 to 1846. Irving died in 1859, just after completing a biography of his namesake, George Washington.

E 1809
Ephraim McDowell, the pioneer of abdominal surgery, died of appendicitis.

The son of a Kentucky judge, Ephraim McDowell had had some medical training but lacked the money to finish his education and earn a degree. Still, he became known as the best surgeon west of Philadelphia.

In December 1809 he rode 60 miles on horseback to help a farmer's wife named Jane Crawford deliver the twins she thought were overdue. When McDowell examined Mrs. Crawford, however, he found that she was not really pregnant — she had a huge ovarian tumor that would probably have killed her within two years.

Medical wisdom at the time held that removing the growth would mean a quick death from "inflammation." Nevertheless, McDowell scheduled surgery for Christmas Day. He hoped that the prayers of the local congregation would help him succeed. Instead, the townspeople thought that he was doing the devil's work by "butchering a woman." A mob gathered outside his office, ready to hang him if the operation failed.

Inside, Mrs. Crawford, who had only opium pills for her pain, recited psalms. As the mob howled, McDowell removed a 20-pound tumor through a foot-long incision. Amazingly, his patient was out of bed in five days and lived 32 more years.

McDowell later performed similar surgery on the wife of a friend of Andrew Jackson. Old Hickory himself served as his reluctant assistant. "I'd rather fight a passel of Indians in ambush," Jackson said.

McDowell did the same operation on 11 other patients and "lost but one." He also removed bladder stones from 17-year-old James K. Polk, who became the 11th president of the United States 33 years later.

Although most doctors of the time criticized McDowell's operations, the University of Maryland gave him an honorary degree in 1825, and his pioneering techniques paved the way for modern abdominal surgery. He died at 58 of what experts now believe was appendicitis. 🔔

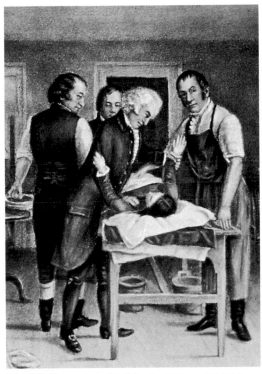

With his assistants, Ephraim McDowell (right) performs the first ovariotomy.

T 1812
The first overland expedition across America was led by explorers Lewis and Clark. A tenderfoot clerk conducted the second.

Wilson Price Hunt and a party of 64 men set out from St. Louis, Missouri, in September 1810 on a trek to the mouth of the Columbia River in Oregon. There, in virgin forest rich with beaver, they were to meet the crew of the *Tonquin*, a ship owned by the wealthy fur trader John Jacob Astor. Their plan was to construct Fort Astoria, a fur-trading post that would serve as the headquarters of Astor's newly established Pacific Fur Company.

Astor had offered Hunt, a city-bred businessman with no wilderness experience, a partnership in the company. Aided by guides, Hunt traced the route that explorers Lewis and Clark had taken along the Missouri River. Then Blackfeet Indians threatened them.

Hunt moved to a safer, more southerly course through the Rocky Mountains. At the Snake River in present-day Idaho, the group unwisely decided to leave their horses behind and build canoes, hoping to reach the Columbia by water. After several days, white water claimed at least one canoe and its steersman. Hunt's men saw that they could navigate no farther, so they traveled on foot through the frozen mountains.

Cold and hungry, the men ate dogs and even their own shoes to survive.

Hunt and his party finally reached Astoria in February 1812. After all the hardships they had endured on the journey, the fort stayed only briefly in American hands; it was turned over to the British after the War of 1812. Hunt's expedition was not fruitless, however. It opened up the Oregon Trail, and the fort's short existence helped lay the basis for America's claim to the lower Columbia River and the Oregon Country. 🔔

Fort Astoria never became the hub of fur trading that it was meant to be.

A *1812*
severe earthquake once made the Mississippi River run backward.

In the winter of 1811–12, three major earthquakes — and 1,874 separate shocks — rocked the Mississippi River valley in the worst series of quakes in American history. The first, on December 16, 1811, caused the ground in New Madrid, Missouri, to pulse in waves several feet high. Shocks reached as far south as Charleston, South Carolina, and as far north as Quebec City in Canada.

Earthquakes made traveling on the Mississippi treacherous.

The February 7, 1812, earthquake was even bigger, having since been measured as 8.7 on the Richter scale. The bed of the Mississippi River was lifted up, and the rising land formed a barrier in the river's path, forcing the water back upstream. As a result, for a few hours the river actually ran backward. The effects of the two quakes, plus one that occurred on January 23, were felt over 1.5 million square miles.

Fortunately, casualties were few. Property damage was so severe, however, that by 1815 Congress passed the first national disaster relief act. **▲**

T *1812*
he War of 1812 was so controversial that the New England states considered secession.

The New England states were so bitterly opposed to the War of 1812 — or "Mr. Madison's War," as it was known — that they threatened to leave the Union. They were not the only states that were opposed to it. After two weeks of tense debate, the U.S. Senate passed the war bill by a slim margin of only six votes.

The chief causes of the conflict were Britain's interference with America's shipping trade and its seizure of American ships and seamen. Another cause was American expansion. As they moved westward, settlers met resistance from American Indians armed by the British. The United States not only wanted to control the West and its fur trade, it also had designs on Canada. Realizing that hostility was growing, England agreed, on June 23, 1812, to end restrictions on American trade. But it was too late; the United States had already declared war on Great Britain.

The war divided the nation. When Federalist newspapers railed against it, pro-war factions attacked their offices. Many American citizens actually sold provisions to the enemy. In addition, the country was ill prepared. The navy had few good ships, and the army had only 6,750 men. Most Revolutionary War veterans were old and unfit, and capable officers were the exception.

Supplies were low, and sanitation inadequate. America lost seven times more men to disease than to battle. Moreover, British blockades of American ports brought almost all sea trade to a halt. If the blockades were not lifted soon, the American economy would be in serious trouble.

Luckily the British became weary of the war. The conflict was supposed to have been a small one, and the British had counted on defeating the Americans easily. Instead, their offensive campaigns produced few victories, and valuable military resources were being depleted with little gain.

The war ended in a draw after 2½ years. Ironically, the Treaty of Ghent did not even address the questions of blockades and impressment that had triggered the fighting. **▲**

The Battle of the Thames, north of Lake Erie, was a key American victory in the War of 1812.

1812

The battleship *Constitution* gave America its first big naval victory (and a great morale boost) in the War of 1812.

On July 16, 1812, the American ship *Constitution* was stranded in light winds off the New Jersey coast. Spotting five British ships, including the *Guerrière*, Capt. Isaac Hull tried to keep the *Constitution* out of shooting range in a slow-motion chase. On the second day a squall arose. Hull quickly shortened sail and escaped. By the time the British, who had been caught in the storm, put their vessels in order, the American ship was almost out of sight.

A little more than a month later, the *Constitution* encountered the *Guerrière* once again. But this time Hull did not run. Instead, he gave chase and after a quick, fierce clash won the battle. The British ship surrendered in such bad condition that it had to be blown up. Although the destruction of the *Guerrière* did little to damage the Royal Navy, it was nevertheless an important victory for the Americans, as it provided a much-needed boost to morale.

After surviving other battles, the *Constitution* (nicknamed Old Ironsides because cannonballs seemed to bounce off its sides) was declared unseaworthy in 1830. Today it remains the oldest commissioned warship afloat in the world. ▲

*The **Constitution** engaged the Guerrière in a fight that lasted just 2½ hours. Today the **Constitution** is docked at the Boston Naval Shipyard.*

Freedom's Second Challenge

Although in some ways considered a failure, the War of 1812 helped to reconfirm that America would no longer tolerate British interference in its affairs. Some of the key events and dates:

1812 An American attempt to invade Canada at the Battle of Queenstown Heights results in a humiliating defeat.

1813 Commodore Oliver Hazard Perry's small, improvised fleet defeats a slightly weaker British force and gains control of Lake Erie for the rest of the war.

The British, retreating northward from Detroit, are overtaken by the Americans and defeated at the Thames River. Casualties include the great Indian leader Tecumseh, a British ally.

1814 After routing the Americans at Bladensburg, just east of Washington, D.C., the British occupy the American capital and burn the president's mansion and other public buildings.

American naval forces defeat the British fleet at Lake Champlain, and ground forces repulse all British land attacks; the British retreat into Canada.

The British and Americans sign a peace treaty at Ghent in the Netherlands, restoring prewar boundaries and arranging to settle, by negotiation, all outstanding disputes.

1812

The Russians built an outpost in California in 1812. Nearly 30 years later they sold it to the man who started the California gold rush.

Although the Russians monopolized the fur trade in Alaska, they lacked food and supplies there. In 1806 entrepreneur Nicholas Rezanov sailed to San Francisco for help. He was received warmly enough (California was under Spanish rule), but at first he could not obtain provisions, because the governor and commandant had received explicit orders not to trade with foreigners.

A dramatic turnaround occurred when Rezanov and the commandant's teenage daughter, Concepción, fell in love. The betrothal of the two ensured food and supplies for the Russians in Alaska. Rezanov left with the provisions and promised to come back for his fiancée. Unfortunately, he could not keep his promise; he died 10 months later while he was traveling across Siberia.

The Russians placed a high value on the fur of the California otter.

Although Rezanov's primary motive for going to San Francisco had been to procure food for his starving countrymen, he also intended to hunt the plentiful sea otters, trade with the Spanish, and expand Russian territory in North America by establishing settlements there.

His plans did not die with him. In 1812 the Russians returned to California and built Fort Ross (a form of the word *Russia*) 18 miles north of Bodega Bay. It was the largest, most southerly Russian colony on the U.S. mainland. Aided by Aleuts, the Russians hunted the sea otters almost to extinction. They also traded with both Spaniards and Mexicans.

Fort Ross eventually became a financial liability, and the Russians tried to sell it — first to the Hudson's Bay Company and then to Mexico. Both refused the offer. Finally, in 1841, the Russians sold the fort to John Sutter. Seven years later gold was discovered on Sutter's land, triggering the great California gold rush. ▲

Congress awarded Perry a gold medal for his victory at Lake Erie.

1813

When his ship was too disabled to finish the battle, Oliver Hazard Perry, dressed as an ordinary seaman to deceive sharpshooters, rowed through a hail of gunfire to another ship.

Sent to gain control of British-occupied Lake Erie in February 1813, young Oliver Hazard Perry had to provide his own ships. Because they had to be constructed quickly, the shipbuilder, Noah Brown, ordered that the vessels were to have "no extras; plain work, plain work, is all we want." Perry had nine ships by August, and pulled them over a sandbar into the lake. If the British captain Robert H. Barclay had attacked the American vessels as they were being hauled, he might have destroyed them. But Perry succeeded in his mission.

Captain Barclay met up with Perry near Put-in Bay on the morning of September 10. There Perry's flagship, the *Lawrence*, flying a banner with the slogan "Don't Give Up the Ship," engaged six British warships in a close and bloody fight. The *Niagara*, another large American brig, inexplicably hung back.

The flagship fought until it was a wrecked hulk, with all but about 20 of its crew members dead or wounded. But Perry, dressed as a common seaman to fool enemy snipers, remained calm and unharmed. Seamen rowed him through a hail of gunfire to the *Niagara*.

Replacing Jesse Duncan Elliot, the ship's commander, Perry sailed back to the British line. His crew, firing guns from both sides of the *Niagara*, was too much for the exhausted enemy. Barclay surrendered his fleet, and Perry sent home a dispatch to Gen. William H. Harrison, commander of the army in the Northwest: "We have met the enemy, and they are ours." British control of Lake Erie had ended. 🔔

1813

The great Indian leader Tecumseh was willing to die to achieve his dream of a united Indian nation that would fight American expansion into Indian lands.

The Shawnee leader Tecumseh was deeply alarmed at the rate at which the white man, backed by U.S. government policies, was encroaching on Indian territory and scattering the tribes. He believed that only a grand alliance of Indian peoples would be strong enough to stop the white man's expansion westward. Tecumseh and his brother, Tenskwatawa, a holy man known as the Prophet, traveled thousands of miles, rallying support from many different tribes. In a voice that one white onlooker said "resounded over the multitude . . . his words like a succession of thunderbolts," Tecumseh called for a great Indian nation west of the Ohio River. Indians would be forbidden to sell their land, because Tecumseh believed that the land was for everyone to share but for no one to own.

Tecumseh and Tenskwatawa set up a model village in Indiana at Tippecanoe, where Indians from many tribes gathered. In 1811 an American force under Indiana Territory governor William Henry Harrison (who 30 years later would become the ninth president of the United States) approached the village while Tecumseh was away spreading his message of unity. Tecumseh had been an obstacle to

Tecumseh's name means "Shooting Star" in Shawnee.

Harrison in his attempt to take over Indian lands, and his absence provided a perfect opportunity for attack.

Using a minor brawl between some Indians and nearby white settlers as an excuse for intervention, Harrison marched into the village with 900 troops. Tenskwatawa panicked, and promising his warriors that the white man's bullets would not harm them, ordered an attack. Harrison razed Tippecanoe, and the surviving Indians, demoralized by the defeat, disbanded. With the breakup of the village went Tecumseh's dreams of a multitribal alliance.

Still hoping to drive the Americans from the West, Tecumseh joined the British in the War of 1812. In October 1813 he was covering the retreat of the British after their defeat at Lake Erie. Tecumseh stopped at Canada's Thames River and forced his allies to turn and face the enemy. The Shawnee visionary battled his old nemesis for the last time. William Henry Harrison once again prevailed, and Tecumseh fell. Although Tecumseh had been a dangerous adversary, Harrison praised him as "one of those uncommon geniuses which spring up occasionally to produce revolutions and overturn the established order of things." 🔔

W *1814*
hile most of Washington's residents fled from the British, Dolley Madison stayed behind to protect the nation's treasures.

With Napoleon's defeat in 1814, the British were free to concentrate on the war in America. In August they sent some 4,000 seasoned veterans under Gen. Robert Ross to the Chesapeake Bay. On August 24 ill-trained U.S. troops and inexperienced militia attempted to make a stand against the British troops at Bladensburg, Maryland, but were unsuccessful.

President Madison spent that day bravely, but ineffectively, at the front. His wife, Dolley, remained six miles away at their official home in Washington (not yet called the White House), packing documents and a few prized possessions. In late afternoon a free black man named James Smith rode up to the house, urging all to flee. Mrs. Madison stayed at her task, however, and refused to leave until she had secured Gilbert Stuart's famed

The British caused less damage to the president's house than some Washington citizens who "ran all over . . . and stole . . . whatever they could lay their hands on."

portrait of George Washington. Before escaping, she asked two men from New York to carry the painting to safety. Sadly, local people then looted the house.

By the time the British general Ross rode into Washington that evening, resistance was almost nonexistent. The officers finished the food and wine left on the Madisons' table, while Ross himself stole the couple's love letters. He then proceeded to burn the city. One of the few buildings spared was the Patent Office, whose director pleaded for the safety of the holdings stored there. Although heavy rains slowed the fires, many government facilities, including the Capitol and the Navy Yard, were severely damaged. Dolley Madison made it safely to a friend's house, and the next day she was reunited with her husband.

A *1814*
seamstress, a prisoner, and an amateur poet all played a part in the birth of our national anthem.

In 1813 the commander of Fort McHenry in Baltimore requested an American flag large enough for the British to see from a distance. Naval pennant-maker Mary Pickersgill complied, sewing for him a huge 30- by 42-foot banner.

The following year the Royal Navy closed in on Baltimore, carrying in its flagship Dr. William Beanes, a prisoner of war. Beanes's friend, Francis Scott Key, a lawyer and amateur poet, got permission from President James Madison to negotiate the doctor's release. Key arrived at the flagship in a small boat on September 13, 1814, only hours before a British assault on Fort McHenry.

A remnant of the actual star-spangled banner.

He was told that Beanes would be released only after the attack. Key and his party were held on their vessel at a safe distance from the fighting.

The British shot rockets at Fort McHenry all night long. As Key watched, he began to compose a poem. The attack seemed sure to overwhelm the fort, but as dawn broke, Key saw Pickersgill's flag still waving. The fort had held. While being rowed to shore, Key finished what we now call "The Star-Spangled Banner."

Key's brother-in-law, a Baltimore judge, had the poem printed immediately and set to the music of a British drinking song. Soon, "The Star-Spangled Banner" was heard in taverns all across the country, and by the 1860's it was a standard tune of military bands. It became the American national anthem in 1931.

Andrew Jackson (on the white horse) at the Battle of New Orleans.

A *1815*
ndrew Jackson's victory at New Orleans lifted American spirits. But the battle occurred two weeks after the Treaty of Ghent had ended the war.

As the veteran British army approached New Orleans in 1814, Andrew Jackson mustered a defending force. To his own few men he added militia, including many free blacks. Even the pirate Jean Laffite provided men, ammunition, and his knowledge of the swamps around the city.

Landing in December, British general Edward Pakenham and his men proceeded slowly through the marshy terrain to the Mississippi River. Jackson, knowing that there was only one dry approach to New Orleans and that Pakenham would take it, built earth embankments along an abandoned canal that lay across the route. On one side of the route was the Mississippi River, and on the other side was a swamp.

By the time Pakenham reached the barricaded canal, Jackson was ready for him.

At dawn on January 8, 1815, 4,000 red-coated soldiers advanced on the Americans. Jackson's force, strengthened by Tennessee riflemen, opened fire. The British fell in waves, and in less than an hour some 2,000 men were lost, including Pakenham. Soon the British were sailing home, with Pakenham's body preserved in a cask of rum (a method used to preserve the remains of distinguished people until they could be buried in their homeland).

Only 71 Americans were killed or wounded in the Battle of New Orleans. The victory won Jackson fame and Laffite's men a pardon, but it accomplished little else. Unknown to any of the combatants in those days of slow communication, the Treaty of Ghent had officially ended the war two weeks earlier.

A *1816*
volcanic eruption halfway around the world caused a "year without a summer."

In 1815 the Indonesian volcano Tamboro erupted, hurling enough ash into the stratosphere to send dust clouds circling the globe. The following year, odd atmospheric effects and bizarre weather were reported in America as well as in northern Europe. In the northeastern United States, it remained so chilly that 1816 has ever since been called "the year without a summer."

Frosts hit the region well into May, delaying the planting of summer crops. Then, after a brief warming, snow fell suddenly from June 6 to 8. Freezing temperatures continued for several days, killing the new corn crop. Encouraged by a spell of warmer weather, optimistic farmers planted again.

At the end of the first week of July, however, what might have seemed like a warn-

ing occurred, when frost killed the vegetables growing in northern New England. The rye and wheat were not affected, although the weather remained cool. Then, twice in late August and again in mid-September, killing frosts struck the entire region.

The corn crop was devastated, and a host of economic problems followed. The price of corn shot up, then the price of cattle that fed on corn plummeted, ruining many farmers. During the winter the cost of all grains rose, and many people were threatened with hunger and were forced to scavenge for wild food. Happily, a normal summer and a bountiful harvest followed in 1817. It was not until the 20th century that scientists connected the volcano's explosion to the peculiar weather.

IN THEIR OWN WORDS

❝ I well remember the 7th of June . . . dressed throughout with thick woolen clothes. . . . On the 10th of June, my wife brought in some clothes that had been spread on the ground the night before, which were frozen stiff as in winter. On the 4th of July I saw . . . men pitching quoits in the middle of the day with thick overcoats on. . . . **❞**

Chauncey Jerome of Plymouth, Connecticut, recalling the summer of 1816.

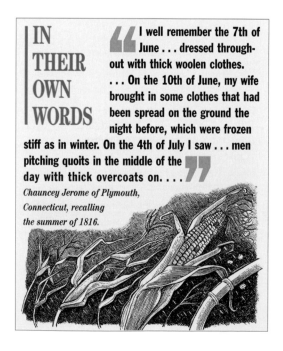

E *1817*
ven though the Erie Canal was derided as Clinton's Ditch, it made New York rich and spurred the growth of the Midwest.

Skeptics called the Erie Canal Clinton's Ditch, after New York governor DeWitt Clinton. Although he had promoted the project for years, when the first shovel of earth was turned over on July 4, 1817, many still believed it would never work. Yet when it was completed, the canal was the most significant engineering feat yet accomplished in the United States; it rose 688 feet through 83 locks over the 363 miles between Buffalo and Albany.

Laborers, many of them Irish immigrants, had worked with shovels, blasting powder, and huge stump-pulling machines to dig the canal. Its 4-foot depth and 40-foot width crossed rivers and streams on 18 aqueducts. Alongside the canal

A commemorative plate celebrating the completion of the Erie Canal.

was a towpath for the mules that pulled the barges.

At the 1825 opening ceremony, Clinton poured into New York Harbor two kegs of water that had been shipped down the canal from Lake Erie. The waterway was an immediate success, as travel time and shipping costs across New York State diminished. It now took only 6 days to travel from Buffalo to New York City, cutting the journey by a full two weeks, and the price to ship a ton of grain dropped from $100 to less than $15. Earlier, travel back and forth from the East Coast to the rest of the United States had been by wagon over tortuous roads. But when the canal was finished, Midwestern products could be floated east with ease. New York Harbor boomed, and cities like Rochester and Syracuse sprang up along the canal's route. Settlers streamed west on barges, heading for the rich lands of Ohio, Indiana, and Illinois.

A *1817*
s a young man, John Trumbull drew accolades for his artistic renditions of the Revolution. His skills had greatly deteriorated, however, when he was commissioned to paint scenes in the Capitol rotunda years later.

Despite being blind in one eye, John Trumbull wanted to be an artist. But when, at the age of 15, he asked his father for permission to study under the painter John Singleton Copley, he was sent away to Harvard College instead. After graduation Trumbull served under George Washington in the Continental Army, but resigned in a fit of pique over a minor clerical error involving his commission.

Free to pursue his dream of being a full-time artist, Trumbull traveled to England in 1780 to study with Benjamin West (who had taught American painters Gilbert Stuart and Charles Willson Peale). But Trumbull's stay in England was cut short. Imprisoned for seven months in retaliation for the execution of British spy Maj. John André in America, he returned home following his release to wait until relations improved between England and the United States.

The young artist first came to the public's attention because of a full-length portrait of George Washington, which he painted from memory. Engravings of the work were sold throughout Europe and

were the first real likenesses of Washington available there. In 1784 Trumbull began painting scenes of the Revolutionary War.

Two of his works, "The Death of General Warren at the Battle of Bunker's Hill" and "The Death of General Montgomery in the Attack on Quebec," inspired Thomas Jefferson to suggest that Trumbull produce a series commemorating key moments in the Revolution. Jefferson furnished the artist with a sketch from memory for what is probably his best-known painting, the "Declaration of Independence." Trumbull, wanting to get everything just right, caught likenesses of most of the signers by actually visiting them and drawing them from life. His attention to accuracy ended there; 13 signers were not shown, and 4 men whom he included in the painting did not actually sign the Declaration.

In 1817 Congress commissioned Trumbull to paint four large Revolutionary scenes inside the rotunda of the new Capitol. Unfortunately, by that time Trumbull's skills had deteriorated, and the paintings proved extremely unpopular. They were soon

At the age of 21 John Trumbull painted this self-portrait.

removed. But Trumbull's smaller studies continued to be admired and were widely reproduced. To this day his paintings and drawings serve as a valuable visual record of the Revolutionary period.

1818
The Missouri Compromise put the slavery question to rest — but just for a while.

When the Missouri Territory applied for statehood in 1818, there were an equal number of senators from the North and the South. The Northerners in Congress sought to ensure that Missouri would be a state into which no slaves could be brought and where all future children born to slaves would be free upon reaching the age of 25. The Southerners, however, viewed the admission of Missouri as a states' rights case and a threat to regional balance. If the federal government could curb slavery in this instance, they argued, Washington might eventually place other restrictions on the states. As the debate grew more heated, both sides threatened to secede from the Union.

It was Rep. Henry Clay of Kentucky who masterminded what came to be called the Missouri Compromise in 1820. The territory could be admitted as a slave-holding state if Maine, formerly part of Massachusetts, was welcomed as a free state. This compromise would maintain the balance of free states and slave states, with 12 of each. In addition, Congress drew a line across the Louisiana Territory at latitude 36 degrees 30 minutes — roughly Missouri's southern border — and declared that except for Missouri itself, slavery would be forbidden north of that boundary.

Missouri became a state on August 10, 1821, and the slavery issue was temporarily resolved. But some observers recognized that the skirmish over Missouri's entry into the young union was a worrysome harbinger of much greater growing pains to come. "This momentous question, like a fire bell in the night, awakened and filled me with terror," Thomas Jefferson wrote of the debate surrounding the compromise. John Quincy Adams agreed, calling the issue "a mere preamble — a title page to a great, tragic volume."

1821
Believing that women had a right to a good education, Emma Willard established the first institute of higher learning for women in the United States.

As a young girl Emma Hart had thirsted for knowledge. Encouraged by her father — and unlike most girls of her time — she read the classics and participated in family discussions on serious topics ranging from religion to politics.

Emma became a teacher, moving in 1807 to Middlebury, Vermont, where she met and married John Willard, a prominent doctor and politician. Their household also included her husband's nephew, a Middlebury College student. Through him, she discovered the world of higher education — a world that at the time was closed to women.

She was determined to make things change. In 1814 she opened a school for young women in her home. In an era when girls were expected to concentrate on learning homemaking skills, and to gain only a rudimentary knowledge of reading and writing, the curriculum included such topics as mathematics and philosophy.

With the encouragement of Gov. DeWitt Clinton of New York, who had read her proposal for advanced education for females,

Rejecting the idea that higher education made girls "puny and nervous," Willard paved the way for academies such as this one, where schoolgirls celebrated May Day.

Willard established a school in Waterford, New York. When the state legislature refused it funds, she feared that the academy might have to close.

The people of Troy, New York, then came to her rescue, offering financial assistance. In 1821 the Troy Female Seminary opened with Willard at its helm.

The school's curriculum of college-style courses was unprecedented. Its graduates fanned out across the expanding United States to spread the idea of women's education, and the school became a model for women's colleges throughout the United States as well as in Europe.

Willard eventually left the seminary in the care of her only child, John Hart Willard, and his wife. The Troy Female Seminary was renamed the Emma Willard School in 1895, and it remains in operation today as a college preparatory school.

1821

James Fenimore Cooper, a gentleman farmer, wrote his first novel on a dare from his wife. His second book brought him literary acclaim and changed his vocation.

Although it was quickly forgotten, the first book by James Fenimore Cooper, America's first best-selling novelist, whetted his appetite for a literary career. He published *Precaution* in 1820, after his wife had challenged him to improve on the dull English novel he was reading aloud to her.

Unlike *Precaution*, Cooper's second book, *The Spy*, was an immediate success when it came out in 1821. The adventure story about a double agent during the Revolutionary War captivated readers. His next work, *The Pioneers* (1823), introduced readers to Cooper's most endearing character, Natty Bumppo, the ideal frontiersman who would appear in all five Leatherstocking Tales, for which Cooper is best known.

Cooper took his inspiration from his youthful adventures in the forests near his father's estate on Otsego Lake in upstate New York. Expelled from Yale University for a prank at the age of 16, he served four years in the U.S. Navy before marrying and settling down in 1811 for what he thought would be a quiet farm life. Cooper was 30 when he started writing.

After publishing *The Last of the Mohicans* (1826), Cooper moved to Paris. He wanted to ensure his four daughters a good education and to capitalize on his literary renown. When he returned to America after seven years, Cooper was disillusioned. He felt that the country had been corrupted, that vulgarity was commonplace, and that Jacksonian Democrats were to blame.

Cooper attacked his opponents and filed libel suits against his critics. Readers shunned him until he wrote *The Pathfinder* (1840) and *The Deerslayer* (1841), his last Leatherstocking tales. By the time he died in 1851, Cooper had written 39 novels and was one of America's best-known authors. ▲

An illustration by N.C. Wyeth for a 1925 edition of Cooper's best-seller The Deerslayer.

1821

A small-town Missouri businessman with good luck and excellent timing became the father of the Santa Fe Trail, a major trading route for two decades.

In September 1821, William Becknell of Franklin, Missouri, set out to trade with the Plains Indians. When his expedition made its way through the rugged Raton Pass, in present-day southeastern Colorado, Becknell learned from Mexican soldiers that Mexico had just won its independence from Spain. That change opened up many opportunities for American traders along what would become the Santa Fe Trail.

The next spring, Becknell struck out again, trekking through the Cimarron Desert. The dust was so thick that his men could scarcely see or breathe. Then, as luck would have it, a buffalo that had just drunk from the Cimarron River wandered across their path. They killed the buffalo, and water recovered from its stomach sustained them until they reached the river.

Travel expanded rapidly on the trail soon after Becknell's initial foray. Americans traded mules and such manufactured goods as finished cotton and cutlery for the furs and gold and silver coins offered by the merchants of Mexican-owned Santa Fe.

Setting out in May from Independence, Missouri, the traders banded together to fend off Indian attacks. Oxen or mule teams pulled the long columns of wagons. At night, the columns would often form an enclosed square with men and animals inside.

Besides threats from the Indians, traders faced problems from the terrain and the weather — the rough landscape destroyed the hooves of oxen, and the spring rains turned prairies into muddy quagmires. In addition, dust storms, intense summer heat, and hailstones plagued travelers crossing the 800-mile route. Still, the caravans continued to grow each year until 1843, when high tariffs and the imminent threat of war with Mexico brought trade to a virtual standstill.

Travel on the Santa Fe Trail was so well organized that only eight men died en route in the first 10 years. The thoroughfare became a model for future pioneers heading overland across other wagon trails and led to American annexation of New Mexico. ▲

The Santa Fe Trail cut across the treacherous, 50-mile-wide Cimarron Desert.

1821

The only person in history known to have invented a writing system single-handedly is Sequoyah, a self-taught Cherokee who had to overcome ridicule from his own tribe.

Although Sequoyah never learned to speak or read English, he was convinced that being able to communicate in writing was an important source of the white man's power. The son of a part-Cherokee woman and most likely an English trader, he believed that the Cherokees could not preserve their proud and ancient heritage without a written language of their own. He determined to create a writing system from scratch that would ultimately contain more than 20,000 words.

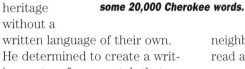
Sequoyah developed symbols for some 20,000 Cherokee words.

Sequoyah began in 1809 by carving pictographs in bark, later switching to parchment. He doggedly pursued his work, refusing to give up even after an arsonist burned down his cabin with all his papers in it.

Eventually Sequoyah developed a syllabary with 86 characters (adapted from English, Greek, and Hebrew letters he had seen in books at a mission school), each standing for sounds or syllables in the Cherokee language.

Most of Sequoyah's tribe regarded his mysterious labors with suspicion, and some even accused him of practicing witchcraft. To convince them of the value of his syllabary, Sequoyah knew that he quickly had to find someone who was willing to learn his writing system.

By sheer accident, Sequoyah discovered that Ayokeh, his six-year-old daughter, was the pupil he had been seeking. After assembling a council of chiefs in 1821, he eliminated their doubts when Ayokeh, in a clear, firm voice, read aloud a message written in her father's symbols.

Almost immediately, thousands of Cherokees in Kentucky, Tennessee, and several neighboring states learned to read and write their native language. To show its appreciation, his tribe gave Sequoyah a silver medal and an annuity. Soon books were published in Cherokee, and in 1828 a newspaper, the *Cherokee Phoenix,* rolled off the presses with articles in English and Cherokee.

Sequoyah's achievement made him a well-respected spokesman who helped maintain tribal unity even after the Cherokees were pushed out of their homeland. Living tributes to his enduring legacy include Sequoia National Park in California and a genus of giant redwood trees. ▲

1822

Honoring his father's deathbed wish, Stephen Austin established the first Anglo-American settlement in Texas.

Born in Virginia and raised in Missouri, Stephen Austin had already worked as a storekeeper, manager of a lead mine, bank director, militia officer, and newspaper editor when his father died in 1821. Reluctantly, the 27-year-old agreed to fulfill the dream of his father, who had received a land grant from Mexico. As he had promised the dying man, Austin gave up his American citizenship to found a settlement in Mexican-owned Texas. He persuaded Mexican authorities to give him a choice site that encompassed 11 million acres on a coastal plain bordering on the Gulf Coast.

In 1822 Austin founded the colony with 300 carefully chosen immigrants. For the next few years, he was a benevolent dictator, serving as judge, lawgiver, and chief executive — as well as head of the military. Even after the colonists voted in their own democratic constitution, his voice remained powerful. He arranged for land surveys and prepared titles, saw to the building of schools and sawmills, and helped pass a law protecting homesteaders from past debts.

As the colony's unofficial ambassador to the Mexican government, Austin tried to strike a balance between the Anglos' demands and Mexican laws. His success was mixed. Briefly imprisoned in 1833 in Mexico City, where he had gone to ask that Texas be

A messenger brings Austin word of an Indian raid.

made an independent Mexican state, Austin returned to his colony to discover that the Texans wanted their own separate country.

Despite his efforts, war broke out. After Texas won its independence in 1836, Austin ran for president of the republic, but he lost to Sam Houston, who appointed him secretary of state. Austin served less than three months; he died of pneumonia at the age of 43. ▲

1822

In Charleston, South Carolina, a slave rebellion that never took place had tragic consequences.

As a young man Denmark Vesey, an African-American slave, had sailed the Caribbean with his master, Capt. Joseph Vesey. He had seen firsthand the rewards of rebellion in Haiti, an independent nation ruled by former slaves. After buying his freedom with the winnings from a lottery, he joined a community of free slaves in Charleston, supporting himself as a carpenter and becoming a Methodist minister. Fiercely religious and a forceful speaker, he used his pulpit to advocate insurrection. As many as 9,000 blacks, both freemen and slaves, may have joined his cause. Vesey reasoned that if they took Charleston, the revolt would spread from the city to the countryside. A plot was devised for the night of July 14, 1822.

It was not to be. In May a slave alerted his master, and word soon spread. Vesey and his lieutenants worked quickly to salvage the plan, but to no avail. Hundreds of blacks were rounded up by the city's authorities. Vesey himself was arrested after a three-day search. Tried under slave law, he was sentenced to death and hanged with five of his followers on July 2. In all, 35 of the conspirators were executed, 48 were flogged, and about 35 sold to West Indian plantations. Some of the bodies were left to hang for a number of days to serve as a warning to others. Throughout the lower South, repressive new laws were enacted to restrict the black freemen and slaves — underscoring the cruelty of slavery and adding fuel to the abolitionists' fire. ▲

Denmark Vesey conducts a clandestine meeting in a church.

President Monroe shapes American foreign policy with his Cabinet.

1823

A mainstay of U.S. foreign policy to this day, the Monroe Doctrine asserted a young republic's power in the New World.

In an address to Congress on December 2, 1823, President James Monroe issued a warning to the European powers: "The American continents, by the free and independent condition which they have assumed and maintain, are henceforth not to be considered as subjects for future colonization." While asserting a policy of noninterference in Europe, Monroe stated that any attempt to reassert colonial dominion from abroad would be viewed by the United States as "dangerous to our peace and safety."

Known as the Monroe Doctrine, the principles set forth that day did much to reassure the American people. Although U.S. sovereignty had been an established fact for some time, government officials worried that the colonial ambitions of European countries might lead them to reassert their authority over the newly independent nations in Latin America. To the west the Russian presence in Alaska, long an irritant to Washington, represented a threat of further expansion. Underneath it all lay Monroe's desire to recognize infant democracies in the Western Hemisphere and to distance the United States from the Old World and its web of monarchical rivalries.

In fact, Americans had little to fear. Despite some aggressive posturing, neither France nor Spain had the resources to reassert their power across the ocean, and Russian interest in the Northwest was tepid at best. But just the idea of European interference was enough. Monroe had inadvertently defined American foreign policy for generations to come, establishing hemispheric independence from Europe and bolstering the status of the United States as the principal power in the New World. ▲

119

A
1823
mericans long believed that the Great American Desert sprawled west of the Mississippi River.

Just as some imaginative Old World cartographers showed dragons lurking at the edges of the unknown, maps of the early 19th-century United States often labeled the vast region between Canada and Texas, and between the Missouri and Mississippi rivers and the Rocky Mountains, as the Great American Desert, so called because it was thought to be barren and uninhabitable.

The "desert" was described as early as the mid-16th century by Francisco Vásquez de Coronado, who explored the North American interior for Spain. But it was explorers Zebulon Pike and Maj. Stephen H. Long who called the vast expanse the Great American Desert. "I do not hesitate in giving the opinion, that it is almost wholly unfit for cultivation," wrote Long in an 1823 report.

Titian R. Peale, the youngest son of American painter Charles Willson Peale, painted this view of the Missouri River (part of the Great American Desert) in 1820.

For the next 40 years, maps of North America bore the designation. The region itself was occupied mostly by Plains Indians and a few mountain men, trappers, and fur traders. By the late 1860's the "desert" boasted a booming cattle industry. The area, although arid, was not a desert, and irriga- tion combined with mechanized equipment eventually made successful farming possible.

Although the label Great American Desert has vanished from U.S. maps, the region, now known as the Great Plains, remains one of America's most sparsely pop- ulated areas. ▲

Many foreigners abstained from the "American form of tobacco vice."

B
1820's
y the early 19th century, both presidents and ordinary people alike indulged in a distinctly American habit — chewing tobacco.

In the nation's earliest days, only seafarers and laborers chewed tobacco — a custom they had adopted from the Indians of the Caribbean. Later, during the Revolu- tionary period, more and more colonists took up chewing, scorning the Euro- pean practice of taking snuff as an Old World habit. By the 1820's chewing was a wide- spread pastime, with even the more affluent and fashionable Americans indulging in it.

Cultural reasons aside, chew- ing tobacco had practical advan- tages over smoking cigars or pipes: it left a man's hands free for clearing land, plowing fields, or performing the myriad tasks necessary to build a nation. Westerners who had little access to a dentist believed that tobacco had medicinal qualities that could prevent cavities or stop a toothache.

Chewing was not limited to rural outposts, however. Spit- toons, or cuspidors, could be found everywhere, even in the halls of Congress.

By 1890 consumption of chewing tobacco had reached its peak: nearly three pounds per year for every American. After that, it declined, replaced by the pipe and then the newly popular cigarette. ▲

A 1824

At the invitation of Congress, the Soldier's Friend returned to the nation he had helped found and embarked on a triumphal tour.

In August 1824 the Marquis de Lafayette arrived in New York to a display of public welcome never before seen. Cannons boomed above the cheering throng, and aging Revolutionary War veterans gathered around him. The general was nearly overcome, and tears streamed from his eyes. In the years since he had left America, Lafayette had seen his fortunes wax and wane. While America had thrived, France had traveled a much rockier road to democracy, and Lafayette had suffered political isolation, exile, and a five-year imprisonment for his liberal ideas. But all that was forgotten the moment he set foot on American soil. The last of the Revolutionary War generals had returned.

Lafayette's reception in New York proved just a foretaste of the adulation that would be heaped upon him during his 14-month stay. Traveling some 5,000 miles, he visited all 24 states, and everywhere he went, the roads were lined with admiring well-wishers. He was feted in Boston, and in Philadelphia he shook so many hands that his own became swollen and bruised. In a tearful ceremony, he visited Mt. Vernon and the tomb of his mentor, George Washington, then spent a week with his old friend, the 81-year-old Thomas Jefferson, who was in retirement at Monticello. He next traveled to Montpelier, the estate of James Madison, and spent four days with the former president, who was 74 years old at the time.

Lafayette went on to Washington, D.C., where he was praised in Congress and awarded $200,000, land in Florida, and honorary American citizenship. He then toured the South and the West, stopping in Nashville, Natchez, and Baton Rouge; in New Orleans he met a group of free blacks who had fought in the War of 1812. The one serious mishap in his entire trip occurred when the steamboat on which he was traveling sank in the Ohio River.

Lafayette delayed his return to France long enough to celebrate his 68th birthday at the White House, and when he finally embarked for France, the nation was saddened. Lafayette knew he would never lay eyes

This ticket admitted the bearer to a Masonic dinner given in honor of Lafayette.

on his beloved America again, but in the hold of his ship lay cases of earth from Bunker Hill, so that one day he could be buried in American soil. ▲

K 1824

Known as "the Indian general," the great Choctaw chief Pushmataha was buried in the Congressional Cemetery in Washington, D.C., with full military honors.

"When our fathers took the hand of Washington," Pushmataha once said, "they told him the Choctaw would always be friends of his nation, and Pushmataha can not be false to their promises."

Throughout his life the great Choctaw chief lived up to this pledge.

A ferocious combatant, Pushmataha distinguished himself as a young man in tribal wars against the Osages, earning the name Eagle. In 1805, at the age of 40, he was elected chief and embarked on a course of improving relations with whites, winning favor in Washington, and consolidating his power at home. At a series of council debates in

A portrait of Pushmataha in 1824.

1811, he spoke eloquently against Shawnee chief Tecumseh's plan to unite the northern and southern Indian tribes in an alliance against the United States. During the War of 1812, Pushmataha — true to his pledge of loyalty to the white man — led his 500 braves against the Seminoles and the Creeks, who had sided with the English. Serving under Maj. Gen. Andrew Jackson in the Pensacola campaign, he acquitted himself well and was rewarded with the rank of brigadier general in the U.S. Army. Jackson, who knew him affectionately as Push, spoke highly of the chief. "He was," said Jackson, "the greatest and bravest Indian I have ever known."

An able statesman, Pushmataha negotiated several treaties, one of which provided for the cession of tribal lands to Mississippi and Alabama in exchange for $500 and an annual annuity of $150 as long as he remained chief. Despite Pushmataha's strong relationship with the U.S. government, his was the first tribe forced to give up its remaining lands. In 1824 he led a delegation to Washington, D.C., meeting with President James Monroe and French general Marquis de Lafayette, who was on a triumphal tour of the United States. During this trip Pushmataha, then in his 60th year, fell ill. Within 24 hours he was dead. A mile-long funeral procession followed him to his final resting place in the Congressional Cemetery. ▲

1825

Although Robert Owen's utopian community at New Harmony, Indiana, lasted only a few years, it left an enduring legacy.

New Harmony was the dream of Robert Owen, a British manufacturer and social reformer who believed that education was the cure to every social problem. An admirer of Owen predicted that the experimental community would embrace "the spirit of equality, without the smallest fear of deception, overreaching, or cheating." Beginning in April 1825, Owen attracted some 900 people to the village and the surrounding 20,000 acres he had acquired in Indiana.

At Owen's invitation, a group of educators and scientists known as the Boatload of Knowledge descended on the colony in February 1826 to help implement the utopian plan and make the village a center of advanced thought. The result was a nasty cultural clash. The Boatload people snubbed the original residents as being "rough uncouth creatures." The residents, in turn, hated the newcomers.

Owen's economic program called for a paternalistic cooperative in which laborers accumulated credits at a community-run store. The

Because of dissension, an experiment in communal living in New Harmony, Indiana, foundered within three years.

quantity of food and other supplies they were permitted to buy was based on the amount of work they performed. The founder fully intended that his "community of equality" would become financially self-sufficient.

Owen's lofty expectations were never realized, however, and in 1827 he decided that New Harmony would have to be dissolved. Some people blamed its failure on Owen's frequent absences, while others pointed to the founder's rejection of organized religion and private-property rights. Still others felt that the experiment failed because Owen did not use good judgment in recruiting members. Owen's son described the population as a "collection of radicals, enthusiastic devotees of principle . . . and lazy theorists, with a sprinkling of unprincipled sharpers thrown in."

Despite its short life span, the experiment in communal living left the United States with a rich educational heritage, the first trade school, the first free library, the first kindergarten, and the first community-supported public school in the nation. ▲

1825

Thirty-five years before the fabled Pony Express sped mail from Missouri west to California, an eastern Pony Express was inaugurated.

Established by the federal government to deliver mail along the East Coast of the United States, the eastern Pony Express served mainly newspaper editors and commodities traders who needed news in a hurry. The speedy publication of fluctuating cotton prices would end, as one newspaper editor put it, "the system of speculation which has lately been so extensively practised by individuals of one commercial town on those of another who were not possessed of the same means of information."

For about a year, from 1825 to 1826, riders delivered mail from Boston to Augusta,

Georgia. Few clients signed up, however, and service was discontinued. Then in 1836 it started up again, revitalized and expanded. Soon horseback riders were racing to and from such business centers as New York, Mobile, Charleston, and New Orleans.

Overnight delivery was not a goal of this 19th-century precursor of Express Mail. Success meant, for example, reducing the New York–New Orleans route from 13 days to 6 days. But with steamboats and railroads, the regular mail was also gaining speed and beginning to compete successfully. In 1839, after three years of operation,

the Post Office shut down the eastern Pony Express. (In contrast, the western Pony Express raced across the plains for just 18 months, from 1860 to 1861.) ▲

The eastern Pony Express delivered this unstamped letter.

Jedediah Smith, shown in South Dakota's Badlands, pushed the nation's border westward.

J 1826
Jedediah Smith was the first white man ever to enter California overland from the eastern boundary.

A hunter and trapper in the flourishing Rocky Mountain fur trade, Jedediah Smith was known for his gentlemanly demeanor, devotion to the Bible, and perhaps most of all, his courage. A story was often told of Smith's encounter with a grizzly bear that mauled him badly. Smith ordered his hunting companions to sew up the gash on his scalp and to reattach the ear that was hanging loose so that he could quickly get back to hunting.

Intending to head for California and then to Oregon to trap beaver, Smith left Utah in August 1826. He arrived in the San Bernardino Valley three arduous months later, having crossed the searing Mojave Desert on his trek from the Great Salt Lake.

Although the friars received him graciously when he arrived at the San Gabriel Mission near Los Angeles on November 26, 1826, the Mexican governor of California was less enthusiastic. The governor, perhaps wary of future invasions of his territory, ordered Smith and his hunting party to leave the region. Instead of going to hunt in Oregon, as he had planned, Smith headed northeast.

He returned to California the next year after a difficult trek across the Sierra Nevada. Although Smith lost half of his contingent in an Indian attack, he pressed on to Oregon. When Smith was killed by Indians in 1831, one admirer declared, "Among the mountain men, he stands alone."

S 1829
So many of Andrew Jackson's supporters tried to join the president at his inaugural reception that they almost destroyed the White House.

It was March 4, 1829, a clear and balmy day, as Andrew Jackson rode to his inauguration amid a "great agitated sea" of well-wishers. Tall, thin, and dignified, the war hero was sworn in by Chief Justice John Marshall. After this solemn moment the time for celebration was at hand, and what a celebration it was! Jackson, on horseback, led a crowd of some 20,000 from the Capitol to the White House. For days people had been streaming into Washington in anticipation. When hotels and boardinghouses ran out of rooms, Jackson's supporters slept on floors or even on billiard tables.

What had been planned as a modest reception suddenly turned into bedlam. Men with muddy boots stood on satin-upholstered chairs just to catch a glimpse of the president. Eager to shake hands with "Old Hickory," hundreds of people surged forward. Jackson was practically "pressed to death and almost suffocated and torn to pieces," according to one onlooker.

Food spilled, glasses shattered, and fights broke out. Although Jackson managed to escape through a back entrance when some friends formed a phalanx around him and shepherded him to a nearby hotel, the mob continued to enjoy itself, eating, drinking, and perpetuating mayhem. A congressman described the gathering as "one uninterrupted stream of mud and filth." Not until some clever person thought of moving the punch and ice cream out to the lawn did the rampage come to an end.

The rowdy festivities marked the dawn of a new era — the beginning of a populist, democratic government. Indeed, as contemporary sages put it: "It was the People's day, and the People's President, and the People would rule."

IN THEIR OWN WORDS

“After a dignified, sweeping bow, the President commenced his address. His manner was simple and emphatic. His voice was distinct and audible at a considerable distance. The address being finished, another acclamation rent the air. There was now a general rush among the foremost to reach the President's hand. But his Excellency, withdrawing into the Capitol with his suite, the crowd was soon seen moving down the Avenue towards the President's house. . . . High and low, old and young, black and white, poured in one solid column into this spacious mansion. Here was the corpulent epicure grunting and sweating for breath — the dandy wishing he had no toes — the tight-laced Miss, fearing her person might receive some permanently deforming impulse — the miser hunting for his pocketbook — the courtier looking for his watch — and the office-seeker in an agony to reach the President.”

A newspaper account of Andrew Jackson's inauguration, March 4, 1829.

THE NATION GROWS
(1830 TO 1860)

Industrialization, westward expansion, and immigration transformed the United States during the middle decades of the 19th century. In 1830 most artisans and craftsmen— furniture makers, shoemakers, butchers, coopers, and blacksmiths — were self-employed, producing their wares in their own shops. Then in the 1830's and 1840's, competition forced artisans to reduce costs by parceling out relatively simple tasks to low-paid unskilled workers. Shoemakers, for example, sent out the tops and soles to women who, working at home, would sew them together into shoes. Eventually, manufacturers gathered the piece-work laborers under one roof, creating factories.

The evolution from craft shop to factory floor took place first in northern port cities like New York and Philadelphia. By 1850 in Philadelphia, only 1 in 10 workers still labored in artisan shops; most wage earners toiled in factories producing clothes, tools, machines, and other goods.

Similar changes were transforming rural areas. In 1830 most farmers were self-employed and self-sufficient. Sons helped their fathers raise crops and tend livestock, while mothers and daughters cooked and preserved food, tended gardens, and made clothes. But after 1830 this independent life became harder to sustain. As settlement became denser and land costlier, families wanting to give children a good start in life had to raise more cash to buy them farms of their own. An economic boom in the early 1830's ran headlong into a financial panic in 1837, followed by a national depression in the early 1840's. Many young adults found that emigration was the only way to obtain land.

AMERICANS HEADED WEST by the thousands, pouring
into Ohio, Indiana, Illinois, and into territories that soon became states: Michigan in 1837, Iowa in 1846, and Wisconsin in 1848. One out of three people born in Connecticut and New Hampshire had left home by 1860, most of them going west. Southerners generally aimed for slave states such as Alabama, Louisiana, and Arkansas — but not always. In the free state of Indiana, more than 40 percent of all residents in 1850 were from the South.

Native Americans also joined the exodus, though not by choice. The U.S. government forcibly expelled them from their lands in the East. Before the 1830's, the federal government had recognized Indian tribes as sovereign nations; their members lacked citizenship, but at least they controlled their own affairs. Then, in 1831, the Supreme Court declared Indians to be "domestic dependents" with no right to sue in Federal court. When the government decided to expel the so-called Five Civilized Tribes from their ancestral lands in the Southeast, they had no legal basis to resist. Nearly 4,000 Cherokees died on the Trail of Tears in the mid 1830's, trudging west beyond the Mississippi River to Indian Territory in present-day Oklahoma. Casualties among the Seminoles, Choctaws, Creeks, and Chickasaws were equally horrifying. The estimated 100 million acres that Native Americans surrendered opened the entire Mississippi Valley to white settlement.

In settling the West, developers often got there first.

The Western states soon became a prosperous region of commercial farming. The bustling demand of textile factories in England and New England drove up the price of cotton. Settlers in Western slave states turned former Indian lands into cotton plantations. Migrants to Western free states transformed the prairies into a corn belt, and sold their produce to Southern planters, who used it to feed slaves.

It took a vast transportation network to carry Southern cotton to Northeastern factories, Western foodstuffs to Southern plantations, and goods manufactured in the Northeast across the nation. The United States built more than 2,000 miles of canals in the 1830's; but railroads were already overtaking canals. The nation had 3,328 miles of railbeds in 1840, mostly in the Atlantic states. By 1860, a latticework of some 30,000 miles of iron rails stretched over the Appalachians into the West.

The revolution in transportation created new cities and new industries. Chicago, Minneapolis, Des Moines, and St. Louis sprang up where rivers converged or emptied into lakes. Old cities grew also, as canals and railroads connected them to rural hinterlands. Railroad construction, along with new agricultural machines, such as Cyrus McCormick's grain reaper and John Deere's steel-faced plow, increased the demand for iron. In no time, iron forges and factories sprang up throughout the country.

This frenetic economic activity reflected a burgeoning population. Between 1820 and 1860, New York City grew from 124,000 people to 1,080,000; Philadelphia, from 113,000 to 566,000; New Orleans, from 27,000 to 169,000. High wages in these port cities attracted thousands of immigrants, many fleeing famine in Ireland and repression in Germany. Some 400,000 newcomers disembarked in New York in 1855 alone. The nation's population rocketed upward from 9.6 million in 1820 to 31.4 million in 1860.

As The Nation Grew in size and industrial might, it

began to develop a unique, particularly American national culture. Writers like Nathaniel Hawthorne, Ralph Waldo Emerson, Walt Whitman, Henry David Thoreau, and Herman Melville celebrated the dignity of the common man. At the same time, many citizens began to question whether the United States was living up to its ideals as the world's first modern democracy.

In the North, a fledgling labor movement struggled for better wages and the right to organize. The federal government used force in a labor dispute for the first time in 1834, when President Andrew Jackson sent troops to subdue angry canal workers. But labor won a critical victory in 1842, when the Massachusetts Supreme

Irish and German immigrants were sometimes accused of rigging big-city elections.

Court declared trade unions and strikes by labor to be lawful.

Several crusades that had originated in the 1820's began producing concrete results. The temperance movement flourished, and by 1835 some 5,000 antidrinking societies claimed 1 million members. Public education spread as states in the Midwest established common schools. At Seneca Falls, New York, several hundred proudly determined women gathered in 1848 to declare that "all men and women are created equal" — and thus lay the foundations of the nation's first women's rights crusade.

No cause loomed larger in American political life than the movement to abolish slavery. England had long since outlawed the trade in human lives at home and in its Caribbean colonies. In the United States, most Northerners considered slavery a disgrace, especially in the "land of the free," where all men are created equal. But in the South, the "peculiar institution," as people called it, was the basis of social and economic life.

Henry Ward Beecher, fiery abolitionist parson.

The anti-slavery campaign took on new militancy on January 1, 1831, when Boston abolitionist William Lloyd Garrison published the first issue of his inflammatory *Liberator*. The Reverend Henry Ward Beecher condemned the institution from his pulpit in Brooklyn, New York. Former slaves like Frederick Douglass and Harriet Tubman gained national fame through their writings and lectures. In 1835 the American Anti-Slavery Society, the nation's first organized group to demand abolition, began operation. Abolitionists hoped that their appeals to conscience would awaken Americans to the need to end both slavery and racial discrimination.

The movement provoked violent opposition — beginning, oddly enough, in the North. Mobs attacked anti-slavery meetings and rampaged through neighborhoods where free blacks lived. In 1837 abolitionist editor Elijah Lovejoy was murdered in Alton, Illinois. The earliest battles between pro-slavery and anti-slavery forces took place in Northern cities.

Opponents of slavery disagreed about what should — or could — be done. Some argued for swift and total abolition. Others, hoping to prevent further violence, wanted to start by forbidding slavery in the new territories. Still others believed that Americans faced a clear-cut choice: either slavery must go, or the United States would not survive as one nation. Given the alternative, they opted for Union.

In the slave states, attitudes steadily hardened. Although only one in four Southerners owned slaves, many believed that abolition would destroy the very fabric of society. Moreover, blacks outnumbered whites in some locales, causing Southerners to fear a slave rebellion. In 1831 Nat Turner, a Virginia slave, led a two-day rampage in which about 70 whites were killed.

Early defenders of slavery had often stressed economic necessity. Later the arguments became more stridently racist, based on the supposed inferiority of blacks. Indeed, some slaveholders claimed that slaves were incapable of surviving without a master's benevolent protection. This view of slavery was self-serving and contradictory, but it persuaded Southerners that the South was a unique society with its own values and virtues.

DESPITE THE GROWING polarization between North and South, the nation had a vibrant two-party system that cut across sectional lines. In 1834 an uneasy coalition of Northern businessmen, evangelical Christians, and Southern planters and merchants formed the Whig Party. Its main source of unity was a shared dislike of Jacksonian Democrats; the Whigs also joined in support of a national bank, tariffs to protect industry in the North, and prison and education reforms. The Whigs ran candidates in five national elections and won twice, with two war heros: William Henry Harrison in 1840, and Zachary Taylor in 1848.

Politicians such as Sen. Henry Clay of Kentucky searched tirelessly for compromises that might help resolve the conflicting demands of both sides. Others, like John C. Calhoun of South

Log cabin miniatures helped send W. H. Harrison to the White House.

An enamel pin depicts Henry Clay, the Great Compromiser.

Carolina, took increasingly rigid stands.

Reacting to the Whig-imposed tariffs of 1828 and 1832, Calhoun developed the notion of "nullification." He pointed out that the tariffs discriminated against the South by raising the cost of its imports while at the same time protecting Northern manufacturers. Faced with this kind of treatment, he argued, a state could disregard, or "nullify," any federal law it opposed. When President Jackson threatened to collect tariffs by military force, if necessary, Calhoun argued for a state's right to secede from the Union.

Calhoun eventually backed down. But the fateful issues of states' rights and secession had entered the political arena.

WEST OF MISSISSIPPI the nation acquired vast new territories. American settlers in Texas, having battled to free the region from Mexico, joined the Union in 1845. The following year President James K. Polk pressured Great Britain into ceding the Oregon Country below the 49th Parallel, and also provoked a controversial war to acquire more land from Mexico. In 1848 the defeated Mexicans ceded the huge expanse between Texas, Oregon, and the Pacific Ocean. The Garsden Purchase of 1853 added land south to the Rio Grande. The country now stretched from sea to sea.

Americans generally supported expansion, believing it was their "manifest destiny" to occupy the entire North American continent. Many traveled along the Oregon, Santa Fe, and California trails, hurrying west to carve out homesteads in the new territories. Mormons, led by Brigham Young, moved to what they considered their Promised Land in Utah Territory. After gold was discovered in California in 1848, tens of thousands rushed to the West Coast.

As each new territory filled with settlers and applied for statehood, the nation's basic political dispute erupted anew: would the territory enter the Union as a slave state or a free one? Pro-slavery forces had spent nine years trying to win statehood for Texas. They succeeded in 1945 when President-elect Polk proposed a way to bypass the two-thirds majority required for Senate approval.

"FACTORY GIRL"

THE NEXT BATTLE began when California applied to join the Union. Only a carefully engineered set of trade-offs, known as the Compromise of 1850, resolved the crisis. The compromise included these provisions: California would join as a free state; the slave trade, but not slavery, would be outlawed in Washington, D.C.; the Fugitive Slave Law would be strengthened to facilitate the capture of runaways; the status of slavery in Utah and New Mexico would be determined by "popular sovereignty" — meaning settlers would decide for themselves.

Opponents of slavery condemned what they called a capitulation. They feared that popular sovereignty would open the way for the unchecked spread of slavery, even to territories established as free in the Missouri Compromise of 1820. Just four years later, they were proved right.

In 1854 Senator Stephen A. Douglas of Illinois proposed creating two territories, Kansas and Nebraska, north of the Missouri Compromise line: popular sovereignty would decide the slavery question in each one. So Congress passed the Kansas-Nebraska Act. Even before the act was signed, thousands of armed Missourians began crossing into Kansas. They helped set up an illegitimate pro-slavery government, based on the outcome of an election in which a small minority of voters cast ballots, most of which were fraudulent. Anti-slavery settlers, who made up the true majority, then installed a rival government of their own. Fighting broke out. By 1856, the troubled land had earned the name "Bleeding Kansas."

The Kansas-Nebraska Act tore the Whigs apart and gave rise to the Republican party. Its commitment to prohibiting slavery in the territories was a rallying point for Whigs, Democrats, and a group known as Free Soilers, who were dedicated to free labor, not slavery,

To abolitionists, the slave trade was the ultimate human outrage.

in the territories. The Kansas-Nebraska Act only deepened the chasm between advocates and enemies of slavery throughout the United States. Southerners talked more frequently of a separate nation. Some abolitionists hoped for a slave uprising. One of them, the zealot John Brown, seized the U.S. armory at Harper's Ferry (now in West Virginia) in 1859. His plan for a black revolt failed completely, to be sure. But after he was captured, tried, and hanged, he was hailed as an anti-slavery martyr.

Poet Walt Whitman, shown here late in life, celebrated freedom.

The pro-slavery U.S. Supreme Court also played a part in escalating tensions. In *Dred Scott* v. *Sandford,* the Court declared the Missouri Compromise unconstitutional. It decided that Congress could not deprive a citizen of property anywhere in the United States — and slaves were property. The 1857 decision enraged opponents of slavery.

ABRAHAM LINCOLN, a former Whig, came to national attention in 1858 when, as the Republican candidate for the Senate from Illinois, he debated Stephen Douglas, the powerful Democratic incumbent. Lincoln proved himself an eloquent spokesman for the middle ground between the radical and moderate wings of the Republican party: while denying that he sought social equality for black people, he insisted that slavery was morally wrong and should not expand into the new territories. Douglas won the election, but it was increasingly clear that his policy of popular sovereignty satisfied neither supporters nor opponents of slavery.

Lincoln and Douglas faced each other again in the presidential campaign of 1860. Douglas's chances looked bleak because the Democratic party had split into two contending factions. Southerners ran their own candidate, John C. Breckinridge, who called for protecting slavery. Since Breckinridge had no chance of winning, Southerners readied themselves for Lincoln. For most, this meant preparing to leave the Union. When Lincoln arrived in Washington for his inauguration on March 4, 1861, seven Southern states had already seceded. The Union no longer existed.

1830

The male publisher of *Godey's Lady's Book*, the preeminent women's magazine of the 19th century, banned any mention of the wrenching political turmoil that culminated in the Civil War.

Pledging to bring "unalloyed pleasure to the female mind," Louis Godey launched his monthly magazine, *Lady's Book* (later renamed *Godey's Lady's Book*) in July 1830. Godey and his editor, Sarah Josepha Hale, offered poetry, fiction, and essays, as well as tips on housekeeping, health (get plenty of fresh air, play archery and croquet), and fashion. The formula for a women's periodical proved to be a successful one: by 1858 its circulation had reached some 150,000, an amazingly large readership for the time.

Controversial or racy topics were taboo for the magazine. Mrs. Hale, the author of the children's poem "Mary Had a Little Lamb," took care not to shock readers by mentioning anything as indelicate as the word breast. Even if the offending body part belonged to a chicken or a turkey, the word bosom was substituted.

Discussion of politics was strictly off-limits, for Godey believed that the "fairest portion of creation" had no interest in such topics. As a result, Union and Confederate soldiers on the front lines who obtained copies could read about homemaking and child care but

Fashions for July 1842.

not about the Civil War — the magazine never mentioned the conflict.

Fearing that men would not be attracted to women who wanted the right to vote, Mrs. Hale did not support women's suffrage, but she did launch crusades for causes that would ease women's financial difficulties. These included creating a fund for widows of lost seamen and a campaign to broaden educational options for women so that they could be self-supporting. 🐃

The July 1842 issue of *Godey's Lady's Book* featured the latest fashions.

1830

If evangelist Charles G. Finney had followed his first instinct, he never would have started the great religious revival in Rochester, New York.

Presbyterian evangelist Charles G. Finney had just turned down a post as a pastor in Rochester, New York, because the ministry there was mired in a bitter squabble. Then, ashamed at his reluctance to take on a challenge, he decided to accept.

Finney's change of heart produced one of the most dramatic religious revivals in 19th-century America. Between September 10, 1830, and March 6, 1831, the inexhaustible minister preached 98 sermons, sometimes three in a day.

Some revival meetings lasted from 6 A.M. to the late evening. On one occasion, so many people packed into a church that the building shifted under their weight, and the fear of its imminent collapse set off a stampede of fleeing worshipers.

Finney, who had practiced law before his own conversion, pioneered a technique that came to be known as the "anxious seat." Clearing some benches in the front of the church, the minister would ask all those who were willing to accept his message to come for-

ward "and offer themselves up to God, while we make them subjects of prayer."

The high point of the service would arrive when occupants of the anxious seats declared their renewed faith. Their public testaments had, Finney observed, a very good effect on the rest of the congregation. Some observers did object to his changing a private spiritual experience into a public spectacle, however.

Finney's impact on daily life extended well beyond the church services. High school classes were interrupted during the day for prayer sessions. Businesses closed early so that tradesmen could return home to pray with their families. Fired with religious zeal, residents embraced a temperance campaign so enthusiastically that many liquor-store owners emptied their stock into the Erie Canal.

Before long, new converts had joined churches of all denominations in Rochester and towns up to 100 miles away. Indeed, Finney's success in upstate New York touched off a religious awakening that spread throughout the United States. 🐃

The impact of Finney's sermons in upstate New York was felt nationwide.

1830

The Bowie knife proved such a lethal weapon that some states actually outlawed it.

Jim Bowie, the epitome of the rough-hewn fighter and inventor of the Bowie knife, didn't like to see a lady treated discourteously. So when a male smoker on a stagecoach refused a female passenger's request to put out his pipe, Bowie placed his enormous knife blade at the man's throat. The pipe was quickly extinguished.

Bowie designed his namesake weapon after he had cut himself with a knife during a fight. It had a heavy curved blade, like a butcher knife, which was honed razor sharp to a double-edged point; in some versions the blade measured up to 15 inches long. With a handle of wood or bone and a heavy brass handguard, the knife was perfectly balanced. It could be used to stab, slash, and chop, and it could be thrown with deadly precision. In 1830 Bowie gave his knife to an Arkansas blacksmith to copy, and the design quickly became a favorite of adventurers. A skilled fighter could hurl the "Arkansas toothpick" faster than he could reload his rifle.

"Use a Bowie and save ammunition" went one boastful bit of frontier wisdom. No one used the knife better than Bowie himself, right up to the moment of his death at the Alamo in 1836. Bedridden from typhoid pneumonia, Bowie is said to have lifted himself from his cot to stab Mexican soldiers to death before he was killed himself.

This version of the Bowie knife has a scooped-out curve on its upper edge.

IN THEIR OWN WORDS

The house was very much packed, filled to its utmost capacity in every part. . . . I heard something which I supposed to be the report of a gun, and the jingling of glass as if a window had been broken by it. . . . The congregation in a moment fell into a perfect panic, and rushed for the doors and the windows as if they were all distracted. One elderly lady held up a window in the rear of the church, where several, as I was informed, leapt out into the canal. The rush was terrific. Some jumped over the galleries into the aisles below. . . . Some of them had their dresses torn off around near the bottom; and bonnets, shawls, gloves, handkerchiefs, and parts of dresses were scattered in every direction.

A description of the near collapse of a church during one of Charles Finney's sermons.

1831

John Quincy Adams did something no president before or since has ever done after leaving the White House: he served as a U.S. congressman.

After Andrew Jackson defeated incumbent John Quincy Adams in the 1828 presidential election, Adams's political career seemed at an end. He returned home to Quincy, Massachusetts, where to his astonishment he found that his neighbors wanted him to run for the House of Representatives. Adams rejected the notion that serving in the House was beneath the dignity of a former president: "No person could be degraded by serving the people as a Representative to Congress."

Winning a Congressional seat, Adams returned to Washington in December 1831. Sen. Henry Clay warned Adams, who was then 64 years old, that he would find the workload demanding. "I well know this," he responded, "but labor I shall not refuse so long as my hands, my eyes, and my brain do not desert me."

For nearly a decade, Adams championed the antislavery cause, speaking out so forcefully that he won the nickname Old Man Eloquent. His argument that the government had a right to free slaves in wartime provided a legal foundation for the Emancipation Proclamation.

Adams's career ended on February 21, 1848, when, still fighting against slavery, he collapsed of a stroke in the House. He was carried to the speaker's room, where he died two days later. In tribute, one admirer asked, "Where could death have found him but at the post of duty?"

Fellow congressmen try to aid John Quincy Adams, who suffered a stroke at his desk.

W *1831*
illiam Lloyd Garrison was the first newspaper editor in America to call for an immediate end to slavery.

The firebrand founder of the *Liberator,* William Lloyd Garrison, assured his readers in the first issue, on January 1, 1831: "I will not equivocate — I will not excuse — . . . and I will be heard. The apathy of the people is enough to make every statue leap from its pedestal, and to hasten the resurrection of the dead." Indeed, Garrison made himself heard: he awakened a nation's conscience and turned the abolitionist movement into a crusade. He fumed over what he perceived as indifference to the slavery question in the North.

Garrison aimed his fierce criticism not only at slave owners but at those abolitionists who favored ending slavery gradually. His hatred of the institution evolved directly from Garrison's conviction that slavery violated God's law. "It was not on account of your complexion or race, as a people, that I espoused your cause, but because you were the children of a common Father, created in the same divine image," he told a meeting of blacks in 1865.

The *Liberator* attracted attention far beyond its modest-size audience, which was comprised mostly of free blacks in the North. The publication gained notoriety when Southerners attacked the paper as an instigator of insurrection, and some even offered a reward to anyone who would arrest Garrison.

Threats to Garrison's life and property didn't slow his printing press.

The crusading New England editor shrugged off threats and insults. "Hisses are music to my ears," he once remarked. Garrison kept publishing the *Liberator* until 1865, when the country finally accomplished the goal he had been seeking: passage of the 13th Amendment, which abolished slavery.

B *1831*
efore Edgar Allan Poe enjoyed any fame for his mastery of the macabre, he found himself court-martialed and dismissed from West Point.

Penniless and alone, Edgar Allan Poe enrolled at West Point out of desperation. He thought that graduating from the academy would earn him the respect of his foster father, who had repeatedly rejected him, and would provide the income with which he could someday launch a writing career.

Poe had already served with distinction in the U.S. Army for two years when, at the age of 21, he won admission to the military academy. Arriving at West Point in June 1830, he discovered that the regimen was much more rigorous than he had expected.

The workday began at 5:30 A.M. Much of the routine was monotonous or grueling. During artillery drills, for example, the cadets were strapped into leather harnesses so that they could pull heavy guns.

Excelling in his studies, particularly mathematics and French, Poe also enjoyed entertaining classmates with satirical verses that mocked his professors. But it was clear that he was not cut out for the military.

Poe read voraciously, wrote poetry, and drank excessively. As one of his fellow cadets noted: "His great fault was his neglect of and apparent contempt for military duties. His wayward and capricious temper made him at

Poe's refusal to abide by the rules earned him a court-martial.

times utterly oblivious or indifferent to the ordinary routine of roll-call, drills, and guard duties."

When he enrolled, Poe had assumed that he could breeze through the academy and become a lieutenant in six months, instead of the standard four years. Realizing his mistake after several months, he decided to withdraw from West Point. His foster father refused to allow it, however, and without his consent, Poe was stuck there. So the unhappy cadet engineered his dismissal by refusing to take part in military formations. A court-martial was held on January 28, 1831, and on March 6 he was discharged from military service.

Although Poe was regarded as a loner, his satires were so popular with his classmates that he persuaded many of them to contribute funds for a book he was writing. Believing that Poe would publish cutting satires of the military academy, many of his fellow cadets contributed 75 cents each, for a total of $170.

Instead of the expected collection of biting humor, the book that Poe published was a volume of poetry. His classmates' reaction was "a general expression of disgust," but the future author of such haunting poems as "The Raven" and "Annabel Lee," and the father of American detective fiction, had at last found his real calling.

1831

Frenchman Alexis de Tocqueville used the excuse of studying prisons in the United States to view democracy in action. His book of insights and criticism became a classic.

When Alexis de Tocqueville arrived in the United States in May 1831, his official mission was to report on the American prison system to the French minister of justice. But the real impetus for the 25-year-old Frenchman was the chance to educate himself about the U.S. political system and to report on it to his countrymen.

Along with Gustave de Beaumont, a friend and fellow magistrate, Tocqueville covered 7,000 miles in nine months, traveling by stagecoach, on horseback, and by boat. When he returned to France, Tocqueville began work on his two-volume *Democracy in America*, one of the most perceptive books ever written about this country.

Looking ahead, Tocqueville predicted that dissension over slavery would lead to a civil war and that competition would arise between the United States and Russia for world dominance. He also studied grassroots political organizations and the relationship between government and religion.

Tocqueville had some reservations about democracy, sus-

Beaumont made sketches as he traveled the country with Tocqueville.

pecting that majority rule would lead to mediocrity and to what he called, in one of his most famous phrases, the "tyranny of the majority." He had faith in the good sense of ordinary citizens — but not in their leaders.

"I was surprised to find so much distinguished talent among the subjects and so little among the heads of government," he wrote. "It is a constant fact that, at the present day, the ablest men in the United States are rarely placed at the head of affairs."

Moving from the political to the personal, Tocqueville praised Americans as hardworking but found them incredibly greedy: "I know of no country, indeed, where love of money has taken a stronger hold on the affections of men." *Democracy in America* was published in Paris and translated into English in 1835.

An ad for McCormick's reaper showed endless fields of golden grain.

1831

The invention of the McCormick reaper not only opened the way for America's expansion westward but indirectly catapulted Abraham Lincoln to the presidency.

Schoolchildren singing "America the Beautiful" praise "amber waves of grain," but without Cyrus McCormick's reaper, those vast fields of ripening grain throughout the Midwest would never have been harvested. And without McCormick's ongoing legal battles to protect his patent, attorney Abraham Lincoln might have had to forgo important speaking dates. One of Lincoln's clients was a competitor who was waging a patent war against McCormick. Lincoln used the $1,000 he earned in fighting his client's suit to underwrite his debates with Stephen Douglas, debates that helped lead to his election in 1860.

McCormick understood the need for a time- and labor-saving reaper, since his father was one of many who had tried to develop a harvesting machine. In July 1831 the 22-year-old McCormick demonstrated his first horse-drawn reaper, then spent several years working on the design. In 1847 he began making reapers in a factory in Chicago, which helped transform that small Midwestern town into one of the nation's major grain shipment centers.

IN THEIR OWN WORDS

An American attends to his private concerns as if he were alone in the world, and the next minute he gives himself up to the common weal as if he had forgotten them. At one time, he seems animated by the most selfish cupidity; at another, by the most lively patriotism. The human heart cannot be thus divided. The inhabitants of the United States alternately display so strong and so similar a passion for their own welfare and for their freedom, that it may be supposed that these passions are united and mingled in some part of their character. And indeed, the Americans believe their freedom to be the best instrument and surest safeguard of their welfare: they are attached to the one by the other.

Alexis de Tocqueville describes the American character in Democracy in America, *published in 1835.*

1832

Treating victims of the first cholera epidemic in the United States, doctors prescribed everything from electric shock to calomel, a mercury compound that often made the symptoms worse.

In June 1832 an Irish immigrant living in New York City developed diarrhea, vomiting, and cramps. Soon his wife and children fell ill. Within a week the entire family had succumbed, becoming some of the first victims of cholera in the United States.

Doctors recognized the classic symptoms of the acute diarrheal disorder that had recently arrived in Western Europe from India, where it had been a scourge for centuries. American medical experts had watched with apprehension as the devastation struck Russia, France, Germany, and then Great Britain.

Afraid of inducing panic, the New York City Board of Health tried to keep the first cholera fatalities a secret, but to no avail. What was all too apparent was that a person who was healthy in the morning

This cartoon warns of filthy water.

could be dead by nightfall. Doctors prescribed such useless antidotes as electric shock, the purgative calomel, arsenic, phosphorus, rhubarb, and other substances that often made the symptoms worse.

Ignorance about cholera's cause intensified the hysteria. Some believed that the contagion was airborne, while others saw it as a punishment for what they considered the vices associated with poverty: cholera most often developed in the poorest neighborhoods.

The disease traveled rapidly, killing 5,000 in New Orleans and thousands more in St. Louis. Mercifully, by the late summer of 1832, the worst was over, although outbreaks occurred for several years. It was not until the mid-1850's that a British doctor discovered that cholera is spread through sewage-contaminated drinking water. This led to improved sanitation, clean water supplies, and public health laws. Finally, in 1883, scientists identified the bacteria that causes the disease. 🐃

1832

Sam Houston's career in public office straddled four sovereign entities: the United States, Mexico, the Republic of Texas, and, very briefly, the Confederate States of America.

By the time he rode into Texas to negotiate with Indian chiefs in December 1832, 39-year-old Sam Houston had already amassed an amazing record. In 1814 he had fought with Gen. Andrew Jackson against the Creeks. Switching from the military life to politics, he won elections as attorney general of Tennessee in 1819, as congressman in 1823, and as governor in 1827. Standing six feet two inches tall, the courageous, quick-tempered Houston was given to baring his battle-scarred chest and proclaiming himself "a humble republican soldier who wears his decorations here!"

At the age of 17, Houston had left home and lived with the Cherokees for three years. He went back to the tribe in 1829, when his bride of three months abruptly left him; he stayed with them for another three years, marrying a Cherokee and drowning his troubles in drink.

When President Jackson needed someone to negotiate a settlement between the Comanches and Cherokees in Texas, he turned to Houston. Texas was still officially

A wounded Sam Houston accepts the surrender of General Santa Anna at San Jacinto.

part of Mexico, and Houston arrived in 1832 to find a spirit of revolution brewing.

Four years later Texas declared its independence, and Houston was chosen to command the new republic's armed forces. He led them to victory in 1836 at the Battle of San Jacinto, crushing a Mexican force in just under 20 minutes.

Twice elected president of the Texas Republic, Houston later served as the state's first U.S. senator and then as its governor on the eve of the Civil War. When Texans voted to secede from the Union in 1861, Houston, who had fought to prevent that outcome, refused to join the Confederacy and was deposed from office. 🐃

A 1833 shortage of carpenters, an abundance of mass-produced nails, and an innovative "balloon frame" building skeleton ushered in a new age of urban architecture.

Until the 1830's home building in America relied on labor-intensive English techniques that had changed little since the Middle Ages. Heavy foot-square beams were joined with wooden pegs and then hoisted into place. Such structures, though sturdy, were relatively expensive, and specialized carpentry skills were needed for their construction. For a rapidly growing country, where there was plenty of wood but not enough carpenters to go around, these structures took too long to build.

Two developments made possible the dramatic, rapid advance in home construction known as "balloon framing": cheap, machine-made nails and the smaller cuts of lumber produced by the steam-driven circular saw.

Easy-to-build balloon-frame houses helped settlers cope with a chronic shortage of skilled carpenters.

Debuting in Chicago, balloon frames used the modern truss system of studs — mostly two-by-fours — nailed together in a basketlike skeleton and faced with brick, stucco, or clapboard. St. Mary's Catholic Church in Chicago was probably the first such structure. It was built in three months in 1833 for approximately $400. Traditional building methods would have cost twice as much and taken twice as long.

Although critics scoffed at these supposedly flimsy structures, the houses proved inexpensive, easy to build, and rugged, too. What's more, almost anyone with a saw, hammer, nails, and a set of plans could build one. And they were easy to transport — owners could literally pick up and move, taking their houses apart and reassembling them at a new site.

In Chicago more than 600 balloon frames were erected in 1833, with an average construction time of one week. Within 20 years these houses dominated the Western urban landscape. "If it had not been for the knowledge of balloon-frames," said one newspaper editor, "Chicago and San Francisco could never have arisen, as they did, from little villages to great cities in a single year."

A 1834 s the demand for beaver-skin top hats vanished, so did the era of the swashbuckling mountain man.

For a quarter of a century, hardy, self-sufficient men had ranged through the Rocky Mountain wilderness, trapping beavers for pelts, the "soft brown gold" prized by clothiers.

In 1834, for the first time in a decade, the trappers' annual summer rendezvous found the mountain men complaining of a dismal catch. Meanwhile, hats produced from imported Chinese silk had begun replacing beaver hats in the well-dressed man's wardrobe.

Seeing the handwriting on the wall, millionaire John Jacob Astor, owner of the hugely successful American Fur Company, sold his business in June 1834. Soon another major fur company shut down when the year's fur harvest was too skimpy to cover expenses.

Without the big commercial outfits, individual traders and trappers engaged in cutthroat competition, cheating each other and angling for control of

Changes in the fur trade forced mountain men out of the Rockies.

fur trapping in the Rockies. "There is here a great collection of scoundrels," muttered one trader as he left the summer rendezvous. By 1840 many trappers had become buffalo hunters, trading-post managers, or wagon train scouts.

IN THEIR OWN WORDS

> If movement and the quick succession of sensations and ideas constitute life, here one lives a hundred fold more than elsewhere; all is here circulation, motion, and boiling agitation. Experiment follows experiment; enterprise succeeds to enterprise.... Riches and poverty follow on each other's traces.... Fortunes last for a season: reputations, during the twinkling of an eye. An irresistible current sweeps away everything, grinds everything to powder, and deposits it again under new forms. Men change their houses ... their party, their sect; the States change their laws, their officers, their constitutions.

Frenchman Michel Chevalier marvels at the American lifestyle on a visit in 1834.

A fake banknote (top) and a real one issued during the Panic of 1837; the two sides of an 1835 coin.

1835

For the first and only time in its history, the United States erased its national debt.

Enriched by the sale of public lands and revenue from the Tariff of 1833, which taxed imported goods, the federal government managed to pay off its debt completely — making the United States the only major nation in modern history to accomplish this extraordinary feat. In January 1835 the national debt was a big, round zero.

During the boom years from 1835 to 1837, the government found itself in the embarrassing position of running a substantial surplus, with a great deal of money still pouring in. Unable to spend it fast enough, Congress in 1836 decided to turn over the riches — some $28 million — to the states.

Most of the money went to railroad, highway, and canal construction, stimulating an economy already overheated by cheap money, easy credit, and a speculative exuberance. In the meantime, Congress did little to interfere; indeed, many members were only too happy to join the speculators who were buying up thousands of acres of Western land, anticipating huge profits.

Alas, the wheel of prosperity turned all too quickly. As President Andrew Jackson watched the nation's acreage being converted to banknotes, he became increasingly concerned. Jackson had always distrusted paper currency, which he felt had no intrinsic value, and toward the end of his presidency he issued a directive that only gold and silver coinage, or notes backed by gold or silver, could be used to buy federal lands.

Jackson's aim was to cool the engines of speculation; instead, he brought the economy to a crashing halt as investors raced to withdraw their funds from banks. In the ensuing financial panic, hundreds of banks and businesses went broke, and the United States suffered its worst depression to date. The boom had gone resoundingly bust, and by 1838 America had rejoined the ranks of debtor nations.

1835

In Vicksburg, Mississippi, honest citizens rose in revolt and chased the gamblers out of town.

With the advent of steam-powered boats on the Mississippi River, gambling began to flourish both on shore and on riverboats. By July 1835 the full-time card cheats who inhabited the riverside city of Vicksburg, Mississippi, had exhausted the patience of decent townsfolk. After a series of confrontations and the suspicious disappearance of a wealthy young planter who had patronized a gambling house, the town issued a decree: Anyone who couldn't prove he made his living honestly must leave within 24 hours or suffer 39 lashes at the public whipping post. Although most of the town's 200 sharpsters promptly fled, five of them refused to budge. When a scuffle broke out and a citizen was killed, the five miscreants were dragged to a gallows and hanged on the spot.

The Vicksburg revolt dampened the atmosphere of lawlessness in towns up and down the Mississippi for a time, but by the early 1840's, gambling was thriving again both on land and on the river. The more elaborate boats, virtually floating palaces, carried land speculators, wealthy planters, and other potential victims. During the heyday of gambling in the 1850's, an estimated 2,000 full-time card cheats preyed on travelers on the river between St. Louis and New Orleans.

Despite popular portrayals of the professional gambler as an elegant dandy who flaunted a gold watch and diamond jewelry, the reality was usually plainer. Con men were more likely than not to wear dirty clothes and appear disheveled. Most of them blended in with the crowd, some posing as tradesmen, farmers, and even clergymen.

Often the scam artists worked in pairs, boarding boats at different stops and pretending to meet one another for the first time over the

Riverboat gamblers played Crown and Anchor with this game set.

poker table or at a "harmless" game of three-card monte. Falling into their trap could be an expensive — even deadly — proposition. More than one passenger who made the mistake of protesting his losses was never heard from again. Some people who suddenly discovered that they were penniless pitched themselves overboard in despair. As one sharpster later recalled: "A sucker had no more chance against those fellows than a snowball in a red-hot oven."

W *1835* **ith pomp and ceremony, the first railroad train to enter Washington, D.C., marked a transportation milestone.**

The first scheduled passenger train to pull into the nation's capital, the pride of the Baltimore and Ohio Railroad, arrived just after noon on August 25, 1835. Drawn by four upright boiler engines named George Washington, John Adams, Thomas Jefferson, and James Madison, 17 cars of invited guests, including the governor of Maryland and members of the legislature, left Baltimore just after 9 A.M.

Stopping in Bladensburg, Maryland, where other officials met the procession, the trains continued on to Washington.

Guests on the first passenger train to Washington received a rousing welcome.

Cannons roared in greeting, and thousands of people turned out to witness their arrival — among them President Andrew Jackson, his cabinet, and a legion of other dignitaries.

A military band led a parade to two hotels, where the hon-ored guests celebrated at banquets. At 4:30 P.M. the travelers left the Washington Depot for the 2-hour, 20-minute journey back to Baltimore. Regular passenger service was soon underway between the two cities.

In the next few years, special excursion trips marked the opening of each new rail line throughout the country. On these highly publicized inaugural voyages, well-wishers lined the tracks to get a glimpse of this novel mode of transportation. As one early passenger on the Baltimore and Ohio Railroad noted, "It is enough to excite a special wonder to behold a row of long houses roaring along the road, borne at the rate of thirty miles an hour by the snorting engine."

Third Parties: The Dark Horses of American Politics

Although most presidents have won election supported by a major political party, underdogs have periodically made inroads. The following list includes some of the third parties founded in the 19th century, along with their candidates for president.

Anti-Masonic Party – Born of distrust of the secretive Masonic order, the Anti-Masonics nominated their first presidential candidate, William Wirt, in 1831.

Free-Soil Party – This group sought to ban slavery in the territories acquired from Mexico. Its 1848 candidate was former president Martin Van Buren.

American Party – Advocating tougher immigration policies, the American Party in 1856 nominated former president Millard Fillmore.

Liberal Republican Party – Members of this splinter group of the Republican Party were nicknamed Mugwumps, an Algonquian term for "big chief," to ridicule them for using complicated language to explain their positions. They supported Democratic candidate Grover Cleveland in 1884.

People's (Populist) Party – Founded in 1892, the Populists supported a graduated income tax, nationalization of the railroads, and the unlimited coinage of silver. James B. Weaver was the party's 1892 presidential candidate.

A *1835* **reform faction within New York City's Democratic Party was named for a type of matches, the Loco Focos. Their influence became so pervasive that for two decades, Democrats across the nation were called Loco Focos.**

The New York political scene had always been volatile, but rarely had it reached such chaotic levels as it did on October 29, 1835, when the Democratic Party's liberal and conservative wings locked horns at Tammany Hall. For months the two factions had tussled over such matters as paper currency, the Bank of the United States, and the granting of franchise monopolies, all of which liberals reviled. After the bitterly contested city elections early in 1834, a group of dissidents on the left formalized their insurgency, calling themselves the Equal Rights Party and adopting a Jacksonian platform: pro-labor, anti-bank, and anti-monopoly.

In 1835, when Democrats convened to nominate candidates for state elections, a shouting match ensued. Ruled out of order, the Equal Righters stormed the stage and expelled the so-called Bank Democrats. Moments later Tammany Hall was plunged into darkness — someone had turned off the gas that provided fuel for the lamps. The Equal Righters, expecting a trick, had come prepared with candles and self-lighting matches known as Loco Focos.

A caricaturist's Loco Foco.

The splinter group nominated its own candidates by candlelight and adjourned for a torchlight parade through the city. The Equal Righters' election bid proved unsuccessful, but the Loco Focos — a name given in mockery by their rivals — won a more lasting victory. Originally linked with boisterous, reform-minded New Yorkers, the principles of Locofocoism eventually had such a broad impact that for two decades the name was commonly used to refer to the national Democratic Party.

1835

In wild and woolly Texas, bands of roaming "rangers" gave new meaning to the expression "frontier justice."

Although they rarely numbered more than 500 men, never wore uniforms, and refused to salute their officers, the Texas Rangers were among the most feared and respected fighting units in American history. They date back to 1823, when Stephen Austin, who recruited settlers to the Texas Territory and headed its government, hired 10 men to help keep the law in Texas.

In 1835 revolutionaries seeking independence from Mexico hired them to guard the frontiers, and they acquired the name Texas Rangers. Traveling the Texas plains, the Rangers battled Comanches, patrolled the border with Mexico, and rounded up bandits and rustlers. They often dispensed frontier justice by hanging miscreants on the spot.

The Rangers' signature sidearm, the Colt six-shooter revolver, gave them weaponry second to none; they soon gained a reputation for the deadly accuracy of their aim. Adding to their fearsome image

A Ranger with his lasso, rifle, revolver, knife, and tomahawk.

was their Texas-size swagger.

It was said that a Ranger had to "ride like a Mexican, track like a Comanche, shoot like a Kentuckian, and fight like the Devil." According to one story, a town that had been pestered by a mob of hoodlums sent for the Texas Rangers, but only one of them showed up. When the town's mayor asked why the rest were missing, the Ranger replied, "You've only got one mob, haven't you? Let's go."

1836

Had Jim Bowie obeyed Sam Houston's orders to tear down an old, decaying mission building, no one would remember the Alamo.

The battle for Texas independence reached its climax in the early spring of 1836. Mexican Gen. Antonio Lopez de Santa Anna, determined to put down an insurrection by American colonists, marched an army of several thousand crack soldiers across the Rio Grande and headed for San Antonio. The Texas commander in chief was Sam Houston, who was still trying to muster his troops. Realizing he could never defend San Antonio, Houston sent his friend Jim Bowie to evacuate the city and demolish its main fortress, a nearby former mission called the Alamo.

Bowie did neither. Primed for adventure, the famous knife-fighter barricaded himself inside the Alamo with nearly 200 co-defenders, including Davy Crockett and some fellow Tennessee Mountain Volunteers. Santa Anna arrived at San Antonio on February 23 and took the city. He then turned his cannon on the Alamo.

The siege lasted 13 days. Col. William B. Travis, who shared the command with Bowie, sent out a stream of couriers with appeals for reinforcements. On the second day he dispatched a now-famous letter: "To the People of Texas & all Americans in the world . . . . I call on you in the name of Liberty, of patriotism & everything dear to the American character, to come to our aid, with all dispatch . . . VICTORY OR DEATH." No help arrived.

During lulls in the Mexican bombardment, Crockett sawed on his fiddle while John McGregor, a Scotsman, played his squealing bagpipes. The final attack began at 4 o'clock on March 6, a chilly Sunday morning. An army that had swelled to between 1,800 and 2,400 men burst through the Alamo's defenses. More than 200 Mexican soldiers died at the Alamo, and another 400 men were wounded there.

All 189 male defenders of the garrison died, but about 15 people — women, servants, and children — survived. Santa Anna sent 22-year-old Susanna Dickerson east to describe the terror and destruction she had witnessed during the siege. If the general hoped to defuse the rebellion by spreading fear, his strategy backfired. Texan rebels, led by Sam Houston and shouting "Remember the Alamo!" overwhelmed Santa Anna's forces on April 21 at San Jacinto. Texas had won its independence.

The last hours at the Alamo, as Texas artist Robert Onderdonk imagined it, shows Davy Crockett flailing away at his attackers with an empty rifle.

1837

In his shop on the Illinois frontier, blacksmith John Deere made an earth-shattering discovery that would soon transform prairies into fertile farms.

Hurt by a recession, blacksmith John Deere left a once-thriving business in Vermont and moved west in 1836. Setting up shop in the small town of Grand Detour, Illinois, he kept busy shoeing horses and repairing farm equipment.

It didn't take long for Deere to notice that the local farmers had problems with their traditional cast-iron plows. The rich loam of the Illinois prairie was so heavy that farmers had difficulty cutting long furrows; they had to stop every few feet to scrape the sticky soil from the blade's rough surface.

Thinking that polished steel might be stronger, less adhesive, and lighter, Deere took a discarded steel saw blade and in 1837 fashioned the first self-cleaning plow. "I cut the teeth off with a hand chisel, with the help of striker and sledge," he recalled, "then laid them on the fire of the forge and heated what little I could at a time and shaped them as best I could with the hand hammer." Using his device, farmers could turn the soil much faster than before. Deere began to produce plows as quickly as he could get the sheet steel he needed, which often meant awaiting shipments from England.

Deere moved to Moline, Illinois, to open a factory on the Mississippi River, which offered a source of water power and a shipping route. The factory produced 1,600 plows in 1850 and 10,000 in 1857.

John Deere and Co., Which made "the plow that broke the prairies," was well on its way to becoming one of the world's largest agricultural implement manufacturers.

A reconstruction of Deere's first plow.

IN THEIR OWN WORDS

"A farmer from across the river drove up. Seeing the plow he asked: 'Who made that plow?'
'I did, such as it is, wood work and all.'
'Well,' said the farmer, 'that looks as though it would work. Let me take it home and try it, and if it works all right, I will keep it and pay you for it. If not I will return it.'
'Take it,' said I, 'and give it a thorough trial.'
About two weeks later, the farmer drove up to the shop without the plow, and paid for it, and said, 'Now get a move on you, and make me two more plows just like the other one.'"

John Deere recalls selling his first steel-bladed plow in 1837.

1837

Despite some educators' worries that a classical education would harm the female mind, a small college in rural Ohio became the first institution in the United States to grant degrees to women.

Oberlin College, with its stump-ridden campus freshly cut from the woods of northern Ohio, was an innovator from its very beginnings in 1833. Oberlin offered the first American college curriculum available to women.

Unfortunately, this groundbreaking "ladies' course" omitted such subjects as higher mathematics and classical languages, topics that were considered too rigorous for "delicate" female minds. Graduates of the four-year course received a certificate, not a degree.

That all changed in 1837 when four pioneering young women were accepted into Oberlin's baccalaureate degree program. At the time, many educators claimed that such demanding studies would leave women "masculinized" and unappealing to potential suitors. Mary Hosford, Mary Kellogg, Elizabeth Prall, and Caroline Rudd hoped to prove the critics wrong when they entered the freshman class on September 6.

Only occasionally did the women warrant special consideration. When a professor used a corpse in "a state of perfect preservation" for a physiology demonstration, the coeds were excused from class. Other forms of bias were more blatant. Although the women could study rhetoric, they were prohibited from public speaking or debate. Men and women were restricted to separate library hours, and in classrooms a wide aisle separated the men's and women's seats.

Three of the four original coeds completed the program in 1841, establishing once and for all that there was a place for women on college campuses. And the fears that no suitor would find them attractive proved unfounded: three of the alumnae married Oberlin men soon after graduation.

The first female graduates of an American college were, from top, Elizabeth Prall, Mary Hosford, and Caroline Rudd.

Graham's wafers started a health-food trend.

1837

Sylvester Graham, a self-styled nutritional moralist, earned the wrath of bakers but the devotion of many early health-food advocates.

Sylvester Graham, a Presbyterian minister, rose to fame in the 1830's as a sharp-tongued critic of the American diet of red meat, refined breads, condiments, and seasonings. In his *Treatise on Bread and Bread-Making,* published in 1837, Graham targeted the nation's commercial bakers, who used highly sifted and refined flour because it was easier for them to work with.

Graham accused the bakers of stretching their flour by adding chalk and plaster of Paris. His crusade attracted such notables as inventor Thomas Edison and newspaper publisher Horace Greeley.

The nutrition educator wanted people to start eating baked goods made from what came to be called Graham flour, a coarsely milled and unadulterated product. The first Graham crackers were crumbly, dry whole-wheat wafers.

When Graham appeared in Boston for a lecture in 1847, irate bakers crashed through police lines at his hotel. Graham's followers saved him from an attempted lynching by pouring slaked lime on his attackers from hotel windows.

1838

The Trail of Tears carried Cherokee Indians from their homeland to desolation.

Before 1838 the Cherokee Indians cultivated 40,000 acres of farmland on the Georgia-Tennessee border, operated sawmills, owned thousands of cattle, and ranked among the country's wealthiest tribes. They developed their own writing system, published a newspaper in their native language, and possessed the only written constitution of any American tribe.

All those accomplishments meant nothing, however, when the federal government enforced the Indian Removal Act of 1830, a shameful piece of legislation that passed Congress by one vote. The removal act "solved" the ongoing conflict between land-hungry whites and Native Americans by relocating five major tribes in the southeastern United States from their territory to desolate tracts on the plains 1,000 miles to the west.

On May 23, 1838, the deadline for their exodus, 17,000 Cherokees still refused to leave, and U.S. Army troops began arresting them. Soldiers, armed with rifles and bayonets, marched into the fields and seized men as they plowed their land.

"Women were dragged from their homes," wrote Pvt. John Burnett, a participant in the roundup who had spent his childhood in the area. "Children were often separated from their parents and driven into the stockades, with the sky for a blanket and the earth for a pillow." In the wake of the soldiers came thieves who looted houses and dug up graves in search of valuables.

After spending the summer in dysentery-ridden camps where hundreds died, the Cherokees began their trek to Indian territory west of the Mississippi River. Starting in October, most traveled on foot without adequate supplies of food and other necessities. They endured heavy rains, bitter cold, and endless misery.

The forced pace allowed the refugees no time to stop and care for the aged and the sick, or even for pregnant women about to give birth. (Childbirth took place unattended, on the side of a road.) The Cherokees called this trek *nunna-da-ul-tsun-yi,* "the trail on which they cried." By March 1839, when the last Cherokees reached what is now Oklahoma, some 4,000 had died.

A modern-day Cherokee artist depicts the suffering endured by his tribe on a forced march that uprooted thousands of Indians.

Tracing the Trail of Tears

Forced by the Indian Removal Act to leave their ancestral homes in the Southeast, some 17,000 Cherokees tramped westward during the winter of 1838-39. The route of this heartbreaking journey was called the Trail of Tears.

1838

A dynamic European-born Jesuit missionary crossed the Atlantic Ocean 16 times to garner support for missions he founded in the desolate, unsettled Great Plains and Pacific Northwest.

They called Pierre Jean De Smet "Samson" when he was growing up in Belgium because of his physical strength. When he later served as a Jesuit missionary to the Indians in the United States, beginning in 1838, his ruggedness served him well. For several weeks he survived in the wilderness by eating plant roots and acorns.

Between 1838 and 1846 De Smet was instrumental in opening missions, hospitals, and schools among the Potawatomi, Flatheads, Kalispels, Coeur d'Alenes, and other tribes in the Midwest and Pacific Northwest.

He traveled 180,000 miles, including 16 transatlantic voyages, to drum up support for his work. Playing up the exotic appeal of the American West, De Smet encouraged European Jesuit novices and priests to establish missions in the United States.

In 1844, four years before he retired from active missionary work, De Smet described the joy of celebrating Christmas among the Flatheads in Oregon: "Here, indeed, the Indian missionary enjoys his greatest consolations: here he obtains his strength, his courage, his zeal to labor to

Feelings of trust and respect were mutual, as this drawing from De Smet's 1843 book indicates.

bring men to the knowledge of the true God, in spite of the poverty, the privations of every description, and the dangers with which he has to contend."

The Indians, who called De Smet "Blackrobe," had enormous respect for him, and he was often able to mediate between tribes or between Indians and whites. His greatest feat as a negotiator came in 1868, when, at great personal risk, he helped arrange a peace treaty between Sioux chief Sitting Bull and the federal government.

1838

Actress Fanny Kemble made the world a stage for her opposition to slavery.

When Fanny Kemble, the leading English actress of the early 1830's, arrived in the United States on tour, debutantes copied her clothing and bachelors wooed her. Who could have guessed that this show-business celebrity would achieve perhaps her greatest success as a social critic who condemned America's "peculiar institution" of slavery?

Pierce Butler, a Philadelphian who was the heir to a rice and cotton fortune, was Kemble's most persistent suitor. After they married in 1834, she retired from the stage. Four years later, when the couple moved from Philadelphia to Butler's Georgia plantations, Kemble got her first close-up look at slavery. It was quite a shock.

Appalled, Kemble kept a journal during that winter of 1838–39. She openly expressed her revulsion to Butler, who forbade Kemble to publish her journals and

Although Kemble's husband tried to silence her, she finally aired her antislavery views.

came to regard her as a danger to his family's business.

Butler tried to justify slavery as an economic necessity, but Kemble rejected his views. During an argument with him, Kemble declared that she would prefer returning to the stage (which she had never really liked) rather than continue "eating the bitter bread of slavery!" They were divorced after 15 years of marriage.

While the Civil War raged in the United States, Kemble was back in England, having resumed her acting career. The emergence in Britain of strong support for the Confederacy upset Kemble, and she decided that it was high time to publish her writings. Published in 1863, her *Journal of a Residence on a Georgian Plantation,* a riveting firsthand account of slavery, made the English see the Southern cause in a new, unflattering light. Partly due to Kemble's revelations, Britain never officially recognized the Confederate government.

1838

Brooklyn's Green-Wood Cemetery was for years a showcase for both the living and the dead.

As New York City's population burgeoned through the 1800's, many church graveyards were running out of space. To remedy the problem, Henry E. Pierrepont, the chairman of Brooklyn's new city planning commission, proposed that 200 acres of farmland — a tract that included the highest point in Brooklyn — be transformed into a new cemetery.

Green-Wood Cemetery, incorporated in 1838, boasted scenic views, rolling hills, lakes, and picturesque drives. Over time it expanded to 478 acres, making it the world's largest landscaped cemetery for many years.

In the 1850's the park that was called the Garden City of the Dead drew 100,000 visitors annually. New Yorkers came to pay tribute to their loved ones and to admire the views while

New Yorkers enter Green-Wood Cemetery to enjoy a holiday promenade in 1899.

riding in horse-drawn carriages.

While many visitors appreciated the natural sights, others were even more intrigued by Green-Wood's memorial art. The Brown monument, for example, offers a marble representation of the sinking of the *Arctic,* a steamship that went down with six of the Brown family members. The sepulchral home of John Matthews, the inventor of seltzer water and the owner of hundreds of New York soda fountains, includes a canopy depicting an array of soda fountain equipment.

Included among the 520,000 people buried at Green-Wood are artists George Catlin and Louis Comfort Tiffany, gangsters Joey Gallo and Albert Anastasia, and newspaper publisher Horace Greeley. "It is the ambition of the New Yorker," observed *The New York Times* in 1866, "to live on Fifth Ave., to take his airings in the [Central] Park, and to sleep with his fathers in Green-Wood."

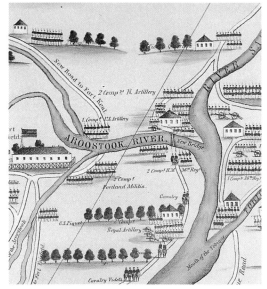

An eyewitness drew this map of the opposing forces' positions in the Aroostook War.

1839

Only fists flew in the Aroostook War.

"A more foolish and ridiculous quarrel never, never before took place between two such great nations as England and the United States," wrote Maine clergyman Caleb Bradley of the 1839 Aroostook War.

The trouble started in 1783, when the treaty ending the Revolutionary War left in dispute the boundary between Maine (then part of Massachusetts) and New Brunswick. Disregarding British claims to territory in Aroostook County, Maine granted land to settlers in the disputed region, which was rich in valuable white-pine timber. Matters went from bad to worse when Britain decided to build a military road that would cut through the territory, and lumberjacks on both sides of the border grew incensed at the trespasses of the other side.

In January 1839 Rufus McIntire, a Maine land agent, entered the contested region to evict a crew of 205 New Brunswick loggers. When the Canadians placed McIntire under arrest, New Brunswick and Maine officials swapped irate letters, and each called up their local militia. Under pressure from New Englanders, Congress authorized President Martin Van Buren to dispatch 50,000 federal troops.

In the end no shots were fired, and the only injuries were a few bloody noses suffered by lumberjacks exchanging punches. Britain's Lord Ashburton traveled to Washington, D.C., to discuss the matter with Secretary of State Daniel Webster. Their compromise gave Maine 7,000 of the 12,000 square miles in dispute, and the British won the right to build their military road.

1839

The most commonly used Americanism is OK, an abbreviation of unclear origin that has traveled around the world.

The earliest known appearance of OK in print, in a March 23, 1839, edition of Boston's *Morning Post,* explains its meaning as "all correct," spelled "oll korrect." But as the years passed and the expression gained wide circulation, speculation grew about OK. Was it the abbreviation for Old Kinderhook, which was President Martin Van Buren's nickname (he was from Kinderhook, New York)? Did it refer to Old Keokuk, an Indian chief who signed treaties with his initials? Or perhaps it came from the Finnish word *oikea,* which means *correct?*

OK reached the West Indies by 1847, England a few years later, India by 1883, and the Philippines around 1908. American soldiers carried it to Japan and Korea in the mid-20th century. OK is now part of the language nearly everywhere, no matter how it is spelled — *o.k., O.K., okay, okey, oke,* or even *okeh.*

A cartoonist suggests that OK was a nickname for President Van Buren.

1841

Seeing firsthand the cruel living conditions of mentally ill prisoners turned a former schoolteacher into a social reformer.

When Dorothea Dix went to teach a Sunday school class at a jail in East Cambridge, Massachusetts, in 1841, she was shocked to find four mentally ill women locked up in a cell that was cold, dark, and filthy. Suddenly her life gained a new purpose.

Dix left the prison determined to change the way Americans cared for the insane. She spent nearly two years visiting the mentally ill in Massachusetts jails and almshouses. At the time, a common practice was to imprison the insane along with vagrants, drunks, and other criminals or to put them in poorhouses, side by side with mentally competent men, women, and children. Dix was horrified to find people who were beaten, chained, and kept naked and caged. One person had been confined to a "close stall" for 17 years.

Widening her investigations, Dix discovered that the insane received atrocious

Dix refused to believe the jailer who claimed that female lunatics couldn't feel the cold.

care in jails nationwide and urged that state-funded asylums be established. In a petition to Congress to lobby for federal legislation, Dix described the hundreds of mentally ill prisoners she had seen "bowed beneath fetters and heavy iron balls attached to drag chains, lacerated with ropes, scourged with rods, and terrified beneath storms of profane execrations and cruel blows; now subject to gibes and scorn and torturing tricks . . . or subject to the vilest and most outrageous violations."

Combining thorough research, persistence, and graphic descriptions of the appalling conditions, Dix persuaded many state legislatures to allocate funds for improving mental-health care. Due largely to her efforts, the United States had 123 mental hospitals by 1880.

On several occasions from 1854 to 1857, Dix traveled to Europe, where she advocated better treatment for the insane there. She met twice with Pope Pius IX, once to tell him of the abysmal conditions at prisons close to the Vatican and again, after an investigation validated her charges, to hear the pope's assurances that he would work on the problem. She was credited with the founding of several European mental institutions.

1841
The settlers on the first wagon train to California had no idea how to get there.

In May 1841 a group of 69 men, women, and children gathered in Sapling Grove, Kansas, to move west together. Their enthusiasm far surpassed their experience — not one of them knew the way to California. Many had been lured by a veteran fur trader's tales of a fertile land, full of natural wonders, and one whose residents were so generous that travelers never had to pay for food or lodging. Raring to go, the westbound pioneers got as far as Weston, Missouri, where they delayed their journey in order to join a band of missionaries who had chosen the fabled guide Thomas Fitzpatrick to lead them from St. Louis to Oregon.

Fending off hostile Indians and a stampeding herd of buffalo, Fitzpatrick led the group as far as Soda Springs, Idaho, on the Bear River. There they split into two parties. One followed Fitzpatrick and pioneered the Oregon Trail. The other party set out on its own: the 33 settlers knew only that their destination lay to the west. They skirted the Great Salt Lake but encountered the Sierra Nevada, where they abandoned their wagons in order to cross the mountain range. When their food ran out, the travelers resorted to eating their mules and oxen.

The Oregon Trail *by Albert Bierstadt shows a wagon train wending its way westward.*

In November the settlers made it to the San Joaquin Valley, not realizing that they had reached California. Some were arrested and jailed in San Jose. After explaining that they were not troublemakers, they were freed to seek legal status as California residents.

1842
A five-month tour of the United States turned British novelist Charles Dickens from an admirer into a critic.

When American writer Washington Irving wrote Charles Dickens a fan letter in 1841 and urged him to visit, that was all the persuasion the famed British novelist needed. The 29-year-old Dickens made plans to see the United States, write a travelogue, and express his kinship with the young nation.

When Dickens and his wife arrived in

Dickens's tour opened his eyes to the rough edges of the American character.

Boston, their first stop, on January 22, 1842, the reception was nothing short of tumultuous. Reporters, admirers, and well-wishers besieged them. Finally able to set off on his own, an ebullient Dickens explored the city after midnight, literally running up and down the streets.

After enjoying celebrity treatment in Boston, Dickens traveled to New York, Philadelphia, Washington, and as far west as St. Louis and north to Buffalo, New York. At every stop, dignitaries and writers greeted him.

Dickens had expected to love the United States because of its democratic principles. Before long, however, the exuberant outpourings of his fans began to wear on his nerves. Spirited public displays of enthusiasm intruded on his privacy. Where he had once idealized the common man's desire to avoid pretentions, he recoiled at his firsthand experience of common vulgarity. The practice of spitting especially upset him.

Perhaps what most shattered his illusions were the storms the author stirred up when he spoke out in favor of international copyright laws. Dickens had lost considerable income because American publishers

regularly pirated his works. Newspaper editorials that condemned his defense of copyright laws depressed him, and the pace of the tour exhausted him. He was relieved when his visit ended in June.

Back home, Dickens wrote a restrained travelogue, but he unleashed his true feelings in *The Life and Adventures of Martin Chuzzlewit.* In the 1844 novel Dickens describes Martin junior, the grandson of the title character, arriving in the United States and fending off crowds unrestrained by British manners or decorum.

Dickens's sojourn abroad left an unexpected and deep imprint on him. In America, he later said, "I discovered I was an Englishman."

E **1842**

ther began to gain acceptance as a medical painkiller after a doctor in rural Georgia hosted an "ether frolic."

Getting high on laughing gas, or nitrous oxide, was a popular form of entertainment in the 1840's; soon it would become a subject of interest to the medical profession.

Intrigued by a demonstration of laughing gas, some friends of Dr. Crawford W. Long of Jefferson, Georgia, urged him to have a "nitrous oxide frolic." He couldn't obtain any laughing gas for the party, but Long offered an alternative, sulphuric ether. His friends agreed to try it.

"I had inhaled it myself and considered it as safe as the nitrous oxide gas," Long wrote several years later. After the party, the doctor noticed several bruises on his body, but he didn't immediately know how he had gotten them.

Recalling the giddy party, Long made a connection between inhaling ether and bumping into objects without feeling pain. He began to wonder whether ether could obliterate the agonizing pain of surgery.

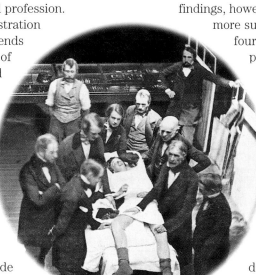
A reenactment of the first medical use of ether anesthesia.

Anxious to test ether as an anesthetic, Long convinced a patient, James Venable, to inhale it before he removed a tumor from Venable's neck. The operation, performed on March 30, 1842, went well, and Long continued to use ether; he held off publishing his findings, however, until he could do more surgery. Over the next four and a half years, Long performed eight operations using ether, even anesthetizing his wife for childbirth.

Meanwhile, unaware of Long's findings, other doctors and dentists began using anesthetics. Three of them became embroiled in a dispute over who deserved credit for discovering anesthesia. Horace Wells, a dentist whose public demonstration of ether failed, committed suicide. Dr. William Morton took out a patent but died a pauper while defending his claim. Dr. Charles Jackson went insane. Credit for the first surgical use of ether anesthesia went to Long in 1849, when a medical journal published Long's account of his pioneering work.

R **1842**

hode Island, the nation's smallest state, once had two separate state governments, each with its own governor.

In the early 1840's a spirit of egalitarianism was sweeping the country, but Rhode Island was out of step. Still governed by its 1663 charter, the state limited voting rights to landowners and their eldest sons.

Led by political activist Thomas Dorr, reformers demanded change. In 1841 they drew up a People's Constitution that dropped property requirements for voters. The incumbents, unwilling to relinquish power, simply modified the old constitution. Both plans were submitted to the voters, and the liberal constitution won easily. When the incumbents refused to accept the new charter, the reformers, known as Dorrites, elected Dorr governor.

In May 1842 Dorrites tried to seize the state arsenal in Providence, but their cannons failed and they retreated. In June Dorr's second effort was repulsed, and his forces disbanded. Responding to public pressure, the lawmakers finally gave voting rights to adult white males; black men also got the vote, a token of thanks for defending Providence.

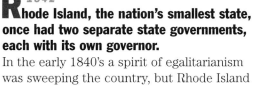
Brandishing a sword, Dorr took up arms to expand voting rights in Rhode Island.

IN THEIR OWN WORDS

"One after another, one after another, dozen after dozen, score after score, more, more, more, up they came: all shaking hands with Martin. Such varieties of hands, the thick, the thin, the short, the long, the fat, the lean, the coarse, the fine; such differences of temperature, the hot, the cold, the dry, the moist, the flabby; such diversities of grasp, the tight, the loose, the short-lived, and the lingering! Still up, up, up, more, more, more: and ever and anon the captain's voice was heard above the crowd — 'There's more below; there's more below. Now, gentlemen, you that have been introduced to Mr. Chuzzlewit, will you clear, gentlemen? Will you clear? Will you be so good as clear, gentlemen, and make a little room for more?' Regardless of the captain's cries, they didn't clear at all, but stood there, bolt upright and staring."

In Charles Dickens's novel The Life and Adventures of Martin Chuzzlewit, *the title character's grandson, Martin junior, gets a suffocating dose of American hospitality.*

1843
A young man's desire to return home to his mother helped open Japan to the West.

Manjiro, a 14-year-old Japanese boy, was working as a fisherman to support his widowed mother in 1841, when a storm shipwrecked him and his four companions on a deserted Pacific island. For five months they survived by eating shellfish, seaweed, and albatross. Then one day a New England whaling ship appeared on the horizon.

W. H. Whitfield, the captain of the whaler, rescued the castaways and took them to Honolulu, his next port of call. During the voyage Manjiro so impressed the captain with his intelligence and cheerful disposition that Whitfield offered to take the youth back to the United States.

On May 7, 1843, the two arrived in Fairhaven, Massachusetts, just a few miles from the bustling whaling village of New Bedford. There Manjiro entered school and learned English, mathematics, and navigational skills.

Although he enjoyed his new life, Manjiro longed to be reunited with his mother. In 1846 he tried to return home by joining a whaling expedition, but the effort was in vain.

The Gold Rush gave Manjiro another chance to reach his native land. After several months prospecting in California, he booked a passage home, even though he knew that Japanese law mandated the execution of citizens who returned after visiting foreign lands. When he arrived in Japan in 1851, Manjiro was imprisoned, but the widespread interest in his story saved his life. Finally, after more than a year, he was reunited with his mother.

In Japan, Manjiro served as a self-appointed cultural ambassador for the country where he had been so well treated. His enthusiasm for America helped pave the way for Commodore Matthew Perry's visits in 1853 and 1854, which opened U.S.–Japanese trade relations.

Manjiro's anti-isolationism worried conservative Japanese lawmakers, who prevented him from meeting Perry. At last Manjiro got a job that suited him well: in 1860 he was chosen interpreter for the first Japanese embassy in the United States. 🐃

Manjiro sketched this view of Boston during his stay in Massachusetts.

1844
If Samuel F. B. Morse had succeeded as a painter — his chosen calling — he might not have revolutionized worldwide communications by inventing the telegraph.

As an artist in training, Samuel F. B. Morse studied painting in London, specializing in depictions of Roman mythology. On his return to the United States, he was dismayed to find that American interest in artists was limited to portrait painters. Unable to sell the paintings he liked best — historical and mythological subjects — Morse turned to portraits and managed to eke out a meager living.

His greatest artistic triumph, a national commission to paint the marquis de Lafayette, a Revolutionary War hero, was marred by the death of Morse's wife midway through the work. Soon afterward his mother and father also died.

Morse went to Europe to recover from

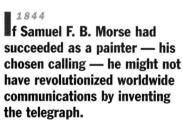

Morse used a painter's canvas stretcher for the first telegraph.

his grief. On his return voyage in 1832, a conversation with a fellow passenger triggered the idea for the telegraph. At first he did not pursue it, turning instead to a career in New York politics. He ran — unsuccessfully — for mayor.

When Morse finally began to develop the telegraph, he enlisted the aid of several prominent scientists in the hope of beating out his European rivals, who were at work on similar projects. Ultimately, Morse's most important contribution to the telegraph was a system of relays to keep signals strong over long distances. He also developed the dot-dash system of the alphabet that became his namesake code.

Morse continued to straddle the worlds of art and industry until 1837, when, stung by the rejection of his bid to paint a portrait in the Capitol rotunda and tired of struggling to make ends meet, he gave up painting altogether. The artistic impulse lingered, however, and in an 1849 letter to a friend, Morse lamented, "The very name of *pictures* produces a sadness of heart I cannot describe."

Congress approved funds for a trial telegraph line from Baltimore to Washington in 1843. On May 24, 1844, Morse sent the first message, "What hath God wrought!" In the following years, Morse enjoyed the fame and fortune that had eluded him as a painter. 🐃

H 1844

Horace Mann set off a tidal wave of public-education reform in Massachusetts that eventually engulfed the whole nation.

In 1837 Horace Mann resigned as president of the Massachusetts senate in order to serve on the state's first board of education. Mann believed that a good education not only would provide the three R's but would allow "the vast treasures of human talent and genius [to] be developed."

As a state education official, Mann had little authority, but working 15 hours a day, seven days a week, he rallied public support for better schools through numerous speeches and articles. When he launched his campaign, a third of the state's children did not attend school, and some teachers were so poorly trained that they couldn't even do their multiplication tables. Corporal punishment was still a widely accepted form of discipline.

Mann gave some schoolteachers failing grades.

One teacher who strongly objected to the use of the whip was Henry David Thoreau, who would later become famous for his essay on civil disobedience and his solitary life beside Walden Pond in Massachusetts. "Cowhide was a nonconductor," Thoreau commented, as he resigned his teaching job after only two weeks.

Mann's goading led to the founding of the first three teachers' colleges in the country, the doubling of appropriations for schools in Massachusetts, and 50 new high schools in the state, but his work also earned him enemies. In September 1844, 31 Boston schoolteachers reacted furiously to Mann's largely critical annual report. After months of attacks and counterattacks, Mann finally prevailed. Four of the 31 protesting teachers were fired, several were transferred, and corporal punishment became less common. His ultimate victory was that many other states began adopting his reforms.

J 1844

James K. Polk, the first dark-horse presidential candidate, was also the first president not to seek reelection.

A former governor of Tennessee and former U.S. representative, James K. Polk was chosen as the Democratic presidential candidate in 1844 on the ninth ballot. His sudden selection broke the deadlock between former president Martin Van Buren and Lewis Cass of Michigan. The Whig candidate, Henry Clay of Kentucky, mocked his nomination with the slogan, "Who is James K. Polk?" The jokes ended in November 1844, however, when Polk defeated Clay.

In fact, Polk was far from unknown. Nicknamed Young Hickory, he was a protégé of Andrew Jackson and had served as Speaker of the House during his 14 years in Congress. But unlike Jackson, he was not a man of the people. Polk was dour, suspicious, and devoid of warmth or charm. He mistrusted his own Cabinet appointees.

James and Sarah Polk in what is probably the first daguerreotype of a presidential couple.

One of Polk's election strategies was to tap into expansionist sentiments, stressing "manifest destiny." On taking office, he again pledged "immediate reannexation of Texas" and "reoccupation" of the Oregon Territory (jointly occupied by the United States and England). In 1846 Polk signed a treaty that gave the United States sole rights to the area as far north as the 49th parallel.

Polk provoked Mexico into war in 1846. A defeated Mexico gave up Texas and territory in seven other states. During his term Polk added more than 1 million square miles to the Union, an expanse of land greater than the Louisiana Purchase. He also kept his campaign promise to reduce the tariff and set up an independent treasury.

Uninterested in a second term, Polk became the first president not to run for reelection. The dark-horse candidate left office with a solid record of accomplishments.

Presidential Nicknames

James Polk was known as Young Hickory, for his devotion to his fellow Democrat Andrew Jackson, who was fondly referred to as Old Hickory. Here are some of the other nicknames attached to U.S. presidents.

Martin Van Buren — The Little Magician, for his tall silk hat, and The Red Fox, for his hair color.

William H. Harrison — Old Tippecanoe, for an Indiana river where he led a victorious battle against Indians.

Abraham Lincoln — The Great Emancipator, for his 1863 proclamation freeing slaves in Confederate states.

Ulysses S. Grant — Unconditional Surrender, for the terms he offered Confederates seeking an end to the Civil War.

Rutherford B. Hayes — His Fraudulency, for winning the presidency in a disputed election.

Chester A. Arthur — The Dude President, for his sartorial splendor.

Theodore Roosevelt — Rough Rider, for the cavalry regiment of adventurers he led during the Spanish-American War.

William H. Taft — Big Bill, for his huge waistline—he weighed more than 300 pounds.

Calvin Coolidge — Silent Cal, for his tendency to say little or nothing at all.

1845

Frederick Douglass, one of the most powerful abolitionist speakers in America, had to seek refuge in England to avoid being returned to slavery when his autobiography was published.

Born into slavery in Maryland in 1818, Frederick Douglass was virtually abandoned by his mother and never knew his white father. With the help of his master's wife, he learned to read and secretly bought a book when he was 12. He later taught himself to write and do arithmetic. At the age of 20 he escaped, arriving in New York disguised as a sailor. There he changed his name from Bailey to Douglass, after the hero of Sir Walter Scott's novel *The Lady of the Lake.*

In 1841 Douglass gave a speech at an antislavery convention in Massachusetts that launched his five-decade career as an orator and a social activist. Not inclined to tread lightly, at one point he described prejudice as "no less than a murderous, hell-born hatred of every virtue which may adorn the character of a black man." A powerful speaker, Douglass sometimes provoked outrage, scorn, and even attacks by mobs in the North.

Douglass wrote his autobiography, *Narrative of the Life of Frederick Douglass, an American Slave,* because few people believed that such an articulate crusader could ever have been a slave. When the book was published on May 1, 1845, he was so fearful that his life was in danger that he left for Europe. While he was in England, Douglass determined that he would have to fight to achieve justice and equality, as well as to abolish slavery.

When Douglass returned to the United States in 1847, he finally had enough money to buy his freedom — after nearly 30 years, he was no longer a slave. In December 1847 he founded the abolitionist newspaper *North Star,* for which he served as editor-publisher.

Abolitionist Frederick Douglass waged a lifelong fight against slavery.

IN THEIR OWN WORDS

> Just here is our sin: we have been a slave; we have passed through all the grades of servitude, and have, under God, secured our freedom; and if we have become the special object of attack, it is because we speak and act among our fellow-men without the slightest regard to their or our own complexion; and further, because we claim and exercise the right to associate with just such persons as are willing to associate with us, and who are agreeable to our tastes, and suited to our moral and intellectual tendencies, without reference to the color of their skin.

Frederick Douglass on the nature of prejudice, in the North Star, *June 1850.*

This 19th-century painting idealizes the nation's westward expansion.

1845

The term Manifest Destiny, a rallying cry for America's westward expansion during the mid-19th century, was coined by a long-forgotten magazine editor.

John L. O'Sullivan was an Irish-American who was born in Europe on a British warship. Optimistic by nature, he was described as "always full of grand and world-embracing schemes." In 1837 he founded the *United States Magazine and Democratic Review* "to strike the hitherto silent string of the democratic genius of the age and country."

It was a period when many Americans hoped to bring the territories of Texas and Oregon into the Union. O'Sullivan went even further, advocating U.S. control of all of North America and Cuba.

O'Sullivan coined a phrase for Americans to rally around in July 1845 when he used "manifest destiny" in his magazine to justify the annexation of Texas. In a newspaper editorial that December, O'Sullivan wrote that it "is by the right of our manifest destiny to overspread and to possess the whole of the continent which Providence has given us for the development of the great experiment of liberty and federative self government entrusted to us."

Thomas Hart Benton, the influential senator from Missouri, picked up and popularized the phrase. It seemed to embody the nation's growing self-confidence and pride.

During the 1840's, expansion in the name of Manifest Destiny added more than 1 million square miles to the United States. It was used to justify the acquisition of California, Alaska, Texas, and Oregon and helped vindicate efforts to take over Mexico and Cuba in the 1850's. The phrase was revived in the 1890's to support American expansion into the Pacific.

A *1845*

An unsuccessful mutiny aboard a U.S. naval vessel prompted the creation of the U.S. Naval Academy.

Although three presidents and six navy secretaries had voiced support for a naval academy in the early 1800's, Congress had defeated some 20 bills authorizing such a school. Its opponents felt that it would be too expensive, that it would be dangerous for the nation to create an elite corps of naval officers, and that seamen should be trained at sea rather than on land.

In the 1820's, schools offering classes for midshipmen on shore leave operated in New York, Boston, and Norfolk, Virginia, but attendance was voluntary and discipline was lax. Chaplains on board ships were to oversee the formal education of seamen, but studies often got short shrift.

As technology improved, the need for naval officers with an engineering background increased. Then, in 1842, the lack of discipline among midshipmen suddenly became an issue of nationwide concern. A mutiny aboard the *Somers* led to the court-martial of three mutineers, who were hanged from the ship's yardarm.

The notoriety surrounding this event convinced Navy Secretary George Bancroft to act. He persuaded the army to turn over an obsolete fort overlooking the harbor at Annapolis, Maryland. Without asking Congress, Bancroft earmarked money for the new school from the navy budget. The U.S. Naval Academy opened on October 10, 1845.

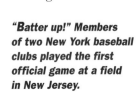

A U.S. Navy Academy cadet proudly displays his blue uniform jacket and wide-brimmed hat.

M *1845*

Members of the New York Knickerbockers made sports history not by inventing baseball but by helping turn it from a children's game into an adult sport.

The Knickerbockers, 28 well-to-do New Yorkers who got together for "health, recreation and social enjoyment," took their name from the volunteer fire company to which many of them belonged. In 1845 Alexander J. Cartwright, a bank teller who was one of the Knickerbockers, mapped out the first set of baseball rules for adults. These regulations called for the game to be played on a diamond with bases roughly 90 feet apart. Cartwright may also have made other lasting contributions as well, such as placing the batter beside home plate rather than in front of it, assigning each player his own position, and outlawing plugging — the dangerous practice of putting a player out by hitting him with the ball.

June 19, 1846, is often cited as the date of the first official baseball game; a score book listed the players and gave the score. The Knickerbockers had decided against playing in Manhattan, which was becoming too congested for ball games, so the contest was held in the Elysian Fields, across the Hudson River in Hoboken, New Jersey.

What is known today as baseball evolved from the British games of cricket and rounder. Since 1744, children's books in America provided rules for a version of rounder called baseball. A similar game, called town ball, was played in Camden, New Jersey, in 1831, but it was so closely linked with children's games that adults who played it were often ridiculed for indulging in youthful amusements. In other areas of the country, adaptations were known by such labels as sting ball, burn ball, and soak ball.

Some Knickerbocker rules that still apply allow the batter three strikes before he is out and permit each side three outs per inning. (Rules that have fallen by the wayside include fining a player for swearing and playing until one team scored 21 runs.) The Knickerbockers' way of playing came to be known as the New York game, and it spread nationwide during the Civil War. The first professional baseball club, the Cincinnati Red Stockings, was organized in 1869.

"Batter up!" Members of two New York baseball clubs played the first official game at a field in New Jersey.

1845
Just one year before moving to Walden Pond, Henry David Thoreau accidentally set fire to the nearby woods.

Twenty-seven-year-old Henry David Thoreau, a Harvard graduate and an avowed nature lover, lived with his family in Concord, Massachusetts, about two miles from Walden Pond. One April morning in 1844, while camping near the pond with a friend, Edward Hoar, Thoreau was unable to douse their campfire. When the flames spread and all efforts to extinguish them failed, Thoreau ran for assistance. Then, rather than help the villagers fight the fire, Thoreau climbed a cliff and watched as 300 acres burned. Thoreau was never charged with the crime, possibly because his

Thoreau's cabin near Walden Pond.

camping companion belonged to one of the town's more prominent families.

In July of 1845, Thoreau built a cabin in the woods near the pond. Tilling a small garden there, he quietly devoted his time to his journals. "I went to the woods because I wished to . . . see if I could not learn what it had to teach, and not, when I came to die, discover that I had not lived," he later wrote in a book that resulted from his self-exile. The book, *Walden, or Life in the Woods,* went on to become his best-known work. During his lifetime, however, Thoreau's writings meant little to some of his Concord neighbors, who only remembered the fire and dismissed him as merely a "damned rascal."

1846
Explorer John Charles Frémont helped a ragtag group of California rebels gain independence from Mexico.

John Charles Frémont, an officer in the U.S. Topographical Corps, was a painstaking and energetic explorer. The vivid reports of his first expedition to the Rockies and his second expedition to California became popular literary works and led to increased interest in the West.

But Frémont had an independent streak (he took a cannon on his second trip, in defiance of a government directive not to do so), and by his third expedition, it was clear that his interest went beyond mere exploration. When war with Mexico seemed inevitable, Frémont was sent by the War Department on a third survey of the West. To this end he took 62 well-armed mountain men and quickly made his way to Sutter's Fort in California, doing little or no real exploring along the way. When Frémont and his men moved from Sutter's Fort to San José, the Mexicans, suspicious of their motives, ordered them out of the territory. Instead of leaving, Frémont defiantly raised the American flag. His actions and support inspired the American settlers in the Sacramento Valley to rise up against Mexican rule.

On June 15, 1846, the rebels at Sonoma raised a flag with the image of a grizzly bear on it. The so-called Bear Flag republic was to last only three and a half weeks. Taking charge of the American forces in early July, Frémont enlisted the enthusiastic Bear Flaggers into a "California battalion" and then went on to help liberate the entire state.

The Bear Flag was incorporated into California's state flag.

1846
The Smithsonian Institution, the world's largest museum, came into existence because of the mysterious generosity of an Englishman who never set foot in the United States.

James Smithson was born in 1765, the illegitimate son of the British duke of Northumberland, Hugh Smithson, and Elizabeth Hungerford Keate Macie, who was a descendant of King Henry VII. Attending Oxford, Smithson studied science and graduated at the top of his class in chemistry. Although Smithson enjoyed a successful career, writing numerous papers, identifying a new ore (now called smithsonite), and becoming a member of Britain's Royal Society, the stigma of his birth haunted him: "The best blood of England flows in

" Picture to yourself, reader, a calm and mirrorlike sea, and our ship rolling to and fro on it. . . . Here and there about the decks, you see the sailors trying to jog the tardy wings of time, by courting sleep, or humming some idle hymn to Bacchus . . . when of a sudden the man at the masthead cries out in a faint and tremulous voice, as if he half doubted his own vision, 'There — she blows!'

As soon as the boats touch the water, every man is at his oar. . . . Until the whale is either actually dead, or spouting blood, the officers seem to be perfect maniacs. At first, they will beg you to pull, and then curse you. 'Oh! do pull, my dear fellows. Do pull. Pull you d—d lubbers; pull, or I will heave this lance through your heart. Pull, my boys. — I've just got five sisters at home, and if you will get that whale, I'll give each of you a wife. Pull, I will give you my voyage for that whale.' In this way they will rave during the whole time of the chase. "

Sailor Ben-Ezra Stiles Ely describes chasing a whale in February 1845.

my veins . . . but this avails me not." Yet he was determined, somehow, to be a part of posterity.

Smithson died in 1829, leaving $500,000 to his nephew, his only surviving heir. There was an unusual stipulation in his will, however: if his nephew died without leaving an heir, the remains of his fortune were

to be given to the U.S. government in order to establish an institution, bearing Smithson's name, for "the increase and diffusion of knowledge among men."

In 1835 his nephew died, leaving no children; three years later 105 bags containing 100,000 gold sovereigns were shipped to the United States. Smithson's reasons for choosing to bestow his wealth on a country he had never visited are not known. Some speculate that he admired America and its new democracy and wanted to contribute to it in some way.

Whatever his reasons, Smithson's legacy threw the Congress into an eight-year debate over the propriety of taking the money. Congress finally accepted it in 1846 and set aside 19 acres for the creation of Smithson's institution, which opened in 1855.

The Smithsonian Institution includes 16 museums and galleries and the National Zoo.

A 1846 New England seaport village became the worldwide center of whaling.

In 1847 the small town of New Bedford on the coast of Massachusetts sent out 254 sailing ships — more than a third of the entire American whaling fleet — to chase and kill whales. The whalers returned with the raw materials of a lucrative industry: sperm oil for lamps, spermaceti for candles, ambergris for expensive perfumes, and bone for such items as corset stays and buggy whips.

The whaling industry in America was at its zenith, and New Bedford was its center. For some 30 years America dominated the industry, with ships ranging from the North Atlantic to the Pacific in search of sperm whales. At its peak in 1846, whaling employed 70,000 people and produced $70 million in revenues. New Bedford had one of the highest per capita incomes in the world, with virtually all of its adult inhabitants involved in the industry in one way or another. Whaling was so much a part of the town's economy that the local ministers and teachers were paid in casks of oil instead of cash.

Ambitious seamen sailed around the world, killing sperm whales and then processing the oil aboard ship. (One sperm whale provided 65 to 80 barrels of oil.) Fortunes were made, but whaling was a dangerous and often heartbreaking profession. It took bravery and

Typical 19th-century sailors' epitaphs: "Carried overboard by the line, and drowned"; "Towed out of sight by a whale."

skillfull seamanship to kill a whale. The favored sperm whale, whose average length is about 60 feet, was a fierce fighter when provoked, capable of destroying small boats and sometimes even ships.

Because the best hunting grounds for these giant mammals were found in the Pacific, whalers spent an average of 42 months away from home, and their wives and children often received no news of them for three to five years. Some houses in New England whaling towns were built with rectangular platforms, nicknamed widows' walks, so that wives could keep a lookout for their husbands' return — hoping to spot a familiar sail on the distant horizon.

1846

Because they followed the advice of an unreliable guidebook, the Donner party spent a winter trapped in the Sierra Nevada.

In April 1846 George and Jacob Donner, two prosperous Illinois farmers, led 89 men, women, and children westward, believing that they would be in California by early fall. The Donners were trusting an unreliable guidebook, *Emigrants' Guide to Oregon and California*, in which author Lansford Hastings claimed

James and Margaret Reed managed to survive the ordeal of the Donner party.

a new shortcut bearing west-southwest. Unknown to the Donner party, Hastings had touted an untested route. Although a mountain man had advised them to stick to longer, better-known routes, the Donners ignored his warnings.

The shortcut was far more difficult than promised. The wagon train moved haltingly through boulder-strewn canyons and a desert described as only 40 miles wide that was actually 80 miles across. As the threat of winter snows

increased daily, the Donner party pushed on through the Sierra Nevada foothills, climbing higher into the mountains.

Howling blizzards trapped them in a mountain pass in early November with little food or shelter. By mid-December the party, their supplies exhausted, could still go nowhere. They began boiling ox hides for soup; then they ate twigs and tree bark. One after another, the pioneers perished of starvation and exposure. Finally, out of desperation, the survivors ate the frozen corpses of those who had died.

On February 19, 1847, a rescue party found 47 emigrants still alive; one of them, a half-crazed woman, cried out, "Are you from California or from heaven?" "We're from California," came their reply.

1847

Thousands walked across plains and over mountains to reach a "New Zion" in Utah, founded by Mormon leader Brigham Young.

Traveling from Illinois to the Great Salt Lake valley in July 1847, Mormon leader Brigham Young's advance party looked out over "the paradise of the lizard, the cricket, and the rattlesnake." Some scoffed at the dubious fertility of the arid desert. Mountain man Jim Bridger supposedly mocked Young, offering him $1,000 for the first bushel of corn grown there.

Young's dream of a Mormon state called Deseret included all of what is now Utah and Nevada, parts of Idaho, Wyoming, Colorado, Oregon, New Mexico, Arizona, and even a strip of coastal California. Out of the shadow of the U.S. government, the Mormons could found a "New Zion" — a safe haven from religious persecution.

Despite initial setbacks due to crop failure and scarce food supplies, the Mormon empire grew over the next decade. European converts arrived in Boston or New York, then traveled by train to Iowa City, where they were given wagons and horses to make the 1,300-mile trip to Salt Lake City. When church funds dwindled, Young ordered his flock to "come on foot with handcarts or wheelbarrows."

From 1856 to 1860 some 3,000 new followers piled their belongings onto two-wheeled handcarts and pushed them across the plains and over the mountains to Utah. The first three "handcart brigades" made the long over-

land trek and arrived to a celebratory welcome. Only 11 out of the 497 people had lost their lives.

Subsequent brigades were not so lucky. Numerous breakdowns and early blizzards caught travelers 300 miles from the Great Salt Lake. Although they inched on, cold and starvation took more than 200 out of 1,076 lives before rescue parties found them. Bolstered by food and warm clothing, some people even managed to sing their unofficial anthem, "Some Must Push and Some Must Pull" as they trundled into "Zion."

One of the travelers painted this record of a handcart brigade making its way westward.

A 1847

war wound did not stop journalist George Kendall from becoming the world's first great war correspondent.

In addition to having the instincts of a newspaperman, George Kendall was an adventurer. In 1841 he was captured by the Mexicans and jailed for taking part in an ill-fated Santa Fe expedition. When the Mexican War broke out in 1846, Kendall accompanied the army to the front lines and assigned other reporters to cover specific military operations. Before Kendall, newspapers relied on government dispatches and letters from people near the front to provide readers with the news. It could take weeks for the story of a battle to make it into print on the East Coast.

Kendall organized an ingenious communications system to transmit news to his readers. Couriers, known as Mr. Kendall's Express, took dispatches by horseback to the Gulf of Mexico, where boats carried them to New Orleans. The *Picayune* published them, then sent the dispatches on by rail and Pony Express to Baltimore, where they were telegraphed to Washington.

Through this dangerous system — one of his couriers was killed and one was injured — Kendall's dispatches not only often arrived ahead of the official government reports, but provided the most complete and well-written news about the war. He brought the information to the country faster than anybody else and earned the title "the father of the scoop."

His biggest scoop turned out to be the news of the end of the war. On the last day of fighting, September 14, 1847, Kendall was wounded in the knee. His injury did not prevent him from writing a 1,200-word story on the Mexican surrender while lying stretched out on a cot. 🐃

People crowd around to hear the latest news about the Mexican War.

A 1848

lthough Mormons witnessed the first gold discovery in California, they found a greater fortune in Utah.

When James Wilson Marshall picked up a shiny object near John Augustus Sutter's sawmill on January 24, 1848, he realized he held no ordinary rock. Henry Bigler, one of the Mormon workers who helped build the sawmill, wrote in his journal: "This day some kind of mettle was found in the tail race that looks like goald, first discovered by James Martial, the Boss of the Mill."

The Mormons had traveled north to Sutter's Mill in California's Coloma Valley a few months earlier, after their enlistments as soldiers in the Mexican War had expired. Now they had first chance at the rich gold deposits there. But it seemed that only 32-year-old Bigler was bitten by the gold bug. Other Mormons tried panning, but despite promising finds along the American River, their interest was short-lived. By the summer of 1848, a group of 67 decided to join their families in Utah's Salt Lake valley, where the Church of Jesus Christ of Latter-day Saints was laying its foundations.

A shortage of food and supplies in the newly settled valley caused Mormon leader Brigham Young to worry about the new community's future. He made every effort to dissuade his people from deserting: "We are gathered here," he declared, "not to scatter around and go off to the mines, or any other place, but to build up the Kingdom of God."

Young himself soon learned the value of gold. The path the Mormons forged over the Carson Pass in the summer of 1848 became the route that thousands of fortune hunters followed on their journey west. On the way, they stopped at the Mormon settlement in Utah to rest, eat, and sell or abandon burdensome machinery and goods. These emigrants were the Mormons' "gold mine," helping the previously floundering church to thrive. 🐃

Flight to Freedom: The Mormon Exodus

To escape religious persecution in Illinois, Mormon leader Brigham Young led his people on a 1,300-mile trek across the frontier to the valley of the Great Salt Lake in Utah. There, Mormon settlers formed the thriving community of Salt Lake City.

WY

Fort Laramie

Council Bluffs

Nauvoo

NE

IA

Salt Lake City

Fort Bridger

UT

IL

The Mormon Trail ▬

A *1848*
housewife and a Quaker sowed the seeds of feminism at a controversial meeting in Seneca Falls, New York.

Lucretia Mott, a founder of the Female Anti-Slavery Society, and Elizabeth Cady Stanton, a mother of seven who had insisted on omitting the word "obey" from her wedding vows, had the shock of their lives in the summer of 1840. At an international antislavery convention in London, they were denied seats because they were women. Mott, Stanton, and others, awakened by this outrage, began to draw parallels between the treatment of American women and that of slaves. Like slaves, women did not have the right to vote.

The antislavery movement was an entry into American politics for many women, who, like Mott and Stanton, became some of the most effective and zealous advocates for human rights. They chaired meetings, prepared agendas, and debated issues in the face of immense opposition from the public.

In the years following their London trip, Mott and Stanton corresponded and eventually decided to hold a convention

Lucretia Mott (top), and Elizabeth Cady Stanton with her son.

"to discuss the social, civil and religious rights of women." The meeting was to be held in Seneca Falls, New York, where Stanton lived. An ad was placed in the local newspaper on July 14, 1848, inviting women to Wesleyan Chapel on July 19. Some 300 people (40 of whom were men) showed up at the little chapel, only to find the doors locked. Apparently, the minister had had second thoughts about hosting such a controversial gathering. But the feminists were not easily deterred: Stanton's young nephew was boosted through a window so that he could open the doors. At the historic meeting that followed, Stanton presented the Declarations of Sentiments and Resolutions, which stated that men and women are created equal, that women must understand the laws "under which they live," and that women should be free to speak in public without stigma. The most controversial resolution — which even Mott was reluctant to put forward so soon — was that women should have the right to vote. In the end, 68 women and 32 men signed the declaration, and the women's rights movement was born. 🐃

T *1848*
he acting governor of California sent astonishing news of gold discoveries to Congress, tempting thousands of people West to make their fortunes.

Capt. John Augustus Sutter was elated when his mill hand, James W. Marshall, discovered gold near his Coloma Valley property in January 1848. Sutter immediately made Marshall his mining partner and secured a treaty with the local Indians for sole rights to dig on the South Fork of the American River. Then he dispatched a messenger to Monterey with a letter for Col. Richard B. Mason, the new military governor of the state. Sutter wanted Mason to validate his lease with the Indians, but the governor refused.

In June Mason decided to see for himself just how much gold was near Sutter's Fort. When he got there, he could barely believe what he found. "I have no hesitation now in saying there is more gold . . . than will pay the cost of the war with Mexico a hundred times over," Mason wrote. He sent his report to President James K. Polk on August 17, with maps of the area and gold samples worth some $4,000 packed in a Chinese tea caddy.

On December 5 the president included news of Mason's report in his annual address to Congress. Soon it was published in newspapers all over the world as well as in thousands of pamphlets. It was stunning confirmation of previous articles about gold in the West that many Easterners had treated with skepticism. The following year more than 40,000 people made their way to California to mine more than $10 million worth of gold. And that was only the beginning. The Gold Rush was on! 🐃

This prospector carries all manner of mining tools.

IN THEIR OWN WORDS

❝ The recent rush to California . . . appears to me to reflect the greatest disgrace on mankind. . . . So many are ready to get their living by the lottery of gold-digging without contributing any value to society. . . . The philosophy and poetry and religion of such a mankind are not worth the dust of a puffball. The hog that roots his own living, and so makes manure, would be ashamed of such company. . . . It makes God to be a moneyed gentleman who scatters a handful of pennies in order to see mankind scramble for them. Going to California. It is only three thousand miles nearer to hell. ❞

Henry David Thoreau rails against the Gold Rush in an 1852 journal entry.

C *1848*
ontrary to popular belief, many of those rushing to find gold traveled to California by boat instead of by land.

To many Americans the Gold Rush conjures up the image of stagecoaches and covered wagons making their way across the prairies. This picture is accurate, but the Gold Rush was also a major maritime event. By mid-December 1848 adventurers were swarming into New York, Boston, and other harbors.

Unlike those who opted for overland travel, sea voyagers did not have to wait for the warm weather to depart. Their journey was often rough, however. One route headed south to stormy Cape Horn at the tip of South America, rounded it, and then traveled north along the West Coast. The entire trip took an average of six months, during

This 1849 lithograph lampoons the way people might try to join the Gold Rush.

which the danger of shipwreck was all too real. Passengers endured long bouts of seasickness, and accommodations were cramped. After weeks at sea, any fresh produce rotted, leaving a regular diet of salted meat, fish, wormy biscuits, and beans, with "two bugs for every bean," as one passenger wrote. Aside from all the physical discomforts, the travelers' main enemy was boredom, with reading, gambling, and singing as the main diversions.

Alternative routes via Panama, Nicaragua, and Mexico were especially popular with those in a hurry. Sailing from the East Coast to the Caribbean side of Panama, passengers would trek and canoe across the country's jungle-covered isthmus, risking such diseases as yellow fever and typhoid. Upon reaching the Pacific, they would set sail for California in another vessel.

Ships advertising the trip sold out within hours, as voyagers were promised arrival in a matter of weeks. Many travelers found, however, that when they arrived at the Pacific, there were not enough ships to take them north to California. Thousands were stranded in Panama for months. Once the ships finally reached their destinations, passengers and even crew members ran off in a frenzy to line their pockets with gold.

P *1848*
osing as a white master and a slave, Ellen and William Craft made a daring and ingenious escape to freedom.

When he was a child, William Craft saw his entire family being taken away and sold to new owners. His wife, Ellen, was the daughter of her white owner and a slave mother. Although they were fairly content in Macon, Georgia — he as a cabinetmaker and she as an expert seamstress — the Crafts' happiness was marred by their fear of being sold and separated, and they resolved to escape. The couple had saved enough money for tickets to Philadelphia, and

Ellen Craft in her disguise as a man.

because Ellen could easily pass as white, she decided to disguise herself as a man traveling north with his slave — William — in tow.

Ellen sewed herself a pair of trousers, and William supplied the rest of her attire from local shops. Because she needed to disguise her beardless face as well as her inability to write, Ellen made a poultice for her jaw and a sling for her arm. A large beaver hat and green spectacles to hide her eyes finished the ensemble.

On December 21, 1848, the two sneaked out before dawn and made their way to the railroad station. For most of the trip, Ellen feigned illness so that she wouldn't have to talk to her fellow travelers, while William rode in the Jim Crow car as her servant. There were close calls along the way. At the Customs House in Charleston, an official told Ellen to register by signing her name; she tried to stay calm and pointed to her sling. Luckily, a fellow passenger offered to sign for "Mr. Johnson and slave." When they reached their destination on Christmas morning, they were deeply relieved.

By 1850 slave hunters were on their trail, and the Crafts fled to England. There they became influential abolitionists and published *Running a Thousand Miles for Freedom*. In 1870, five years after the end of the Civil War, the Crafts were finally able to return to the South.

A **1848**

young entrepreneur from Maine took sticky tree resin and turned it into a popular American treat.

As a 21-year-old swamper, John B. Curtis's job was to clear underbrush in the woods near Bangor, Maine. One day, while watching resin ooze from the trunk of a spruce, he had an idea: why not sell the gooey substance for chewing? After all, Indians and woodsmen had chewed it for centuries; perhaps Curtis could find a way to make it more palatable. When he explained his idea to his father, the elder Curtis was dubious. Why, he asked, would people pay for something they could get free from the trees?

In 1848 John Curtis went ahead with his idea anyway, and soon the pungent aroma of spruce resin was wafting from the family's Franklin stove. The raw gum was

The stationery letterhead from Curtis and Son Chewing Gums.

boiled into a molasseslike substance, and then, as bits of bark and other impurities rose to the surface, they were skimmed off. The sticky mixture was poured out onto a slab, rolled into a sheet, and chopped into chewable pieces. Dipped in cornstarch and covered with tissue paper, the first batch of State of Maine Pure Spruce Gum was ready for America's jaws.

By 1850 the Curtises were successful enough to set up a small factory in Portland. In its first year, Curtis and Son rang up a substantial $6,000 in profits. Soon tastier paraffin-based gums were being produced, with names like "Four-in-Hand," "Sugar Cream," and "Licorice Lulu." Curtis and Son lost its monopoly on the chewing-gum business in the 1870's when New York inventor Thomas Adams entered the business. Adams used chicle, which came from the elastic sap of Central America's sapodilla tree, to produce his gum. In 1892 Chicago soap salesman William Wrigley also jumped into the "gum wars," introducing a spearmint flavor. Despite the competition, Curtis's own business empire flourished, and he died a wealthy man in 1897, at the age of 69.

B **1849**

reaking the gender barrier, Elizabeth Blackwell became the first woman to earn a medical degree in America.

When Elizabeth Blackwell was 24, a dying friend told her that "If I could have been treated by a lady doctor, my worst sufferings would have been spared me." Blackwell, a North Carolina schoolteacher, tried to put the notion of becoming a doctor out of her mind, but it "gradually assumed the aspect of a great moral struggle."

Blackwell applied to the Harvard University School of Medicine, but the dons concluded that she was "either mad or bad" and rejected her application. In time she was rejected by every medical school in New York and Philadelphia. Many men feared that a medical education, with its "ghastly rituals" and "blood and agony" in the

dissection room, would make women too hardhearted to raise children. Others thought women lacked the courage and intellect that the profession required. Finally, in 1847, after applying to 30 colleges, Blackwell was accepted at Geneva College, a small medical school in upstate New York.

As it happened, the reason for her acceptance was that the students, when asked by the faculty to vote on her application, found the idea of a woman in their midst hilarious. Believing it to be a practical joke

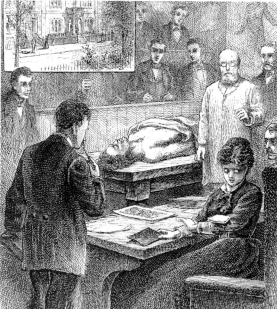

Elizabeth Blackwell attends class in the operating room of her medical school.

played by another school, they glibly voted her in.

Once in school, Blackwell endured constant ridicule. The townspeople labeled her "queer" and immoral, and initially she was barred from anatomy classes. Finding consolation in her work, she managed to graduate in January 1849 at the top of her class — thus becoming the first American woman to earn a medical degree. After furthering her education abroad, Blackwell returned to New York, where her fierce determination was called upon again. Hospitals barred her from practicing on their staffs, and landlords were unwilling to rent office space to a woman doctor. By 1857, however, Blackwell had raised enough money to open the New York Infirmary for Women and Children, aided by another female doctor — her sister Emily. The New York Infirmary became the world's first teaching hospital for women.

1849

If the leader of California's constitutional convention had had his way, the state would have included most of the western United States within its boundaries.

Even though the California territory was ceded to the United States at the end of the Mexican War, Congress was slow to grant it statehood. As a result, California's newly arrived inhabitants had to make their own rules. Military governor Bennett Riley decided the best and quickest way to bring about self-government was to hold a constitutional convention.

On September 1, 1849, the first of 48 delegates started trickling in to the convention site at Monterey. Seven were native Spanish-speaking Californians, and the rest were newcomers — some from slave-holding Southern states, others from the free North. The task of bringing them all to a consensus fell to the chairman of the constitutional committee, William M. Gwin, an ambitious Southern politician.

With few law books in town, the delegates used the Iowa and New York constitutions as models, then proceeded to pass a unique body of laws. A provision banning slavery "unless for the punishment of crimes" was unanimously passed, despite the presence of 15 Southern delegates. Another section guaranteed a woman's entitlement to

The great seal of California.

her property after marriage, one of the first times this right was granted in a state constitution.

The most controversial issue concerned California's boundary. Gwin envisioned its borders to include the huge expanse of land now occupied by California, Nevada, Arizona, Utah, and parts of Wyoming, Colorado, and New Mexico. Many objected, however, on the grounds that such a huge state would be too hard to govern and would never be admitted by Congress. Ultimately, Gwin was voted down, and the border was drawn largely along the state's present boundaries.

1849

Juliet Brier's strong will and inner strength brought her and her family across one of the most treacherous spots in North America — Death Valley.

The Brier family was part of a group of 250 people who planned to settle in California. When the travelers gathered in Provo, Utah, on October 9, 1849, many voiced their concern about the approaching winter. With the story of the ill-fated Donner party still fresh in their minds, some decided to take a detour going south. Along the way, some members of this group, including the Briers, took what they thought would be a shortcut. Instead, they got lost.

On Christmas Eve Juliet Brier, her husband Rev. John Brier, and their three small sons descended into Death Valley. Juliet, who is believed to be the first white woman to enter the valley, stumbled through the choking dust, while her husband went ahead to search for water. Night fell, and making her way by starlight, Juliet followed ox tracks to the camp. The men there suggested that she stay behind while they continued on. "Every step I take will be towards California," she replied. Drawing upon all her tenacity and faith, Juliet struggled on. She watched as men with black, swollen tongues and skeletal frames lay down and waited for death. Praying to God for strength, she admonished them so severely for quitting that they stood up and pressed on.

When the party finally emerged from the 130-mile-long valley, they entered the Mohave Desert. A few weeks later, Juliet Brier led her ragged, starving family out of the San Gabriel Mountains and into Los Angeles.

A contemporary drawing shows travelers attempting to coax their reluctant horses and pack mules into the heat of Death Valley.

1850

The first pictures of the heavens were taken by an enterprising studio photographer with the help of a Harvard astronomer.

John A. Whipple was no stranger to innovation: he had, with a partner, successfully created a new technique for making paper prints from glass negatives. Now he was looking for a way to distinguish himself from his Boston competitors in the brand-new trade of studio photography.

Across the river in Cambridge, William Cranch Bond, the director of the Harvard College Observatory, had just purchased and installed the largest telescope in the world. It is not certain who approached whom, but on October 23, 1847, the two men combined their resources and began photographing the sky through Bond's telescope. Their first effort failed when the sun's rays, aligned in the telescope's lens, set Bond's coat sleeve

on fire. But in July 1850, after a string of unsuccessful attempts, they finally produced a daguerreotype of the star Vega. Less than a year later Whipple captured images of the moon that were, he boasted, "a better representation of the Lunar surface than any engraving."

Flush with the excitement of their success, the two men made a triumphant trip through Europe. Bond visited observatories, handing out copies of the now-famous daguerreotypes. Whipple won a medal for one of his lunar images at London's Great Exposition: their celestial pictures were, without a doubt, the best in the world.

An 1852 daguerreotype of the moon.

1850

Henry Clay may have forestalled the Civil War for a decade with his last act of political wizardry.

In 1848 71-year-old Henry Clay failed in his final bid for the presidency and retired to his 600-acre farm in Ashland, Kentucky. After devoting his life to public service, however, it was difficult for him to stay away from Washington, D.C., where so much turmoil was brewing. While the Northern and Southern states clashed fiercely in Congress over the slavery status of several new Western territories, Clay was elected one last time to the U.S. Senate.

If anyone could have prevented a rift, it was Clay. Working in Congress for nearly five decades, he had become the most beloved statesman in America. Known across the country as the Great Compromiser, he nonetheless possessed a fierce devotion to principle. It was Clay who once said, "I had rather be right than be president," a consolation he sorely needed

Henry Clay: "The Great Pacificator."

after losing his bid for that office five times.

Back in the Senate, Clay argued passionately for the preservation of the Union and warned the South against splitting with the North. The Constitution, he said, was made "for posterity — unlimited, undefined, endless, perpetual posterity." He then sponsored a series of bills and helped push them through Congress. Called the Compromise of 1850, these laws admitted California into the Union as a free state, abolished the slave trade in Washington, D.C., and strengthened the existing Fugitive Slave Act, a law that penalized citizens for assisting runaway slaves.

For the time being, both the North and the South were pacified.

Clay died in office two years after his final success. His most famous speech in the Senate, delivered in 1848, could well have been his epitaph: "I know no North, no South, no East, no West, to which I owe any allegiance. The Union, sir, is my country."

1851

Capitulating to an army of petitioning teetotalers, a number of states banned the sale of alcohol during the 1850's.

Convinced that the demon rum was the root of all the social ills in his state, Neal Dow appeared at the door of the Maine legislature with a 59-foot petition that called for lawmakers to ban the sale of intoxicating drink. Five years later, in 1851, when Dow became mayor of Portland, he sponsored a law that made Maine the first dry state in the Union. By 1855 the rest of New England and much of the Midwest had followed suit.

The roots of Dow's movement can be traced to Saratoga, New York, where a group of men gathered in 1808 to swear off rum, whiskey, gin, and wine — except "by advice of a physician or in case of actual disease." Later temperance advocates held themselves to stricter standards. The American Temperance Society,

W¹⁸⁵¹**hen it was first published, *Moby Dick* was both a critical and commercial flop.**

By his late twenties, Herman Melville had thoroughly captivated the reading public. After nearly four years as a sailor in the South Seas, he had returned home, transforming his experiences of mutinous sailors, exotic climes, and noble savages into a series of highly successful novels, among them *Typee* (1846) and *Omoo* (1847). By the time Melville began *Moby Dick*, he was one of the highest-paid writers in America.

Moving to a farm in the Berkshire Hills in Massachusetts, Melville wrote daily in his study that looked out on Mount Greylock, a granite mountain that resembled the hump of a whale. The result of his efforts was *Moby Dick*, a long meditation on man's struggle with fate, with a vengeful tyrant as

The great white whale sends a sailor hurtling skyward in this 1892 illustration from Moby Dick.

its central figure. The book failed both critically and commercially — it held none of the allure of Melville's previous works. After its publication in 1851, it sold only about 100 copies per year for the next decade.

The author was devastated. His publisher refused to give him another advance, and two years later a fire consumed the plates of all his books and most of the unsold copies of *Moby Dick*.

With his popularity in decline, Melville became a customs inspector in New York City. After his retirement in 1886, he began writing *Billy Budd*, finishing it just three months before he died. It wouldn't be until the 1920's, when tales of the South Seas enjoyed a sudden vogue, that Melville's works would be rediscovered and recognized as masterpieces. 🐃

founded in Boston in 1826, convinced 1 million repentant drinkers to become teetotalers within the following 10 years and to sign pledges embossed with a capital T, for total abstinence.

By many indications, the crusaders had their work cut out for them. In the early 19th century, the average American consumed up to four gallons of pure alcohol yearly, nearly twice the intake of post-Prohibition drinkers.

Temperance crusaders attacked the demon rum with a host of tracts and public lectures, usually maintaining that alcohol was the main cause of crime, poverty, and the dissolution of the family. Lyman Beecher, a Presbyterian minister, exhorted people in the 1820's to save their communities from "rum-selling, tippling folk, infidels and ruff-scruff." The most famous piece of temperance propaganda was the

book *Ten Nights in a Barroom and What I Saw There*, by Timothy Shay Arthur. Published in 1854, it was second in sales only to *Uncle Tom's Cabin*. *Ten Nights in a Barroom*, which chronicled the degradation of a small town because of liquor, was turned into a popular melodrama that played for decades across the country.

The tale also became an entertainment staple in lecture and church halls from the mid-19th century on, where it was told with a series of graphic slides depicting the dire consequences of wanton drunkenness.

By the 1850's the

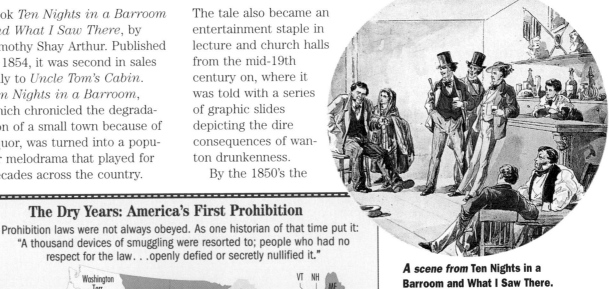

The Dry Years: America's First Prohibition

Prohibition laws were not always obeyed. As one historian of that time put it: "A thousand devices of smuggling were resorted to; people who had no respect for the law. . .openly defied or secretly nullified it."

☐ **No Prohibition**
■ **Full Prohibition**
▨ **Partial Prohibition**
(localities have option to vote dry)

A scene from Ten Nights in a Barroom and What I Saw There.

movement could claim a number of converts, in both taverns and legislatures, but drinking remained widely popular. Within a decade most state prohibition laws had been repealed, declared unconstitutional, or ignored. Nationwide prohibition was left to the crusaders of another era. 🐃

157

K *1851*
arl Marx, the champion of communism, worked as a foreign correspondent for an American newspaper.

In 1848 New York *Tribune* newsman Charles Dana was in Germany covering European revolutions when he got the opportunity to spend an afternoon with the radical German socialist Karl Marx. Three years later Dana convinced his publisher, Horace Greeley, to increase foreign coverage in the newspaper. He wrote to Marx, offering $5 apiece for articles on European politics. Marx, who was unemployed at the time, quickly accepted; he and his family were living in poverty, existing on handouts from friends, including fellow socialist Friedrich Engels. The new job would provide money and give Marx a chance to test out socialism on Americans.

The first of Marx's articles on European political events appeared in October 1851, and over the next 10 years, hundreds more followed. Greeley published his ideas (even the ones he disagreed with) and ran some as though they were his own editorials. Little did he know, however, that some of the editorials had actually been written by Engels, to allow Marx time for his "other work" — a book that would become the cornerstone of modern communism — *Das Kapital.* In fact, much of what he wrote for the *Tribune* appeared in that historic volume.

During the Civil War, Greeley decided to devote most of the *Tribune's* pages to the conflict. Marx's last dispatch for the newspaper ran in 1862.

Sheet music for "Old Folks at Home" memorialized the Suwanee River in both a souvenir issue (top) and in a first edition.

S *1851*
tephen Foster's best-known song almost began with the words, "Way down upon the Pee Dee River."

Looking for a river with a two-syllable name, songwriter Stephen C. Foster picked Florida's Suwanee River from a map. He had already rejected other Southern streams like the Pee Dee and the Yazoo because they just didn't sound right. He shortened the Suwanee to Swanee and in 1851 he finished his most famous song "Old Folks at Home."

It was immensely popular, but Foster was unable to take credit for it. Following a practice commonly used to publicize new compositions, he sold the authorship rights to minstrel-show operator Edwin Christy in exchange for $15 in ready cash. (Eventually Foster would recover $1,500 in royalties; and in 1879, when the copyright was renewed, Foster would finally be listed as the song's writer and composer.)

Sadly, one-sided business deals of this sort were common for Foster, who could not seem to manage his own success. Born in Pittsburgh in 1826, he had shown an early talent for music. By his early twenties he had written such popular songs as "Oh! Susanna," and had decided to become a professional songwriter. In 1850 he married Jane McDowell, but his happiness was short-lived; he began to drink and borrow heavily, and his wife soon left him. He moved to New York City in 1860, but despite his fame he could never sell his songs for more than a few dollars each. Then in 1864, in the charity ward of Bellevue Hospital, the composer of "Jeanie With the Light Brown Hair," "Beautiful Dreamer," and "De Camptown Races" died, at the age of 37, with only 38 cents to his name.

Popular 19th-Century American Songs

Stephen Foster's "Old Folks at Home"– or "Swanee River," as it is better known – is perhaps the most famous American song to come out of the mid 19th century, but it wasn't the only popular tune of its day. The following are some of the favorite songs of that era, many of them also written by Foster.

1848 Oh! Susanna
Old Uncle Ned

1849 Nelly Bly

1850 De Camptown Races

1851 Old Folks at Home
Wait for the Wagon

1852 Lilly Dale
Massa's in de Cold, Cold Ground

1853 Hazel Dell
My Old Kentucky Home
Old Dog Tray

1854 Jeanie With the Light Brown Hair
What Is Home Without a Mother?

1855 Come Where My Love Lies Dreaming
Listen to the Mocking Bird
Rosalie, the Prairie Flower

1856 Darling Nellie Gray
Root, Hog, or Die

1857 Jingle Bells
Mrs. Lofty and I

1860 Dixie
Old Black Joe
'Tis But a Little Faded Flower

In an effort to cool the sickrooms of his patients, Dr. John Gorrie stumbled upon a way to manufacture ice.

While caring for malaria victims in an Apalachicola, Florida, hospital, Dr. John Gorrie noticed that his patients experienced high fevers on hot nights. Convinced that he could relieve some of their suffering by lowering the temperature of the sickrooms, he began seeking ways to cool the air.

Initially, Gorrie suspended buckets of ice over his patients' beds. Air from a ceiling vent blew over the ice and then flowed over the feverish patients. Because the ice had to be shipped from the North, however, it was expensive

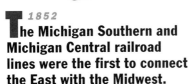

This peculiar-looking machine is the 1851 patent model of Dr. John Gorrie's ice maker.

and scarce. Gorrie decided to find another method that did not rely on ice. Using his knowledge of physics, he built a steam-powered machine to compress and cool the air.

One night the machine was left running by accident. When Gorrie came in the next morning, he found the pipes that carried the cool air to be clogged with ice. Gorrie retired from his medical practice to work full-time on his new invention.

News of Gorrie's machine did not reach the public until 1850, when the French consul scheduled a banquet but could not obtain ice to chill his champagne. There was none available in town — or so the guests thought — until waiters entered the banquet hall carrying buckets full of champagne on ice, compliments of Dr. Gorrie.

Gorrie patented his ice maker in 1851, then spent months trying to raise money to build a factory. He found no investors, and one newspaper even ridiculed him as "a crank . . . (who) claims he can make ice as good as God Almighty." A defeated Gorrie returned home and died in 1855. His ideas, however, helped lead to modern refrigeration, and the world's first ice plant was later built near Apalachicola.

The Michigan Southern and Michigan Central railroad lines were the first to connect the East with the Midwest.

"With the use of a map any person can see that all the [rail]roads and branches that we have noticed, aim at Chicago," proclaimed the editors of the Chicago *Daily Democratic Press* in 1852.

Indeed, in the next five years Chicago became the center of a burgeoning railroad system. The Galena and Chicago Union line reached 80 miles northwest of the city to Rockford, while the Illinois Central spanned the entire state from north to south. Lines such as the Chicago and Rock Island and the Chicago, Burlington and Quincy stretched toward the Mississippi River. These trains traveled into the rural sections of the Midwest, allowing farmers to send greater quantities of their products to Chicago by rail than they could ever have transported by wagon.

The railroad lines that extended to rural Midwestern outposts were necessary to support the growing economy there, but even more important were the trains that stretched east toward New York City. For the first time, on February 20, 1852, a train from the Michigan Southern railroad line arrived in Chicago from New York. Along with the Michigan Central line, the Michigan Southern railroad would be critical in establishing Chicago as the major junction between Eastern markets and the vast agricultural resources of the Midwest.

An Illinois Central train chugs along the lakeshore in Chicago in 1865.

The network of railroad lines originating from and passing through Chicago helped local farmers and manufacturers sell more of their products and greatly stimulated the economy of the city itself. A comparative study showed that some Chicago businesses doubled in

value between 1854 and 1856.

Travel from New York to Chicago now took two days, rather than two weeks, and there were other benefits as well. Mail delivery was faster, and the latest news from back East was no longer stale by the time it arrived in Chicago.

A¹⁸⁵² lthough she had little firsthand experience with slavery, Harriet Beecher Stowe wrote a book that helped doom the institution.

Passage of the 1850 Fugitive Slave Act outraged most Northerners. "Now, Hattie, if I could use a pen as you can," a Boston minister's wife said in a letter to her sister-in-law, "I would write something that would make this whole nation feel what an accursed thing slavery is."

Hattie was Harriet Beecher Stowe, the 39-year-old daughter of minister and reformer Lyman Beecher and the author of a number of short stories. Drawing on her brother Charles's recollections of the South, slave narratives, and the experiences of her own black servants, Stowe produced the epic novel *Uncle Tom's Cabin; or, Life Among the Lowly*. Centered around such characters as the dignified but doomed Uncle Tom, the angelic plantation owner's daughter, little Eva, and the cruel overseer, Simon Legree, the book was published in weekly magazine installments between June 5, 1851, and April 1, 1852, and also as a two-volume work. Within a week of publication, it had sold 10,000 copies; by the end of a year, 300,000 copies — making it second in popularity only to the Bible.

Southerners were incensed by Stowe's harsh depiction of slavery. But Northerners, many of whom had no idea of the true brutality of the slave system, were moved to activism by such heart-stopping scenes as the slave girl Eliza courageously carrying her infant to freedom across the ice-choked Ohio River. By 1860 more than 1 million copies of *Uncle Tom's Cabin* had been sold, and its impact on the public was clear. When, in the midst of the Civil War, Stowe visited the White House, she was greeted by President Lincoln: "So you are the little woman who wrote the book that made this great war," he said.

135,000 SETS, 270,000 VOLUMES SOLD.

UNCLE TOM'S CABIN

FOR SALE HERE.

AN EDITION FOR THE MILLION, COMPLETE IN 1 Vol., PRICE 37 1-2 CENTS.
" " IN GERMAN, IN 1 Vol. PRICE 50 CENTS.
" " IN 2 Vols., CLOTH, 6 PLATES, PRICE $1.50.
SUPERB ILLUSTRATED EDITION, IN 1 Vol., WITH 153 ENGRAVINGS,
PRICES FROM $2.50 TO $5.00.

The Greatest Book of the Age.

An 1860 advertisement for Uncle Tom's Cabin.

A¹⁸⁵² ppalled at the poor quality of medicine he encountered aboard ship, a young naval surgeon took up a lifetime crusade for pure drugs in America.

Two years out of medical school, in 1847, Edward R. Squibb was commissioned as a medical officer in the U.S. Navy. While at sea, Squibb became ill and required a dose of medicine. When the medication made his condition worse, he suspected that the purity and standardized strength of the commercial drugs were not reliable. He tested the medicine he had taken and discovered that it was spoiled. Examining the rest of the supplies, he found that most were contaminated with everything from sand to worms. He promptly tossed the drugs overboard.

In 1852, assigned to the naval hospital in Brooklyn, New York, Squibb convinced the Navy to establish its own laboratory for the manufacture of pharmaceuticals and chemicals; he became its director a year later. Before lack of funds forced the closing of the laboratory in 1857, Squibb and his group created a steam-heated anesthetic ether that had more reliable results than previous ethers; they also developed processes for the production of numerous other drugs, always emphasizing the need for strict quality control.

After leaving the Navy, Squibb set up his own drug manufacturing firm and helped draft a pure food and drug law that was adopted by New York in 1879 and by the federal government in 1906, six years after his death.

Ether was first stored in bottles; later it was kept in cans.

IN THEIR OWN WORDS

" A thousand lives seemed to be concentrated in that one moment to Eliza. Her room opened by a side door to the river. She caught her child, and sprang down the steps towards it. The trader caught a full glimpse of her . . . and throwing himself from his horse . . . he was after her like a hound after a deer. In that dizzy moment her feet to her scarce seemed to touch the ground, and a moment brought her to the water's edge. Right on behind they came; and, nerved with strength such as God gives only to the desperate, with one wild cry and flying leap, she vaulted sheer over the turbid current by the shore, on to the raft of ice beyond. It was a desperate leap, — impossible to anything but madness and despair. . . .

The huge green fragment of ice on which she alighted pitched and creaked as her weight came on it, but she stayed there not a moment. With wild cries and desperate energy she leaped to another and still another cake; — stumbling, — leaping, — slipping, — springing upwards again! Her shoes are gone, — her stockings cut from her feet, — while blood marked every step; but she saw nothing, felt nothing, till dimly, as in a dream, she saw the Ohio side, and a man helping her up the bank. "

An account of how the slave girl Eliza escaped to freedom, from Harriet Beecher Stowe's Uncle Tom's Cabin.

George Catlin paints himself painting a Mandan Indian chief.

C 1852
Congress rejected the purchase of George Catlin's unparalleled collection of paintings of Native Americans by a single vote.

Between 1829 and 1838, self-taught Pennsylvania-born artist George Catlin ceaselessly traveled throughout the West, painting some 600 portraits of American Indians. He had dedicated his life to "rescuing from oblivion the looks and customs of the vanishing races of native man in America."

Catlin produced the first and only complete record of the Plains Indians, neither sentimentalizing nor idealizing his subjects, but portraying them as "free, proud . . . aristocratic lord[s] of the land." After publishing several books of his experiences among the tribes, and touring the United States and Europe with his collection of Indian paintings, Catlin, deeply in debt, sought to sell them to the federal government for $50,000.

Although such senatorial stalwarts as Henry Clay and Daniel Webster lavishly praised the artist's work, the purchase was defeated in the Senate by just one vote during the 1852–53 session. Thereupon one of the artist's creditors claimed the collection. It wasn't until more than a century later that Catlin's paintings were given a proper exhibition at the Smithsonian Institution. 🐃

F 1853
For more than 200 years Japan had been closed to most foreign trade — until Commodore Perry arrived to open the nation to the West.

On July 8, 1853, four tall black ships flying the American flag sailed into Yedo Bay, Japan; the squadron's commander, brusque 59-year-old navy veteran Matthew C. Perry, was carrying letters from President Millard Fillmore to Japan's reclusive emperor. A small fleet of boats maneuvered near the American vessels, one bearing a sign that read in French: "Depart immediately and dare not anchor!"

With the exception of Dutch traders permitted on an island off Nagasaki, all foreigners had been barred from Japan since 1638. The United States wanted to open a port there for several reasons, one being a fueling station for ships bound for China. Realizing that their defenses were not strong enough to hold off Perry's military force, the Japanese allowed him to come ashore on July 14 and present his message — a request for a commercial treaty that would guarantee the safety of any American seamen landing on Japan's shores. The treaty would also open one or more Japanese ports for trade and allow for the refueling and provisioning of American ships.

A detail of a Japanese scroll shows Perry.

Perry, who had immersed himself in Japanese culture in preparation, shrewdly judged that his reluctant hosts needed time to consider the proposal and quickly departed from Japanese waters. He announced, however, that he would be back the following spring for an answer.

News that Russian and French warships were headed for Japan to make their own trade agreements caused Perry to return on February 14, 1854, earlier than he had promised. When told that Japanese laws forbade meeting the American demands, Perry persisted, offering a copy of a trade agreement that the United States had made with China. In the meantime, Perry presented the negotiators he met at Yokohama with gifts for the emperor, including books, clocks, firearms, liquor, and a miniature steam railroad that soon had a crowd jostling for rides at 20 miles per hour around a 350-foot track. For more than a week the Japanese entertained the Americans with sumo wrestling matches and sightseeing tours, while the Americans reciprocated with banquets and ship tours. After two more weeks of deliberation, the Japanese relented, and on March 3 Perry had his treaty. 🐃

1853
The Crystal Palace Exhibition in New York City was the first international fair held in the United States.

The Exhibition of the Industry of All Nations, more commonly known as the Crystal Palace Exhibition, opened in New York City on July 14, 1853. Housed in an iron and enameled glass building, it was, according to Theodore Sedgwick, one of the exhibition's organizers, a world's fair of "the choicest products of the Luxury of the Old World and the most Cunning Devices of the Ingenuity of the New."

Despite the fact that it had contributed to less than half the exhibits, America still took center stage. Along with Cyrus McCormick's reaper and Samuel F. B. Morse's telegraph were inventions for making chain links and barrel staves.

The hundreds of exhibits at the Crystal Palace astonished its many thousands of visitors. Some people marveled at such grand technological breakthroughs as the reaper and the telegraph; others were impressed by the machines for domestic use. "We had nearly lost our faith in Washing-Machines, . . . " wrote New York *Tribune*

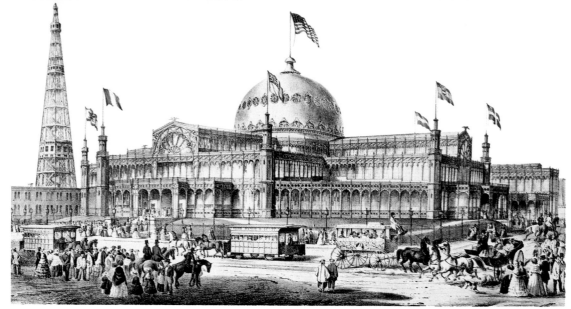

Harper's New Monthly Magazine *praised the Crystal Palace: "at night . . . it is a scene more gorgeous and graceful than the imagination of Eastern storytellers saw."*

editor Horace Greeley in his column on the fair, "but there is a rough-looking customer lately brought into the Exhibition, which revives it."

The washing machine had been designed to replace the washboard and tub, and it held out the promise of similar time-savers: mechanization could help with tedious and often exhausting household chores. Priced at $50 — or $75 if one wanted the model

"with a boiler above for rinsing" — Greeley noted that the washer was here to stay.

The exhibition closed on December 1, 1853, and due to lack of financing, it was never reopened. It had served its purpose, however: "We have grown tired of hearing that we were such a great nation," said the editor of *Harper's New Monthly Magazine*, "but the Crystal Palace inclines us to tolerate the boast."

1854
Driving a herd of cattle more than 2,000 miles from Texas to New York City, Tom Candy Ponting gave Easterners their first glimpse of longhorns.

Young and adventurous, cattle drover Tom Candy Ponting left England to seek his fortune in America. Once settled in Illinois, Ponting lost no time in getting into the American cattle trade. He and his partner, Washington Malone, traveled to Texas in the fall of 1852 with an ample supply of gold, using it to purchase a herd of 700 cattle. The trip back to their base in Illinois that spring proved to be a difficult one. Heavy rains made river crossings treacherous. Nervous about traveling through Indian country, Ponting spent many sleepless nights on horseback, watching his herd.

In this 1874 newspaper illustration, Texas longhorns stampede through the streets of New York City, creating total chaos.

Finally, the partners reached Illinois, where they wintered their cattle. In the spring of 1854, after selecting 150 of the best animals, they headed east. At Muncie, Indiana, the cattle were loaded onto railroad cars for the trip to New Jersey. After a ferry ride across the Hudson River, the animals were herded to the

Hundred Street Market in Manhattan. They arrived on July 3, 1854, concluding a two-year trip of 1,500 miles on foot and 600 miles by rail and boat.

The partners were richly rewarded. Good beef cattle were extremely marketable in the industrialized sections of the East; the herd Ponting had purchased for approximately $9 a head cost less than $20 a head to drive from Texas to New York, where the animals sold for $80 to $100 each. Yet pride was as important as profit. "We had the satisfaction of knowing that we had the best bunch of cattle in the market that day," Ponting later wrote in his autobiography.

Most authors just dream of writing rave reviews of their own work. Walt Whitman actually did just that to help win recognition for a collection of his poetry.

Born in 1819, the second of nine children, Walt Whitman spent his early adult life working for New York City area newspapers. In 1855, after several years of producing mostly mediocre short stories and poems, Whitman published *Leaves of Grass,* establishing the theme of his verses in the preface: "the United States themselves are essentially the greatest poem." When the work failed to attract the attention of booksellers, Whitman wrote his own anonymous reviews, proclaiming in one, "An American bard at last!"

Ralph Waldo Emerson, one of America's foremost poets, read the dozen poems in *Leaves* and sent Whitman a congratulatory letter: "I find it the most extraordinary piece of wit and wisdom that America has yet contributed." Whitman seized upon these words to promote his book. Public response to *Leaves* remained disappointing, however, even hostile. Whitman's own mother said the book was "muddled," and critics found his frank references to sexuality offensive. Even Emerson later distanced himself, calling the younger man's poetry "a singular blend of the *Bhagavat Ghita* and the New York *Herald,*" and Whitman "a wayward, fanciful man."

Eventually *Leaves of Grass* became an American classic, appearing on required reading lists in many schools. Later editions were expanded by Whitman and published in many languages. The 150 original copies that are still known to exist are rare collector's items.

Whitman's fame continued to increase, often through his own efforts. An 1872 newspaper article written to mark the poet's appearance at a Dartmouth College commencement compared Whitman to Homer and Shakespeare. The article's author? Walt Whitman, of course.

Walt Whitman on the frontispiece of the first edition of Leaves of Grass.

A Southern congressman claimed that he was defending his family's honor when he beat a Northern senator unconscious in the Senate chamber.

On May 19, 1856, in the first part of a two-day speech, Massachusetts senator Charles Sumner stood on the Senate floor and condemned Southern proslavery activity in Kansas as "the rape of a virgin territory." Not content with this denunciation, he then launched a personal attack on South Carolina senator Andrew Butler, calling him the Don Quixote of slavery, who had "chosen a mistress to whom he has made his vows, and who, though ugly to others, is always lovely to him."

Under the Southern gentleman's code, Butler (who was not present that day) was bound to defend his honor. But he was an elderly man. One of his younger relatives, Rep. Preston Brooks, was present, however, and angered by Sumner's character assassination, decided to take matters into his own hands.

On May 22 Brooks, clutching a walking stick, entered the Senate chamber after the day's adjournment and strode to Sumner's desk, where the senator was busy with paperwork. The South Carolina congressman announced that he had come to take revenge for Sumner's attack on his relative and began to beat him. Sumner tried to rise, but eventually fell to the ground, bleeding and unconscious.

Northern newspapers and citizens blasted Brooks, and a special House investigating committee recommended that he be expelled. But the House, voting 121 to 95 along regional party lines, failed to achieve the necessary two-thirds majority needed for the ouster. Brooks resigned his seat anyway, although his South Carolina constituents soon reelected him to the job. The South hailed Brooks as a hero, in fact, and many supporters presented him with new canes to replace the one he had smashed. Sumner's wounds may have been more damaging psychologically than physically; he did not return to the Senate for another 2 ½ years.

IN THEIR OWN WORDS

" As you will learn by Telegraph that I have given Senator Sumner a caning. . . . Sumner made a violent speech in which he insulted South Carolina and Judge Butler grossly. The Judge was and is absent and his friends all concurred . . . that the Judge would be compelled to flog him. This Butler is unable to do as Sumner is a very powerful man. . . . I felt it to be my duty to relieve Butler and avenge the insult to my State. . . .

I . . . went to the Senate and waited until it adjourned. . . . I then went to S's seat and said. 'Mr. Sumner, I have read your Speech with care and as much impartiality as was possible and I feel it my duty to tell you that you have libeled my State and slandered a relative . . . and I am come to punish you for it.' At the concluding words I struck him . . . and gave him about 30 first rate stripes with a gutta percha cane . . . . Every lick went where I intended. . . . I have been arrested of course and there is now a resolution before the House the object of which is to result in my expulsion. . . . "

In a letter to his brother, dated May 23, 1856, Preston S. Brooks describes his attack on Sen. Charles Sumner.

1856

The sewing machine was the first household appliance to come into wide use in the United States.

In the mid-19th century, several men independently invented sewing machines. By the 1850's inventors Elias Howe and Isaac Singer were two of several men who were entangled in a web of lawsuits claiming patent infringement. Finally, in 1856 Singer and his

Howe's machine removed the stigma of sewing at home.

lawyer, Edward Clark, suggested calling a truce and forming a patent pool. Such an arrangement, the first of its kind in the United States, allowed several participating companies to share all licensing fees, although Singer and Howe gained the most profits.

Once the pool was in place, Singer and Clark concentrated on selling the sewing machine to a skeptical American public. The two proved to be marketing geniuses. They set up franchised showrooms with attractive women sewing in the storefront

display windows, a public relations strategy aimed at overcoming resistance to women working on machines.

Singer and Clark introduced the first installment-buying plan, a must for the family wishing to purchase a $100 machine on an average annual household income of $500. Before long the sewing machine, the first important labor-saving device not invented for factories or farms, was cherished by millions of women, who could now produce better-quality clothes faster than if they sewed them by hand. 🐃

1857

A secret society saved a festive New Orleans tradition.

The French, who founded New Orleans in 1718, brought with them the tradition of celebrating Mardi Gras, or what is known today as Shrove Tuesday. Beginning in 1837, the citizens of New Orleans kicked off the pre-Lenten carnival party season with a public parade. Party-goers wearing elaborate masks thronged the streets; subsequent events included revelers riding on floats.

As part of the fun, the people riding on floats tossed beads and trinkets into the crowd. By the 1840's, however, innocent revelry was turning into mayhem. Rowdy spectators began shooting off guns and heaving mud, lime, sticks, and bricks at the costumed participants and into the crowd. Dismayed at this breach of civic decorum, the press joined with outraged citizens in calling on public officials to abolish the festival.

When it looked as if the Mardi Gras tradition might disappear entirely, a group of citizens got together and decided to stage their

own private parade. Only members of their secret society, called the Mistick Krewe of Comus (the pagan god of mirth), would be allowed to take part in the parade. Mysteriously worded newspaper ads announced the meetings, which were often held in remote places.

Crowds throng balconies in New Orleans as the Mistick Krewe leads a parade in 1858.

The theme of the first parade, which began as a torchlight procession after dusk on February 24, 1857, was "Demon Actors in John Milton's *Paradise Lost.*" Revelers dressed as Satan and Comus paraded through the streets on carts while masked devils, fates, furies, and fallen angels danced alongside. The procession ended at a theater, where more than 3,000 invited guests waited beneath festoons of flowers and wreaths.

The Mistick Krewe's first New Orleans Mardi Gras parade was such a success that it reinvigorated the holiday tradition. In the following years more secret societies were formed, and each sponsored a parade and a ball. Exotic parade themes included "The Missing Links in Darwin's Origin of the Species," "The Hindu Heavens," and Egyptian mythology. 🐃

A *1857*
slave who lost a legal battle to gain his freedom brought the nation one step closer to the brink of the Civil War.

Dred Scott was the slave of an army doctor, who took him from the slave state of Missouri to the free state of Illinois, and then to Wisconsin, a territory that had been declared free under the Missouri Compromise. When he returned to Missouri, Scott sued for his freedom, claiming that living in Illinois and Wisconsin had changed his status from slave to freeman.

On March 6, 1857, 11 years after Scott had filed his lawsuit, the Supreme Court ruled 7 to 2 against him. Expressing the opinion of the majority, Chief Justice Roger Taney held that Negroes, whether enslaved or free, were not citizens, and thus they had no right to sue in a federal court. The issue was so heated that each justice filed an opinion or comment.

Dred Scott.

Reaction was swift. One New York newspaper blasted the ruling as the "moral assassination of a race." Northerners concluded that a slave-owning faction controlled the federal government. (Most of the justices on the Court were Southerners.) In the South the decision reaffirmed the slaveowners' belief in slavery. The political repercussions widened the gulf between North and South.

Incumbent Douglas, seated at Lincoln's right, accepted a challenge to debate.

T *1858*
he famous Lincoln–Douglas debates pitted two articulate Senate candidates against each other and set the stage for the losing contender to become president.

The race to represent Illinois in the U.S. Senate in 1858 brought together a pair of candidates with contrasting looks, different oratorical styles, and opposing beliefs. The first of their seven scheduled debates, on August 21, attracted some 12,000 people to the town of Ottawa in northern Illinois.

The incumbent, Democrat Stephen Douglas, was short (5 feet 4 inches) and stocky, but he took great pride in his appearance. He dressed for the occasion with a ruffled shirt, blue coat, shined shoes, and a wide-brimmed hat. His tall (6 feet 4 inches) challenger, Republican Abraham Lincoln, topped his lean frame with a stovepipe hat and wore pants that were too short to hide his dusty old boots. (The press labeled them the Little Giant and the Tall Sucker.)

Under a scorching sun in Ottawa, the crowd listened for three hours. The two debaters were well matched. "I felt so sorry for Lincoln while Douglas was speaking," one listener observed. "Then to my surprise I felt so sorry for Douglas when Lincoln replied."

The candidates' views on the most significant issue of the day were diametrically opposed. Lincoln wanted slavery to be forbidden from western territories. He declared that the Union "cannot endure permanently half slave and half free" and

argued that "there is no reason in the world why the negro is not entitled to all the natural rights enumerated in the Declaration of Independence."

Douglas viewed slavery as an issue for citizens, not the federal government, to decide. He called Lincoln a radical bent on destroying the Union and later declared that "this great republic can exist forever divided into free and slave states."

In the end Lincoln lost the Senate seat, but the published version of the debates gave him the national recognition he sought. In 1860 he became president of the United States in a landslide victory over Douglas. And in 1863 he signed the Emancipation Proclamation that gave Southern slaves their freedom.

IN THEIR OWN WORDS

❝ Has anything ever threatened the existence of this Union save and except this very institution of Slavery? What is it that we hold most dear amongst us? Our own liberty and prosperity. What has ever threatened our liberty and prosperity save and except this institution of slavery? If this is true, how do you propose to improve the condition of things by enlarging Slavery — by spreading it out and making it bigger? You may have a wen or cancer upon your person and not be able to cut it out lest you bleed to death; but surely it is no way to cure it, to engraft it and spread it over your whole body. That is no proper way of treating what you regard as wrong. ❞

Abraham Lincoln in his debate with Stephen Douglas, October 15, 1858.

R¹⁸⁵⁹**ich deposits of gold and silver on a windswept mountainside lured thousands of fortune seekers to Nevada and created a thriving, densely populated city almost overnight.**

Beginning with the first stakeout on June 12, 1859, the abundant ore of the Comstock Lode brought hordes of hopefuls to Mount Davidson, part of the Virginia Range east of the Sierra Nevada. Prospectors combed virtually every inch of the canyons and ravines, "digging and delving into the earth like so many infatuated gophers," as

life, a community of tents, sheds, and shanties gave way to sturdy wood cabins, solid brick homes, business offices, 150 saloons, and three churches. A visitor in 1863 marveled at the number of brick houses, some of them four stories high, that lined the streets.

Further expansion brought an opera house, a library, and four theaters (in which Sarah Bernhardt and Lillian Russell performed). Circus impresario P. T. Barnum visited Virginia City, bringing Tom Thumb and the India Rubber Woman to

Between 1859 and 1879 miners at the Comstock Lode in Virginia City dug a half-billion dollars' worth of gold and silver ore. This framework shored up loose soil.

one observer put it.

Between 1859 and 1860, 10,000 people arrived in Virginia City, which became prosperous so rapidly that it was known as Queen of the Comstock. Virginia City's mines were the richest in the United States at that time.

As successive finds transformed the miners' hardscrabble

town. Mark Twain worked on one of the city's eight newspapers. But within 20 years of its founding, the veins of gold and silver in nearby mountains were depleted, the rollicking boomtown atmosphere vanished, and its population declined. By 1900 Virginia City had become a has-been among frontier towns.

A¹⁸⁵⁹**n obscure Pennsylvania town provided America with its first oil gusher.**

One of the few natural resources of Titusville, Pennsylvania — a town on the banks of Oil Creek, some 40 miles southeast of Erie — was a salt-brine well. To the annoyance of its operators, the well brought up not only valuable salt brine but a greasy, smelly brown substance that had to be extracted before the brine could be changed to salt.

The Seneca Indians, a local tribe, liked the thick gooey liquid, using it as a medicine and as an ingredient in their war paint. The Indians extracted the substance by soaking a blanket in it, then wringing it out and collecting the liquid.

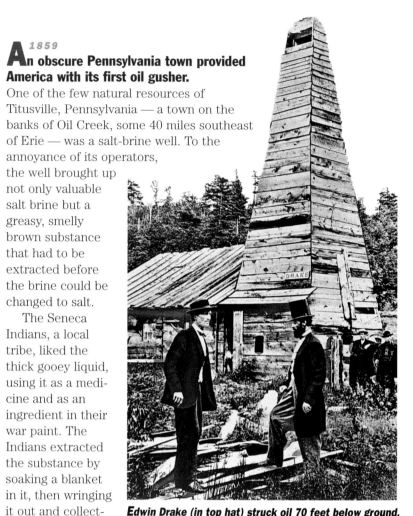

Edwin Drake (in top hat) struck oil 70 feet below ground.

Local farmers prized the extract as a horse rub with a noxious odor that kept away flies, while snake-oil hawkers dubbed it "The Most Wonderful Remedy Ever Discovered."

In 1858 a group of speculators sent Edwin Drake, a retired railroad conductor living in New Haven, Connecticut, to see if he could find a way to get more oil out of Titusville. It took the former trainman a little more than a year to devise a derrick that did what he wanted. Finally, on August 28, 1859, Drake's patience paid off. The nation's first working oil well marked the birth of the petroleum industry.

Suddenly Titusville recalled the California gold rush: boomers crowded the streets; shanties and saloons sprang up. Within two years a forest of derricks was pumping oil out of the ground at the rate of 2,000 barrels a day. At first the oil was used chiefly to illuminate lamps and to lubricate machinery in steel mills; it wasn't until later in the century that it become valued as fuel.

Fortunes were made and lost. John D. Rockefeller, who never even saw Titusville, amassed the largest oil fortune of all. As for Edwin Drake, he earned only a small sum for his pioneering effort and lost it all speculating on Wall Street. He was rescued from poverty late in life, however, when Pennsylvania granted him a small pension.

1859

Millionaire industrialist Peter Cooper founded a college to give future generations the education he had never received.

An inventor and industrialist who believed that education should be "as free as air and water," Peter Cooper prospered in several endeavors, including building an ironworks for the Baltimore and Ohio Railroad. Despite his success, however, Cooper always regretted that his formal schooling had been limited to less than a year.

Cooper spent some 30 years formulating a plan for a school for the working class. His credo: "the duty and pleasure of every rich man is to do something in a public way for the education and uplifting of the common people." Cooper became a role model for Andrew Carnegie and other philanthropists.

When The Cooper Union for the Advancement of Science and Art officially opened in Greenwich Village in New York City on November 2, 1859, students clamoring for admission almost created a riot. (The name was later shortened to Cooper Union.) The institution's mission was to provide free scientific and technical schooling, a vision unique in American education at the time. No wonder, then, that men and women,

Peter Cooper designed his school's first building.

ranging in age from 16 to 59, immediately filled every class in chemistry, physics, mathematics, drawing, and applied mechanics.

Not wanting students to have to choose between earning a living and advancing their education, Cooper saw to it that courses were offered at night.

When Cooper decided to merge his institution with an existing women's school and teach "usefull arts" like lithography and engraving, he did so to ensure that women could earn a living "and especially be kept from marrying bad husbands."

The school's reading room was the first in New York open to the public. Its lecture hall featured such speakers as Mark Twain, Susan B. Anthony, and Abraham Lincoln. It was there in February 1860 that Lincoln gave the speech that he later said got him elected president.

A detail of Frederic Remington's The Coming and Going of the Pony Express.

1860

The Pony Express set an enviable record of service: during its 18-month life, only one mail sack failed to reach its destination.

When the Pony Express began recruiting employees to carry mail between St. Joseph, Missouri, and Sacramento, California, the job description was explicit: top-notch young horseback riders weighing less than 120 pounds and "willing to face death daily." Besides such hazards as blizzards, mud slides, floods, and heat waves, riders would be targets for Indian attacks and other assaults. (After an encounter with Indians in Nevada, one rider covered 120 miles with an arrow wound in his arm and a jaw broken by a second arrow.)

Service began on April 3, 1860; every 75 miles riders handed their *mochila* — a lightweight leather blanket with pockets sewn on all four corners — to a new rider. As a rule, they changed horses every 10 to 15 miles, and company agents, alerted to a rider's approach, would have a horse saddled and ready to go. Riders were allowed two minutes to change horses, but many could do so in only 15 seconds.

The Pony Express cut the time for delivering mail from 22 days overland to 10 days or less. With the advent of a daily stagecoach that carried mail and the rapid growth of the telegraph, however, the Pony Express went out of business in October 1861. The young men who had covered 650,000 miles of desert, prairies, and mountains, delivering 34,753 pieces of mail and losing just one sack, were unemployed.

> ## IN THEIR OWN WORDS
>
> "A black speck appears against the sky.... In a second or two it becomes a horse and rider, rising and falling, rising and falling — sweeping toward us nearer and nearer — growing more and more distinct, more and more sharply defined — nearer and still nearer, and the flutter of the hoofs comes faintly to the ear — another instant a whoop and a hurrah from our upper deck, ... and man and horse burst past our excited faces, and go winging away like a belated fragment of a storm!"
>
> *Mark Twain describes an encounter with the Pony Express in Nevada.*

THE CIVIL WAR AND ITS AFTERMATH

(1861 TO 1877)

Ripped apart by irreconcilable differences, the American republic careened toward civil war. By late spring 1861, 11 Southern states had seceded from the United States and established an independent nation called the Confederate States of America. They chose Jefferson Davis, an experienced military leader and politician, as president. Richmond, Virginia, became the capital.

The Confederates compared themselves to the American colonists who had struggled against Britain. They believed they were fighting for independence against an oppressive power — the North. The Northern states, known as the Union, believed that they were putting down an insurrection. They saw the Southerners as rebels who had no right to secede from the United States. Both sides thus pointed to secession as the immediate issue. But the causes of the war ran deeper, and included disputes over states' rights, economic interests, preservation of the Southern way of life, and — most contentious of all issues — slavery.

Despite his opposition to slavery, President Abraham Lincoln insisted in 1861 that emancipation was not a goal of the war. Only a minority of Northerners wanted to abolish slavery, and Lincoln himself shared a widespread belief that the Constitution prohibited the federal government from attacking slavery in states where it already existed. He also thought the Border South — slave states such as Delaware, Maryland, Kentucky, and Missouri that decided to remain in the Union — was critical to the war. Keeping the North united and the Border South loyal were among Lincoln's most difficult tasks.

AS BOTH SIDES MOBILIZED for war, Northerners expected to triumph quickly. The North seemed to have decisive advantages. It outnumbered the South by more than 2 to 1 in population, 7 to 1 in industrial firms, and 5 to 1 in miles of railroad track. The North even outstripped the South in agriculture, producing twice as much corn and four times as much wheat. For its part, the South hoped that a defensive war would more than compensate for such advantages. The North would need a huge army to wage an offensive war in enemy territory, while the South could dig in and resist.

The South's advantages also included a strong military tradition, talented commanders, and the conviction that it was fighting to protect its homeland. Most important, the South had King Cotton on its side. Britain's textile mills depended heavily on Southern cotton. Confederate strategists reasoned that when cotton supplies ran short, all British industry would feel the pinch, and England would leap to the South's defense. That turned out to be a miscalculation: unsure of the war's outcome, England stayed out of America's turmoil.

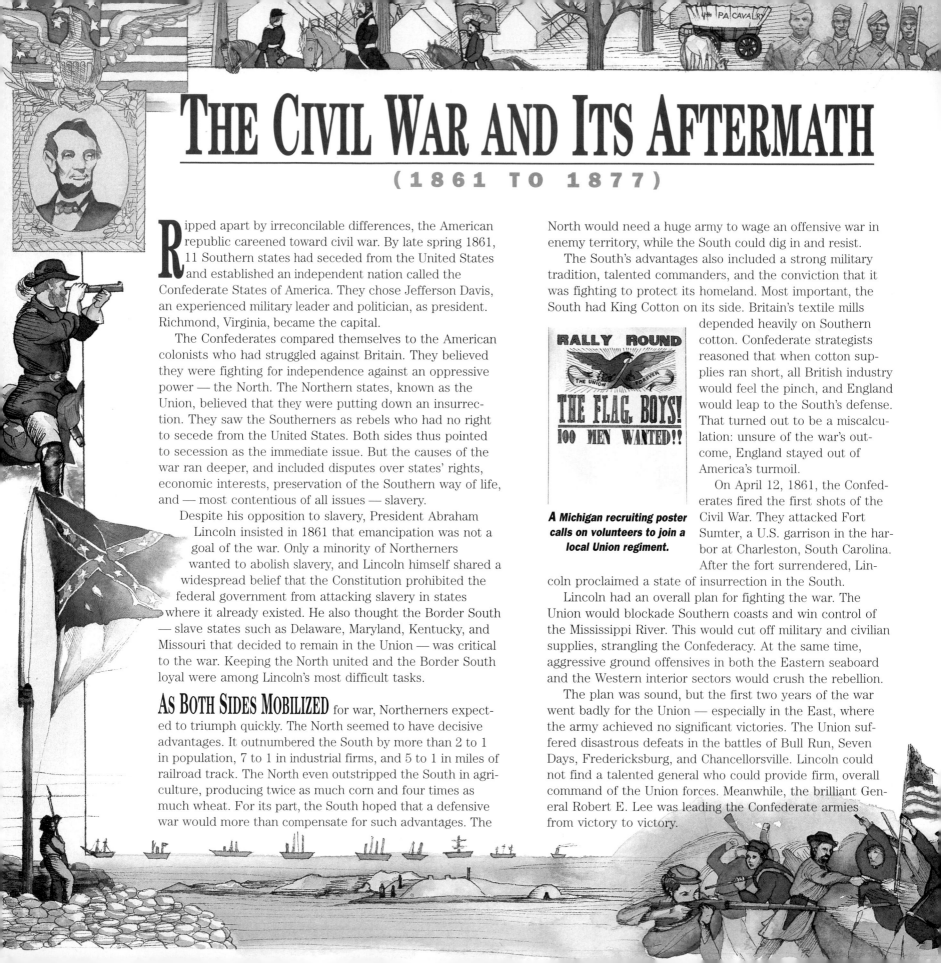

A Michigan recruiting poster calls on volunteers to join a local Union regiment.

On April 12, 1861, the Confederates fired the first shots of the Civil War. They attacked Fort Sumter, a U.S. garrison in the harbor at Charleston, South Carolina. After the fort surrendered, Lincoln proclaimed a state of insurrection in the South.

Lincoln had an overall plan for fighting the war. The Union would blockade Southern coasts and win control of the Mississippi River. This would cut off military and civilian supplies, strangling the Confederacy. At the same time, aggressive ground offensives in both the Eastern seaboard and the Western interior sectors would crush the rebellion.

The plan was sound, but the first two years of the war went badly for the Union — especially in the East, where the army achieved no significant victories. The Union suffered disastrous defeats in the battles of Bull Run, Seven Days, Fredericksburg, and Chancellorsville. Lincoln could not find a talented general who could provide firm, overall command of the Union forces. Meanwhile, the brilliant General Robert E. Lee was leading the Confederate armies from victory to victory.

Lincoln's military difficulties soon turned into political problems. The cost of the war in human lives shocked the public. The Union was suffering as many as 16,000 casualties — dead, wounded, and captured — in a single battle. Lincoln's critics in Congress and the press called him inexperienced and incompetent. Dissension in his cabinet and profiteering by contractors and officials in the War Department also called Lincoln's leadership into question.

Regimental colors from South Carolina.

Abolitionists denounced him for not targeting slavery, which, they argued, was the root cause of the war. Freeing the slaves would disrupt civilian labor in the South, they believed, and entice former slaves to join the Union army.

In September 1862 Lincoln revealed his plan. Using his authority as commander in chief, he declared that all slaves in the Confederacy would be free, unless the rebel states rejoined the Union by January 1, 1863. Lincoln exempted the Border South, Tennessee, and those parts of Virginia and Louisiana occupied by Union troops.

A California cavalry unit bore this flag. In effect, the decree freed slaves where it could not be enforced but exempted areas where it could. Still, Lincoln had made emancipation an aim of the war. From that day forward, Union victory meant the end of slavery.

LINCOLN SIGNED the Emancipation Proclamation on New Year's Day, saying, "If my name ever goes into history, it will be for this act." In addition to provisions on emancipation, the proclamation sanctioned enlisting black troops. In the summer of 1863, as free blacks filled regiments in New England, slaves in the Border South fled to Union lines offering their services to the military in return for freedom.

While Lincoln worked out his plan for emancipation, the war in the West shifted in favor of the Union. Early in 1862 the army secured Kentucky, western Tennessee, and Missouri. In April a naval squadron commanded by David

The hand-driven Confederate submarine Hunley sank a Union warship in 1864.

Farragut captured New Orleans. Farragut's bold maneuver set the stage for winning control of the Mississippi. Over the next two years, as Union forces made steady progress in the West, Lincoln found the aggressive commanders he had long sought: Ulysses S. Grant and William T. Sherman. Grant finally gained control of the Mississippi on July 4, 1863, when Vicksburg surrendered.

The Union's fortunes in the Eastern sector took a turn for the better in a titanic battle at Gettysburg, Pennsylvania. More than 170,000 troops clashed on July 1. Three days later, 51,000 men lay wounded or dead, including 28,000 Confederates. Robert E. Lee's daring foray onto Northern soil had failed. The victories at Gettysburg and Vicksburg turned the tide of the war.

TRAVELING TO GETTYSBURG in November, the president attended the dedication of a military cemetery. After the main speaker's two-hour oration, Lincoln read a two-minute speech on the meaning of the Civil War. The nation's founders, he said, had begun a great experiment based on two premises: all people have an equal right to freedom, and all people have a right to govern themselves. The terrible war would decide whether this experiment could survive.

In March 1864 Lincoln appointed Grant commander of all the Union armies. Grant quickly mapped out a strategy to end the war. He planned to launch three simultaneous offensives in order to prevent the Confederate armies from reinforcing one another. In the Western campaign, Union troops in New Orleans would make their way to Mobile, Alabama; and Sherman would drive from Chattanooga, Tennessee, south to Atlanta, a key railroad hub. In the East, Grant hoped to crush Lee's forces between two Union armies. Grant would attack Lee in northern Virginia, while another force menaced Richmond from the South.

Grant began his offensive in Virginia on May 3. The next day, Sherman descended into Georgia. Despite desperate conditions in the South — shortages of food and clothing, inadequate troop replacements, crippled transportation and communication systems — Lee's army held. A month later, Grant

FREEDOM TO SLAVES!

had lost 60,000 troops without achieving his objectives.

Northerners grew increasingly frustrated with the long war. They protested the carnage, and the antiwar movement gained ground. Everyone, including Lincoln himself, doubted that he could win reelection in November. Then on September 2, 1864, Sherman captured Atlanta. The news electrified the North, uniting Republicans behind Lincoln and sowing dissension among antiwar Democrats. Lincoln would win reelection after all. Meanwhile, Sherman set out on a dramatic March to the Sea. He would prove the North's ability to operate at will in the heart of the Confederacy, maximizing his army's mobility and destructive power by cutting loose from supply lines and living off the civilian populace.

On April 9, 1865, Lee finally met Grant in a tiny Virginia town called Appomattox Court House to discuss terms of surrender. The war was over.

THE UNION HAD BEEN PRESERVED, and slavery abolished.

But the nation had paid dearly: as many as 620,000 Americans dead, more than in all other wars combined. Over half died of disease or conditions suffered in prison. One of every three Confederate soldiers perished. The South — its cities, towns, factories, farms — lay in ruins. The bitterness between North and South would endure for generations.

The collapse of the Confederacy posed the most elementary political problems: how to reestablish agricultural production, the rule of law, and the South's place in the Union. What system of labor would replace slavery? Who would enforce laws that the South had repudiated while in secession? Questions like these forced Americans to revise such basic principles as the rights of citizenship and the balance of power between the states and the federal government.

Lincoln wanted Reconstruction carried out "with malice toward none; with charity for all." A leader of his skill might have accomplished this. Tragically, on April 15, 1865, six days after Lee's surrender, Abraham Lincoln lay dead, the bullet of a Southern extremist lodged in his head.

THE JOB OF RECONSTRUCTION fell to Lincoln's successor.

Andrew Johnson, though a former slaveholder, was also a staunch Unionist. At the end of May, he unveiled his plan. States could return to the Union after they repudiated secession and accepted the 13th Amendment abolishing slavery. Confederate officials and large slaveholders could not vote unless they obtained a pardon from the president. Many Republicans regretted that Johnson made no provisions to give former slaves the vote but took heart that the South's prewar leadership was disfranchised.

By summer, Johnson had granted hundreds of pardons to disfranchised rebels. Many promptly ran for office and won. The North was especially galled to see Confederate vice president Alexander Stephens elected to the U.S. Senate. At the end of 1865, several Southern states enacted repressive Black Codes that reduced former slaves to virtual peonage. The North became convinced that it could ensure former slaves their civil rights and prevent Confederate leaders from regaining control of the South only by repudiating Johnson and starting over.

ANGRY REPUBLICANS in Congress took charge in 1866.

They divided the South into five districts, each under military control, and required states to ratify a new 14th Amendment before returning to the Union. The amendment vastly increased the power of the federal government, guaranteed equality before the law, and provided for universal male suffrage. It made the federal government the guarantor of Constitutional rights instead of the states, made anyone born or naturalized in the United States a citizen, and extended the vote to black men by penalizing states that prohibited them from voting.

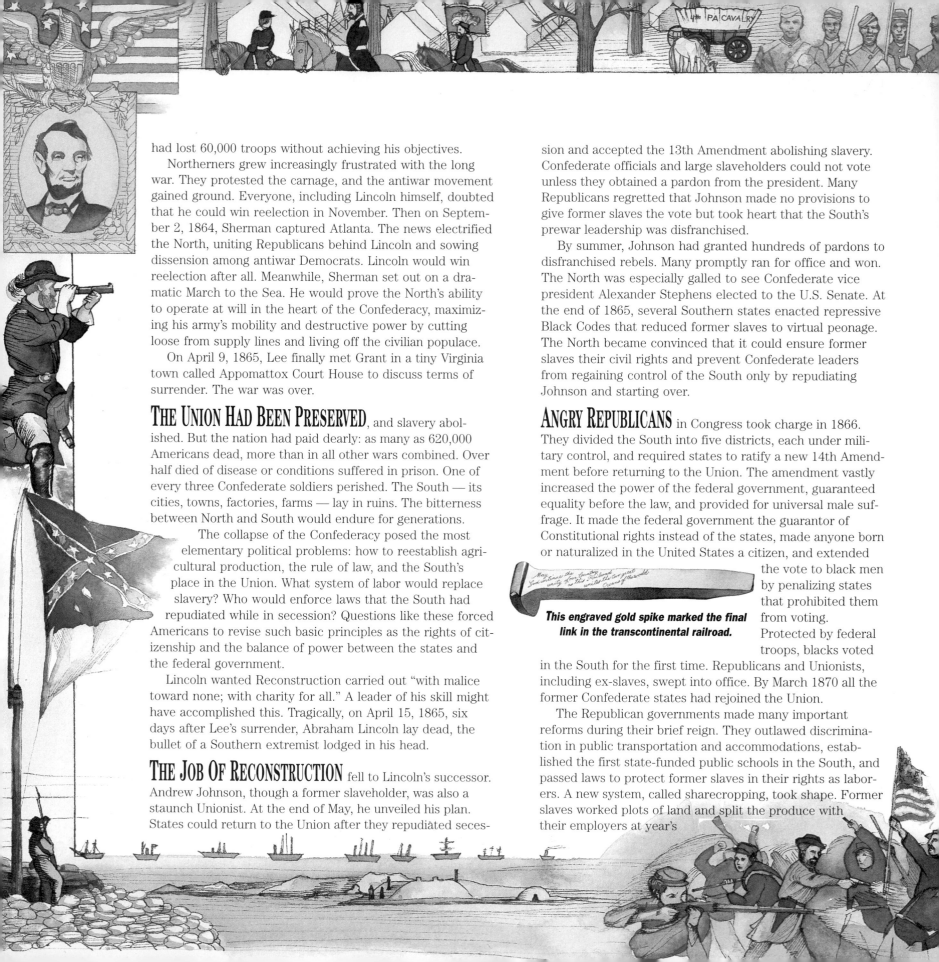

This engraved gold spike marked the final link in the transcontinental railroad.

Protected by federal troops, blacks voted in the South for the first time. Republicans and Unionists, including ex-slaves, swept into office. By March 1870 all the former Confederate states had rejoined the Union.

The Republican governments made many important reforms during their brief reign. They outlawed discrimination in public transportation and accommodations, established the first state-funded public schools in the South, and passed laws to protect former slaves in their rights as laborers. A new system, called sharecropping, took shape. Former slaves worked plots of land and split the produce with their employers at year's

The Statue of Liberty's torch was displayed in Philadelphia in 1876.

end. Sharecropping relieved planters from paying wages in cash, and it afforded former slaves the independence they needed to expand the families, churches, and fraternal and political groups they formed after emancipation. More than 600 blacks, most former slaves, held political office in the South during Reconstruction.

The Republicans faced formidable opposition. Many whites could not abide living under conditions of equality with former slaves. The Ku Klux Klan, founded in 1866, spread throughout the South in the next two years. The KKK intimidated, assaulted, and killed Republicans, primarily blacks. Federal authorities took decisive action. Republican Ulysses S. Grant, elected president in 1868 and again in 1872, used military arrests and federal court trials to break up the Klan across the South.

The 1876 presidential election ended Reconstruction. The Grant administration had been marred by scandal and corruption, and the Democrats won a majority of the ballots counted. But the election was close, and hinged on results in the three Republican states in the South. Both Republicans and Democrats claimed victory in those states. Southern Democrats and agents of the Republican candidate, Rutherford B. Hayes, struck a bargain. Democrats would recognize Hayes as the winner of the presidential election, and Hayes would recognize the Democrats in the state elections in South Carolina, Louisiana, and Florida. A reaction set in. Over the next 25 years, Democrats created a rigid system of segregation and white supremacy across the South.

In the North the war had given a tremendous boost to industrial development. Output of iron, coal, and

On the cattle trail: the birth of an American legend.

textiles had reached unprecedented heights. Industrialization promoted mechanized agriculture, and that in turn allowed the North to feed its army and at the same time to double its exports of wheat, corn, pork, and beef. When the conflict ended, factories churned out many consumer goods, like shoes and ready-made clothing, that Americans had made by hand before the war. Industrial production in 1877 was 75 percent above its level in 1865.

INDUSTRIAL EXPANSION

was a powerful impetus to settlement west of the Mississippi. Workers finished the first transcontinental railroad in 1869. Railroads, in turn, promoted the open-range cattle industry. Cowboys drove herds of several thousand cattle thousands of miles to railroad towns in the central Plains — and in the process created an enduring American icon. As it happened, the age of the cattle drive lasted just 20 years. Settlers, determined to obtain land and plow it under, fenced out the cowboys.

The settlers also squeezed out the Native Americans. The government had promised many tribes vast lands west of the Mississippi where they could hunt unmolested. But the Homestead Act of 1862 offered the same land to white settlers for little or no money. As farmers swarmed over the Great Plains and other pioneers moved into the Southwest, federal troops fought a new round of wars with the Sioux, Arapaho, Comanche, Cheyenne, Kiowa, Modoc, Apache, and Nez Percé

Sitting Bull led Sioux warriors against the 7th U.S. Cavalry.

tribes. The tribes struggled desperately for greater freedom but, as before, suffered defeat. Those who returned to the reservations faced poverty and disease.

Cynics had long predicted that a republic as large and diverse as the United States was doomed to self-destruction. Such was clearly not the case. The young nation had proved phenomenally successful in securing economic growth and individual rights. It had extended the ranks of citizenship (if not always the rewards) to its former slaves. It had survived a Civil War, and in 1876 it celebrated the centennial of its birth. ☙

FREEDOM TO SLAVES!

1861
The diary of a Southern housewife offers a revealing look at Confederate politicians and details a very personal objection to slavery.

Mary Boykin Chesnut moved in the highest Confederate political and social circles. At the side of her husband, James Chesnut, Jr., Mary was a witness to the formation of the Confederacy at Montgomery, Alabama, in February 1861; the firing on Fort Sumter in Charleston harbor in April; and the transfer of the Confederate headquarters to Richmond early in June. There James Chesnut became an aide to and confidant of President Jefferson Davis. To relieve what she considered the tedium of life in Richmond during the war, Mrs. Chesnut held open houses for dancing, playing parlor games, and exchanging news and gossip.

Mrs. Chesnut began a diary on February 18, 1861. "This Southern Confederacy must be supported now

Although often confined to bed by illness, Mrs. Chesnut continued to write.

by calm determination and cool brains," the 37-year-old housewife wrote in her first entry. Mrs. Chesnut belittled Davis's detractors, writing: "Everybody putting their mouths in, nothing sacred, all confusion of babble, crimination, and recrimination."

Although she enjoyed the convenience of having servants in her home, Mrs. Chesnut denounced slavery as "a monstrous system." She objected to the common practice of slave women giving birth to children whose fathers were the slave owners. "Our men live all in one house with their wives and their concubines," she wrote, "and the mulattoes one sees in every family partly resemble the white children."

Chesnut's *Diary From Dixie* was first published in 1905, nearly 20 years after her death. With its intimate portraits of the South's leaders and frank discussion of events, the book has been praised as more revealing than any fiction inspired by the war. 🔫

1861
Rumors of an assassination attempt forced Abraham Lincoln to steal into the capital under cover of darkness for his inauguration ceremony.

After bidding farewell to his hometown of Springfield, Illinois, on February 11, 1861, the president-elect boarded a special train for a 12-day whistle-stop journey to Washington. People wanted to hear what he had to say about the secession crisis that his election had brought about. Already seven Southern states had left the Union, choosing Mississippi's Jefferson Davis to head their Confederate government.

On February 21 private detective Allan Pinkerton came to Lincoln's hotel room in Philadelphia with disturbing news: there appeared to be a conspiracy to assassinate the president-elect when he passed through Baltimore. At first Lincoln shrugged off the news as just another anonymous threat, but when Frederick

A cartoonist lampoons Lincoln's stealthy arrival in Washington.

Seward, the son of Sen. William Seward of New York, informed him of a planned assassination in Baltimore, Lincoln reluctantly agreed to a surreptitious entry into the capital. First, though, he insisted on giving speeches scheduled the next day in Philadelphia and Harrisburg.

Accompanied only by a friend who was well armed, Lincoln quietly boarded the sleeper of a regularly scheduled train about 11 P.M. and jammed himself into a berth. After an uneventful transfer in Baltimore — the only disturbance being a drunk singing "Dixie" on the station platform — the president-elect arrived in the capital at 6 A.M. on February 23 and headed to a hotel suite.

On March 4, 1861, Lincoln stood against the backdrop of the unfinished Capitol dome to deliver an inaugural address appealing to the South. "Though passion may have strained, it must not break, our bonds of affection," he declared. 🔫

1861

Charles Francis Adams, U.S. minister to Great Britain and heir to a political dynasty, did as much to ensure a Confederate defeat as any Northern general.

On March 19, 1861, soon after being reelected to the U.S. House of Representatives for his second term, Charles Francis Adams headed to London. Appointed minister to Great Britain, he was following in the footsteps of both his grandfather, John Adams, and his father, John Quincy Adams, who had served there as diplomats before their elections to the presidency of the United States.

Arriving in London on May 13, Adams learned that Queen Victoria had just issued a proclamation of neutrality recognizing the Confederacy's rights as a belligerent. Confederate envoys in Britain were already playing up that country's dependence on Southern cotton to keep its clothing mills humming. The British ruling class and many businessmen were generally sympathetic to the South, so it was up to Adams to keep England out of the war.

In November 1861 a U.S. warship stopped the British mail packet *Trent* en route from Havana, Cuba, to London, and the captain removed two Confederate agents as war prisoners. The North was jubilant; Britain threatened war. Adams intervened and the agents were released. Adams also managed to persuade the British government to hold off recognizing the Confederacy, which France had already done.

In 1863 Adams learned that two ironclad ships were being built in Britain for the Confederacy. Allowing the vessels to leave the Liverpool shipyard meant war, he told the British government. The ironclads were detained. Henry Adams later said of his father's diplomatic coup, "The years of struggle were over, and Minister Adams rapidly gained a position which would have caused his father or grandfather to stare with incredulous envy."

French Impressionist Edouard Manet depicted the sinking of a Confederate blockade runner attempting to leave England with supplies for the South.

Ellsworth's Zouave unit practices its famed precision drill.

1861

The commander of one of the volunteer militia units known as Zouaves was the North's first Civil War casualty.

Among those who responded to President Lincoln's call on April 15, 1861, for 75,000 volunteers to put down the Southern rebellion was Elmer Ellsworth, a 24-year-old man who had worked in Lincoln's Springfield, Illinois, law office. Ellsworth had campaigned for Lincoln during the fall of 1860 and then moved to Washington after Lincoln was elected president.

Before he worked for Lincoln, Ellsworth had established himself as the leader of a precision drill team, the U.S. Zouave Cadets of Chicago, who performed throughout the Midwest and the East. The troop was as renowned for its costumes as its intricate drill formations: the cadets' uniform, modeled after the Algerian troops known as Zouaves, included a braid-trimmed blue jacket over scarlet pants (white pants in the summer) and a tassled red fez.

Shortly after the Civil War broke out, Ellsworth went to New York to assemble a regiment. Within four days, he had recruited some 1,100 firemen for a new unit, the 11th New York Fire Zouaves.

On May 23, 1861, Colonel Ellsworth's Zouaves joined a night march across a Potomac bridge to occupy Alexandria, Virginia. At sunrise on May 24, Ellsworth was preparing to seize a telegraph office when he noticed a Confederate flag hanging from an attic window of the Marshall House hotel. Impetuously, the officer entered the hotel, charged upstairs to the attic, and grabbed the rebel banner.

As Ellsworth started downstairs, the hotel proprietor shot him in the chest. The colonel became the first Union soldier killed during the war. One of Ellsworth's men then shot and killed the hotel owner.

The incident had repercussions nationwide. The South grieved for the loss of the hotel proprietor, who had "perished a'mid the pack of wolves," as one newspaper proclaimed. Ellsworth was hailed as a martyr for the North who had been "assassinated by a rebel," and his body lay in state in the White House.

1861

The mystery of the daring young soldier from Michigan who suddenly deserted his army post remained unsolved for nearly a quarter century after he vanished.

When she was in her mid-teens, Sarah Emma Edmonds left her home in Canada to escape an arranged marriage. Under the name Franklin Thompson, Edmonds worked as a Bible salesman in Michigan.

At the outbreak of hostilities, Frank Thompson, not yet 20, was inducted into the U.S. Army in Detroit on May 25, 1861. The next month his unit, the 2nd Michigan Infantry, was sent east to defend Washington, and Thompson was assigned to hospital duty. Nursing the wounded at the First Battle of Bull Run on July 21, he barely managed to escape capture by the victorious rebels.

Early in 1862 Thompson was named regimental mail carrier, an assignment that masked his true work as a spy. Assuming the guises of a black man, an Irish peddler woman, and an escaped female slave,

Thompson combined bravery with subterfuge.

Thompson gathered vital information as he slipped between the Union and Confederate camps during several campaigns in Virginia. He had a number of close calls, one of which he later described as dodging "a perfect blaze of both musketry and artillery."

While he was in Kentucky the following year, Thompson contracted malaria. Realizing that hospitalization would reveal his secret identity, he donned another disguise and slipped off into the night.

In 1864, when Edmonds published an account of her exploits as a war nurse and spy, she omitted the fact that she had disguised herself as a man. Two decades later, by then a married woman, she asked for a military pension. Her former army cohorts agreed to write testimonials to her dedication and good moral character, and Congress authorized her pension. Before her death in 1898, the Grand Army of the Republic, the Union veterans' organization, made Edmonds a member — the only woman so recognized.

All Aboard

The face of the nation was changed forever as the iron horse began thundering across the land. Inspired by Britain's first experimental steam locomotive in 1804, Americans soon caught up with their British counterparts. Here are some important dates in the development of the U.S. railroad industry.

1830 Passenger service begins on the South Carolina Railroad, America's first steam-powered line.

1830 Engineer and steamboat designer Robert L. Stevens invents the modern rail, along with railroad spikes and roadbeds of wooden ties set in gravel.

1836 The world's first railroad sleeper carries passengers between Harrisburg and Chambersburg.

1840 A railroad building boom begins in the United States. Total track mileage grows from 5,000 in 1840 to 30,000 in 1860.

1857 The first refrigerated railway car leaves Chicago with beef stored in ice compartments.

1859 George Pullman's sleeping car goes into service.

1861 The first railroad-assisted military victory in U.S. history coincides with the first land battle of the Civil War. Some 3,000 Union troops board two trains at Grafton, West Virginia, on June 2, travel several miles, march to nearby Philippi, and rout the Confederates.

1869 The transcontinental railroad is completed. Union Pacific rails from the East meet those of the Central Pacific from the West at Promontory, Utah.

The 14th West Virginia Infantry flag.

1861

The 35 counties in Virginia that broke away to form the free state of West Virginia achieved the only successful — and permanent — secession of the Civil War.

For years, Virginians west of the Allegheny Mountains had protested the Tidewater aristocracy's domination of their state's politics and control of its spending. These mountaineers, who grew no tobacco or cotton and held few slaves, resented that eastern counties were given the lion's share of railroads, canals, and other public-works projects.

On May 23, 1861, shortly after Virginia seceded, voters in the western part of the state chose to remain in the Union. Members of a spontaneous grassroots movement soon decided to form an independent state. When representatives of the western counties gathered at Wheeling on June 11, they faced a big hurdle — a provision in the U.S. Constitution that forbade a new state's formation from part of an old one without the consent of the legislature. To sidestep this obstacle, they named themselves the "restored government" of Virginia, called the Confederate legislature in Richmond illegal, elected their own governor, and sent congressmen to Washington.

The North moved promptly to establish military control of the breakaway counties, and its support made possible a referendum on statehood on October 24, 1861. On June 20, 1863, West Virginia was admitted to the Union as the 35th state.

A *1861*
dour, tightfisted merchant from New York struck it rich as a key fund-raiser for the transcontinental railroad.

Stranded for three months in Panama en route to California to mine gold in 1849, Collis P. Huntington trudged back and forth across the isthmus trail selling food and wares that he carried on his back. By the time he arrived in San Francisco, he had quadrupled his capital. A single day of mining convinced Huntington that gold digging was not for him. In partnership with Mark Hopkins, another forty-niner, he established a hardware business in Sacramento.

On June 27, 1861, Huntington and Hopkins joined grocer Leland Stanford and dry-goods merchant Charles Crocker in incorporating the Central Pacific Railroad. Building east from Sacramento, the

A timetable for the Central Pacific's first riders.

men — later known as California's Big Four — planned to meet the Union Pacific tracks being laid west from Omaha in order to form the nation's first transcontinental railroad. Huntington masterminded the partnership, lying to get federal construction loans, bribing congressmen, and forgetting details when called before an investigating committee.

Huntington was not the only businessman who skirted the law; few others, however, were as frank in admitting to such practices. He once complained that the competition among those bribing public officials was so stiff that the cost of doing business with Congress had risen to between $200,000 and $500,000 a session. Unlike Stanford, who endowed Stanford University, and other robber barons, Huntington gave almost nothing to charity or philanthropies.

T *1861*
he Battle of Bull Run was the first major conflict of the Civil War — and the one the North expected would end the Southern rebellion.

As bands blared and banners waved, the 30,000-man Union army, commanded by Brig. Gen. Irwin McDowell, marched out of Washington, D.C., on July 16, 1861. Twenty-five miles ahead, a 22,000-man Confederate force commanded by McDowell's West Point classmate Gen. P.G.T. Beauregard was all that stood between him and Richmond, the Confederate capital.

In a lighthearted mood that one observer compared to "a political club marching to its annual outing and clambake," the troops festooned their saddles with streamers and their cannons with flowers. Anticipating an easy victory, Union politicians and society women followed a few days later to watch the events unfold, their carriages stocked with food and drink for picnic lunches. By Sunday morning, July 21, 1861, the rival

This contemporary sketch of the First Battle of Bull Run conveys the widespread panic.

forces were lined up on opposite sides of a meandering stream called Bull Run, just north of the important railroad junction at Manassas (the Confederates called the conflict the Battle of Manassas).

Each general planned to attack his enemy's left flank, which would have had them circling like waltzers on a dance floor. But the arrival of 9,000 more Confederate soldiers from the Shenandoah Valley — the first wartime troop movement by rail — had wiped out the Union's numerical advantage.

McDowell attacked first. When Beauregard saw the threat to his left, he rushed the newly arrived troops to that sector. With the Confederates' left flank giving way, legend has it that one Southern general pointed to a Virginia brigade led by Gen. Thomas J. Jackson. "There stands Jackson like a stone wall," he shouted to his men. "Rally on the Virginians!"

It was a haphazard contest between poorly trained, disorganized troops. Eventually, the outnumbered, exhausted Union forces began a withdrawal that soon turned into a confused retreat. The exodus did not end until the troops — and the shocked spectators — were safely back across the Potomac River.

In what came to be known as the First Battle of Bull Run, the Union lost 2,896 men; the Confederates, 1,982. Sobered by the defeat, President Lincoln asked Gen. George B. McClellan, who had won some minor engagements in West Virginia, to take command of the troops around Washington.

1861
When John Tyler ended his 15-year hiatus from politics, he became the only U.S. president to serve in the Confederacy.

After President William Henry Harrison died of pneumonia in April 1840, just a month after taking office, Vice President John Tyler was sworn in as president, the first to gain the position through the death of his predecessor. In 1845, after the completion of the term, Tyler returned to his plantation in Sherwood Forest, Virginia. The unpopular politician described himself as eager to "seek repose in the quiet enjoyments of rural life." In 1860, however, with Abraham Lincoln's election as president further inflaming tensions between the North and the South, Tyler, who was then 70 years old, found himself on the verge of relaunching his political career.

When Southern states began to secede from the Union, Tyler organized a peace convention in Washington in February 1861. Delegates from 13 Northern states and 7 border states attended, and they elected him president of the convention. When Tyler could not get the delegates to reach an accord, he returned to Virginia. There he added his voice to the movement for secession. On April 17, 1861, Virginia became the eighth state to leave the Union.

Soon after the Civil War began, Tyler won an election that sent him to the Confederacy's Provisional Congress. In the fall of 1861, the only former U.S. president to serve as a Confederate official was elected to the Confederate House of Representatives. He died in 1862, before taking office.

Viewed as a traitor in Washington, Tyler was honored with a state funeral in Richmond, Virginia, and his casket was draped in a Confederate flag. It was not until 1915, 53 years after his death, that Congress voted to erect a memorial stone over his grave. 🔫

The unrest leading up to the Civil War brought Tyler out of retirement.

Brother versus brother: Confederate George Crittenden (left) and Thomas Crittenden, a Union general.

1861
The Civil War divided families as well as the nation, sometimes pitting brother against brother.

Virginian Robert E. Lee wrote to his sister in 1861 about the most difficult decision of his life: he had resigned from the Union Army, in which he held the rank of colonel, and would serve the South.

Although he did not believe in slavery or a state's right to secede, Lee could not "raise my hand against my relatives, my children, my home." The former superintendent of the U.S. Military Academy at West Point went on to become the South's greatest military hero.

Many families on both sides of the conflict were divided, including that of President Abraham Lincoln. His wife, Mary Todd Lincoln, had three half-brothers who fought for the Confederacy. And Varina Davis, the wife of Confederate president Jefferson Davis, had a brother who was an officer in the Union navy.

About 54,000 white Southerners fought in the Union Army; more than 100 became high-ranking officers. One such officer was Gen. George H. Thomas, known to his troops as Old Pap and The Rock. He earned the last nickname at the Battle of Chickamauga in 1863, when he rallied his troops and held his position while many other Union forces fled in panic.

General Thomas's military accomplishments for the Union led his Virginia family to disown him. His sisters turned his picture to the wall, burned his letters, and sent back his many gifts unopened. They even refused to attend his funeral in 1870, an event whose mourners included President Ulysses S. Grant. "George died to us in '61," one of the sisters said.

In countless other families the loss of loved ones on opposite sides of the conflict did little to heal the rifts. William Rufus Terrill, for example, a native Virginian related to Robert E. Lee, outraged his father when he decided to honor his pledge to the Union army after he graduated from West Point.

"Do so and your name shall be stricken from the family records," William Terrill's father wrote. William's brother, James, served as a colonel in the Confederacy. After both brothers died in battle, the family erected a memorial with the inscription "God Alone Knows Which Was Right." 🔫

Among the thousands killed at the Battle of Antietam were these Rebels, who fell at Hagerstown Pike.

M¹⁸⁶¹ore American lives were lost in the Civil War than in any war before or since.

From 1861 to 1865, during the four years of carnage that led to the abolition of slavery in the United States and the preservation of the Union, about 618,000 Americans lost their lives. The toll included 360,000 troops on the Union side. Although figures for the South's losses are especially difficult to ascertain, about one out of four white males of military age in the Confederacy died — approximately 258,000 soldiers.

The cost in lives lost was higher than in any other American conflict including World War II, in which 405,399 Americans died. In fact, nearly as many Ameri-

cans died in the Civil War as in all the other wars the United States has fought combined. The First Minnesota regiment had the highest percentage loss of any regiment in the war: 224 of its 262 men at Gettysburg were killed or mortally wounded.

One reason for the war's fearsome mortality rate was that advances in the killing power of weapons had outpaced progress in medicine or hygiene. Physicians unaware of the importance of antiseptic practices or the underlying causes of diseases could do little to help soldiers wounded by powerful new guns or languishing in disease-ridden camps. Some 400,000 of all wartime deaths were from disease.

The Confederate States of America

Although 11 states seceded from the Union, 4 others that permitted slavery (Delaware, Kentucky, Maryland, and Missouri), did not join the Confederacy.

State	Date of Secession
● South Carolina	**Dec. 20, 1860**
● Mississippi	**Jan. 9, 1861**
● Florida	**Jan. 10, 1861**
● Alabama	**Jan. 11, 1861**
● Georgia	**Jan. 19, 1861**
● Louisiana	**Jan. 26, 1861**
● Texas	**Mar. 2, 1861**
● Virginia	**Apr. 17, 1861**
● Arkansas	**May 6, 1861**
● North Carolina	**May 20, 1861**
● Tennessee	**June 8, 1861**

S¹⁸⁶¹tandard sizing for men's clothing was born of the need to mass-produce uniforms for Civil War troops.

The men who fought in the first battles of the Civil War wore an assortment of different cuts and styles of uniform. Not only were some of the more stylish outfits ill suited for fighting, but the variation in attire often made it difficult for soldiers to distinguish between friends and foes.

Early in the war, Union officials realized that the government would have to develop a reliable, efficient method for producing uniforms. Before it could turn out thousands of uniforms quickly, however, the military had to address the problem of sizing. To design an accurate sizing grid, the Union army abandoned the early-19th-century practice of using the measure of one body part as the basis for all of a person's clothing. Instead, the military took full body measurements of more than 1 million inductees to calculate average sizes.

In 1861 the first "statistical data regarding the form and build of the American male" became the basis for standard patterns for uniforms. The release of the army's sizing charts to clothing manufacturers helped set a precedent.

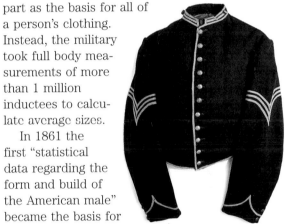

This jacket belonged to a Union cavalry officer.

At the same time, the growing acceptance of machine-made garments contributed to making standard-size suits the popular attire for men in all walks of life. The stigma attached to wearing ready-made men's clothing, which previously had been associated with the lower classes or laborers without wives, was disappearing. By the end of the century, standard sizing for women's clothing was also developed. Machine-made garments would soon become an important part of the American wardrobe.

1862

When the sounds of battle receded, Civil War soldiers on both sides sang familiar tunes including their favorite: "Home! Sweet Home!"

Music making was so prevalent during the Civil War that Confederate general Robert E. Lee asserted, "I don't believe we can have an army without music." Soldiers gathered around campfires to sing, often accompanied by harmonica and banjo players. Marches were frequently occasions for singing, and regimental bands performed concerts from time to time.

One of the few things shared by the North and the South was a similar taste in music. By and large, the troops rejected battle songs for sentimental standards about home, hearth, and affairs of the heart.

In addition to "Home! Sweet Home!" which was composed in

The original song sheet for the Civil War soldiers' best-loved tune.

1823 and was the favorite song on both sides of the Mason-Dixon line, "Annie Laurie" (1835), "'Tis the Last Rose of Summer" (1813), and "Listen to the Mockingbird" (1855) were

all popular tunes. When it came to patriotic songs, Confederate soldiers preferred "Dixie" (1860), which had actually been written by a Northerner named Dan Emmet for a minstrel show in New York City. Union soldiers favored the old Revolutionary War tune "Yankee Doodle." Of the music written specifically for the War Between the States, however, Northerner Julia Ward Howe's stirring march "Battle Hymn of the Republic" (1862) has turned out to be the most enduring song.

The Civil War also saw the introduction of the lone bugle melody that is commonly known as "Taps." Daniel Butterfield, a Union major general, adapted the melody from a French bugle call in 1862, and by 1867 it had become the official sign-off for the military day.

Melodies of War

The Civil War inspired thousands of marches, hymns, and sentimental songs. The lyrics often described dramatic war events, the soldiers' longing for home, or their loved ones' yearning for their safe return.

1861 The Battle Cry of Freedom

1861 The Bonnie Blue Flag

1861 Maryland, My Maryland

1862 Battle Hymn of the Republic

1862 Kingdom Coming

1863 All Quiet Along the Potomac Tonight

1863 When Johnny Comes Marching Home

1863 When This Cruel War Is Over

1864 Tenting on the Old Camp Ground

1864 Tramp! Tramp! Tramp!

1862

The ironclad ship that fought the *Monitor* was not officially called the *Merrimack.*

When the U.S.S. *Merrimack,* a sturdy three-masted wooden ship, was burned and sunk by Union forces retreating from Norfolk, Virginia, in 1861, Stephen Mallory, the Confederate secretary of the navy, saw an opportunity. Unable to obtain any of the ironclads that the French and English navies had available, Mallory ordered the *Merrimack* pumped out, raised, and put into dry dock. There the Confederate Navy transformed the Union frigate into an armored terror by adding an iron-plated casemate with 10 heavy guns and an iron ram. The rebuilt vessel was christened the C.S.S. *Virginia* but was still known to some as the *Merrimack.*

The *Virginia* proved its worth on its first trial. On March 8, 1862, while engaging a blockading squadron at Hampton Roads, Virginia, the ironclad rammed one Union warship and destroyed another by gunfire. The next day, however, as the *Virginia* stalked the rest of the blockading fleet, it met its match with the Union's ironclad vessel — the U.S.S. *Monitor.* Notable for a revolving gun turret on a flat deck, the *Monitor*'s unique design earned it the nickname "Yankee cheese box on a raft." Smaller and more maneuverable than its Confederate counterpart, it was no less impervious to shells.

The two ironclad ships dueled for more than four hours, then

The first battle between Union and Confederate ironclad warships

broke off the battle. Despite the stalemate, the encounter had demonstrated the value of ironclad warships, and both the North and the South scrambled to build more armored vessels, ushering in a new chapter in the history of naval warfare.

D**espite its fierce advocacy of states' rights, the Confederacy — not the Union — was the first government to enact a military draft.**

1862

In his message to the Confederate Congress in March 1862, President Jefferson Davis recommended conscription in the face of declining troop strength, weapons, and morale. Davis faced a double-edged sword: the combination of several military defeats and the impending expiration of his soldiers' 12-month tour of duty. He proposed that all nonexempt white males between the ages of 18 and 35 serve in the army for three years. Davis made the recommendation at the urging of his secretary of war and his generals; Gen. Robert E. Lee, for one, had predicted that disbanding the army would prove "highly disastrous."

FREEMEN!
AVOID CONSCRIPTION!

The undersigned desires to raise a Company for the Confederate states service, and for that purpose I call upon the people of the Counties of Jefferson and Hawkins, Tenn., to meet promptly at Russellville, on **SATURDAY, JULY 19th, 1862,** and organize a Company.

By so doing you will avoid being taken as Conscripts, for that Act will now be enforced by order of the War Department. Rally, then, my Countrymen, to your Country's call.

S. M. DENNISON,
Of the Confederate States Army.

CHARLESTON, Tenn., JUNE 30, 1862.

The draft measure provoked bitter debate among Southern politicians, and the controversy dogged Davis throughout the life of the Confederacy. Arguing against the draft, one senator said, "We can accomplish our deliverance without violating our fundamental law." This was a minority view, however. On April 16, 1862, the House approved the measure by a margin of 2 to 1, and the Senate by 4 to 1. (The Union enacted conscription the following year.)

took place at Hampton Roads, a deep channel off the Virginia coast.

Ironically, neither the *Monitor* nor the *Merrimack/Virginia* survived the year. The *Virginia* was deliberately destroyed in May 1862 when the Confederates abandoned Norfolk, the ship's home port. The *Monitor* sank in a storm off Cape Hatteras in December.

C**ongress passed the Homestead Act with farmers' needs in mind but unwittingly gave speculators a golden opportunity to buy land.**

1862

Signed into law on May 20, 1862, the Homestead Act allowed any citizen (or immigrant who intended to become a citizen) to acquire up to 160 acres of public land between the Mississippi River and the foothills of the Rockies. The requirements were simple: $10 and a promise to settle on the land for five years and improve it. After that time a small additional fee would provide ownership.

Although the act was intended to aid struggling settlers and turn "the Great American Desert" into an agricultural paradise, it was fraught with problems. The easterners who wrote the legislation did not understand what farming the Great Plains would require. In the East, 80 acres provided a comfortable living for a family; on the parched prairies it took at least 360 acres.

Land speculators were quick to seize on the loopholes in the act and, in so doing, worsened the plight of the cash-poor

South Dakota tried to lure settlers with offers of "cheap deeded lands" and free homes.

farmer. The act, for example, allowed homesteaders to stake a claim by constructing a house that was 12 by 14; but the law failed to specify a measure, so some speculators built homes in inches. Some also constructed houses on wheels, which they moved from claim to claim. Meanwhile, trees were so scarce that homesteaders were forced to build small houses out of sod, which often meant coping with infestations of vermin.

Speculators commonly hired witnesses to testify that they had seen a house on a piece of property, even if it was only a few shingles fastened to the side of a tent. The law allowed homesteaders to buy their land after six months for $1.25 an acre, but few of the new settlers could afford to do this. Speculators could turn a quick profit by buying up acreage, paying so-called nominees to hold the titles, then transferring the property to large landowners.

The railroads, which transported thousands of farmers, also were eager to exploit legal loopholes, often hiring "dummy" homesteaders to claim the best land. Yet even with all its flaws, the Homestead Act succeeded in turning the Great Plains into one of the world's most productive farm belts.

1862

Despite being timid and high-strung, Clara Barton showed great courage in the face of danger; her devotion to wounded Civil War soldiers earned her the nickname "angel of the battlefield."

Hearing that a regiment from her home state of Massachusetts was billeted in the Senate chamber just after the Civil War broke out, Clara Barton rushed over from the U.S. Patent Office, where she worked as a clerk. Barton was delighted to greet her "boys," some of whom she recalled from her years as a schoolteacher, but she was also distressed that their supplies of food, blankets, and other necessities were inadequate. She immediately solicited contributions for the regiment from their families. Soon Barton was seeking donations of supplies for other Union troops.

Before long Barton began visiting hospitals and invalid camps, where she discovered wounded men dying of neglect. Some soldiers had to wait so long for treatment that gangrene set in and their feet had to be amputated. Her proper place, Barton decided, was in the field, "between the bullet and the hospital."

"If I can't be a soldier, I'll help soldiers," vowed Clara Barton, the devoted nurse who founded the Red Cross.

In the summer of 1862, she went to the site of the Second Battle of Bull Run, where the carnage had been devastating. Some 3,000 wounded survivors, many of them starving, awaited medical evacuation from a field. As soldiers were lifted into an ambulance, Barton tried to provide each one with food and drink. The men began to call her the "angel of the battlefield."

Although Barton had always been somewhat shy and prone to depression ("pursued by a shadow," as she once put it), she was unflappable in the face of suffering and willing to risk her own life. At Fredericksburg, Virginia, for example, a shell ripped through the door of a room where she was caring for the wounded; while others ran for cover, Barton remained at her post.

On a visit to Switzerland in 1869 to recuperate from an illness, Barton learned of the work of the Swiss philanthropist Jean-Henri Dunant, who was the guiding force behind the founding of the International Red Cross. Following his example, in 1881 Barton decided to found the American Red Cross. 🛏

1862

The South came within hours of capturing Washington, D.C., and perhaps winning the Civil War because of Confederate spy Thomas Nelson Conrad.

For years a mansion in the heart of Washington, D.C., served as the headquarters for a major espionage ring set up by Capt. Thomas Nelson Conrad. With the help of Southern sympathizers in President Lincoln's War Department, Conrad was able to ferret out many important Union Army secrets and pass them to the Confederates in Richmond, Virginia.

Conrad launched his espionage activities in 1860 when, as the headmaster of a boys' school in Georgetown, he recruited students to relay notes to Confederates across the Potomac River in Virginia. Later, as a chaplain in the Third Virginia Cavalry, Conrad would enter Union camps in his preacher's garb, offer spiritual guidance, and elicit information.

Operating as a spy, Conrad got what could have been a fateful break soon after the Second Battle of Bull Run, which was fought from August 29 to August 31, 1862. Conrad was elated to learn that Union general George McClellan and his troops had departed from Washington to reinforce Gen. John Pope's battered forces in Manassas, Virginia — leaving the capital unprotected.

Conrad desperately tried to get word to Gen. J. E. B. Stuart, who commanded the Confederate cavalry, but because Union troops were on the move, all the usual routes were unsafe. Despite his haste, Conrad chose a circuitous path through Fredericksburg and into the Blue Ridge Mountains, where he hoped to run into Stuart but never did.

By the time word reached the Confederates that the capital was vulnerable, it was too late: federal forces once again surrounded Washington. Had Conrad succeeded, the South might have captured Washington and won the Civil War. 🔫

Spies Who Wore Skirts

During the Civil War dozens of women knowingly risked their lives serving as spies. Those who used their charm, beauty, and wits to advance the cause of the North or the South include the following:

W. H. Baker (Union)
Revealed Confederate plans to use a submarine and torpedoes to attack squadrons blockading Southern ports, thereby saving Union ships.

Belle Boyd (Confederate)
Described Union positions so well that Gen. Thomas J. "Stonewall" Jackson was able to make a decisive attack at Front Royal, Virginia.

Pauline Cushman (Union)
Acting as a Southern sympathizer, she infiltrated Confederate fortifications in Kentucky and Tennessee, then passed valuable information to the Union Army.

Antonia Ford (Confederate)
Helped at the First and Second Battles of Bull Run. Entrapped Union general Edwin H. Stoughton, leading to his capture at Fairfax, Virginia.

Rose O'Neal Greenhow (Confederate)
The head of the capital's first spy network, "Rebel Rose" led a courier service of 50 spies and helped Confederates win the First Battle of Bull Run.

Elizabeth Van Lew (Union)
Ran a relay system to a Union military information officer, Gen. George H. Sharpe, in Richmond and installed her servant in Jefferson Davis's home to spy. Often disguised herself as a crazy old woman.

Loreta Juanita Velazquez (Confederate)
Pretending to be a Union spy, she revealed Union battle plans and smuggled goods to Confederates in Canada.

An officer who survived the bloodbath at the Battle of Antietam sketched the battlefield, then re-created the grisly scene in a series of paintings.

S *1862* **eptember 17, 1862, the date of the Battle of Antietam, was the single bloodiest day of the Civil War.**

The Confederacy was winning the war in the fall of 1862. Rebel troops had advanced north in every major theater, while overseas, leaders of several European nations were considering recognition of the new nation. As Confederate general Robert E. Lee boldly marched his army northward through Union-held Maryland, the federal high command decided that Lee must be stopped. And stopped he was, but at a terrible price.

Sheer luck determined the battle's location. Union troops in an abandoned Confederate campsite chanced upon a package of cigars wrapped in paper. The wrapping turned out to be a copy of Lee's orders detailing planned troop movements.

Union general George B. McClellan, commander of the Army of the Potomac, confronted Lee's Army of Northern Virginia at Sharpsburg on Antietam Creek. In a fog-shrouded field at daybreak on September 17, 1862, Union troops launched their assault on the Confederate line. The next 12 hours would account for more fatalities than any other single day of the war.

Although they had sustained devastating losses, the Union soldiers fought savagely to gain possession of the field, only to be pushed back by counter-assaults. In the surrounding woods soldiers shot each other at close range and grappled hand to hand. Confederate soldiers died in piles several men deep defending a sunken road. The site has been known ever since as "bloody lane."

When the day was over, no one was victorious. The death toll was appalling: of the 70,000 Union troops, about 12,350 men had perished. The Confederates lost approximately 13,700 soldiers out of 39,000.

Forced to abandon his invasion, on the night of September 18 Lee led his troops back across the Potomac River into Confederate territory. The Battle of Antietam had been a draw from a tactical standpoint, but strategically it marked a turning point. The Southern campaign had faltered, the North had gained momentum, and European statesmen decided to stay on the sidelines. 🔫

A *1862* **s the head of Union intelligence during the early years of the Civil War, detective Allan Pinkerton unknowingly provided much erroneous information.**

When Maj. Gen. George B. McClellan, commander of the Army of the Potomac, needed someone to run his intelligence operations, he looked to the nation's foremost detective, Allan Pinkerton. A Scottish immigrant who founded the first national private detective agency in 1850, Pinkerton was already celebrated for nabbing counterfeiters, solving train robberies, and guarding president-elect Abraham Lincoln en route to his inauguration in 1861.

Unfortunately for the Union, Pinkerton was out of his depth when it came to gathering military intelligence. Although his agents managed to slip behind Confederate lines, they were all too ready to believe exaggerated reports of enemy troop strength from unreliable sources. Pinkerton regularly overstated Confederate troops by two or three

Lincoln meets with his chief spy, Pinkerton (left), and Gen. John McClernand at Antietam.

times their numbers. McClellan trusted the erroneous counts and passed up several opportunities for routing the enemy because he was convinced that his troops were outnumbered.

Distressed at the outcome of the Virginia peninsula campaign and the Battle of Antietam in 1862, Lincoln relieved McClellan of his command. Pinkerton went back to running his detective agency. His business flourished, although he would later be embroiled in controversy when his employees used brutal force to break up strikes. 🔫

R *1862*

hett Butler admitted to being a mercenary whose illegal Civil War occupation, blockade-running, was highly profitable.

In Margaret Mitchell's *Gone With the Wind*, Scarlett O'Hara was shocked to learn Rhett Butler's motives for daring to run ships past the Union blockade: "Blockading is a business with me and I'm making money out of it." Indeed, many in his line of work made fortunes while aiding the Confederate cause.

The Union blockade of Confederate ports went into effect in April 1861, when President Lincoln warned that any vessels attempting to enter or leave Southern harbors would be subject to capture and confiscation. By the early summer of 1862, four federal squadrons patrolled the long coastline from Virginia to Texas. As a result, in order to get supplies from Europe or

Nassau (a way station for the illicit trade), brought $1,700 a ton in the South. Freight rates and crew wages were similarly inflated, with ships' captains netting $5,000 and shipowners sometimes pocketing $150,000 for a single trip.

Carrying military supplies and consumer goods, blockade runners risked capture and destruction of their vessels. To improve their odds of success, they traveled at night in small craft that could sneak into secluded coves; even so, by the war's end, some 1,500 vessels had been captured.

Although the Union blockade succeeded in strangling the Confederate economy — and may have done more to end the

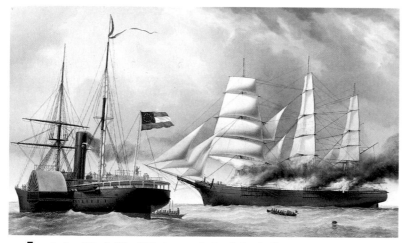

The gunboat **Nashville,** *flying an early Confederate flag, rescues prisoners from the burning Union merchant ship* **Harvey Birch.**

to carry away exports, the Confederacy had to depend on adventurous seamen willing to slip past the Union fleet.

Goods smuggled through the blockade commanded outrageous prices. Salt, valued at $6.50 a ton in the Bahamas at

war than the Union's military victories — many blockade runners went away wealthy. In the words of Rhett Butler, "There is just as much money to be made out of the wreckage of a civilization as from the upbuilding of one."

T *1862*

he Union's daring Balloon Corps provided the North with a psychological advantage over the South, rather than any military gains.

In April 1861, a week after the firing on Fort Sumter, Thaddeus Lowe traveled 900 miles in a nine-hour balloon flight from Ohio to South Carolina. Lowe, a bold and imaginative balloon designer, had built and flown several balloons, but this time his mastery of air currents won him a president's admiration — even though the flight landed him briefly in prison as a suspected Union spy.

When he was released from jail, Lowe went to Washington to see President Abraham Lincoln. Impressed by Lowe's engineering know-how and his ability to send air-to-ground telegraph messages, Lincoln created the Union's Balloon Corps and placed Lowe in charge of it. The War Department provided labor and some technological help for the construction of seven observation balloons.

During Gen. George McClellan's offensive against Richmond in 1862, Lowe's balloon unit carried out aerial reconnaissance from an altitude of approximately 300 feet above ground. In the Battle of Fair Oaks, which was fought between May 31 and June 1, 1862, and the Battle of Fredericksburg, on December 13,

Lowe ascends in a balloon to view enemy lines.

1862, Lowe used his new portable hydrogen-gas generators; these allowed the balloonists to cover much more territory than when they had to rely on a stationary gas source. Weather permitting, the balloonists went aloft daily.

During their 3,000 missions those manning the balloons coped with snagged telegraph wires and Confederate cannons aimed high enough to serve as primitive antiaircraft weapons. The largest balloon had a volume of 32,000 cubic feet, making it an easy target.

In 1863, because of a change in military command, reductions in the budget of the corps, and the loss of his autonomy, Lowe resigned and the corps was disbanded. Although the information its observers gleaned was of little practical value, the possibility that the balloonists could indeed bring back accurate reports sent the Confederates scrambling to conceal their troop movements.

1862

Nearly half a million soldiers in the Union Army were foreign-born.

During and after the Civil War, Southerners accused Northerners of hiring immigrants to face the bullets while they stayed home and reaped the profits of war. While many foreign soldiers did enlist in the Union Army (and comparatively few joined the Confederates), foreigners comprised only about one-fourth of the Union forces.

Soldiers from different countries brought with them the military expertise that many Americans lacked. Lured by bounties and, frequently, the desire to become American citizens, Europeans from the British Isles to the Caucasus joined the federal cause. One colonel had 15 different nationalities in his regiment.

Germany contributed the most men, some 200,000, to the Union cause; many Germans had emigrated to Northern states before the war.

This green banner identifies an Irish regiment.

Germans were prized for their discipline, respect for authority, and technical expertise in artillery and engineering. An estimated 150,000 Irishmen were the second-largest foreign-born contingent of soldiers. The Chicago archdiocese urged its parishioners to rally to the cause of the first country the Irishman ever had "that he could call his own." The Hibernians flaunted their nationality proudly, forming their own units and wearing shamrocks on their uniforms. Gen. Thomas Meagher's Irish Brigade won national attention for its heroism (and loss of lives) at Antietam and Fredericksburg in 1862.

While some foreign soldiers had their own units, most were tossed into the melting pot of army life. Despite the occasional fistfight, discipline generally prevailed. Through their dedication to preserving their adopted country's unity and their personal sacrifices, these soldiers sealed their right to citizenship.

1863

The Emancipation Proclamation had special meaning for a group of former slaves who lived off the coast of South Carolina.

Throughout the first half of the Civil War, abolitionists had urged President Lincoln to put an end to slavery, but Lincoln held off. He felt he could not afford to alienate the slave-owning border states that supported the Union. In the first year of the war, his speeches focused on reuniting the nation.

After the North gained a military advantage at the Battle of Antietam in September 1862, Lincoln saw an opportunity to take a stand on slavery. He warned that if the states in rebellion did not return to the Union by January 1, he would proclaim that the slaves living there would be "forever free." On New Year's Day, 1863, the president delivered on his promise. The Emancipation Proclamation declared freedom for slaves in states that had seceded but not for those in the border states or those areas of the South under Union control.

On January 1, 1863, some 5,000 people, including former slaves, their families, and friends, gathered for a celebration on Port Royal Island off the coast of South Carolina. For several months the island had been the site of an "experiment" that demonstrated how former slaves could work as freemen

on a cotton plantation and on farms. During the ceremonies a local planter read aloud the Emancipation Proclamation.

When the speaker was finished, a flag was presented, and a black person in the audience started singing "My Country 'Tis of Thee." Many blacks chimed in. "I never saw anything so electric," said one observer. "It seemed the choked voice of a race at last unloosed. . . . Tears were everywhere."

Despite its limited scope, the proclamation marked a step toward freedom from which there was no turning back. It led to the passage of the 13th Amendment in 1865, which made slavery illegal in all states. The proclamation also encouraged freed slaves to join the Union forces. By the end of the war, some 135,000 former slaves who had fled to the North for freedom secured it by fighting for a Union victory.

Freed blacks celebrate their emancipation.

Abraham Lincoln calls for an end to slavery in the Confederate states in his Emancipation Proclamation, dated January 1, 1863.

1863
William Tecumseh Sherman was the first (and only) general to charge a reporter with treason before a court-martial.

During the Civil War the new telegraph and railroad systems that linked the country's most distant points allowed the press unprecedented speed and access. The result was that Southern generals could track Union troop movements simply by reading New York's daily newspapers.

Many of the newsmen reported on morale problems or inept generals; as a result, tensions between the military and war reporters ran high. Gen. George Meade, known as Old Snapping Turtle, paraded a reporter through his camp with a sign labeling him a "libeller of the press" as a band played "Rogue's March." One commander ordered a reporter to be executed by a firing squad. (Gen. Ulysses S. Grant reduced the sentence to banishment from the army.)

War correspondents celebrate Christmas near the battlefield in 1864.

Early on, federal authorities censored reports and ordered press blackouts, but such tactics backfired: journalists merely circulated gossip and tall tales. Ultimately, the government left the decision up to the generals in the field. In 1862 Gen. William Tecumseh Sher-

man, smarting from reports questioning his sanity, banned reporters from all contact with his troops. Convinced that the Union Army had lost battles because of reckless press coverage, Sherman viewed journalists as spies and traitors with the "impudence of Satan."

On January 18, 1863, Sherman was incensed to find the entire front page of the *New York Herald* devoted to his defeat at Chickasaw Bayou, with the headline "Vicksburg Disaster." Reporter Thomas Knox had sneaked onto one of Sherman's steamboats at Memphis, heading downriver. Fearing Sherman's wrath, Knox stayed away from the battlefield. Based on secondhand information, Knox's reports mixed facts and errors, but his animosity toward Sherman was evident. The general decided to have Knox court-martialed as a deterrent to other journalists.

Although Knox was acquitted of spying and treason and only convicted on a minor charge, Sherman did manage to keep the press at bay afterward. In 1864, he marched from Atlanta to the Atlantic Ocean without any newspaper divulging his plans. 🔫

1863
The first Congressional Medals of Honor were awarded to six Union army volunteers for their daring raid on a Confederate railway connection.

Twenty-two Union army volunteers, led by civilian scout James J. Andrews, infiltrated deep into Southern territory in April 1862. Intent on sabotaging a vital Confederate communication link between Atlanta, Georgia, and Chattanooga, Tennessee, the Union men commandeered several cars of a northbound train in Big Shanty, Georgia. The Confederates soon followed in hot pursuit.

The volunteers burned bridges and cut telegraph lines as they fled, but mud and rain-slicked tracks hampered them. The Confederates captured the raiders after a 90-mile chase. Andrews and seven

Medal of Honor winner Sgt. William Carney.

others were tried and hanged. Eight escaped, and the remaining six were freed in March 1863 in a prisoner exchange.

The six men arrived in Washington, D.C., on March 25, 1863, where Secretary of War Edwin M. Stanton awarded them Congressional Medals of Honor. They later had a special meeting with President Lincoln.

These six were among more than 1,500 Civil War heroes who received the nation's highest military recognition for bravery. On December 21, 1861, Congress had approved a Medal of Honor for enlisted men of the Navy and Marine Corps, and on July 12, 1862, for the Army and Volunteer Forces. African-Americans were acknowledged, as were boys as young as 12 years old. 🔫

1863
Confederate soldiers' desperate need for shoes inadvertently led to the Battle of Gettysburg, the decisive confrontation of the Civil War.

By the summer of 1863, Gen. Robert E. Lee's Confederate Army of Northern Virginia had advanced deep into Union territory, within striking distance of Harrisburg, the capital of Pennsylvania. In contrast to the army's boldness was the precariousness of the Confederate economy. The South was staggering under the twin burdens of inflation and severe shortages of food and other supplies for both the military and civilians. So poorly equipped were the rebel troops that some were forced to go barefoot.

Dismayed that he had to fight a war under such constraints, Lee ordered his men to seize food and clothing from nearby towns. On July 1, 1863, one division marched east toward the village of Gettysburg in search of a shoe factory. They found the Union cavalry instead. The ensuing

T 1863
Thanks to a mail clerk's compassion for postal patrons, the U.S. Post Office began free home-delivery service.

Before 1863, standing in a long line at the post office was an inconvenience that city residents had come to take for granted. Wealthy citizens could hire private carriers to fetch their mail, but everyone else had to wait their turn to reach a mail clerk's window.

As Civil War casualties mounted during the winter of 1862–63, the line of people waiting outside post offices in the bitter cold grew longer. Joseph Briggs, a window clerk at a small Cleveland post office, found the situation troubling. Also distressing were such painful scenes as an official death notice arriving with a packet of unopened letters or with the slain soldier's blood-stained prayer book.

In order to eliminate the long wait in line, Briggs started delivering soldiers' letters to their families at home. Soon he was campaigning for free home mail delivery. At first the idea of door-to-door service was considered too expensive, but he eventually convinced his superiors in Cleveland and Washington that he could devise a successful system. Free home delivery for city residents in Cleveland and some 40 other cities began on July 1, 1863.

Veterans were among the first letter carriers.

By July 4, 1863, the Battle of Gettysburg was over, and with it the South's hopes of winning the war.

son's Ridge, Seminary Ridge, Cemetery Hill, Cemetery Ridge, Culp's Hill, Little Round Top, the Peach Orchard, Devil's Den.

On July 4, the day after Confederate general George E. Pickett led a disastrous charge against Meade, Lee was forced to retreat. Together, the two armies had suffered more than 50,000 casualties, including about 3,200 Union deaths and 3,900 Confederate deaths. With the almost simultaneous Union victory at Vicksburg, Mississippi, the Battle of Gettysburg marked the turning point of the war. As needy as Lee's troops had been before the battle, their condition would only grow worse as the Union divisions closed in on them.

clash marked the start of the greatest battle of the Civil War.

Union general George Meade led the full strength of his Army of the Potomac against Lee's invading forces. By the end of the first day, the outlook for the Union appeared grim, but over the next two days Lee failed to drive the Union forces from their positions. Savage fighting raged across places whose names are etched in history: McPher-

A 1863
n account of her experiences as a nurse in the Civil War was the first commercial success for Louisa May Alcott, the author of *Little Women.*

Although she had written fairy tales, poems, and plays, Louisa May Alcott was still uncertain about what career to pursue. When the War Between the States broke out, she decided to volunteer at Union Hospital in Washington, D.C., where she became known as the "nurse with the bottle" for the lavender water she dispensed to block the stench of unsanitary conditions.

In the letters home that formed the basis for her 1863 book, *Hospital Sketches*, Alcott described the hospital as a "perfect pestilence box." (Throughout Alcott's writing career over the next quarter century, she was plagued by ill health, a result of the

Working in this Washington hospital helped launch Alcott's writing career.

typhoid fever she contracted there.)

Critically well received for its vivid portrayal of wartime hospital horrors, *Hospital Sketches* brought its author literary notice. It wasn't until the publication of *Little Women* in 1868–69, however, that Alcott became famous. Readers became so devoted to the fictional March family that Alcott was

prompted to write sequels, including *Little Men* in 1871.

Although *Little Women* depicts old-fashioned values and domestic virtues, its unmarried author was something of a radical. She endorsed women's rights and the suffrage movement, and was outspoken on other controversial issues. Alcott had acquired some of her social and political beliefs from her father, Bronson Alcott.

A nonconformist who set up a commune that failed, Bronson Alcott espoused unorthodox religious beliefs and supported the temperance movement. His unconventional views, and perhaps his emotional instability, made Bronson unable to support his family. Luckily, Louisa's prolific writing and her popularity here and abroad enabled her to provide for both her parents and herself.

T 1863
hanksgiving Day became a national holiday during the Civil War.

On October 3, 1863, President Abraham Lincoln declared the last Thursday in November to be Thanksgiving Day, a decision no doubt swayed by the recent Gettysburg victory and a 36-year campaign by magazine editor Sarah Josepha Hale.

Hale's motives for the holiday crusade were both sentimental and political. She had begun by voicing regrets that the United States had too few national holidays. Then, in 1835, she wrote, "There is a deep moral influence in these periodical seasons of rejoicing in which whole communities participate. They bring out, and together, as it were, the best

Turkey: a Thanksgiving symbol.

sympathies of our natures."

As the clouds of war gathered in the 1850's, Hale, the editor of the popular magazine *Godey's Lady's Book*, was convinced that the celebration of a national day of thanks would actually help avert a war. In a magazine editorial in November 1859, Hale posed the question, "If every state would join in Union Thanksgiving on the 24th of this month, would it not be a renewed pledge of love and loyalty to the Constitution of the United States which guarantees peace, prosperity, progress and perpetuity to our great Republic?" After another three years of letter writing and intense lobbying of state and federal officials, Hale's wish was finally granted.

The War That Saved the Union

From 1861 to 1865 the United States was locked in the throes of civil war. A bloody culmination of years of tension between Northern and Southern states, it would unite, once and for all, the disparate states of the Union under one federal government. The following are some of the most important events.

1861 On April 12 Confederate forces attack Fort Sumter off Charleston, South Carolina, marking the start of the Civil War.

Union troops are defeated on July 21 at the First Battle of Bull Run, near Manassas, Virginia, ending the North's hopes for a short-lived war.

1862 Troops under Gen. Ulysses S. Grant capture Fort Henry and Fort Donelson in February, opening the Tennessee and Cumberland rivers to Union offensives.

A Union fleet under Flag Officer David G. Farragut captures New Orleans, the South's most important seaport, on April 28.

Gen. Robert E. Lee's first foray into the North ends in retreat after the Battle of Antietam near Sharpsburg, Maryland, on September 17.

1863 Lee's second attempt to invade the North meets with disaster at the Battle of Gettysburg in Pennsylvania, July 1–4, marking the turning point in the war.

On July 4, after weeks of siege, Vicksburg, Mississippi, falls into Northern hands, opening the way for Union dominance of the Mississippi River and the West.

1864 Beginning on May 5, the Union mounts an 11-month offensive to take Richmond, Virginia, suffering heavy losses at the battles of the Wilderness, Spotsylvania, and Cold Harbor and at the Siege of Petersburg.

On September 2, Atlanta, Georgia, falls to Gen. William Tecumseh Sherman, who then marches to the coast, capturing Savannah, Georgia, on December 22.

1865 After having evacuated Petersburg and Richmond a week earlier, Lee is forced to surrender on April 9 at Appomattox Court House, Virginia.

T¹⁸⁶⁴ he battle cry "Damn the torpedoes! Full steam ahead!" referred to what are known today as mines, not torpedoes.

In Civil War terminology torpedoes were actually mines. These explosive devices were buried underground or submerged underwater to be detonated by pressure or remote control. Despite outcries from those who considered mines cowardly and uncivilized, both the North and the South used them. The Confederacy often relied on mines to defend its harbors and rivers.

The devices became a part of American legend on August 5, 1864, at the Battle of Mobile Bay, Alabama. Union Rear Admiral David Farragut was eager to capture Mobile, the last

key Confederate port on the Gulf of Mexico. The waters there were thick with mines.

As Farragut steered into Mobile Bay, one of the mines sank a Union ship, causing the fleet to hesitate. Although fire from the guns of Fort Morgan raked his ships, the indomitable Farragut, lashed to the rigging of his flagship *Hartford*, is said to have shouted: "Damn the torpedoes! Full speed ahead!"

The fleet maneuvered past the guns and the minefield. Then, despite a fierce defense from the Confederate ironclad *Tennessee*, Farragut obtained Mobile's surrender. His battle cry has become a catchphrase for courage in the face of deadly danger. ⚔

G¹⁸⁶⁴ en. William Tecumseh Sherman was called the Attila of the West.

As commander of Union forces in the West, Gen. William Tecumseh Sherman captured and burned Atlanta, Georgia, then took 62,000 troops on an eastward march to Savannah on the Atlantic coast. During this virtually unopposed "march to the sea," which began on November 15, 1864, his men spread out across a 60-mile-wide front, destroying or seizing anything of value to the military.

The troops ripped up and burned railroad ties, softening the rails over fires so they could twist them around trees in shapes known as "Sherman's hairpins." More than just malicious mischief, this virtually ensured that the Confederates

Sherman compared war to a thunderbolt that spares nothing.

could no longer use the tracks. Marauding gangs followed the army's path, robbing and burning at will.

Stunned by Sherman's destructiveness, Southerners called him the Attila of the West, comparing him to the savage leader of the Huns, who had scourged the Roman Empire in the fifth century. But Sherman had a deliberate rationale for attacking civilian and military property alike. He wanted to hasten the war's end by cutting the supply lines to the Confederate forces farther north. He also wanted to demoralize the enemy by inflicting suffering on areas previously spared the horrors of war. In his words, he wanted to "make Georgia howl."

After capturing Savannah on December 21, Sherman sent season's greetings to President Lincoln: "I beg to present you, as a Christmas gift, the city of Savannah, with 150 heavy guns and plenty of ammunition, and also about 25,000 bales of cotton." Sherman continued to wreak havoc in North and South Carolina, finally resting when the Confederate forces capitulated, shortly after Lee's surrender in April 1865. ⚔

Admiral Farragut climbs into the rigging of his ship to see over the smoke in the hard-fought battle for Mobile Bay.

Men drafted into the Union army could pay substitutes to fight for them, leading to criticism that it was "a rich man's war and a poor man's fight."

1864

To make the unpopular military draft more acceptable, the laws authorizing conscription allowed a reluctant draftee into the Union army to hire a substitute. Brokers matched draftees who were willing to pay but unwilling to fight with men who agreed to go to the front; but those who took the money were often no more eager to go to war than those who paid them.

Some soldiers enlisted over and over again. These bounty jumpers, as they were called, pocketed the cash incentive offered by the government (usually about $300 per enlistment) and disappeared. The record holder may have been John "Jumping Jack" O'Connor, who deserted the Union Army 32 times after enlisting on each occasion for a bounty.

Cash payments enticed army volunteers in the North.

Daring bounty jumpers resorted to such measures as flinging themselves off the trains taking them to military camps, tunneling out of army stockades, or fleeing from guard posts by shinnying down ropes of knotted sheets. Seeking to discourage the practice, some local officials tried public humiliation: bounty jumpers wearing placards were marched handcuffed through the streets of Indianapolis in 1864. A Rhode Island doctor developed a more scientific approach, which involved marking the backs of new recruits with silver nitrate. If the soldier tried to reenlist, the chemical could be detected during the induction physical. The process prompted widespread criticism, however, largely because of its unappealing name — branding. As a result, the army discontinued the practice, and bounty jumping remained a problem up to the end of the Civil War.

Confederate arsonists tried to burn down New York City in retaliation against Union triumphs in Georgia and Virginia.

1864

With Confederate fortunes looking increasingly grim in the fall of 1864, a small band of Southern agents headed by Col. Robert M. Martin came up with a desperate plan to revitalize the Southern cause: in a single night, they would torch all of New York City.

On November 25, 1864, the rebels did manage to set fire to some waterfront barges, more than a dozen hotel rooms, and several buildings, but the blazes neither consumed the city nor sparked an uprising of Southern sympathizers, as the plotters had anticipated. The arsonists had left the windows closed in the hotel rooms, and without a proper draft the blazes were easily extinguished. Although they had only themselves to blame for the fiasco, the plotters attributed the failure to sabotage, claiming that a chemist had deliberately given them a defective incendiary mixture.

All eight of the arsonists escaped to Canada. Then one of them, Robert Cobb Kennedy, was later captured as he crossed the border on his way back to the United States. Tried as an arsonist and spy, Kennedy was convicted and hanged. He was the last Confederate soldier executed by the U.S. government during the Civil War.

1865

Opposing generals Ulysses S. Grant and Robert E. Lee were old battle comrades.

When Robert E. Lee and Ulysses S. Grant faced each other at Appomattox Court House on April 9, 1865, to discuss terms for ending the Civil War, it was not their first meeting. During the Mexican War (1846–48) Robert E. Lee had served under Gen. Winfield Scott, who called the Virginian "the very best soldier I ever saw in the field." Grant, who was 15 years Lee's junior, had distinguished himself in campaigns under Gen. Zachary Taylor and was transferred to Scott's army, where Lee and Grant met very briefly.

The Union general's first words to his Confederate counterpart, who had waited half an hour for Grant's arrival, recalled their previous encounter, which dated back nearly two decades. Said Grant: "I met you once before, General Lee, while we were serving in Mexico. . . . I have always remembered your appearance, and I think I should have recognized you anywhere." The distinguished-looking Lee replied, "Yes, I know I met you on that occasion, and I have . . . tried to recollect how you looked, but I have never been able to recall a single feature."

Grant reminisced at length about their service in Mexico, until Lee finally reminded him that the purpose of the meeting was to draw up the terms of surrender. Grant generously released Lee and his soldiers on their honor, removing the specter of a prison term that had haunted Lee. In a remarkable gesture of conciliation, Grant allowed all Confederate soldiers who owned their horses or mules to "take their animals home with them to work their little farms."

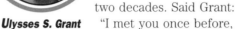
Ulysses S. Grant

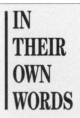
Robert E. Lee

1864

The Sand Creek Massacre of Cheyennes was so brutal that it shocked even the most hardened frontiersmen.

At dawn on November 29, 1864, Col. John M. Chivington, the military commander of Colorado, and his soldiers silently surrounded an Indian encampment at Sand Creek, near Fort Lyon, Colorado. By the afternoon the regiment had killed some 200 Cheyennes, two-thirds of them women and children.

Clashes between the settlers and the Indians had been escalating ever since gold was discovered on Cheyenne and Arapaho hunting grounds in the late 1850's. In an effort to protect their people from all-out war, Chief Black Kettle and Chief White Antelope had traveled to Fort Lyon in the summer of 1864 to surrender and entrust their people to the protection of John Evans, the governor of the Colorado territory.

Evans betrayed them, however. Unable to secure rights to the Indians' mineral-rich land through negotiation, he ordered Chivington to clear out the territory by force. Chivington, a former Methodist minister nicknamed the Fighting Parson, was fanatical in his hatred of Indians.

Telling his men to take no prisoners, Chivington and his soldiers fell upon the sleeping village, killing and scalping, mutilating the bodies of the dead, and committing other atrocities. Black Kettle escaped, but White Antelope was shot to death, unarmed and wearing the peace medal that President Lincoln had given him.

Initially, news of the massacre sparked celebrations among Colorado residents. A local theater displayed scalps as trophies of war. Gradually, however, as more details emerged, the public reaction shifted to outrage. Said Kit Carson, a frontiersman not known for his kindness to Indians: "No one but a coward or a dog would have had a part in it."

Two congressional investigations and a military commission that probed the massacre were unanimous in condemning Chivington. One congressional committee reported that he had "planned and executed a foul and dastardly massacre which would have disgraced the veriest savage among those who were the victims of his cruelty."

Although such criticism derailed Chivington's plans for a political career, he managed to escape prosecution. It was discovered that his commission had expired before the incident, so he was beyond the reach of a military tribunal.

Seeing a white flag of truce on Black Kettle's tent did not deter state militiamen from massacring Indians at Sand Creek, Colorado.

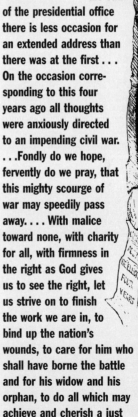

IN THEIR OWN WORDS

"Fellow Countrymen: At this second appearing to take the oath of the presidential office there is less occasion for an extended address than there was at the first . . . On the occasion corresponding to this four years ago all thoughts were anxiously directed to an impending civil war. . . .Fondly do we hope, fervently do we pray, that this mighty scourge of war may speedily pass away. . . . With malice toward none, with charity for all, with firmness in the right as God gives us to see the right, let us strive on to finish the work we are in, to bind up the nation's wounds, to care for him who shall have borne the battle and for his widow and his orphan, to do all which may achieve and cherish a just and lasting peace. . . .

Abraham Lincoln's Second Inaugural Address, March 4, 1865.

1865

Abraham Lincoln's fondness for the theater provided his assassin with an opportunity for murder.

A devotee of *Hamlet* and *Macbeth*, President Lincoln would occasionally relax from the burdens of his office by slipping unannounced into a theater. Despite having had little formal education, Lincoln was a cultured man who particularly enjoyed attending plays. To the amazement of White House guests, from time to time he would recite from memory long passages from Shakespeare. So impassioned were these spontaneous performances that one observer suggested that the president might have missed his calling.

On Good Friday evening, April 14, 1865, President and Mrs. Lincoln went to Ford's Theater in Washington to see the popular actress Laura

Keene in a British comedy, *Our American Cousin*. The occasion was a festive one, celebrating the surrender of Robert E. Lee's Confederate army earlier that week, and Lincoln's plan to attend the performance was reported in the press. During the second scene of the third act, as the audience howled with laughter at an especially funny line, the sharp blast of a pistol was heard. For a moment no one realized what had happened. Some in the theater thought that the noise was part of the performance. Then a man shouting *"Sic semper tyrannis"* ("Thus be it always to tyrants") leaped from the president's box to the stage, and Mrs. Lincoln cried out, "The President has been shot. Is there a surgeon here?"

Lincoln died early the next morning. Ironically, his assassin was a Shakespearean actor, John Wilkes Booth. 🔫

Lincoln on his deathbed, surrounded by friends and aides who grieved for their leader.

1865

Confederate president Jefferson Davis tried to elude Union cavalry draped in his wife's shawl.

Jefferson Davis fled the Confederate capital at Richmond, Virginia, on April 3, 1865, shortly after receiving a warning from Gen. Robert E. Lee that the city was about to fall. Davis planned to cross the Mississippi River and set up a new base for Confederate operations. Pursued by Union troops, he sped southward and was reunited with his wife and children, who had left Richmond before him.

Two cavalry units caught up with Davis near Irwinville, Georgia, on May 10, 1865. In the confusion that ensued, the Union troops fired on each other and two men were killed. As Davis tried to escape on foot, his wife, Varina, hurriedly tossed her shawl around

Cartoonists mercilessly ridiculed Davis, who fled from pursuers in his wife's shawl.

his shoulders, a gesture that later made Davis the butt of cartoonists' jibes.

Captured almost immediately, the former president of the Confederacy spent the next two years imprisoned at Fort Monroe, Virginia. There, Davis was treated so inhumanely by his jailers that even Northerners protested, among them prominent journalist Horace Greeley and railroad tycoon Cornelius Vanderbilt. Both men contributed to the $100,000 bail that secured Davis's release from jail in May 1867.

Federal officials wanted to try Davis for treason and complicity in Lincoln's assassination, but legal complications made it impossible. After his release from prison, Davis never once asked for amnesty. As a result, the Confederate president never regained his U.S. citizenship. 🔫

Presidents Who Died in Office

Assassins and illnesses claimed the lives of these U.S. presidents before their terms expired:

William Henry Harrison – Contracted pneumonia a month after his inauguration. Died on April 4, 1841.

Zachary Taylor – Suffered acute gastroenteritis, but the cause of death is unknown. Died on July 9, 1850.

Abraham Lincoln – Shot on April 14, 1865, by John Wilkes Booth in Washington, D.C. Died on April 15, 1865.

James A. Garfield – Shot on July 2, 1881, by Charles Guiteau in Washington, D.C. Died on September 19, 1881.

William McKinley – Shot on September 6, 1901, by Leon Czolgosz in Buffalo, New York. Died on September 14, 1901.

Warren G. Harding – On his return from a trip to Alaska, he contracted food poisoning in Seattle on July 27, 1923, then developed pneumonia, and suffered a stroke in San Francisco, where he died from an embolism on August 2, 1923.

Franklin D. Roosevelt – Died on April 12, 1945, in Warm Springs, Georgia, from a cerebral hemorrhage.

John F. Kennedy – Allegedly shot by Lee Harvey Oswald in Dallas, Texas. Died on November 22, 1963.

C¹⁸⁶⁵

onfederate general Robert E. Lee was not pardoned for his role as a rebel leader until 105 years after his death.

Like other Confederate leaders, Robert E. Lee was excluded from the Proclamation of Amnesty and Reconstruction of 1865 and had to apply personally for a pardon. On June 13, 1865, he petitioned President Andrew Johnson "for the benefits and full restoration" of his civil rights. Later, when he learned that regaining citizenship also meant signing an oath of allegiance to the United States, he sent a document, dated October 2, 1865, to complete the process.

Through a bizarre twist of fate, his application went astray. Secretary of State William Seward received the document but mistakenly assumed that Lee's oath had already been recorded elsewhere. Seward innocently gave Lee's oath of allegiance to a friend as a souvenir, who placed it in the pigeonhole of his desk. Since he had received

no response, Lee interpreted the silence as a sign that no pardon would be granted.

By then Lee had returned to private life. The same day that he signed the oath of allegiance, he was sworn in as president of Washington College in Lexington, Virginia. He soon expanded the school's curriculum to include practical disciplines such as business, agriculture, chemistry, engineering, and journalism — skills that were vital, Lee felt, to rebuilding the South.

Under his leadership "General Lee's school" grew from just a few dozen students to more than 400 in two years. A man of deep religious and moral convictions, Lee introduced the honor system and demanded that "every student must be a gentleman."

At his death in 1870, Lee was buried in the campus chapel, and Washington College was renamed Washington and Lee University in his honor. A hundred years later, Lee's oath of allegiance — signed and duly notarized — turned up in a bundle of papers at the National Archives. In 1975 Congress voted to restore his citizenship. 🔫

T¹⁸⁶⁵

he last Confederate general to surrender in the Civil War was a Cherokee Indian who turned in his sword two months after the war had officially ended.

Shortly after the War Between the States broke out, Confederate general Albert Pike received a mandate to recruit Indians in the West. He promised the Cherokees and other tribes that the Confederacy, once it had vanquished the Union armies, would establish a state for those who had been expelled from their native lands in the East.

Stand Watie, a Cherokee and Confederate army officer.

Stand Watie, a Cherokee leader of great strength and courage, responded to Pike's entreaty by recruiting a volunteer regiment, the Cherokee Mounted Rifles. An expert in guerrilla warfare, Watie engaged in numerous battles throughout the war and, in 1864, attained the rank of brigadier general.

Unaware of Gen. Robert E. Lee's surrender to Gen. Ulysses S. Grant on April 9, 1865, at Appomattox Court House in Virginia, Watie continued skirmishing with Union troops in Indian Territory (an area that later became Oklahoma). Watie commanded a menacing force of some 2,000 Cherokee, Creek, and Choctaw Indians.

Although Watie learned of Lee's surrender in late May, Union officers feared that this powerful adversary might still lead a raid into Kansas. Watie finally surrendered on June 23, 1865, but not until federal authorities agreed to sign a separate treaty with the Cherokee nation. This pact officially ended the Confederate Indians' war against the United States. 🔫

Even after Lee conceded defeat, his troops never wavered in their loyalty.

1865

Ironically, the discriminatory statutes known as black codes, passed by several Southern legislatures after the Civil War, were termed civil-rights legislation.

The Mississippi legislature passed the first "black codes" of the Reconstruction era in November 1865. Although these laws recognized the rights of freedmen to marry, to sue, and to acquire property, their general tenor was racist and oppressive. Legislators entitled the first law "an Act to confer Civil Rights on Freedmen."

Playing on the widespread belief that former slaves would work only if made to do so, the Mississippi law declared that all freedmen 18 years or older who were not employed by January 1866 would be classified as vagrants, fined, and sentenced to 10 days' imprisonment. Those too poor to pay the $50 fine would be hired out to anyone who paid the fee in their stead.

Freedmen in Mississippi who had jobs were forbidden to quit. A laborer who left before his contract ran out forfeited his wages and was subject to arrest; a bounty of $5 was offered for bringing back a wayward freedman. Other offenses subject to fine and imprisonment included making "seditious speeches," using "insulting gestures," and "exercising the function of a minister of the Gospel without a license."

Mississippi's black codes — closely followed by passage of similar statutes in South Carolina — evoked stern outcries above the Mason-Dixon line. Many Northerners took the codes as confirmation that the South was trying to reinstitute slavery. A Chicago newspaper vowed that "The men of the North will convert the State of Mississippi into a frog pond before they will allow such laws to disgrace one foot of soil in which the bones of our soldiers sleep and over which the flag of freedom waves." With congressional oversight of Reconstruction in the offing, eight Southern states passed less restrictive codes, and Mississippi repealed its most offensive statutes within the year. 🔫

Dollar bills issued in 1862 (top) and in 1865.

1865

The end of the Civil War brought a brief experiment with a new national currency to a controversial conclusion.

The Legal Tender Act of 1862 created the first national paper money. Designed to help finance the war, the law permitted up to $150 million in greenbacks, or paper money, to be circulated at the outset. Greenbacks, named for their color, were not backed by specie, or gold. By the end of the war, more than $440 million in paper money, worth 40 percent of gold currency, had replaced a dizzying array of notes issued by state banks as currency before the war.

The advent of the greenback created some strange types of small change. Removed from circulation were pennies, 5- and 10-cent pieces, and gold and silver. In their place Americans made change by circulating postage stamps and bills known as shinplasters, which were pieces of paper or cardboard. Those who patronized saloons, barbers, merchants, and others would get shinplasters; many of those who issued them, however, had no intention of redeeming them. One satirist created a so-called conversion chart for the new currency. Ten beer tickets from a local tavern make one shinplaster, he said, and a "handful of shinplasters . . . make a man cuss."

Between 1865 and 1875 the federal government took paper currency out of circulation and replaced it with gold, or hard currency. This move brought protests from farmers and laborers, who were then required to pay off debts of inflated greenbacks in precious gold. For the next two decades controversy raged over whether gold, silver, or paper currency should serve as the nation's money. 🔫

In some states a jobless freedman could be fined for vagrancy, then sold at an auction.

1865

Some defeated Southerners established Confederate colonies in Mexico after the Civil War.

Unwilling to live under what they considered the dictatorship of the hated Yankees, thousands of Confederates chose to emigrate. Among those fleeing to Canada and Central and South America when the Civil War ended were military and government leaders who feared punishment for their wartime activities, and zealots who vowed undying loyalty to the lost cause. A majority of the exiles went to Mexico.

In 1862, knowing that the Union was preoccupied with the Civil War, French emperor Napoleon III had invaded and occupied Mexico, flouting the provisions of the Monroe Doctrine that prohibited such aggression; he then installed Austrian archduke Maximilian as Mexico's emperor. In mid-1865 Confederate cavalry general Joseph O. Shelby led several hundred of

Confederate generals who fled to Mexico after the Civil War.

his men to Mexico City, where they offered their services as a foreign legion. The emperor declined, but he granted them land to found colonies.

Although prices were reasonable at first, speculation quickly drove up the cost of land ownership. Most of the tiny colonies consisted of little more than ramshackle buildings and farms carved out of the jungle. Still the exiles tried to retain their aristocratic Southern customs. Women organized book clubs, and weekly dance cotillions were held at the Confederate, the largest hotel in the city of Cordoba.

In 1867 Confederate colonization in Mexico ended. Mexican resistance fighters forced the French troops to withdraw and executed Maximilian. The Confederate exiles, fearing persecution as collaborators, fled. Some sought sanctuary in other countries, but many returned home. ☙

A Show Business Hit

From the 1880's to the 1930's, vaudeville was America's most popular entertainment. Many of the stars, who went on to careers in radio, movies, theater, and television, are still remembered fondly.

1882 The 13-year-old W. C. Fields gets his first job in vaudeville, as a juggler.

1889 At the age of 11, George M. Cohan is introduced to vaudeville as part of his family's act, "The Cohan Mirth Makers." He goes on to become famous as a composer of songs ("Yankee Doodle Dandy" and "Over There") and a theatrical star.

1891 Harry Houdini, whose name is synonymous with the tricks of escape and illusion, first performs on the vaudeville stage.

1899 After working in the theater, Al Jolson begins to perfect the minstrel show that will become his trademark.

1905 Will Rogers launches his career at a vaudeville theater in New York City, doing his stylish rope tricks.

1906 Seven-year-old Fred Astaire begins his career dancing with his sister, Adele. A few years later, they are described as the "most talented youngsters who [have] yet graced the vaudeville stage."

1911 Jack Benny disappointed his father, who wanted him to become a classical violinist. Instead, he uses the instrument as a comedy prop throughout his career; he makes his debut in a vaudeville show entitled *From Grand Opera to Ragtime*.

1921 English acrobat Archie Leach (later Cary Grant) comes to the United States and tours in vaudeville.

1923 George Burns and Gracie Allen begin the successful professional partnership that takes them from vaudeville to radio and television.

VAUDEVILLE

1865

A circus entertainer "invented" vaudeville as an alternative to the types of shows in saloons and theaters that no decent women or children would go to see.

The variety show named for the town of Vau-de-Vire, France, made its American debut in 1865 at Tony Pastor's Opera House in New York City. Unlike such popular burlesque acts of the era as Lydia Thompson and her British Blondes, vaudeville offered wholesome fun for the entire family.

Pastor, a former circus performer who became known as the father of American vaudeville, worked very hard to attract crowds. At one point he even gave away dresses to female ticket buyers. His shows entertained the entire family with jugglers, magicians, animal acts, acrobatic daredevilry, comedy, dramatic sketches, and song and dance routines.

Vaudeville came of age in the 1870's. Under the leadership of American businessmen Benjamin Franklin Keith and Edward Franklin Albee, it became the country's most popular form of entertainment. In its heyday from the 1880's to the early 1930's, theaters offered between 2 and 12 shows daily, sometimes running from 9:30 A.M. to 10:30 P.M.

Dozens of show-business greats including Lillian Russell, Will Rogers, George Burns, and the Marx Brothers got their start on the vaudeville circuit. Some youngsters virtually spent their childhoods onstage: Judy Garland was 2½ years old when she first performed, and Groucho Marx joined a vaudeville trio at the age of 10. The Great Depression and the introduction of talking pictures sent vaudeville into a decline after more than a half-century of nonstop entertainment. ☙

1866
Henry Bergh's crusade for the humane treatment of animals led to the founding of the ASPCA.

The heir to a shipbuilding fortune, Henry Bergh served in Russia as a secretary in the American legation during the Civil War. While there, he watched in horror as peasants cruelly beat their horses in the streets. After meeting in London with the president of Britain's Royal Society for the Prevention of Cruelty to Animals, Bergh decided to found a similar organization in America. "At last," said the would-be champion of defenseless beasts, "I have found a way to utilize my gold lace."

The American Society for the Prevention of Cruelty to Animals, chartered by the New York state legislature on April 10, 1866, was the first organization of its kind in the Western Hemisphere. As its president for the next two decades,

Bergh's crusade made him an easy target for caricaturists.

Bergh tirelessly devoted himself to enlightening the public about animal abuse. Always nattily dressed in a top hat and starched collar, Bergh set to work — raiding cockfights and slaughterhouses, staying the hands of teamsters who beat their horses in the streets, establishing the first ambulance service for horses (two years before one was provided for humans), and arresting the perpetrators of the most flagrant animal abuses.

Branded "the great meddler" and subjected to howling derision in the press, Bergh's crusade was nevertheless effective: within five years, 19 states and the Dominion of Canada had founded similar societies. In 1874 Bergh expanded his efforts to include a sister organization in New York, the Society for the Prevention of Cruelty to Children. 🐾

IN THEIR OWN WORDS

" During the day the ladies devote themselves to making shirts, knitting stockings, &c. . . . These . . . are to be offered for sale at the great fair, which . . . is to come off at Seattle. . . . In the evening the young people either gather round the piano . . . or go up on the hurricane deck. . . . With the exception of the first night at sea, we have enjoyed the most delightful weather. . . . Fresh sea breezes have made the air cool and pleasant, while old mother moon has looked smilingly down, casting her soft, quiet rays over the little groups gathered together to while away the time in pleasant gossip. At the close of the evening they all declare that they have had (what a young lady would say) a most magnificent time. "

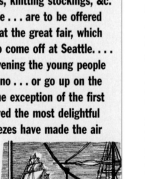

A correspondent for The New York Times *describes life aboard ship on the Mercer expedition.*

1866
Women were so scarce in the Far West that many bachelors resorted to mail-order matchmaking.

As a professor and president of Seattle's Territorial University, Asa Mercer understood well the laws of supply and demand. While women in the Pacific Northwest were so rare that lonely men would travel for days just to glimpse one, Mercer knew that, a continent away, the Civil War had depleted New England's stock of eligible bachelors. Mercer hatched a scheme to capitalize on the imbalance. In early 1865 he placed an ad in a Seattle newspaper offering to secure any man a wife for the sum of $300. Within days Mercer received some 500 orders and set sail on the long journey via the Isthmus of Panama to gather a group of brides.

Many of the women who signed on claimed that landing a husband wasn't their primary motive, and that, like many Ameri-

cans, they were curious about the West. Whatever their reasons, about 100 women left with Mercer for the four-month return trip. When they arrived in San Francisco, 11 of them received marriage proposals and stayed behind. Then something close to a riot ensued as lonely men stormed the ship for the others. When at last they reached Seattle, on May 29, 1866, Mercer left them on the ship while he made sure that the town was ready for newcomers.

He needn't have bothered; the taverns were closed, the buildings had been freshly whitewashed, and Seattle's lovelorn lumberjacks and prospectors were all nervously waiting in their Sunday finest. A week later the first wedding took place, and in time nearly all of "Mercer's brides" were married. Mercer himself was no less vulnerable to Cupid's dart — among the earliest marriages was his own, to Annie Stephens of Baltimore. 🐾

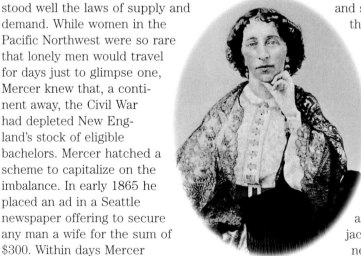

Lizzie Ordway, the only Mercer girl not to marry.

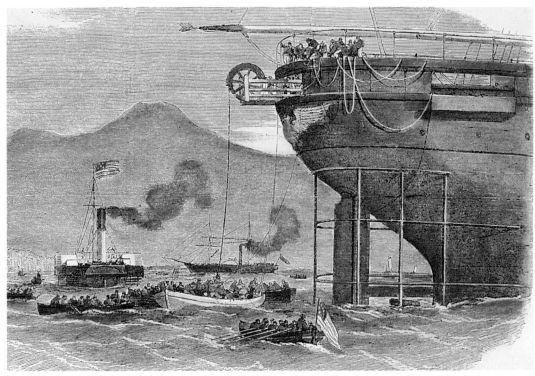

The **Great Eastern** *lays the first transatlantic cable; by 1900, 15 cables crossed the Atlantic Ocean.*

B¹⁸⁶⁶ **randed both a fool's errand and a heroic struggle, the linking of America to Europe by cable revolutionized communication.**

After four foiled attempts, Europe and America were finally permanently connected by wire on July 27, 1866, when the ship *Great Eastern* arrived in Trinity Bay, Newfoundland, trailing 1,896 nautical miles of cable from her stern. Unlike earlier efforts, which were bedeviled by storms, sabotage, and just plain bad luck, the operation had proceeded perfectly, much to the relief of team leader Cyrus Field. A wholesale paper dealer, Field had had to raise the funds to make his dream of a transatlantic link a reality.

Once ashore, Field discovered that the wire connecting Newfoundland with New York was broken, but repairs were quickly made, and soon news was streaming back and forth across the Atlantic. Queen Victoria sent the first official message from England over the wire to President Andrew Johnson: "The Queen congratulates the President on the successful completion of an undertaking which, she hopes, may serve as an additional bond of union between the United States and England."

Shortly afterward, a second cable that had been severed on an earlier attempt was recovered 600 miles off the Newfoundland coast; this doubled the capacity of the transatlantic link and guaranteed that the Old and New Worlds would never again lack for news of one another.

Q¹⁸⁶⁶ **ueen Emma of Hawaii, the first royal matron to visit the United States, captivated the American people.**

Despite its democratic traditions, America was thrilled to receive a visit from the dowager queen, widow of King Kamehameha IV. Although it was officially billed as a pleasure trip to take her mind off her husband's death, the queen's visit was not without its political undertones. At the time, both Britain and the United States had their colonial sights set on Hawaii. Queen Emma's visit to Britain the year before had set America scrambling to forge closer ties with the Hawaiian monarchy. Urged to travel to the United States by her brother-in-law, King Kamehameha V, Emma arrived in New York on August 8, 1866.

Described as "well formed and graceful," the exotically beautiful young widow quickly mesmerized Manhattan society. Emma's next stop was Washington, where she was received by President Andrew Johnson and his wife, Eliza. Even Johnson, deeply immersed in the quagmire of post–Civil War politics, was said to brighten in the presence of the handsome queen. From Washington, Emma and her retinue traveled to Niagara Falls and made a brief visit to Canada; the trip was cut short, however, by the news that her adoptive mother had suddenly died. Grief-stricken once more, she returned to Hawaii on an American warship — which carried her, in the words of her escort, Admiral H. K. Thatcher, "as a queen should go."

Although her visit to America had been a pleasant one, Emma hoped, with the help of Great Britain, to prevent the United States from annexing Hawaii. She never succeeded to the throne and was unable to make an agreement with England to protect her islands. In 1885 Queen Emma died, well before Hawaii became a permanent part of the United States.

Queen Emma of Hawaii.

1866

Audiences were wowed and scandalized by *The Black Crook,* the first large-scale American musical comedy.

The crowds that filled Niblo's Garden in New York for opening night on September 12, 1866, had never laid eyes on anything like *The Black Crook.* Although the plot was thin — a mishmash of classical myth and melodrama — the 5½-hour production more than compensated with a dazzling parade of Amazon warriors, fairies and nymphs, elaborate sets and musical numbers, spectacles of fire, and a chorus line of demons who, as a *New York Times* reviewer noted, "wore no clothes to speak of."

The production's haphazard quality was no accident; the sets, costumes, and dancers were all hand-me-downs from New York's Academy of Music, which had burned down on the eve of a production of its own. While a few reviewers blanched at the scantily clad dancers in their flesh-colored leotards and close-fitting pantaloons, the revealing costumes accounted in large measure for the play's appeal. The theater manager, William Wheatley, even printed a schedule of the play's racier numbers so that gentlemen could drop in just in time to glimpse a favorite pair of legs in action.

Among the many who flocked to Niblo's Garden was Mark Twain, who wrote rapturously of the play's

Daringly clad Amazons from The Black Crook.

sets but professed to be shocked by the girls who had on "just barely enough clothes to be tantalizing." Immoral or not, the play had 475 performances, making it the longest-running production on Broadway up to that time, and the second longest of the 19th century.

1866

It took less than 15 minutes for a gang of thieves to pull off America's — and the world's — first train robbery.

On an October evening in 1866, two members of the Reno gang boarded an Ohio & Mississippi Railroad train in Seymour, Indiana. As it chugged out of town, the two met on the passenger car's outside platform and donned masks.

The men then headed for the express car, which carried all the mail and valuables, and inched along the running boards to its sliding door. Finding it unlocked, they entered and aimed their Colt revolvers at the surprised clerk's head. They quickly opened a safe and grabbed the contents. Then one of the robbers yanked the emergency bell rope. As the engineer slowed the train in

response to the bell, the two thieves leaped to the ground.

One of the men shouted "All right!" to the engineer, who, believing the two had just

needed to get off after missing their stop, threw open his throttle. In less than 15 minutes, the robbers had escaped with $10,000 in gold coins.

Bypassing the passenger car, bandits lost no time in finding the train's express car, where most of the valuables were kept.

Allan Pinkerton of the Pinkerton Detective Agency quickly went to the scene of the crime in Indiana and recommended that the railway company bolt all its safes to the floor and start locking the express car doors.

Detectives caught the bandits within a week, and they were imprisoned at Missouri State Prison, where gang leader John Reno allegedly bragged of his exploits to another inmate, a member of the James gang. When the inmate was released, he went straight to Jesse James with insider tips on the art of robbing trains. That must have had a profound effect on Frank and Jesse James, who became folk heroes as train robbers, frustrating squads of law enforcers.

Thaddeus Stevens, the most radical of the radical Republicans in Congress, wanted to confiscate rebel lands and turn them over to freed slaves.

At an age when most of his contemporaries had settled into a comfortable retirement, 74-year-old congressman Thaddeus Stevens was still a force to be reckoned with.

Despite his physical frailty, he had emerged as the most ardent voice in Congress on behalf of radical reconstruction of the South, and although he failed to engineer a complete overhaul of Southern society, he managed to push his party and the nation closer toward his goals.

In February 1867 during a heated debate in Congress over the Reconstruction Act, Stevens, speaking so softly that his colleagues had to crowd around him to hear, implored the Congress not to treat the South with kid gloves. The resulting bill carved up the South into five military districts and made black suffrage a requirement for readmission to the Union. The legislation passed, and Congress overrode a veto by President Andrew Johnson.

His goal partially accomplished, Stevens next acted to obtain land for the newly freed blacks, stating that "homesteads to them are far more valuable than the immediate right of suffrage." In March 1867, a month after the Reconstruction Act was passed, Stevens introduced a new bill calling for the confiscation of all Southern estates worth more than $5,000. The land would be divided into 40-acre farms and given to black families. The bill failed, and Stevens died the following year. 🔫

Stevens wanted to recast the South in the "image of a perfect Republic."

When a friend asked Secretary of State William Seward (seated at left) what his most significant achievement was, he replied, "The purchase of Alaska! But it will take the people a generation to find that out."

Alaska, considered by some to be a waste of money, was a greater bargain than the Louisiana Purchase.

"I see the Russian as he busily occupies himself by establishing seaports and towns and fortifications on the verge of this continent, . . ." said Secretary of State William Seward in 1860, "And I can say, 'go on and build up your outposts all along the coast and even up to the Arctic Ocean — they will yet become the outposts of my own country — monuments to the civilization of the United States.' " However noble Seward's intentions, he still drew jeers both from the Congress and from private citizens when he negotiated the purchase of the Alaska Territory from Russia in 1867. One congressman said that the land could sit there "until the last echo of the trump of time had faded away among the hills of eternity" before he would approve the purchase.

Alaska's frigid wilderness, falling partially within the Arctic Circle, was considered by many Americans to be a barren land, of little value because it could not be farmed, and overpriced at $7.2 million. In terms of sheer size, however, Seward had reason to be proud of the deal. Acre for acre, the Alaska Purchase was an even greater bargain than the Louisiana Purchase. The federal government paid France $15 million in 1803 for the 828,000 square miles of the Louisiana Territory, amounting to about 3 cents an acre. But Alaska, which comprises 586,000 square miles, was only about 2 cents an acre. Seward himself traveled through Alaska in August 1869, extolling the virtues of its abundant forests and marine life when he returned to the United States.

Even so, the Alaska Purchase, known to its critics as "Icebergia," "Walrussia," "Seward's Icebox," and most popularly, "Seward's Folly," did not prove its worth to many Americans until 1896, when gold was found in the Klondike. Since then, natural resources — including abundant fisheries, vast timberlands, natural gas and oil, and pristine landscapes — have made Alaska (which gained statehood in 1959) a true national treasure. 🔫

1867

Milwaukee printer Christopher Latham Sholes produced the practical typewriter, one of the world's most utilitarian inventions.

The typing machine of Christopher Latham Sholes had no lowercase letters, could only be used with tissue paper, and was exasperatingly difficult to operate. But it did possess one singular virtue: it could print faster than a man could write. Even so, Sholes's invention was hardly an overnight success.

After securing the financial backing of fellow printer James Densmore in 1867, Sholes worked six arduous years in order to bring his invention up to marketable standards. He tested the machine over and over by typing the campaign slogan of Republican presidential candidate Ulysses S. Grant: "Now is the time for all good men to come to the aid of their party." To solve the problem of jamming keys, he scattered the most frequently used letters in their widest possible configuration. His arrangement, known as QWERTY, is still used today on most word processors and computer keyboards.

The patent model for the Sholes typewriter, 1868.

In 1873 E. Remington & Sons agreed to manufacture the typing machine, and although sales were initially slow, by the turn of the century they reached 100,000 units a year. One of the earliest devotees of Sholes's "type-writer" was Mark Twain, who plunked down $125 for one of the earliest Remingtons and produced history's first typewritten manuscript, *Life on the Mississippi*. To thousands more — especially women, who found a new role in the business world as "typewriters" — the machine invented by Sholes was one of the century's most liberating devices. 🖋

1867

More hired hand than hero, the cowboy embodied the spirit of the American West.

An Abilene, Kansas, newspaper editor looked out his office window one day and was staggered. His small town had become "an island in a sea of cattle." The year before, in 1867, entrepreneur Joseph G. McCoy had established Abilene as a central depot for Texas cattle. For the next 20 years, Abilene, as well as other cow towns such as Ellsworth, Cheyenne, and the notorious Dodge City, would play host to a thriving livestock industry and the men who played an essential part in it — the cowboys.

The romantic image of the cowboy — the hero who saves the town and then rides off into the sunset, or the remorseless outlaw who terrorizes good citizens — has been mostly the stuff of fiction. The typical cowboy in the late 1860's was a loyal hired hand who worked long, hard hours riding the range. Confederate Civil War veterans, ex-slaves, Mexican migrants, and the like comprised much of the cowboy population in the West. The average cattle driver and ranch hand did not make a habit of wearing six-shooters, and many of them relieved the tedium of the trail by reading.

Railroads, Cow Towns, and Cattle Trails

WYO. TERR. · Ogallala · NEBR. · IOWA · Chicago
Cheyenne · Denver · KANS. · St. Joseph · ILL.
Ellsworth · Abilene · Sedalia
Pueblo · Kansas City · St. Louis
COLO. · Dodge City · Baxter Springs · MO.
Santa Fe · INDIAN TERR. · ARK.
N. MEX. TERR. · TEXAS · MISS. · LA.
MEXICO · San Antonio · Houston

— Goodnight-Loving Trail   — Chisolm Trail
— Western Trail   — Sedalia Trail

"The cowboy's life is a dreadful life/He's driven through heat and cold . . ." went one popular 19th-century range song.

Rarely staying more than seven years on the job, cowboys battled Indian attacks, disgruntled farmers, blizzards, and floods in order to move their "dogies" up such trails as the Goodnight-Loving, Western, Chisholm, and Sedalia. As soon as the herds were delivered, many of the cattle drivers, flush with pay (usually $25 to $40 a month), galloped into town looking for a bath and a good time. Some did ride their horses through the swinging doors of saloons or charge drunkenly through the streets, firing their six-shooters. But not all cowboys joined in, and some found the wild behavior offensive.

By the mid-1880's cattle drives were on the wane. The once open ranges had become overgrazed, and a series of harsh winters killed thousands of cattle. With the end of the great drives came the end of the careers of most of the true American cowboys, but their mythical counterparts live on — in Wild West shows, dime novels, and western movies. 🔫

A **1867**
s breathtaking as they were destructive, raging grassland fires on the Western plains posed an annual threat to settlers.

"One of the finest spectacles we have ever witnessed is a prairie on fire," wrote an editor of the *Nebraska City News* in 1858. "Upon all sides of us . . . the lambent flames are licking up the prairie grass, and causing the heavens to be all aglow with their reflected brilliancy."

Beautiful, yes — but terrifying, too. Among the many hardships that nature visited upon settlers on the Western plains, few were as awesome as prairie fires. The worst burned for weeks, blackening hundreds of square miles and blotting out the sun with dense, choking smoke. Autumn was the most dangerous time; the grass was dry then, and lightning or a stray ember could ignite it, starting a

D **1867**
uring his lifetime hundreds of dime novels were written about William F. Cody, best known as Buffalo Bill, the flamboyant showman of a spectacular Wild West show.

William F. Cody claimed he was christened "Buffalo Bill" in 1867 after he killed 4,280 buffalo during a 17-month stint as a buffalo hunter for a railroad. E.Z.C. Judson, a prolific pulp fiction writer, seized on the nickname, writing hundreds of dime novels glamorizing Cody as one of the West's grander heroes.

At 14, Cody rode for the Pony Express. Later, he was a Union soldier, drove a stagecoach, fought in Indian wars, and served as a scout for the U.S. Cavalry. As the frontier was settled, Cody refashioned himself into a master showman.

In 1883 he mounted a spectacular traveling show, later renowned as "Buffalo Bill's Wild West and Congress of Rough Riders of the World" — featur-

One newspaper called Buffalo Bill's Wild West show "more than realism — it is reality."

ing hundreds of performers. While some of the acts, such as the Pony Express ride, were fairly accurate, others were pure fiction. In one episode, for instance, Cody falsely depicted himself and a band of cowboys as being moments away from rescuing Custer's 7th Cavalry at the Little Bighorn. In another, Cody took revenge for Custer's

raging fire. Farmers quickly learned to plow fireguards around their properties. Fires sometimes flared up so quickly that the only way to dodge them was to burn off a small plot of land in the path of the conflagration and wait there until it roared past. People huddled in dugouts, dived down wells, and attempted to beat back the flames with gunnysacks.

Soldiers at Fort Stevens were among the lucky ones. When a great firestorm bore down on their post in the Dakota Territory in November 1867, they were able to exinguish the flames and save themselves. Other people were not so fortunate. Although surprisingly few lives were lost, the devastation was often complete, as farms, livestock, grain stores, valuable timber, and sometimes whole communities were consumed in the flames. 🔫

defeat by staging a mock hand-to-hand knife fight with a Cheyenne warrior. Audiences often accepted Cody's exaggerations as the unvarnished truth.

Showmanship, Cody knew, was what audiences wanted: he insisted that everything he put on stage was true. The money rolled in.

It poured out just as fast. Cody lived high on the hog and made ruinous investments in get-rich-quick schemes. After he went on a series of drinking sprees, a business partner demanded that he stay sober while the show was on the road. He agreed, but threatened at season's end to "get on a drunk that is a drunk." He became known for eccentric behavior. He once claimed that his wife had tried to poison him.

Cody finally went bankrupt, and in 1913 creditors took the Wild West show away from him. He died in January 1917, still tangled in lawsuits over money — and still determined to put his show back on the road. 🔫

1867

Despite their epithets, not all those called carpetbaggers and scalawags were scoundrels.
In the post–Civil War South, no insult was greater than to be called a "carpetbagger" or a "scalawag." Carpetbaggers were Northerners who traveled South, supposedly carrying all of their possessions in a carpet-bag, eager to get rich quick in a devastated land. They were said to gain personal advancement through political corruption and commercial chicanery. Scalawags were Southern white Republicans who collaborated with the carpetbaggers.

There was, however, another side to the story. Many so-called carpetbaggers were not mere opportunists but rather businessmen, teachers, and Union army veterans who promoted social and political reform. Although many hoped for personal prosperity, some were also motivated by an idealistic desire to build a new, more equitable South. They founded public schools, hospitals, and charitable institutions to help former slaves realize the promise of freedom.

From 1867 to 1877, during the period known as Radical Reconstruction, carpetbaggers, who were Republicans, came to dominate the Southern state governments. They were elected mainly by former slaves whose right to vote was enforced by federal troops. Once in office, the Northerners tried to combat racial discrimination, make taxation more just,

A 19th-century carpetbag.

rebuild roads, and promote railroad development. It is true that some were corrupt, but so were many politicians of the time, including a number who had sat in the same statehouses before the Civil War.

As for the Southern whites who helped them — the so-called scalawags — many were former planters, businessmen, and Confederate army veterans who had opposed secession from the start. Others were yeoman farmers who had steadfastly resisted the domination of the planter aristocracy.

Still, most whites of the former Confederacy continued to oppose racial equality, and they despised the Reconstruction laws that Congress forced upon them after the war. By 1877, when the last federal troops left the South, Democrats who had sided with the Confederacy began to replace Republicans in the state governments, and the climate for carpetbaggers and scalawags became increasingly hostile.

Drovers herd Texas longhorns into a boxcar in Abilene, Kansas, in 1871.

1867

"The Nation's Slaughterhouse" could very well have been St. Louis instead of Chicago.
After the Civil War, Texas ranchers had difficulty shipping cattle to Northern markets. None of the nation's railroads reached that far into the Southwest. In addition, Kansas and Missouri were enforcing quarantine laws to protect their livestock from Spanish fever. Drovers who tried to take their animals over routes that ran through those states met with harassment from farmers.

In 1867 Illinois entrepreneur Joseph McCoy thought of a way to help the ranchers and make some money for himself. Why not build a new rail line through Kansas, west of the settlement area and connected to Texas by the Chisholm Trail? So McCoy approached the Missouri-Pacific Railroad, with offices in St. Louis, and invited the line's president to go into business with him. The answer was a resounding no. Undaunted, McCoy struck a deal with another railroad, the Hannibal and St. Joseph, to transport his cattle to Chicago.

McCoy's instincts proved correct, and the result of his venture was a resounding success. Northern markets could not get enough of the Texas beef. The herd-driving cowboy became the stuff of legend, as did the Union Stock Yards of Chicago, the city that became the slaughtering and meatpacking capital of the nation.

IN THEIR OWN WORDS

...The genus carpet-bagger is a man with a lank head of dry hair, a lank stomach and long legs, club knees and splay feet, dried legs and lank jaws, with eyes like a fish and mouth like a shark. Add to this a habit of sneaking and dodging about in unknown places — habiting with negroes in dark dens and back streets — a look like a hound and the smell like a polecat....

Our scallawag is the local leper of the community.... Once he was respected. ... Now, possessed of the itch of office and the salt rheum of Radicalism, he is a mangy dog, slinking through the alleys, defiling with tobacco juice the steps of the Capitol, stretching his lazy carcass in the sun on the Square, or the benches of the Mayor's Court.

An 1868 newspaper article expresses the hatred felt toward carpetbaggers and scalawags in the postwar South.

A *1868*
ndrew Johnson is the first American president to have been impeached — yet he still served out his term in office.

The struggle between President Andrew Johnson and the radical Republicans over Reconstruction reached crisis proportions during the last months of 1867. Johnson had consistently undermined congressional policy in the South, and he had already withstood two impeachment attempts.

In the first attempt, a member of the House, James Ashley of Ohio, became so obsessed with the president's obstructionist tactics that he publicly advanced the theory that Johnson had been involved in a plot to assassinate Lincoln. Although few took Ashley seriously, radical Republicans in Congress had come to believe that Reconstruction could not proceed while Johnson remained in the White House.

In order to impeach the president, the Congress needed evidence that the chief executive had committed "high crimes and misdemeanors." In early 1868 the legislators had their chance after Johnson fired Secretary of War Edwin Stanton and replaced him with Ulysses S. Grant. Johnson had acted without Sen-

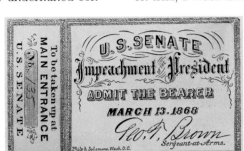

A ticket to Johnson's impeachment trial.

ate approval — a requirement of the Tenure of Office Act, a piece of nuisance legislation that Congress had passed in 1867 for the primary purpose of undermining Johnson's authority. As a consequence, the House voted on February 24, 1868, to put the president on trial; a week later it adopted 11 articles of impeachment, charging Johnson with violating the Tenure of Office Act, assaulting the authority of Congress, and attempting to bring it "into disgrace."

On March 13 the Senate met to hear the charges of impeachment. Johnson himself stayed away from the proceedings, preferring to let his lawyers deal with the matter. Johnson's defense was that he had the right to remove Stanton, while the prosecution argued that he did not. Although many members of Congress believed that Johnson was totally unfit for office, no charge of "high crimes and misdemeanors" was found. The momentum to oust Johnson lost steam, and when the Senate voted in late May the count fell one short of the two-thirds majority required for conviction. By then, the country wanted to hear no more of the affair. ☙

A *1868*
steamboat captain who knew nothing about cattle became the first great rancher in Texas.

Richard King received this piece of advice from his friend Robert E. Lee: "Buy land, and never sell." King did exactly that, and in the process became a Texas legend. Having amassed a fortune during the Civil War by trading Confederate cotton to Mexico for livestock and guns, he built an empire of more than half a million acres along the Santa Gertrudis Creek in south Texas, 45 miles southwest of Corpus Christi. So vast was King's operation that he imported

an entire Mexican town to run it. (Descendants of these people still work on the ranch.) He also maintained riflemen to fend off rustlers from both sides of the border.

King's operation might never have reached its titanic dimensions without the arrival of the Atchison, Topeka, and Santa Fe Railway in 1868. Passing through Kansas, the railroad connected the Western grasslands with Eastern markets hungry

for beef. King soon began driving his cattle north to Kansas so that he could ship them from the railway stations there, and by 1875 he was driving as many as 60,000 head a year to Kansas.

After King's death in 1885, his heirs continued to expand the ranch, and at its peak "King's Kingdom" covered an astonishing 1.2 million acres of coastal plain — nearly 2,000 square miles. Although reduced now to 825,000 acres, it is still one of the largest ranches in the world and universally recognized as the birthplace of the modern beef ranching industry. ☙

This modest frame house would grow to be a two-story building with 10 bedrooms — a true measure of Richard King's success.

1869

A preacher with a passion for the great outdoors almost single-handedly turned the Adirondacks into one of the East's most-favored vacation spots.

Twenty-nine-year-old Rev. William Henry Harrison Murray was much admired for his impassioned sermons at Boston's Park Street Congregational Church. Although he worked hard, he managed to find time for vacations. Murray spent his summers 150 miles away in the Adirondack Mountains, in pursuit of trout and small game.

In the spring of 1869, he published *Adventures in the Wilderness*, a small volume about the joys of the sporting life. It had a greater impact than all his sermons. Part travel guide and part paean to nature, the book offered something for everyone, giving advice on what routes to take, what clothes to wear, and what prices to expect. The frugal camper learned, for example, that he could spend a month in the mountains for just $125.

Schroon Lake, one of hundreds of camping sites in the Adirondacks.

In a matter of months, thousands of copies of *Adventures in the Wilderness* were sold at $1.50 each. Railroads gave them away with the purchase of a round-trip ticket. Thousands of people gave up their summer plans to follow Murray's suggestions.

The press grew cynical about the hype and dubbed the eager sportsmen "Murray's Fools." But fools or not, the Eastern elite had caught the camping bug. By 1892 nearly 25 percent of the Adirondacks was owned by private clubs and individuals with names like Morgan, Vanderbilt, and Rockefeller.

In the meantime, Murray moved on. He gave up his ministry for other vocations: raising horses in Connecticut, ranching in Texas, running a restaurant in Montreal. Thirty-five years later he was chagrined to learn that his pristine hills had been "civilized by the axe and the plough, and that the divine silence of the Sabbath air is jarred into discord by the clang and rattle of a chapel bell!"

IN THEIR OWN WORDS

❝Back and forth, round and round that pool he flashed . . . until at last . . . he rolled over upon his side and lay panting upon the surface. . . . I paused a moment to admire. A bluish-black trout he was, dotted with spots of bright vermilion. His fins, rosy as autumnal skies at sunset, were edged with a border of purest white. . . . A trout in color and build rarely seen, gamy and stanch.❞

The Reverend William Murray describes one of his frequent encounters with Adirondack trout.

1869

National pride soared with the completion of a railroad that stretched across America.

Construction on the transcontinental railroad began in early December 1863, with Union Pacific crew members laying track at Omaha, Nebraska. Mostly Irish immigrants and Civil War veterans, the workers performed the backbreaking work of hefting and dropping 700-pound rails onto the railbed, all under the threat of Indian attacks.

As they moved across the Great Plains, the construction teams built sordid tent cities that were often derided as "Hell on Wheels." Saloons and dance halls sprang up overnight, and violence and vice abounded. "They used to 'have a man for breakfast here every morning' as they pleasantly spoke when chronicling the nightly murders in the town . . . " said one observer of a tent city.

Meanwhile, starting in Sacramento, California, Central Pacific crews had been working since January 1863, pushing the railbed up through the ice and granite of the Sierra Nevada. Laborers had to hang from baskets to drill blasting holes into the sides of the mountains, and blizzards and avalanches were often a threat. Immigrants from Canton, China, each man weighing an average of 110

The official meeting of East and West at Promontory, Utah, 1869.

1869

The British-born manager of the first professional baseball team, the Cincinnati Red Stockings, brought innovations to the game that are still used today.

By the time the Cincinnati Red Stockings began their first national tour in 1869, baseball was already more than a national pastime: it was also a profession. Players for the Philadelphia Athletics and the Brooklyn Atlantics were being given a percentage of the gate receipts. One team, the New York Mutuals, had been paying each player a yearly salary under the table. The Red Stockings earned between $600 and $1,400 a year — at a time when an average worker's annual salary was only $490.

The Red Stockings' British-born manager, Harry Wright, joined the team in 1867 as "probably the trickiest pitcher in the United States." Good as he was, his true talents lay in his ability to recognize the business potential in baseball.

Wright took the game to new heights, drilling the players in organized practice sessions and admonishing them to "keep good hours and abstain from intoxicating drinks and tobacco." He also demanded that players behave with decorum while on the field.

The original members of the Cincinnati Red Stockings.

Perhaps his most enduring innovation was the modern baseball uniform. Deciding that knickerbockers would be more practical than long pants tied off at the cuffs, Wright commissioned a seamstress to make identical white flannel knickers and shirts for each member of the team. Two daughters of a prominent Cincinnati family knitted dozens of bright red stockings to complete the outfit.

The "invincible Red Stockings" went on to wow their fans, winning an unbroken string of 65 games in the 1869 season. They seemed all but unstoppable. Then in their final game of the season, the Brooklyn Atlantics defeated them before some 15,000 wildly cheering New Yorkers. Fans abandoned the team, investors cut off support, and the team broke up. Wright, however, refused to be beaten. He merely gathered together his best players and moved his ball club east, where they became the Boston Red Stockings.

---

pounds, comprised much of the Central Pacific team. Skeptics scoffed that the hard work would crush the Chinese body and spirit, but they were soon silenced when the industrious newcomers proved their mettle by working with amazing skill and speed.

On May 10, 1869, six years and 1,775 miles later, a gold spike was driven into the final railroad tie at Promontory, Utah: the transcontinental railroad was completed. People cheered as two locomotives, one from the East and one from the West, ceremonially met, cowcatcher facing cowcatcher, setting off a tumultuous celebration across America. An entire continent, joined by muscle, blood, and iron, rejoiced.

1869

John Wesley Powell led an exploration of the last uncharted region in America.

In 1540 Spanish explorers ventured partway into the vast chasm of the Grand Canyon, then turned back, writing it off as a "useless piece of country." Three centuries later, a geology professor who had lost an arm in the Civil War decided to find out for himself.

On May 24, 1869, John Wesley Powell set out to explore the Colorado River with nine other men in four specially designed wooden boats. Powell, a devoted naturalist, was entranced by the canyons that surrounded him. He wrote in his journal that it was "a world of grandeur," bounded by cliffs "from which the gods might quarry mountains."

Then just 16 days into the trip, the picturesque journey turned dangerous. One of the boats splintered on a boulder, and the crew watched a third of their provisions disappear into the roiling waters. By the 11th week of the trip, they were left with barely a month's worth of

During a break in his expedition, Powell poses with a Paiute Indian chief.

mildewed flour, rancid bacon, and a soggy sack of coffee. In the pages of Powell's journal, the canyon had become a "granite prison."

On the evening of August 27, after the haggard crew opened the last bag of flour, three of the men told Powell that it was suicidal to follow the river any farther. They decided to take their chances and climbed out of the canyon, where they ran into an angry band of Shivwit Indians and died in a barrage of arrows. On August 29, after 14 weeks and a 900-mile journey, Powell and the others floated safely out of the gorge, the first white men to navigate the Colorado River through the Grand Canyon. "The river rolls by us in silent majesty," Powell wrote; "the quiet of the camp is sweet; our joy is almost ecstasy."

Powell returned to civilization a famous man. He would take a second trip to the canyon before becoming head of the U.S. Geological Survey and starting the herculean task of mapping the topography of the entire country.

1869

Sixty years before Black Tuesday, there was Black Friday — and four years after that, the Panic of 1873.

In June 1869 money barons Jay Gould and James Fisk collaborated with Abel R. Corbin, the brother-in-law of President Ulysses S. Grant, to corner the gold market. A few months later, on Friday, September 24, their manipulations to raise and lower gold prices drove thousands of gold speculators to financial ruin. The gold scam was the most serious financial crisis in the young country's history, and the infamous day on which it began became known as Black Friday.

Almost four years later, on September 18, 1873, another panic occurred. Prompted by the collapse of the banking house of Jay Cooke & Company, overinvestment in the nation's infrastructure, and an international monetary devaluation, the disastrous Panic of 1873 caused the ruin of 5,000 businesses and a financial depression the likes of which would not be seen again until the 1930's. So severe was the blow to the economy that the New York Stock Exchange was closed for 10 days to stabilize prices.

The Panic of 1873 increased support for paper money, or "greenbacks." Rather than being backed by gold and silver, currency would be printed as needed by the government.

For some people, the panic presented opportunity. A young man named Henry Clay Frick bought vast amounts of coal-rich land in Pennsylvania at a reduced rate. Over the next few decades, his investment would make him rich enough to rival Black Friday's Jay Gould. ☙

Hard Times: America's Financial Panics

Their causes may be simple or complex, but financial panics have occurred periodically. The following list highlights some of America's financial low points.

1819 A sudden drop in cotton prices bursts a speculative bubble. As a result, banks fold, Western real estate depreciates, and credit tightens.

1857 A short-lived financial panic is set off by several factors, including a drop in food prices, the failure of the Ohio Life Insurance and Trust Company, and the loss of $2 million in gold when the uninsured ship *Central America* sinks on her way from California.

1873 A financial crisis in Europe results in the withdrawal of investments in the United States, the failure of Jay Cooke & Company (a prominent banking house), and the closing of some 100 banks.

1893 U.S. gold reserves fall below a safe minimum. As a result, the securities on the New York Stock Exchange fall to their lowest point ever. Some 600 banks close and thousands of businesses fail.

1907 A run on New York's Knickerbocker Trust Company forces the bank to close its doors. Other banks follow suit. Further panic is averted by financier and banker J. P. Morgan's swift intercession.

1929 Following an alarming decline in stock prices beginning on October 21, the market, which had been buoyed by speculative trading, collapses on October 29. It triggers a 10-year depression, the worst in the country's history.

1987 On October 19 an apparently healthy market plummets. When the stock market closes at the end of the day, it has lost some $500 billion in value.

1869

The Wyoming Territory was the first location in the United States to grant women the right to vote.

When Col. William H. Bright introduced the bill for women's suffrage to the Wyoming legislature in November 1869, some lawmakers saw it as a joke. But the ratio of men to women over the age of 21 in the territory was a disheartening six to one, and the chance to attract more women to Wyoming by taking a pro-suffrage stance proved a powerful incentive for the legislators. The bill to give women the vote was passed "amid the greatest hilarity."

The legislators, who were mostly Democrats, assumed that Wyoming's straight-laced Republican governor, John A. Campbell, would veto the measure. But Campbell, not wanting to be blamed for standing in the way of social progress, signed it into law on December 10.

The experiment with female suffrage propelled women into positions of real civic importance in the

Wyoming women exercise their right to vote in the 1888 presidential election.

Wyoming Territory. In February 1870 Esther Morris was appointed justice of the peace in South Pass City — the first female ever to hold such a position in the United States. An advocate of women's rights, Morris officiated for eight and one-half months, overseeing some 70 cases. In March 1870 six women were called to jury duty in Laramie, another first in American history. Although initially reluctant, the female jurors proved scrupulous in their judgments and remarkably tough when handing down convictions.

Social constraints soon prevailed, however. Female jurors were ridiculed, and some men thought jury duty too taxing for women. Just one year after it began, the experiment that allowed women in the courtrooms ended. Esther Morris completed her term as judge in November 1870 and was not reappointed.

Oddly enough, the right to vote did nothing to attract more women, as was originally hoped. Nevertheless, the population supported suffrage, and in 1890, when Wyoming became a state, it had the first state constitution giving women full voting rights. ☙

1869

His first official invention was a practical failure, but Thomas Edison went on to patent more ideas than any other scientist in American history.

In 1869 Thomas Alva Edison was flush with pride over his first patented invention. His electric vote recorder, he thought, would surely find admirers in local legislatures. But Edison had never considered that the speedy recording of votes would interfere with one of the lawmakers' most cherished institutions — the filibuster. No legislators wanted his vote recorder, and not a single one was purchased.

Edison moved to New York, resolved never again to waste his time inventing unmarketable machines. Two years later, with a $40,000 windfall from the sale of a stock ticker, he opened a research lab designed to produce inventions to order. Amazingly, the "old man," as his workers liked to call him, had no formal education in theoretical science. He read Newton's *Principia* at age 15 and later remarked: "It gave me a distaste for mathematics from which I have never recovered."

Thomas Edison with his phonograph, the most popular exhibit at the Paris Exposition in 1889.

Practicality, not pure science, drove Edison's "invention factory." Over the course of 40 years, he amassed 1,093 patents, an average of more than two a month; these included the incandescent electric light, the phonograph, and a forerunner of the movie projector and camera. Once the need for a particular device became clear, Edison would commit unlimited resources. In 1880 he spent $100,000 to come up with the perfect material for a light bulb filament. (He used a strain of bamboo found in the Amazon.) To Edison, trial and error were simply part of the invention process. "Well," he remarked after testing models for a storage battery 8,000 times, "at least we know 8,000 things that don't work."

For all of their modern efficiencies, Edison's factories could not help but take on their creator's spirit. One mechanic reminisced that after finishing an invention, Edison would "jump up and do a kind of Zulu dance." And particularly long workdays often ended with a concert by the factory's makeshift band, which boasted a zither, a violin, several tin pans, and Edison himself on the organ. 🔫

1869

The first apartment building constructed in New York City more closely resembled a luxury hotel than a permanent residence.

To answer the needs of a rapidly growing middle class, urban housing underwent many transformations. In the 1850's and 1860's, spacious and private "apartment hotels" provided a comfortable alternative to the more common form of long-term communal living, the boardinghouse. With six-room suites that included private bathrooms and kitchens, as well as public dining rooms and maid service, buildings such as the Stuyvesant Apartments, built in New York City in 1869, more closely resembled modern-day luxury hotels than the independent residences now known as apartments.

Many apartment hotels and other early apartment buildings disguised their function as communal living centers through their mansionlike designs. It wasn't until the end of the century that tall apartment towers, with residences stacked atop one another, were built.

At the same time laborers and immigrants were offered a similar but less enticing type of residence — the tenement. Commonly known as "tenant houses" and "railroad tenements," these were narrow multiroom structures that often lacked adequate sanitation and ventilation. 🔫

The Stuyvesant Apartments in New York City had such amenities as elevators and telephone service.

1870

Lured west by the promise of a better life, many homesteaders met with hardship and failure.

The immense prairies of the United States were being settled at an increasing rate. Spurred by the promise of virtually free land (provided in the Homestead Act of 1862) and the expansion of the railroads, prospective farmers moved west in vast numbers by 1870. Immigrants with little experience traveled along with seasoned Eastern farmers to a place where, according to one railroad advertisement "all become prosperous, and many will acquire fortunes in a short period."

Once they arrived, many new homesteaders were in for a bitter disappointment. Legal loopholes in the Homestead Act and other land legislation enabled speculators and rich planters to grab the choicest real estate. Also, the railroads received large tracts from the government, leaving the small farmer with inferior parcels of land. The less fortunate settlers worked long hours just to survive, with periods of drought adding to their difficulties.

Even when the land was good, farmers could not always come up with the capital to pay for tools and livestock, and they often had to take on extra jobs or assume debt just to get started. In addition, because they provided virtually the only means of transporting goods, the railroads charged the farmers exorbitant prices to move their products.

At the mercy of the railroads, small-time farmers organized themselves into social and political groups, the most prominent of which was the Patrons of Husbandry, or the Grange. Founded by postal clerk Oliver Hudson Kelley in 1867, the Grange's original purpose was to disseminate information that would improve the farmer's lot, but it soon took on the responsibility of breaking the railroad's monopolistic practices, arguing that public businesses like railroads were subject to state regulation. Its efforts were so effective that states soon enacted new shipping and warehousing rates that benefited the farmers. But even with better rates and the invention of more efficient tools, farming as a profession was on the wane. Between 1870 and 1910 the number of farmers in the United States dropped from more than half of the population to less than one-third.

Numbering nearly 800,000 members nationwide, the Grange had units in almost every state.

As late as 1913 more than 200,000 one-room schools, such as this one in Hecla, Montana, still existed in America.

1870

Although teaching was an acceptable profession for women, it was filled with many hardships — especially on the frontier.

By 1870 female elementary school teachers outnumbered males by two to one in most settled areas. Women were considered by some administrators to have more agreeable natures and better morals than their male counterparts and to be "infinitely more fit than males to be the guides and exemplars of young children." Women, moreover, could be paid lower wages than men.

For female teachers on the Western frontier or at an isolated rural outpost, the lower wage must have seemed especially unfair. Forced to make do in a one-room schoolhouse that often lacked paper, desks, and blackboards, many "schoolmarms" nevertheless had to teach a variety of subjects to a group of students ranging from 6 to 16 years old. In addition to being cramped and dark, the schoolhouses were filled with physical discomforts. Students and teachers alike endured leaky roofs, bitter cold, reptiles, vermin, fleas, and rickety outhouses. Older male students were at times an intimidating presence, and much of the schoolteacher's time was spent disciplining the rowdy pupils.

The teacher's trials did not end with the school day. Although her salary usually included room and board, her accommodations, provided by the community, were often less than adequate, "My bedroom was an unfinished attic room with an outside stairway which at times was slick with ice and snow," recalled one South Dakota teacher. The teacher was often forced to move from home to home, and privacy was at a premium. Despite the obvious drawbacks, some women saw teaching as the only career choice. Wrote one Nebraska teacher in her memoirs, "I *was* going to be respectable and *was* going to earn a living. So, I became a teacher."

M

1871

Massive fires in Chicago and three other major U.S. cities resulted in stricter safety codes and better city planning.

Comprised mostly of wooden structures and governed by deficient fire codes, Chicago was a disaster waiting to happen. In October 1871 it did. The Great Chicago Fire (which may or may not have been started by Mrs. O'Leary's cow kicking over a kerosene lamp) raced through some 18,000 buildings in a 3½-mile radius, killing 300 people and causing $200 million in damage.

The next year a fire in Boston's business district raged for nearly two days, killing 13 people and causing $75 million in damage to some 65 acres of cityscape. Boston's fire companies had been hindered because most of the horses that pulled the trucks were sick, and the district's congested street plan made it easy for flames to spread across the rooftops.

In 1904 the Great Fire of Baltimore destroyed most of the downtown area, but the damage did not equal that of the conflagration touched off by the San Francisco earthquake in 1906. For three days the fires burned, destroying two-thirds of the city and displacing hundreds of thousands of people.

Although the four cities were rebuilt with surprising speed, the terrible toll the fires had taken emphasized the need for better urban planning and effective fire-safety legislation. Eventually, more stringent building codes were enforced, and fireproof building materials like concrete and asbestos became more commonly used. 🖎

This remnant of a once-elegant building stands testament to the grim destruction of the Great Chicago Fire.

A

1871

A little-known blaze in the North Woods of Wisconsin killed four times as many people as the Chicago Fire — on the very same night.

Peshtigo was a thriving logging community nestled deep in the heart of Wisconsin's North Woods. Built around a single sawmill, the town logged 150,000 feet of fresh pine each day, sending most of it 250 miles south for sale in Chicago.

On the night of October 8, 1871, as people rested from their Sunday dinners, a peculiar crimson glow lit the sky in the distance. The woods, brittle from three months without rain, rumbled with a strange deep roll. Here and there, pockets of gas in the air exploded into sudden balls of fire. Then the winds came, whipping up a murderous firestorm.

The town's one piece of equipment, a hand-drawn pumper, quickly broke down, and bucket brigades were useless against the inferno. Within minutes huge walls of fire engulfed the town. Pine sidewalks burst into flames, chimneys toppled, and roofs were torn from houses. Hundreds of people crowded into the tiny Peshtigo River that bisected the area, beating the water with their arms to keep the flames away. In a single hour the town, except for one house that still stood the next day, was completely destroyed.

Two days passed before word of the disaster reached the capital at Madison. The only telegraph wire connecting Peshtigo to the world had burned before a message could be sent. At the time, workers were preparing to send relief trains south to Chicago, where 300 people had died the same night in the "fire of the century." The relief workers, sent to Peshtigo instead, found that 1,200 people and 1 million acres of trees had been destroyed in a blaze that history would soon forget. 🖎

IN THEIR OWN WORDS

❝The air was no longer fit to breathe, full as it was of sand, dust, ashes, cinders, sparks, smoke, and fire. . . . Some were hastening towards the river, others from it, whilst all were struggling alike in the grasp of the hurricane. A thousand discordant deafening noises rose on the air together. The neighing of horses, falling of chimneys, crashing of uprooted trees, roaring and whistling of the wind, crackling of fire as it ran with lightning-like rapidity from house to house — all sounds were there save that of the human voice. People seemed stricken dumb by terror. They jostled each other without exchanging look, word, or counsel. The silence of the tomb reigned among the living; nature alone lifted up its voice and spoke.❞

The Reverend Peter Pernin recounts his harrowing flight from the Great Peshtigo Fire of 1871.

1871

Legendary showman P.T. Barnum was not just known for his famous circus.

Entertainment impresario Phineas Taylor Barnum was a master at harnessing the full power of the press to draw huge crowds to his uniquely American entertainments. His first foray into show business, at the age of 25, was as an exhibitor of Joice Heth, a woman alleged to be George Washington's 161-year-old slave nurse. When interest in Heth waned, Barnum used his knowledge of the press, gained in a short stint as a newspaper publisher, to spread the rumor that she was a machine. That was enough to get thousands of people to return to see if they had been "humbugged."

The public's yen for amazements like Heth intensified over Barnum's lifetime. Beginning in 1842 his five-story American Museum in New York City satisfied that hunger with thousands of "curiosities,"

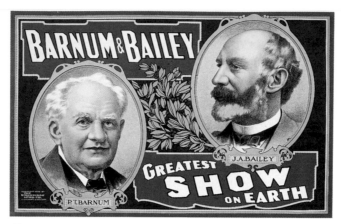

Phineas Taylor Barnum and James Anthony Bailey joined forces to create the first three-ring circus performed under electric lights.

including the famous midget, Tom Thumb, and the country's first public aquarium. The tour of Swedish singer Jenny Lind, highly publicized by Barnum, made his name a household word.

The showman was already 60 years old and famous when his first three-ring circus was launched under the Big Top in 1871. James A. Bailey, his most successful competitor, became his partner 10 years later. Said Barnum: "If you can't lick 'em, join 'em." The Barnum & Bailey Circus, dubbed "The Greatest Show on Earth" by none other than Barnum himself, was only the last of his larger-than-life spectacles.

Barnum's circuses, museums, and tours were the grand entertainments of their time. At the end of his career, he admitted that "without printer's ink, I should have been no bigger than Tom Thumb." With it, he invented a uniquely American way of amusement.

1872

When the Russian czar's son visited the United States, the highlight of his trip was a buffalo hunt on the Great Plains.

For a few days during the cold winter of 1872, some Americans were treated to a rare event: royalty "roughing it" on the Western frontier. The Grand Duke Alexis Romanov, on a tour of the United States, had decided his education in American culture would not be complete without a buffalo hunt.

On January 13, 1872, the 21-year-old Alexis arrived on the plains of southern Nebraska, with a Smith & Wesson revolver strapped to his belt. Gen. Philip Sheridan, the Civil War hero and Indian fighter, accompanied him into camp, where the grand duke was greeted by two companies of infantry and two of cavalry — an impressive escort even for a foreign dignitary. That night, a group of 100

On a hunt with Plains Indian chiefs, the Grand Duke Alexis delivers the coup de grace to his first buffalo.

Sioux Indians entertained the royal visitor with mock battles and a war dance. The next morning, the most publicized hunt in American history began.

A team that included Col. George Armstrong Custer and "Buffalo Bill" Cody shepherded the grand duke through the first days of the outing; by the time the party moved on to Colorado, Alexis was hunting with great enthusiasm. One day, he and Custer came barreling over a hill after a couple of wounded buffalo, only to realize that they were firing right at Sheridan. A moment later, after the bullets stopped flying, Sheridan delivered a tirade. The grand duke apparently was having too good a time to be offended. He

promptly went back to his business, brought down a dozen or so buffalo, and celebrated with champagne.

After the hunt, Alexis embarked on a tour of the South with Colonel Custer. General Sheridan returned to Chicago, where he received a medal from the czar of Russia for his noble service.

1872

The first woman to run for president, Victoria Woodhull nearly spent Election Day in jail under obscenity charges.

Victoria Claflin Woodhull was not, by any standards, a typical candidate for the office of president of the United States. The daughter of a snake-oil salesman and a spiritualist, Woodhull worked as a clairvoyant in her early twenties. At 32, she opened a Wall Street brokerage with her sister, Tennessee. With characteristic irreverence, the sisters published a weekly newspaper that ran ads for brokers and banks on its front page, while printing the first American version of the *Communist Manifesto* inside.

As a dabbler in the more extreme doctrines of her day, such as socialism, spiritualism, and sexual freedom, Woodhull could easily have been ignored as an eccentric. But she also believed in legal equality. In January of 1871 she went before the Judiciary Committee of the House of Representatives to sue for women's suffrage. Her exceptional oratory skills and beauty captivated the audience, which included renowned suffragist Susan B. Anthony.

Despite her radical ideas,

Woodhull is lampooned as a female demon for her radical ideas.

Woodhull ran for president in 1872. In the midst of her campaign, she came under attack by the Reverend Henry Ward Beecher, the dean of the liberal clergy and a friend of the suffrage movement. Woodhull, he charged, was "either insane or the hapless victim of malignant spirits." In response, Woodhull used her newspaper to expose an alleged affair Beecher was conducting with the wife of a young aide. The exposé landed her in New York's Ludlow Street Jail, charged with distributing obscene matter through the U.S. mail. Out on bail within two days, she was barred from the polls by election officials. Thus Woodhull could not even cast a vote for herself during her historic candidacy.

1873

San Francisco's Andrew Hallidie successfully operated the first cable car in America, launching the spread of mechanized public transportation across the nation.

On August 2, 1873, Andrew Smith Hallidie and a few hopeful investors gathered in the morning fog atop San Francisco's Nob Hill. Below them, a mile of wire rope from Hallidie's cable factory snaked to the bottom of the hill through a groove in the street. Attached to the rope by a single metal clamp was the world's first cable car. The driver supposedly took one look down the 307-foot drop and declined the job, muttering something about his wife and children. Undaunted, Hallidie climbed into the car and disappeared into the mist, returning safely within a matter of minutes.

Hallidie's creation, based on plans proposed by various inventors since 1812, was an instant hit. Within two years some 150,000 San Franciscans were braving "the rope" monthly. Before long, cable rails crisscrossed 28 other American cities, including New York, Chicago, and St. Louis.

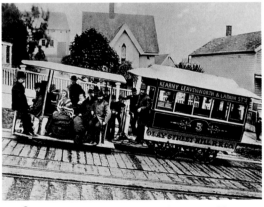

Curious San Franciscans test the new cable car technology on the Clay St. Hill Railroad in 1874.

The cars launched a revolution in transportation. Horse-drawn streetcars became obsolete, streets grew quieter, pavements became cleaner, and property values soared. As H. H. Windsor, the secretary of Chicago's first cable car company, dryly pointed out, "The value of removing from a street the voidings of two or three thousand horses is a matter not to be lightly estimated."

By the turn of the century, however, efficient electric railways had swept the cable cars off most city streets. In San Francisco the great earthquake and fire of 1906 left the tracks a twisted mass of iron and concrete. Shingled and fitted with indoor plumbing, leftover cars housed some of the 300,000 people left homeless by the quake. A mere 8.8 miles of cable and some 40 cars survived into the 1960's, when they were declared the country's first moving national monument — an honor that stands to this day.

1874

The city of Philadelphia welcomed 3,000 visitors to the grand opening of the first chartered zoo in America.

It was an exotic experience: for a mere 25 cents, visitors to the new Philadelphia Zoological Garden, which opened on July 1, 1874, were treated to a truly international menagerie. The African contingent included six giraffes. From the South Pacific came a diverse collection of colorful birds. Australia contributed an odd assortment of wombats, dingoes, wallabies, and kangaroos, along with a Tasmanian devil.

Although Europeans had seen this kind of display after the age of exploration had created interest in the world's wildlife, Americans were stunned by the creatures in Philadelphia. "The kangaroos," wrote S. Weir Mitchell, a local physician and writer, "are manifestly bits of two animals put together at the midriff." Amusement was not always the most common reaction. Jennie the elephant, who lumbered to and fro across from the bear pits, sent many visitors scrambling before they realized she was chained at the leg.

Philadelphians quickly warmed to the new entertainment. During the zoo's second year, some 420,000 people paid to gawk at the many oddities. In the years to follow, the zoological garden would distinguish itself with a number of "firsts." It founded the first laboratory for animal research in 1901. It successfully bred the first wild animals in captivity, including an orangutan and a cheetah.

And in 1938 it started the first children's zoo in the nation. Now, more than a century after it opened, the Philadelphia zoo plays host to about 1.5 million visitors each year.

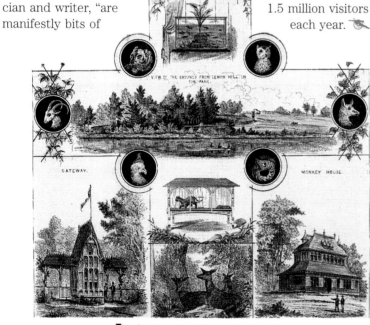

*The front page of **The Daily Graphic** celebrates the opening of the Philadelphia zoo.*

A Nebraska farmer vainly swings his hatchet at the rapacious "hoppers" of 1874.

1874

In the summer of 1874, hordes of grasshoppers swarmed through the plains, leaving total destruction in their wake.

The grasshoppers would come with little warning. First, "strange silvery spots" would appear in the sky, and the sun would become veiled with what looked like a thick, gray cloud. Then the cloud, sounding like a distant waterfall, would approach. Unfortunately, the noise was not a waterfall, but the beating wings of "hoppers."

Forced by drought to leave their usual feeding grounds, the grasshoppers — or, more accurately, Rocky Mountain locusts — descended upon the pastures of the West and Midwest like a living plague. Farmers struggled to save what crops they could, but to no avail; the hoppers, which traveled in swarms up to 100 miles wide and 300 miles long, ate everything. They devoured blankets. They gnawed through wood. One report had them eating a harness while it was still on a horse. Once inside a house, they would shred curtains and crawl into beds. Only constant vigilance prevented the hoppers from eating the clothes off a person's back. There was little defense; killing them was futile since they formed a living carpet four to six inches deep. Powerful trains were brought to a halt when the tracks became slick with crushed hoppers.

The worst of the grasshopper plague began in the summer of 1874, but the unwelcome visitors reappeared the next three summers, voraciously eating their way through $200 million worth of crops in an area that reached from the Dakota Territory to Texas and from the Rocky Mountains to the Mississippi River.

Since nothing was safe from the grasshoppers, most people had little choice but to watch their food, crops, and belongings vanish. The pests stayed until there was nothing left to eat, usually a few days. Then they moved on, carried by the wind, to the next victims, leaving, as one rueful farmer put it, "nothing but the mortgage."

1874

Martha Dunham Summerhayes followed her husband, an army lieutenant, to uncharted Western territory and wrote a moving account of life on the frontier.

Brought up in a well-to-do Nantucket family, Martha Dunham caught a glimpse of military life when she spent two years abroad in Hanover, Germany, in 1871. She was feted by young Prussian soldiers at dances, garden parties, and other social events and was dazzled by the dashing uniforms and the apparent glamour of military life. Although she was warned by an older officer's wife that it was all just "glittering misery," Martha Dunham returned home, and two years later, in 1874, married John Wyer Summerhayes, a second lieutenant with the Eighth Infantry.

Soon after their wedding, the newlyweds were sent to Fort Russell, in Wyoming Territory. There, the inexperienced Mrs. Summerhayes got her first real taste of life on a military post when she moved into the "forlorn" quarters assigned to the couple. Far from the parties of Hanover and the comforts of Nantucket, the new officer's wife struggled to make a home.

No sooner had the Summerhayes settled in than the regiment was ordered to Arizona Territory — a "dreaded and then unknown" land filled with Apache Indians who, in an attempt to survive total destruction by the U.S. government, had become increasingly brutal in their treatment of the white man. Despite sandstorms, rattlesnakes, lack of water, and treacherous mountain passes, Mrs. Summerhayes maintained her stamina — all the more astonishing because she was pregnant throughout the journey.

In 1876, nine weeks after giving birth to a son, Mrs. Summerhayes was on the move again with her husband and his regiment. Her health was failing, however, so she returned to Nantucket, determined never to set foot in Arizona again. Eight months later, her health now improved, she changed her mind. Returning to her husband at Fort Mac-Dowell in Arizona, she spent the rest of his career crisscrossing the Southwest, setting up housekeeping in a number of army posts. "I had cast my lot with a soldier," she wrote in her book, *Vanished Arizona,* which was published in 1908, "and where he was, was home to me." 🖋

Martha Summerhayes was encouraged to "place the army wife and her fortitude on record."

IN THEIR OWN WORDS

> ... The grasshoppers would alight in the middle of the day for their 'siesta.' ... They flew up like a swarm of bees at one's step. They had the most voracious appetites. ... One or two would begin on a melon ... others came, and the melon would soon be eaten down to a shell. Onions and beets were a luxury to them, but my husband saved ours, by turning a furrow over them. ... The grasshoppers stayed so long that they destroyed the newly sowed fields of wheat. ... We could get mosquito netting. ... The netting went, like other things, down the throats of the pests. ... It was difficult even to save the clothes on the line. ...

Anne E. Bingham describes how hoppers destroyed her Kansas farm in 1874.

1875

Initially a showcase for the state's horse-breeding industry, the Kentucky Derby has become an institution in American horse racing.

On May 17, 1875, a black man named Oliver Lewis rode his horse Aristides to victory in the first Kentucky Derby in an astonishing 2 minutes and 37¾ seconds — the fastest time yet for a three-year-old horse in the United States.

The Derby, founded by Louisville sportsman Col. M. Lewis Clark, was modeled after a similar contest for three-year-olds at England's Epsom Downs. It was Clark's intent to showcase the horses and boost Kentucky's breeding industry, which had fallen on hard times after the Civil War. Devoting himself to every detail, he personally selected the winner's silver bowl, and he set up a ladies' committee to sew silk purses for holding the prize money. Kentucky society flocked to Churchill Downs, Clark's handsome new track; the Derby's fame spread far and wide. There was only one problem: most years, the race lost money. By the century's end, its glory days appeared to be over. Then in stepped Matt J. Winn, a local businessman and promoter.

Winn made the Kentucky Derby America's premier horse race. Pouring on all his charm, he wooed high-rolling Eastern horse owners and famous sportswriters such as Grantland Rice and Damon Runyon. Mint juleps and track-side picnics became race day institutions. An enthusiast to the end, Winn attended every Derby until his death in 1949. 🖋

First Derby winner Oliver Lewis.

S *1876*
elf-ordained minister Dwight Moody caused a near riot when thousands flocked to hear him.

In the last few seconds of New Year's Eve 1875, Dwight Lyman Moody, a former shoe salesman and self-appointed deputy of the Lord, looked out upon his congregation. "Should any people faint," he said, "I hope the ushers will carry them right out." Fainting was quite possible in the crowded auditorium where thousands had come to hear the special brand of preaching that had brought Moody fame.

Two years after his own conversion in 1856, Moody founded a successful Sunday school in Chicago and later preached to Union soldiers in the Civil War. In 1870, as president of the Young Men's Christian Association (Y.M.C.A.), he

Hand raised to heaven, Moody calls for converts.

heard a delegate, Ira Sankey, sing at a convention. Recognizing that a musical accompaniment would give his sermons a powerful effect on a crowd, Moody enlisted Sankey.

Touring England in 1875, the two men went from being obscure revivalists to international sensations. They drew 3 million people during their four months in London. A true presence at more than 200 pounds, Moody promised instant salvation, delivering sermons and inspirational stories about miracles, deathbed conversions, and struggles with Satan, while all the time pounding his lectern and waving his Bible. Ira Sankey, who at 240 pounds rivaled Moody in size, stirred the crowd with songs of inspiration.

By the time they returned to America, Moody and Sankey were so popular that even President Ulysses S. Grant attended a meeting. In February 1876 the two nearly caused a riot when a crowd of 15,000 people surged into the Hippodrome in New York City to see them. In the next two decades, they crisscrossed the country, making millions of dollars and giving most of it away to Sunday schools. By the time they ended their ministry, Moody and Sankey had traveled 1 million miles and preached to 100 million people. 🖎

T *1876*
he largest crowd ever assembled up to that time in the United States gathered for the opening of the Centennial Exhibition — a patriotic celebration of American industry.

The opening ceremonies on May 10, 1876, said it all: the Centennial Exhibition in Philadelphia was the event of the year. A 150-piece orchestra and a choir of 1,000 voices entertained a crowd so huge that the state militia had to maintain order. Excursion trains arrived every 30 seconds with visitors. The dignitaries included President Ulysses S. Grant and Emperor Dom Pedro of Brazil. Total admissions numbered 186,672 people by official count — the largest crowd ever assembled in America, according to the New York *Tribune.*

The mobs who swarmed through the gates were in for a remarkable experience. First there was the exhibition's sheer size — 30,000 exhibits housed in 167 buildings scattered across 450 acres. The Main Building, with 11 miles of walkways, was the largest piece of architecture in the world. In Machinery Hall visitors gaped and gasped at an awesome display of industrial age inventions, including a lamp that operated on nothing but electricity. Almost completely

The 40-foot-high Corliss Engine operated 13 acres of machinery at the exhibition.

ignored among the rows of chugging, clanking machinery was Alexander Graham Bell's telephone.

Pavilions dedicated to some 50 different nations gave Americans a glimpse into the exotic and far away. People could watch 6,000 Chinese silkworms hard at work, visit the largest soda fountain in the world, drool over a 200-pound vase of solid chocolate, or view the cancan sideshow — an "exhibit" that was raided several times. Surely the most practical facility was the Department of Public Comfort — a rest station for the weary. Footsore fairgoers could also seek relief by riding around the grounds on a narrow-gauge railroad, zooming along at the dizzying speed of eight miles an hour.

Amid all of the inventions and displays, the true reason for the exhibition was not forgotten. The centennial's motto — "1776 with 3 million people on a strip of seacoast; 1876 with 40 million people from ocean to ocean" — was a proud reminder of the first 100 years of a growing nation. When the Centennial Exhibition closed, after six months and a total of 8 million visitors, everyone agreed that it had all been an overwhelming success. 🖎

1876

The candidate who received the most popular votes in the 1876 presidential election did not become president.

Were it not for a bizarre quirk of electoral history, Samuel J. Tilden would have been the 19th president of the United States. With 4,288,546 votes in the 1876 general election, Tilden, a New York Democrat, won over Ohio Republican Rutherford B. Hayes, who gained only 4,034,311 votes. Unfortunately for Tilden, the voting returns in South Carolina, Louisiana, Florida, and Oregon were all in dispute, and without them he did not have a clear majority of electoral votes.

The final decision was left to a special electoral commission consisting of seven

Centennial-year campaign pins for Hayes (left) and Tilden (right).

Republicans, seven Democrats, and one independent Supreme Court judge. In February 1877 the commission voted to give Hayes all the disputed states' electoral

votes. As a result, Hayes ended up winning the election with an electoral vote of 185 to Tilden's 184.

The results outraged Southern Democrats, who considered it another example of Northern Republican arrogance. To keep peace, Hayes agreed to the Compromise of 1877, which effectively ended Reconstruction by withdrawing the last federal troops from the South. As for Tilden, he took his defeat philosophically: "I can retire to private life with the consciousness that I shall receive from posterity the credit of having been elected to the highest position in the gift of the people, without any of the cares and responsibilities of the office."

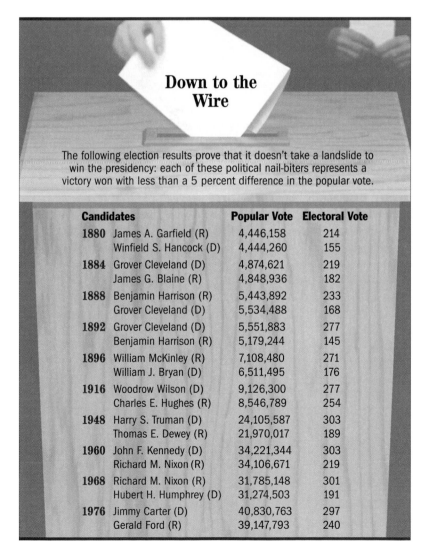

Down to the Wire

The following election results prove that it doesn't take a landslide to win the presidency: each of these political nail-biters represents a victory won with less than a 5 percent difference in the popular vote.

Candidates	Popular Vote	Electoral Vote
1880 James A. Garfield (R)	4,446,158	214
Winfield S. Hancock (D)	4,444,260	155
1884 Grover Cleveland (D)	4,874,621	219
James G. Blaine (R)	4,848,936	182
1888 Benjamin Harrison (R)	5,443,892	233
Grover Cleveland (D)	5,534,488	168
1892 Grover Cleveland (D)	5,551,883	277
Benjamin Harrison (R)	5,179,244	145
1896 William McKinley (R)	7,108,480	271
William J. Bryan (D)	6,511,495	176
1916 Woodrow Wilson (D)	9,126,300	277
Charles E. Hughes (R)	8,546,789	254
1948 Harry S. Truman (D)	24,105,587	303
Thomas E. Dewey (R)	21,970,017	189
1960 John F. Kennedy (D)	34,221,344	303
Richard M. Nixon (R)	34,106,671	219
1968 Richard M. Nixon (R)	31,785,148	301
Hubert H. Humphrey (D)	31,274,503	191
1976 Jimmy Carter (D)	40,830,763	297
Gerald Ford (R)	39,147,793	240

1876

The merciless cartoons of Thomas Nast not only helped turn the public against corrupt New York official "Boss" Tweed but also aided the police in his capture.

With his timely illustrations in *Harper's Weekly* magazine, German-born artist Thomas Nast fought for such causes as the emancipation of slaves, the preservation of the Union, and the destruction of the Tweed Ring. The ring, headed by William Marcy "Boss" Tweed, consisted of corrupt political leaders who controlled New York City government. During the late 1860's Tweed had used fraud and patronage to steal at least $45 million of city and county funds.

Nast's caricatures, as well as exposés in *The New York Times*, made Tweed infamous. In 1871 that same combination, plus a public confession of fraud by the city controller, defeated most of the Tweed Ring in the November elections. Tweed himself was reelected to the state senate, but the next month he was convicted of forgery and larceny. Sentenced to 12 years in prison, he gained early release in 1875 through a legal loophole. Shortly thereafter he was jailed for trying to recoup stolen funds, but he soon escaped to Spain. Nast's cartoons had earned such notoriety, however, that in August 1876 Tweed was recognized and returned to the United States. He died in prison before he could be prosecuted.

A vulturous Tweed waits out the storm in this Nast cartoon.

A 1877
lthough a defeat for the unions, the first national railroad strike gave birth to the modern labor movement.

In March 1877, after four years of steady reductions in the wages of railroad workers, the Erie, Pennsylvania, Baltimore & Ohio, and New York Central railroads imposed an additional system-wide 10 percent cut in pay. Three months later, when the Baltimore & Ohio levied its own wage cut, workers in West Virginia struck. The work stoppage, known as the Great Uprising, spread over 14 states and disrupted railroad service for 10 days, making it the first national strike in U.S. history.

Marked by violent demonstrations in Baltimore, Chicago, Pittsburgh, and St. Louis, the uprising caused numerous casualties. In Pittsburgh strikers went on a rampage and destroyed the train depot

Under the protective cover of the militia, a construction gang props up railroad cars that had been overturned by angry strikers in Corning, New York.

after local police and militia fired into the crowds of protesters, killing dozens of bystanders. President Rutherford B. Hayes called in federal troops to quell the "insurrection." Nevertheless, workers were galvanized and the strike spread south to Texas and west to California.

The railroad men eventually returned to their jobs, but the brutal treatment of the laborers clearly emphasized the division between the owners and the employees. Workers became convinced of the need for representation through labor unions. Recalling one of the Great Uprising's bloody encounters, one labor leader wrote, "Pittsburgh, with its sea of fire caused by burning freight cars, roundhouses, and depots, was the calcium light which illumined the skies of our social and industrial life."

N 1877
icodemus offered a Kansas home to African Americans fleeing the harsh conditions of the South.

Willianna Hickman first saw her new home of Nicodemus, Kansas, in 1878. She later wrote that she noticed "various smokes coming out of the ground. . . . The families lived in dugouts. . . . I began to cry."

Many of the African Americans from Kentucky, Tennessee, and Mississippi who began settling in Nicodemus in 1877 were surprised by the primitive living conditions. Drawn by posters addressed to "Colored people of the United States" and alarmed by the harsh racial climate of the post-Reconstruction South, they joined thousands of "Exo-

A family of "Exodusters": (clockwise from left) Mrs. America Bates and her daughters Sarah, Martha, Rose, and Eliza.

dusters" heading west. However unsatisfactory they found things, the new settlers made do.

Nicodemus — believed to be named after a 17th-century slave who bought his own freedom — quickly outgrew its beginnings as a collection of sod houses and prided itself as the largest African-American colony in the Midwest. Its founders envisioned an even larger town, but it was bypassed by the railroads in the 1880's. The population stalled at about 600 people and then declined for the next 100 years. Still, the town remains a focus of African-American pride, attracting many descendants of the original settlers to its annual homecoming event.

N 1877
ez Percé Chief Joseph's 1,600-mile trek to escape the U.S. Cavalry ended in his capture 40 miles from the Canadian border.

The Nez Percé Indians had long dwelt in the area where Oregon, Washington, and Idaho meet. An 1855 treaty had promised them a reservation in their homeland, but a gold rush five years later had brought miners and white settlers onto their land. Some Nez Percé leaders agreed to move to a small reservation in Idaho; but others, including the southern Nez Percé in the Wallowa Valley, refused.

The Nez Percé leader, Chief Joseph (later dubbed the "Indian Napoleon" by the press), would not even consider moving to Idaho until 1877, when bloodshed seemed inevitable. But before his people could depart, some Nez Percé warriors killed several hostile whites in the region.

When that attack brought an advance of federal troops under Gen. Oliver Otis Howard, Chief Joseph's 700 Nez Percé headed east to seek assistance from the

R*1877*
eplacing the old-fashioned dry goods merchant, the department store offered a wide variety of merchandise under one roof.
The department store was first imagined as a palace of genteel service to the growing middle class. Eliminating the sometimes perfunctory air of the dry goods stores and specialty shops, department store owners encouraged customers to browse, reasoning that people would appreciate the chance to consider their purchases carefully.

Customer service was just one aspect, however. Middle- and lower-class consumers had more money to spend on more products, and Philadelphia merchant John Wanamaker was keenly aware of this. Wanamaker's Grand Depot opened in 1877 and was touted as the "largest space in the world devoted to retail selling on a single floor." It was divided into separate areas for everything from crockery to lace, and every item was sold at a haggle-free fixed price. Customers shopped amid luxurious interiors,

Wanamaker first called his Philadelphia store the "Grand Depot"; then he decided to name it after himself.

replete with gaslights and stained-glass windows, dined at the restaurant, and enjoyed personal services like home delivery.

Macy's department store in New York City rivaled Wanamaker's in its huge variety of merchandise. In an effort to draw customers, founder Rowland Hussey Macy experimented with selling everything from garden tools and fancy groceries to magazines and potted plants. In Chicago, Marshall Field's salespeople gave VIP treatment to every shopper because the store's owner, businessman Marshall Field, believed that making customers feel special was the best way to keep them coming back. Credited with ordering a surly clerk to "give the lady what she wants," Field provided such amenities as a "goods-on-appproval" return policy, and female lingerie clerks to make women feel more comfortable.

By the turn of the 20th century, department stores had sprung up nationwide, becoming the mainstay of American shoppers.

Crow Indians. With Howard in pursuit, they trounced U.S. troops at White Bird Canyon, Idaho, and survived a horrendous attack at Big Hole Valley, Montana. "Few of us will

Hinmaton-Yalaktit of the Nez Percé, more commonly known as Chief Joseph.

soon forget the wail of mingled grief, rage and horror which came from the camp . . . when the Indians returned to it and recognized their slaughtered warriors, women and children," wrote Col. John Gibbon, the leader of the attack. The survivors managed to slip through Yellowstone National Park and reach the Crows. The Crows refused to help, however, so Chief Joseph led his band — many of them sick or wounded — north in a last-ditch attempt to reach Sitting Bull and his tribe of Sioux in Canada.

After trekking 1,600 miles, to within 40 miles of the border, the Nez Percé stopped to rest near the Bear Paw Mountains in Montana. Federal troops surrounded their camp, and Chief Joseph, hoping to save his people from further trial, decided to surrender. "I will fight no more forever," he vowed.

The survivors, numbering more than 400, were exiled to Indian Territory (now Oklahoma). Chief Joseph eventually returned home and died in 1904 at the Colville reservation in Washington Territory — "of a broken heart," his doctor reported.

PROGRESS AND PROSPERITY

(1878 TO 1918)

As the 19th century drew to a close, the United States grew into the world's leading industrial power. In the space of one generation, daily life was radically transformed. The electric light bulb turned night into day, the skyscraper changed the skyline of the modern city, and affordable consumer goods — sometimes gathered under one roof at a department store — began flooding the market.

Population growth provided a powerful thrust for industrial development. In just two decades, from 1880 to 1900, the number of Americans surged from 51 million to 76 million, partly because of an increase in immigration. More than 8 million foreigners arrived, mostly from Germany, Ireland, Italy, Eastern Europe, and Sweden, and they tended to settle in urban areas. By 1900, New York, Chicago, Philadelphia, St. Louis, Boston, and Baltimore had more than 500,000 residents each.

TECHNOLOGICAL INNOVATIONS gave added impetus to

economic expansion. Electricity and combustion engines greatly increased the scale and productivity of industrial enterprises. Steel producers adopted the Kelly-Bessemer method to make steel strong enough to hold up suspension bridges and skyscrapers. Electric power moved people from floor to floor in multistory buildings by elevator, and from one neighborhood to another by subway and streetcar. In 1903 Orville and Wilbur Wright soared a few hundred feet across

Orville Wright stayed aloft for over an hour in his 1908 model Flyer.

a North Carolina beach in the first heavier-than-air flying machine. A nation of four prototype automobiles in 1895, the United States had nearly 5 million on the road in 1917, thanks in large measure to the moving production line in Henry Ford's auto plants.

An economy of small local manufacturers gave way to huge industrial corporations that sold staples like sugar or new consumer goods like cigarettes and telephones nationwide. By the early 1900's, the United States was turning out more factory goods than any other nation. Transportation became easier with an expanding railroad network, which grew from 93,000 miles of track in 1870 to 193,000 miles in

Steel magnate Andrew Carnegie, said to be the world's richest man.

1890. Leading the spurt in growth was the volume of steel production, which in 1900 exceeded that of England and Germany combined.

These spectacular economic achievements created gross inequalities — unprecedented wealth for a few and devastating hardships for many. The industrial empire builders — Jay Gould in railroads, John D. Rockefeller in oil, Andrew Carnegie in steel, among others — were known as captains of industry to their admirers and robber barons to their critics because of their ruthless (and often illegal) business methods. Mark Twain dubbed this period the Gilded Age, skewering both the vulgarity of the well-to-do and the ephemeral nature of their prosperity.

Imitating Europe's nobility, the richest Americans flaunted their wealth. They bought jewels and antiques, and built magnificent urban mansions and palatial country estates. Meanwhile, the gap between the rich and the poor was widening. In 1890 the richest 1 percent of Americans owned more than half the country's property and income.

In an economy structured to benefit the rich, farmers earned a precarious living. The cost of shipping farm produce by rail could make or break a farmer, and the railroad

barons kept their prices high. Fees paid to the owners of grain elevators and mills also shrank farm earnings. Tight money policies, which enhanced the investments of bankers, forced many farmers to default on their mortgages. In addition, the new technology that increased farm production likewise decreased the need for human labor. In the 1870's and 1880's, hard-pressed farmers set up groups like the Grange and the Farmers' Alliance to negotiate better prices for crops and supplies, but such cooperatives as these generally failed to make farming profitable.

URBAN LABORERS did not fare much better. Most worked
in dark, airless factories where wages were miserly, conditions dangerous, and 60-hour workweeks routine. Mothers often labored alongside young sons and daughters in "sweatshops." At the end of the day, parents and children went home to small houses or to tenements — blocklike buildings of cramped apartments with inadequate ventilation where disease spread swiftly. Immigrant workers faced the added burden of prejudice, or even hatred, from native-born Americans.

Unemployment was a fact of life for industrial workers. Joblessness swelled during the economy's lapses into depression: in 1882, 1893, 1907, and 1913. Even in good times, about one in four heads of households was out of work for several months a year. Working conditions were so bad that, in spite of high unemployment rates, unions arose to win better treatment.

In the 1880's both unskilled and skilled workers joined the Knights of Labor. But a bloody confrontation between workers and police in Chicago's Haymarket Square in 1886 stoked antilabor sentiment. The ensuing wave of arrests and vilification of union activitists decimated the Knights. At the same time the American Federation of Labor, founded by Samuel Gompers to represent skilled workers,

A bilingual handbill announces the 1886 Haymarket labor rally.

gained strength from its willingness to go on strike for union recognition and higher wages. The nation's employers, determined to undermine the fledgling labor movement, fought back with sometimes lethal violence. The railroad strike of 1877, the Homestead steelworkers' strike of 1892, and the 1894 Pullman strike left dozens dead.

Neither urban workers nor farmers got help from the federal government. When the Pullman strike paralyzed train traffic in Chicago, a major hub of the national rail network, President Grover Cleveland sent federal troops to quell labor unrest. When that didn't work, he used a court injunction and jailed union leader Eugene V. Debs.

Until the 1890's Congress kept money tight and tariffs high (which meant higher prices for consumers). At every level of government, politicians traded favors and government jobs for money and votes, although several presidents pressed for moderate reforms to curb big business and government corruption. James A. Garfield, for example, promoted civil service reform by reserving specific government jobs for qualified applicants instead of handing them out to political loyalists. A frustrated office seeker assassinated him in 1881, only months after his inauguration. In 1883, Garfield's successor, Chester A. Arthur, won passage of the Pendleton Act, which created the Civil Service Commission. President Cleveland won Congressional approval in 1887 for an Interstate Commerce Commission to regulate business, but the courts quickly rendered the agency powerless.

NEITHER REPUBLICANS NOR DEMOCRATS were doing
much for ordinary people, so workers and farmers began looking elsewhere. Some joined socialist groups committed to transferring power from industrialists and bankers to working people. In 1890 reformers interested in uniting Southern rural whites, Midwestern and Western farmers, and industrial workers set up the Populist party. In just two years Populists took over several Western states, won a million votes in the presidential election of 1892, and looked like a serious threat to replace the Democrats as the number two party.

The Populist party's star fell as quickly as it had risen. Black and white farmers both embraced populism, and sometimes they worked together under its auspices. But many populist leaders laced their oratory with racist taunts and blamed the farmers' predicament on shadowy Jewish bankers. When the Democratic party nominated William Jennings Bryan, a firebrand reformist, for president in 1896, it stole much of the Populists' thunder.

BRYAN BASED HIS CAMPAIGN on one narrow plank in the populist program, namely, "free silver." Advocates argued that the unlimited coinage of silver would inflate U.S. currency, raise the prices that farm products fetched in the market, and allow farmers to pay off their debts in cheap currency. Free silver may have been shaky economics, but Bryan parlayed it into lofty political rhetoric. Over time, Bryan became an icon of a vague reform spirit, and the Democrats nominated him as their standard-bearer in four consecutive presidential contests — none of which he won.

Bryan lost in 1896 and 1900 to William McKinley, a Republican sympathetic to big business. During McKinley's first administration, Congress passed a record-high tariff. Industrial monopolies grew in size and power. But in 1901, at the start of his second term, an anarchist assassinated McKinley; and when Vice President Theodore Roosevelt (TR) took charge, a new era dawned.

The word "progressive" has come to describe the period between 1901 and 1917. Writers such as Ida Tarbell, Sinclair Lewis, and Lincoln Steffens were called "muckrakers" for exposing abuses in industry and government. In response, local, state, and federal officials enacted reforms dealing with a broad range of issues, including unhealthy food and drugs, union organizing, child labor, mine safety, unscrupulous trade practices, and electoral corruption. Citizen reformers like Dorothea Dix, Jane Addams, and Frederic C. Howe worked alongside government agencies as they provided services for the poor and the mentally ill. Women pressured and protested until they won the right to vote in the 19th Amendment to the Constitution.

Eight-year-old boys sorted lumps of coal in the nation's mines.

A Teddy Roosevelt rag doll fairly bristles with energy.

Reformers found a sympathetic ear at the White House in Teddy Roosevelt, who pioneered a new, activist presidency. At age 42 he was the youngest man ever to assume the nation's highest office, and he set to work with energy and dramatic flair. He became the first American president to intervene in a labor dispute on behalf of workers when, in 1902, he took the side of striking coal miners who were protesting dangerous conditions and low wages. During his two terms in office, TR brought two dozen antitrust suits against powerful businesses. These widely publicized acts gave him the reputation of a trust buster. But unlike many progressives of the era, Roosevelt had no desire to break up the corporate giants. He thought that their economic might was good for the country, but that they should be bridled and reined in whenever they strayed too far.

ROOSEVELT WAS THE FIRST president to make conservation of natural resources a priority; he established wildlife refuges, created national parks, and turned 125 million acres of public land into forest reserves. He also supported a progressive tax and a tax on inheritance that would make the rich pay their fair share.

Although progressive reformers could neither eliminate poverty nor guarantee workers basic rights on the job, they did manage to curb some of the worst excesses of the nation's growth spurt. They also gave citizens a measure of control over powerful new institutions, like trusts, and introduced new standards of social justice that Americans could use as a benchmark for judging their leaders. Those standards did much to push Roosevelt and his immediate successors, Republican William Taft and Democrat Woodrow Wilson, in the direction of reform.

In the South, these were years of wrenching change but little reform. In 1900 the South's share of U.S. manufacturing had doubled in 20 years, with textiles, tobacco, iron, and steel its major products, but the average Southerner's income was still less than half the average Northerner's. The New South, as economic promoters dubbed the region, found new ways to manage relations between blacks and

whites. Cities like Montgomery, Alabama, passed laws establishing separate neighborhoods, railroad cars, and waiting rooms in train stations. Denied the right to vote and frozen out of white society, blacks resisted segregation with boycotts and lawsuits. But in 1896, the U.S. Supreme Court put its stamp on "separate but equal" facilities in the notorious *Plessy* v. *Ferguson* case.

IN THE WEST,
Native Americans lost the final battles to protect their land and preserve their way of life. In government-organized "land grabs," tens of thousands of white settlers claimed tribal territory in South Dakota, Oklahoma, and Montana. By the turn of the century, the great American frontier — as white scholars termed it — was closed. It was no longer possible to draw an unbroken line from north to south marking the limit of white settlement.

As the continental frontier disappeared, many Americans turned to a global frontier. In 1898 the Spanish-American War began under President McKinley as a venture to help Cuba win independence from Spain; it ended with the U.S. acquisition of Spain's "possessions" — Puerto Rico, Guam, and the Philippines. The United States annexed the Hawaiian Islands that same year and divided up the Samoan Islands with Germany the next year. In 1903 President Roosevelt obtained a swath of land across the isthmus of Panama for building and operating a canal.

These imperial forays were controversial at home, although not with most businessmen. Eager for new markets and new sources of raw materials, industrialists and merchants gener-

An explosion sinks the U.S.S. Maine in Havana harbor, setting off the Spanish-American War.

ally favored expansion worldwide. And many people believed that American imperialism, unlike the European variety, would bring democracy to the colonized.

Dissenters objected on moral grounds to subjugating other people, and they worried about the brutal costs of militarism. More Americans died putting down an insurrection in the Philippines than died in the Spanish-American War. President Wilson, too, had grave misgivings about the United States joining the territorial rivalries that kept Europe endlessly at war. He opposed a foreign policy that catered to private economic interests. When war broke out in Europe in 1914, he resolved to stay on the sidelines. Even when German U-boats began torpedoing American ships, he opted for neutrality. But as the "war to end all wars" dragged on, Wilson began to fear the consequences for the United States of Britain's possible defeat. In 1917 he asked Congress for a declaration of war against Germany and the other Central Powers.

Uncle Sam calls for an end to civil unrest in Panama so he can dig the canal.

THE WAR MOBILIZATION
lasted only 18 months, but it reached deep into American society. It drew 4 million conscripts into the army, 1 million women into the workforce, and 75,000 "four-minute men" into the streets to drum up support with short patriotic speeches. The government arrested hundreds of pacifists and political radicals who opposed the war. On the battlefield, the U.S. Army soon convinced German military leaders and officials that their cause was doomed. American losses were comparatively small, totaling 112,000; Europe tragically lost an entire generation of men. Ten million had perished; 20 million more were wounded, many crippled by poison gas.

The United States emerged from the war preeminent in world politics as well as in industry. Even so, many Americans regarded the peace as unstable, and many hoped for a return to the isolationism of prewar days. Meanwhile, the causes of the war — imperialist rivalries, militant nationalism — remained intact. They would surface again in the years ahead, and America would be called once more to assume a role of world leadership. ☀

1879

To protect her business, cattlewoman Lizzie Johnson Williams made her husband, Hezekiah, sign a prenuptial agreement.

Before she took up ranching, Elizabeth Johnson taught school, wrote magazine and newspaper articles, and kept account books for cattlemen. Investing her earnings in livestock, she expanded her herd with maverick cattle, which had multiplied freely in South Texas while ranch hands and cowboys had been away fighting the Civil War. In 1871 she registered her own brand.

When she got around to marrying, in 1879, she made her cattleman fiancé, Hezekiah Williams, sign a prenuptial agreement. No matter what, all her property and earnings would remain hers alone.

The new Mrs. Williams had a good eye for cattle, and she personally chose the steers for both their herds. She also, it was said, sometimes rounded up her husband's unmarked calves and branded them as her own. Still, Lizzie seems to have loved him after a fashion. She bailed him out of debt several times, and when he was kidnapped by bandits in Cuba, she paid a $50,000 ransom to get him back. And when he died, she spent $600 on his coffin — a minor fortune in those days. "I loved this old buzzard this much," she scrawled across the undertaker's bill when she paid it.

Hezekiah and Lizzie Johnson Williams on their wedding day.

1881

Emerging unscathed from the gunfight at the O.K. Corral, full-time gambler and sometime lawman Wyatt Earp became one of the most unlikely legends of the West.

Why popular lore has chosen the hot-headed Wyatt Earp to represent the force of law on the frontier remains a mystery. Far from the righteous gunslinger of celluloid fame, the real Wyatt Earp had a distinctly checkered career.

Although in 1875 he served as a minor officer of the law in Wichita, Kansas, he was fired after a year for brawling; a later stint as a deputy in Dodge City yielded no more evidence to substantiate the Earp myth. Very likely, he spent most of his days at the Long Branch Saloon, where he moonlighted as a faro dealer and made the acquaintance of such shady characters as Luke Short and John (Doc) Holliday, a bad-tempered dentist with a drinking problem who would later sustain two bullet wounds at the O.K. Corral.

Wyatt Earp   *Morgan Earp*

In 1879 Earp moved from Kansas to Tombstone, Arizona, with his brother Virgil, who became the town marshal. True to legend, Tombstone was a rough and rawboned place, and before long the Earp brothers

1879

Frank W. Woolworth's first enterprise, The Great Five Cent Store, was a total flop.

One morning in 1878, his boss at the dry goods store ordered Frank W. Woolworth to hand-paint a sign: "Any Article on This Counter, Five Cents." By nightfall, the counter had been stripped bare of handkerchiefs, harmonicas, washbasins, and a host of other items. Delighted with the bargains, customers clamored for more, and Woolworth's boss quickly telegraphed for a rush new shipment of the inexpensive merchandise. A spark lit up in Woolworth's rapid-fire business mind.

Believing that a store stocked solely with five-cent items would be a success, Woolworth borrowed $300 from his boss and started his own business on February 22, 1879. Only five months after it opened, however, Woolworth's Utica, New York, store closed; it had been a flat-out failure. Customers, initially curious about nickel prices, had lost interest in the cheaper goods. In addition, the store

F. W. Woolworth's first 5 and 10¢ store in Lancaster, Pennsylvania.

was on a side street, a poor location.

Undaunted, Woolworth borrowed another $300 and set up a second shop in Lancaster, Pennsylvania, on June 21, 1879. First-day sales were $127.65 — considerably better than the $9.00 the Utica store had taken in on its first day. Within a month, the new store's complete stock had turned over three times.

In 1880 Woolworth added goods priced at a dime to satisfy customers' tastes for higher-quality merchandise. He changed the sign to "Woolworth's 5 and 10¢ Store."

Expanding rapidly, he added 12 stores throughout the Northeast by 1888, hiring relatives, friends, and former coworkers as managers. He often spot-checked his stores, looking for carelessness and issuing detailed critiques to the managers.

By 1913, with nearly 700 stores and annual sales of $66 million, Woolworth spent $13.5 million in cash to erect a 60-story Manhattan skyscraper, at the time the tallest building in the world.

Virgil Earp

found themselves embroiled in a feud with some cattle-rustling cowboys under the leadership of Ike Clanton. As a showdown loomed, Virgil hastily deputized his brother Wyatt, a third brother, Morgan, and Wyatt's old friend Doc Holliday. They confronted the Clanton gang on the afternoon of October 26, 1881. Accounts differ as to who fired first. Either way, in a 30-second hail of gunfire, all of the Clanton gang except Ike himself were killed; on the other side, while all survived, only Wyatt escaped injury.

The bloodshed horrified the people of Tombstone, and Wyatt and Doc Holliday were arrested for murder. When they were later set free, the Clanton gang moved quickly to settle the score. Virgil, ambushed outside the Oriental Saloon in Tombstone, was shot and crippled for life. Three months later, in January 1882, Morgan was shot and died instantly. Wyatt immediately organized a posse to avenge his brothers and went on such a wild shooting spree that a second posse chased him out of the state. Eventually he retired to California, and although he disliked discussing the events of the O.K. Corral shootout, by the time he died in 1929 at the age of 80, Wyatt Earp had lived to see his name immortalized in dime novels as one of the frontier's most romantic figures. 🌟

The Mansions of the Very Rich

In the era of industrial fortune-making, one way for a plutocrat to announce his wealth was to build an expensive townhouse and match it with an equally expensive "cottage" by the sea or in the mountains. They were the utmost in conspicuous consumption; one social critic dubbed them "a sort of visible bank balance." Here are a few.

1885 Bertha Honoré Palmer's brand new medieval castle dominates Chicago's Lake Shore Drive — much as Mrs. Palmer herself dominates Chicago society. The mansion will be razed in 1950.

1892 William K. Vanderbilt completes Marble House in Newport, Rhode Island. It reputedly costs $7 million to build and $4 million to furnish. It continues to stand today.

1895 Biltmore, in Asheville, North Carolina, becomes the obsession of George Washington Vanderbilt, brother of William K. The house takes five years to finish and includes 40 master bedrooms.

1898 Isabella Stewart Gardner begins Fenway Court in Boston. She hangs her art collection there and stipulates in her will that the house be made into a museum.

1901 Andrew Carnegie builds his New York mansion at Fifth Avenue and 91st Street. It is now a museum.

1919 William Randolph Hearst constructs San Simeon on the California coast, using stones, furniture, and art brought over from Europe. Hearst died in 1951, before completion of construction. The mansion is now open to the public.

1883

To gain the approval of New York society, Mr. and Mrs. William K. Vanderbilt threw one of the most extravagant parties in American history.

When she married William K. Vanderbilt in 1875, the young Alva Smith landed not only a husband but an empire. The second son of William H. Vanderbilt and the grandson of railroad tycoon Cornelius Vanderbilt, William K. stood to inherit a huge fortune — $105 million — easily one of the largest amassed in America up to that time.

Such wealth carried no guarantee of acceptance in the halls of New York's high society. For that, Mrs. Vanderbilt needed the blessing of Caroline Astor, who was married to William Astor, the grandson of fur and real estate magnate John Jacob Astor. But the blessing was not forthcoming. Rich though they were, the Vanderbilts were not "old New York," and a publicized dispute over a will had tainted the family with scandal. For eight years Mrs. Vanderbilt tried to gain Mrs. Astor's approval only to be snubbed each time.

To win her over, Mrs. Vanderbilt made plans for a party that would be her greatest triumph, a

Alva Vanderbilt in her ball attire.

masquerade ball to be held on the evening of March 26, 1883, at the recently constructed Vanderbilt mansion at 660 Fifth Avenue. Some 1,200 invitations went out, with two very pointed omissions — Caroline Astor and her beloved youngest daughter, Carrie. When word of Caroline Astor's displeasure reached Mrs. Vanderbilt, she explained that she considered it improper to invite anyone who hadn't paid her a call at home. Within hours Caroline Astor's card was deposited on the silver plate at 660 Fifth Avenue, and a butler was dispatched with an invitation.

The party itself was a conspicuous display of pomp unequaled even by the prodigal standards of the Gilded Age. In all, the Vanderbilts spent some $250,000 on costumes for the guests, catering, champagne, flowers, and music — mostly to gain the attention of one woman. Alva Vanderbilt's efforts did not go unrewarded. Amidst the festivities, she was seen chatting with Caroline Astor, and New York society gave a collective, knowing nod. Alva Vanderbilt had won her victory. 🌟

Officials appear to be obeying the safety guidelines on the sign (center) as they inspect progress on the Brooklyn Bridge.

1883

Fourteen years in the making, the Brooklyn Bridge opened on May 24 and was instantly hailed as the Eighth Wonder of the World.

It was an unparalleled achievement. Spanning more than a mile, one-third of it 130 feet above the turbulent waters of New York's East River, the Brooklyn Bridge did more than connect two cities: it connected America with the future. On opening day, May 24, 1883, as President Chester A. Arthur began his ceremonial walk from Manhattan to Brooklyn, cannons boomed, factory whistles blew, and church bells rang out over the waterfront in joyous cacophony.

Ironically, absent from the inaugural festivities were the bridge's designer, John A. Roebling, and his engineer son, Washington. The elder Roebling, a German-born engineer who had conceived of the bridge while stranded on an icebound Brooklyn–Manhattan ferry in 1853, had died of tetanus resulting from a freak waterfront accident just as construction was getting underway. Washington, who had taken over for his father, had been stricken with caisson disease (the bends) while working in the underwater chamber used to dig the bridge's foundations. For 11 years he had been forced to supervise the project from the window of his Brooklyn home.

The Roeblings were not the only casualties: some 20 men had died during construction, and countless more were injured. Still, on that jubilant opening day, the bridge's triumphs, not its costs, were celebrated. The longest suspension bridge constructed up to that time, it was indeed an engineering marvel. But to all who beheld its arched Gothic towers and spidery array of wires, the Brooklyn Bridge seemed even more: it was poetry in steel. America's romance with the bridge was best captured by Brooklyn mayor Seth Low, who told the crowds, "No one who has ever been upon it can ever forget it." More than 100 years later, it remains the most celebrated span in the nation, and one admired throughout the world. ☀

1883

To regularize railroad schedules across the country, the railroad industry established Standard Railway Time, resulting in the four time zones still used today.

Even before the golden spike linked the transcontinental railroad at Promontory Point, Utah, in 1869, the rail industry faced a daunting task: how to get the trains to run on a reliable schedule. The problem lay not in the quality of the trains but in the varieties of time observed throughout the country. Because each town set its clock by the noonday sun in the public square, a distance of a few miles could mean a difference of minutes per day from one place to the next.

When most U.S. citizens made their living from the land, the day was governed by sunrise and sunset, not minutes. With the rise of industry in the 19th century, however, minutes mattered — not just to railroads but to factories, offices, and weather-reporting stations. And so, on November 18, 1883, after years of debate, a group of railroad owners, scientists, and businessmen launched a uniform time system called Standard Railway Time. It instituted a set of four time zones across the country, replacing the countless local time belts that marked time in every small town in America.

For the next three decades, Standard Railway Time was widely accepted. But a few cities and states ignored it, and it was challenged in the state supreme courts. Finally, in 1918 the federal government ended the controversy with the passage of the Standard Time Act, legalizing Standard Railway Time. Progress had triumphed over the dictates of the noonday sun. ☀

When U.S. time zones were reduced from 80 to 4, railroad watches such as this one had to be reset much less often.

Standard Railway Time

If this map of Standard Railway Time looks familiar, it's because these demarcations were the precursors of our modern time zones.

8 A.M. PACIFIC	9 A.M. MOUNTAIN	10 A.M. CENTRAL	11 A.M. EASTERN

Missouri River →

Chicago

Salt Lake City

San Francisco

← Denver

Topeka   St. Louis

Boston

Philadelphia   New York

Mississippi River

Rio Grande River

New Orleans

Charleston

B *1884*
uffalo herds that had roamed the Great Plains for centuries vanished almost completely in the course of a few decades. People had worried about the buffalo for a long time. George Catlin, an artist of the American West, predicted "the buffaloe's doom is sealed." Even if they heard Catlin's dire predictions, Indians and white men alike might have found it hard to believe that the huge herds could ever vanish from North America.

By the early 1830's, however, white hunters began to kill the buffalo — or, more accurately, the American bison. Long considered a Native American delicacy, buffalo tongue had become a favorite of the white man, and a market soon emerged. In addition, there was a great demand for pemmican. A combination of dried buffalo meat, fat, and berries that could keep for long periods of time without spoiling, pemmican pro-

Hunters were not the only enemy of the rapidly disappearing bison. Disease, lack of food, water shortages caused by drought, and natural enemies such as wolves greatly diminished the buffalo population. And sportsmen, attracted to the prairies during the 1850's, shot this primitive-looking beast simply for the fun of killing.

By 1884 rail shipments had decreased to only 300 buffalo hides.

In 1872 an army officer in Kansas watched as "three (excited) English gentlemen . . . bagged more buffalo than would have supplied a brigade."

vided food for trappers at remote outposts. Buffalo skins were also valuable. In 1850, 100,000 robes were shipped through St. Louis alone. The demand for hides increased over the next 20 years until between 1872 and 1874 more than 4 million buffalo hides were sent east from the Great Plains.

Three years later, officials at the Smithsonian Institution, worried that the buffalo was headed for extinction, rushed an expedition to Montana territory. All they managed to round up was a small group of wild buffalo — but the report they issued helped save the American bison from complete disappearance. ☀

S *1884*
eventy years before Rosa Parks made her famous bus protest, Ida B. Wells refused to leave her seat in a "whites only" train compartment. When 21-year-old Ida B. Wells, traveling on the Chesapeake, Ohio, and Southwestern Railroad in 1884, was told to leave her comfortable seat in the first-class car and move to a car reserved for "colored" passengers, she refused to budge. The conductor grew surly and tried to drag her to the car, so she bit him. As a result, she was unceremoniously thrown off the train. After the incident Wells

did what any angry red-blooded American would do: she sued. Although her circuit court victory was eventually overturned by the Tennessee supreme court, her stand was to be the first of many that the Memphis schoolteacher — whose parents were born slaves — would take on behalf of civil rights.

As a part-time journalist for several black-owned newspa-

As a young woman, Ida Wells fought for equality.

pers, Wells loudly denounced the shameful conditions of black schools. When the Memphis school board refused to renew her contract in 1891, she turned to writing full time, later acquiring a financial interest in the Memphis *Free Speech*. Later, when the newspaper's offices were destroyed by a mob of whites opposed to her ongoing antilynching efforts,

Wells moved north to New York, and then to Chicago, where she married Ferdinand Lee Barnett, a newspaper editor and lawyer who would become an Illinois assistant state's attorney.

While raising four children, Ida B. Wells-Barnett continued her work as an activist, writer, and advocate for racial justice. She founded many associations and social clubs — among them the Negro Fellowship League, one of the first black women's clubs in Chicago, and the Alpha Suffrage Club, the first organization to lobby for the right of black women to vote. ☀

1884

For those late 19th-century visitors who wished to observe proper etiquette, a well-placed calling card was an absolute necessity.

Taking their cue from the mannerly rituals of high society, middle-class Americans spent a large portion of their leisure time exchanging afternoon calls.

Proper form demanded that each visit be announced — in advance — with a calling card.

The basic tool of social intercourse, calling cards were imprinted with the owner's name, and often a personal design, making them — as *The Art of Correspondence* put it in 1884 — "the representative of the individual." A would-be visitor left his or her card at the front door with a servant, who might place it on a silver "card receiver." The lady of the house would then decide to accept the visit, decline it, or put it off, softening the rebuff by sending her own card to the caller the next day. Conversely, a would-be hostess would distribute cards declaring herself to be "At Home" on a certain day.

Leaving a card was a way to introduce oneself to society or to one's neighbors. Even in the college dorms at Bryn Mawr, proper young ladies arranged meetings by slipping cards under each other's doors. People also sent cards to fulfill social obligations and maintain existing friendships: "The annual visits are made and returned with peaceful regularity," Mark Twain wryly noted in *The Gilded Age*. "It is not necessary that . . . two ladies shall actually see each other oftener than once every few years."

Men presented cards to schedule business meetings, announce address changes, offer congratulations and — when the chance arose — to meet young ladies.

After World War I the widespread use of telephones and automobiles, along with more relaxed social standards, led to a decline in formal visiting and its herald, the calling card. "Formal visits and 'duty calls' savor of dullness," proclaimed a 1923 book called *Gracious Hostess*, "and we refuse to be dull." ✴

Visitors deposited their calling cards — some plain, others artfully ornate — in a more or less elaborate "receiver" in the front hall.

1885

Mark Twain's *Huckleberry Finn*, roundly condemned as "no better in tone than the dime novels," was banned near Boston.

When Samuel Langhorne Clemens — a.k.a. Mark Twain — published *The Adventures of Huckleberry Finn* in February 1885, he was already a famous humorist. Short stories such as "The Celebrated Jumping Frog of Calaveras County" (1865) and longer works like *The Innocents Abroad* (1869), a collection of travel letters, nestled conspicuously in bookshelves across the nation. But *Huckleberry Finn* raised hackles everywhere. Many readers felt that Twain's satirical treatment of race relations — his novel related the fictional adventures of young Huck and his friend Jim, a runaway slave — was just not suitable reading for growing boys. The *Springfield Republican*, a prominent Massachusetts daily, condemned Clemens for having "no reliable sense of propriety"; the public library at Concord, a town near Boston, banned the book entirely. Fellow writer Louisa May Alcott, the author of *Little Women*, criticized: "If Mr. Clemens cannot think of something better to tell our pure-minded lads and lassies, he had best stop writing for them."

A century later *The Adventures of Huckleberry Finn* continues to raise debate. To some critics, the book is racist; others consider it immoral. When it was published, Twain himself cautioned against reading too much into his novel: "Persons attempting to find a motive in this narrative will be prosecuted," he warned in a "notice" to readers. ✴

1885

The world's first "skyscraper" was only 10 stories tall.

After the Great Chicago Fire of 1871, the commercial heart of the city lay devastated. Then, as people began to rebuild, land values in the downtown "Loop" area rose steeply. By 1890 prices had reached $900,000 per quarter acre, and businessmen cast about for ways to cram the most usage into their high-priced real estate. At that very moment, engineer William Le Baron Jenney proposed a new kind of building — a so-called skyscraper.

Up until then, buildings were constructed with the outside walls supporting all the weight. But this "bearing wall" technique was

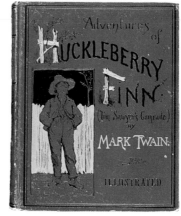

A first edition of Huckleberry Finn *shows the youthful hero in a jaunty pose.*

1886

Pharmacist John Styth Pemberton invented Coca-Cola over an open fire in his Atlanta backyard.

On May 8, 1886, when John Styth Pemberton mixed the flavors of the African cola nut with the South American coca leaf and stirred the boiling syrup with a boat oar, he happened upon one of the most successful recipes of all time. Full of excitement, Pemberton took his caramel-colored brew to Jacobs' Pharmacy and asked Joseph Jacobs, the proprietor, to taste it.

After first mixing the syrup with ice water, the men then tried it with carbonated water. Jacobs declared the result delicious. Delighted with his sweet, bubbly concoction, Pemberton decided to market it as a carbonated drink. His bookkeeper, Frank Robinson, suggested calling it Coca-Cola, jotting down the name in a distinctive sloping script that is still used today.

This elaborate urn (c. 1893) dispensed Coca-Cola syrup.

The new beverage went on sale in Jacobs' Pharmacy, doubling as a soft drink and headache tonic. By the end of the month, the first newspaper advertisements promoting the elixir hit the stands: "Coca-Cola. Delicious! Refreshing! Exhilarating! Invigorating!"

Despite the ads, the public was slow to respond. In the first year Pemberton sold only 50 gallons of syrup, charging a mere $1 per gallon. Two years later, in failing health, he sold the formula to a friend, pharmacist Asa Candler.

Although its inventor never shared in the profits, Coke would become one of the world's most recognized brand names. It is consumed by hundreds of millions daily. ✳

both costly and limiting: the higher a building rose, the more masonry was needed to strengthen the ground-floor walls. In addition, because of Chicago's swampy soil, buildings there had to be kept light to prevent them from sinking or tilting.

In Jenney's design the masonry walls were "hung" like curtains on an iron and steel skeleton, resulting in lighter — and cheaper — structures. As a result, architects could design to unprecedented heights. In 1885 Jenney's innovative 10-story Home Insurance Building opened up a lofty new perspective of wondrous possibilities.

A few years after the Home Insurance Building went up, structures twice as tall began to grace Chicago's skyline. Jenney had started a race for height that goes on to this day. ✳

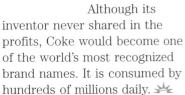

The Home Insurance Building, hailed as the first skyscraper.

Tall, Taller, Tallest

In the late 19th century the skyscraper began to be an integral part of the American cityscape. By the 1930's, with the advance of construction technology and the invention of the high-speed elevator, buildings reached breathtaking heights. The mid 20th century saw a new direction in high-rise design when the monolithic curtain-walled office tower began to dominate the city block. Today, many of these buildings still exist, a visual history of American urban architecture.

1885 William L. Jenney is the first to use "skyscraper construction" on his 10-story Home Insurance Building in Chicago.

1891 The nine-story (plus an attic) Wainwright Building is completed in St. Louis. It is considered to be the first tall building where the exterior design takes the shape of the interior frame, initiating the idea that form must follow function.

1895 The Reliance Building is completed in Chicago. At 16 stories and 200 feet, it is the first tall building in which steel columns and rivets are used.

1913 The 792-foot Woolworth Building in New York City is completed. The tallest building to date, it is also the first to use a high-speed elevator system operated by a switchboard.

1930 The 1,046-foot Chrysler Building is completed in New York City.

1931 The Empire State Building is completed in New York City. At 1,250 feet, it has a tower for mooring dirigibles, which is used only once. For the next 42 years it remains the world's tallest building.

1952 The Lever House is completed in New York City. Although not tall compared with other buildings of the time, the glass and metal curtain-walled office tower will become a prototype for modern skyscrapers of the late 20th century.

1970 The 1,127-foot John Hancock Center is completed in Chicago. Nearly half of its 100 floors are residential, making it the tallest multiuse building in the United States.

1973 The World Trade Center is completed in New York City. Comprised of "Twin Towers" that are 1,368 and 1,362 feet tall, it thrusts well above the Empire State Building.

1974 The Sears Tower is completed in Chicago. At 1,454 feet it becomes America's tallest building.

1977 New York's 60-story Citicorp Center is completed. Distinguishable by its sloping roof, it is built on four piers that rest above a sunken plaza.

1984 AT&T (now Sony) headquarters is built in New York City. Believing that "the only rule is that there are no longer any rules," its architect, Philip Johnson, tops the 660-foot skyscraper off with a whimsical 30-foot-high broken pediment.

1886

It took a full year and thousands of U.S. soldiers and civilian militiamen to capture Geronimo, the last of the Apache chiefs.

When Geronimo and a band of his fellow Chiricahua Apaches fled the San Carlos, Arizona, reservation in the spring of 1885, white settlers trembled in fear. They had heard stories about the renegade medicine man and prophet, and newspaper headlines carried dire predictions of massacres to come.

In fact, what Geronimo least desired was direct contact with white settlers, and he had left the reservation because of a rumor that he was about to be arrested and hanged; he was, in effect, fleeing for his life. Making a beeline for Mexico, the Apaches were pursued by an American force commanded by Gen. George Crook. Crook's orders left little room for misinterpretation: kill Geronimo and his followers or force them to surrender. Meanwhile, Mexican

A downtrodden Geronimo (front row, third from right) and his fellow Apache prisoners rest outside a train en route to Florida.

forces had gathered in the Sierra Madre to greet the Apaches with gunfire. Caught between certain death in Mexico and a chance for reconciliation north of the border, Geronimo surrendered to Crook on March 25, 1886. Then a few days later, he and 30 of his warriors broke away from Crook's encampment.

Severely reprimanded for allowing the Apaches to escape, Crook resigned. His replacement, the more militant Brig. Gen. Nelson Miles, gathered a force of 5,000 army regulars and thousands of civilian militiamen to hunt down the renegades. For months Geronimo eluded capture. Then in August 1886 he was cornered in the Sierra Madre, and on September 4 he surrendered for the last time. He was deported to Florida, and later to Fort Sill, Oklahoma. Although a prisoner of war, Geronimo enjoyed an unusual celebrity status and even rode in President Theodore Roosevelt's 1905 inaugural parade.

1886

The model for the Statue of Liberty's face was sculptor Frédéric-Auguste Bartholdi's mother, who had a reputation as a bigot.

One evening in 1865 at a Paris dinner party, the guests of historian Édouard de Laboulaye came up with a monumental idea: give the United States a physical symbol that would celebrate the ties forged between the two nations during the American Revolution. Sculptor Frédéric-Auguste Bartholdi was asked to build it — much to his delight. He could now realize his long-held dream of making a lighthouse shaped like a torch-bearing woman.

Bartholdi spent more than a decade creating a huge copper statue, while anticipation mounted on both sides of the Atlantic. In France private donations paid for the sculpture itself, while in the United States, Hungarian immigrant and newspaper editor Joseph Pulitzer used the pages of his New York *World* to generate enthusiasm and raise the funds needed to construct the statue's pedestal on Bedloe's Island.

When he came to create the statue's face, the sculptor chose his mother, Auguste-Charlotte Bartholdi, as a model — a distinctly eccentric choice, considering her character. She was a notorious bigot, who ran her family with such an iron fist that Frédéric, afraid of incurring her wrath, did not dare to marry until he was 42. His brother, Charles, is said to have gone insane trying to hide the fact that he was in love with a Jewish woman. What she lacked as a mother, however, Charlotte made up for

The similarities between the face of Madame Bartholdi (left) and that of the Statue of Liberty are unmistakable.

as a model, and from her stern countenance her son Frédéric fashioned a likeness that would forever be synonymous with liberty.

Finally completed in 1885, the 225-ton Statue of Liberty was disassembled and shipped to the United States. It was unveiled in New York Harbor on a rainy October 28, 1886, in front of 1 million spectators. The sculptor himself pulled the cord that dropped the French tricolor from Lady Liberty's face, while a roar went up from the crowd and, as *The New York Times* wrote, "a hundred Fourths of July broke loose."

1886

As founder and first president of the American Federation of Labor, Samuel Gompers laid the groundwork for the modern labor movement in the United States.

The son of a Dutch-Jewish cigar maker from the slums of London, Samuel Gompers emigrated to New York City with his family in 1863 at the age of 13. He went to work immediately in his father's trade, joining the Cigarmaker's Union Local 144 and earning $4 for every 1,000 cigars he made. In the teeming sweatshops and tenements of New York's manufacturing districts — a backbreaking world of 100-hour workweeks, unsafe conditions, and miserly wages — Gompers drew strength from his dream of an all-encompassing federation that would include all the nation's trade unions.

Samuel Gompers, the scourge of industrialists and the president of the American Federation of Labor.

Gompers worked hard for his fellow laborers, rising through the ranks and making the Cigarmaker's Local the model for other unions. In 1886 he was elected president of the American Federation of Labor (AFL), a position he held every year but one until his death in 1924.

Under his leadership, the AFL moved away from violent confrontation with management, focusing instead on economic goals and workers' rights. "Labor and management are man and wife," he would explain, "and somehow they've got to sleep together." Gompers fought for, and won, numerous reforms, including laws to protect minors and women in the workplace, the widespread use of the eight-hour workday, the first workmen's compensation statutes, and the creation of the U.S. Department of Labor. ☀

1887

The nation's first female mayor was elected to office after her name was placed on the ballot as a prank.

In tiny Argonia, Kansas, a group of "wets" decided to embarrass the local chapter of the Women's Christian Temperance Union — and keep them out of town politics once and for all — by putting the name of the group's secretary on the ballot for mayor. Surely, they reasoned, no one would vote for a woman. And what woman would want the job anyway?

Susanna "Dora" Salter proved them wrong on both counts. On election day, April 4, 1887, the 27-year-old wife of the town clerk was elbow-deep in laundry suds and attending to her four children when the town's Republican Party chairman stopped by to tell her that she had been named as a candidate.

Over her husband's objections, Salter launched a vigorous half-day campaign, and by sundown was swept into office with a stunning two-thirds majority. Only one woman in town voted against her.

Letters of congratulation poured in from as far away as Austria, and reporters from all over the country descended on Argonia to watch the nation's first female mayor in action. Although some observers claimed Argonia's experiment in gender-blind politics would forever cure women of the desire to hold office, most reviews were favorable. Salter quickly won the support

Salter modestly declined to vote for herself when running for mayor.

of the town's all-male city council — which included three of the original pranksters.

During her one-year term, for which Salter received just a dollar in compensation, alcohol became so scarce in Argonia that many of the "wets" left town. Salter also made headlines when she became the nation's first mayor to give birth while in office. Sadly, the child lived just 11 days. And although the town's Republican Party asked her to seek reelection, the grief-stricken mayor declined, choosing to return to her life as a wife and mother. ☀

_1888_

The country's most famous baseball poem, "Casey at the Bat," went largely unnoticed until it became a vaudeville staple.

Only 25, Ernest Lawrence Thayer was the new humor columnist on William Randolph Hearst's *San Francisco Examiner*. Trying his hand at poetry, Thayer wrote a 13-stanza lament about the new American pastime — baseball. Entitled "Casey at the Bat: A Ballad of the Republic, Sung in the Year 1888," it told the tale of the hapless team from the mythical town of Mudville that suffers ignominious defeat when its star slugger, Casey, strikes out. The poem, published on June 3, 1888, under the pseudonym Phin, earned Thayer $5.

Only after popular vaudevillian William DeWolf Hopper decided to recite the poem between acts did it gain wide recognition. Although Hopper's melodramatic rendition of "Casey at the Bat" never earned Thayer any royalties, it did make the trials of "the Mudville nine" part of American folklore and the lament "no joy in Mudville" the common cry of any fan whose team loses a close game. ☀

The "Mighty Casey" reposes in bronze in Cooperstown, N.Y.

_1888_

A new invention — the telephone — created a new job for women: they became telephone operators, known as Hello Girls.

When the first commercial telephone exchange opened in New Haven, Connecticut, in 1878, teenage boys were engaged to operate the switchboards; it was the worst possible choice. Prone to rude and boisterous behavior, the young lads brawled with each other constantly, leaving the phone lines unattended as they fought. Even worse, they heaped so much profane abuse upon subscribers that the more timid customers gave up using the telephone.

To remedy the situation, the manager of Boston's Telephone Dispatch Company hired America's first female operator, Emma Nutt, in 1878. It turned out to be a wise decision,

New York City operators in 1888.

and women phone operators soon outnumbered males. Dependable on the job, blessed with good manners and soft, pleasant voices, women operators made "Number, please?" a household phrase.

By 1888 there were 3,000 women working at telephone exchanges nationwide.

It was highly respectable employment for any young woman. Still, she often made two-thirds the salary of her male counterpart — even though the work was taxing and the responsibility could be great. Often, a single operator handled an entire town's telephone lines.

Until direct dialing became widespread, Hello Girls — also known as "the Voices With a Smile" — kept the industry humming, connecting millions of telephones across the nation. ☀

_1889_

During the Great Oklahoma Land Rush, 2 million acres were claimed by settlers on a single afternoon.

In 1879 Elias C. Boudinot, a Cherokee Indian who had broken with his tribe, declared in a Chicago newspaper article that some 14 million acres in Indian territory really belonged to the American public. Boudinot, an attorney, represented several railroad companies eager to expand westward.

Although Boudinot's claims were exaggerated, 2 million acres of unassigned lands had in fact been ceded by the Creeks and Seminoles to the U.S. government for use by other Indian tribes. Over the next decade white farmers in search of land made repeated incursions into Indian territory, only to be sent back by federal

troops. In the meantime, railroad lobbyists, Western congressmen, and private land agents pressured Congress to open the lands to settlement. In January 1889 the Creeks and Seminoles surrendered their rights to the unassigned lands for the sum of $4,193,799.

Three months later, on April 22, the region was opened for white settlement. At the appointed hour, as U.S. Cavalrymen gave the signal with a synchronized volley of pistol shot, eager homesteaders burst over the border. By sunset all 2 million acres had been claimed.

1889

In little more than an hour, the worst flood in 19th-century American history claimed more than 3,000 lives and left $17 million in damages.

The rain began to fall on Johnstown, Pennsylvania, on Thursday afternoon, May 30, 1889. By 11 P.M. it had evolved into the worst storm anyone in the steelmaking community could remember.

Upstream on the South Fork of the Little Conemaugh River, 14 miles above town, the water was rising in a man-made lake used by the exclusive South Fork Fishing and Hunting Club for sport and recreation. Holding in the lake was a 300-yard-wide, 72-foot-high earthen dam, 40 years old and poorly maintained. At dawn on Friday, a young engineer named John Parke, worried about the buildup in pressure, measured the water level. The

The Johnstown flood surges forward, destroying everything in its path.

lake, which was three miles long and up to a mile wide, had risen two feet.

Efforts to clear debris from the dam's spillway proved futile, and big leaks appeared in the face of the structure; by

11:30 that morning, water was lapping at the top of the dam. Parke rode to the nearest railroad signal tower to send a warning to the 30,000 people downstream, but the telegraph lines were out. Returning to the lake, he watched in horror as the dam gave way in what one witness recalled as "one big push."

Moving at speeds of up to 40 miles an hour, a wall of water coursed down the narrow valley and wiped out everything in its path: trees, homes, factories. A young man helping his bride out of a derailed train said the flood was "a seething, turbulent wall of water, whose crests seemed mountain-high." A great mass of debris became lodged at an arched stone bridge in Johnstown, and fire broke out. Some 300 people who were trapped in the congestion burned to death.

Another 60 perished when the four-story brick hotel in which they had sought refuge collapsed. By the time it was all over, at 4:20 P.M. on May 31, the disaster had claimed at least 2,200 lives. An additional 1,000 people were missing, their bodies never found.

America quickly reached out to help the stricken community. Within 24 hours of hearing the news reports, Pittsburgh had organized a 20-car relief train. Clara Barton, the 67-year-old veteran nurse of the Civil War, arrived to set up a hospital unit of her newly formed American Red Cross. Everyone from Wall Street financiers to schoolchildren donated money; more than $3 million was raised to provide relief for the flood victims. Over the years legends about the great flood continued to grow, until the phrase "run for the hills, the dam has busted" became a part of the American language. ⚡

In just a few hours, cities such as Guthrie, Stillwater, and Oklahoma City sprang from the wilderness, and the once-virgin Oklahoma prairie was dotted with the encampments of 50,000 new arrivals. Not everyone managed to stake a claim, though. The Great Oklahoma Land Rush left hundreds out in the cold, and some overeager homesteaders who had jumped the gun (known as Sooners) were forced to give up their claims. Other land rushes occurred in the years ahead, and by 1906 the Oklahoma Territory comprised the area covered by the state today. ⚡

Land attorneys advertise their services in the makeshift village of Guthrie, Oklahoma.

IN THEIR OWN WORDS

❝I was sitting in the tower, and all at once, I heard a roar. I looked up the track, and I seen the trees and water coming. I jumped up and throwed the window up, and climbed out on a tin roof around our office and walked around on it . . . and I heard voices; I could hear somebody hollering, but I couldn't see them, and I walked around until the drift came down, and . . . I saw a man standing on a house roof. He looked over and seen me and recognized me.

He says, 'Mineral Point is all swept away, and the people swept away, and my whole family is gone.' I says, 'Is that so?' and I says, 'Do you know anything of my family?' and he says, 'No, I don't; I think they were all drowned.'

Christ Mongomery was his name, and I says, 'Cheer up, Christ, don't give up; as long as you're on top, there's hope!' . . .

After I cheered him up, I turned around to walk [back] into my office . . . I didn't have more than fifteen feet to walk, but I almost fainted [after Christ Montgomery had] told me my whole family was drowned.❞

W. H. Pickerell (whose family did, in fact, survive) relates his experiences in the Johnstown flood.

A young boy is dwarfed by a gauge for measuring snowfall.

1890

A **new bureau in the Department of Agriculture was formed to monitor one of the least predictable aspects of American life — the weather.**

"The weather is always doing something," Mark Twain said, and he was right. In fact, the United States experiences more severe storms and damaging floods than any other country in the world, and before the days of modern meteorology, blizzards, tornadoes, hurricanes, and other life-threatening weather events could arrive with little or no warning.

In 1870, after a series of violent storms battered the New England coast, President Ulysses S. Grant authorized the Army Signal Service to take over the task of charting the nation's weather. President Benjamin Harrison reassigned the job to the Department of Agriculture in 1890, creating the Weather Bureau (since renamed the National Weather Service) that still exists today.

Using temperature and precipitation data provided by a nationwide network of civilian volunteers, the bureau soon got a fix on the nation's weather picture. Over the following decades the bureau became responsible for issuing hurricane, tornado, and flood warnings, as well as flight bulletins. (Orville Wright checked with the bureau before making his first powered airplane flight at Kill Devil Hill, North Carolina, in 1903.) By the 1960's, with the advent of weather satellites, the bureau was able to deliver much more accurate storm predictions and, as a result, save many lives. ✺

1890

T**he murder of a New Orleans policeman who had stumbled upon a secret Sicilian society resulted in a horrifying display of vigilante justice.**

A group of Sicilian immigrants, playing out a centuries-old battle from across the ocean, in January 1899 murdered a New Orleans man of Neapolitan descent named Vincenzo Ottumvo. While investigating this and similar homicides, police chief David Hennessy repeatedly heard (sometimes in guarded whispers) about the involvement of a "secret society" called the Mafia. He confirmed the rumors by writing to Sicilian authorities; they wrote back, telling him "that more than one hundred escaped convicts are in New Orleans." Vowing to "break the Mafia . . . [and] tear it out by the roots," Hennessy prepared to testify against the Matrangas, one of the two families involved in the blood feud.

The determined police chief never got the chance to take the witness stand. On October 15, 1890, Hennessy was cut down by shotgun blasts just minutes away from his home. Before he died, he told his friend, Capt. William O'Connor, that "the Italians" were responsible.

A. Scaffidi

A. Bagnetto

J. P. Macheca

J. Matranga

In February 1891 nine men (five of whom are shown at right) went to trial for Hennessy's murder. Two weeks later, to the shocked dismay of many New Orleans citizens, all nine were acquitted. The jurors had found the prosecution's case weak. (There were rumors that the Mafia had paid off some of the jury.) Incensed by the verdict, thousands of citizens marched to Parish Prison, where the prisoners, awaiting release, were being held. Along with the 9 acquitted men, 10 others who had been indicted in connection with the murder remained locked in the jail. The vigilante mob stormed the prison, hanging or shooting 11 of the 19 men, even as some of them begged for their lives. When it was over, the vigilante leader,

P. Monastero

William S. Parkerson, a respected lawyer and well-known politician, gave his benediction: "I called you together for a duty. You have performed that duty. Now, go home and God bless you."

Although the Mafia in New Orleans lost some of its power, it had not been destroyed. The organization grew nationally, fanning out to such cities as St. Louis and New York. By World War I the Mafia controlled much of the country's waterfront property and made millions of dollars in illegal trade — setting the stage for a fabulously profitable bootlegging business during the 1920's Prohibition era. ✺

B **1890** **y the end of the 19th century the virtually limitless land of the Western frontier had dwindled considerably.**

Although the 1890 U.S. census revealed that the nation had reached a population of 62.9 million, with no sign of leveling off, new land for the growing number of Americans was no longer available; nowhere did a section exist with fewer than two people per square mile — the government's definition of a frontier. Gone were the vast stretches of land that had beckoned explorers and pioneers for nearly 300 years. People would now have to build farms and towns on already settled land.

With this in mind a historian named Frederick Jackson Turner offered a view for the century to come. In 1893, at the meeting of the American Historical Association,

A tamed and settled West is seen in this late 1880's lithograph.

THE GREAT WEST

the 32-year-old Turner, a University of Wisconsin professor, offered a paper entitled "The Significance of the Frontier in American History." In it he argued that the frontier had represented a powerful force in molding the American character. It had helped the United States to develop a sense of self-reliance, optimism, and perseverance that had allowed the nation to weather economic depressions and had made it a world power.

The "Turner thesis" greatly influenced 20th-century thinking. Over the years it touched American life at many levels, from politics to popular culture, from John F. Kennedy's hopeful "New Frontier" to the television show "Star Trek," which always opened with the announcement, "Space, the final frontier. . . ."

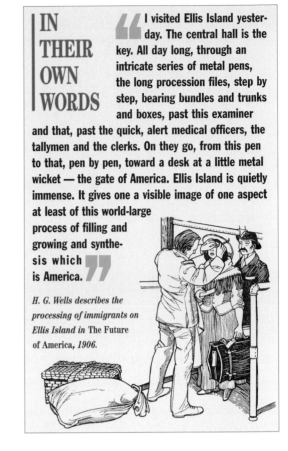

Immigrants wait in the steerage area of an ocean liner as it arrives in New York.

A **1892** **doorway opened to millions of would-be Americans when the Ellis Island Immigration Station began operation.**

On New Year's Day, 1892, 15-year-old Annie Moore of Cork County, Ireland, was the first immigrant to arrive at the Ellis Island Immigration Station; she was welcomed with speeches and a $10 gold piece. In 1954 a Norwegian seaman named Ivan Pederson was the last immigrant to be processed. In the intervening decades, Ellis Island welcomed some 12 million newcomers from all over the world. For most people the process was stressful but swift, taking only a few hours; for those who were detained because of ill health, lack of funds, or suspected mental incompetence, it could be a harrowing ordeal that dragged on for days or weeks, with the specter of deportation always preying on their minds.

During the peak years from 1910 to 1914, the station processed 2,000 to 5,000 immigrants daily, and spectacular chaos greeted all who made it to the Great Hall — described by one journalist as "a sea of straining immigrant faces . . . a babel of languages and dialects, heavily clad women in babushkas clutching in one hand a saucer-eyed child and in the other a knotted bedsheet bulging with the possessions of the first half of life." In all, 98 percent of the new arrivals were admitted, and today 4 out of 10 Americans can claim an ancestor who passed through the Great Hall on Ellis Island.

1892

More than a century after the laying of its cornerstone, the world's largest Gothic cathedral is still incomplete.

Choosing from more than 60 entrants in a competition, the Episcopal diocese of New York selected the architectural firm of Heins and LaFarge to design a "House of Prayer for all people." The site was Morningside Heights, 13 acres of largely uninhabited woodland in upper Manhattan. On this bucolic plot a cathedral was planned that, when finished, would contain the largest cubic footage of any Gothic structure in the world. Two football fields long, it would be tall enough to shelter the Statue of Liberty under its central dome.

The cornerstone was laid on December 27, 1892, the feast day of St. John the Divine, for whom the cathedral is named. But serious work on the foundation did not begin for another two years. Then, piece by piece, the cathedral rose. The first eight granite columns — each weighing 250,000 pounds — were erected behind the site of the main altar. The side chapels took shape, as did four huge granite arches for the transept. In 1916 construction of the nave began.

Two world wars and the Great Depression slowed and then halted construction. Meanwhile, the surrounding neighborhood slowly gave way to urban decay. The Episcopal diocese, not wishing to appear insensitive to its low-income neighbors by continuing to lavish funds on such a costly structure, put the project on hold. Only in 1982, after a four-decade hiatus, was building resumed. Ten years later, just short of the cathedral's centenary, lack of money forced yet another halt. New Yorkers began referring to the partly built edifice as St. John the Unfinished.

Even as the cathedral gained a reputation for tardy completion, it became known for being proudly ecumenical. Besides the traditional saints depicted on its stained-glass windows are historical figures such as the ancient Greek physician Hippocrates and French scientist Louis Pasteur. Master carvers have chiseled the cathedral's stone into bears, skyscrapers, Indian totem poles, and the likenesses of Abraham Lincoln and South African president Nelson Mandela. Its pulpit has held everyone from Bishop Desmund Tutu of South Africa to Tibet's Dalai Lama, from Jerusalem mayor Teddy Kolleck to Czechoslovakian president Vaclav Havel, from author Kurt Vonnegut to homeless people and teenage mothers. "It's a place of wonderful contradictions and odd juxtapositions that somehow manage to work out in the end," St. John's former dean, the Very Reverend James Parks Morton, philosophized. "It's a place with something for everyone." ✺

Though still far short of its final design — indicated here by the superimposed drawing — the Cathedral of St. John the Divine stands resplendent.

1893

A renowned expert on early education left a unique legacy: a song cowritten with her sister that is among the world's best known.

In 1893 Patty Smith Hill, a teacher in Louisville, Kentucky, and her sister Mildred, a church organist, published *Song Stories for the Kindergarten*. The first song in the book was a four-line ditty of welcome entitled "Good Morning to All." Later Patty wrote new lyrics, changing the title to "Happy Birthday to You."

Patty Smith Hill

"Happy Birthday" remains one of the most popular songs in English; it is also sung in Spanish, Dutch, Italian, Swedish, and other languages. The lyrics, finally copyrighted in 1935 — and so protected until the year 2010 — still earn as much as $1 million annually for use in plays, movies, and TV shows. Patty Smith went on to head the department of kindergarten education at Columbia University Teachers College, where she gained further acclaim by devising new methods for teaching kindergarten. ✺

Mildred Hill

Federal troops riding special patrol trains such as this one were used to break the Pullman strike.

1894
The Pullman strike was a triumph of union solidarity, yet it failed to fulfill workers' demands.

In the midst of a national depression, workers at the Pullman Palace Car Company factory near Chicago voted to strike against their employer. Frustrated by recent wage cuts and the high living costs in factory owner George Pullman's company town, they appealed for help to the newly organized American Railway Union. The union responded by asking its members across the country not to handle trains hauling Pullman sleeping cars. Since this involved nearly all trains, the boycott, launched on June 26, 1894, succeeded in shutting down most of the nation's rail traffic. The 260,000 boycotters included not only union members but thousands of unaffiliated coworkers determined to show solidarity.

Siding with the nation's railroad owners, the U.S. attorney general secured a court injunction against boycotting the trains, on the grounds that the strike interfered with mail delivery. When the union refused to comply with the court order, federal troops and state militia were sent to enforce it. In a clash between soldiers and strikers at Chicago in early July, 13 people were killed and more than 50 wounded. Violent confrontations broke out in 26 states, from Maine to California. By mid-July, when the strike was crushed, 34 people had been killed. The leader of the American Railway Union, Eugene V. Debs — later to be a Socialist Party candidate for president — was sentenced to a term in prison for ignoring the court order.

Although the Pullman strike failed to win its immediate goals, it demonstrated that strikes could be organized and coordinated on a national scale. As one railroad worker put it, the strike showed that "the laboring men . . . must get together; that no single organization can win." ☀

1895
An unemployed sea captain set sail in a rebuilt sloop on the first solo voyage around the world.

A sailor from the age of 16, Joshua Slocum had made and lost fortunes as a shipmaster plying the Pacific from San Francisco and China to Japan and Australia. He was down on his luck and barely making a living working in shipyards and organizing chartered fishing parties, when in 1894 he came up with the idea of circling the globe alone. Slocum rebuilt the *Spray*, a 37-foot-long oyster boat he had found rotting in a pasture near Fairhaven, Massachusetts. Stocking it with tinned food and salted meat, he sailed from Boston on April 24, 1895. The *Spray* had no engine and only one compass, one sextant, and a few navigational charts.

Slocum crossed the Atlantic Ocean, only to learn at Gibraltar that pirates threatened his planned route through the Mediterranean and Red Seas. To avoid confrontation, he recrossed the Atlantic to Brazil, navigated the treacherous Strait of Magellan, and made his way to the Pacific Ocean, arriving in April 1896. During the next two years, the intrepid sailor visited Australia, crossed the Indian Ocean to South Africa, then returned to the Atlantic. He dropped anchor at Newport, Rhode Island, on June 27, 1898.

Joshua Slocum poses on the Spray during a stopover in a South American port, c. 1896.

Slocum's epochal voyage was overshadowed by the Spanish-American War, but he earned a bit of money from his memoirs and by showing off the *Spray* to tourists. Determined to begin a new adventure, Slocum sailed from Martha's Vineyard on November 14, 1909, bound for South America. Neither he nor the *Spray* was ever seen again. ☀

A 1895
Massachusetts bottle-cap salesman had an inspiration that made shaving safer, easier, and cheaper.

When shaving, men of the late 19th century relied on straightedge steel blades that had to be painstakingly sharpened before each use, and which often inflicted painful nicks. One morning in 1895, King Camp Gillette, a 40-year-old traveling bottle-cap salesman, saw to his dismay that his razor was worn out and once again had to be taken to a barber or cutler for professional sharpening. As he stared at the useless blade in his home in Brookline, Massachusetts, the idea of the safety razor with a disposable blade took form.

Gillette envisioned a three-piece device: a thin piece of steel sharpened on both sides, a handle, and a clamp to center the blade over the handle. When the inexpensive blade was worn out, it could be thrown away and replaced with a new one at minimal cost. It took Gillette nearly eight years to perfect the device and put it on the market. The first year (1903) his company sold only 51 razors, each with 20 disposable blades, at $5 apiece. Despite the poor sales, Gillette secured a patent, bought a factory building in South Boston, and expanded production. By the end of 1905, Gillette had sold 250,000 razor sets and 100,000 blade packages. Although annual sales of razors remained constant at between 300,000 and 400,000 over the next decade, blade package sales zoomed to 7 million.

A 1917 government order for 3.5 million razors and 36 million blades for World War I servicemen gave an enormous boost to the business — but by that time Gillette had sold his interest in the company, moved to California, and bought an orange grove. ☀

The original Gillette razor and blade packet was patented in 1904.

Hanging by her teeth, a turn-of-the-century aerialist performs a daredevil act at Dreamland, Coney Island.

A 1895
An internationally renowned aquatic daredevil came up with the idea of an "all-in-one" amusement park.

New Yorkers had been going to Coney Island in Brooklyn, New York, for summer vacations since the first beach hotel was built there in 1829. By the 1840's the narrow five-mile-long spit of land was drawing such luminaries as Daniel Webster, Herman Melville, Henry Clay, and Walt Whitman. At mid century it attracted so many visitors that a plank road was built to facilitate the 11-mile journey from mid Manhattan. Over the next few decades, dance pavilions and beer halls sprang up, and bathhouses were built to accommodate those who came for the new sport of ocean bathing.

"Did you ever see such high light and motion before?" a writer at *Harper's* rhapsodized in the 1880's. "The shining white pine buildings, glittering windows, sea foam, dazzling sand and spray . . . the fluttering of countless flags . . . the restless crowd." While well-to-do visitors enjoyed the "high light and motion" in luxury hotels, at a safe distance from the crowds, day visitors engaged in all manner of amusement on the beach and boardwalk. They sampled raw clams and "red hots" (later dubbed "hot dogs" by a newspaper that questioned the origin of the meat), visited Gypsy fortune-tellers and vaudeville shows, and took rides on the "switchback railway," an earlier, gentler cousin of the Cyclone roller coaster.

By the 1890's it was clear that Coney Island was not just a resort but also an amusement park, and that the biggest attractions were the rides. With names like the Witching Waves, the Scrambler, the Tickler, and the Human Toboggan Slide, dozens of rides dotted the park, most designed to toss passengers about until they shrieked with delight. Then international daredevil stuntman Capt. Paul Boyton came up with the idea of grouping the rides together and charging one admission.

On July 4, 1895, Boyton opened Sea Lion Park to accommodate his aquatic circus. In it he offered other popular attractions such as a Shoot-the-Chutes water ride, the Flip-Flap, and in 1901, a Loop-the-Loop roller coaster. The popularity of Boyton's single enclosed amusement park soon brought competitors to Coney Island, including Dreamland, Steeplechase, and Luna Park. By 1900 as many as 100,000 fun-seekers were drawn to Coney Island on summer Sundays. ☀

1896

The only Supreme Court justice to dissent from the decision to uphold racial segregation was a former slave owner.

Army colonel John Marshall Harlan, born into a family of slaveholders, strongly supported the Southern system of slave ownership. At the same time, as a native of Kentucky and an officer in the U.S. Army, he fought for the Union during the Civil War — believing with equal conviction that the South should not be allowed to secede.

After the war his views on race began to change, and he became a lifelong advocate of civil equality for freed blacks. Appointed to the Supreme Court in 1877, he often found himself alone in his opinions, including his support for racial equality. Defending justice as he saw it, Harlan continued to speak out as a minority of one.

His most famous dissent occurred in the case of *Plessy* v. *Ferguson* in 1896. By a vote of seven to one — Justice David J. Brewer

Justice Harlan served as a Supreme Court justice for 34 years.

did not particpate in the voting — the Supreme Court upheld a Louisiana state law allowing racial segregation on railroads. The majority ruled that legal separation of the races did not "necessarily imply the inferiority of either race," and that the Louisiana statute's provision for "equal but separate accommodations" was constitutionally acceptable. Harlan dissented, forcefully stating that "our Constitution is color-blind." Calling racial segregation "a badge of servitude," he argued that "the thin disguise of 'equal' accommodations . . . will not mislead anyone, nor atone for the wrong this day has done."

The decision on *Plessy* v. *Ferguson* allowed legally sanctioned racial segregation (enforced by Jim Crow laws in the South) to become even more deeply entrenched. Not until *Brown* v. *Board of Education* in 1954 did the Supreme Court overturn the doctrine of "separate but equal," at last vindicating Harlan's lonely dissent.

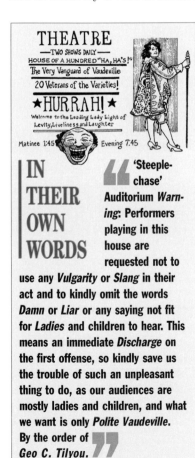

IN THEIR OWN WORDS

'Steeplechase' Auditorium *Warning*: Performers playing in this house are requested not to use any *Vulgarity* or *Slang* in their act and to kindly omit the words *Damn* or *Liar* or any saying not fit for *Ladies* and children to hear. This means an immediate *Discharge* on the first offense, so kindly save us the trouble of such an unpleasant thing to do, as our audiences are mostly ladies and children, and what we want is only *Polite Vaudeville*. By the order of Geo C. Tilyou.

A sign at George C. Tilyou's Steeplechase Park on Coney Island.

1896

Presidential candidate William Jennings Bryan gave the most famous convention speech in American history, yet he lost the election.

Former Nebraska congressman William Jennings Bryan was only 36 years old when he was chosen to defend the cause of free silver at the 1896 Democratic National Convention in Chicago. There, Bryan joined the debate over whether America should base its currency on gold alone, or on the value of both gold and silver. His powerful plea for silver coinage transformed the debate into a battle for the soul of the nation: "Our war is not a war of conquest," he declared; "we are fighting in the defense of our homes, our families, and posterity. . . . "

Bryan adhered to the familiar argument that only prosperous financiers wanted a gold standard, because it would maintain the high value of their money. Debt-ridden farmers and other struggling people, he claimed, would benefit from the free and unlimited coinage of silver, because it would allow them to pay off their debts in cheaper currency. Bryan delivered his message in brilliant rhetoric: "You shall not press down upon the brow of labor this crown of thorns, you shall not crucify mankind upon a cross of gold."

The day after the speech, convention delegates named Bryan as Democratic candidate for president. Despite a hard-fought campaign, he and the free-silver platform lost to Republican William McKinley, who sup-

Bryan's Cross of Gold speech was criticized as blasphemous because it mixed politics with biblical imagery.

ported the gold standard. Running again in 1900 and in 1908, Bryan again lost, fated to be remembered not for his deeds, but for his words.

C 1896
leveland industrialist Mark Hanna entered politics not as a candidate but as a kingmaker determined to choose the next president of the United States.
In the three decades since he had gone into business with his father-in-law, Marcus Alonzo Hanna had made a fortune in coal, iron, shipbuilding, and banking. But all this was not enough to satisfy his ambition or harness his energy. Early in 1895, at the age of 57, he set out to win the presidency for his friend William McKinley, a former U.S. congressman and two-term governor of Ohio. Together, the clever but stiffly formal Hanna and the affable, easygoing McKinley (it was said) made one perfect politician.

An 1896 cartoon of Hanna, dressed in a dollar-sign suit, raiding Wall Street for donations.

Hanna used $100,000 of his own money to secure the Republican nomination for McKinley, then lobbied the business community to raise an unprecedented sum — estimated at between $6 million and $7 million — to put his man over the top on Election Day, November 3, 1896. It was the largest amount of money spent on a presidential campaign up to that time, twice as much as the Republicans had spent in 1892 and six or seven times what the Democrats spent on their losing candidate, William Jennings Bryan. McKinley's victory proved one of Mark Hanna's favorite adages: "Politics are one form of business and must be treated strictly as business." ☀

The Sears, Roebuck and Co. catalog for spring and summer 1896.

A 1896
nything — from a mustache cup to a glass eye for your horse — could be ordered from a Sears, Roebuck catalog.
To supplement his income as a railroad agent in North Redwood, Minnesota, Richard Sears bought a jeweler's rejected batch of gold-filled watches in 1886 and began selling them through a telegraphed announcement to other agents. After making a profit of $5,000, Sears quit his job, moved to Chicago, and teamed up with

watchmaker Alvah Roebuck to sell timepieces and other jewelry through mail-order catalogs. In 1896 the pair issued their first large general catalog. The 753-page book offered a wide variety of merchandise, including furniture, small machinery, and clothing — all guaranteed by the name that would define retailing for the next several decades: Sears, Roebuck and Co. The catalog appealed mainly to rural residents whose shopping alternatives were mostly distant general stores and small emporiums. (Its one real competitor was Montgomery Ward & Co., a mail-order house founded in 1871 that also catered to rural customers.)

Amply illustrated with practical but enticing woodcuts, the early catalogs generated sales of nearly $1 million a year. The catalog soon became known as the nation's wish book, hooking readers with such inducements as "Look what 5¢ will buy!"

Beginning in 1908, a Sears, Roebuck house catalog sold tens of thousands of prefabricated houses. Actresses Gloria Swanson and Lauren Bacall modeled for the regular catalog, and Tarzan's creator, author Edgar Rice Burroughs, wrote copy. So complete was the wish book that when asked at Sunday school for the source of the Ten Commandments, a student is said to have cried, "From Sears, Roebuck, where else?"

The Sears, Roebuck catalog remained a treasure trove for consumers until changing shopping habits and rising production costs ended its publication in 1993. ☀

The Nation's Wish Book

"It is the Policy of Our House to Supply the Consumer Everything on which we can save him money," stated the Sears, Roebuck and Co. catalog. Judging from the selection of merchandise offered to the mail-order customer, this seemed to be completely true. The following are just a few of the items offered for sale in the pages of the 1897 Sears Wish Book.

• No. 1 house broom	$0.22
• 1 oz. Sears-brand perfume extracts	$0.25
• 5-lb. box of fancy chocolate creams	$0.70
• 1 child's extra-fine Madras cloth dress	$0.58
• Webster's Unabridged Dictionary	$1.68
• Nickel-plated watch	$1.68
• Spalding's basemen's mitt	$2.55
• 1 pair of ladies' Paris kid button shoes	$2.98
• Silver-plated 4-piece tea set	$4.50
• Men's extra-fine combination Mackintosh coat	$6.98
• 5-piece overstuffed parlor set	$15.00
• Acme dry-air refrigerator	$17.60
• Sears, Roebuck and Co. special piano No. 71	$125.00

A 1898

Although Spain was accused of sinking the battleship _Maine_ — an event that helped ignite the Spanish-American War — the allegation may have been untrue.

On February 15, 1898, a tremendous explosion rocked the U.S. battleship _Maine_ as it lay anchored in the harbor of Havana, Cuba. The blast quickly sank the vessel, killing 260 men. Many people assumed that a Spanish mine had destroyed it.

The warship had steamed into a hotbed of intrigue and local rebellion. A number of Americans favored armed intervention on behalf of the Cuban rebels who had been fighting for years against oppressive Spanish rule. Some prowar advocates hungered for the commercial possibilities of an indepen-dent Cuba; others wanted to gain an overseas empire for the United States. The yellow press, especially the sensational-ist newspapers of William Randolph Hearst and Joseph Pulitzer, craved the increased circulation that war headlines would bring.

By early 1898 the United States lacked only a provocation to touch off war with Spain, and the sinking of the _Maine,_ on a purportedly friendly

The wreck of the U.S.S. Maine _in Havana harbor as it appeared in 1900._

visit to Cuban waters, provided one. Spain denied responsibil-ity, but an investigation by the U.S. Navy concluded otherwise, and on April 25 war was declared.

Later inquiries revealed that a minor blast of unspecified origin had set off an ammunition magazine. In the rush to "Remember the _Maine!_" the fact that its sinking might have been an accident was almost completely ignored. ✷

T 1898

The Spanish-American War was one of our nation's shortest conflicts, but it still took a major toll.

A "splendid little war" is how Secretary of State John Hay character-ized America's four-month-long conflict with Spain. It seemed a fit-ting description for a war that consisted of little more than a pair of naval engagements and a hand-ful of land battles in the spring and summer of 1898. Yet by the time the Spanish-American War was over, the United States had gained an empire.

America's speedy victory was largely due to the sorry state of the aging Spanish navy. Spain's fleet proved to be antiquated and in poor repair. In swift, one-sided battles in Manila Bay and off the coast of Cuba, American ships swept down on their outmatched Spanish oppo-nents and literally blew them out of the water.

U.S. ground forces faced a much tougher time, however. After a chaotic embarkation from Tampa, Florida, 17,000 troops under Maj. Gen. William R.

The Rough Riders and black troopers of the 10th Cavalry engage the Spanish near Santiago, Cuba, in 1898.

Shafter landed in Cuba in June of 1898 and began their march on Santiago. Along the way they risked defeat at the Battle of San Juan Hill, where inadequate training, obsolete artillery, and blistering tropical heat nearly undermined the American offensive. The 300-pound Shafter was virtually incapacitated by the extreme tempera-ture, leaving subordinate officers to carry out his orders and attack. Among them was Lt. Col. Theodore Roosevelt, who along with his Rough Riders gained lasting fame in the battle that followed.

Despite their difficulties, U.S. troops prevailed in Cuba by mid-July. Subsequent landings in Puerto Rico and the Pacific spelled defeat for the Spanish forces, and on August 12 an armistice was signed. A formal treaty in December gave the United States an overseas empire of former Spanish pos-sessions: Puerto Rico, Guam, and the Philippines. Hawaii was also taken, almost by after-thought, as a refueling stopover for naval vessels.

America's victory had been decisive, but the cost was high: more than 6,700 servicemen lost their lives. Amazingly, fewer than 10 percent died in combat, many of them at the Battle of San Juan Hill. The remaining men were victims of illness. Diseases such as malaria, yellow fever, and typhoid infected as many as 80 percent of the troops. Additionally, an unappetizing diet of hardtack, spoiled tinned meat, and corrosive coffee felled thousands of soldiers with dysentery. It was a shameful legacy for a "splendid" war. ✷

A *1898*
monarchy, then a republic, Hawaii was annexed by the United States despite its monarch's efforts to maintain its sovereignty.

When Queen Liliuokalani came to the throne in 1891, the Hawaiian Islands were a constitutional monarchy ruled from the Iolani Palace in Honolulu. The queen was admired for her dignity, piety, and musical talent; she composed the well-known song "Aloha Oe." But she clashed with the local community of rich and powerful American sugar investors.

The crisis boiled to a head in 1893, when Liliuokalani substituted a new constitution that increased her royal powers and limited the influence of Hawaii's American residents. The move provoked a revolution in which the queen was overthrown.

A provisional government headed by American businessman Sanford B. Dole took control. Dole, backed by the sugar interests, sought admission to the United States, but President Grover Cleveland blocked the proposal. He insisted on restoring Liliuokalani to the throne.

Dole defied Cleveland by refusing to step down, instead proclaiming Hawaii an independent republic. Several months later Liliuokalani decided to renounce her royal claims.

The Spanish-American War demonstrated the strategic value of maintaining a U.S. naval base at Pearl Harbor. President William McKinley convinced Congress to annex Hawaii, and on August 12, 1898, the annexation ceremony was held. ☀

Pint-size cowgirl Lucille Mulhall more than held her own against brawny cowboys.

W *1899*
hen humorist Will Rogers saw 14-year-old Lucille Mulhall perform at her father's Wild West show, he gave her a thrilling new title: *cowgirl.*

Lucille Mulhall, the daughter of Oklahoma rancher Col. Zack Mulhall, was riding fences and roping calves by the time she was 10. The next year her father offered her any calf that she could rope, tie, and brand. But he quickly called off the deal: Lucy had placed her "LM" on nearly two-thirds of his herd.

Will Rogers met Zack Mulhall and his talented daughter at a riding and roping contest that Mulhall staged in St. Louis in 1899. And so Rogers discovered "the first cowgirl, one that could do anything — not pose, but ride and rope." The humorist, who later became famous for his own rope tricks, was lavish in his praise for her rope-handling ability.

Theodore Roosevelt was another admirer. A family friend and occasional visitor to the Mulhall ranch, Roosevelt once challenged little Lucille to rope a lobo wolf that had been menacing the cattle. She not only lassoed the creature, but killed it with a stirrup iron. When Roosevelt became president in 1901, he took the wolf pelt that Lucille gave him to the White House and displayed it prominently.

Although Lucille's cowpunching skills made her father proud, Mulhall might never have allowed her to perform in public if the future president had not talked him into it. When Roosevelt and his Rough Riders entered a Wild West extravaganza in Oklahoma City, Lucille joined in, riding a wild steer. So impressed was Roosevelt, according to observers, that he urged Mulhall to showcase Lucille's talents. And so America's first true cowgirl rode out to glory — in Mulhall's Wild West Show.

At a county fair in San Angelo, Texas, in 1901, 16-year-old Lucille earned $1,000 for roping and tying a 1,000-pound steer, and her father won a small fortune in bets from onlookers who didn't believe she could do it. In 1904 the bashful, freckle-faced slip of a girl — she weighed only 100 pounds in her stocking feet — electrified the crowd at an exposition in St. Louis by jumping on the back of a wildly bucking steer and riding it instead of roping it. Lucille Mulhall continued to delight rodeo crowds with her daredevil stunts for a decade and a half. ☀

The raising of the U.S. flag at the Royal Hawaiian Palace in 1898 was a sad occasion for former queen Liliuokalani, the territory's last monarch.

1900

The influx of women enrolling in college evoked hostility from male students on campuses nationwide.

Between 1870 and 1900 the number of women attending colleges and universities rose nearly eightfold. By the turn of the century, 85,000 women were enrolled, comprising 37 percent of the 230,000 students working toward degrees.

Women often found campus life an uphill struggle. A Columbia University debating team refused to compete against the Cornell team because the latter included a coed. One Columbia student voiced his concern that "a girl would have the advantage every time because she could immediately prejudice the

Turn-of-the-century coeds at Cornell had to fight for fair treatment.

judges in her favor." Male students at the University of California at Berkeley objected to the mere presence of coeds. At the University of Chicago, enrollment by women increased from fewer than 200 students to more than 1,000 in four years. This dramatic upsurge aroused worries in certain circles that women would begin to exert a strong influence on campus.

Ignoring the hostility of men on some campuses, many women organized their own clubs and lobbied for the construction of female dormitories. One dean described these coeducational institutions as "little Edens of liberty" that opened the lives of women to the world beyond home and hearth. ☀

1901

President William McKinley was shot by an assassin, and his well-meaning doctors then helped kill him.

At 4 o'clock in the afternoon on September 6, 1901, William McKinley, the 25th president of the United States, began greeting supporters at the Pan-American Exposition in Buffalo, New York. Because anarchists had threatened to kill the president and four other world leaders, security was tight. Incredibly, no one paid much attention to a slim man who approached the president with a dirty handkerchief wrapped around his hand.

Suddenly, shots rang out, and President McKinley lay sprawled on the floor. He was badly wounded and covered with blood, but alive. Leon Czolgosz, an unemployed mill worker and outspoken anarchist, had fired twice. One bullet was stopped by a button on the president's suit; the other had lodged in his stomach.

Within a few hours McKinley went into shock. He was taken to the Exposition's hospital, which was little more than a first-aid station. A prominent Buffalo surgeon, Dr. Matthew D.

Mann, was summoned. Despite rudimentary equipment and inadequate lighting, Mann decided to operate. As he cut into the president's abdomen, Mann had such a difficult time seeing what he was doing that one of his assistants had to hold a mirror to reflect sunlight into the incision.

Mann hunted long and hard, but was unable to find the bullet. Concluding that wherever it had lodged it could do no further damage, he proceeded to sew up the president's stomach. But, following surgical practice of the time, he made no provision for draining the wound.

Infection and gangrene soon set in. As McKinley's health deteriorated, doctors prescribed enemas and laxatives in a misguided attempt to "purge" the president of infection. Nothing seemed to work.

McKinley expired on September 14, 1901, eight days after the shooting and two days after his final purge. The fatal bullet was never discovered. ☀

This photograph of McKinley was taken minutes before the assassination.

IN THEIR OWN WORDS

❝ A little girl was immediately ahead of him in the line, and the President, after patting her kindly on the head, turned with a smile of welcome and extended hand.

The assassin thrust out both of his hands, brushed aside the President's right hand with his left hand, lurched forward, and thrusting his right hand close against the President's breast, pulled the trigger twice. . . .

At the first shot the President quivered and clutched at his chest. At the second shot he doubled slightly forward and sank back. It all happened in a moment. . . . A detective clutched the assassin's right hand, tore from it the handkerchief, and ❞ seized the revolver.

An eyewitness account of President McKinley's assassination, September 6, 1901.

1901

The youngest man ever to become president, Theodore Roosevelt brought a passionate vitality to the White House.

Republican boss Mark Hanna had vociferously opposed the selection of Theodore Roosevelt as William McKinley's running mate in 1900: there would be but one life, Hanna said, "between that madman and the Presidency." Roosevelt had pushed through so many reforms as governor of New York that some party stalwarts, hoping to prevent further changes, wanted to elevate him to a national post where he could do no harm. Then on September 14, 1901, Hanna's nightmare came true. McKinley was assassinated and Roosevelt took the oath of office.

Replacing the childless McKinleys were Theodore, 42 years old; Alice, his 17-year-old daughter by his first wife; Edith, his second wife; and their five rambunctious children. There was a menagerie of exotic pets.

For exercise, Roosevelt boxed, practiced jujitsu, rode horseback, and took vigorous hikes that left his companions thoroughly exhausted. He was the first president to ride in an automobile (a Columbia Electric Victoria), fly in an airplane, go undersea in a submarine, win a Nobel Prize, and visit a foreign country while in office — this last being his trip to Panama, where the canal he had insisted upon was being built.

For him the White House was a "bully pulpit" from which to preach a wide-ranging agenda of trust-busting, land conservation, federal intervention in labor disputes, regulation of food and drug supplies, and world power status for the United States. He talked incessantly, wrote volumes of letters, and was author of a shelf full of scholarly books. He took every opportunity he could to promote his presidential achievements. An old friend, Henry Adams, summed up the president's exuberant and brash style, saying, "Theodore is drunk with himself." ✸

Ebullient as ever, Theodore Roosevelt engages in one of his favorite activities, public speaking.

1901

"I won't say goodbye, it's just *au revoir*," the portly woman said as she prepared to go over Niagara Falls in a wooden barrel.

Watching circus performers as a young girl, Annie Edson resolved to do something that would catch the world's attention. A half-century later — by then she was a widowed teacher of 63 — Anna Edson Taylor conceived the stunt that she hoped would bring her fame and fortune. Strapped inside an oak barrel bound with iron hoops and kept upright by a 200-pound anvil, she would plunge over the 158-foot Canadian cataract of the Niagara River.

On October 24, 1901, Taylor climbed into the barrel, which was released some distance upriver from the drop. Onlookers cheered as the vessel neared the precipice and disappeared. Some 15 minutes later, anxious lookouts spied the bobbing barrel, towed it ashore, and pried off the lid.

"I'd sooner be shot by a cannon" than repeat the stunt, a dazed Taylor admitted. She suffered a three-inch scalp wound but was otherwise unharmed. Although she toured the East and the South, Taylor never made money from the feat and was destitute at her death 20 years later. ✸

A wide-eyed Taylor clings to the barrel as she is towed out to the falls.

Over the Edge: The Niagara Daredevils

The challenge of cheating death has lured more than one daredevil to Niagara Falls. Listed here are some of those who have knowingly tempted fate in the perilous 180-foot fall to fame, as well as two persons who took the plunge by accident.

October 24, 1901 Annie Edson Taylor is the first person to attempt a barrel ride over Niagara Falls. She emerges gashed and shaken.

July 25, 1911 Bobby Leach survives his ride over Niagara Falls in a steel barrel but breaks his jaw and kneecaps in the process.

July 11, 1920 Charles Stephens dies during his attempt to conquer the falls in a wooden barrel.

July 4, 1928 Jean Lussier survives his plummet over the falls in a large rubber and steel ball.

July 4, 1930 George Stathakis survives the drop but is suffocated when his wood-and-steel barrel is trapped behind the cascading water for 22 hours.

August 5, 1951 William "Red" Hill, Jr., dies when his flimsy craft of inner tubes, fishnet, and canvas breaks apart in the falls.

A
1901
dinner party and a golf game led to the formation of the first billion-dollar corporation.

Two weeks before Christmas 1900, some of New York City's most prominent businessmen assembled for a dinner party at the prestigious University Club. The guests included John Pierpont Morgan, who was America's leading financier and industrialist, and Andrew Carnegie, king of the nation's steel industry. The two titans of American business, both in their sixties, had taken divergent paths to wealth and power, but they understood that the time might be right for a joint business venture.

The keynote speaker at the dinner was Charles W. Schwab, president of the Carnegie Steel Company. Schwab spoke of the need for a consolidation of competing steel interests in order to regulate and expand the industry. After the speech, Morgan, who was involved in nearly every major corporate-finance deal in the country at the time, approached Schwab to learn how he could participate in such a merger.

Morgan already knew that before other steel manufacturers would agree to a merger, the all-powerful Carnegie — Schwab's boss — would first have to give up control of Carnegie Steel. So at a second meeting, Morgan urged Schwab to pursue the matter, declaring, "If Andy wants to sell, I'll buy.

When financial wizard J. P. Morgan created the U.S. Steel conglomerate, he acquired this Homestead Steel plant in Pittsburgh.

Go and find his price."

Schwab, who knew that Carnegie was considering retirement, consulted his boss's wife to see how best to pose the delicate question of a buyout. She suggested that, in order to set the right mood, Schwab should invite Carnegie to play a round of golf, then have lunch at a country club.

At the lunch meeting, the steel magnate responded to Schwab's inquiry on his willingness to sell by scribbling out a figure, which Morgan later accepted without a single objection. So in 1901 Carnegie handed over his steel company to Morgan's newly formed U.S. Steel Corporation for $492 million in stocks and bonds. With assets of $1.4 billion, the new industrial giant was the largest corporate enterprise of its day, the first ever to pass the billion-dollar mark. ☀

July 9, 1960 Roger Woodward, who is swept over Niagara Falls after a boating accident, survives with only a life preserver to protect him.

August 19, 1985 The youngest of the Niagara daredevils, 22-year-old Steven Trotter takes his first trip over the falls in a homemade rubber barrel.

October 5, 1985 John David Munday, whose first attempt is foiled by authorities, makes it the second time, encased in a steel barrel. On September 26, 1993, Munday becomes the first person to survive two plunges when he goes over the falls in a steel diving bell.

September 27, 1989 Peter DeBernardi and Jeffery Petkovich, riding in a steel barrel, become the first pair of daredevils to survive the drop.

June 18, 1995 Joining Steven Trotter in his second successful trip over the falls is newcomer Lori Martin. They ride in a capsule of fiberglass, Kevlar, and Styrofoam.

October 1, 1995 Robert Overacker, from Camarillo, California, drowns after he tries to ride a jet-propelled craft over the brink of Niagara's Horseshoe Falls and his parachute fails to open.

B
1902
y refusing to shoot a black bear cub, Theodore Roosevelt gained immortality.

Outdoorsman, Rough Rider, and president, Theodore Roosevelt was enjoying a Mississippi hunting trip in 1902 when he came upon a black bear cub that his hosts had trapped and tethered for him to kill. Roosevelt, horrified, put up his gun.

Roosevelt's gesture of mercy and sportsmanship inspired Morris Michtom, a Brooklyn candy-store owner, and his wife to design a plush toy bear with movable parts as a way to honor the president. Roosevelt gave Michtom permission to use his nickname, and Teddy's Bear, a stuffed animal with button eyes, became an instant hit.

At about the same time, German toy manufacturer Margaret Steiff introduced a similar stuffed bear. When her company displayed the toy bear at the Leipzig Fair in 1904, it became another standard version of what would become the most popular toy of the early 20th century. ☀

A chained-up cub is no target for T.R. in this widely circulated 1902 cartoon by Clifford Berryman.

1903

Jack London rose from a hand-to-mouth existence on the Oakland, California, waterfront to become the best-known and highest-paid writer of his time.

By the time he sold his first short story in 1898, 22-year-old Jack London had worked in a cannery and as an "oyster pirate" in San Francisco Bay, crossed the country as a hobo, spent time in jail for vagrancy, sailed to Japan and Siberia, dropped out of college, and joined the Klondike gold rush. The last adventure provided the backdrop for his 1903 masterpiece, *The Call of the Wild*. By then, the prolific writer had already published eight books and dozens of magazine articles and short stories.

The Call of the Wild earned London a following around the world. It also ushered in a new literary style — sentimentality was out, realism was in. Lon-

London's 1903 novel describes wolves' harsh struggle to survive.

don's novel about a dog that abandons human civilization to lead a wolf pack conveyed the author's own restlessness — his yearning for freedom combined with an abiding respect for society's norms.

By 1905 London was probably the nation's highest-paid writer. The shift from grinding poverty to sudden wealth did nothing to quench his wanderlust, however. Roaming far and wide, London lectured on socialism, sailed to the South Pacific, and popularized the sport of surfing — all the while writing nearly nonstop. He periodically returned to California, where he tried to become a gentleman rancher.

Eventually, his frenetic lifestyle took its toll: he lapsed into alcoholism and became dependent on sedatives for liver disease and other ailments. On November 22, 1916, just short of his 41st birthday, London died following a drug overdose.

1903

The first World Series between the National and American leagues would have been the last post-season contest ever if the cranky manager of a National League team had had his way.

In 1903 no one was certain how many fans cared to see the Boston Pilgrims of the upstart American League play the National League's Pittsburgh Pirates in a best-of-nine series. Amazingly, more than 16,000 people turned out for the game on that cold, damp October 1 in Beantown.

Outside Boston, few people expected much of the Pilgrims. Although their star pitcher, the great

Cy Young, had won 28 games in the regular season, the Pilgrims had gained only three years of experience playing together as a team. The well-established and respected National League champion Pirates, powered by the bat of shortstop Honus Wagner, were heavily favored to win.

When the series began, however, Wagner was hurt, and two of Pittsburgh's best pitchers were out of commission: one with a sore arm, the other on his way to an insane asylum. Deacon Phillippe, a 25-game winner, ended up pitching five complete series games. (He was the first — and last — pitcher ever to do so.) Three of those games Phillippe won, and they were Pittsburgh's only victories.

So Boston triumphed, thus establishing the American League as a worthy opponent. But the series had not been sanctioned by the new baseball commission, and so in 1904, when the victorious Boston Pilgrims challenged the National League-winning New York Giants to a match-up, Giants' manager John McGraw refused.

"We are champions of the only real major league," grumbled McGraw. In 1905 the commissioners and the team owners adopted rules mandating an annual series between the leagues.

Boston fans pour onto the playing field just before the first World Series game.

1903

The United States encouraged an insurrection against Colombia in order to get a regime receptive to its goal of building the Panama Canal.

The Spanish-American War left the United States with new territories to protect in the Pacific and the Caribbean. Such responsibilities made President Theodore Roosevelt eager to build a canal across the narrow Isthmus of Panama, thereby providing a shortcut between the Atlantic and Pacific oceans.

Standing in the way was Colombia, which owned Panama and was reluctant to give up any portion of its territory. So U.S. and Colombian officials negotiated a long-term treaty that would have allowed the United States to lease a 10-mile-wide strip of land across Panama in return for a fee of $10 million, plus annual payments of $250,000. The Colombian senate refused to ratify the treaty, however, and by the summer of 1903, all hope for the canal seemed lost.

1903

Lasting a mere 12 seconds, the first successful flight of the Wright brothers' flying machine was four years in the making.

On December 17, 1903, an Ohio bicycle maker named Orville Wright rode a wood, canvas, and metal machine called the *Flyer* off the sandy hills of Kitty Hawk, North Carolina. In that 12-second voyage, with little fanfare, Orville and his brother Wilbur achieved what they had spent four years working toward: the world's first engine-powered controlled flight in a heavier-than-air machine.

The Wrights became interested in designing a flying machine in the 1890's, after reading about the gliders of German aviator Otto Lilienthal. They also learned about experiments with motor-driven airplanes, notably those of the distinguished American scientist

On the sands at Kitty Hawk, Wilbur Wright watches as his brother Orville lifts off in the **Flyer.**

Samuel P. Langley. Although Langley's government-subsidized flying machines flopped conspicuously, his experiments suggested that powered flight was possible.

The Wright brothers also turned to nature for inspiration. Taking careful observations of birds in flight, they noted how a buzzard twists its wings as it banks, turns, dives, and climbs. An airplane would also need to bend its wings in order to maneuver successfully, they reasoned. And so the brothers devised the box-kite design of the historic *Flyer,* which had built-in controls for flexing the wings. (In modern aircraft, ailerons produce the equivalent effect.)

With no corporate or government support, the Wrights worked out of their bicycle shop, where they built kites and gliders. Fittingly, the day of their first successful flight at Kitty Hawk was pretty much like any other day. There were no reporters to witness the momentous event, and only a single photographer to record an image for posterity. Had it not been for a telegraph operator who called a newspaper reporter, there would have been no published account of the "monster bird" that ushered in the age of flight. ⋇

Meanwhile, behind the scenes, plans were being hatched for a Panamanian revolt against Colombia. A major instigator was Philippe Bunau-Varilla, a former director of a French company that had earlier tried without success to build

Roosevelt digs a canal in Panama as U.S. warships patrol.

a Panama canal. The company hoped to sell its assets to the United States.

Although Panamanian businessmen supported the insurrection, it probably would never have occurred without the tacit approval of the United States, which sent three naval vessels to the area with instructions to land troops if necessary.

The revolution came on November 3, 1903. Discouraged by the American presence on land and sea, Colombia made little effort to regain control.

Three days later, the United States recognized the new Republic of Panama.

American and Panamanian representatives soon signed a treaty that gave the United States control of the canal zone on the same terms that Colombia had rejected previously. The Panama Canal, a 40-mile-long complex of locks, lakes, and a channel through the Continental Divide, opened for shipping in 1914. In 1921 the United States paid Colombia $25 million for its loss of territory. ⋇

Aviation Milestones

Some 400 years after Leonardo da Vinci sketched airborne machines with wings, the Wright brothers made aviation history by powering their double-winged *Flyer* on a 12-second flight over the beach near Kitty Hawk, North Carolina. Here are some other high points in the development of manned flight.

1909 American pilot and aircraft designer Glenn Curtiss sets an air-speed record of 47.06 miles per hour at the first international air race, held in Reims, France.

1911 American aviator Calbraith Rodgers completes the first transcontinental flight across the United States, a series of short hops that included 3 days 10 hours 4 minutes of airborne travel spread over 49 days.

1914 The Benoit Company's St. Petersburg–Tampa air boats initiate the world's first scheduled airline service, ferrying one passenger at a time.

1927 Charles A. Lindbergh flies from Long Island, New York, to Paris in 33$\frac{1}{2}$ hours, the first solo nonstop transatlantic flight.

1933 American pilot Wiley Post makes the first solo flight around the globe, covering 15,596 miles in 7 days 18 hours 49 minutes.

1947 U.S. Air Force captain Charles Yeager becomes the first pilot to break the sound barrier.

A *1903*
lthough the Buick was the cornerstone upon which the General Motors Corporation was built, its designer, David Buick, became a mere footnote in automobile history.

David Buick was a successful plumbing-supply manufacturer when he decided to try building cars. By 1903, the year he incorporated the Buick Motor Company in Flint, Michigan, two of his engineers had developed the valve-in-head engine that gave his car superior power and hill-climbing capabilities. Unfortunately, Buick could not translate his vision into a commercial success. He sold only 6 cars in 1903, and the following year, a mere 37.

Buick was on the verge of bankruptcy in 1904, when marketing dynamo William

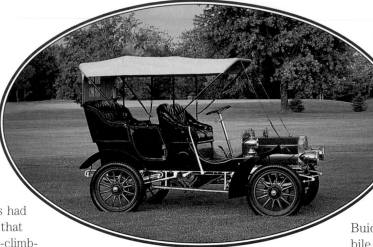

A 1905 Model C Buick.

Crapo Durant bought him out. With the boldness and business acumen his predecessor lacked, Durant forged ahead, and by 1908 the Buick assembly plant was the world's largest. Durant sold more than 8,000

cars that year, marketing them through a nationwide network of dealerships that he had created.

Soon the Buick was the vehicle of choice for buyers of medium-priced cars. The publicity-conscious Durant sparked interest in his car with such tactics as entering the Buick in a national automobile race, where it easily outclassed the competition.

Encouraged by his success with the Buick, Durant bought other small automobile firms and in 1908 renamed his enlarged company General Motors. Unfortunately, David Buick was not part of the success story — he had resigned from Durant's company in 1906. At the time of his death in 1929, the entrepreneur who helped launch an auto-industry giant was employed as a clerk in a Detroit vocational school. ☀

I *1905*
t could take as many as three men to fill the tank of an early automobile.

Turn-of-the-century drivers couldn't just pull into a gas station and call out "Fill 'er up." Motorists had to drive to fuel depots, where gasoline was stored in steel drums. Sometimes a three-man crew was needed to help a driver fill a five-gallon container with gasoline, remove any extraneous material, strain the liquid through a cloth into a funnel, and then pour it into the gas tank.

Sylvanus Bowser of Fort Wayne, Indiana, came up with a better idea. He adapted the equipment he had developed for pumping kerosene so that it would pump gasoline instead and record the amount sold. Before long, Bowser quit his job as a traveling salesman to peddle gas pumps full-time.

In 1905, after the pump had been encased in a tall wooden cabinet, one of Bowser's salesmen dubbed it a "filling station," and the name stuck. These stations heralded a new era in automobile travel. Motorists took to the road with the assurance that they could easily fill their tanks on the way home if their fuel supply ran low. In fact, so many drivers refueled at the curbside pumps, affectionately called Bowsers, that they soon created one of the most hated byproducts of the automobile age: traffic jams. ☀

Roadside gas pumps helped boost the popularity of car travel.

T *1906*
he huge fires touched off by the San Francisco earthquake caused more damage than the tremor itself.

The great earthquake that rocked San Francisco on April 18, 1906, caught residents sleeping — quite literally. The first tremor pulsed through the city at 5:13 in the morning. Registering a devastating 8.3 on the Richter scale, it lasted 40 seconds; after a pause of 10 seconds, a second tremor jolted the city for 25 seconds.

Police sergeant Jesse Cook, walking with a friend at dawn, watched in amazement as the street buckled in front of him. "It was as if the waves of the ocean were coming toward me, and billowing as they came," he recalled. Blocks of tenements built on unstable landfill toppled instantly, millionaires' mansions on Nob Hill crumbled, and giant redwoods were uprooted.

Even worse damage resulted, however, from the huge fires that followed the earthquake. Ruptured gas and electric lines caused San Francisco's mostly wood-frame buildings to ignite. The city's 585-man fire force could only stand by helplessly, since the earthquake had broken the water mains. On Telegraph Hill, an Italian neighborhood, residents tried quenching the flames with some 1,000 gallons of wine. Smoke from the fires could be seen 100 miles away.

At last, after three days, the wind changed course and the great conflagration burned itself out. More than four square miles of the city, the heart of its business district, smoldered in ruins; some 28,000 buildings had been destroyed, among them San Francisco's new $6 million City

After the quake, soldiers patrolled San Francisco's Market Street to restore calm and discourage looters.

IN THEIR OWN WORDS

San Francisco is gone. Nothing remains of it but memories and a fringe of dwelling-houses on its outskirts. . . . Before the flames, throughout the night, fled tens of thousands of homeless ones. Some were wrapped in blankets. Others carried bundles of bedding and dear household treasures. Sometimes a whole family was harnessed to a carriage or delivery wagon that was weighted down with their possessions. Baby buggies, toy wagons, and go-carts were used as trucks, while every other person was dragging a trunk. . . . They held on longest to these trunks, and over their trunks, many a strong man broke his heart that night. The hills of San Francisco are steep, and up these hills, mile after mile, were the trunks dragged. Everywhere were trunks, with across them lying their exhausted owners, men and women.

An account of the quake and its aftermath by Jack London in Collier's *magazine, May 5, 1906.*

Hall. Estimates of property damage ran as high as $500 million. The death toll was put at more than 700 people, some of whom were looters summarily executed on the streets while martial law was in effect.

Still, the people of San Francisco refused to let the devastation shake their belief in the city's future. Barely eight months after the quake, optimistic residents pledged $4 million so that they could bring an exposition celebrating the Panama Canal to their recovering city in 1915. 🌟

M *1906*
rs. William Corey's highly publicized divorce from her wealthy industrialist husband established Reno, Nevada, as a mecca for divorce seekers.

Nevada's legislators decided to establish a state residency requirement of six months to accommodate the needs of their transient population of miners and entrepreneurs.

This brief waiting period for residency and the state's liberal grounds for divorce inadvertently transformed Reno into a mecca for couples who wanted to end their marriages.

One would-be divorcée who traveled to Reno to take advantage of the six-month rule was Laura Corey, a Pittsburgh resident.

Mary Pickford with her second husband, Douglas Fairbanks.

After her husband, U.S. Steel Corporation president William Corey, left her for a dancer, Laura filed for divorce. The two-timing industrialist fought his wife's lawsuit in vain. On July 30, 1906, a judge awarded Laura a staggering $2 million divorce settlement, which made headlines nationwide.

Of the other unhappily married spouses who followed Laura's lead, the most famous one in the early part of the century was silent-screen star Mary Pickford, who divorced her first husband in Nevada in 1920 and promptly married Douglas Fairbanks. Seeing the prosperity that the divorce trade was bringing to Nevada (flourishing enterprises included dude ranches for the soon-to-be-single), neighboring states began to change their own residency rules. Not to be outdone, Nevada reduced its residency requirement to three months in 1927 and to six weeks in 1931. 🌟

1906

It was intended to foment social change, but Upton Sinclair's best-selling novel *The Jungle*, about the meat-packing industry, altered food-safety laws instead.

After six weeks of living among Chicago's immigrant meatpacking workers, 27-year-old socialist writer Upton Sinclair was appalled at their plight. They lived in squalor, contracted deadly diseases, labored long hours in filth, and sometimes were killed while using unsafe equipment. Hired by a socialist newspaper to write a report, Sinclair believed that his exposés would open the nation's eyes to the misery and injustices faced by many workers in slaughterhouses.

Sinclair's 1905 series of articles appeared in the socialist weekly *Appeal to Reason,* and then, slightly revised, in 1906 as a novel, *The Jungle.* The widely read book brought about change, but it was not the kind the author had hoped for.

It was the horrors of the food-preparation process, not the fictionalized misfortunes of immigrant Jurgis Rudkus and his family, that scandalized readers. Sinclair offered vivid scenes of men butchering diseased and pregnant cattle, using toxic chemicals to "prepare" beef entrails, adding rats to sausage, and watching workers fall into vats and end up as lard.

One horrified reader was President Theodore Roosevelt. Moving decisively, Roosevelt ordered an investigation of food-preparation standards and practices that resulted in the passage of federal meat inspection laws and the Pure Food and Drug Act of 1906.

Despite the food-safety laws, Sinclair considered his muckraking effort a dismal failure. The man who wanted a more humane, socialist form of government, not more government regulations, lamented: "I aimed for the heart and by accident I hit the stomach instead." ⚡

Upton Sinclair's portrayal of the unsanitary conditions in Chicago meatpacking houses such as this sausage factory ignited protests and changed eating habits.

Preservationist John Muir (right) helped convince President Theodore Roosevelt (left) to set aside vast forest preserves.

1907

Although the term *environmentalist* had yet to be coined, Theodore Roosevelt was the nation's most vocal advocate for preserving America's natural resources.

As much as he enjoyed wielding political power, Theodore Roosevelt seemed to relish the great outdoors even more. He was a rancher, hunter, and naturalist first, a politician second. Before becoming president, Roosevelt had published two books on hunting, and he continued to write magazine articles on the outdoors while in office.

Roosevelt's love of nature resulted in major federal measures to conserve America's natural resources. Under the 1902 National Reclamation Act, he allocated proceeds from the sale of public lands to construct dams and irrigate arid terrain in Nevada, Arizona, Colorado, and other Western states. (By 1920 this program had opened about 1.2 million acres to cultivation.)

In 1907 Roosevelt made another lasting contribution to conservation. Fearing that unrestrained development would deplete the nation's timber, he added nearly 150 million acres of public land to the national forest reserves; the additional lands covered an area slightly larger than France. The farsighted chief executive also set aside vast regions for mining and for generating water power many decades before the nation encountered its first energy crisis.

In addition to promoting the intelligent management of natural resources for practical needs, Roosevelt cared about preserving land for its recreational value, potential scientific importance, and sheer beauty and grandeur. He created five new national parks, two national game preserves, 16 national monuments, and 51 wildlife refuges. Fittingly, the only national park that is named after an individual is Theodore Roosevelt National Park, which protects a section of rugged North Dakota badlands that its namesake cherished. ⚡

R¹⁹⁰⁸

Robert La Follette weathered parliamentary maneuvers and food poisoning to give one of the Senate's longest speeches.

At 12:20 A.M. on May 29, 1908, Sen. Robert La Follette of Wisconsin took the floor of the Senate. A proposed bill to back public currency with private railroad bonds had fired up the Populist legislator, who feared corporate control of the U.S. economy.

Tempers and the temperature were both sweltering on

The seven-minute roll calls during his filibuster gave La Follette time to eat.

the day of the filibuster. Periodically, the senators would leave the stifling chamber to rest on the coatroom's couches. La Follette brought them back for 32 roll calls.

To keep up his strength, La Follette drank a concoction of milk and eggs. One such mixture nearly ended the filibuster, when the senator gagged on the foul-tasting liquid. "Take it away; it's drugged," he cried out. Tests later showed that the ptomaine from a rotten egg or spoiled milk would have killed him if he had finished the glass.

La Follette spent the next two hours of quorum calls doing battle with a mild case of food poisoning. His opponents used a flurry of parliamentary maneuvers to disrupt the filibuster, all in vain. Finally, at 7:05 A.M. on May 30, La Follette left the floor, yielding to his ally, William Stone of Missouri.

Thomas Gore of Oklahoma, who was blind, took over at 2 A.M. After two hours, he yielded the floor, expecting that Stone would continue, but Stone had left the room. The measure was quickly brought to a vote and passed easily. ✦

Long-Winded Senators

Although the House of Representatives decided in the 19th century to limit the amount of time a member could monopolize the floor, the Senate has no such restriction. The following are some of the longest filibusters by individual senators in the 20th century and the legislation they were intended to block.

Senator/Date	Time/Subject
Strom Thurmond August 28–29, 1957	24 hours 18 minutes *Civil Rights Act of 1957*
Wayne Morse April 24–25, 1953	22 hours 26 minutes *Tidelands oil bill*
Robert La Follette, Sr. May 29–30, 1908	18 hours 23 minutes *Currency bill*
William Proxmire Sept. 28–29, 1981	16 hours 12 minutes *Public debt ceiling limitation*
Huey P. Long June 12–13, 1935	15 hours 30 minutes *National Industrial Recovery Act*
Alphonse D'Amato October 5–6, 1992	15 hours 14 minutes *Tax bill*
Robert C. Byrd June 9–10, 1964	14 hours 13 minutes *Civil Rights Act of 1964*

T¹⁹⁰⁸

The arrival of a Chicago film company transformed a tiny community in California into the movie capital of the world.

At the turn of the century, the 500 residents of Hollywood, California, were enjoying their oasis of tranquility in a rapidly changing world. Mostly pious Midwestern retirees, they declared their town dry in 1901 and banned theater, dance, and other amusements.

In 1908 director William Selig's camera crew arrived from Chicago and set up near Hollywood to finish filming *The Count of Monte Cristo.* Before long, the word was out: Los Angeles offered a variety of terrain, including desert for on-location Westerns, and open-shop laws that kept unions out and wages low. The weather was extraordinary — 350 days of sun every year, according to the Chamber of Commerce. Motion picture companies flocked to Los Angeles, only too happy to vacate their Manhattan rooftop studios, where hailstorms and pigeons made shooting outdoors a hazardous occupation.

In October 1911 the movie invasion hit Hollywood proper. The Nestor production company set up shop in an old roadhouse on Sunset Boulevard. A nearby barn was turned into a film-developing studio, thus shortening production time. Word of Nestor's success traveled quickly, and soon 15 companies were shooting motion pictures in and around the Hollywood area.

One of the first film crews to shoot in the Hollywood Hills.

The townspeople referred to the newcomers as "movies," apparently unaware that the term referred to the product, not its creators. Aggravated residents complained that director D. W. Griffith's cowboys were running across their lawns and that the Keystone Kops' chases staged by Mack Sennett were disrupting their daily lives. Suspicious of the Easterners, the locals kept them out of country clubs and exclusive apartment complexes. One hotel posted a sign that read, "No dogs, no actors."

Before long, however, nearly the whole industry had moved westward, and local resistance began to break down. By 1919 the movie business was the fifth largest in the country, with revenues of approximately $700 million a year. ✦

D *1908*
espite fears that it could become a national police force, the FBI was authorized to conduct federal investigations.
Theodore Roosevelt's presidency, from 1901 to 1909, saw a marked expansion of government power — including the birth of America's first federal detective agency. Convinced that he needed an investigative body to enforce federal law, Roosevelt overrode protests from congressmen — many of whom worried that such an agency would abuse its mandate — until he got his way. In 1908 Attorney General Charles Bonaparte set up the Bureau of Investigation within the Department of Justice.

It didn't take long for the dire predictions to come true. During and after World War I, the bureau shifted from catching crooks to spying on suspected radicals — including such dyed-in-the-wool American patriots as social reformer Jane Addams and New York City mayor Fiorello La Guardia. So in 1924 the bureau was reorganized and its authority curbed. A new director was appointed: 29-year-old J. Edgar Hoover.

Hoover built the bureau into a more professional organization while at first keeping its role limited. But as an organized-crime wave swept the nation in the 1930's, Hoover moved to expand the bureau's investigative reach. In 1933, under President Franklin D. Roosevelt, it was again reorganized and its powers increased. Two years later it was renamed the Federal Bureau of Investigation, or FBI.

The bureau continued to grow in size and authority. By the time of Hoover's death in 1972, it had become an autonomous agency of 10,000 agents, with jurisdiction over some 180 matters, including espionage, sabotage, kidnapping, bank robbery, interstate gambling, civil rights, and fraud.

With such extensive power came new abuses, including illegal break-ins and wiretaps. In 1973, after the Watergate scandal involving President Richard Nixon's reelection campaign, the FBI was once more reorganized to prevent its being used to serve political interests. ☀

One of the first badges worn by Bureau of Investigation officers.

T *1909*
he first published blues tune originated as a campaign song for a Memphis mayor.
William Christopher Handy came of age in the Bible Belt in Alabama, where a trombone was "the devil's pitchfork." Handy's father, a Methodist preacher, once told him, "Son, I'd rather follow you to the graveyard than to hear you had become a musician."

His father's threat notwithstanding, W. C. Handy pursued his natural bent, playing the organ in church, studying music theory in school, singing in minstrel troupes, and composing music nonstop. When he got together with his friends, he would often turn to music making,

improvising a set of drums with milk pails and tin pans.

Cornet in hand, Handy left home at 18 to make a living as a musician. He worked as a music teacher and a bandleader in minstrel shows. For inspiration he drew on everything from the "baptisin'" and "death-and-burial" songs of his father's congregation to the music of the black songsters who hawked snake oil at medicine shows in the South.

By 1909 the man who would one day be known as the Father of the Blues was writing music and running a music-publishing firm in Memphis, Tennessee. That same year a candidate for mayor, Edward Crump, hired him to compose a campaign song. Handy wrote a tune called "Mister Crump" and played it at rallies across the city. When Crump won the election, Handy's star rose.

One music historian dated the birth of the blues to the time when Handy "returned to

Beale Street [in Memphis] and set his pen to music paper." Soon the composer had a chain of bands with as many as 90 men playing at a time, belting out the distinctive blues sound — part loneliness and heartbreak, part triumph and survival. In 1912 Handy published "Mister Crump" as "Memphis Blues," and the rhythms of black folk music began their climb into the world of popular song. His best-known piece, "St. Louis Blues," followed in 1914.

Four years later Handy moved to New York City, where he wrote, performed, and published music. He eventually reached the pinnacle of a musician's career — playing at Carnegie Hall. But Handy never forgot his musical roots. Much of his inspiration, he would later recall, came from the "Negro roustabouts, honky-tonk piano players, wanderers, and others, of their underprivileged but undaunted class." ☀

W. C. Handy and a song that changed music history.

C *1910*
hinese immigrants endured interrogations and prolonged detention at the Angel Island Immigration Station because federal policy deemed them undesirable.

The American West was developed in part by the labor of Chinese immigrants. But their willingness to work for low wages rankled many Americans, and in 1882 Congress passed the Chinese Exclusion Act, aimed primarily at limiting the number of laborers.

By January 21, 1910, when a new entry facility opened on Angel Island in San Francisco Bay, the guidelines had grown more restrictive. Only select groups, such as teachers and tourists, were welcomed. So for the next 30 years they funneled through the Angel Island Immigration Station, attempting to prove their suitability.

Some would-be immigrants, carefully coached and armed with forged documents, posed as the offspring of Chinese-American citizens, becoming "paper sons and daughters" of nonexistent parents.

Immigration officials often made it difficult for Asians to stay in the United States.

But U.S. government officials closely interrogated anyone they thought was trying to sneak in, and an applicant who offered imprecise responses was usually rejected. As the regulations stated, "in every doubtful case the benefit of the doubt shall be given . . . to the United States."

Immigrants could be held for questioning at Angel Island for weeks or even years. Behind locked doors in stark quarters, detainees had to limit their activities mostly to reading or listening to opera on a Victrola. Some immigrants inscribed anguished poems on the walls; a few committed suicide.

In the 1920's, conditions improved and visitors were permitted. One regular visitor was Deaconess Katherine Maurer, who was known as the "angel of Angel Island" for her efforts in helping detainees to write letters and learn English. In 1940 a fire closed the immigration facility, but it had served its purpose: in California alone, the Chinese population had decreased from 8.7 percent of the state's total in 1880 to only 0.6 percent. ✳

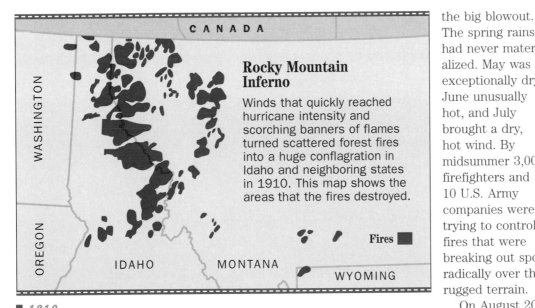

Rocky Mountain Inferno

Winds that quickly reached hurricane intensity and scorching banners of flames turned scattered forest fires into a huge conflagration in Idaho and neighboring states in 1910. This map shows the areas that the fires destroyed.

Fires ■

I *1910*
n a matter of 48 hours, raging fires engulfed 3 million acres of drought-ridden forest in the Northwest.

In the summer of 1910, prospectors, loggers, and homesteaders in Idaho's Coeur d'Alene National Forest nervously awaited the big blowout. The spring rains had never materialized. May was exceptionally dry, June unusually hot, and July brought a dry, hot wind. By midsummer 3,000 firefighters and 10 U.S. Army companies were trying to control fires that were breaking out sporadically over the rugged terrain.

On August 20 a gale-force wind known as a chinook blew in from the southwest at 70 miles an hour. Suddenly, the whole forest seemed to burst into flames, and ash blotted out the sky.

A U.S. Forest Service supervisor, William Weigle, ordered the railroad to ready two evacuation trains in Wallace, the region's largest town. Speeding through the mountains while trestles burned behind it, the evacuation train saved 1,000 people.

Entering the forest to gauge the progress of the fire, Weigle almost became a victim himself. Encircled by the flames, he drenched himself with water from a mine, then buried himself in the sand with only his neck and back exposed. "The flames seemed to whip back and forth over me in sheets," he recalled after escaping, badly burned but happy to be alive.

After midnight on August 22, rains began to fall on the forests of northern Idaho, eastern Washington, and western Montana. The chinook faded to a light breeze, and the fire burned itself out. In time the scale of this disaster would lead to federal relief and a law for the permanent protection of forest land. But the survivors had little reason for consolation. The destruction to the fire-ravaged 3 million acres would shut down the logging industry, one of the area's economic mainstays, for decades to come. ✳

During the evening rush hour in 1895, Chicago's Randolph Street station bustled with activity.

By the early 20th century, the railroad **1910** industry had become the nation's largest employer and its greatest user of natural resources.

As new technology like the air brake and automatic coupler made trains faster, safer, and more economical, the nation's growing industries increasingly relied on the "iron horse" to transport Texas cattle, California produce, Chicago packed meat, Twin City flour, and other goods. Tracks were hurriedly laid down through mountain passes and across deserts; between 1865 and 1916, the nation's total network of rails increased from 35,000 miles to 254,000 miles.

With all this expansion, the railroad business became the nation's largest industry. No enterprise used more natural resources — chiefly iron and coal — or employed more workers — 1.7 million in 1910.

At the same time, corruption and monopolistic practices flourished as railroad tycoons inflated securities, forced competitors into bankruptcy, and set discriminatory freight rates. When the Interstate Commerce Commission, formed in 1887, introduced regulations to curb such abuses, it provoked outrage in the rich and powerful. A senator from Rhode Island denounced the commission as "an empty menace to great interests, made to answer the clamor of the ignorant and unreasoning."

More than a few U.S. senators considered it their duty to defend the unfettered growth of big business, of which railroads were the biggest. Muckraking journalist William Allen White wrote that in the 1880's one senator represented the interests of the Union Pacific Railroad; another, the New York Central; and several senators from the West fought fiercely for the Southern Pacific. After World War I — when trolleys, automobiles, buses, trucks, and eventually airplanes began to compete with railroads — such blatant flouting of the public trust became less commonplace. ✳

Juliette Low, rejected first by her mother **1912** and then by her husband, found worldwide acceptance as the guiding spirit behind the Girl Scouts.

Juliette (Daisy) Low was the daughter of a well-to-do Georgia cotton broker and his egocentric wife, who once declared her adorable young child to be "as ugly as ten bears." Juliette's marriage to William Mackay Low, a wealthy Englishman, did little to prop up her battered self-image. Moving to England with her husband, she soon found out he was being unfaithful. When Low died in 1905, he left his fortune to his mistress, with whom he had lived in the house he shared with his wife.

Girl Scout founder Juliette Low (standing, center) with one of the first troops.

Adrift and downhearted, Juliette Low discovered a friend in Sir Robert Baden-Powell, a hero of the Boer War. Baden-Powell had founded the Boy Scouts in 1908 to acquaint young boys with the manly rigors of outdoor life and to teach them proper discipline. When some 6,000 girls applied to join, he put his sister in charge of setting up a separate group. Juliette was only too happy to help her.

Baden-Powell insisted on calling the new group Girl Guides. Using the term *scouts,* he feared, would foster "a race of tomboys," and he could imagine "nothing more objectionable."

On March 12, 1912, back home in Savannah, Georgia, Low signed up 18 young girls for the first Girl Scout troop and began taking them on hikes and camping trips. But it wasn't just for fun. The girls had to prove their merit by earning badges for such practical skills as cooking outdoors, treating snakebites, and stopping runaway horses.

Although some people considered her eccentric (she wore huge hats decorated with parsley and loved to stand on her head), Low's charm won her many admirers as she traveled from city to city, drumming up support for her cause. When she died in 1927, the ever-loyal Low was buried in her Girl Scout uniform. ✳

1912

Massachusetts enacted the country's first minimum-wage law.

Beginning in 1894, when New Zealand passed a minimum-wage law, the idea that workers should be guaranteed a basic living wage gained acceptance in many nations, including the United States. In the early 20th century, unskilled American mill hands working 12 hours a day earned barely enough to support their families. Living in squalid tenements, they had to rely on the labor of their wives and children to make ends meet.

In response to such conditions, former president Theodore Roosevelt made a minimum wage part of the platform of his Progressive, or "Bull Moose," Party in 1912.

In May 1912 some 15,000 women marched along New York's Fifth Avenue seeking improved working conditions.

That same year Massachusetts became the first state to enact a minimum-wage law; it covered women and children who worked for private companies.

Federal laws were slower in coming, with the Supreme Court repeatedly striking down proposed legislation as unconstitutional. Not until 1938, during the Great Depression, did the Fair Labor Standards Act succeed in setting a nationwide minimum wage.

The new law excluded many types of laborers, such as domestics and farm workers, and the minimum wage for the first year was only 25 cents per hour. Still, the United States had taken a major step toward guaranteeing the right of workers to make a decent living from their labors. ☀

1913

A large number of Americans got their first look at contemporary European art at an exhibit in New York, and many were shocked at what they saw.

Believing that nonacademic artists on both sides of the Atlantic were being neglected, a group of American painters and sculptors mounted the International Exhibition of Modern Art in the vast Sixty-Ninth Regiment Armory in New York City. Beginning on February 17, 1913, in New York, and later in Chicago and Boston, 300,000 people went to see what was in effect a cultural time bomb.

Some 1,000 works of young American artists like John Sloan and Maurice Prendergast were displayed, along with about 500 paintings and sculptures by Europeans, including cubist canvases by Pablo Picasso and Georges Braque and abstractions by Wassily Kandinsky and Marcel Duchamp. Perhaps the most talked-about painting was Duchamp's "Nude Descending a Staircase." Its multiple renderings of a human shape in motion provoked public outrage, and it was widely derided as "an explosion in a shingle factory."

One *New York Times* art critic, who vilified Paul Cézanne as a painter, reserved his most poisonous venom for Henri Matisse. He called Matisse's vibrant canvases "repellent" and shuddered at what he saw as a "sudden

backward jump toward savage art." The critic did admit that what was "hideous to our unaccustomed eyes" might be viewed differently in the future. And in that one respect, he was right.

Although Matisse and the sculptor Constantin Brancusi were hanged in effigy in Chicago, their works and many others exhibited at the Armory Show are now regarded as masterpieces of the 20th century. Meanwhile, the academic art they dared challenge gathers dust in museum storerooms. ☀

IN THEIR OWN WORDS

❝ We come reluctantly and holding back, to Matisse. . . . We enter a stark region of abstractions that are hideous to our unaccustomed eyes. . . . We may well say in the first place that his pictures are ugly, that they are coarse, that they are narrow, that to us they are revolting in their inhumanity. ❞

A New York Times art critic singles out the works of Henri Matisse, including "The Red Studio," 1911 (right), as among the worst paintings at the 1913 Armory Show.

1913

In a game that changed football forever, two Notre Dame players made the forward pass a permanent part of gridiron strategy.

When the Fighting Irish of Notre Dame tumbled off the train that brought them from Indiana to West Point, New York, they hardly looked like the so-called gridiron powerhouse from the Midwest. Notre Dame's 18 players boasted only 14 pairs of cleats. The West Point cadets outweighed them by an average of 15 pounds per man. To add to the sorry state of affairs, the Fighting Irish had to rely on the cadets to pay their travel expenses.

True, the team from South Bend had won its first three games of the season; but the competition had been mediocre at best. The game against the formidable U.S. Army Military

Rockne dashes for the end zone in 1913.

Academy was sure to be much tougher — unless, of course, the Fighting Irish had a secret weapon. And that's exactly what they did have.

Notre Dame quarterback Charles (Gus) Dorais and left end Knute Rockne had spent the summer perfecting a little-used play, the forward pass,

throwing and catching at a beach in Ohio where they both worked as lifeguards. Although the pass had been officially sanctioned in December 1905, it was considered a gimmick in what was essentially a ground game. When autumn arrived, Dorais had mastered the "spiral," a way of hurling the ball with newfound accuracy.

The Notre Dame–Army game on November 1, 1913, started out like any other gridiron contest, with players slowly battering their way up and down the field. Then quarterback Dorais huddled with his team and made a call that changed football forever: "Let's open up."

Rockne repeated a ploy he had used several times already, limping downfield as if he were injured. Suddenly quarterback Dorais lofted the ball. A very healthy Rockne reached up, grabbed the pass, and crossed the goal line.

From then on, *The New York Times* reported with amazement, "the yellow leather egg was in the air half the time." Dorais threw an unprecedented 17 passes, 14 of which were completed for 243 yards. The final score was Notre Dame 35, Army 13.

The final impact was much greater than the upset victory, of course. Notre Dame's wide-open forward pass offensive proved that football could be a more exciting game when played their way — in the air as well as on the ground. ✳

1913

Elsie de Wolfe published America's first interior decorating book and launched a design revolution.

As a little girl in New York City, poor Elsie de Wolfe desperately wanted to be pretty, but everyone told her how plain she really was. So imagine their surprise when de Wolfe grew up to become America's first interior decorator and the 20th century's leading arbiter of good taste, directing a self-styled "revolt against ugliness."

She began as a theater actress in New York. Onstage she wore the very latest fashions from Paris. Designers flocked to see her, clutching their sketch pads.

After 10 years of performing, de Wolfe knew it was time for a change. Choosing the unheard-of field of interior decoration, she sent business cards to friends who had admired the smart decor of her New York townhouse. Then in 1906 she won a commission from an exclusive women's club — and launched a design revolution.

Flinging aside the dark Victorian clutter then in vogue, de Wolfe replaced it with light, elegant furni-

"A living factory of chic" is what photographer Cecil Beaton, who painted this likeness, called de Wolfe.

ture, bright fabrics and wallcoverings, and lots of mirrors. She made chintz, a patterned fabric popular in England, a design essential. Reproduced in newspapers and magazines across the country, her work caused a sensation. As she herself put it, she "opened the doors and windows of America and let in the air and sunshine."

In 1913 de Wolfe's trendsetting book on American interior decoration, *The House in Good Taste,* was published. An instant success, it offered low-cost comfort for budget-conscious homeowners, along with her sure sense of refinement. Her signature touches soon appeared in thousands of residences: parquet floors, reclining chaise lounges, cabinet covers for radiators, and needlepoint pillows with witty sayings. Married at age 60 to a British Embassy attaché in Paris, de Wolfe continued designing even as she moved onto an international stage, entertaining prominent financiers, politicians, and artists at gala parties in Paris, London, and New York. ✳

A 1914 mericans initially welcomed the idea of an income tax.

It took half a century for the United States to adopt a permanent income tax. But when the new levy finally came to pass, it was popular because it affected so few — only the richest 1 percent of the population. Families paid no tax if they earned less than $4,000 a year ($3,000 for an unmarried person). That was enough, said one congressman, "to maintain an American family according to the American standard and send the children through college."

Most people believed that the income tax would replace the tariffs and excise taxes that had driven up the price of food, clothing, and other necessities, burdening the poor and middle classes. The ratification of the 16th Amendment in October 1913 removed the constitutional barriers that had stood in the way of earlier income tax laws. The income tax became a permanent fixture in American life.

The first Form 1040 returns (1040 was the next number in the Bureau of Internal Revenue's book of forms) were due at midnight on March 2, 1914. Many people waited until the last minute to file — the scurrying of procrastinators in New York was front-page news the next day.

No money changed hands on filing day that first year. Once its agents had examined the

Paying the new income tax in 1914 was considered by some to be an honor.

returns, the bureau sent out bills. The top tax rate under the new law was 7 percent.

Although a *New York Herald* report took note of "the young man who overstates his income in order to be among those who are obliged to pay an income tax," such enthusiasm was short-lived. By 1919, to pay off U.S. debts incurred during World War I, the maximum tax rate had risen to 77 percent; in World War II it soared to 90 percent for those with incomes over $200,000.

T 1914 he death of the last passenger pigeon in a Cincinnati zoo marked the extinction of what may once have been the most common bird species in eastern North America.

Painter and naturalist John James Audubon likened passenger pigeons in flight to a solar eclipse; one flock he observed contained an estimated 1 billion birds. They traveled in such numbers that they used up local food sources, and so had to keep moving: they were birds in perpetual passage.

These dovelike creatures were also a highly prized delicacy on human tables, and because of their nesting habits they were easy targets for hunters. Once a small flock settled into an area, millions joined them; breeding grounds became so crowded that a single tree might hold as many as 90 nests. Young squabs, which made particularly good eating, could be

Passenger pigeons flourished when John James Audubon drew these colorful birds.

poked from their nesting places with long poles.

Hunters soon found even faster methods of slaughter. They lured thousands of birds to hidden nets by sprinkling an area with salt, a substance the adult pigeons craved after the breeding season. So-called stool pigeons were also used. A trapper would capture a bird, sew its eyes shut, fasten it to a long pole, and hide behind a bush. When a flock of pigeons flew by, the trapper shook the pole so that the captive would flutter and caw, attracting others. Then he could scoop them all up into his net.

Conservationists warned that the pigeon population was being depleted, but no one bothered to listen. Destruction of their natural habitat, beech and oak forests, also contributed to the birds' demise. So on September 1, 1914, nature's last passenger pigeon, Martha, died in her cage at the Cincinnati zoo.

A 1914
Automotive innovator Henry Ford stunned America by doubling his workers' wages; but for the men building his cars, the offer was a mixed blessing.

December 1913 was a troubling time for Henry Ford. Although the Ford Motor Company's revolutionary assembly line had reduced from 12 hours to 1½ hours the time needed to produce a chassis for the Model T, workers were quitting the factory in droves. They found that performing the same simple task all day long was both monotonous and exhausting.

As the rising costs of hiring and training employees began to eat into Ford's record-setting profits, he knew that he had to find a remedy. On January 5, 1914, Ford announced that his company would henceforth pay its workers $5 a day — nearly double the going rate.

Other industrialists expressed outrage at what seemed to be a wild extravagance, but Ford's rationale was purely practical. The unprecedented pay hike would discourage staff turnover and unionization, he reasoned, while attracting the auto industry's best workers. In addition, Ford reduced the workday from nine hours to eight. This change would not only ease wear and tear on employees but allow for three daily shifts, thereby increasing production. By the end of 1914, annual output had reached 300,000 vehicles.

Model T Fords roll off the assembly line.

For Ford's workers, who had previously earned $2.34 a day, it all seemed too good to be true — and in some respects it was. The basic daily wage remained the same; only after six months' tenure could a worker qualify for the additional $2.66 a day. And the bonus arrived in the form of profit sharing, not take-home pay.

A worker's eligibility for the $5 a day pay package also required a pledge not to join a union and adherence to strict standards of conduct on and off the job. Inspectors from the company's sociological department investigated workers and their families to ensure that they led "a clean, sober, and industrious life."

The biggest drawback, however, was still the work itself. Many assembly-line workers labored for eight straight hours to meet the grueling production schedule. One former Ford employee, who lasted only a week on the line, bitterly described his job as "a form of hell on earth that turned human beings into driven robots." ☀

W 1917
Woodrow Wilson unwittingly shaped American foreign policy for several decades by telling Congress that "the world must be made safe for democracy."

In 1914, when the nations of Europe plunged into the bloody maelstrom of World War I, President Woodrow Wilson insisted at first that the United States remain neutral — an isolationist stance that had been the core of American foreign policy since the days of George Washington. Unlike the president, however, American public opinion and commercial interests readily took sides.

Merchants and bankers did more business with Britain, France, and the other Allies than with Germany and the Central Powers. When German submarine attacks led to American deaths at sea, the losses stoked flames of anger against the German Kaiser. Even so, Wilson won reelection to a second term in 1916 with the slogan "He kept us out of war."

Early in 1917, Germany announced that it would lift all restrictions on submarine warfare. More American ships were torpedoed and more lives lost. On April 2, 1917, Wilson finally called upon Congress to declare war. He argued that the United States must fight not only to protect the principle of freedom of the seas, but to defend the democracies of Britain and France against the autocratic empire of Germany.

"The world must be made safe for democracy," said Wilson. "Its peace must be planted upon the tested foundations of political liberty." Congress agreed, and the United States entered what was being called the Great War. American isolation had come to an end. ☀

GEE !! I WISH I WERE A MAN I'd JOIN The NAVY
BE A MAN AND DO IT
UNITED STATES NAVY RECRUITING STATION
The nation's late entry into war made recruiting a priority.

IN THEIR OWN WORDS

" The question upon which the whole future peace and policy of the world depends is this: Is the present war a struggle for a just and secure peace, or only for a new balance of power? If it be only a struggle for a new balance of power, who will guarantee, who can guarantee the stable equilibrium of the new arrangement? Only a tranquil Europe can be a stable Europe. There must be, not a balance of power but a community of power; not organized rivalries but an organized, common peace. . . . a peace without victory. "

An excerpt from President Wilson's "Peace Without Victory" speech, delivered to the Senate on January 22, 1917.

P *1917*
Pacifist Jeannette Rankin, the first woman elected to the U.S. Congress, was the only voice on Capitol Hill to vote against America's entry into both world wars.

Born on a ranch in Montana Territory in 1880, Jeannette Rankin was an early supporter of a woman's right to vote. Her home state's passage of a women's suffrage law in 1914, for which she had actively lobbied, inspired her to run for Congress in 1916. Commenting on her election victory, she announced, "I will not only represent the women of Montana, but also the women of the country, and I have plenty of work cut out for me."

Less than a week after she took her congressional seat — in March 1917 — President Woodrow Wilson pressed for the entry of the United States into World War I. Rankin joined 56 other representatives in voting against the war resolution. She did so because, she stated, "The first time the first woman had a chance to say no to war she should say it."

That position doomed her chances of reelection, and Rankin spent the next two decades as a peace activist. But when isolationism became a popular issue in Montana in 1940, she again won election to Congress. Then in December 1941, the Japanese attacked Pearl Harbor.

This time Rankin was the only member of either the House or the Senate to vote against a declaration of war. "As a woman, I can't go to war, and I refuse to send anyone else," she said. Again, her decision to put principles above politics made her reelection impossible.

Rankin remained true to her pacifist ideals, working for organizations that promoted peace and participating in antiwar protests until she was well into her eighties. She remained a strong voice against war until her death in 1973. ✵

Jeannette Rankin receives a flag that flew over the House when women's suffrage was passed.

F *1917*
Father Flanagan, in founding a home for orphans, ended up creating an entire town for destitute children.

When Spencer Tracy gave an Oscar-winning performance as Father Edward J. Flanagan in the 1938 film *Boys Town,* millions got to know the Roman Catholic priest. Long before Hollywood celebrated his achievements, however, Flanagan had been working to give homeless children a better life.

Born in Ireland in 1886, Flanagan settled in the United States in his teens. After his ordination he opened a men's hostel in Omaha, Nebraska. Three years of working with vagrants convinced him that his calling lay elsewhere. "I knew that my work was not with these shells of men," he later recalled, "but with the embryo men — the homeless waifs who [had] nowhere to turn, no one to guide them."

In 1917 he opened a house in Omaha to shelter five boys: two down-and-out newsboys and three charged as delinquents. Within two years he was caring for nearly 100 children, most of whom would otherwise have ended up in reformatories, living on the streets, or imprisoned. Besides giving his wards an education, Flanagan stressed the importance of building relationships based on mutual trust. "There is no such thing as a bad boy," was his slogan.

Father Flanagan accepted boys of all races and religions, becoming a pioneer in what is now known as intergroup relations. At a time when racial tensions ran high in the Omaha area, with at least one lynching and occasional Ku Klux Klan incidents, Flanagan made a point of circulating photographs that showed a black boy and a white boy living in harmony at his residence.

Flanagan eventually moved the home to a 160-acre Nebraska farm he named Boys Town, which was later incorporated as a separate municipality. A skilled fund-raiser and publicist, Flanagan expanded the facilities and gained attention worldwide. Today, the Boys Town organization serves more than 20,000 boys and girls through its group homes, foster-care programs, hospital, and other services. ✵

In the spirit of brotherhood, a Boys Town resident gives a ride to a younger friend.

American troops in Archangel, Russia, man a machine gun in the winter of 1918.

While the world celebrated the end of World War I, American soldiers were battling the Red Army in the frozen wasteland of northern Russia.

1918

On September 4, 1918, 5,000 American troops steamed into the port of Archangel, where the Northern Dvina River reaches the White Sea, about 100 miles south of the Arctic Circle. There they joined 10,000 Allied troops. Their mission was to keep both the Germans and the Bolsheviks, who had gained control of Russia in a 1917 revolution, from capturing arms and supplies that the Allies had sent to Russia's previous rulers.

There was another pressing reason for the foray into the forbidding land — Germany's anticipated expansion of its operations in Finland. The Allies feared that the Germans might seize the city of Murmansk, which remained ice-free year-round, and establish a submarine base there.

Fanning out from Archangel, the Allies sank into a morass of swamps and bogs. Winter brought immobilizing snowfalls and interminable Arctic nights, with temperatures of 40° below zero. And then there was the Red Army. On November 11, 1918, as the armistice was signed in Europe, the Communists slipped gunboats up the icy Northern Dvina and launched an attack that forced some Allied troops to abandon their outposts.

In February 1919 President Woodrow Wilson announced to the peace conference in Versailles that Allied troops were "doing no sort of good in Russia." A young British Cabinet officer, Winston Churchill, disagreed. Speaking unofficially, Churchill replied that without the Allies, "an interminable vista of violence and misery was all that remained" for Russia.

Wilson was adamant, however, and in June 1919 the Americans left the frozen tundra for good. After engaging in several skirmishes, the British departed in September. ☀

The death toll from the devastating influenza pandemic made World War I casualties pale by comparison.

1918

Although it eventually rivaled the plagues that decimated Europe and Asia in the 6th and 14th centuries, there was no general alarm over what began as a small localized outbreak of the disease in the United States. In March 1918 an army cook checked into a hospital with a fever, sore throat, and minor aches and pains. Five weeks later some 1,100 fellow soldiers at Fort Riley, Kansas, received treatment for the same malady, one that would later be identified as the Spanish influenza. Only 4 percent of the infected soldiers died, but when the troops left Fort Riley for France, they spread a devastating disease on both sides of the trenches.

It took several more months before the pandemic hit the United States full force. On September 7, 1918, a soldier at Camp Devens, Massachusetts, complained of a backache, sore throat, and fever. The next day a dozen of his fellow infantrymen were treated for similar symptoms. By September 20, medics were stretched to their limits as they logged in 1,543 new cases on that one day.

October 1918 brought widespread deaths from influenza in the United States. In Philadelphia 13,000 had died by the end of the

A trolley car conductor and passenger don face masks, hoping to protect themselves from flu germs.

month, a tally nearly five times as high as combat deaths, which claimed 2,700 Americans that month. In a single week the flu accounted for 21,000 deaths throughout the United States.

City authorities in San Francisco ordered people to wear gauze veils in public places, even though the thin material provided no protection against the highly contagious virus. Public funerals were prohibited in Chicago, and in New York some 500 people were charged with the crime of sneezing in public without using a handkerchief.

Eventually influenza killed 548,452 American soldiers and civilians, 300,000 Germans, 350,000 Italians, 500,000 Mexicans, up to 20 percent of the population on some South Pacific islands, thousands of Eskimos, and at least 5 million people in India.

The pandemic began to abate in the spring of 1919. By then the worldwide toll exceeded 21 million victims. The flu claimed another 100,000 victims in the United States in 1920. ☀

The United States in World War I

1914 Archduke Ferdinand of Austria-Hungary is gunned down on June 28 in Sarajevo by an assassin with ties to Serbia.

On July 28 Austria-Hungary declares war on Serbia; its armies attack the next day, igniting World War I.

1915 The United States warns Germany against attacks on American shipping. Three months later a German submarine sinks the U.S. tanker *Gulflight*, taking two American lives.

The British passenger ship *Lusitania*, on a journey from New York to Liverpool, is torpedoed off the Irish coast by a German U-boat. Of the 1,198 dead, 124 are American.

1916 Congress passes the National Defense Act, strengthening the U.S. Army.

1917 Germany resumes unrestricted submarine warfare after a respite of 16 months; on April 6 the United States declares war.

Advance units of the American Expeditionary Force arrive in France in June and are assigned to a relatively quiet sector. In November, German troops successfully raid the U.S. positions.

1918 The 28th Infantry Regiment [1st U.S. division] recaptures and holds the village of Cantigny.

In early June, the U.S. 2nd and 3rd Infantry divisions halt a German advance toward Paris in heavy fighting around Château-Thierry, Belleau Wood, and Vaux.

During the 2nd Battle of the Marne, in July and August, eight American divisions spearhead a successful French counteroffensive, thwarting the last major German offensive.

With another offensive in mid September, American forces clean out the Saint-Mihiel salient.

Americans fight through heavily defended German positions to cut the vital Strasbourg-Bruges railhead at Sedan during the Meuse-Argonne autumn offensive.

On November 11 an armistice is signed; the war is over.

Infantrymen hug the ground in France's battle-scarred Argonne forest.

S *1918*
ome 120,000 Americans were killed or wounded in the Meuse–Argonne campaign, one of the last major battles of World War I.

The battles of World War I were among the fiercest that American soldiers had ever known. None cost more lives than the Meuse–Argonne campaign, the last major American offensive along the western front. Launched in northern France on September 26, 1918, the campaign called for the First American Army of Gen. John Pershing to advance on either side of the Argonne forest.

The goal was to cut off the railroad from Strasbourg, France, north to Bruges, Belgium, and thus sever a vital route used by the Germans to move troops and supplies. The terrain was ideal for the defending Germans and a nightmare for attackers. Hills, bluffs, steep ravines, and forests were part of a 12-mile-deep German defensive network. German guns commanded the heavily fortified heights.

The absence of roads made moving artillery and supplies especially arduous. Despite suffering heavy losses, by mid October the Americans had cleared the Argonne forest. By early November they had advanced even farther, cutting off a vital railroad between Metz and Mézières.

The success of British, French, and Belgian troops along the Hindenburg Line, a well-fortified string of trenches reaching across northern France and Belgium, contributed to a decisive setback for Germany. Meanwhile, Germany's allies — Austria–Hungary, Turkey, and Bulgaria — had suffered disastrous defeats in Italy, the Balkans, and the Middle East.

The Meuse–Argonne campaign helped to bring about Germany's surrender, which became official with the signing of an armistice on November 11, 1918. Of the 1.2 million Americans who participated in this campaign, 26,000 were killed and 96,000 wounded, approximately 10 percent of the total. ⚡

D *1918*
uring World War I, sauerkraut became "liberty cabbage," as German foods were renamed or disappeared from grocery shelves.

While U.S. soldiers were battling the Germans in Europe, many other Americans did what they considered their patriotic duty at home. Besides observing the government's food rationing — meatless Tuesdays, for example — Americans showed their hostility toward the enemy by relabeling or avoiding German foods. Sauerkraut became known as liberty cabbage, German toast turned into French toast, and pretzels, a traditional German food, vanished from lunch counters.

Among the other forms of anti-German sentiment that surfaced during the war were boycotts of German operas and bans on teaching German in schools. ⚡

Patriotic citizens ate sparingly during World War I.

BOOM, BUST, WAR, AND VICTORY

(1919 TO 1945)

When World War I ended, so did an era of American idealism and social reform. Democratic President Woodrow Wilson lost the political support he needed to promote peace abroad and reforms at home. As a result of the November 1918 midterm elections, which produced Republican majorities in both houses of Congress, many of Wilson's programs faced stiff resistance.

The Senate refused to allow the United States to join the League of Nations—the "government of governments" that Wilson hoped would resolve international disputes. The senators had powerful reasons for rejecting the multinational league: not only would membership place limits on U.S. sovereignty, but the very idea of entering a foreign alliance ran counter to a growing isolationist mood among American voters. The European allies united to form the league on their own, but the absence of the United States seriously weakened its effectiveness.

Another major disappointment for Wilson was the World War I peace treaty. He had argued for a non-punitive peace settlement, but the other victors were determined to weaken Germany forever. They imposed unilateral disarmament and demanded exorbitant reparation payments. For the next 15 years, a humiliated Germany struggled to free itself from economic chaos; ultimately, the entire world paid the price.

A new distraction, the movie palace, captured the nation.

IN DOMESTIC POLITICS the mood of the nation shifted

dramatically. Intense nationalism, intolerance, and materialism characterized the new decade. The Bolshevik seizure of power in Russia touched off a wave of revolution in Europe and a Red Scare at home. In 1920 Attorney General A. Mitchell Palmer conducted raids across the nation, jailing thousands in the name of quelling the "red menace." Recent immigrants, trade unionists, radicals, and dissenters of all kinds became targets of arrest, deportation, even mob attack.

Another sign of the times was the revival of the Ku Klux Klan in the South and Midwest, where its members won some local elections. In addition to blacks, the KKK aimed its politics of hate against Catholics, Jews, and foreigners.

Opponents of modernist thinking sought to stifle ideas that offended traditional sensibilities. Christian fundamentalists launched an attack on science. In a famous 1925 trial, the state of Tennessee successfully prosecuted John T. Scopes for teaching Darwin's theory of evolution

Republicans Harding and Coolidge set the mood.

in a public school. Government authorities attacked many avant-garde literary works as immoral. They went so far as to seize some works by foreign writers — for example, James Joyce's *Ulysses* — at the border to keep them from reaching a U.S. audience.

Ironically, an era of prejudice and repression gave rise to such contradictory trends as increased social freedom and artistic experimentation. People eventually called the decade the "Roaring Twenties" and the "Jazz Age" in tribute to the exuberant spirit that prevailed. Americans drove around in their new cars, listened to radio broadcasts, flocked to lavish movie palaces, and tried out each "shocking" new clothing style or dance fad that came along. Women married later and had fewer children. The "flapper" look — bobbed hair and short skirts — reflected their new, if still limited, freedom.

Musicians such as Louis Armstrong, Duke Ellington, George Gershwin, and Benny Goodman created a legacy for generations of listeners. Meanwhile, writers like Theodore Dreiser, F. Scott Fitzgerald, Ernest Hemingway, Sinclair Lewis, and Eugene O'Neill were opening new pathways in literature and drama.

Nothing summed up the contradictions of the time better than Prohibition. The 18th Amendment to the Constitution, ratified in 1919, prohibited the sale and transport of alcoholic beverages. The measure drew support from many quarters, including nativists suspicious of recent immigrants and Protestants hostile to Catholics. Joining these conservative groups were progressives and feminists, who believed that alcohol caused poverty and domestic violence.

Mah-jongg tiles: the game was hugely popular.

PROHIBITION PRODUCED the opposite of what was

intended. A huge illicit business sector sprang up to smuggle liquor into the United States and to produce and sell it clandestinely. Many police officers, politicians, and judges winked at the lawbreakers — and patronized their businesses. Crime flourished. Finally, in 1933, tired of waging a losing battle against corruption and lawlessness, the states approved the 21st Amendment, repealing Prohibition.

While citizens wrestled with a paradoxical world — bursts of repression on the one hand and of hedonism on the other hand — the Republican party kept a firm grip on national politics. GOP senator Warren G. Harding easily won the 1920 presidential election. His administration defined government ideology and general policy for the decade. Under Harding and then presidents Calvin Coolidge and Herbert Hoover, the federal government retreated from the progressive ideals of the prewar era and made a sharp right turn in the direction of the nation's big-money interests. "The chief business of the American people is business," declared Coolidge in 1925. At the same time, Washington carefully avoided imposing controls over the operations of private enterprise.

The Republicans raised tariffs, lowered taxes for corporations and the wealthy, and encouraged monopolies. Meanwhile the courts helped employers sabotage the labor movement. The judiciary restricted picketing, used court injunctions against strikers, and invalidated child-labor laws and minimum wages.

THE REPUBLICANS PROMISED prosperity, and, in a lop-

sided fashion, they delivered. Technical advances made mass production more sophisticated, brought cheap electric power to factories, and boosted productivity and profits. "Scientific management" brought modern methods of accounting, budgeting, and marketing to industry. A booming auto industry spurred production and employment in basic industries like steel, glass, copper, rubber, and oil. The 1920's introduced mass consumption to the United States. Americans bought electrical appliances — toasters, refrigerators, irons, and vacuum cleaners — to ease the domestic workload, and they used their automobiles to bring within reach a new range of leisure activities.

Unemployment was a modest 5 percent to 7 percent in the 1920's, inflation was almost nil, and per capita income shot up by a third. For anyone who cared to see, however, structural problems lurked beneath this facade of prosperity. As farm prices tumbled from wartime highs, farmers' real purchasing power fell by one-fourth. Wages of unskilled laborers rose barely at all. Workers' average annual income was only $1,500, tottering between subsistence and poverty. Meanwhile, industrial output rose 60 percent; the productivity of agricultural workers, 15 percent. Americans' income lagged far behind their productivity. They simply could not buy all the goods they produced.

A 1920's refrigerator carried its cooling coils on the top.

African Americans and Native Americans were the least likely to enjoy the prosperity of the period. Confined to reservations too small for hunting and with soil too poor for farming, Native Americans lived in abject misery. The government did not even recognize them as full citizens until 1924.

Meanwhile, four out of five blacks lived in the segregated South, where poverty prevailed. Many hoped that service by thousands of black men in World War I would gain

African Americans the full civil rights due every American citizen. But, despite individual successes, the doors of opportunity remained closed.

The distance between the bottom of the social ladder and the top looked greater than ever when the entire edifice suddenly collapsed. Anxious about inflated values on the stock market, investors set off a selling panic in October 1929. One-third of the value of stocks listed on the New York Stock Exchange vanished into thin air. The crash laid bare the weakness beneath the facade of prosperity. Many major industries — textiles, coal, railroads — had already fallen on hard times. The Great Depression had begun.

President Hoover mounted an unprecedented effort to stimulate the economy with government expenditures on public building and agricultural price supports. But these innovations proved inadequate for what was increasingly seen as a national catastrophe. He stubbornly opposed direct federal aid to indigent families, and insisted the economy would right itself. Worse, in June 1930 Hoover signed the highest tariff bill in history, the Hawley-Smoot Tariff Act, which strangled commerce further, as nations around the world raised trade barriers in retaliation.

THE ECONOMY ground to a near halt. In the next three years, 9,000 banks failed. The gross national product shrank from $104 billion to $56 billion. Farm prices dropped another 50 percent. Many Americans could not pay their rents or mortgages; they lost their homes and farms. Desperate for food and shelter, they waited in bread lines, begged in the streets, and slept inside makeshift shacks clustered in what became known as "Hoovervilles." Some rioted; others died of disease brought on by malnutrition.

By the 1932 presidential election, one of every four workers was jobless. The relatively modest sums that Hoover had allocated to stimulate job creation did little good, and he persisted in his belief that direct aid to individuals would destroy their initiative. As condi-

Hollywood chic: sexy Jean Harlow helped take America's mind off the Depression.

tions worsened, he became the object of widespread derision and contempt. Americans began to wonder whether the Democratic contender, Franklin Delano Roosevelt (FDR), might possibly save the nation.

Roosevelt had revived his political career in 1928, despite having been crippled by polio seven years earlier. As governor of New York, he pushed through such reforms as unemployment insurance, old-age pensions, and child-labor laws. As a candidate for president, FDR communicated confidence and hope. "I pledge you, I pledge myself, to a new deal for the American people," he declared in ringing tones, and he won by a landslide.

ROOSEVELT HOPED to accomplish four tasks: provide immediate relief to individuals, revive the economy, correct the structural flaws that had caused the Depression, and provide for the citizens' future security. He took a pragmatic approach to ending the Depression: try something, and if it doesn't work, try something else. Unlike the Republicans, he believed that government should play a major role in the economy. The day after his inauguration, Roosevelt began inundating Congress with proposals. During his first three months in office — the famous Hundred Days — he signed more than a dozen major pieces of legislation. Several programs provided direct aid to workers and farmers. Projects like the Public Works Administration (PWA) and the Civilian Conservation Corps (CCC) created jobs and wages for millions of people, setting them to work planting trees and building everything from bridges and dams to hospitals and schools. Other government agencies provided credit and crop insurance to farmers.

Social welfare programs gave money to laid-off workers and pensions to the elderly — thus combining humanitarian principles with practical purposes. In distributing funds to the needy, such programs softened future economic downswings by allowing the unemployed to continue buying goods and services.

Wartime gas shortages closed many filling stations.

Other New Deal innovations transformed the conditions of private enterprise. Banking regulations outlawed the irresponsible practices that had helped precipitate the Depression. The Securities and Exchange Commission regulated investments and the stock market. New legislation set a nationwide minimum wage, outlawed child labor in factories, and guaranteed workers the right to join labor unions.

FDR's efforts to end the Depression made him immensely popular with most Americans. First lady Eleanor Roosevelt's support for the rights of blacks and labor won her the respect and gratitude of millions. Voters in the 1936 election gave FDR his second landslide victory. At the same time, the president won the enmity of powerful opponents: fiscal conservatives, employers hostile to labor reform,

Women made up one-third of the workforce during World War II.

Northern Republicans, and Southern Democrats opposed to racial reforms. A conservative Supreme Court declared several New Deal programs unconstitutional, including much of the National Recovery Act (NRA), which had allowed sweeping government intrusion into private businesses.

The New Deal did not end the Great Depression, but it restarted the economic engines and provided relief to a desperate nation. It also preserved the American commitment to democracy by showing that a democratic government could weather a seemingly terminal economic crisis.

ACROSS THE OCEAN it was a different story. Swamped by

their own economic problems, Germany, Italy, Spain, and Japan sought relief in the siren call of charismatic dictators, who promised national renewal through armed military aggression. Germany under Adolf Hitler set out to conquer Europe, with a bit of help from Italy's Benito Mussolini. In Asia, the warlords of imperial Japan laid claim to a so-called Co-Prosperity Sphere that included most of the Far East.

War once again engulfed much of the world.

Roosevelt, understanding that freedom everywhere was at risk, set about coaxing a reluctant Congress to begin rearming America. Hitler overpowered Austria in

a bloodless coup and sent his armies rolling into Eastern Europe. Denmark and Norway fell, then Holland, Belgium, Luxembourg, and France. FDR cajoled and maneuvered to get aid to Britain. When Americans voted in 1940 to give him an unprecedented third term, they implicitly acknowledged that he would lead them into war.

Just 13 months later, on December 7, 1941, Japanese bombers destroyed the U.S. naval base at Pearl Harbor, Hawaii, plunging the nation into war. By then Germany controlled all continental Europe, and Japan occupied much of Asia. Then at the Battle of Midway in June 1942, the United States turned the tide of battle in the Pacific. American forces advanced toward Japan, island by island, in two years of bloody fighting. Meanwhile, American and British troops landed at Normandy, surprising Hitler and taking his army by storm. They freed Paris on August 25 and moved on into Germany.

The United States and its allies finally forced Germany and Japan to surrender in the summer of 1945. The war had united all America in "the good fight" to rescue the free world, bringing millions of women into the labor force to take over jobs vacated by men who had gone to battle. It also ended the Depression — but at a horrific price. More than 50 million people lost their lives: 17 million troops, including 405,399 Americans; 20 million Soviet civilians and 10 million Chinese; and 6 million Jews slaughtered in Nazi death camps. Thousands of Japanese died in an instant when atomic bombs hit Hiroshima and Nagasaki.

Although Roosevelt won an unprecedented fourth term in 1944, he did not live to see the war's end. He died of a

August 6, 1945: the world's first nuclear weapon demolished Hiroshima.

cerebral hemorrhage on April 12, 1945. Americans mourned the man who had led the country through its worst crises since the Civil War. Vice President Harry S Truman took the oath of office determined to continue FDR's work. The New Deal had laid the foundation for years of widespread prosperity. But with the use of the atomic bomb, the war had opened the gate to a new kind of conflict.

F*1920*

Fear of Communist propagandists and revolutionaries prompted U.S. Attorney General A. Mitchell Palmer to authorize the invasion of many homes and the arrest of thousands.

The Russian Revolution of 1917 had struck fear in the hearts of many Americans, who worried that it would inspire political radicals in the United States. In the spring of 1919, fear gave way to terror when radicals set off a series of explosions throughout the country. A bomb said to be "big enough to blow out the entire side of the County-City Building" was addressed to the mayor of Seattle, who had been speaking out against the so-called Red Menace.

Soon afterward, the Post Office intercepted some 30 packages containing bombs addressed to such wealthy businessmen as John D. Rockefeller and J. P. Morgan. In June 1919 eight bombs exploded almost simultaneously in different parts of the country. One of them blew off the front of Attorney General A. Mitchell Palmer's house.

Palmer was convinced that the bombings were part of a conspiracy fomented by hordes of radicals. Hoping to advance his political career by destroying this Red Menace, he authorized the search of both private houses and labor headquarters on January 1, 1920.

Sweeping through radical groups in 33 cities, the raiders arrested several thousand people. Many of them were Russians, but few were Communists. In Detroit alone, 300 were arrested on false charges and held for a week. Some 500 foreigners were deported; most of the other detainees were soon released.

Although the raids were aimed at discovering a secret arms cache, only three pistols were confiscated, and no dynamite was found. Palmer suffered another setback when he warned that a group planning to overthrow the U.S. government would create havoc on May 1, 1930. The day came and went uneventfully.

Massachusetts residents arrested in a Palmer raid forlornly make their way to an emigration station in Boston.

A cartoon entitled "The End of the Climb" heralds the adoption of the 19th Amendment, which gave women the vote.

B*1920*

Because of a Tennessee legislator's devotion to his mother, American women won the right to vote.

Tennessee became the crucial 36th state to ratify the 19th Amendment to the Constitution, which gave women suffrage. Harry Thomas Burn, a 24-year-old state representative who had originally rejected the measure, cast the swing vote on August 18, 1920. He had just gotten a letter from his mother.

"Don't forget to be a good boy," wrote Febb Ensminger Burn. "Vote for suffrage." Harry Burn did just that, and when he was attacked by antisuffragists, Tennessee's youngest lawmaker dutifully replied: "I know that a mother's advice is always safest for her boy to follow."

If Tennessee had not approved the amendment, women might have had a long wait for the franchise, since lawmakers in the states that had not yet voted were firmly against the amendment. (In 1984, at the insistence of female state legislators, Mississippi voted for ratification, becoming the last state to do so.)

A pivotal event in the struggle for woman suffrage had been the Seneca Falls, New York, convention that Elizabeth Cady Stanton and Lucretia Mott organized in 1848. The delegates passed a resolution that "it is the duty of women of this country to secure to themselves their sacred right of the elective franchise."

Those who opposed giving women the vote feared that empowering women would upset the political status quo. Such fears proved groundless, at least at the outset. Only 26 percent of the 26 million eligible women (21 years of age or older) went to the polls to choose between Warren G. Harding and James M. Cox in the 1920 presidential election.

1920

Even the sharpest business-men fell for the get-rich-quick scheme that swindler Charles Ponzi masterminded.

Charles Ponzi, the man whose name is synonymous with financial scams, opened the Old Colony Foreign Exchange Company of Boston in 1919. He sold International Postal Union money orders to investors at depressed foreign currency rates, promising a 50 per-cent profit on their money within 90 days. The profit would come from favorable currency exchange rates, he said.

At first business was slow, but as news circulated of the high returns being paid, millions of dollars came pouring in. Sud-

Ponzi's smile masked a swindler's heart.

denly Ponzi was a rich man.

Ponzi flaunted his newfound wealth, buying a mansion and expensive clothes and riding around in a chauffeur-driven limousine. Boston business-men admired his Midas touch, and the Italian–American community revered him as a genius.

What no one real-ized was that Ponzi was using the money acquired from new investors to honor pay-ments on old deposits, at the same time keep-ing a generous sum for himself. As long as new money kept arriving, he could pay Paul with Peter's dollars.

Then local reporters blew the whistle. They learned that less than $60,000 in international money orders had been printed in the United States in the pre-vious year, but that in the same time Ponzi had sold $20 million worth of orders. Federal and state investigators found that Old Colony had no assets what-ever and that its liabilities exceeded $2 million.

Old Colony was shut down in August 1920, and Ponzi was tried and convicted of mail fraud. He went to prison, where he served four years. Released on appeal, he headed to Florida, where he got involved in shady real estate deals. When he lost his appeal, Ponzi served nine more years in prison, after which he was deported to his native Italy.

1920

Babe Ruth brought the "big bang" to baseball and gave the national pastime its first bona fide celebrity.

The Boston Red Sox had never had it so good. They had won three out of four World Series championships between 1915 and 1918. True, 1919 had been a disappoint-ment, but a rebound seemed assured.

For one thing, George Herman (Babe) Ruth, the team's star pitcher, had been moved to the outfield, and he had responded by swatting an unheard-of 29 home runs. Meanwhile, H. Harrison Frazee, a showman whose first love was Broadway, had bought the Red Sox. Eager to raise money for the theater, Frazee let it be known that anyone willing to pay his price could have any one of his players.

In 1919 Col. Jacob Ruppert, owner of the New York Yankees, bought Babe Ruth for $125,000. It is difficult to overstate the effect that Ruth's 1920 season had on the game. In that one year he smacked 54 homers — more than the total hit by the

entire roster of any other team in the American League. He batted .376, and hit for a slugging average of .847 (a number calculated by dividing the total bases he reached by the number of times at bat). That slugging record has never been equaled or even approached.

People were flocking to see the Babe: base-ball had never known such a personality. The Yankees became the first team to attract a million fans in a season, and they soon outgrew the Polo Grounds, their home field. Its replacement was Yankee Stadium, the House that Ruth Built, which opened in the Bronx on April 18, 1923.

Ruth takes a swing in batting practice.

Before long Ruth's larger-than-life exploits off the field also began to catch the public eye. His breaking of training rules — especially drinking — became com-mon knowledge. His appetite was legendary. After one hot-dog-eating binge in 1925, he needed abdominal surgery. The Yankees slipped to seventh place in the American League during the Babe's weeks of recuperation.

Ruth retired from the Yankees in 1934, still holding both pitching and batting records. Two years later he was one of the first play-ers elected to the Baseball Hall of Fame.

1921

When the first Miss America pageant was held, the modestly revealing swimsuit contest provoked gasps from spectators along Atlantic City's Boardwalk.

Each summer the seaside resort town of Atlantic City, New Jersey, was crowded with visitors, but as soon as Labor Day had passed, the tourists vanished. In 1921 local businessmen, eager to entice vacationers to extend their stays, came up with a novel solution: a pageant that would include a "bathers' revue." A reporter for the *Atlantic City Press,* who was publicizing the event, suggested the title Miss America.

The pageant organizers set themselves the task of choosing "the most beautiful bathing girl in America." Newspaper editors loved the idea, and tabloids from nearby cities began sponsoring competitions. On the second weekend in September, eight young women who had already won earlier beauty contests paraded along the beach

The first Miss America gets the key to Atlantic City.

between the Grand Pier and the Steel Pier.

The authorities relaxed the rules governing proper beach attire, which the lifeguards normally enforced. Contestants strolled on

the hot sand wearing skirted bathing suits, rolled-down stockings, and stylish headbands. Although most onlookers were wearing bathing suits too, many watched in amazement. Some gasped, some applauded.

On September 7, 1921, Margaret Gorman, a petite 16-year-old student from Washington, D.C., was crowned the first Miss America. Wearing a Statue of Liberty tiara and an American flag robe, the blonde, blue-eyed victor with a dazzling smile — and measurements of 30-25-32 — received her prize: a gilt mermaid figurine. She then went quietly home to finish high school.

But the pageant had generated so much welcome publicity that organizers quickly decided to make the next one more elaborate. The following year contestants paraded along the Boardwalk on rolling wicker chairs, led by King Neptune, who wore a seaweed robe and was carried by "sea monsters" on a giant seashell.

The Unknown Soldier is interred at Arlington Cemetery in 1921.

1921

The first unknown soldier was buried in Arlington National Cemetery with greater honors than any American president.

At 8:30 A.M. on November 11, 1921 — Armistice Day — a horse-drawn caisson carried the body of an unidentified soldier from the Capitol rotunda to a grave at the plaza of Memorial Amphitheater at Arlington National Cemetery in Virginia. The unknown doughboy (slang for soldier in World War I) had died in combat in France.

His burial was meant as a symbolic tribute to the 53,000 other doughboys who lost their lives in World War I, many of whom were buried where they fell. Thousands of mourners, including dignitaries from foreign countries, clustered around the gravesite.

After delivering a speech that moved some listeners to

tears, President Warren G. Harding stepped forward with the Medal of Honor in one hand and the Distinguished Service Cross in the other. He pinned the medals on the flag-draped coffin. The casket was then lowered into the ground and sprinkled with a two-inch layer of French soil.

Today the heavily visited site is marked by a white marble sarcophagus with the inscription: "Here rests in honored glory an American soldier known but to God." Alongside him lie unknown warriors from World War II and the Korean War. The 3rd Infantry Regiment, one of America's elite military units, stands guard.

Day and night, a sentinel paces back and forth, marching 21 steps each time. His routine symbolizes a 21-gun salute, the highest military honor.

E 1922
Emily Post's book on etiquette broke new ground by insisting on a commonsense approach to good manners.

Having achieved success as a fiction writer, Emily Post was surprised when an editor suggested that she write a book on etiquette. Preoccupation with manners seemed to her pretentious or just silly. But after reading the nonsense in some of the books on the subject — "to eat an olive correctly is proof of culture," one read — Post decided to take a stab at the topic.

Her 692-page *Etiquette* was published in the summer of 1922 and quickly became a bestseller. When she learned that hordes of customers were asking bookstore clerks for "Emily Post," she mused, "I might be a cosmetic or a ship or a fancy dessert." Librarians complained that her book was frequently pilfered: only the Bible was stolen more often. Post went on to host a radio show and to write a syndicated newspaper column. She received 250,000 letters annually seeking advice on matters ranging from wedding protocol to handling an obstinate child.

Post believed that what was socially proper was simple and straightforward behavior. "Nothing is less important than which fork you use," she declared. "Etiquette is the science of living. It embraces everything. It is honor. It is ethics."

Although the first edition of *Etiquette* focused on the rich, updates addressed the concerns of the average American as well. The country was in the midst of a postwar boom, and as more Americans were becoming wealthy enough to achieve social mobility, they needed to know how to behave.

But the ways of middle-class life were largely unfamiliar to Post, who came

Post: a paragon of proper decorum.

from a well-to-do, socially prominent family. Curious to find out how a hostess could give a dinner party without a maid, a butler, and a cook, the resourceful author found out by trying it herself.

Post never hesitated to do her own research or to ask questions. To answer a reader's query about the correct way to word an invitation, she decided to inquire at Tiffany's, a New York store with an elite clientele. The clerk told her that he would have to check the answer in a book he kept under the counter. It was a copy of *Etiquette*.

President and Mrs. Coolidge (second and third from left) attend the national tree-lighting ceremony.

C 1923
Calvin Coolidge was the first president to light a national Christmas tree on the grounds of the White House.

Like many Americans, U.S. presidents had typically celebrated Christmas Eve by lighting a decorated tree in the privacy of their homes. But on December 24, 1923, Calvin Coolidge took the custom a step further. He invited the public to a tree-lighting ceremony on the White House grounds.

Some 6,000 spectators gathered to watch Coolidge press a button that lit up a gigantic Vermont spruce. Then everyone joined the president and his wife for Christmas carols. The tree glimmered on, its twinkling lights augmented by a searchlight beamed from the Washington Monument. A national tradition was born, and every president has kept it up.

Once it was almost broken. The year was 1941, and the nation had just been swept into World War II. A nightly blackout was in effect, and the Secret Service warned President Franklin D. Roosevelt that a lit tree could pose a security risk. Security aides were especially concerned because the White House had an important visitor — British prime minister Winston Churchill.

Roosevelt insisted. As a precaution, the tree was set up inside the protective fence surrounding the South Lawn and the guest list was kept small. Roosevelt pushed a button, the lights blinked on — and the first Christmas Eve of World War II was ushered in with a proud blaze of seasonal glory.

1924

Composer George Gershwin rushed to write his masterpiece, *Rhapsody in Blue,* so that he could enter a prestigious contest.

One day in early January 1924, composer George Gershwin and his brother, Ira, were patronizing their favorite pool hall in Manhattan when Ira came upon a newspaper article announcing that George would soon present a new jazz concerto. This came as a complete surprise to George.

It seemed that Paul Whiteman, a popular bandleader, was organizing a concert called An Experiment in Modern Music, and George was slated to be one of the contributors. A panel of distinguished musicians, including Sergei Rachmaninoff, the famed composer, conductor, and pianist, and violinist Jascha Heifetz, was to judge the entries, then formulate a definition of American music.

At the age of 25, George had already written his first hit song, "Swanee." Many other Gershwin tunes had been performed in Broadway musicals, including "Somebody Loves Me" and "Do It Again." Being measured against some of the nation's most eminent composers was a daunting challenge, however. With less than six weeks remaining until the concert, he began creating the work that would become *Rhapsody in Blue.*

Gershwin, who had said that he could hear music "in the heart of noise," found his inspiration in the sound of a train's wheels clicking along the track as he rode to Boston. "I heard it as a musical kaleidoscope of America, of our vast melting pot, of our national pep, of our blues, our metropolitan madness," he later said.

On February 12, 1924, despite the cold, snowy weather, Aeolian Hall in New York was packed to the rafters. Concertgoers listened to 21 other musical compositions before a clarinetist sounded the first notes of *Rhapsody.* Restless members of the audience, who had begun leaving the hall, quickly returned to their seats. Gershwin's distinctive, jazz-inspired rhythms and unique harmonies were riveting.

Gershwin vied against such music-world luminaries as Victor Herbert — and won the contest.

Although some critics carped, most listeners were wildly enthusiastic. "The audience was stirred," said a reviewer for *The New York Times,* "and many a hardened concertgoer was excited with the sensation of a new talent finding its voice." Since that day, perhaps no other piece in the 20th-century concert repertory has been played as often as *Rhapsody in Blue.*

Weissmuller parlayed his success as an Olympic swimmer into a second career as a silver-screen Tarzan.

1924

Johnny Weissmuller, who won three gold medals for the United States at the 1924 Paris Olympics, may have been ineligible to compete.

Swimming champion Johnny Weissmuller was a man of distinctly mysterious origins. His parents had immigrated to the United States from Europe, and his father claimed that his oldest son had been born in Chicago. Later, Johnny called Windber, Pennsylvania, his hometown. In truth, according to the magazine *Sports Illustrated,* Weissmuller was born in the hamlet of Freidorf, in what is now Romania.

If the magazine were correct, Weissmuller — who had never been naturalized — would have been ineligible to compete for the United States in the Olympics. To remedy this problem, the baptismal certificate of the swimmer's American-born younger brother, Peter, was allegedly altered to make it appear to be a record of Johnny's own birth.

After winning three gold medals in swimming during the 1924 Paris Olympics at the age of 20, Weissmuller won two more at the 1928 games in Amsterdam. During nine years of competitive swimming, he won 52 national championships, set 67 world records, and captured every freestyle record from 100 yards to the half mile.

When his athletic career ended, the handsome, well-built Weissmuller shifted easily into a new role — Hollywood's most famous Tarzan. He was the fourth actor to play the part, and the first to speak on screen. (The first three Tarzans appeared in silent films.) Twenty-year-old Maureen O'Sullivan played opposite him as Jane in *Tarzan the Ape Man.*

For his film debut in 1932, the movie studio billed the scantily clad swimmer as the "only man in Hollywood who's natural in the flesh and who can act without clothes." Weissmuller had no illusions about the quality of his acting, however. The key to his success, he said, was his grunt.

C *1924*

artoonist Harold Gray's idea for a new comic strip featuring a male street urchin named Little Orphan Otto got sidetracked, and Otto was reborn as Annie.

When Joseph Patterson became publisher of the New York *Daily News*, he decided he needed a brand-new comic strip for his fledgling newspaper. Chicago cartoonist Harold Gray came up with the idea

Comic-strip immortals: Sandy and Annie.

of a comic strip centered around a parentless boy named Otto, but Patterson had other ideas and transformed Otto into Annie.

Gray discovered the model for the curly-haired waif on a Chicago street. "I talked to this little kid and liked her right away," Gray recalled. "Her name was Annie."

Patterson gave Gray strict guidelines for "Little Orphan Annie," which debuted on August 5, 1924. "Make it for

grownup people, not for kids," the publisher demanded. "Kids don't buy papers. Their parents do." The comic-strip moppet developed into a feisty youngster with a "heart of gold and a fast left," as Gray put it.

Among Annie's legions of devoted fans was auto magnate Henry Ford. When her faithful canine companion, Sandy, got lost, Ford wired the newspaper: "Please do all you can to help Annie find Sandy. We are all interested." For years "Little Orphan Annie" remained one of the nation's most popular comic strips, spawning a radio serial, two movies, and a Broadway musical.

H *1924*

. L. Mencken's *American Mercury* ridiculed every sacred cow of the day — and became the nation's most influential magazine.

Baltimore-born writer and editor Henry Louis Mencken had already earned his journalistic credentials as a reporter for two Baltimore newspapers and as the literary editor of the magazine *Smart Set.* Then in 1924 he co-founded the *American Mercury.* He called his new mission "an agreeable duty to track down some of the worst nonsense prevailing and do execution upon it."

In the *Mercury,* Mencken and George Jean Nathan, his co-editor, railed against all manner of people, places, and concepts that offended them: religion, capitalism, the Ku Klux Klan, censorship, Prohibition, even Southerners. Mencken saved his harshest comments for politicians, whom he considered "plainly and depressingly inferior, both in common sense and in common decency," to their constituents. He detested all modern presidents, but Calvin Coolidge may well have topped his list. Silent Cal's sole talent, Mencken claimed, was that he "slept more than any other President, whether by day or by night."

Although he was a gifted satirist and commentator, Mencken sometimes went beyond the boundaries of good taste, veering into intolerance, cruelty, and personal vendettas. He liked to make people laugh, but he had a pessimistic view of the human race. He once described mankind as perhaps "a local disease of the cosmos — a kind of pestiferous eczema or urethritis."

The *American Mercury,* which attracted some of the nation's finest fiction writers and satirists, became the most influential magazine of its time. Mencken also made a name for himself with his groundbreaking three-volume study, *The American Language* (1919–48), which covered such topics as the differences between English usage in the United States and Great Britain. In 1927 political writer Walter Lippmann called him "the most powerful personal influence on this whole generation of educated people." In 1955, the year before he died, Mencken was immortalized as the irascible E. K. Hornbeck, a character in the play *Inherit the Wind.*

A portrait painter captures Mencken in an oddly mellow mood.

H. L. Mencken: King of the Curmudgeons

Baltimore's most famous literary son, H. L. Mencken gained fame and notoriety with his biting criticism of religion, politics, and his fellow man. Here are a few of his observations:

- No one ever went broke underestimating the intelligence of the American People.
- Conscience is the inner voice that warns us somebody might be looking
- The New Deal began, like the Salvation Army, by promising to save humanity. It ended, again like the Salvation Army, by running flophouses and disturbing the peace.
- The older I grow, the more I distrust the familiar doctrine that age brings wisdom.

- Puritanism. The haunting fear that someone, somewhere, may be happy.
- Say what you will about the Ten Commandments, you must always come back to the pleasant fact that there are only ten of them.
- The typical lawmaker of today is a man wholly devoid of principle— a mere counter in a grotesque and knavish game. If the right pressure could be applied to him he would be cheerfully in favor of polygamy, astrology, or cannibalism.

1925
The debut of air conditioning in a Broadway movie theater attracted hordes of summertime viewers who had previously shunned the stifling film houses.

The real star at the Rivoli Theater on Memorial Day, 1925, was not an actor in the silent film *Old Home Week* or the accompanying vaudeville acts. It was an air conditioner, the first to be installed in a New York City movie house. Previously, some theaters had shut down during the summer because the heat was so intolerable that few people attended the shows.

Engineer Willis Carrier had designed this great leap forward in creature comfort — a centrifugal refrigeration machine — to keep cinema patrons cool. Carrier, who had worked all night on May 29, 1925, supervising the installation of his 133-ton-capacity machine at the Rivoli, waited anxiously for the reaction of movie magnate Adolph Zukor, who was in the audience. Exiting the theater, Zukor glanced over at Carrier and predicted, "Yes, the people are going to

The Rivoli Theater on Broadway was the first to offer patrons a cool interior.

like it." He was right. Within five years, 300 movie theaters had air conditioners.

Carrier had developed his cooling system as a young engineering school graduate in 1902. At first its use was limited to controlling heat and humidity in textile and candy factories, printing and meat-packing plants, and other establishments that required tight temperature controls.

It took a while before the inventor devised a system that could cool people. But in 1924, to help keep shoppers at big-city department stores from fainting in summertime heat, Carrier developed central air conditioners for stores. He installed the first ones at J. L. Hudson in Detroit — much to the delight of customers, who flocked to Hudson's bargain-basement summer sales. In 1928 and 1929 air conditioning was installed in the U.S. Capitol. After World War II the availability of air conditioners in homes and office buildings contributed to a massive population shift as residents left the Northeast and Midwest for the Sun Belt.

1925
At the height of the Florida land-speculation frenzy, an issue of the Miami *Daily News* ran 504 pages of real estate advertisements — a record for a single newspaper.

In 1910 Miami was a sleepy hamlet of 5,471 people. Some 15 years later the population had mushroomed to 75,000 as get-rich-quick dreamers poured into the state. At the height of the boom, real estate prices seemed to go up by the minute.

One investor happily recounted that his property was worth "$30,000 at nine o'clock this morning. But at ten o'clock, the lot next to mine sold for $40,000, so I suppose it ought to bring about $50,000, as it is now ten minutes past twelve." In the summer of 1925, the Miami *Daily News* contained a record-setting 504 pages of real estate advertisements.

The knowledge that some of the land was undrained swamp in subdivisions that existed only on paper did not quench the speculators' thirst. Promoters promised that the boom would last forever — or until the sun stopped shining and the Gulf Stream "ceases to flow," as one Florida real estate board officer put it. But by 1926 the cost of land had become so inflated that investors could no longer resell their property at a profit. Panic followed as speculators tried to unload their real estate at any price.

Seeking their fortunes in Miami real estate, would-be investors head out to inspect potential home sites during the 1920's Florida land boom.

To make matters worse, on September 18, 1926, a hurricane with winds of more than 125 miles an hour tore along the Florida coast, destroying what remained of the land boom. Miami Beach was virtually under water, and 13,000 homes between Miami and Fort Lauderdale were damaged or destroyed. A visitor to Florida observed in 1928: "Whole sections of outlying subdivisions are composed of unoccupied houses, past which one speeds on broad thoroughfares as if traversing a city in the grip of death."

1925
The Grand Ole Opry opened with an 80-year-old fiddler and went on to become the longest-running radio show in history.

On Saturday night, November 28, 1925, Uncle Jimmy Thompson sat in front of a carbon microphone in WSM's tiny Nashville studio and played straight through the station's first hour-long *WSM Barn Dance*.

When Thompson laid down his fiddle, the program's host, George D. Hay, asked if he was tired. "Why, shucks," said the octogenarian, producing a blue ribbon that he had recently won at an eight-day-long fiddling contest, "a man don't get warmed up in an hour."

George Hay launched **The Grand Ole Opry,** *a radio hit.*

Little did anyone know that this humble event heralded the beginning of a musical empire. In 1926 Hay renamed his show *The Grand Ole Opry,* after the grand opera that aired before his *Barn Dance.* Recognizing that his audience liked the program's down-home atmosphere, Hay's marketing campaign promised "the unique entertainment that only Tennessee mountaineers can afford."

Despite the fact that some of the *Opry*'s performers were city dwellers, Hay stuck them in cornfields or dressed them in overalls for publicity photos. He fashioned countrified names for his acts, like the Possum Hunters and the Gully Jumpers.

In 1939 *The Grand Ole Opry* gained a slot on the NBC radio network, becoming a Saturday night institution for millions of listeners. By the 1950's, the show had attracted a nationwide audience. It brought country music to the cities of America and turned Nashville into a worldwide hub of the country-music industry.

Eventually, overalls gave way to less rustic attire on the stage of the *Opry*. In 1974 President Richard Nixon dedicated a new Opry house at a theme park called Opryland, which also includes water rides, shops, and restaurants. Despite the changes in their surroundings, performers still chatted with the audience as if they were family members, telling old jokes and announcing the birth of babies onstage. "*The Grand Ole Opry,*" George Hay had once said, "is as simple as sunshine."

1925
Clara Bow, the movies' It Girl, transformed herself from a poor Brooklyn teenager into "the hottest jazz baby in films."

Clara Bow was supporting her impoverished family — her handyman father and her mentally ill mother — by working as a Brooklyn doctor's receptionist when her life suddenly changed. As a tomboy whose shabby clothes, she recalled, made her the "worst-looking kid on the street," 16-year-old Clara nevertheless won a beauty contest. The prize was a small film role, and she headed for Hollywood. In 1925, at the age of 19, she rose to stardom in *The Plastic Age,* a romance about Jazz Age youth.

Offscreen, Bow played the role of Hollywood starlet to the hilt, cruising the streets in a red convertible, accompanied by seven chow dogs whose fur matched her own flame-colored tresses. She wore trousers before they were considered proper attire for women, ran up enormous gambling debts, and flaunted her affairs with Gilbert Roland and Gary Cooper, the hottest male sex symbols of the day.

In 1927 she landed a starring role as the It Girl, playing the woman with that indefinable quality that drives men wild with desire. Fan letters poured in at the rate of 45,000 a month, and Bow became a bona fide Twenties icon. Novelist and screenwriter F. Scott Fitzgerald called her the quintessential flapper, "pretty, impudent, superbly assured, as worldly-wise, briefly-clad and 'hard-berled' as possible."

By 1933 her career was in decline. The talkies had revealed her thick Brooklyn accent, for one thing. Then a lawsuit by the wife of one of her lovers, charging Bow with alienation of affection, created an aura of scandal. Even worse, the Great Depression caused her carefree flapper persona to seem crude and irrelevant. The world's favorite jazz baby, now married to a part-time actor who owned a Nevada ranch, made a brief comeback attempt. Then once and for all she closed the book on her movie-star life.

Clara Bow: sex appeal and girl-next-door innocence.

1925

The novel *The Great Gatsby* portrayed the dissolute underside of the Roaring Twenties, even while it held out hope for the American Dream.

As a Princeton undergraduate, Minnesota-born F. Scott Fitzgerald encountered many of the excesses of the Jazz Age. In 1920 he captured his experiences in his first novel, *This Side of Paradise.* The book was written in part to impress his future wife, Zelda Sayre, an attractive but unstable Alabama belle whom he had met during his tour of duty in World War I.

In 1925 *The Great Gatsby* — a work that would earn

F. Scott Fitzgerald wrote several novels, but Gatsby was the best.

the author a permanent niche as the great romantic of the Jazz Age — was published to mixed reviews and mediocre sales. Its depiction of a world of money run amok was one that Scott and Zelda knew all too well. By then the couple was drinking excessively, participating in nude bathing parties, and periodically getting thrown out of swanky hotels.

The Fitzgeralds lived the precarious life of the characters in *Gatsby,* who understood that "the rock of the world was founded securely on a fairy's wing." Despite the shallow morals and careless behavior of the novel's rich wastrels, neither Fitzgerald nor the book's narra-

tor, Nick Carraway, abandoned the dream that allowed a young nobody named Jimmy Gatz to transform himself into the flamboyantly successful Gatsby.

On and off during the 1920's, the Fitzgeralds were part of an enclave in Paris of expatriate American writers disillusioned by post–World War I American culture. Among those whose paths they crossed in Parisian cafés and bars were novelist Ernest Hemingway, poet e.e. cummings, *New Yorker* journalist Janet Flanner, and writer Gertrude Stein. It was Stein who gave the talented but rootless writers a name when she gently scolded Hemingway: "You are all a lost generation."

1926

Physicist Robert H. Goddard, who launched the first liquid-fuel-propelled rocket into space, labored most of his life in obscurity.

On March 16, 1926, Robert H. Goddard arrived at his Aunt Effie's farm in Auburn, Massachusetts, with some metal tubing, fuel cylinders, and an engine. Along with two colleagues from nearby Clark University, where he taught physics, Goddard put the pieces together near a cabbage patch.

As one of the men lit an igniter with a blowtorch and ducked behind an iron barrier, Goddard's wife stood by with a movie camera to record the event. The world's first liquid-fuel rocket hovered just long enough for Esther Goddard's film to run out, then took off with a whoosh. After just two and a half seconds in the air, it nose-dived into the frozen ground 184 feet away.

Mankind took its first step toward outer space that day — and the event barely turned a head. Goddard had already published a paper in 1919 predicting that a rocket would one day be sent to the moon. *The New York Times* ridiculed the notion, stating that Goddard lacked the "knowledge ladled out daily in our high schools."

Goddard grips the frame that held his successful rocket, launched at a farm in rural Massachusetts.

After the successful rocket launch, Goddard continued his work on space flight in relative obscurity, partially funded by the Smithsonian Institution. Single-minded in his devotion to flight beyond the earth's gravitational pull, Goddard once remarked of himself, "God, pity a one-dream man."

In time, copies of his 1919 paper found their way to Germany. As World War II neared its end, a group of Americans asked some German scientists who had defected about the technology behind the long-range ballistic missiles in Hitler's arsenal. To their surprise, the response was: "Ask your own rocket scientist, Robert Goddard."

In August 1945, 16 years before astronaut Alan Shepard left the earth's atmosphere in a NASA rocket ship, Goddard died. He was granted more than half of his 214 patents posthumously for such inventions as a gyroscopic stabilizer, a jet-driven propeller, a resonance chamber, and other devices used in or adapted for the space program. In 1960 the federal government awarded his widow $1 million. And in July 1969, as *Apollo 11* rocketed toward the moon, *The New York Times* retracted its criticism of the visionary physicist.

W *1926* **ill Rogers, the most American of humorists, made even the dourest of presidents beam with delight.**

When Calvin Coolidge invited Will Rogers to the White House in 1926, the humorist bet a friend that he could make the taciturn president laugh within 20 seconds. As the entertainer was introduced to the chief executive, Rogers looked puzzled, stuck out his hand, and exclaimed: "Excuse me, I didn't quite get the name." Coolidge couldn't suppress a wide grin. Rogers won the bet.

It was a typical Will Rogers joke — warm, gently satirical, and distinctly American. It was the kind of humor that, by the 1920's, had turned the affable, part-Cherokee country boy from Oklahoma into one of the most quoted men alive.

Rogers started in show business as a rope artist and rough rider in a circus that played in South Africa and Australia. Back home, he was hired to appear in *The Ziegfeld Follies,* where he managed to steal the show from the dancers.

"I'm just out here while the girls make a change," he deadpanned. "Imagine, changin' from nothin' to nothin'!"

Rogers: a beloved humorist.

In the early 1930's Rogers's newspaper column and his comic films made him the highest-paid entertainer in the country. His quick wit, anchored in common sense, was comforting in the dark days of the Depression. "Too many people spend money they haven't earned to buy things they don't want to impress people they don't like," he once quipped.

Rogers, who claimed that he had never met a man he didn't like, was an early fan of air travel. Boasting that planes were safer than trains, Rogers flew about 500,000 miles in seven years.

In 1935, while circling the globe with aviator Wiley Post, his plane stalled and crashed into an Alaskan stream, killing both men. Millions mourned him. "A smile has disappeared from the lips of America," a friend lamented.

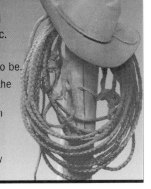

Will Rogers: The Cowboy Comic

With his shy grin and fractured grammar, Will Rogers would shrewdly unmask pretentions and undercut political rhetoric. Here are just a few of his offhanded quips:

- A politician is not as narrow-minded as he forces himself to be.
- You have to have a serious streak in you or you can't see the funny side of the other fellow.
- We don't have secret diplomacy. American diplomacy is an open book — generally a check book.
- Everybody is ignorant, only on different subjects.
- I'll bet you the time ain't far off when a woman won't know any more than a man.

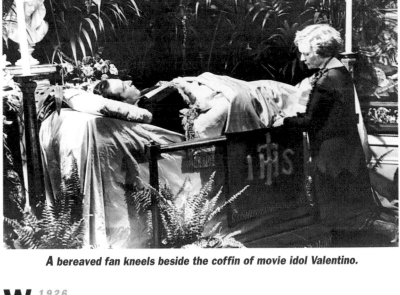
A bereaved fan kneels beside the coffin of movie idol Valentino.

W *1926* **hen movie star Rudolph Valentino died suddenly of appendicitis, publicists helped send his distraught fans into agonized outpourings of grief.**

In July 1926 Rudolph Valentino arrived in New York City and fought his way through screaming crowds to attend the glittering premiere of his film *The Son of the Sheik.* Valentino had reached the height of his popularity. The critic H. L. Mencken described the silent screen's Latin lover as "a young man who was living daily the dream of millions of other young men."

Just weeks after the premiere, Valentino was stricken by appendicitis. Pleurisy developed after surgery, and on August 23, 1926, "the world's greatest lover" died at the age of 31.

Reports of uncontrolled grief poured in. A London dancer committed suicide. A New York housewife shot herself while clutching a sheaf of the star's pictures. Two Japanese women were seen jumping into a volcano. In New York a thrashing, screaming mob smashed a plate-glass window at the funeral home.

The mourning melodrama was not without its offstage cues. The undertaker's press agent paid 30 people a dollar each to line up outside the mortuary. After a crowd had gathered, the funeral director sent an honor guard of swarthy, menacing-looking men to stand by the bier. A liberal group then began to protest, allowing the director to ban the "fascists" from the premises with a righteous flourish.

Meanwhile publicists at United Artists, distributor of *The Son of the Sheik,* sent 20 professional weepers to the funeral. The spokesmen also relayed the sheik's last words — "Let the tent be struck!" — to the press. Unfortunately, the line closely resembled Robert E. Lee's deathbed utterance and had to be changed.

271

1927

Aviator Charles Lindbergh became the first man to fly nonstop across the Atlantic alone and incommunicado; he didn't even have a radio.

Just before 8 A.M. on a rainy May 20, 1927, a lanky airmail pilot named Charles Lindbergh cleared Roosevelt Field, Long Island, and headed east over the Atlantic Ocean. Flying a custom-built nine-cylinder monoplane, the 25-year-old aviator was bound for Paris. His plane, the *Spirit of St. Louis,* was stripped down to reduce its weight and to increase fuel efficiency. It had navigating instruments but no radio.

Lindbergh hoped to capture the $25,000 prize that New York hotel owner Raymond Orteig had offered in 1919 to the avia-tor who could fly non-stop from New York to Paris. Just that month two French pilots had died vying for the prize, and several others had been killed or injured previously.

Just before 10:30 P.M. on May 21, 1927, three hours ahead of his expected arrival, Lind-bergh landed at Le Bour-get Field near Paris. He had traveled 3,600 miles in 33½ hours, some of it through snow and sleet.

Sheer determination, good instincts, and the ability to stay alert for a day and a half had brought him through the ardu-ous flight. To the crowd of cheering onlookers who wel-comed him, he

Detail of a tapestry honoring Lindbergh.

stated simply: "Well, I made it."

News of Lindbergh's arrival touched off a virtual stampede. Nearly 100,000 Frenchmen stormed the small landing field to get a glimpse of their new hero. Lindbergh had earned a place in history books and also a nickname, the Lone Eagle.

1927

Hailed as an engineering marvel, the Holland Tunnel between New York and New Jersey was the first mechani-cally ventilated underwater tunnel for cars and trucks.

A holiday spirit united both banks of the Hudson River on that chilly November 12, 1927. The crowd, which numbered in the tens of thousands, listened to speeches marking what New York governor Al Smith called "the wedding" of New York and New Jersey.

At 4:55 P.M. the same gold telegraph key that had triggered the Panama Canal's opening turned on electricity to unfurl two giant American flags from each of the tunnel entrances.

In the next hour 20,000 pedestrians walked the 1.6-mile-long tubes, eager to see New York City's latest engineering miracle. Up to that time, dozens of overloaded ferries had han-dled traffic between the two states. The ferries carried 22,000 vehicles daily, weather per-mitting; on the opening day for cars, November 13, 1927, the tunnel served some 52,000 vehicles.

The tunnel had posed a serious engineering problem for its designer, Clif-ford Holland. It would require a complex ventilation system to keep

The opening of the Holland Tunnel created a major traffic jam.

Al Jolson drew on his vaudeville rou-tine when he made the first "talkie."

1927

The Jazz Singer revolutionized the movie industry, becoming the first money-making film to merge the spoken word and the moving on-screen image.

As early as 1890 Thomas Edison's laboratory had produced one device to record sound and another to depict moving images: the phonograph recorded sounds on a wax cylinder, and the kine-tograph captured pictures on a piece of celluloid. Several decades elapsed before engineering break-throughs allowed for such improvements as syn-chronized sound and image, however. Even then, other barriers remained.

Many of the era's movie moguls, who had invested heavily in silent films, actors, and the-aters, saw no use for pictures that talked. "To have conversation," said film-studio executive William Fox, "would strain the eyesight and the sense of hearing at once, taking away the restfulness one gets from viewing pictures alone." Legend has it that when Sam Warner presented the idea to his brother, Harry, the movie producer bellowed: "Who the hell wants to hear actors talk?"

The farsighted Sam Warner prevailed. On Octo-ber 6, 1927, Warner Brothers' *The Jazz Singer* opened to rave reviews; the audience actually burst into applause at the end. It was the first narrative film to feature spoken words, and the first commercially successful "talkie."

Al Jolson's first line of film dialogue, a saying he had used onstage for years, seemed prophetic. "Wait a minute," he quipped, "you ain't heard nothin' yet." By 1929 more than 1,000 theaters were wired for sound, and the silent era was all but dead. "If I were an actor with a squeaky voice," wrote one critic, "I would worry."

motorists from succumbing to carbon-monoxide fumes.

Holland's solution was to build four 10-story-high air towers housing a total of 84 powerful fans, which pumped a steady stream of air under the roadway; vents let the air pass into the vehicular level. The system, it was said, kept the air in the tunnel cleaner than the air in midtown Manhattan.

Construction of the world's first mechanically ventilated underwater car tunnel was hazardous: 13 of the workers died while digging through the Hudson River silt. The tunnel also buried its designer, who had worked nonstop for seven years, despite his doctors' warnings that his heart could not take the strain. Holland died of overwork at the age of 41. His death came just two days before the ends of the tunnel met beneath the river.

D *1928* isillusioned and down on his luck, Walt Disney allowed his masterpiece, the first animated film with a successful sound track, to open at only one New York theater.

In the fall of 1928, Walt Disney, the creator of Mickey Mouse, was in New York with a great idea but little cash. A 26-year-old cartoon artist and entrepreneur, Disney wanted to add music and sound effects to Mickey's third film, *Steamboat Willie*. The first two silent adventures starring Mickey, *Plane Crazy* and *Gallopin' Gaucho*, had never been released.

After a week in New York, where his efforts to work out a deal with a film distributor had fallen flat, Disney was tired and broke. "Personally I am sick of this picture *Steamboat Willie*," he wrote to his brother Roy, who managed the struggling animation studio in California. "This damn town is enough to give anybody the heebie jeebies."

Before long, Walt decided to make a personal sacrifice, selling his beloved Moon roadster and other possessions to pay for recording the film's score. After several distributors failed to show interest, Disney gave *Steamboat Willie* to the Colony Theatre for a two-week run.

Suddenly Mickey was a movie star. One reviewer praised the cleverly synchronized sound track; another called the film a "riot of mirth." Disney, who provided Mickey's voice, spent his evenings in the back of the theater, reveling in the laughter.

The talking rodent acquired a devoted following nationwide, and soon the Mickey Mouse Club had 1 million members. He became an international pop-culture icon; his image was enshrined in wax at Madame Tussaud's Wax Museum in London. Mickey also appeared on

The original poster for Steamboat Willie, *Disney's first box-office hit.*

notebooks, handkerchiefs, and watches.

As Mickey grew in popularity, Disney altered the mouse's personality to suit his audience. The first Mickey was a cocky, cruel adolescent with a wicked sense of humor. "No one has ever been softened after seeing Mickey," observed British novelist E. M. Forster, "or has wanted to give away an extra glass of water to the poor." But soon Mickey had become everybody's favorite underdog — who, said Disney, "gets in scrapes through no fault of his own but always manages to come up grinning."

Lights! Camera! Action!

From the earliest years of moviemaking, American films have had a blockbuster impact on the industry worldwide. Some American film firsts:

1903 The first westerns, *Kit Carson* and *The Pioneers,* are shot in the Adirondack Mountains in New York.

1903 Ex-cavalryman Frank Hanaway, who can fall off a horse without getting hurt, wins a part in Edwin S. Porter's *The Great Train Robbery*, becoming the movies' first stuntman.

1912 A film with an all-black cast, *The Railroad Porter,* is directed by African-American filmmaker Bill Foster.

1922 The first 3-D feature film is Nat Deverich's *Power of Love*, about a young 19th-century sea captain.

1927 The first talkie — a feature film with spoken words — is *The Jazz Singer* starring Al Jolson.

1928 An animated cartoon with a synchronized sound track that actually works stars Mickey Mouse in *Steamboat Willie.*

1929 The first musical with an original score, *The Broadway Melody,* debuts. Its advertising slogan: "All-Talking! All-Singing! All-Dancing!"

1929 The Academy of Motion Picture Arts and Sciences holds its first awards ceremony. *Wings,* starring Gary Cooper and Clara Bow, wins for best picture.

The St. Valentine Day's Massacre all but ended the career of Capone's rival.

1929
The St. Valentine's Day Massacre lasted eight long minutes, yet gunmen still missed their main target, gangster Bugs Moran.

The battle over profits in Prohibition bootlegging made the top gangs of Chicago mortal enemies. Headed by Al Capone and Dion O'Banion, the gangs were constantly fighting turf wars and hijacking each other's supplies as they competed for sources of illegal liquor.

Capone had moved to Chicago from Brooklyn in 1920 at the invitation of gangster Johnny Torrio, who needed a right-hand man to expand his flourishing illegal-liquor business. At the age of 21, Capone had already committed a string of crimes, many of them as a member of New York's infamous Five Points gang. He wasted no time making his mark on the Windy City and eventually supplanted Torrio as the head of a group of murderous thugs.

The Capone gang rose to the top of the heap in 1924, when it murdered O'Banion in his Chicago flower shop, but mob conflicts between Capone and the O'Banion gang's new leader, George (Bugs) Moran, continued throughout the decade. By 1927, according to U.S. Treasury Department estimates, Capone had 1,000 workers on his payroll, and his mob's income from prostitution, graft, and boot-legging operations generated about $100 million, of which Capone's profit was nearly $10 million.

In 1929 Capone contrived an elaborate hoax as a way to eliminate Moran. At 10:30 A.M. on February 14, a front man from Detroit was supposed to unload a shipment of hijacked liquor. Instead, a Cadillac pulled up to the curb outside the Moran gang's garage, and three men dressed as policemen and two others emerged.

The fake police officers asked the gang members to lay down their arms and stand up against the garage wall. Then the machine-gun and shotgun blasts began. Eight minutes later, five of Moran's men and one bystander were dead. A sixth gang member died a few hours later at a hospital. Ironically, Moran himself, sensing trouble at the sight of the policemen, had fled and emerged unharmed.

1929
Only 250 people attended a banquet in Hollywood to honor winners of a new award for excellence in the film industry — an event that later came to be known as the Oscars.

Movie executive Louis B. Mayer had helped create the Academy of Motion Picture Arts and Sciences in 1927, not only to confer status on the burgeoning film industry, but also to diffuse growing tension among the industry's workforce. By stressing the creative mission shared by various elements of the movie business, Mayer's group hoped to prevent dissatisfied workers from forming a union.

On May 16, 1929, the academy bestowed the first of its annual awards. Gold-plated 13½-inch-tall statuettes went to 21-year-old Janet Gaynor for her performances in *Seventh Heaven* and two other films; to renowned German actor Emil Jannings for his work in *The Last Command* and *The Way of All Flesh;* and to the film *Wings,* an epic war drama. The award for best director of a drama went to Frank Borzage for *Seventh Heaven.* Lewis Milestone received the award for best director of a comedy, *Two Arabian Knights.*

Charlie Chaplin was given a special award for "his genius and versatility" as writer, actor, director, and producer of *The Circus.* Another special award went to Warner Brothers for *The Jazz Singer,* which was to revolutionize the industry.

Televised since 1953, the annual awards ceremony has honored hundreds of artists and technicians. *Ben Hur* (1959) and *Titanic* (1997) have won the most awards for a single film, garnering 11 Oscars each.

Walt Disney won the most awards in all categories with 26 regular Oscars and 6 special trophies. The only actor to receive a statuette with the wrong name was Spencer Tracy, whose 1938 best-actor award read "Dick Tracy."

Although several people have claimed that they gave the statue its name, credit for the choice goes to Margaret Herrick. A secretary at the academy, Herrick said that the statuette looked like her uncle Oscar.

Douglas Fairbanks presents a radiant Janet Gaynor with the first Oscar for best actress.

A 1929

Although Black Tuesday marked the greatest crash in stock market history, not everyone grasped its seriousness immediately.

More than 16 million shares of stock were sold and about $15 billion was lost in the greatest crash in New York Stock Exchange history, on Black Tuesday, October 29, 1929.

The crash capped a two-month decline in stock prices and came only days after a steep slide on October 24. At the market's low point in mid-November, the value of stocks listed on the Exchange had fallen by some $30 billion.

Black Tuesday by itself did not cause the Great Depression that followed, but because the economy was already shaky, the crash opened the door to a national catastrophe. Contributing factors were years of overproduction in industry and agriculture, plus easy credit that allowed many consumers, investors, and businesses to pile up excessive debt.

At first, business, finance, and government leaders generally downplayed the event, as did most newspapers. Industrialist Andrew Mellon saw "nothing in the present situation that is either menacing or warrants pessimism." President Herbert Hoover loudly proclaimed that "the fundamental business of the country is sound." A headline in *The Wall Street Journal* of October 30, 1929, sounded equally reassuring: "Stocks Steady After Decline: Spokesman Expresses View Hysteria Is Passing."

The show-business periodical *Variety* put it differently: "Wall St. Lays an Egg." Within months of the crash, thousands of businesses were crippled or bankrupt, banks had failed, and unemployment had spread like wildfire.

Black Tuesday marked the end of a Wall Street boom.

Wall Street Speak

Stockbrokers use a special jargon all their own, replete with bulls, bears, and other wildlife.

Bear – A pessimist who believes that the price of a security or the direction of the market will continue to drop.

Blue chip – The stock of a large corporation with a record of strong profits and good management. (In poker, a blue chip is often the most valuable.)

Bull – An optimist who believes that the price of a security or the direction of the market will continue to rise.

Cats and dogs – speculative, high-risk stocks that do not have a market history.

Churning – Excessive buying and selling of a customer's holdings to earn extra commissions for the broker.

Float – The number of shares available for public trading. A thin, or small, float is risky because it means a large buy or sell order can drastically change the price.

Pure play – An investment in a company that specializes in one industry or business only.

R 1929

Richard E. Byrd became the first person to fly over both the North and South poles.

By 1912, the year Richard E. Byrd graduated from the U.S. Naval Academy, overland expeditions had already reached both poles. The American Robert E. Peary arrived at the North Pole in April 1909, and the Norwegian Roald Amundsen made it to the South Pole in December 1911. For Byrd, however, there was still the challenge of reaching the poles by air.

After commanding a naval air squadron in World War I, Byrd resigned from active duty to organize his first polar expedition. From a base in Spitzbergen, Norway, Byrd and pioneer aviator Floyd Bennett flew 1,600 miles round-trip over the Arctic ice cap on May 9, 1926, in their Fokker monoplane, to a spot they believed was the North Pole. They beat Amundsen's dirigible flight by three days.

When Byrd and Bennett returned to the United States, Congress awarded them the Medal of Honor. Before long, Byrd started planning the more difficult flight over the South Pole. Not only was the pole 1,000 miles from any habitation, but some of the mountains en route rose higher than 14,000 feet.

Late in the afternoon of November 28, 1929, the intrepid Byrd bundled up in his fur-lined parka — he knew that he would have to take his bearings through an open window in punishing arctic temperatures.

An N. C. Wyeth painting of Byrd's North Pole flight.

With three others, Byrd left their camp at Little America in the Ford trimotor plane *Floyd Bennett,* named for Byrd's North Pole pilot, who had died of pneumonia the previous year.

At 1:55 A.M. on November 29, Byrd radioed that they had reached the "almost limitless" plateau of the South Pole and were heading back north. After stopping at a refueling dump, the crew reached Little America at 10:10 A.M.

Only then did Byrd report the hazards of the flight. The crew had jettisoned food to lighten the plane so that it could ascend to the proper altitude. Air currents had tossed the plane about "like a cork in a washtub" as it flew over glaciers that snaked through the mountains. But it had been worth the risks. The Antarctic landscape, Byrd said, "was the most magnificent sight I have ever seen."

1929

Prohibition didn't end the consumption of alcohol — it just made drinking more expensive and dangerous.

During his first year in office, President Herbert Hoover appointed a commission to study the effects of the 18th Amendment — the "great social and economic experiment, noble in nature," as he called it, that prohibited the manufacture, sale, and transport of alcoholic beverages. But after almost a decade, it was clear that Prohibition was an experiment gone awry.

By 1929 booze was more popular than ever. Backyard distilleries operated around the clock. According to one government study, the production of corn sugar, a key ingredient of home-brewed liquor, had increased sixfold between 1919 and 1929. And thanks to big-time gangsters like Al Capone and "Dutch" Schultz, bootleg whiskey flowed over the border from Canada and Mexico in crates

Federal agents dump barrels of beer in Hackensack, New Jersey, in 1930. Three years later, passage of the 21st Amendment repealed Prohibition.

labeled "farm equipment" and "olive oil."

Government agents ran themselves ragged attempting to enforce the law — raiding speakeasies, breaking up stills, and pouring liquor down sewers. Nearly 10,000 agents made 75,000 arrests annually, at a cost to taxpayers of $20 million. It all made little difference — except to inflate

the price of a drink. During Prohibition, the cost of a beer shot up from 5 cents to 50 cents.

Another consequence of Prohibition was the large number of fatalities from adulterated booze. Unscrupulous bootleggers might stretch their product with paint thinner, ether, gasoline, or antifreeze. Home tipplers sometimes gulped down equally dangerous brew: bay rum, hair tonic, wood alcohol, Sterno. The result could be blindness, paralysis, or even death.

And still the party continued. Despite the expense and danger — and the certain knowledge that they were breaking the law — Americans guzzled alcohol at an astounding rate. When New York's most notorious speakeasy owner, Texas Guinan, greeted customers with her famous "Hello, sucker!" it was all just part of the fun.

1929

Edward Bernays, called the father of public relations, founded a new profession when he publicized a play on a taboo subject.

While he was editing a medical journal, Edward Bernays rallied behind a theatrical producer who was worried about putting on a play that dealt with venereal disease. Bernays marshaled the support of businessmen, society matrons, and civic leaders. They endorsed the play and helped attract a large audience.

The unexpected success of this campaign convinced Bernays to give up editing and become a publicist. Among his

Bernays promoted soap, celebrities, even the nutrients in bananas.

many promotions were soap-carving contests for Procter & Gamble, intended to make children enjoy taking baths with Ivory soap. His celebrity clients included ballet star Vaslav Nijinsky, opera singer Enrico Caruso, and many actors. Eleanor Roosevelt and Dwight D. Eisenhower hired Bernays to buff up their images.

Bernays defined his work as "the technique and method of reaching the public, with particular emphasis on the newspaper, the periodic press, the pulpit," and other outlets. In sum, he declared it was "public relations," and Bernays soon

became known as its father.

Thomas Edison was also a client — a fact that made newspaper editors skeptical about a celebration Bernays had arranged in 1929 to honor him. Bernays had convinced the Post Office to issue a stamp depicting a lamp. Many wondered if the event was staged to promote the electric-light industry.

When Czech leader Tomás Masaryk told Bernays that he was about to declare his nation's independence, Bernays offered some advice. Announce the decision on a Sunday, a slow day for news, to get more press coverage. "But that would be making history for headlines," Masaryk protested. In what may be a summary of his philosophy, Bernays replied, "Headlines make history."

1930

Bobby Jones captured the open and amateur championships in both the United States and Great Britain, becoming the only person to win the Grand Slam of golf.

When Bobby Jones returned to the United States after winning the British Amateur and Open championships in the spring of 1930, New York City honored him with a tickertape parade. Jones scored his next victory at the U.S. Open. Then, on September 27, 1930, he won the U.S. Amateur championship.

Jones had triumphed in the four most prestigious contests in golf. The golfing world created a title for the four-part event, known ever since as the Grand Slam. No one had done it before, and although the individual events have changed, no one has done it since.

Jones's final victory took place at the Merion Cricket Club outside Philadelphia — where, as it happened, he had first qualified for the U.S. amateur championship, in 1916, at age 14.

For all his promise as a teenage golfer, Jones had trouble controlling his temper. Some fans doubted that he would ever win a tournament. The doubts vanished in 1923. Jones took the U.S. Open, the first of an extraordinary 13 U.S. and British championships — a record that stands to this day.

Bobby Jones on his way to winning the Grand Slam of golf.

IN THEIR OWN WORDS

"My husband and me just started traveling around, for about three years. It was a very nice time, because when you're poor and you stay in one spot, trouble just seems to catch up with you. But when you're moving from town to town, you don't stay there long enough for trouble to catch up with you. It's really a good life, if you're poor and you can manage to move around.

I was pregnant when we first started hitchhiking, and people were really very nice to us. Sometimes they would feed us. I remember one time we slept in a haystack and the lady of the house came out and found us and she said, 'This is really very bad for you because you're going to have a baby. You need a lot of milk.' So she took us up to the house.

She had a lot of rugs hanging on the clotheslines because she was doing her house cleaning. We told her we'd beat the rugs for her giving us the food. She said, no, she didn't expect that. She just wanted to feed us. We said, no, we couldn't take it unless we worked for it. And she let us beat her rugs. . . . When we left, she filled a gallon bucket full of milk, and we took it with us."

Peggy Terry recalls what it was like being homeless in Oklahoma during the Depression in Hard Times: An Oral History of the Great Depression *by Studs Terkel.*

At the height of the Depression, apple sellers clogged city sidewalks.

1930

An excess supply of fruit provided an enduring symbol of the Depression — the 5-cent-apple salesman.

In the autumn of 1930, the International Apple Shippers Association was feeling the effects of the Depression. To unload inventory, the trade association sold crates of apples on credit to the unemployed, who hawked them for a nickel apiece. Apple sellers soon dotted the street corners of major cities. By November, New York City alone had 6,000 fruit peddlers.

Apple selling was only one of many survival tactics. Some down-and-out residents in the state of Washington set forest fires in order to create jobs for themselves — as firefighters.

The unemployed and underemployed learned to make the most of what little they had. They stretched the life of shoes by inserting pasteboard, and they stuffed newspapers under shirts to ward off the winter cold. Depression-era cooks made tomato soup by adding hot water to ketchup.

In New York, Chicago, and other cities, friends of a person who was about to be evicted would raise money by holding a "rent party"; future jazz greats like Fats Waller sometimes provided the entertainment. The mayor of Detroit turned over vacant city-owned land to people willing to grow produce in so-called thrift gardens.

Although President Herbert Hoover tried to sponsor programs to deal with poverty and unemployment, the major impetus came from his successor, Franklin D. Roosevelt, who was elected in 1932. Of the many "alphabet" programs initiated by Roosevelt to get people on payrolls and to restart the economy, one of the most effective was the Civilian Conservation Corps (CCC). Begun in 1933, when the nation's jobless reached a peak of some 13 million, the CCC put young men to work on public conservation projects in return for food, lodging, and a small stipend.

1930

Sinclair Lewis was awarded the Nobel Prize for literature — the first U.S. citizen so honored.

After a dozen years of disappointing literary efforts and restless travels nationwide, Sinclair Lewis achieved celebrity at the age of 35 with the publication in 1920 of *Main Street*. Set in a prairie town based on his birthplace of Sauk Centre, Minnesota, the novel stripped bare the pretensions and pressure for conformity in American society. In subsequent novels, Lewis examined business ethics (*Babbitt*, 1922), doctors (*Arrowsmith*, 1925), evangelism (*Elmer Gantry*, 1927), and marriage (*Dodsworth*, 1929).

Lewis disdained the Pulitzer Prize.

Not surprising for a critic of the status quo, Lewis defiantly rejected the Pulitzer Prize he was offered for *Arrowsmith*. This award, he said, only made American authors "safe, polite, obedient, and sterile." But the Nobel Prize, announced on November 5, 1930, was a welcome honor, the ultimate grand finale to a decade of critical and popular acclaim.

In his acceptance speech at the awards ceremony in Stockholm, Sweden, Lewis praised such American writers as Eugene O'Neill, Ernest Hemingway, and William Faulkner — each of whom would follow in his footsteps to Stockholm to collect the prize for literature. He envisioned a glorious future for a country whose writers would produce works as monumental in scope as its mountain ranges and "endless prairies."

Sadly, his moment of triumph as a Nobel laureate turned out to be the peak of Lewis's career. During the next two decades, he wrote little or nothing of lasting merit. Lewis died in Rome in 1951, all but cast aside in the wake of a new generation of postwar literary brilliance.

IN THEIR OWN WORDS

"I have, for the future of American literature, every hope and every eager belief. We are coming out, I believe, of the stuffiness of safe, sane, and incredibly dull provincialism. There are young Americans today who are doing such passionate and authentic work that it makes me sick to see that I am a little too old to be one of them. There is Ernest Hemingway . . . Thomas Wolfe . . . Thornton Wilder . . . and there are a dozen others, . . . most of them a little insane in the tradition of James Joyce, who, however insane they may be, have refused to be genteel and traditional and dull."

Excerpts from Lewis's acceptance speech for the Nobel Prize for literature.

1932

A decade before their triumphs in World War II, Gen. Douglas MacArthur and Maj. Dwight D. Eisenhower evicted thousands of World War I veterans from a Washington, D.C., demonstration for veterans' benefits.

Many doughboys who enjoyed a warm welcome on their return from World War I found themselves deeply in debt or impoverished during the Depression. Knowing that in 1924 Congress had voted to compensate them for their low wages by awarding them future bonuses didn't help much — the money wasn't due to be paid until 1945, which seemed a lifetime away.

In the hopes of persuading Congress to pay the bonus immediately, 15,000 veterans and their families formed the Bonus Expeditionary Force. They set up camp near the Capitol and in nearby Anacostia Flats, Maryland, and staged a Bonus March in Washington, D.C., in May 1932. The next month the House of Representatives passed a bill approving immediate bonus payments; the Senate promptly voted the measure down, however.

With little beckoning them home, some of the group decided to stay in Washington throughout the summer, camping out in tents and tar-paper shacks. Annoyed by the protesters and worried that radicals had infiltrated their ranks, President Herbert Hoover decided to remove the former soldiers by force.

When police efforts to evict them resulted in the death of two veterans, an angry Hoover called in Gen. Douglas MacArthur, who was then the army chief of staff. A distin-

Bonus Army veterans who refused to leave Washington battle the police.

guished officer with the Allied Expeditionary Force in France during World War I and a former superintendent at West Point, MacArthur also saw the Bonus Army as a threat. Aided by Maj. Dwight D. Eisenhower, who worked in the office of the Assistant Secretary of War, MacArthur mobilized the active army on July 28, 1932.

With tanks, machine guns, and tear gas, the soldiers went about dislodging their former comrades. They set the shanty-towns on fire and rousted out stragglers at bayonet point.

Reports about the callous treatment of the Bonus Army horrified the Depression-weary nation, and the fallout contributed to Hoover's loss of the election in November 1932. Neither MacArthur nor Eisenhower suffered comparable setbacks in their military careers.

P *1932*
Politicians who said the "little woman" from Arkansas couldn't be elected to the U.S. Senate failed to account for the intervention of Louisiana's flamboyant senator, Huey Long.

When Thaddeus Caraway died in November 1931, Arkansas governor Harvey Parnell appointed his widow, Hattie, to Caraway's seat in the U.S. Senate. In a special election the following January, Hattie was chosen to fill out the remaining 14 months of her husband's term — the first woman ever elected to what had been exclusively a men's club.

No sooner did Mrs. Caraway win the special election than Arkansas notables began lining up to enter the August 1932 Democratic primary. For a Democrat, victory in the primary was tantamount to election in the fall campaign.

By the time the incumbent declared her intention to seek a full six-year term, there were half a dozen challengers, including a former governor and a former senator. But Mrs.

Caraway and Long: a winning combination.

Caraway (known as the little woman) had a secret weapon — namely, Sen. Huey Long of Louisiana. In the Senate Mrs. Caraway had supported Long's "share the wealth" program, which pitted the common citizen against what Long referred to as "Wall Street and the pot-bellied politicians."

On August 1 Long entered Arkansas in his blue Cadillac, leading a caravan that included two sound trucks and four vans stocked with campaign literature. Zigzagging across the state for a week, Hattie and Huey drew an estimated 300,000 people to speeches in three dozen towns.

Pundits expected that Mrs. Caraway would get only a sympathy vote. On August 9, 1932, she carried 60 of Arkansas' 75 counties and received as many votes as all of her six opponents combined. Her victory in the general election in November won her the first of two consecutive full terms in the U.S. Senate.

N *1932*
Negro League star Leroy (Satchel) Paige, who some think was the greatest pitcher of all time, won 32 games for the Pittsburgh Crawfords in one season.

Hustling baggage for tips at the railroad depot in Mobile, Alabama, seven-year-old Leroy Paige acquired the nickname Satchel. After spending five years in reform school, Paige emerged as a polished baseball pitcher. In 1926, following two seasons with semiprofessional teams, he signed with the Chattanooga Lookouts, a team in the Negro Southern League. Paige was just 20 years old.

Although there were separate leagues for black and white baseball players, Paige began to receive national attention playing with the Pittsburgh Crawfords in 1931. He pitched his all-black team to 32 victories in 1932 and 31 wins in 1933, a feat few pitchers in any league could equal.

Soon the baseball world was buzzing with tales of his fastball, which soared across home plate looking to hapless batters like a marble in flight. Playing baseball year-round, he pitched in Mexico, Puerto Rico, and Cuba. Paige was

Paige demonstrates his famous "hesitation pitch," which was banned by the major leagues.

eventually credited with 300 shutouts and 55 no-hitters in an estimated 2,500 games. (Record keeping in the black leagues was always a bit relaxed.) After batting against him in an exhibition game, New York Yankee slugger Joe DiMaggio called Paige "the best I've ever faced and the fastest."

After leaving Pittsburgh, Paige played for the New York Black Yankees and other Negro League teams. His cocky, comic showmanship made him a crowd pleaser wherever he played. In 1948, when he was 42, he crossed the color line and became the oldest rookie in the major leagues. He spent three seasons with the Cleveland Indians, then one with the St. Louis Browns, who jokingly put a rocking chair in the dugout for him.

In 1965, at the age of 59, when Paige pitched three innings for the Kansas City Athletics, he set a record as the oldest pitcher ever to play in the major leagues. But his proudest day came in 1971, when he became the first player elected to the National Baseball Hall of Fame because of his outstanding achievement in the Negro Leagues.

Giuseppe Zangara (center) pleaded guilty to shooting Chicago mayor Anton Cermak and was electrocuted in a Florida prison.

1933

Less than three weeks before his inauguration, President-elect Franklin D. Roosevelt barely escaped an assassination attempt.

Franklin D. Roosevelt won a landslide victory over incumbent president Herbert Hoover in the November 1932 election. Taking time out to relax before facing his demanding new job, Roosevelt went on a fishing trip with his friend Vincent Astor. On the evening of February 15, 1933, Roosevelt met reporters aboard Astor's yacht, which was docked in the Miami harbor.

Rather than talk about the crisis of the Great Depression that he would soon face as president, the ebullient ex-governor of New York joked with reporters about the "whale of a fish" that got away during his recent Caribbean cruise. Then, shortly after 9 o'clock, he seated himself in the back of an open touring car for the short drive to Miami's Bay Front Park for a scheduled address.

Roosevelt's car slowed to a halt beside the park bandstand, and the president-elect was hoisted to the top of the back seat — few in the crowd knew how his crippled legs immobilized him. After a few brief remarks, Roosevelt slid back into the seat and stretched out a hand to Chicago mayor Anton Cermak. The mayor was in Miami to arrange a fence-mending meeting with the Democrats' new standard bearer, whose nomination he had opposed.

As Cermak moved away, Roosevelt heard what he thought was a firecracker. In fact, it was the first of five shots fired by an unemployed bricklayer named Giuseppe Zangara. Cermak and four others were hit in the fusillade before a woman standing next to the assailant deflected his shooting arm upward. Roosevelt calmly ordered Cermak placed in his car, and he cradled the bleeding mayor in his arms during the drive to Jackson Memorial Hospital.

On March 4, 1933, Roosevelt, telling his fellow countrymen that "the only thing we have to fear is fear itself," was inaugurated. Two days later, Cermak died.

1933

In the first of many breaks with tradition, Eleanor Roosevelt helped serve at the inaugural buffet for her husband, Franklin.

After Franklin D. Roosevelt was elected president in November 1932, Lou Hoover, the wife of incumbent Herbert Hoover, invited Eleanor Roosevelt to the White House for the traditional preinaugural tour. Disdaining an escort and a car, Mrs. Roosevelt chose to walk from her hotel to her new home.

Five weeks later, on March 4, 1933, the new First Lady helped serve the food at the inaugural buffet. She even told the president that he had to stand in line with the guests.

In the first year of her husband's presidency, the popular first lady received more than 300,000 pieces of mail, and she tried to answer them all. The downtrodden and the underrepresented, including single women, blacks, children, and the poor, were of special concern to her, and she decided to become their advocate.

When Eleanor began to hold her own press conferences, which were open only to female reporters, the move forced editors to hire more women. Mrs. R, as the press called her, permanently altered the public perception of the role of the first lady, moving her away from strictly domestic duties and into the public-policy domain.

As the designated "eyes and ears" for her husband, who was crippled by polio in adulthood, she traveled 38,000 miles in his first year in office, visiting slums, coal mines, sharecroppers' camps, mental hospitals, and jails. Usually the president knew her whereabouts, but once she visited a penitentiary without his knowledge. When he asked for his wife, Roosevelt was told that she was in prison. "I'm not surprised," he said, laughing, "but what for?"

Eleanor Roosevelt's women-only press conferences helped create a female press corps.

A *1933*

s the United States faced its worst crisis since the Civil War — 13 million unemployed, banks going broke, breadlines everywhere — Franklin D. Roosevelt told the nation to take a holiday.

On Monday, March 6, 1933, two days after his inauguration, President Franklin D. Roosevelt issued a proclamation declaring a national bank holiday. To halt the run on banks by depositors, who feared losing their life savings, all banks that had not collapsed would be allowed to shut down temporarily.

Meanwhile, Roosevelt directed his aides to draft legislation that would salvage the nation's financial system. On the morning of March 9, 1933, Roosevelt sent the proposed act to Congress, which he had summoned into a special session.

With members frantically shouting "Vote! Vote!" even before the formal reading of the bill had been completed, the House of Representatives passed the act by acclamation; the Senate approved it a few hours later by a vote of 73 to 7. At 8:37 P.M. the president signed into law the Emergency Banking Relief Act, which no longer required the government to redeem dollars for gold, made hoarding or exporting the precious metal illegal, and extended federal protection to banks sound enough to reopen.

On March 12 Roosevelt gave the first of his "fireside chats" on national radio, reassuring the public that any bank that reopened on the following day was backed by the financial might of the U.S. government. Downplaying his concerns about a financial system on the brink of collapse, Roosevelt told some 60 million listeners that putting money into banks was much safer than stuffing it "under the mattress."

The optimism Roosevelt voiced provided a badly needed morale boost. Within two days, bank deposits exceeded withdrawals. "Capitalism," presidential adviser Raymond Moley said, "was saved in eight days."

I *1934*

n one immense dust storm, some 300 million tons of topsoil was lifted from the farms of the Southern Plains — as much earth as had been dredged to build the Panama Canal.

American farmers had a long-standing tradition of turning Western ranges into farms, stripping away the protective buffalo grass to plant crops. The demand for wheat in World War I and the introduction of larger tractors and combines in the postwar years brought more land under cultivation — 32 million acres for wheat alone between 1909 and 1929.

Then came the drought of 1931, the first of seven years when precipitation levels were as much as nine inches below normal. Wheat, corn, and cotton crops withered. The parched soil turned to powder.

A "black blizzard" blankets a Southwestern town in 1937.

IN THEIR OWN WORDS

"By mid-morning a gale was blowing, cold and black. By noon it was blacker than night, because one can see through night and this was an opaque black. It was a wall of dirt one's eyes could not penetrate, but it could penetrate the eyes, the ears, and nose. It could penetrate to the lungs until one coughed up black. If a person was outside, he tied his handkerchief around his face, but he still coughed up black. . . . When the wind died, and the sun shown forth again, it was on a different world. There were no fields, only sand and eddies that swirled in . . . an autumn breeze."

In the August 13, 1938, issue of The Saturday Evening Post, *R. D. Lusk recalls a "great black blizzard" of 1933.*

The first "black blizzards," which were storms carrying only dust, hit the Southern Plains in January 1932. Winds scattered topsoil over distant Eastern cities and even on ships 500 miles out in the Atlantic Ocean. A storm that struck on May 11, 1934, brought winds that carried away some 300 million tons of topsoil. The turbulence turned day into night and led to such respiratory illnesses as bronchitis, strep throat, and what came to be known as dust pneumonia.

Soon roads west were choked with caravans: an estimated 350,000 farmers and their families fled the area. By spring 1935 these recurring billows had created a 97-million-acre Dust Bowl from western Kansas and southeastern Colorado down through the panhandles of Oklahoma and Texas into northeastern New Mexico.

By 1936 one of every four farms had been abandoned. Those farmers who remained began to profit from the New Deal's conservation programs, which taught them how to rotate crops and how to contour their fields in order to stop erosion. In 1938 the rains finally returned, and in the 1940's the Southern Plains became the nation's prosperous "bread basket" once again.

A **1936**
photograph of Fort Peck Dam in Montana heralded the first issue of a magazine designed "to see life; to see the world; to eyewitness great events."

In 1883 a young entrepreneur named Edward Sandford Martin began publishing a new humor magazine called *Life*. For the next 50 years the magazine entertained American readers with social satire and fine illustrations. Among other classic images, *Life* introduced the Gibson Girl — an ideal turn-of-the-century beauty named for her creator, illustrator Charles Dana Gibson.

But by 1935 the magazine was feeling its age. It took an enterprising publisher named Henry Luce to reinvent the periodical for modern readers. Gambling on America's dual fascination with news magazines and photography,

Luce gave new life to *Life*, with the first issue to hit the stands — November 23, 1936.

Luce had already displayed his publishing genius when he offered *Time*, the nation's first news magazine, to the American public in 1923. *Life* was to be something more, however. Luce aimed not just to report news, but to create a new immediacy of experience, enabling the reader "to see life; to see the world; to eyewitness great events . . . to see and take pleasure in seeing; to see and be amazed; to see and be instructed." For this he drew upon a developing profession, photojournalism, made possible by the recent refinement of hand-held cameras with fast shutter speeds. The first cover photo, of Fort Peck Dam in Montana, taken by staff photographer Margaret Bourke-White,

Photojournalism made its debut in the first issue of Life *magazine.*

set the standard. It typified the work of *Life*'s photojournalists, who captured in a split second the essence of a place, person, or event.

Over the years Bourke-White became one of the magazine's best-known photographers. Her subject matter ranged from Depression-era families, to armed combat, to Gandhi at his spinning wheel. Other major *Life* photojournalists included Robert Capa, W. Eugene Smith, and Alfred Eisenstaedt. The latter's shot of a sailor kissing a young woman in Times Square on V-J Day symbolized the end of World War II for an entire nation.

John L. Lewis drums up support for labor unions at a Massachusetts rally in 1937.

R **1936**
ather than walk out on strike, automobile workers in Michigan sat down at their stations and waited for negotiations to begin.

On December 30, 1936, employees at the General Motors plant in Flint, Michigan, stopped working and sat down. Soon 16 more strikes at General Motors plants closed down production. The auto workers were angry; the company was paying its top officials $200,000 a year and its laborers barely $1,000. What they wanted most — even more than higher wages — was recognition of a new union, the United Auto Workers (UAW). Since the late 1880's the labor movement had been dominated by the craft unions of the American Federation of Labor (AFL). But in 1935 John L. Lewis, the president of the United Mine Workers of America, led a secession unit from the AFL to form the Congress of Industrial Organizations (CIO). The new group organized workers by industry rather than by craft. It aggressively targeted the textile, steel, and auto industries for strikes if management failed to negotiate.

Worried that the unorthodox sit-down strikes might flare out of control, Michigan governor Frank Murphy was on the verge of calling out the National Guard. But first he contacted Lewis. The bushy-browed labor leader told Murphy that he would personally go to the Flint plant, bare his chest to the troops, and be the first to fall if bullets were fired. So great was Lewis's prestige that Murphy tore up the order and forbade General Motors from blocking food delivery to the strikers. Losing profits at a rate of $1 million a day, General Motors finally agreed to recognize the UAW in February 1937.

A *1936*
lthough he was responsible for the construction of more highways than any American in history, Robert Moses never learned how to drive a car.

"Those who can, build," Robert Moses once said. "Those who can't, criticize." And build he surely did. When Robert Moses became park commissioner in 1924, New York was a vast, disconnected maze of islands and neighborhoods, with few public spaces and few major roadways. Moses, a great proponent of urban renewal, leveled large tracts of city slums, developed 2.6 million acres of state parks, and constructed 416 miles of parkways to link Manhattan with the suburbs and the new recreation areas.

During the 1930's, a time of severe economic depression for most Americans, Moses thrived. Rounding up a team of unemployed architects (Moses himself had no architectural or engineering training), he oversaw numerous projects, ranging from building public swimming pools and playgrounds to revitalizing the Central Park Zoo in New York. His greatest achievement was the construction of the Triborough Bridge, a three-way expansion bridge that connected Manhattan, the Bronx, and Queens;

Responsible for reshaping New York City's landscape, Robert Moses called himself the "senior ditchdigger."

it was dedicated in 1936. Ironically, Moses had to be ferried across his new creation in a chauffeured car because he had never learned how to drive.

However civic-minded he may have seemed to the public, Moses could be a tyrant. New York's "master builder" ruled over his projects with autocratic imperiousness — bullying, cajoling, and threatening to quit when things failed to go his way. In addition, he could be ruthless; he razed entire neighborhoods in order to build his highways, in the process displacing some 250,000 people. "I hail the chef who can make omelets without breaking eggs," was his unrepentant response to critics.

By 1968, when Moses left his job as head of the Triborough Bridge and Tunnel Authority, New York had grown into a thoroughly modern metropolis. He had spent more than 40 years changing the landscape of the city. To his credit are 12 bridges, 35 highways, 658 playgrounds, 288 tennis courts, 673 baseball diamonds, and such edifices as Lincoln Center, Shea Stadium, the New York Coliseum, and the United Nations. Moses worked as a consultant for the city right up to his death, in 1981, at the age of 92.

D *1936*
ale Carnegie's book *How to Win Friends and Influence People* showed how "fitting into society" was the key to success.

Seven years into the Depression, almost 17 percent of all Americans were unemployed, and there was little hope of finding a job. Bleak as the future seemed, many people still found hope in the simple philosophy and practical advice of a Missouri-born teacher named Dale Carnegie.

How to Win Friends and Influence People was published in 1936. Before then, Carnegie had taught public speaking and had written a largely unnoticed book on a similar subject. But the widespread hardship of the Depression made people ready for hopeful, practical ideas. It was a relief to read what Carnegie called his "action book,"

full of techniques for success and divided into chapters with titles like "How to Make People Like You Instantly," "How to Interest People," and "Making People Glad to Do What You Want." Carnegie's straightforward good sense was refreshingly easy to follow, all of it centering on one

simple concept: "a vigorous determination to increase your ability to deal with people."

Read by clerks and executives alike, *How to Win Friends and Influence People* became one of the best-selling books of the 1930's. In great personal demand, Carnegie became a popular figure on the lecture circuit, and he wrote a syndicated column. By the time he died in 1955, nearly 5 million copies of his book had been sold.

IN THEIR OWN WORDS

"There is only one way under high Heaven to get anybody to do anything. Did you ever stop to think of that? Yes, just one way. And that is by making the other person want to do it. Remember, there is no other way. Of course, you can make a man want to give you his watch by sticking a revolver in his ribs. You can make an employee give you co-operation — until your back is turned — by threatening to fire him. . . . But these crude methods have sharply undesirable repercussions. The only way I can get you to do anything is by giving you what you want. . . ."

Dale Carnegie on the "The Big Secret of Dealing With People" from his
How to Win Friends and Influence People, *published in 1936.*

The **Hindenburg** *explodes at Lakehurst, New Jersey.*

1937

For a year a dirigible named *Hindenburg* provided elegant passage across the Atlantic, until a fiery crash brought an end to travel by airship.

In May 1936 an airborne palace called the *Hindenburg* made its first flight from Germany to a landing area in Lakehurst, New Jersey. Running on diesel fuel and held aloft by hydrogen gas, the 800-foot airship floated almost silently at 80 miles an hour. With a piano, cocktail lounge, two promenade decks, and a dining room that seated 34 passengers, the *Hindenburg* offered non-Depression luxury and a tenuous link between two former enemies.

For a year the *Hindenburg* traveled between Germany and the United States, transporting more than 1,300 passengers and thousands of pounds of mail and packages. But during a routine landing at Lakehurst, on a rainy May 6, 1937, at 7:23 P.M., the hydrogen gas inside the *Hindenburg* ignited, and the ship exploded and crashed. Thirty-six of the 97 passengers and crew members died in the crash. The moment was preserved for history by magazine and wire-service photographers, as well as by Herbert Morrison, a horrified radio announcer who was on the scene to cover the ship's landing.

After the *Hindenburg* crash, airships were deemed dangerous and were never again used for commercial transport.

1937

Two convicts escaped from the infamous Alcatraz prison — the only escapees who were never found or recaptured.

Established as a maximum-security prison in 1934 on 12 acres of rocky bluff, Alcatraz was surrounded by guard towers, barbed wire fences, and finally, San Francisco Bay.

Escape from the island was a long-shot gamble that 25-year-old Theodore Cole and 29-year-old Ralph Roe dared to take. Cole, who was to serve a 50-year term, and Roe, whose sentence was 99 years, had a history of escape attempts from other prisons.

The weather, at least, was on the convicts' side. On the afternoon of the planned getaway, a dense fog shrouded the island, reducing the tower guards' visibility to zero. The two inmates had secretly sawed through the iron bars of a prison shop window, concealing their progress with a pasty black mixture that hid the cuts. When the guard left the shop on December 16, 1937, the inmates bent back the bars and quietly broke the window. Cole and Roe then shimmied out, opened a gate lock with a wrench, and dashed for a crag, where they leaped into the bay's rolling waters. Twenty minutes later the guards realized they were missing. An intense manhunt followed, but the prisoners were never found.

Did they make it to the shore, more than a mile away? In 1962 the possibility of reaching land was confirmed when the police caught the last escapee from Alcatraz on the shore near the Golden Gate Bridge. If he had gotten that far, perhaps Cole and Roe had too.

IN THEIR OWN WORDS

"Here it comes, ladies and gentlemen, and what a sight it is, a thrilling one, a marvelous sight.... The sun is striking the windows of the observation deck on the westward side and sparkling like glittering jewels on the background of black velvet.... Oh, oh, oh. ... It's burst into flames.... Get out of the way, please, oh my, this is terrible, oh my, get out of the way, please! It is burning, bursting into flames and is falling! This is terrible! This is one of the worst catastrophes in the world! Oh the humanity and all the passengers....I — I — folks, I'm going to have to stop for a moment because I've lost my voice. This is the worst thing I've ever witnessed."

Radio announcer Herbert Morrison's coverage of the Hindenburg *disaster.*

A 1938 view of Alcatraz, also known as The Rock.

1938

King of Swing Benny Goodman and his orchestra played the first swing concert in the history of New York's Carnegie Hall.

On a cold January evening in 1938, Carnegie Hall in New York City hummed with an unaccustomed sound as the tentative opening strains of a Benny Goodman standard, "Don't Be That Way," pulsed through a packed audience. Hepcats and jitterbuggers swayed to the rhythms of Count Basie's piano, Harry James's trumpet, and Goodman's clarinet. Gene Krupa's wild drum solo stirred the crowd to a fever pitch, and by the final ecstatic notes of "Sing, Sing, Sing," even society patrons in tuxedos and evening gowns were dancing in their theater boxes. Swing — the rhythmic, improvisational music born of honky-tonk and hot jazz, and deemed by *The New York Times* to be "dangerously hypnotic" — had become a national sensation.

Left to right: Benny Goodman, Cootie Williams, and Vernon Brown swing at Carnegie Hall in 1938.

Goodman, who took his first music lessons at a synagogue, had costarred with the popular bandleader Xavier Cugat in 1934, on a radio show called *Let's Dance*. Fans in the East would stay up until the wee hours of the morning to listen to their West Coast concerts. In 1935 the King of Swing expanded his following with an appearance at the Palomar Ballroom in Los Angeles.

Rather than play predictable foxtrots, Goodman picked up the pace and improvised with swing rhythms arranged by jazz pianist Fletcher Henderson. His new versions of old favorites were an immediate hit. Three years later, Goodman's concert at Carnegie Hall broadened his appeal and opened the door to a wider audience for swing. Now both older, sophisticated listeners and trendy teenagers were swinging to the music side by side.

1938

Broadcasting from four European capitals and Washington, D.C., CBS's coverage of the Austrian *Anschluss* brought a new urgency to global events.

Sitting alone in his apartment in Vienna on March 11, 1938, Columbia Broadcasting System (CBS) foreign correspondent William L. Shirer considered what to do next. Adolf Hitler had accomplished his *Anschluss* (annexation) of Austria to Germany, and Shirer knew what a tremendous impact any broadcast from Vienna would have. Making his way to the Nazi-controlled Austrian radio station, Shirer was told "Nothing doing. No lines. No broadcast," and was hustled out onto the street.

It was not the first time Shirer had been thwarted. He and his boss, CBS European bureau chief Edward R. Murrow, had repeatedly tried to broadcast news of Hitler's movements only to be told by

CBS president William S. Paley to stick to the weekly children's program of youth choirs to which they had been assigned. Paley, afraid that his station might be seen as taking an editorial stance if he allowed the direct news broadcasts, insisted that a United Press International (UPI) staff writer read the European news from CBS's New York City studio. The bulletins, although factual, lacked the sense of immediacy that on-the-spot reporting provided.

Intent on broadcasting, Shirer consulted with Murrow, and at his suggestion flew to London on March 12. Shirer went on the air at 6:30 P.M. Eastern Standard Time and described the *Anschluss* of the day before, giving American audiences "an uncensored, eye-

witness account." The following day the CBS news director asked Murrow and Shirer to do a 30-minute European roundup, featuring reports from various cities. The correspondents spent the next several hours contacting reporter friends across Europe — not to mention trying to relay the news over cranky shortwave radios and telephone lines. That evening Shirer led off a broadcast from London with accompanying reports from Edgar Mowrer in Paris, Pierre Huss in Berlin, and U.S. senator Lewis Schwellenbach in Washington, D.C. Murrow, whose terse, vivid

news delivery would make his name a household word in America, sent his report out of Vienna.

Edward R. Murrow (left) and William L. Shirer at a Paris café.

Back in the United States everyone, including Paley, was impressed; the radio could bring distant events right into America's living rooms with a sense of immediacy that newspapers could not match. Nightly "world roundups" quickly became the norm, and as Europe lurched toward all-out war, it was the radio, and not the morning paper, that first delivered the breaking news story.

1938
The great September hurricane of 1938 took the Northeast completely by surprise.

The first mention of the storm appeared in the September 18, 1938, edition of *The New York Times*. According to the newspaper, a hurricane had been spotted 450 miles north of San Juan, Puerto Rico, and 900 miles east-southeast of Miami. It was moving at about 20 miles per hour, and small craft were advised to stay in port.

The news attracted little attention, and by the next day the storm seemed to be blowing itself out in mid Atlantic. What no one knew was that unusual atmospheric conditions would draw it inexorably northward; the biggest hurricane of the season was headed straight for one of the most densely populated regions of the United States. The Long Island Express, as it would later be known, was on its way.

It wasn't until 3:00 P.M. on September 21, when the storm had already grazed the Jersey Shore, that the New York City Weather Bureau issued a warning. By then it was too late. Hurling winds of more than 100 miles per hour, the hurricane plowed into Long Island. Residents were caught totally unprepared. Homes collapsed, roadways were flooded, and entire families were lost in the storm's massive tidal surges.

New England bore the full brunt of the hurricane's fury. A wall of ocean roared through downtown Providence, Rhode Island, submerging the city under 12 feet of water. Along the state's coastal resorts, the surging waters smashed houses and drowned dozens of people. From New York to Boston, some 20,000 miles of electric, telephone, and telegraph lines were blown down, cutting off communications and plunging the Northeast into darkness.

By 10:00 P.M. it was all over. Charging up the Connecticut River valley, the storm turned northwest over Lake Champlain, crossed into Canada, and died out. In its wake it left a scene of almost surreal devastation. About 600 people lost their lives, and 60,000 were left homeless. Total property damage amounted to a whopping $400 million.

A house that was swept off its foundation by the hurricane sits placidly in a Long Island bay.

1939
World's fairs on opposite coasts of the United States entertained millions of Americans.

As bells rang out from the 400-foot Tower of the Sun that dominated a sparkling Magic City, the Golden Gate International Exposition opened in San Francisco on February 18, 1939. Built on 400 acres of silt dredged from San Francisco Bay, the Pageant of the Pacific celebrated the achievements of America's Western states and the Pacific Basin countries. Attractions ranged from a $40 million international art exhibit in the Palace of Fine Arts to a 40-acre midway. With some 55 amusements, including a ranch with 47 scantily clad cowgirls, the midway was a popular draw, and *Life* magazine declared the exposition a "gay and charming carnival."

As the San Francisco exposition moved into full swing, across the nation on what had been a marsh in Flushing, New York, another international exhibition was just beginning. With 60 nations participating, the

A souvenir pin with the World's Fair symbols: the Trylon and Perisphere.

New York World's Fair opened on April 30. "The World of Tomorrow" was the fair's theme, and its symbols were the 700-foot-high triangular Trylon and the 200-foot-diameter Perisphere.

Spread out over 1,216 acres were numerous exhibits devoted to technological innovation. Visitors to Futurama got a glimpse of what America would look like 20 years later — express highways, high-rises, and all — and came away with a button declaring "I Have Seen the Future." Along with exhibits featuring nylon stockings, air conditioning, and color photography were a speech synthesizer called the Voder and a walking, talking robot named Electro. On the lighter side, the Amusement Zone provided a 250-foot simulated parachute jump, an aquacade, and skimpily dressed women in shows that had little to do with the future. Despite disappointing revenues and criticisms that it was too highbrow a venture, the New York World's Fair was popular enough to run for two seasons, closing permanently in October 1940.

A leading organizer of the Lincoln Memorial concert, Secretary of the Interior Harold Ickes greets celebrated contralto Marian Anderson.

A *1939* **fter being banned from performing in Constitution Hall in Washington, D.C., African-American contralto Marian Anderson was invited to sing at the Lincoln Memorial.**

Blessed with one of the most electrifying operatic voices of her time, Marian Anderson had applied to sing a recital at the 4,000-seat Constitution Hall in Washington, D.C., the finest concert hall in the capital. When the hall's owners, the Daughters of the American Revolution (DAR), discovered that Anderson was black, they claimed a scheduling conflict, then did not offer another date.

Even those Americans accustomed to segregation laws were shocked at this discrimination against a celebrated artist in the nation's capital. As a tireless campaigner for equal rights, first lady Eleanor Roosevelt was especially outraged at the DAR. In protest, she publicly resigned from the group in her syndicated column *My Day*. "They [the DAR] have taken an action which has been widely talked of

in the press," wrote the first lady. "To remain as a member implies approval of the action."

Through the efforts of Mrs. Roosevelt and a number of supporters, including Secretary of the Interior Harold Ickes, an even more impressive place was found for the recital: the Lincoln Memorial. On Easter Sunday, 1939, Secretary of the Interior Harold Ickes announced to a crowd of 75,000 gathered along the reflecting pool: "I give you Marian Anderson."

Although the concert lasted only 20 minutes, it became a symbol of racial unity for decades to come, proof that the color of a person's skin is no barrier to great art.

W *1939* **uthering Heights was one of Sam Goldwyn's favorite and most successful films — but he could never get the name right.**

Born into a poor Polish family and left fatherless as a small child in Warsaw, 11-year-old Samuel Gelbfisz (who later changed his name to Goldwyn) ran away to England; when he was 13, he entered the United States — probably illegally. Landing a job at a New York glove factory, Goldwyn rose to the position of salesman, and at 18 became a partner in the firm. In 1910 he joined his brother-in-law, a vaudeville producer, in the risky venture of motion-picture production.

Goldwyn's first film, *The Squaw Man* (1913), was America's first full-length movie, and its director was an unknown playwright also destined for Hollywood mogul status: Cecil B. DeMille. The picture was a hit, and when Goldwyn left the company four years later to form Goldwyn Pictures, his share of the enterprise amounted to a princely $900,000.

By the 1920's Goldwyn was established as one of Hollywood's most powerful figures. As an independent producer, he discovered some of Hollywood's greatest stars, including Rudolph Valentino, Pola Negri, and Will Rogers. For the next two decades, Goldwyn produced hit after hit, including *All Quiet on the Western Front* (1930), *The Dark Angel* (1934), *Stella Dallas* (1937), and *Wuthering Heights* (1939), which the producer always mispronounced Withering Heights. This was typical of Goldwyn, who never quite mastered idiomatic English and was prone to hilarious mistakes known as "Goldwynisms."

Merle Oberon and Samuel Goldwyn review costume sketches.

A Sampling of Goldwynisms

Movie producer Samuel Goldwyn was nearly as well known for his sometimes bungled English as he was for his films. The following are a few quotes attributed to him.

- Include me out.
- A verbal contract isn't worth the paper it's written on.
- In two words, im possible.
- I don't think anyone should write his autobiography until after he's dead.
- I was on the brink of an abscess.

- I'll give you a definite maybe.
- Speaking to an ungrateful director: "You've bitten the hand of the goose that laid the golden egg."
- Anybody who goes to a psychiatrist ought to have his head examined.
- You've got to take the bull between the teeth.

1939
After a record-breaking career, Lou Gehrig, the Pride of the Yankees, played his final game.

Lou Gehrig stepped up to bat for the last time on April 30, 1939, but his fans waited until the Fourth of July to pay tribute to one of baseball's all-time greats; on that day 61,808 fans at Yankee Stadium honored the Hall of Famer nicknamed the Iron Horse. The throng had gathered to hail Gehrig for his outstanding career, which included a record-breaking 2,130 consecutive games in a 15-season stint with the New York Yankees. (The figure would stand nearly half a century, until September 6, 1995, when Baltimore Orioles shortstop Cal Ripken played his 2,131st consecutive game.)

The unparalleled string of records started on June 1, 1925, when the 21-year-old Gehrig went to bat as a pinch hitter and swatted a single. Between that day and April 30, 1939, the hard-hitting first baseman filled the record books with statistics. In 1927 and 1936 he was the Most Valuable Player in the American League. In 1931 he set a league record of 184 runs batted in, and in 1934 his batting average was .363, the highest in the league. He played in seven World Series for a total of 34 games, and his lifetime average was a whopping .340. Perhaps the title of the movie about his life says it all — *Pride of the Yankees.*

An emotional moment at Lou Gehrig Appreciation Day.

But in 1939 tragedy struck. Gehrig's health had been mysteriously declining, and he finally decided to withdraw from the team lineup on May 2. Several weeks later he was diagnosed with amyotrophic lateral sclerosis, a fatal illness that attacks the nervous system, and now known as Lou Gehrig's disease. At the Yankee Stadium farewell Gehrig expressed his deep feelings before a hushed crowd: "What young man wouldn't give anything to mingle with such men for a single day as I have for all these years?" he asked the crowd. Then he added: "Fans, . . . today I consider myself the luckiest man on the face of the earth."

1939
Franklin D. Roosevelt was the first U.S. president to appear on television.

The 1920's and 1930's saw great advancement in the field of television technology. In 1923 Vladimir K. Zworykin, a Russian-born American scientist, developed a device that could change light into electric signals and then into a TV image. Three years later Scottish engineer John Logie Baird demonstrated a television system based on photomechanically transmitting moving pictures. Shortly thereafter Philo Farnsworth, a Utah engineer, invented an all-electronic scanning system designed to bring television into individual homes. Transmission tests on experimental stations then began. In the mid-1930's the Radio Corporation of America (RCA), at the direction of its president, David Sarnoff, invested $1 million in television demonstrations.

A television first: FDR opens the New York World's Fair.

The first telecast of a major news event in the United States took place during the New York World's Fair, when President Roosevelt spoke "live" at the opening-day ceremonies on April 30, 1939. In so doing, he became the first U.S. president to appear on the small screen. The broadcast was carried by the National Broadcasting Company (NBC), a subsidiary of RCA, which immediately began regular programming two nights a week.

1939
The Neutrality Act allowed the United States to aid the Allied powers and stay out of World War II at the same time.

Early on September 1, 1939, President Franklin D. Roosevelt received a phone call from Ambassador William Bullitt in Paris. The news was grim: Adolf Hitler, who had signed a nonaggression pact with the Soviet Union eight days earlier, was bombing Poland.

On September 3 France and Great Britain formally declared war on Germany; World War II had begun. Addressing the nation over the radio in one of his famous "fireside chats," Roosevelt assured Americans that the United States intended to remain neutral. At the same time, he explained that true neutrality would probably not be possible: "It is easy for you and me to shrug our shoulders and to say that conflicts taking place thousands of miles from the whole American Hemisphere do not seriously affect the Americas. . . . Passionately though we may desire detachment, we are forced to realize that every word that comes through the air, every ship that sails the sea, every battle that is fought, does affect the American future."

Congress, sharply divided about the war, resolved its differences after bitter debate by passing, on November 3, a Neutrality Act that was also not really neutral. Prior legislation had outlawed the export of war materials to any belligerent nation. The new law removed the embargo on war supplies but stipulated that they had to be purchased on a cash-and-carry basis: the Allies could bring their own money and ships to the United States to buy and transport materials. In this way the United States could help supply Great Britain and France, and at the same time stay out of the war.

A poll conducted by Dr. George Horace Gallup, director of the American Institute of Public Opinion, showed that Americans were squarely behind the sort of compromise the Neutrality Act provided. Out of a cross section of voters from every state, Gallup found that 95 percent of Americans wanted to stay out of the war, but 84 percent hoped for an Allied victory. 🚗

1939

The debut of the first FM station revolutionized the radio broadcasting industry.

The New York Times was downright giddy in its enthusiasm. The world's first "high-powered, thunder-defying" radio station was up and running, it declared in early 1939, and all because of the visionary determination of a college professor turned entrepreneur.

The story began six years earlier when Prof. Edwin H. Armstrong of Columbia University took out a patent for something called frequency modulation (FM). It was an entirely new radio system, better than anything then in use. Unlike amplified modulation (AM), it could send and receive an enormous range of tonality and volume, from the highest tweet of a piccolo to the deep explosive rumble of a bass drum. At the same time FM receivers were largely free of annoying static. Armstrong unveiled his invention at a 1935 meeting of the Institute of Radio Engineers. He then began looking for backers.

He was met by a chorus of polite yawns. His fellow engineers, while impressed by the technology of FM, saw little commercial application. Established AM broadcasters, whom Armstrong hoped would switch to FM, invariably turned him down. So did potential investors. Even David Sarnoff, a onetime friend and the president of the Radio Corporation of America (RCA), said no. While Sarnoff admitted that FM

was indeed "a revolution," he decided that for RCA the future was television.

Realizing that the only way he was ever going to sell FM radio to broadcasters and the public was to do it himself, Armstrong erected a 50,000-watt radio tower in Alpine, New Jersey, directly across the Hudson River from his home in Yonkers. To demonstrate the clarity of FM radio, Armstrong had a friend saw wood, strike matches, and mix cocktails, complete with tinkling ice and fizzing soda water, on the air.

Armstrong's plan worked; word about FM radio began to spread. On July 18, 1939, W2XMN, broadcasting from Alpine, went into commercial operation. That same month General Electric started marketing two types of FM receivers: a

For FM broadcasts, a special tuner could be hooked up to an existing radio.

$70 radio for FM only; and a combination AM/FM model costing $250. By fall the Federal Communications Commission (FCC) had received some 150 applications to build FM stations, and in 1940 the FCC assigned FM broadcasters their very own spectrum on the nation's airwaves. 🚗

1939

Twenty-five-cent double features made the movies a popular Depression-era escape, with the films of director Frank Capra becoming box-office leaders.

The 17,000 movie theaters across the country in the 1930's came in many shapes and sizes, ranging from corner bijous to opulent palaces. Loew's Paradise Theatre in the Bronx, New York, seated 4,000 moviegoers amid paintings, statuary, and a dark blue ceiling that flickered with stars. Even neighborhood movie houses featured handsome lounges and elaborate interiors. Whatever the setting, the program was similar; besides a double feature, there were cartoons, newsreels, travelogues, and on Saturday, serials — all for just 25 cents. But no matter what was showing, the reason for going to the movies was almost always the same: to escape the everyday dreariness of the Depression.

One director who was successful at helping moviegoers take their minds off their worries was Frank Capra. After winning five Academy Awards in 1934 with his screwball comedy *It Happened One Night,* starring Clark Gable and Claudette Colbert, Capra directed a number of socially relevant dramas about the average man's fight for justice and decency: *Mr. Deeds Goes to Town* (1936), *Mr. Smith Goes to Washington* (1939), and *Meet John Doe* (1941). Capra's films pitted bumbling small-town heroes against sophisticated, often corrupt opponents. Audience members could identify with the ordinary fellow, who, possessed of old-fashioned virtues such as honesty and integrity, somehow prevailed.

Mr. Smith Goes to Washington, now hailed as a classic, was originally the source of major national controversy. Intended as an idealistic statement about the American political system, it told how freshman senator Jefferson Smith (played by James Stewart) waged a single-handed battle against government corruption. But when it premiered in October 1939 at Constitution Hall in Washington, D.C., the film so outraged some viewers that one-third of the audience left early. Citizens and members of Congress alike were appalled. Majority Leader Alben Barkley called it a "grotesque distortion" of the way Congress was run — attacking, in particular, its depiction of the Senate as "the biggest aggregation of nincompoops on record." Despite all the criticism, the film went on to be nominated for several Academy Awards, including Best Director. It remains popular to this day.

James Stewart and Jean Arthur peruse a guide to the city in **Mr. Smith Goes to Washington.**

Ida Mae Fuller picks up her landmark retirement check.

1940

Ushering in a New Deal program for America's retirees, Ida Mae Fuller received the first Social Security check.

Ida Mae Fuller had brushed against greatness before. Born in 1874 in the small town of Ludlow, Vermont, she attended school with a sullen young man named Calvin Coolidge; later, she worked as a legal secretary for Vermont attorney John G. Sargent, who would become U.S. attorney general in the second Coolidge administration.

Still, none of this compared to the thrill of opening her mailbox on the chilly morning of January 31, 1940, and finding a check inside: Social Security check #00-000-0001, in the amount of $22.54. Smiling for the cameras, the retired Vermonter held it up for reporters to see. The Social Security Act of 1935, the cornerstone of President Franklin Roosevelt's New Deal, had begun to pay off.

For Fuller, it wasn't just the New Deal, it was a great deal. Under the terms of the Social Security Act, employers and employees each paid 1 percent of the worker's salary into a trust fund, with a maximum contribution of $30 annually. Ida Mae Fuller had been in the system just two years, and from her investment of $22, the retired Vermonter — who lived to be 100 — eventually drew some $20,000 in benefits.

S 1940
Stores were stampeded and silk stockings forgotten on Nylon Day.

The search for a synthetic substitute for silk ended in 1937 when a research chemist at the Du Pont Company discovered a polymerized chemical fiber that would soon be known by its trade name — nylon. It was an essential fabric during World War II, replacing silk in parachutes and fortifying flak jackets and aircraft tires. Consumers soon encountered nylon in hundreds of items, including lingerie and toothbrushes. One of nylon's most dramatic contributions, however, was in the form of hosiery.

To announce the availability of nylon stockings, Du Pont and merchants across the country devised an official debut called Nylon Day. On May 15, 1940, crowds gathered at department store doors hours before opening; at the end of the day, the shelves were empty. Nylon hosiery was a success.

A 1940
American surgeon Charles Richard Drew led the effort to supply blood to injured American GI's, but would have had his own blood rejected because he was African-American.

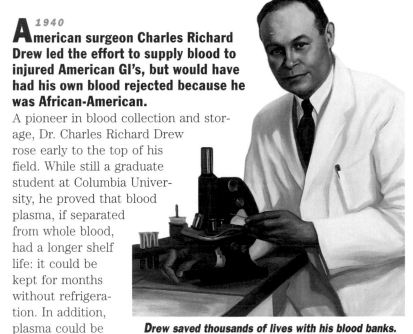

A pioneer in blood collection and storage, Dr. Charles Richard Drew rose early to the top of his field. While still a graduate student at Columbia University, he proved that blood plasma, if separated from whole blood, had a longer shelf life: it could be kept for months without refrigeration. In addition, plasma could be given to patients

Drew saved thousands of lives with his blood banks.

without going through the process of cross-matching or blood-typing. Drew used this knowledge to create the first working blood plasma bank — at Presbyterian Hospital in New York City.

When the national Blood for Britain project was initiated in September 1940, Drew was the logical choice to head it up. Over the next five months he supervised the shipment of some 14,500 pints of lifesaving plasma overseas. Then, in 1941, with the entry of the United States into World War II all but certain, he led the American Red Cross effort to stockpile more than 1 million pints of plasma. Because of Drew, the lives of thousands of GI's were saved, and his system of collection and distribution eventually became the model for the blood donor program of the American Red Cross.

In 1941 Drew was appointed director of the first American Red Cross Blood Bank, but he didn't remain in the position for long. Against all reason, the military decreed that only Caucasian blood could be accepted for storage. The public outcry was immediate, and the military compromised: henceforth, "Negro blood" would be accepted, but it would be kept separate from the "white" blood supply. The racial segregation of the blood banks was more than Drew, who was black himself, could tolerate. He called a press conference. "The blood of individual human beings may differ by groupings," he explained to reporters, "but there is absolutely no scientific basis to indicate any difference according to race."

He was right, of course, but prejudice retained the upper hand, and Drew resigned in protest. He retired to the department of surgery at Howard University in May 1941, and became chief of staff at the medical school's teaching hospital. During the next nine years he trained one-half of the nation's black surgeons, until his death in an automobile accident in 1950.

Eager New York City shoppers queue up for stockings on Nylon Day.

1940
Ernie Pyle's "worm's-eye view" of World War II made him the most widely read war correspondent.

Ernie Pyle wrote his first newspaper column almost by accident. He had taken a three-month sick leave from his editing job at the Washington *Daily News,* and he spent the time touring the country. When he returned to work, the paper's regular columnist was on vacation. So Pyle filled in with his travel notes. His chatty, homespun articles quickly found an audience.

Ernie Pyle taking a break with a group of Marines on Okinawa in 1945.

In 1940 Pyle went to London to cover the Blitz, and from there he followed the Allied forces to North Africa. And there in the desert foxholes, amid the heat of battle, he discovered his real specialty — writing about ordinary fighting men.

Pyle's worm's-eye view of life at war won him an almost legendary status among soldiers and civilians alike. For many at home, his dispatches were like letters from their boys overseas. He wrote of daily discomforts such as sore feet, boredom, and the agonizing slowness of the mail. He also wrote of friendship and loyalty, the thousand daily heroic acts of men at arms, and the grief over fallen comrades. To the combat infantrymen with whom he traveled, Pyle was a true comrade, one of their own.

Eventually, Pyle's columns appeared in 400 newspapers with a combined readership of some 60 million — making him, according to *Time* magazine, "America's most widely read war correspondent."

On April 18, 1945, on the tiny Pacific island of Ie Shima, Pyle's jeep was caught in an ambush; he was shot in the head and died instantly. Where he had fallen, soldiers erected a plain but eloquent marker: "AT THIS SPOT / THE 77TH INFANTRY DIVISION / LOST A BUDDY / ERNIE PYLE." To the end, he was one of them.

1941
The U.S. military expected a possible Japanese strike, but no one thought Pearl Harbor would be the target.

At 7:55 A.M. on December 7, 1941, Commander Mitsuo Fuchida led the first wave of Japanese warplanes over Oahu Island, Hawaii. The American naval base at Pearl Harbor, he reported, was "asleep in the morning mist." Seconds later, it was a cauldron of oily flames and smoke. Some 400 Japanese bombers and fighters, attacking over a two-hour period, reduced most of the U.S. Pacific Fleet to burning wreckage.

Even as the bombs rained down, it was hard to admit what was happening. Adm. Husband E. Kimmel, commander of the Pacific Fleet, stood still and

After being hit at Pearl Harbor, the U.S.S.

1941
Franklin D. Roosevelt and Winston Churchill held their first war conference four months before the United States entered World War II.

By May of 1941, as the fighting raged in Europe, it was clear that the United States could no longer remain neutral. German

FDR and Churchill exchanged some 1,500 messages before they met in 1941.

U-boats, which had been picking off British ships in the Atlantic Ocean, were now targeting American boats.

President Franklin Roosevelt, declaring that the country was in an "unlimited national emergency," arranged a meeting with the prime minister of England, Winston Churchill. While the two heads of state had been corresponding since September 1939, they had not met face to face for nearly 25 years. "I have got to see Churchill myself in order to explain things to him," Roosevelt said.

On August 9, 1941, accompanied by their military staffs, Roosevelt and Churchill began a series of private talks aboard two warships in Argentia Bay, Newfoundland. The Argentia conference produced the Atlantic Charter, which laid out the "common principles" on which the two nations based their "hopes for a better future." By calling for the destruction of Nazi tyranny, the document expressed America's unequivocal support for every nation fighting toward that end.

The Argentia conference cemented the working relationship between the two men. As Roosevelt confided afterward, "I am very confident that our minds travel together."

watched, in momentary shock, as the battleship *Arizona* went up in smoke. When news of the disaster hit Washington, D.C., Secretary of the Navy Frank Knox gasped in disbelief.

Yet only hours earlier American intelligence officers (who had long since cracked the Japanese diplomatic code) had deciphered a radio communique that might have served as warning. Japanese diplomats in Washington had been negotiating a peace accord, and the message abruptly ordered them to break off talks. Some American officials thus suspected that the Japanese might attack. But they thought that the target would be the Philippines.

When he saw the intercepted message, the army chief of staff,

Gen. George C. Marshall, issued a warning to all Pacific commanders to "be on alert." But his orders to Pearl Harbor, sent by Western Union, arrived too late: the attack had already begun. And earlier, when an army radar operator sighted "something completely out of the ordinary" headed straight for Oahu, it was discounted as a routine flight of U.S. B-17's.

Behind the lack of preparedness was a misguided belief that no Japanese government would be rash enough to provoke war with the United States. Mitsuo Fuchida's attack planes proved otherwise. American losses staggered the imagination: nearly 200 airplanes destroyed; 18 ships destroyed or damaged; 2,403 Americans killed; 1,178 wounded. In contrast, the Japanese lost only 29 planes and suffered fewer than 100 casualties.

But in the end the Pearl Harbor attack was a major strategic blunder. It aroused the fury of a once-neutral America, bringing the United States into World War II — and spelling the doom of the Japanese empire.

At a top-secret atomic pile during World War II, physicists monitor a nuclear reaction in this painting entitled "Birth of the Atomic Age."

J 1941
Just one day before the attack on Pearl Harbor, Roosevelt secretly approved the development of the atomic bomb.

Residents of Santa Fe, New Mexico, wondered just what was going on. Truckloads of tight-lipped strangers were moving into the remote Los Alamos Ranch School compound, 35 miles to the northwest atop a 7,200-foot mesa. But who were they? And what were they doing?

Some of the most brilliant scientific minds in America, in fact, were gathering at Los Alamos. Their purpose: to develop an atomic bomb. The $2 million Manhattan Project, authorized by President Roosevelt on December 6, 1941, was the Allied answer to rumors that the Germans already had a nuclear weapon. So men such as the chief scientist J. Robert Oppenheimer, Danish physicist Niels Bohr, and Italian-born physicist Enrico Fermi pulled out their slide rules and went to work. More than 1,000 men and women volunteered to remain confined behind barbed wire under conditions of suffocating secrecy, laboring 18-hour days for the chance to make history.

They succeeded brilliantly. On July 16, 1945, the first nuclear bomb, code-named Fat Man, exploded with the force of 17,000 tons of TNT, bathing everything in a "light that outshone the noonday sun" and blasting a 25-foot-deep crater into the desert near Alamogordo, New Mexico. The target was to have been Germany; but Germany had surrendered two months earlier, on May 7. Another enemy remained, however. On August 6, 1945, Fat Man's airborne brother, Little Boy, was dropped on Hiroshima, Japan, killing 80,000 people instantly. Three days later a second bomb leveled Nagasaki, leaving 40,000 dead. On August 14, Japan surrendered.

West Virginia *goes down in flames.*

U *1942*
ntil a convoy system was created, German U-boats took a terrible toll in the western Atlantic.
Operation Paukenschlag ("Roll of Drums") began the night of January 12, 1942. The British steamship *Cyclops* was sunk 300 miles off Cape Cod, Massachusetts, taking 87 lives. Two days later a tanker off Cape Hatteras, North Carolina, disappeared, and others soon followed. Thirteen vessels — a total of 95,000 gross tons — were lost in the next two weeks of submarine warfare in the western Atlantic. German U-boats were menacing shipping lanes from the Gulf of Mexico to the Gulf of St. Lawrence. In March alone, 48 ships were sunk off the East Coast, with especially heavy losses in the area between Norfolk, Virginia, and Wilmington, North Carolina, where U-boats slipped along in the dark waters picking off ships at will.

The spectacular success of Operation Paukenschlag was as much a consequence of American foot-dragging and inexperience as of German military acumen. During the winter and spring of 1942, a mere dozen U-boats patrolled the Eastern seaboard. Because no

Menace Beneath the Waves

Shortly after America entered World War II, German U-boats subjected Atlantic shipping lanes to a reign of destruction known as the Roll of Drums. The United States lost at least 460 vessels before effective anti-submarine defenses could be mounted.

• **Sunk by U-boats**

Newfoundland
Nova Scotia
New York
Norfolk
Bermuda
New Orleans
Bahamas
West Indies
Galapagos Is.
SOUTH AMERICA
EQUATOR

effective convoy system was in place until summer, ships traveled alone — making them easy targets. In addition, American seamen often talked openly over their radios, unknowingly revealing vital information to the Germans. Perhaps the worst mistake was the failure of American coastal cities to dim their lights. Surfacing near a brilliantly illuminated Miami, one U-boat commander could hardly believe his eyes. "Against this footlight glare" he recalled, "were passing the silhouettes of ships . . . sharp as the outlines in a sales catalogue. Here they were formally presented to us on a plate: please help yourselves!"

By April 1, 1942, a partial convoy system was put into place along the Atlantic coast. Merchant ships received escorts during short day runs and anchored in safe harbors at night. Three months later a full convoy network, stretching from Halifax, Nova Scotia, to the island of Aruba off the northern coast of South America, was fully operational. Meanwhile, a government-mandated coastal blackout dimmed the entire Eastern seaboard, at long last giving Allied ships a fighting chance.

A *1942*
merican soldiers landed in the British Isles in a "friendly invasion."
On January 26, 1942, Pfc. Milburn H. Henke of Minnesota was the first American GI to land on British soil. Over the next two years, nearly 2 million of Henke's fellow servicemen inundated the British Isles. They came from all over the United States, and they brought with them an endearing frankness and a keen desire to win the war.

Small English towns were suddenly transformed into islands of American culture. London swarmed with GI's — most of them overtipping, speaking too loudly, cracking corny jokes, frowning at the warm beer, and talking to British women with an easy flirtatiousness that British men could only marvel at. Still, a Yank was liked for his easygoing ways and such traits as his devotion to his mother and "kid sis."

When they weren't fighting the enemy, American GI's were fighting homesickness and fear. To lessen the distance between the British Isles and home, they held square dances and baseball games, read American comic books, watched American movies, and sang songs like "Deep in the Heart of Texas." Some drowned their woes in the pubs; others fell in love with English sweethearts.

Although most of the British welcomed the American troops — there was a war on, after all — some were not so sure. One

Pfc. Milburn H. Henke, the first American GI to land in England during World War II.

Englishman complained, "I'm beginning to understand what the American Indian went through." However he was received, and however he may have behaved, the GI was in Britain for one purpose, and wasn't leaving until he had finished his task: "Sure I want to go home now, but what good would it do?" declared one homesick soldier. "We'd have to chase out and do it all over again. We've come this far — the only thing to do is to fix it now so it *stays* fixed."

W¹⁹⁴² hile American soldiers fought hard to whip Hitler, Americans at home did their own part to win the war.

"Save your cans, help pass the ammunition" read one wartime poster, and by 1942 Americans had met the call, scouring their attics and basements for the old pots, tin cans, rusted locks, waste paper, and leaky galoshes that suddenly seemed the priceless margin between victory and defeat. Everyone knew the stakes. From one old lawn mower, enough metal could be extracted to make six three-inch shells; from an old rusted shovel, four hand grenades; from a discarded tire, enough rubber for 12 gas masks. So successful were the nationwide scrap drives that by the end of the war, recycled materials accounted for much of the steel and half the tin and paper used to defeat the Axis Powers.

In a hundred other ways Americans pitched in: rolling bandages (2.5 million), entertaining GI's at USO clubs, planting victory gardens. Preparedness became the national watchword. From the largest coastal city to the smallest inland town, civil defense wardens memorized the shapes of enemy aircraft and scanned the skies from towers and rooftops. (All for naught: not a single enemy plane was ever sighted over the continental United States.) Windows were darkened, and regular air-raid drills sent schoolchildren scurrying to the basement with textbooks held over their heads. Red Cross volunteers took first-aid training courses and collected 13.3 million units of blood for plasma during the war.

Perhaps the greatest contribution of all was money. Stoically enduring an additional 5 percent "victory tax," Americans also stuffed federal coffers with cash from the sale of war stamps and bonds. Hollywood celebrities played a vital role in the fund drive, and a few offered unusual bribes to high-rolling purchasers. Betty Grable, whose celebrated pinup decorated thousands of GI barracks, bestowed a pair of her nylons on the high bidder at a bond rally. Hedy Lamarr offered kisses to anyone who purchased a $25,000 bond; one buyer was so overcome by the prospect that he fainted before he could reap his reward. For most purchasers, though, the promise of an Allied victory was reward enough, and by war's end, some $135 billion worth of bonds had been sold.

Betty Grable smiles in a pinup pose that would become a favorite of GI's.

D¹⁹⁴² uring World War II, shortages of rubber, silk, paper, and gasoline made the slogan "Use it up, wear it out, make it do, or do without" second nature to many Americans.

In December 1941, soon after America declared war on Japan, the Office of Price Administration began to plan the rationing of common supplies for the war effort. By the end of the following year, gasoline was rationed through A, B, C stickers, with the most frugal A allowance providing just four, then later three gallons of gas per week. Even if a person had a full tank, he was expected to use his car only for such purposes as getting to work or going to church — even pleasure driving was forbidden for a time. This restriction, along with a 35-mile-per-hour speed limit, saved wear and tear on civilian tires, which were next to impossible to replace. After February 1942 no new cars were produced until the war ended.

Food rationing was also put into effect, and people needed special ration cards to purchase

During the war nearly one-third of America's fresh vegetables were grown in victory gardens.

meat, butter, cheese, fish, flour, sugar, and canned goods. Of course, ration cards did not guarantee that the food would actually be on the grocery store shelves, so substitutes were made: corn syrup, molasses, saccharin, or honey for sugar; margarine for butter; chicory for coffee. War rationing also took its toll on wardrobes. Gone were such luxuries as flap pockets, cuffs, and long skirts — clothing was made with a reduced amount of fabric. Individuals were restricted to three, then later two pairs of shoes a year, and nylon and silk went to the war effort, not into women's hosiery. To compensate, women painted lines down the backs of their calves to make it look as though they were wearing stockings.

Just as they had during World War I, Americans devised ingenious ways to make their newly restricted lives more bearable. For some, there was the black market trade in red coupons for meat and alphabet stickers for gasoline. For others, home canning became a necessity, and meatless, butterless, milkless, and sugarless dishes appeared on dinner tables. Whatever the reason, rationing or shortages, people made do. After all, there was a war going on.

Gen. Vinegar Joe Stilwell leads his troops on a grueling 14-day retreat out of Burma.

1942

As the Japanese smashed through Burma, American general Joseph (Vinegar Joe) Stilwell led his men on a daring 140-mile hike to safety.

"By the time we get out of here," 59-year-old Gen. Joseph Stilwell said, "many of you will hate my guts. But I'll tell you one thing: you'll all get out."

Those who knew Stilwell didn't doubt him. A senior Allied officer in the China, Burma, and India theater, Stilwell was known to be a hard-nosed and stubborn man — and very likely the ablest corps commander in the entire U.S. Army.

In Burma, Stilwell had been dealt an all but impossible hand. Some of his Chinese commanders ignored his orders, and Japanese assaults pushed back the Allied forces. "We are about to take a beating, I think," Stilwell wrote his wife. Finally, on May 6, 1942, with his command about to be overrun, the army's toughest general faced the grim reality of retreat.

With a group of 114 soldiers and civilians representing nine different nations, he headed for a railroad depot — only to learn that the line had been blocked by a wreck. Soon the roads gave out as well. Stilwell ordered everyone to abandon their vehicles and take only what they could carry. They would proceed on foot to India and safety.

In front of them lay mountains, the Uyu River, and some of the densest jungle in Asia; behind them, the murderous advance of the Japanese line. Stilwell informed his men that strict discipline was necessary to succeed, and anyone who didn't like it could leave.

Heatstroke, malaria, dysentery, and blisters took their toll, but Stilwell never eased up. When food ran low, he ordered half-rations and plunged on, driving the group hard and berating those who lagged behind. At last, on May 20, after two weeks and 140 miles of marching, they reached Imphal, India — sick, hungry, exhausted, but as Stilwell had promised, every one of them alive.

1942

For more than 30 years, the man who invented what is thought to be the first electronic computer was neither recognized nor paid for his work.

Devising a way to move from clumsy mechanical computation machines to electronic ones was a leap of inspiration that, John Atanasoff later said, came to him during a long trip from Iowa to Illinois. Driving past vast cornfields, Atanasoff solved the problem of applying a base-two binary format (all information conveyed in combinations of 0 and 1) to electronic systems. It remains the basic architecture for all computers in use today.

A theoretical physicist at Iowa State College, Atanasoff, along with graduate student Clifford Berry, completed a working model of the Atana-

The original Atanasoff-Berry computer.

soff-Berry Computer (ABC) in May 1942. He never put it into production. Instead, he made the mistake of explaining it to John Mauchly, who later gained fame as one of the inventors of the electronic numerical integrator and computer (ENIAC), the first publicly demonstrated general-purpose electronic computer. (The ABC was a special-purpose computer designed to solve systems of linear equations.)

Mauchly applied for, and was granted, a patent for the ENIAC in 1946. In 1973 a federal court invalidated the patent, ruling that Mauchly had invented the ENIAC after carefully studying the ABC during a visit with Atanasoff in 1941. Within the computer community the controversy about who deserves the title "founding father of the information age" remains an unresolved issue.

1942

The American naval victory against the Japanese at the Battle of Midway was achieved without either fleet coming in view of the other.

The decisive turning point in the Pacific war was the Battle of Midway, which ushered in a new kind of naval warfare. Instead of firing at each other, the opposing fleets fought with airplanes launched from the flight decks of their carriers.

The battle began on the morning of June 4, 1942, when a fleet of four Japanese aircraft carriers sent 108 bombers and fighters to attack the vital U.S. naval base on Midway, a tiny atoll northwest of Honolulu.

Americans inflicted irreparable damage on the Japanese fleet at the decisive Battle of Midway.

C 1942

Climaxing one of the greatest rescue missions in modern times, Eddie Rickenbacker and six crewmen were found alive after 24 days adrift in a small life raft in the Pacific.

The last message was grim: compass broken, bearing unknown, only an hour's worth of fuel remaining. Somewhere over the Pacific, Capt. Edward (Eddie) Rickenbacker and a crew of seven were flying their B-17 straight into oblivion.

Family, friends, and fans of the great World War I flyer would have to wait three full weeks for news of Rickenbacker's fate. As a decorated combat pilot, occasional aviator, and race-car driver, Rickenbacker had dodged death many times. Now he was president of Eastern Airlines, doing his bit for the war effort by inspecting American air bases abroad. But while delivering an important message to Gen. Douglas MacArthur, Rickenbacker and his crew were forced to bail out.

As the days dragged on, hopes dimmed. Reluctantly, a number of newspapers printed Rickenbacker's obituary. Then, on November 13, 1942, came astonishing news: after one of the most intensive naval searches in history, a member of the Rickenbacker team had been found alive, bobbing in a life raft. A day later Rickenbacker himself and two others were sighted some 600 miles north of Samoa. Three other crewmen who had made it to a tiny island were also rescued.

Weakened by the ordeal, Rickenbacker told reporters the story of their harrowing 24 days

adrift: the scorching sun and frigid ocean spray, the agonies of hunger and thirst, and the deadly temptation to drink seawater. When a raft overturned, one crew member inadvertently swallowed a mouthful; he died several days later, driven mad by thirst and saltwater poisoning. "Frankly and humbly we prayed for deliverance," Rickenbacker said. Their prayers were answered when a seagull landed on Rickenbacker's head, providing not only a meal but bait for fishing.

Joy over Rickenbacker's rescue was unrestrained. Everyone from Mayor Fiorello LaGuardia of New York City (where Rickenbacker and his wife, Adelaide, maintained a residence) to presidents of rival airlines expressed happiness over the rescue of one of America's favorite heroes.

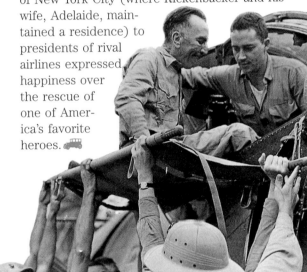

Eddie Rickenbacker is assisted out of a Catalina flying boat after his rescue from the Pacific Ocean.

Adm. Chester W. Nimitz, forewarned by intercepted Japanese messages, was ready to repel the invasion and to launch a counterattack from three of his own carriers.

At first the American counteroffensive went badly, with 35 of the 41 torpedo bombers shot down by the enemy. But a few minutes later, American dive bombers set three of the four Japanese carriers ablaze; the fourth was destroyed later that day. Scores of aircraft, which had been packed on the decks for refueling, sank with the

doomed Japanese carriers. Also lost were many of Japan's best-trained pilots, along with their leaders' hopes for continued dominance at sea.

Before Midway, the Japanese navy had seemed unbeatable, its ships marching steadily on across the Pacific Ocean. After Midway, Japan was on the defensive against a growing and aggressive U.S. Navy. Rear Adm. Raymond A. Spruance, a commander in the battle, recalled thinking: "Here is where we really jump off in a hard, bitter war against the Japanese."

IN THEIR OWN WORDS

> Some of the men began suffering pangs of hunger. . . . They began to talk about food and drink. Each man had his own peculiar desires. Captain Cherry wanted chocolate ice cream. Reynolds mused out loud about soft drinks. . . .
>
> Suddenly there was a familiar taste in my mouth! When I was first working for Duesenberg back in Des Moines, my daily lunch had consisted solely of a chocolate milk shake with an egg in it. I hadn't had one for 25 years, but now I wanted one so badly that I could literally taste it. I felt the cold, thick, sweet sensation in my mouth. My tongue moved involuntarily, and I swallowed. There was nothing there.

In his autobiography, Eddie Rickenbacker recalls his ordeal while adrift in the Pacific Ocean.

1942
German POW's played a crucial role in keeping America's farms and factories operating during World War II.

Few remember them, but from May 1942 to the end of World War II, America played host to an unusual group of guests: some 375,000 German and 50,000 Italian prisoners of war who were housed in isolated camps across the country. A small group were unrepentant fascists; but the vast majority were ordinary foot soldiers, and many found their stay in America surprisingly enjoyable. They learned to speak English, took college courses, read *The New York Times*, played soccer and handball, staged theatrical productions, and dug into a meat-and-potatoes diet that many of them could only dimly recall from their youth. In return, America hoped to procure humane treatment by the Germans for its own POW's.

The prisoners served a useful function in the United States, since they provided a much-needed labor supply. As shortages dictated, POW's picked cotton in Mississippi, logged in New Hampshire, farmed in Nebraska, and worked as clerks at army bases all across America; some handed out furlough papers to American GI's newly home from the front. The prisoners were paid, too: 80 cents a day, as stipulated by the Geneva Convention.

Not everything was wonderful about life in the camps, but it was vastly better than German soldiers had been told to expect. As Hitler's "thousand year" Reich began to crumble, many thought themselves lucky to be sitting out the war. One captive wrote home, "I have never as a soldier been as well off as I am here; we are being treated very decently — much better than by our own officers." At the end of the war, a survey of 20,000 departing prisoners found that an amazing 74 percent "had a friendly attitude toward their captors," and many were so enamored of America that they later returned and became U.S. citizens.

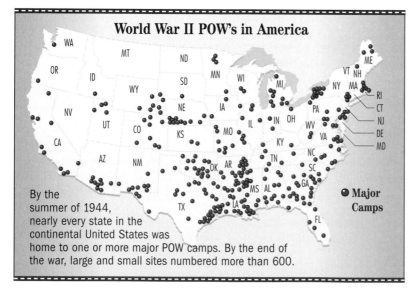

World War II POW's in America

By the summer of 1944, nearly every state in the continental United States was home to one or more major POW camps. By the end of the war, large and small sites numbered more than 600.

● Major Camps

Bob Hope and Frances Langford entertain the troops in North Africa.

1942
From canteens to the USO, celebrities did their part to help the war effort, both at home and abroad.

After the bombing of Pearl Harbor, Hollywood celebrities joined the throngs of ordinary civilians who made their way to the nearest recruiting stations. Actors like Clark Gable, Jimmy Stewart, and Burt Lancaster left behind their glamorous lives as film stars and enlisted in the armed forces. Others used their talents and celebrity status to raise money — and morale — in the war effort.

Stage Door Canteen in New York City and its counterpart, Hollywood Canteen, both established in 1942, were popular places for movie stars and entertainers to do their part. Open to enlisted men only, the canteens offered the ordinary soldier free entertainment and the opportunity to meet and chat with the likes of Betty Grable, Bette Davis, and Marlene Dietrich. No less of an attraction were the hostesses — usually young local women — who served beverages and food with a warm smile and a friendly word.

Of all the efforts to entertain the troops, the United Service Organization (USO) was probably the best known. Entertainers like Bob Hope, dubbed "soldiers in greasepaint," traveled overseas under the auspices of this nonprofit civilian body to help brighten the ordeal of life in the trenches. Sometimes performing dangerously close to the battlefront, Hope and his troupe, which included such regulars as singer Frances Langford and mustachioed comedian Jerry Colonna, relieved boredom and homesickness with their jokes and songs. If they were lucky, the shows took place on a stage; if they were not, there was always a Quonset hut or the back of a truck. In all, the USO put on more than 400,000 shows between 1941 and 1947, with audiences as large as 15,000 and as small as 25. Hope remarked, "I felt good about myself but realized that any contribution I was making was minimal. I was offering time and laughs — the men and women fighting the war were offering up their lives."

1942

The Cocoanut Grove nightclub in Boston passed a fire safety inspection just days before 491 revelers perished there in a devastating blaze.

At 10:00 P.M. on Saturday night, November 28, 1942, the Cocoanut Grove nightclub was packed with patrons. More than 1,000 people, twice the club's legal capacity, crowded its three bars, cabaret, dining room, and dance floor, eager to take their minds off the war for one night.

What lay ahead was just as bad as any battlefield horror. A fire began in the basement lounge, started by a single match struck by a busboy who needed a light in order to change a lightbulb. He fixed the bulb, then tossed the match aside; moments later, one of the lounge's paper palm trees burst into flames. Fire raced across the satin-covered ceiling, and pandemonium erupted. Two hundred patrons bolted for the cramped stairway leading to one of Cocoanut Grove's exit doors. Those who made it to the top of the stairs without being trampled found that the door to the outside had been welded shut to prevent people from sneaking out without settling their tabs.

In the cabaret on the ground floor, cries of "Fire!" and the screams of people trying to escape from the downstairs

Rescue workers pull the dead and the dying out of the burnt ruins of the Cocoanut Grove nightclub.

lounge created a wild panic. The fire reached the cabaret within seconds. People stampeded the club's revolving doors, creating an impenetrable bottleneck. Many people who did not succumb to smoke inhalation were crushed to death. Passersby recoiled in horror as nightclub patrons burst into the street with their clothes and hair aflame. Witnesses later claimed that the screams from inside the club ceased all at once, as if the fire had overcome everyone simultaneously.

When it was over, 491 of the club's patrons had been killed, many burned beyond recognition. Tangled bodies were discovered near the exits, and only 220 people escaped unhurt. Although the club had passed a safety inspection only eight days earlier, virtually all of the doors were found to be either locked, unmarked, or in some way obstructed.

For all its agony and heartbreak, the fire left some positive side effects. Doctors saved lives by applying new and experimental techniques; they injected blood plasma to treat shock, and they used penicillin to stop infections. In addition, fire safety laws were passed in Massachusetts and throughout the country that made such security features as automatic sprinkler systems and illuminated exit signs mandatory.

1943

The infamous Tokyo Rose was not one, but several female radio personalities.

Throughout the war the Axis powers broadcasted English-language radio shows out of Tokyo and Berlin. These broadcasts — often hosted by women — had a specific purpose: to sabotage the Allied war effort.

In the Pacific theater the best-known of the airwave sirens was Tokyo Rose, a nickname given by American GI's to any of a dozen female disc jockeys. Although U.S. government officials later conceded that no one person with the name Tokyo Rose ever existed, the myth of a single radio seductress acquired a life of its own, and after the war a woman named

Iva Toguri, also known as Tokyo Rose.

Iva Toguri was singled out by American authorities and charged with treason.

Toguri, a Japanese-American and a graduate of UCLA, had been visiting a sick aunt in Japan when the war broke out. Poor and hungry, she was unable to find regular employment because she refused to renounce her American citizenship. In 1943 the Japanese authorities ordered Toguri to work at Radio Tokyo, the official government radio station. Her job was to play hit songs and read news from home on an English-language show called *Zero Hour*. The program, laced with Axis propaganda, was supposed to demoralize the Allied troops.

As straight propaganda, *Zero Hour* was a total flop. The show was prepared by Allied prisoners who had also been forced to work for the station, and they urged Toguri to parody the role of a merciless airwaves temptress. Her double-edged chatter and arch delivery went unnoticed by Japanese officials, but made her a resounding hit with Allied soldiers.

Not a single piece of evidence indicated that Toguri was anything but a loyal American citizen caught in a bad situation. Even so, she was convicted on one of eight counts of treason and spent a total of 8½ years in prison. After her release in 1956, she remained in the United States, and in 1977 President Gerald Ford granted her a full and unconditional pardon — forever laying to rest the myth of Tokyo Rose.

1943
The All-American Girls Professional Baseball League kept America's favorite pastime alive during the war.

Concerned that major league baseball might disappear with so many players going off to war, Philip K. Wrigley, chewing gum magnate and owner of the Chicago Cubs, came up with a substitute — professional women's softball. Wrigley sent talent scouts all across America to hire the best women's amateur softball players. He then formed four teams: the Rockford (Illinois) Peaches, the South Bend (Indiana) Blue Sox, the Kenosha (Wisconsin) Comets, and the Racine (Wisconsin) Belles. The All-American Girls' Softball League's first official game, a doubleheader between the Blue Sox and the Peaches, was held on May 30, 1943. Admission was $1, and the Blue Sox took both games.

Although some observers were skeptical, the women, who received very little pay, quickly proved that they could play as hard as any men. Then Wrigley, seeking to reduce competition from established women's softball teams, altered the game so it had a faster pitch, a smaller ball, and longer bases. In 1945 the league's name was changed to the All-American Girls Professional Baseball League.

All over the Midwest, fans flocked to see their favorite players: athletes like fastball pitcher Jean Faut, who compiled a lifetime ERA of 1.24 and threw two perfect games; Dorothy (Kammie) Kamenshek, selected for seven All-Star teams as first baseman and touted by Wally Pipp of the Yankees as "the fanciest fielding first baseman I've ever seen, man or woman"; and champion base-stealer Sophie Kurys, who nabbed 1,114 freebies for the Racine Belles.

Great ballplaying was only part of the attraction. In order to dispel the image that female ballplayers were too masculine, Wrigley deliberately clothed his players in short dresses and required them to take charm lessons from beauty expert Helena Rubinstein. His team members were to represent "the highest ideals of womanhood." They could not travel unchaperoned, could not drink or smoke in public, could not cut their hair shorter than shoulder-length, and could not wear pants or shorts.

The league, which expanded to include 11 more teams, reached its peak in 1948, when nearly a million fans watched 10 women's teams compete. The league was finally disbanded in 1955 — a victim of mismanagement and the popularity of television as entertainment.

Margaret Callaghan of the Fort Wayne Daisies stretches for a fly ball.

General Eisenhower rallies the members of the 101st Airborne on the eve of D-Day.

1944
When D-Day plans were threatened, Gen. Dwight D. Eisenhower had to make the most important decision of his life.

As commander of Operation Overlord, an Allied plan to take back northern France from the Germans, Gen. Dwight D. Eisenhower knew that a victory could bring the war to a much-needed turning point. The plan called for 2,700 ships and 176,000 soldiers to cross the English Channel and storm the beaches of Normandy. The Allies first had to penetrate the "Atlantic Wall" — a line of defenses the Germans had built along the coast. To succeed, the invasion would have to be launched at dawn during low tide, when the beach obstacles would be more visible. Low tide would occur at dawn from June 5 to 7 and from June 19 to 21. But the Allies also needed a full moon to provide light for parachute divisions that would be dropping inland in advance of the ships. A full moon would coincide with low tide only between June 5 and 7.

As June 4, 1944, dawned, the situation did not look promising. A storm raged at sea, causing Eisenhower to postpone the operation for 24 hours. At 3:30 in the morning on June 5, the general awoke to sheets of pounding rain. Afraid he would have to postpone D-Day (a military term for the target day of an operation, the "D" merely being a repetition of the first letter of "day") once again, Eisenhower drove to headquarters to meet with his advisers. There meteorologist Capt. J. M. Stagg offered him some encouraging news: it appeared that a 36-hour window of calm was on its way. But Stagg also believed more bad weather was due on June 7, and 1½ days was not enough time to get all the troops ashore safely.

Eisenhower paced the floor at headquarters. If he postponed the operation again, enemy intelligence would undoubtedly learn of the Allied strategy. Finally, he stood still and faced his staff. "OK," he said quietly but firmly. "Let's go." By dawn on June 6, Allied ships opened fire on a 60-mile stretch of the Normandy coast in the largest seaborne invasion in history.

1944
The only Allied photographs of D-Day were made unforgettable by a film developer's error.

When he accompanied the troops to the invasion of Normandy in June 1944, 30-year-old Robert Capa (born Andrei Friedmann) was already a renowned war photographer. His 1936 photograph of the Spanish Civil War, "Moment of Death (of a Loyalist Soldier)," was one of the most striking images of war ever captured on film. Having covered World War II in Africa and Italy, Capa was anxious to be a part of the Normandy operation. "For a war correspondent to miss an invasion," he said, "is like refusing a date with Lana Turner after . . . a five-year stretch in Sing-Sing."

The D-Day experience was long and torturous. Aboard the U.S.S. *Chase* as it neared Omaha Beach, Capa saw through his viewfinder a frame "filled with shrapnel smoke, burnt tanks and sinking barges." As the troops under attack fell to the ship's floor, a young officer whispered to him, "You know what I see up there? I see my old mother sitting on the porch waving my insurance policy at me."

Capa sent his film, which contained more than 100 individual shots, to *Time* magazine's offices in London. A developer there over-

Capa's "D-Day, Omaha Beach, June 6, 1944," one of the eight photographs that survived the darkroom.

dried the negatives, ruining most of them. Those that survived had a blurred quality that gave them a vivid sense of immediacy. Much more than a clear shot, those shaky images born of a darkroom mistake caught the desperation and danger of the Longest Day.

FDR consults with Fala on the way to his third inauguration.

1944
President Roosevelt's pet, Fala, made the White House his doghouse.

Nobody could have predicted that Fala, a black Scottie sired by Peter the Reveller and whelped by Keyfield Wendy, would grow up to become America's most famous dog.

It was the pooch's owner, not his lengthy pedigree, that made him so well known. Born in 1940, Fala was a gift to President Franklin D. Roosevelt from a cousin, Margaret Suckley. The animal became Roosevelt's constant companion. Wearing the distinguished District of Columbia dog tag number 1, Fala even joined the president and Winston Churchill aboard the U.S.S. *Augusta* in 1941 for the signing of the Atlantic Charter.

The public loved the dog as well, and he became a popular figure in bond drives and an important prop in the 1944 presidential campaign. When Republicans spread a rumor that Roosevelt, after paying a visit to the Aleutian Islands, sent a destroyer back to retrieve a stranded Fala, FDR denied the report in a tongue-in-cheek campaign speech, declaring that Fala's "Scotch soul was furious. He has not been the same dog since."

White House guests looked forward to meeting Fala. When artist Leo Hershfield came for a visit in 1944, he reported that the Scottie performed two tricks before "he dozed off under the full-length portrait of President Garfield."

Fala outlived FDR by seven years, dying two days before his twelfth birthday in 1952.

Executive Pets

Over the years, the presidential mansion has housed an astonishing variety of wildlife:

Thomas Jefferson – Several grizzly bears and a mockingbird named Dick.

Abraham Lincoln – Ponies, rabbits, a pair of goats, and – his favorite – Jack the turkey.

Theodore Roosevelt – A piebald rat, a flying squirrel, kangaroo rats, a hyena, a barn owl, a pig, countless dogs and cats, snakes, and a badger.

Woodrow Wilson – A flock of sheep including Old Ike, a ram who chewed tobacco.

George and Barbara Bush – Millie the cocker spaniel, who wrote a best-selling autobiography.

A *1944*
groundbreaking heart oper-ation on an oxygen-deprived "blue baby" began a new era of lifesaving surgery.

Fifteen-month-old Eileen Saxon was near death when she was wheeled into the operating room at Baltimore's Johns Hopkins Hospital on November 29, 1944. She weighed only nine pounds and had a congenital heart defect called tetralogy of Fallot. Blood was not flowing properly from her heart to her lungs, a condition that prevented oxygen from getting into her blood-stream and caused her skin to take on a bluish hue. In an attempt to save her life, chief pediatrician Helen Taussig and chief surgeon Alfred Blalock agreed to risk open-heart surgery on the baby.

After three hours on the operating table, the child began turning a healthy pink. By rerouting an artery from the aorta, the doctors had formed a duct that would carry more blood and oxygen between the heart and lungs. Eileen soon improved and went home.

It was Dr. Taussig who first believed that the heart defect could be corrected. Dr. Blalock had spent years performing a bypass procedure on dogs with the help of Vivien Thomas, a surgical technician who devised a hand-held oxygen pump vital to the operation.

Before the Blalock-Taussig procedure was tried, open-heart surgery was extremely rare. News of the "blue baby" break-through spread throughout the nation, and the procedure saved thousands of children with con-genital heart defects, launching a new era in cardiology.

J *1944*
Japanese balloon bombs sent over the Pacific killed six people — the only enemy-induced deaths in the continental United States.

On May 5, 1945, Archie and Elsye Mitchell took five Sunday school chil-dren on an outing in the woods about 30 miles from Bly, Oregon. While there, the children discovered a strange object on the ground. As they examined it, the object exploded, killing Mrs. Mitchell and the children.

A hydrogen-filled balloon bomb drifts across the Pacific. A com-plex release mechanism (inset, above) dropped the payload.

The Fu-Go Project, a Japanese plan to bomb North America from balloons, was the reason for these deaths — the war's only enemy-induced casualties on the U.S. mainland. Japan had launched the balloons, which carried incendiary bombs, on November 3, 1944. The wind blew thousands across the Pacific Ocean over the next year.

Japanese leaders hoped to start forest fires and frighten the pop-ulation, but only a few bombs caused any damage. The first one was discovered near Thermopolis, Wyoming, on December 6, 1944. Another, caught on power lines for the Hanford Nuclear Plant in Washington, triggered a security mechanism that shut down the plant for three days. For the most part, however, the balloons drifted harmlessly over the West Coast, the Midwest, and southern Canada, with a few landing as far east as Michigan.

Wartime censorship prevented news of the Fu-Go balloon attacks from spreading. Not until 1987 did they became public knowledge, when seven Japanese women who had helped construct the balloons sent letters of apology to the families of the bombing victims.

G *1944*
Glenn Miller's disappear-ance may have been caused by "friendly fire."

On December 15, 1944, on the way home from an aborted attack on Siegen, Germany, a four-engine Lancaster bomber jettisoned its load of bombs over the ocean. For its British crew it was a fairly routine procedure.

But for U.S. Army Air Force major Glenn Miller — whose orchestra had been the most popular big band before World War II — the routine maneuver probably proved fatal. In 1984, 40 years after the Norseman C-64 in which Miller was flying from England to Paris vanished without a trace, the Royal Air Force navigator and the pilot of the Lancaster made a stunning disclosure. The explo-sion of the bombs they had jettisoned had caused a shock wave that knocked a Norse-man airplane out of the sky. "It was the only Norseman in the area," the pilot said. "The times are exact. That was Glenn Miller crash-ing." The navigator had previously tried to tell his story to the press in 1954, after seeing the film *The Glenn Miller Story*, but was ignored.

The disclosure offered a convincing solution to a mystery that had long haunted fans of the bandleader.

Glenn Miller conducts his band during a tour of U.S. bases and clubs in Britain in 1944.

302

The Glenn Miller Orchestra had entered the scene with its hit song "In the Mood." Popular with lovers of swing music, the band rose to fame on the strength of excellent arrangements, strong vocals, and such tunes as "Moonlight Serenade," "Tuxedo Junction," and "Chattanooga Choo-Choo." By the early 1940's, one out of every three nickels that Americans plugged into jukeboxes set a Miller record on the turntable.

When Miller's plane disappeared, fans everywhere were stunned. The official explanation that bad weather had probably downed the plane gave little solace to those hungry for news of Miller's true fate. The British crew's story helped solve the mystery.

1944
During World War II women made up a major percentage of the workforce in some industries.

With 12 million men overseas on active duty, women at home found themselves courted for jobs formerly reserved for males. Induced by higher pay and instructional brochures like "Can You Use an Electric Mixer? If so, you can learn to operate a drill," as many as 20 million women worked outside the home between 1942 and 1945; by 1944 they made up to 65 percent of the workforce in some industries. Women assembled parts and polished bomber noses in

Rosie the Riveter came to represent all women who rolled up their sleeves for the war effort.

munitions plants, and they painted shells in aircraft factories. They also held jobs in domestic industry — on the auto assembly line, in meatpacking plants, and on the railroads.

Although they performed the same tasks as men, women often found the job titles changed and their wages slashed. They made the best pay in manufacturing jobs — though only about two-thirds as much as their male counterparts. Women also had to endure the barbs of male coworkers. Said one New York machinist: "You had to keep up with the man standing next to you. . . . If you slowed down, they would say, 'we knew these women would be no damn good.' " Still, for some women, working in the plants had a positive side. "I had friends whose mothers went to work in factories," reminisced one woman. "For the first time in their lives, they worked outside the home. They realized they were capable of doing something more than cook a meal."

When the war ended, returning GI's clamored for work, and women were discharged from their wartime jobs and told to return to homemaking. After winning the war on the home front, they drilled, polished, and riveted no more.

World War II: The U.S. in Europe

By 1942 the Axis Powers had swept across Europe and gained control of an area that extended from France in the west to deep inside what was then the Soviet Union, and from Norway to northern Africa. That same year their luck changed, however: American soldiers, fighting alongside British and French troops, defeated German forces in northern Africa. From then until the end of the war, luck resided with the Allies.

1941 Congress passes the Lend-Lease Act on March 11, offering aid to any nation battling the Axis.

Germany and Italy declare war on the United States on December 11; the United States, in turn, declares war on Germany and Italy.

1942 U.S. and British troops land in French North Africa on November 8. Free French forces join them two days later.

On November 30 German troops halt General Eisenhower's advance in Tunisia. The Allies end an unsuccessful offensive on December 24.

1943 From July 9 to August 17 Allied forces invade, then capture, Sicily.

After desperate fighting from September 9 to September 17, the Allies secure a beachhead at Salerno and begin a difficult advance up the Italian peninsula.

1944 Operation Overlord: June 6, D-Day, Allied forces land on the beaches of Normandy.

Operation Dragoon: August 15, the Allies land in southern France.

Battle of the Bulge: Beginning December 16, after initial setbacks, U.S. forces halt a German surprise counteroffensive in the Ardennes, Belgium.

1945 Roosevelt, Churchill, and Stalin meet at the Yalta Conference, February 4 to February 11.

The Allies begin their drive to the Rhine River on February 8.

U.S. and Russian troops meet near Torgau, Germany, on April 25.

The German High Command surrenders unconditionally on May 7. Two days later, at 12:01 A.M., hostilities end in Europe.

R 1945
Raising the flag at Iwo Jima was just the beginning of a long, punishing battle.

One of the most famous photographs of World War II shows four U.S. Marines unfurling the Stars and Stripes atop Mount Suribachi on Iwo Jima. Photographed by Joe Rosenthal of the Associated Press, the flag raising — on February 23, 1945 — marked an early triumph in the bitter campaign to take this tiny, strategically placed volcanic island. More than a month of hard fighting lay ahead.

The American assault began on February 19. A fleet of 800 ships carrying some 80,000 troops steamed in and landed four Marine regiments on the island's southern tip. Resistance was brutal. The Japanese had packed Iwo Jima's eight square miles of mountainous jungle with more than 20,000 troops, all securely dug into pillboxes, trenches, tunnels, and caves. As one American officer noted, the place was "as well-defended a fixed position as exists in the world today."

Yet taking it was essential: Iwo Jima

U.S. Marines raise the American flag on Mt. Suribachi at Iwo Jima.

formed a vital stepping stone on the invasion route to the Japanese mainland.

Mount Suribachi, the highest point, fell after four days of grueling, yard-by-yard combat. The rest was even worse. With Japanese soldiers hiding out in caves and fighting to the death, the Battle of Iwo Jima continued until March 16 — more than a month after the initial assault. It was the bloodiest battle so far of the Pacific war. The Americans sustained about 25,000 casualties: 6,800 killed (among them three of the men who had helped to raise the flag on Mount Suribachi) and more than 18,000 wounded. The island's 20,000 Japanese defenders suffered even more terribly: nearly all were killed, with only about 200 taken prisoner.

H 1945
Harry S Truman stepped into the presidency with only 82 days of training as vice president.

Vice President Harry S Truman was having an afternoon drink with Speaker of the House Sam Rayburn when he was summoned to the White House. As soon as he arrived, Eleanor Roosevelt informed him that her husband, President Franklin D. Roosevelt, had just died of a cerebral hemorrhage in Warm Springs, Georgia. "I felt like the moon, the stars and all the planets had fallen on me," Truman said.

A Missouri native who never attended college, Truman had built a reputation for integrity. During World War II he headed a watchdog committee investigating and overseeing defense fund expenditures. He did such an outstanding job that he was proposed as FDR's running mate. He was voted into office in the November election of 1944, and served as vice president for exactly 82 days. Then came the news that he would be the next president.

He took the oath of office at 7:09 P.M. on April 12, 1945, in the presence of the Cabinet, his wife, Bess, and his daughter, Margaret.

Harry S Truman is sworn in as president of the United States by Chief Justice Harlan Stone.

Only 2 hours and 24 minutes had elapsed since FDR's death. Political opponents, who regarded Truman's qualifications as less than presidential, were stunned.

Nothing daunted him, however. After making the momentous decision to drop the atomic bomb on Hiroshima and Nagasaki, effectively ending the war, Truman met the challenge of helping to rebuild a battle-scarred Europe. He was responsible for the Truman Doctrine and the Marshall Plan (named for the man who introduced it, Secretary of State George C. Marshall). Both projects sent millions of dollars overseas in foreign aid.

On the domestic side, Truman supported civil rights and other liberal causes, many of them based on FDR's New Deal programs. Conservatives fumed, but Truman stood his ground. One of his boldest, most controversial moves was to desegregate the armed forces in 1948. That same year the Democratic Party, with grave misgivings, nominated him as its presidential candidate. He went on to win a dramatic upset victory over the highly favored Republican contender, Thomas Dewey.

1945
The misinterpretation of one word may have altered the course of history.

In Japanese, *mokusatsu* can mean to "refrain from comment" or to "ignore." That linguistic ambiguity may have led to President Harry S Truman's decision to attack Japan with atomic bombs.

As the summer of 1945 approached, Japan was desperate. Its navy was decimated, its highways and bridges were in ruins from U.S. bombings, and food was scarce. Many of the country's military leaders wanted to continue fighting, but a war-weary faction of Japanese diplomats hoped to negotiate a surrender. On June 3 they secretly approached the Soviet Union, which was not then at war with Japan, to help arrange peace with the Allies. The Soviets rebuffed the overture, along with another one that followed on July 12.

On July 26 the United States, Great Britain, and China issued a joint ultimatum, demanding that Japan surrender unconditionally. In Tokyo, Japanese leaders debated about how they should respond. Emperor Hirohito found the ultimatum acceptable because it ensured the continued existence of Japan and of the Emperor himself (the ultimatum strongly hinted that Hirohito would be allowed to keep his throne), but War Minister Korechika Anami argued to reject it. Eventually, the cabinet voted to delay making a final decision because yet another Japanese peace proposal had been sent to the U.S.S.R. just two days earlier.

On July 28 Premier Kantaro Suzuki told reporters that the cabinet had decided to follow a policy of *mokusatsu*. In a hurry to broadcast the message, Japan's official news agency translated Suzuki's statement to mean "ignoring," or rejection of the ultimatum. What Suzuki really intended to say, in fact, was that the cabinet was "refraining from comment" until it could reach a decision. But the die was cast. "Fleet Strikes As Tokyo 'Ignores' Terms," the July 28 headline in *The New York Times* announced. The Japanese diplomatic mission to Moscow failed, and Truman, convinced that the enemy would fight to the bitter end, ordered the atomic bomb to be dropped on Hiroshima on August 6.

The New York Times.

LATE CITY EDITION
Partly cloudy, low humidity today.
Cloudy, showers tomorrow.

NEW YORK, SATURDAY, JULY 28, 1945.

THREE CENTS NEW YORK CITY

Cross Regains
00,000 Packages

FLEET STRIKES AS TOKYO 'IGNORES' TERMS; B-29 CHIEF NAMES 11 CITIES TO BE WIPED OUT; ATTLEE PICKS BEVIN AS FOREIGN MINISTER

1945
Although every soldier knew the meaning of KILROY WAS HERE, his true identity was never discovered.

Throughout World War II the life of the average GI was memorably chronicled by many writers and artists. War correspondent Ernie Pyle lived in the trenches with the soldiers in order to relay their stories to the folks back home, while cartoonist Bill Mauldin sardonically told the soldiers' tale through the characters of Willie and Joe.

Yet no word or image spoke for soldiers as clearly as the phrase KILROY WAS HERE. Lettered onto walls and battleships from Europe to the Pacific from 1941 to 1945, KILROY WAS HERE suggested the persistence of the U.S. soldier and the invincibility of the armed forces. It embodied the spirit of the GI at war.

Two men claimed to be the true Kilroy — Sgt. Francis J. Kilroy of the U.S. Army Air Corps and shipyard inspector James J. Kilroy — but neither identity was ever verified. To this day Kilroy remains what he had always been to anyone wearing a dog tag: a World War II everyman.

World War II: The U.S. in the Pacific

Its Pacific Fleet badly crippled by the Japanese surprise attack on Pearl Harbor, the United States was hard-pressed to stop Japan's push for domination of Southeast Asia and the western Pacific Ocean. But it still had one vital naval asset: U.S. aircraft carriers had been out on patrol, and returning unharmed, they helped turn the tide of war in favor of the Allies.

1941 Japanese carrier aircraft attack Pearl Harbor on December 7.

On December 8, Japan launches a wide offensive across the Pacific and Southeast Asia, hitting hard and decisively at Guam, the Philippines, Thailand, Malaya, Hong Kong, Burma, and Wake Island.

1942 U.S. and Philippine forces on Bataan surrender on April 9. The remaining Allied forces in the Philippines surrender over the next few months.

From June 3 to June 6 the Japanese Navy suffers a decisive defeat at Midway, losing 4 aircraft carriers and more than 200 planes.

U. S. Marines land on Guadalcanal in the Solomon Islands on August 7. Months of brutal fighting follow, until the Japanese are finally driven out in February 1943.

1943 A major Allied counteroffensive begins June 30 in the Southwest Pacific.

1944 On June 19 the Japanese fleet is soundly defeated in the Battle of the Philippine Sea.

The Americans carry out the first B-29 bombing raid on Tokyo on November 24.

1945 U.S. Marines take Iwo Jima on March 26, after nearly four weeks of fighting.

U.S. forces invade Okinawa on April 1. They complete its capture on June 21, after months of bloody fighting.

An atom bomb explodes over Hiroshima on August 6. Three days later a similar bomb is dropped on Nagasaki.

Japan agrees to unconditional surrender on August 14. Its leaders sign the surrender documents on September 2 aboard the battleship USS *Missouri*.

TURMOIL AND TRIUMPHS
(1946 TO THE PRESENT)

Surrounded by the devastation of global war, the community of nations tried once again, as they had after World War I, to create a peacekeeping organization. This time they succeeded. The United Nations was born in October 1945 with full U.S. participation. Yet even as the delegates gathered for the first meeting, tensions were escalating between the world's new superpowers: the Soviet Union and the United States.

Occupying Eastern Europe at the war's close, the Soviet Union set up satellite dictatorships in Poland, East Germany, Hungary, Rumania, Bulgaria, and Czechoslovakia. U.S. President Harry S Truman had expected Soviet domination of Eastern Europe, but he could not accept the Communists' attempts to gain power elsewhere. Hoping to "contain" the spread of Communism, Truman in 1947 issued a foreign policy doctrine stating that the United States would help any nation resisting interference by Communist "armed minorities or outside pressure."

The Soviet Union remained undaunted. In 1948 Soviet armed forces blockaded the Western-controlled zone of Berlin. The United States and its allies responded with a massive airlift of supplies to the city. In 1949 Moscow ended the U.S. monopoly on nuclear weapons by successfully testing its own bomb. That same year Communists took power in China.

The shock of these events swept away the nation's deep-seated aversion to long-term alliances with Europe. In 1948 Truman set up the North Atlantic Treaty Organization (NATO) as a grand political and military

Flags from 185 countries fly in front of the UN Secretariat in New York City.

alliance of the United States, Canada, and Western Europe. At the same time Secretary of State George C. Marshall orchestrated a vast aid program to rebuild Western Europe. The Marshall Plan put Western Europe on the road to prosperity, at the same time forging strong bonds between recipient nations and the United States.

ARMED WITH NUCLEAR WEAPONS too fearsome to use,
the world's two superpowers engaged each other through alternative means — propaganda, espionage, and military and economic aid to client nations around the globe. A state of Cold War hostility took hold, shaping American politics at home and abroad for the next 40 years. On occasion the Cold War turned hot, as in Korea in 1950, when the Communist North invaded South Korea. An alliance of United Nations forces led by the United States pushed the invaders back to the Chinese border. Then China entered the conflict, its troops rolling south in Russian-built tanks while Russian MIG fighter planes screamed overhead; the allies fell back to the 38th geographic parallel, and there they dug in.

On the domestic front, Truman pledged to continue FDR's social reforms. Truman's "Fair Deal" included an increase in the minimum wage, government-sponsored low-income housing, and expanded Social Security coverage. But a coalition of Republican conservatives and Southern Democrats derailed much of his program, including a national health insurance plan and his entire civil rights agenda.

During the 1950's more Americans than ever settled into a middle-class lifestyle. They got bank mortgages to buy homes in new suburban developments; they bought cars, television sets, and household appliances; they spawned so many children that the result was dubbed a "baby boom." As women

More than 76 million American babies were born from 1946 to 1964.

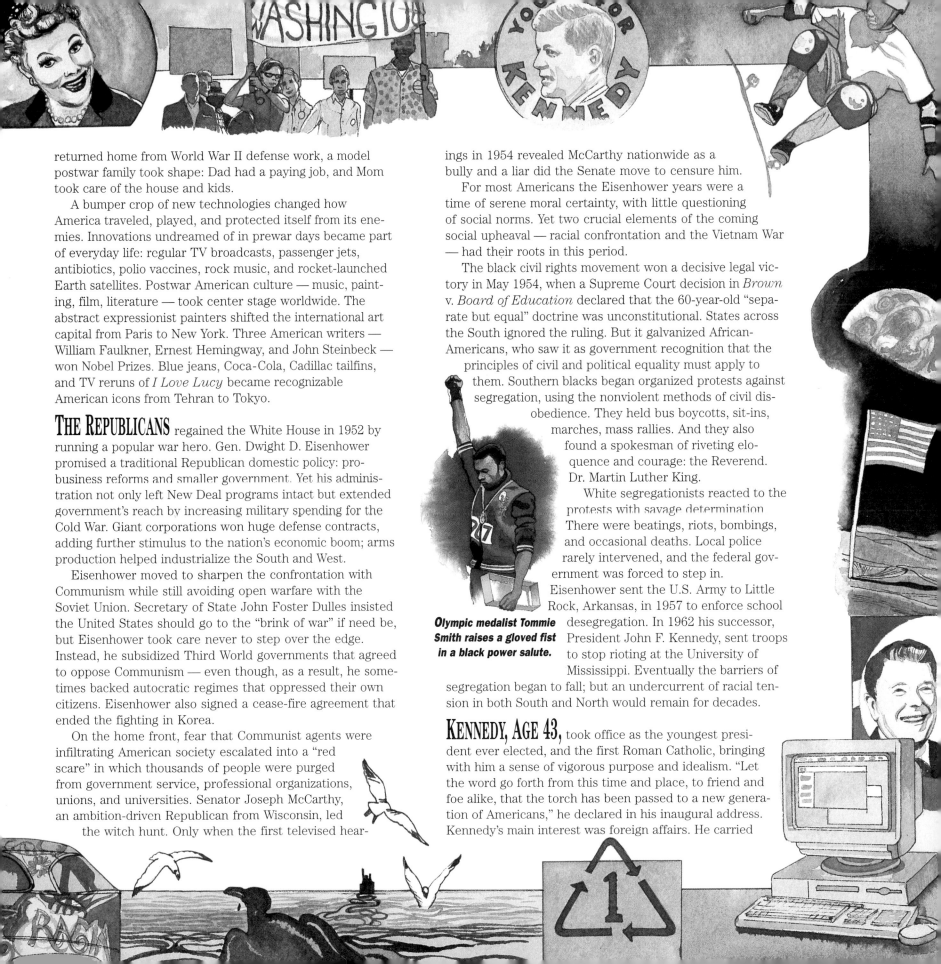

returned home from World War II defense work, a model postwar family took shape: Dad had a paying job, and Mom took care of the house and kids.

A bumper crop of new technologies changed how America traveled, played, and protected itself from its enemies. Innovations undreamed of in prewar days became part of everyday life: regular TV broadcasts, passenger jets, antibiotics, polio vaccines, rock music, and rocket-launched Earth satellites. Postwar American culture — music, painting, film, literature — took center stage worldwide. The abstract expressionist painters shifted the international art capital from Paris to New York. Three American writers — William Faulkner, Ernest Hemingway, and John Steinbeck — won Nobel Prizes. Blue jeans, Coca-Cola, Cadillac tailfins, and TV reruns of *I Love Lucy* became recognizable American icons from Tehran to Tokyo.

THE REPUBLICANS regained the White House in 1952 by running a popular war hero. Gen. Dwight D. Eisenhower promised a traditional Republican domestic policy: pro-business reforms and smaller government. Yet his administration not only left New Deal programs intact but extended government's reach by increasing military spending for the Cold War. Giant corporations won huge defense contracts, adding further stimulus to the nation's economic boom; arms production helped industrialize the South and West.

Eisenhower moved to sharpen the confrontation with Communism while still avoiding open warfare with the Soviet Union. Secretary of State John Foster Dulles insisted the United States should go to the "brink of war" if need be, but Eisenhower took care never to step over the edge. Instead, he subsidized Third World governments that agreed to oppose Communism — even though, as a result, he sometimes backed autocratic regimes that oppressed their own citizens. Eisenhower also signed a cease-fire agreement that ended the fighting in Korea.

On the home front, fear that Communist agents were infiltrating American society escalated into a "red scare" in which thousands of people were purged from government service, professional organizations, unions, and universities. Senator Joseph McCarthy, an ambition-driven Republican from Wisconsin, led the witch hunt. Only when the first televised hear-

ings in 1954 revealed McCarthy nationwide as a bully and a liar did the Senate move to censure him.

For most Americans the Eisenhower years were a time of serene moral certainty, with little questioning of social norms. Yet two crucial elements of the coming social upheaval — racial confrontation and the Vietnam War — had their roots in this period.

The black civil rights movement won a decisive legal victory in May 1954, when a Supreme Court decision in *Brown v. Board of Education* declared that the 60-year-old "separate but equal" doctrine was unconstitutional. States across the South ignored the ruling. But it galvanized African-Americans, who saw it as government recognition that the principles of civil and political equality must apply to them. Southern blacks began organized protests against segregation, using the nonviolent methods of civil disobedience. They held bus boycotts, sit-ins, marches, mass rallies. And they also found a spokesman of riveting eloquence and courage: the Reverend. Dr. Martin Luther King.

White segregationists reacted to the protests with savage determination. There were beatings, riots, bombings, and occasional deaths. Local police rarely intervened, and the federal government was forced to step in. Eisenhower sent the U.S. Army to Little Rock, Arkansas, in 1957 to enforce school desegregation. In 1962 his successor, President John F. Kennedy, sent troops to stop rioting at the University of Mississippi. Eventually the barriers of segregation began to fall; but an undercurrent of racial tension in both South and North would remain for decades.

Olympic medalist Tommie Smith raises a gloved fist in a black power salute.

KENNEDY, AGE 43, took office as the youngest president ever elected, and the first Roman Catholic, bringing with him a sense of vigorous purpose and idealism. "Let the word go forth from this time and place, to friend and foe alike, that the torch has been passed to a new generation of Americans," he declared in his inaugural address. Kennedy's main interest was foreign affairs. He carried

the Cold War banner forward, stumbling at times (a disastrous invasion at Cuba's Bay of Pigs by anti-Communist Cuban exiles), and sometimes in triumph (as when he forced Soviet president Nikita Khrushchev to withdraw ballistic missiles from Cuba). Then on November 22, 1963, during a visit to Dallas, Texas, Kennedy became the first American president in living memory to die by an assassin's hand.

A sober-faced Lyndon B. Johnson took the presidential oath of office aboard *Air Force One,* the presidential jet. On reaching the White House, he launched the most sweeping program of domestic rehabilitation since FDR's New Deal. With a stroke of the pen, Johnson set aside billions of dollars to combat poverty, improve education, provide health care, aid the elderly, and ensure racial justice. Proclaiming a Great Society of "abundance and liberty for all," he signed bills establishing Medicare and Medicaid, a Job Corps, Head Start for disadvantaged preschoolers, and dozens of other trailblazing initiatives. His 1964 Civil Rights Act was the most comprehensive anti-discrimination measure in U.S. history. But for all LBJ's energy and legislative skill, one issue defied solution: the Vietnam War.

American involvement in Vietnam had begun under Eisenhower and Kennedy, who sent arms, money, and military advisers to the South Vietnamese regime battling Communist guerrillas. Johnson dramatically escalated the war in 1965, when he ordered 300,000 troops to Vietnam. It was a decision he quickly came to regret.

As images of burning villages and dying people burst into view on TV screens worldwide, thousands of Americans took to the streets in protest. Students held "teach-ins" at university campuses, staged marches on Washington, D.C., and other cities, and went to jail or fled the country in order to resist the draft. Meanwhile, the fighting continued. Massive bombing of both North and South Vietnam ravaged the

A U.S. Army helicopter platoon assaults a Vietnam rice paddy.

countryside, and the war spread to neutral countries like Laos and Cambodia. At the same time, the Johnson administration regularly issued false reports about the war's progress — deeply compromising the credibility of the U.S. government.

The antiwar movement convinced Johnson not to run for a second term. Violent clashes between police and protestors disrupted the Democratic Convention in Chicago in 1968. That same year, two more assassinations — of civil rights leader Martin Luther King and of presidential contender Robert Kennedy, JFK's brother — rocked the nation. The United States seemed to be headed into chaos.

RICHARD NIXON assumed the presidency in 1969 in the guise of peacemaker, resolved to end the war in Vietnam and "to bring America together" at home. During his first term, with the aid of Secretary of State Henry Kissinger, he engineered a détente, or political thaw, with the Soviet Union; traveled to Moscow to sign an agreement curtailing nuclear armaments (dubbed SALT, for Strategic Arms Limitation Talks); and became the first U.S. president to visit China.

But the Vietnam conflict dragged on and on. Nixon gradually withdrew U.S. forces, reducing the number of troops from 550,000 in 1969 to 30,000 by 1972. The bombings continued, however, and so did the protests. Finally, with the signing of a peace agreement in Paris in 1973, the last American soldiers came home.

Without the U.S. Army, South Vietnam lacked the military might and political will to resist its tenacious adversary. In 1975, South and North were reunited under a Communist regime. And by then Nixon himself had departed in disgrace, forced to resign the presidency because of his role in an ugly intrigue of burglary, cover-up, and perjury called Watergate.

Other reform movements took shape during this period. Women, blacks, and Native Americans sought equality of opportunity in education and jobs. Their struggle achieved some success over the next two decades. Women joined the workforce in dramatic numbers, and many blacks entered the professions and climbed

Two anti-war protestors burn their draft cards.

YOU ARE NOW CROSSING 38TH PARALLEL

TRUMAN FIRES M'ARTHUR

into the middle class. But both groups encountered deep-seated barriers impeding their progress — even as some Americans concluded that enough had already been done to assist them.

Support for social reforms receded as the nation confronted a perilous economic transition. Each year, industrial production was becoming more global. With the aid of computers, investment capital moved around the world with destabilizing speed. Beginning in the 1970's, American industries like steel, autos, and electronics began to face stiff competition from rivals in Western Europe and Asia. Events halfway around the world had profound effects on the nation's well-being: a 1973 embargo by oil-producing nations in the Middle East sent the American economy into a sudden tailspin.

The long, steady rise in American living standards stalled. Many professionals — lawyers, physicians, real estate developers, financiers,

Each year many thousands of immigrants take the oath of citizenship.

among others — flourished in the new environment. But real wages for working Americans stagnated. First industrial employees and then middle-level managers lost their jobs as corporations moved production overseas, where wages were lower. Most households needed two breadwinners to sustain a middle-class lifestyle. For the first time since World War II, young people did not expect to live as well as their parents.

A NEW POLITICAL CONSERVATISM took hold. In 1980 voters elected Republican Ronald Reagan, who promised a return to "traditional values." During his two terms in the White House, Reagan rolled back government intervention in the economy, lowered taxes for corporations and the wealthy, and sharply boosted military spending. Industrial production rose, and the nation's soaring inflation rate abated — but at a price. The gap in income between rich and poor widened alarmingly. And Reagan's successors, Republican George Bush and Democrat Bill Clinton, would be faced with the heaviest budget deficits in the nation's history.

Beginning in 1989, Communist regimes all over the world collapsed from the weight of their internal economic and political failures. The Cold War finally ended, and with it the confrontation of nuclear superpowers that had shaped half a century of world events. Moscow released its grip on the satellite nations of Eastern Europe, and in 1991 the Soviet Union itself split up into more than a dozen independent states.

AMERICA'S POPULATION, meanwhile, was changing in significant ways. The children of the baby boom had grown to adulthood and beyond; most of them now had children of their own. The number of Americans currently stands at about 260 million, almost double the figure of a half-century earlier, and the median age is shifting rapidly upward. So many people are living beyond retirement age — one in every eight Americans are 65 or over — that economists have begun to doubt the financial integrity of government entitlement programs such as Medicare and Social Security.

Adding to the demographic ferment was the largest influx of foreign-born residents since the years before World War II. Refugees from political fear or economic woe have poured in from Vietnam, Hong Kong, the West Indies, Central America, the former Yugoslavia, and the Middle East. By the end of the 20th century some 25 million Americans had been born somewhere else.

As the 21st century approached, the nation throbbed with a productive energy and diversity unlike anything in its 200-year history. Americans earned and spent, labored and rested, in ways that seemed unimaginable just a generation earlier. For all their worries about job

Sneakers carried Americans everywhere — from gyms to the nearest shopping mall.

security, more families than ever drove two cars, owned two TV sets, and took time off at a vacation home. People started businesses, moved to new neighborhoods, ate out, recycled their trash, jogged and bicycled, bought cellular telephones, and learned about a wonderful new thing called the Internet. And if the future seemed uncertain, the world's oldest democracy could take pride in its ability to meet the challenges at hand and move ahead with confidence.

1946

The birth of Kathleen Wilkens just after midnight on New Year's Day gave her a unique claim to fame as the first official baby boomer in the United States.

Baby boomers' parents relied on Dr. Spock for advice.

A surge in the national birthrate was one of the most dramatic impacts of the end of World War II. The so-called baby boom began at exactly one minute after midnight on January 1, 1946, when Kathleen Wilkins came into the world at a Philadelphia hospital. From that moment until the end of 1964, when the birthrate tapered off, more than 76 million babies were born. In the peak year, 1957, the United States experienced a record-setting 4.3 million births.

The unexpected number of babies not only filled hospital maternity wards to capacity and beyond, it also boosted toy sales, diaper-delivery services, and even the casting of bronze-plated baby shoes. School construction tried to keep pace with the influx of students. In the 1950's, for example, a new school opened in California (one of the nation's fastest-growing states) each week for several years.

New parents eager for child-rearing advice turned to Dr. Benjamin Spock's *The Pocket Book of Baby and Child Care,* published in 1946; it sold almost a million copies a year throughout the 1950's. New mothers and fathers drew confidence from Dr. Spock's commonsense approach to child rearing, a welcome departure from the rigid theories of earlier generations.

Dr. Spock urged parents to trust their own instincts about nurturing children. He reminded them that being a mom or a dad could be not just a demanding obligation but a pleasurable experience, too.

1946

When Winston Churchill agreed to speak at tiny Westminster College in Missouri, no one expected a proclamation that would reverberate throughout the Cold War.

The phrase "iron curtain" had been around ever since 1914, when Queen Elizabeth of Belgium used it to express her horror at German aggression. But it was Winston Churchill who made the words famous.

The occasion was a speech at Westminster College in Fulton, Missouri. Churchill had been planning a private visit to the United States when President Truman prevailed upon him to give a lecture to Missouri students. "This is a wonderful school in my home state," Truman wrote; "hope you can do it." Churchill accepted, and a college with only 212 students gained instant fame.

Churchill traveled by train to Jefferson City, the state capital, then continued the 25 miles to Fulton in a motorcade. Ever mindful of his public persona,

the former British prime minister stopped his open-topped car on the outskirts of Fulton so that he could arrive brandishing his trademark stogie. "I can't light my cigar in this wind, and I know the people will be expecting it," he explained.

Advance copies of his speech omitted the iron-curtain phrase. Thus the sudden drama when, on March 5, 1946, Churchill delivered it: "From Stettin in the Baltic to Trieste in the Adriatic an iron curtain has descended across the Continent. Behind that line lie all the capitals of the ancient states of Central and Eastern Europe . . . all these famous cities and the populations around them lie in what I must call the Soviet sphere and all are subject in one form or another, not only to Soviet influence but in some cases to a . . . measure of control from Moscow."

As he was leaving Westminster, Churchill told the college president that he hoped that "he had started some thinking that would make history." Russian aggression in the coming years would soon affirm Churchill's parting wish.

At the urging of President Truman (left), Churchill took the podium.

Hostility in the Nuclear Age

Soon after the end of World War II, the world's leading nations split up into two hostile camps. Here are some milestones in the clash of ideologies known as the Cold War.

1947 President Harry S Truman asks Congress for $400 million in economic and military aid to help stem the spread of Communism.

1949 The United States, Canada, and 10 Western European nations agree to form the North Atlantic Treaty Organization (NATO).

1950 The Korean War begins on June 25.

1961 East Germany seals off the 25-mile border between East and West Berlin and erects a permanent barrier: the Berlin Wall.

1962 The Cuban missile crisis brings the United States and the Soviet Union to the brink of war.

1972 President Richard M. Nixon and Soviet leader Leonid Brezhnev sign treaties on strategic arms limitation (SALT).

1989 The Berlin Wall is torn down.

1991 Boris Yeltsin and the leaders of the Ukraine and Byelorussia announce the breakup of the Soviet Union.

1992 Presidents George Bush and Boris Yeltsin declare an end to the Cold War.

1946

The first atomic bomb tests on Bikini Atoll — one of which spewed a 6,000-foot column of radioactive water onto nearby Navy ships — were broadcast to American radio listeners as entertainment.

With live commentary from Gen. Carl (Tooey) Spaatz, radio stations aired the first peacetime detonation of an atomic bomb by the U.S. government. The two tests, known by the labels Able and Baker, took place at tiny Bikini Atoll in the southern Pacific. They were treated as if they were a movie premiere or a sports contest. Spaatz referred to the bombings as the "main event."

A joint Army-Navy project, Operation Crossroads was billed as a way for engineers to judge the nuclear survival levels of naval vessels, and thus find ways to improve their design. The operation's chief of safety, however, was appalled at the risks. In now-declassified documents, Army colonel Stafford Warren predicted that the tests would jeopardize the safety of 42,000 U.S. servicemen. His warning was ignored, and men who slept unprotected on the decks of nearby observation ships were

An atomic bomb blast near Bikini Atoll: the fifth of a series.

sprinkled by radioactive fallout.

The first explosion, Able, on July 1, 1946, sank only five vessels. Baker, which exploded underwater on July 25, created a mile-wide dome of water and a 6,000-foot column of spray. Unmanned ships that had been moored above the detonation site were drenched in radioactive mist. To decontaminate them, the Navy tried scrubbing them with everything from soap and water to lye and diesel oil. When these attempts failed, the ships were blasted with sand, rice, barley, ground coffee, and ground coconut shells. Nothing worked. Decontamination efforts had to be halted and the crews evacuated.

Residents of Bikini Atoll, the scene of 23 atomic and hydrogen bomb tests between 1946 and 1958, fared badly. They had agreed to vacate the island when the U.S. government promised that they could resettle there after radiation levels dropped. Some returned in 1969, but tests in 1978 showed that Bikini was still too dangerous, and it was abandoned again.

1946

Las Vegas was just a sleepy cow town before Bugsy Siegel and the mob brought bright lights to the Strip.

Nevada legalized gambling in 1931, and for the next several years Reno was the undisputed gambling capital of the state. Las Vegas offered only a few rustic Western gaming resorts downtown and on the outskirts on Route 91 — now a dazzling, neon-lit thoroughfare known as the Strip.

When mobster Benjamin (Bugsy) Siegel arrived in Las Vegas in the early 1940's, he envisioned what the town could be. Lacking the cash to finance his dream scheme, he turned to his colleagues in organized crime. In 1943 he persuaded mobster friends to contribute the initial $1 million he needed to set up a lavish casino.

Siegel and his girlfriend, Virginia Hill, spent more than $6 million to build the Flamingo Hotel and decorate it with the best of everything. Gambling, gorgeous showgirls, and top-name entertainers could not fail to bring in the high rollers to the

Flamingo, Siegel figured. Unfortunately, his big gamble didn't pay off.

Opening night, December 26, 1946, was a dismal flop. The gaming tables gathered dust, and even entertainers like comedian Jimmy Durante and bandleader Xavier Cugat were unable to attract customers.

When mobsters discovered that Siegel and his girlfriend had stashed away in a Swiss bank account some of the money that was earmarked for the casino, Siegel's days were numbered. He died in a fusillade of bullets on June 20, 1947, as he sat in his living room in Beverly Hills.

But as time went on, the Flamingo began attracting gamblers from all over the country, and its success helped turn Las Vegas into one of America's most popular vacation destinations. Star-studded extravaganzas and the lure of instant riches have brought in millions of tourists annually. Visitors can get married by an Elvis impersonator, admire a replica of the Sphinx, and watch a staged sea battle every 90 minutes.

The Flamingo Hotel gave Las Vegas a new image.

1947

When French designer Christian Dior unveiled his spring collection, American women were so enchanted by the "New Look" that they rushed to remake their wardrobes.

The first showing of a collection by a little-known Paris designer named Christian Dior took the fashion world by storm on both sides of the Atlantic. When Dior's models sauntered down the runways in Paris on February 12, 1947, each one wearing yards of flowing fabric and nipped-in waists, women all but stampeded to buy the new designs. *Life* magazine dubbed the collection the New Look.

Editors of fashion magazines hailed Dior's creations as revolutionary and

A sketch of a suit from Dior's 1947 collection.

voluptuous. The most enthusiastic editors urged women to clear out their closets and start acquiring totally new wardrobes. Protesting such an expensive undertaking, some disgruntled spouses formed the "League of Broke Husbands." (Dior originals sold for up to $450, in fact; but people on a budget could purchase off-the-rack copies for as little as $8.95.)

The look introduced in Dior's spring collection seemed like a kind of wonderful emancipation: stringent wartime regulations had

severely restricted the amount of fabric that could be used in clothing. Women's suits had been limited to tailored outfits with skirts just below the knee. Women's shirtmakers had been forbidden to sew breast pockets on blouses because of the extra material that was required.

When Dior dropped hemlines to 12 inches above the floor, some women protested by joining the "Little Below the Knee Club." But they were in the minority. Within weeks of Dior's first Paris show, shoppers had demonstrated their enthusiasm by snapping up more than a million mass-produced copies of the original outfits. Astonished by the success of his new look, the trendsetting designer is said to have asked, "My God, what have I done?"

1947

In order to cross the color barrier in baseball's major leagues, Jackie Robinson had to convince a baseball official that he could field insults as well as ground balls.

Branch Rickey, the president of the Brooklyn Dodgers, had contemplated integrating baseball for several years. In 1945 he finally settled on his first black player: Jack Roosevelt Robinson, of the Negro American League's Kansas City Monarchs. Robinson had shown himself to be an intelligent, uniquely well-rounded minority athlete while he was still at UCLA, where he was the only student to earn varsity letters in track, basketball, football, and baseball.

If he wanted to play in the National League, Robinson would have to endure in silence a heavy barrage of racial slurs. "I want a ballplayer with guts enough not to fight back," Rickey told Robinson before he signed him. "You will symbolize a crucial cause. One incident, just one incident, can set it back 20 years."

Robinson gave the Dodgers' official his word that he would turn a deaf ear to the inevitable verbal and physical assaults. On April 10, 1947, he took his place in the lineup for the first time.

During the first season, he had to dodge pitches that were thrown at his head. Then came the threats to the safety of his family. Robinson was warned that if

he didn't quit the Dodgers his wife and son would be murdered. "I was afraid to accept invitations to parties in strange towns. I worried about getting into a situation that would result in bad publicity," Robinson recalled later. "I was on guard day and night." It seemed that everywhere he turned, Robinson ran into hostility.

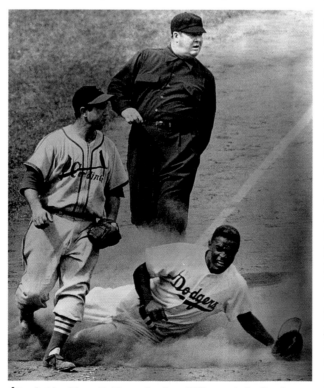

Ignoring hecklers, Robinson kept on hitting and stealing bases.

The Dodgers clubhouse was no exception. Teammate Eddie Stanky, for one, had been dead set against playing beside a black man and had circulated a petition demanding to be traded if the team hired Robinson. Later, he had a change of heart. "You know he's under orders not to yell back at you," Stanky shouted to the manager of the Philadelphia Phillies in Robinson's defense. "Why don't you pick on somebody who can fight back?"

Robinson did fight back — in his own way, and on his own turf. Along with his multiple talents as batter, base runner, and fielder, he burned with a fierce competitive fire. One opposing coach advised players that the only way to beat the Dodgers was to keep Robinson off base. "But how are you going to do it?" asked the manager. "Kidnap him before the game?" At the end of the 1947 season, *The Sporting News,* which had originally opposed the integration of baseball, honored Robinson by naming him its first Rookie of the Year.

1947

A civilian pilot claimed that he saw a chain of thin, round objects careening by his plane — and soon reports of "flying saucers" were pouring in from every direction.

On a bright, sunny June 24, 1947, pilot Kenneth Arnold took the controls of his single-engine plane and headed east from Chehalis, Washington. Flying over the Cascade Range, Arnold was searching for a marine transport plane that had crashed in the mountains.

A veteran flier, businessman, and deputy sheriff, Arnold claimed that nine strangely luminous objects

A publishing first: a flying-disk cover.

flashed by his airplane window at speeds of more than 1,000 miles per hour. The speeding objects were "flat like a pie pan," he said, and flew "like a saucer would if you skipped it across the water."

Journalists quickly dubbed the objects "flying saucers," and the U.S. Air Force set up a task force to investigate possible extraterrestrial threats to national defense. Wide news coverage led to a rapid increase in reports of unidentified flying objects (UFO's).

By 1952 an average of four flying-saucer sightings were being recorded every day, among them two sightings of strange objects on radar screens at the National Airport in Washington and nearby Andrews Air Force Base. The UFO's seemed to be targeting the White House and the Capitol, but forays by Air Force jets in pursuit turned up nothing. The incidents ranged from the verifiable to the wacky: one man claimed that aliens in a flying saucer had taken him from New Mexico to New York.

The U.S. Air Force spent nearly $500,000 investigating reports of flying saucers between 1947 and 1960. In the end, most incidents were dismissed as hoaxes, optical illusions, or misinterpretations of natural phenomena — explanations that some who study UFO's found unsatisfactory.

1947

Former potato fields in rural Long Island became a haven for World War II veterans with growing families.

The postwar housing shortage was so acute that returning GI's were living in converted chicken coops, coal sheds, even renovated trolley cars. Then developer William Levitt came up with a solution.

Using assembly–line construction techniques that he had learned in the Navy in World War II, Levitt built dwellings almost anyone could afford. A four–room Cape Cod–style house, with 721 square feet of living space, cost $6,999. His building site, an area soon named Levittown, sprawled over 1,200 acres of former potato fields on Long Island, east of New York City. With a G.I. Bill loan, a veteran could buy a house for only $65 a month, with no down payment. The first Levittown families took possession of their homes on October 1, 1947.

Operating at peak production, construction teams completed 36 houses a day — one every 15 minutes. An army of building tradesmen worked virtually nonstop for several years turning out cookie-cutter houses. Before long architectural critics and others began to deride the units' boring similarity. "Fresh air slums," said one commentator.

Such criticism didn't halt the growth, however. By 1951, 82,000 people lived in 17,447 new homes. They were in the vanguard of the 1950's demographic shift, as 18 million people moved from central cities to suburbs.

Levitt's assembly-line houses turned cash-strapped veterans into homeowners.

1947

A horseback-riding accident nearly prevented Chuck Yeager from making the world's first manned supersonic flight.

Enlisting in the Army soon after the United States declared war on Japan, Chuck Yeager moved rapidly up the ranks. In 1943 he became a flight officer. By the time the fighting ended in 1945, Yeager had shot down more than a dozen German jet fighters — a remarkable feat for someone who was only 22 when his tour of duty ended.

For the next two years, Yeager worked as a test pilot. His willingness to take risks seemed limitless. It was not surprising therefore that when the Army Air Force was looking for some-

one who could beat the British and German speed records, Yeager was chosen. At 24 years old he was ready, willing, and eager to break the sound barrier.

Two days before the scheduled flight, Yeager decided to go for a late-night horseback ride with his wife, Glennis. Galloping over California's Mohave Desert, Yeager suddenly saw a closed gate looming before him in the moonlight. As the horse smacked into the gate, Yeager toppled off, landing on his right side and breaking two ribs.

Determined not to miss his date with destiny, Yeager said nothing about the accident to

his superiors. On October 14, 1947, still throbbing with pain, he climbed into a bright orange Bell X-1 plane, which he had christened *Glamorous Glennis*. Knowing that his right arm

Yeager's daredevil nature won him a plum assignment; then he almost grounded himself.

would be too weak to close the cockpit door, he slammed it shut with the left, using a sawed-off broomstick that he had sneaked into the plane for just that purpose.

Everything else went pretty much as planned. Yeager soared skyward and into aviation history. Reaching speeds of more than 660 miles per hour, he survived the loss of control from gravitational pull that had made breaking the sound barrier seem insurmountable. After he had used up all his rocket fuel, Yeager descended in a series of twists, turns, and other aerial acrobatics — just for the fun of it.

1948

W hen Russia set up a blockade to drive the Allies out of the Russian zone in the occupied city of Berlin, East Germany, the Western forces organized a heroic 15-month-long airlift.

As a result of a World War II peace agreement, Berlin — a city located deep within the Russian-administered sector of Germany — was jointly occupied by the British, French, Americans, and the Soviets. When Soviet dictator Joseph Stalin learned that his former allies wanted to rehabilitate, not punish, the areas of Germany they administered, he was furious. In retaliation, he decided to drive them out of Berlin by setting up a blockade.

The Soviets closed off all road and train traffic into Berlin, a city of 2.5 million, then confidently waited for the Allies to withdraw. Accepting the fact that resistance might precipitate a war, President Harry Truman vowed, "We stay in Berlin, period."

On June 26, 1948, two days after the borders were sealed, the Berlin airlift began. For the next 15 months, American and British aircraft carried 2.3 million tons of food, fuel, and other supplies to Berlin in 276,926 separate flights.

The airlift demonstrated a high degree of military efficiency and human concern. One airman dropped small packages of candy for the children, earning himself fame as the "chocolate flier." When a need arose for steam rollers at an airfield construction site in the French sector, some pilots balked. None of the planes could hold a steam roller. No problem, said Maj. Gen. William H. Tunner, who had arrived to supervise the airlift for the United States. He ordered the steam rollers sliced apart with an acetylene torch, flown to Berlin, and welded back together. At the height of operations, a plane was landing or taking off in the beleaguered city every 90 seconds. The Soviets finally conceded defeat and lifted the blockade on May 12, 1949.

German children hail the arrival of an American plane as it drops food to hungry Berliners during the 1948 airlift.

Battle for the 38th Parallel

The war fought in the divided nation of Korea pitted U.N., U.S., and South Korean forces against soldiers from North Korea and Communist China. A few of the key events are listed here.

1950 From June 25 to early September, North Korean invaders drive U.S. and South Korean forces south into a perimeter around the port of Pusan. U.N. troops launch a counteroffensive on September 15, landing at Inchon and thrusting north to the Yalu River.

Communist China openly enters the war, attacking on November 25 and pushing U.N. forces south of the disputed 38th Parallel.

1951 Beginning January 25, a U.N. counteroffensive drives the Chinese and North Koreans north of the 38th Parallel.

A Communist spring offensive quickly stalls, and by summer U.N. troops resume the attack. They capture Heartbreak Ridge in the central mountains after 17 days of fighting.

1952 Both sides dig into defensive positions straddling the 38th Parallel. Sharp clashes occur at Bloody Ridge, White Horse Mountain, and Pork Chop Hill.

1953 A cease-fire, signed July 26 at Panmunjom, ends the fighting; Korea remains divided along the armistice line.

1950

President Harry S Truman sent troops to Korea without seeking the approval of Congress, and called the move a police action to avoid violating the Constitution.

President Harry S Truman was vacationing at home in Independence, Missouri, when the North Korean Army, led by a phalanx of Russian-built tanks, crossed the 38th Parallel, a geographical latitude that separated Communist North Korea from U.S.–backed South Korea. Upon hearing the news, Truman hurried back to Washington.

The president acted quickly. Two days later, on June 27, 1950, he ordered Gen. Douglas MacArthur, commander of the U.S. and U.N. forces, to provide air support for the South Koreans and to protect Americans who were evacuated. By the end of the week, Truman had committed thousands of U.S. troops.

Telegrams of praise poured into the White House from Democrats and Republicans alike. "For once he made the right decision," said an Iowa Republican group. Republican senator Robert Taft of Ohio dissented, however, pointing out that by skirting Congress the president had violated the Constitution. Not so, Truman reasoned, because "We are not at war."

In fact, the United States had pressured the United Nations to enter the fray. The U.N. Security Council condemned North Korea and called on its member nations to repel the attack. Truman argued that the U.S. troops, which comprised the majority of U.N. forces, were part of a police action to quell "a bandit raid" on South Korea.

For a time this explanation satisfied a country engaged in a Cold War power struggle with the Soviet Union. But within two years the fighting had bogged down in a grinding battlefield stalemate. In 1952 Gen. Dwight D. Eisenhower, promising to end the Korean War, was elected president.

1950

In the Korean War MASH doctors and nurses brought mortality rates down to an all-time low. They also inspired a TV series that lasted longer than the war.

The U.S. Army called them Mobile Army Surgical Hospitals. Soldiers referred to them as MASH units, medical teams who could set up a makeshift operating room just behind the front lines in no time flat. Performing surgery and treating such diseases as typhoid fever and cholera, they were miracle workers in the brutal war fought by pro-Communist North Korea and American-supported South Korea from 1950 to 1953.

During combat MASH units arrived in a steady stream, evacuating men with severed limbs, gaping stomach wounds, and other life-threatening conditions. Struggling to maintain basic sanitation and hampered by insufficient supplies of blood, surgical teams did their best. When necessary, helicopters airlifted soldiers to a fully equipped hospital in South Korea or Japan for further medical care. "Stitch this, clip that, sponge, stitch, clip, saw — faster, faster," wrote a journalist who was assigned to follow a MASH team.

Surgeons, most of whom were barely out of medical school, often worked two 16-hour shifts in a row, with equally dedicated nurses close by. The teams rushed wounded soldiers from the battlefield into surgery within two to four hours on average; during World War I it had commonly taken 12 to 18 hours. In World War II, the mortality rate from battle wounds stood at 4.5 per 1,000 soldiers treated; by the end of the Korean War the figure had been cut in half, to 2.3 deaths out of every 1,000 combatants treated.

Despite all the obstacles, MASH units became pacesetters in such fields as preventing and treating frostbite and in using new techniques to repair wounded arteries, thus helping to avoid amputation. A feature film and the popular TV series *M*A*S*H* — which ran from 1972 to 1983, four years longer than the entire Korean War — made the medical teams truly unforgettable.

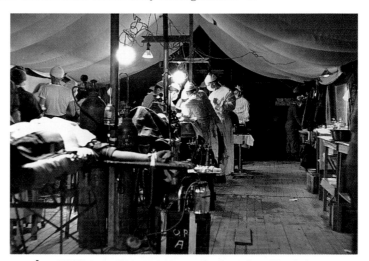

In a MASH operating room, one patient receives blood plasma while surgeons operate on two others.

1950

A **businessman's humiliation when he couldn't pay for his restaurant meal gave birth to a multibillion-dollar industry.**
After enjoying an excellent dinner at a fine New York restaurant, Frank McNamara discovered that he had no cash on hand to pay the bill. His embarrassment that evening inspired McNamara to launch a credit-card business. Thus began America's love affair with buy-now–pay-later financing.

Soon after the dinner, McNamara, the manager of a credit company, borrowed $10,000 from an attorney, Ralph Schneider, and founded Diners' Club on February 28, 1950. By the end of that year, McNamara had persuaded about 200 people to pay $5 annually for a pressed-paper card that was acceptable at a total of 27 New York restaurants. There would soon be other merchants. Although they had to pay Diners' Club a commission of up to 10 percent of sales, more and more businesses signed on, especially when they learned that credit-card users often spent considerably more than those carrying only cash.

At first it was difficult to persuade a skeptical public that membership came with no strings attached. It seemed too good to be true: joining the club required nothing more than filling out an application and paying dues. For a time the company had to resort to costly promotions, such as all-expenses-paid vacations, in order to gain new members.

In fact, Diners' Club was not the first credit card issued in the United States. Fancy New York hotels like the Waldorf–Astoria and the Ritz had offered their best customers such cards in the early 1900's. In the 1920's Filene's department store in Boston and the General Petroleum Company in California had started their own credit-card programs. It's unlikely that McNamara, who sold his share of Diners' Club for $200,000, or any other pioneers in the business envisioned the growth spurt that lay ahead — an estimated $1 trillion in credit-card purchases by the year 2000.

"Charge it" — the first Diners' Club card.

1951

A **n awkward, unknown senator from Tennessee became television's first celebrity politician during a hearing on organized crime that attracted twice as many viewers as the previous World Series.**
Estes Kefauver, the plain-looking, ill-at-ease freshman senator from Tennessee, was an unlikely candidate for the role of media star. But in the spring of 1951, luck was with the ambitious Kefauver. He was winding up 10 months of hearings on the shocking extent of interstate crime in America. Mobsters had infiltrated unions and businesses and had bought off a number of corrupt public officials.

As the hearings drew to a close in March 1951, the senator's staff zeroed in on New York. Earlier hearings had yielded such riveting material that TV producers decided to give the event nationwide coverage. It was, as one TV critic put it, "nothing less than a Hollywood thriller truly brought to life." Nearly three in every four TV sets in New York were turned on. The hearings garnered ratings twice as high as the 1950 World Series had earned.

Heading the cast was Frank Costello, the reputed New York crime boss, who testifed on March 13, 1951. The mobster refused to let his face be seen on camera. "Mr. Costello doesn't care to submit himself as a spectacle," announced his lawyer, so instead the cameras zoomed in on his hands. While Costello refused to answer questions, his fingers fidgeted, drummed nervously on the table, and clutched a water glass. His agitation convinced the jury of TV viewers that Costello was guilty of various sordid crimes.

The performance of Virginia Hill, the blonde girlfriend of the late mobster Bugsy Siegel, nearly topped Costello's. Hill insisted during questioning that underworld figures had given her large sums of money simply because they were her "friends." As she made her way through a swarm of newsmen after the hearing, she slugged one reporter and blasted the rest: "I hope an atom bomb falls on every one of you."

By the time the hearings were over, Kefauver felt that he had uncovered nothing less than a "nationwide crime syndicate . . . guided by an evil coalition of conscienceless mobsters and of cynical . . . businessmen." Unfortunately, the hearings produced no major legal offensive and only three successful prosecutions. They did, however, turn the gentle Democratic senator from Tennessee into an overnight celebrity. Magazines wrote cover stories about him, his book *Crime in America* became a bestseller, and he briefly entered the race to become his party's nominee for president.

The clenched, nervous hands of mobster Frank Costello made a Senate hearing a riveting television event.

W 1951

When President Harry S Truman fired the nation's most beloved general, he found himself in a battle to affirm the civilian control of the military.

For months Gen. Douglas MacArthur, the supreme commander of the U.S. and U.N. forces in the Far East, had been pressing hard for clearance to invade China. MacArthur met strong resistance, however, from his commander-in-chief. President Harry S Truman felt that such an invasion would be a prelude to World War III. When the general refused to back down, Truman announced on April 11, 1951, that he was relieving MacArthur, a revered war hero, of his command.

The outcry was startling. Truman was besieged by hate mail, censured by four state legislatures, and hanged in effigy in several towns. Meanwhile, MacArthur made his way back home from Japan to outpourings of praise.

Honolulu University bestowed an honorary degree on him. Half a million people greeted him in San Francisco, and 300,000 awaited him in Washington, D.C. — where, to Truman's dismay, the general had been invited to address a joint session of Congress.

On April 19, 1951, MacArthur spoke to the assembled senators and representatives. His speech, broadcast on radio to a record audience of 30 million, was interrupted by applause 30 times.

In a series of Senate hearings in May on the administration's policy in Asia, a united stand by the secretary of defense and the joint chiefs of staff blunted MacArthur's attack on Truman. Secretary of Defense Gen. George C. Marshall accused MacArthur of undermining the troops' morale.

Gen. Omar Bradley, a much-respected World War II hero who was chairman of the joint chiefs, delivered a devastating blow. He declared that MacArthur's planned aggression would draw the nation into "the wrong war, at the wrong place, at the wrong time with the wrong enemy."

MacArthur then took to the road, crusading in an era of rabid anti-Communism against the "moral weakness" of American foreign policy. After several months, however, his bravado began to sound shrill and vindictive. In 1952 MacArthur made a permanent retreat, retiring in New York City.

T 1951

The hero of J. D. Salinger's novel, *Catcher in the Rye*, became a role model for a whole generation of teen rebels.

Holden Caulfield, the 16-year-old hero of J. D. (Jerome David) Salinger's first and only novel, *Catcher in the Rye,* flunks out of prep school and winds up in New York City. There he encounters a world of con artists, crooks, and hypocrites.

Catcher in the Rye, published in 1951, caught the spirit of an emerging generation, which would soon develop its own highly charged subculture. Young Americans who came of age during the postwar boom years began to idolize rebellious movie heroes and to imitate singers belting out loud, nerve-jangling songs known as rock 'n' roll. Holden's disaffection with the values of the adults around him struck a chord with many of them. Like him, they grew up skeptical and insecure in a period of conspicuous consumption and Cold War militarism.

Salinger had created "the dialect of a generation," one critic declared. *Catcher in the Rye* went through 14 printings in its first year, and within a decade it had appeared on more high school and college reading lists than any other American novel — despite periodic attempts by some school board members and anxious parents to get the book banned.

A camera-shy Salinger peers out from the book's dust jacket.

1952

The first computer to predict a presidential election would have called the vote almost perfectly if its operators had not mistrusted their own machine.

It was election night, November 4, 1952, and the future was on display. Television was giving the presidential election nationwide coverage, and the special guest star was a $600,000 electronic computer called UNIVAC.

The UNIVAC, which stands for universal automatic computer, was to forecast the results of the election long before the final tally. "Officials of Remington Rand, which built the machine, emphasize that it is not psychic," quipped *The New York Times*.

In fact, its task was purely statistical. Stuffed with figures from the 1944 and 1948 elections, the computer was programmed to compare the early returns in each state with the early returns from the previous two presidential elections.

At 9 P.M. the machine made its first prediction: Gen. Dwight D. Eisenhower, the Republican Party nominee, would defeat Sen. Adlai Stevenson, the Democratic candidate, in a landslide, garnering 33

CBS newsman Walter Cronkite (right) looks at election data from UNIVAC, the first commercial electronic computer.

million popular votes and 438 votes in the Electoral College.

Technicians and statisticians from Remington Rand were shaken. Pundits had predicted a close race. With less than 7 percent of the vote to work with, their mechanical brain must have made a mistake. They told representatives of CBS, the network that was depending on UNIVAC to predict the election results, that the computer would miss its scheduled 9:25 appearance. Then they reprogrammed the machine, which promptly cut Ike's projected total to 317 electoral votes. By 10:30 P.M., after another modification was made, the computer was calling the race a toss-up.

When the election was over, the UNIVAC people could only wince. The total number of both popular and electoral votes cast for each candidate came very close to UNIVAC's first prediction. Eisenhower did, indeed, win the presidency by a landslide. "The trouble with machines," concluded CBS broadcaster Edward R. Murrow, "is people." ✈

1953

A moderate Republican when he took over as chief justice, Earl Warren surprised everyone by leading the Supreme Court into an era of sweeping social changes.

During his years in California politics, Earl Warren was never renowned for being a champion of individual rights. As a county district attorney and then as the state attorney general, he freely denounced radicals and aliens. While governor during World War II, he helped consign Japanese–Americans to internment camps.

In September 1953 President Dwight D. Eisenhower nominated Warren to be the chief justice of the Supreme Court. To his dismay, Eisenhower quickly discovered that Warren's legal and political decisions prior to his appointment provided no clue to the next phase of his judicial life. During his 16 years as chief justice, Warren presided over some of the most far-reaching decisions ever made by the Court.

The Warren justices outlawed school segregation in the famous *Brown* v. *Board of Education* decision. They also barred racial discrimination in voting, curbed wiretapping and unreasonable searches, kept evidence obtained by illegal police methods from being used in trials, extended free legal help to poor defendants, expanded free speech, banned prayer in public schools, and restricted persecution of political radicals. In the important *Miranda* v. *Arizona* ruling, the Court determined that a criminal suspect has the right to see a lawyer before being questioned by the police, and that suspects must be informed of that right.

"On the Court," Warren said, "I saw [things] in a different light." His vision soon became the center of a fiery controversy. While liberals praised him for giving the Court a moral center, conservatives charged that he had launched a social revolution from the bench. Eisenhower told a confidant that naming Warren to the Court was the "biggest damn-fool thing I ever did." ✈

When Chief Justice Earl Warren (left) paid a courtesy call on President Dwight D. Eisenhower in 1953, they still saw eye to eye.

The United States be-
came the first country to
harness nuclear power
to propel a vessel when
it commissioned the
USS *Nautilus.*

1954

A year after the atomic
bomb was dropped on
Hiroshima, Navy captain
Hyman Rickover staked his
career on a revolutionary
idea: nuclear-powered submarines. He was convinced
that such vessels would
prevent nuclear war.

Because nuclear sub-
marines create their own
oxygen, they would be able to
patrol the depths almost indefi-
nitely without refueling, Rickover reasoned. Conventional
subs, by contrast, have to surface in order to get sufficient
oxygen for their internal-
combustion engines and to
recharge their batteries.

It took Rickover six years
to convince Congress to fund
his idea; building the sub took
two more years. The USS *Nautilus* was finally launched on
January 21, 1954.

Driven by steam turbines and
powered by a miniaturized
nuclear reactor, the *Nautilus*

The launch of the USS Nautilus *ushered in a
new era in military-defense strategy.*

soon broke all underwater
endurance records. In 1958 it
traveled beneath the Arctic ice
from the Pacific to the Atlantic
in just five days. Only two years
later, the USS *Triton,* a submarine with two nuclear reactors
aboard, circumnavigated the
globe underwater.

In 1958 the Soviet Union
placed nuclear ballistic missiles
on a conventionally powered
submarine. The United States
responded by building an all-
nuclear submarine fleet. Ever
since, nuclear submarines have
played a key role as seagoing
weapons of deterrence.

A medical researcher launched history's largest public-health
experiment in order to test a new vaccine for polio, the disease
that paralyzed thousands during the 1950's.

1954

For many generations of parents and their children, the warm-
weather months were associated with death and disease. The summer stalker was poliomyelitis, a contagious illness that killed and
crippled thousands every year. Its symptoms included stiffness in
the neck, weariness, nausea, and finally, pain everywhere.

In 1952 a polio epidemic that swept across the United States
claimed some 3,000 lives and crippled more than 50,000.
Some victims could move around with the aid of
crutches, others were confined to wheelchairs; the least
fortunate had to live inside the dreaded iron lung, a
machine that kept people
breathing after paralysis set
in. To help blunt the force of
the epidemic, public officials
shortened school years and
shut down movie theaters,
pools, and playgrounds.

Finally, Jonas Salk, an
associate professor of bacteri-
ology at the University of
Pittsburgh, brought hope. He
launched the largest medical
test in history, which involved
inoculating more than 1 million people with his polio vaccine. Beginning in April 1954,
with the help of 20,000 physi-

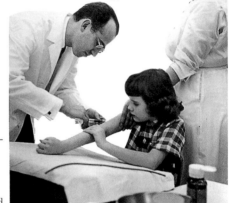

*Dr. Jonas Salk injects an
eight-year-old girl with his polio
vaccine during the field trials.*

cians and public-health aides, Salk vaccinated 400,000 children with
either the killed-virus vaccine or a placebo. On April 12, 1955, the results
of the test were announced. The vaccine was safe and effective.

Shortly after he was acclaimed as a hero, Salk found himself
shunned by other physician researchers, who accused him of courting publicity for personal
gain. Salk insisted that he
never profited personally.

By 1962 Salk was
embroiled in a debate with
Alfred Sabin, who had developed a live-virus oral vaccine
that, unlike Salk's inocula-
tions, offered permanent protection. Eventually, Sabin's
vaccine replaced Salk's in the
United States. In tandem, the
two vaccines nearly wiped out
polio in the industrialized
world within a decade.

Modern Medical Breakthroughs

Progress in the prevention, diagnosis, and treatment of disease has occurred with amazing speed in the United States.
The following are a few of the most dramatic advances in health care in the 20th century.

1902 Surgeon Alexis Carrel develops sutures to close incisions in blood vessels, thus aiding healing and helping to pre-vent infection.

1912 Casimir Funk suggests that certain diseases, such as scurvy and rickets, are due to dietary deficiencies in nutrients that he called "vitamines."

1923 George N. Papanicolaou develops the Pap test, a lifesav-ing procedure for the early detection of uterine cancer.

1943 Biologist Selman A. Waksman discovers the antibiotic streptomycin, which helps eradicate tuberculosis.

1953 American James D. Watson and Briton Francis H. Crick decode the structure of the genetic material DNA.

1954 John F. Enders, a virologist, and Thomas Peebles, a pediatrician, develop a vaccine to prevent measles.

1957 Clarence W. Lillehei, a physician, builds the first pace-maker to stabilize an irregular heartbeat.

1973 Michael S. Brown and Joseph L. Goldstein discover how cholesterol is transported through the body, advancing the treatment of cardiovascular diseases.

1954

In a single stroke the Supreme Court outlawed 60 years of legalized segregation in elementary schools and set off a storm of protest throughout the South.

On May 17, 1954, nine black-robed justices filed into the Supreme Court chambers. With a crowd of reporters scribbling notes as fast as they could, Chief Justice Earl Warren delivered the Court's opinion in the case of *Brown* v. *Board of Education of Topeka.*

"To separate [black children] from others of similar age and qualifications solely because of their race," he said, "generates a feeling of inferiority . . . that may affect their hearts and minds in a way unlikely ever to be undone." The Court ruled unanimously that segregated public schools were unconstitutional, and the following year it mandated that school districts should proceed to inte-

Artist Norman Rockwell views the pain of school integration from a child's perspective.

grate classes "with all deliberate speed."

For Thurgood Marshall, the attorney who argued the case for the National Association for the Advancement of Colored People, the ruling crowned a four-year battle to overturn an 1896 Court decision that segregation was legal. The reaction of the South, however,

soon made it clear that the struggle was far from over.

Ninety-six congressmen issued a Southern Manifesto, charging that the ruling destroyed "the amicable relations" that had been built up "through 90 years of patient effort by the good people of both races." One Southern governor vowed to withhold all funding from the schools.

Across the South segregationists organized Ku Klux Klan cells and White Citizens' Councils to resist enforcement. In a district in Tennessee, it took hundreds of state troopers and seven tanks to get 12 black students admitted to one public school.

School integration would proceed slowly, but the dam had been breached. As one historian put it, "The Court said . . . that when you stepped on a black man, he hurt. The time had come to stop." 🦋

1954

Just a few years before he was anointed the King of Rock 'n' Roll, Elvis Presley played the opening of a drugstore, performing from the back of a flatbed truck for $10.

In 1954 Elvis Presley was paying his dues. After cutting his first single at Sam Phillips' Sun Record studio in Memphis, Elvis toured the South in a Lincoln. He earned $10 to $20 a night for playing at school gymnasiums, roadhouses, even on the back of a flatbed truck for the opening of a pharmacy. But no matter how modest the venue, he electrified the crowd, leaving legions of screaming fans in his wake. In November 1955, when Sun Record sold his contract to RCA, a major recording company, Elvis's career took off.

Hailed as the King of Rock 'n' Roll, Elvis delighted teenagers and horrified most parents. It was not just the sound — a fusion of blue-eyed country-and-western with the soulful rhythm and blues of black musical groups — that set adults' teeth on edge. No, it was the unabashed sexuality of his performances, particularly his swiveling hips. While *The New York Times* grumbled that "Mr. Presley has no discernible singing ability," Ed Sullivan pronounced him "unfit for a family audience."

Yet soon even Ed Sullivan caved in, booking him for three performances on his popular television variety show. Elvis's first appearance drew a record TV audience of 82.6 percent. By April 1956, sales of Elvis records were grossing $75,000 a day. The thousands of young women who flocked to his concerts sobbed and swooned. A performance in Jacksonville, Florida, ended in a riot when Elvis closed the show with the teasing invitation, "Girls, I'll see you all backstage." And in New Orleans six desperate fans bound and gagged an elevator operator so that they could hold their idol captive between floors for an hour.

In time rock 'n' roll passed Elvis by. The King retreated to recording ballads, appearing in Las Vegas nightclubs, and making movies, but his fans never gave up. When Elvis died in 1977, such recordings as "Hound Dog," "Blue Suede Shoes," and "Love Me Tender" had sold some 150 million copies. Within a few years his Memphis mansion, Graceland, had become second only to the White House as the most visited home in the United States. 🦋

Elvis in mid gyration — a swivel-hipped stance that caused Ed Sullivan to show him from the waist up.

1955

The opening-day extravaganza at the fairy-tale kingdom of Disneyland turned into a real-life fiasco.

Walt Disney, the cartoon creator and entrepreneur, had worried that the opening of Disneyland would fail to reach his high expectations, so he was elated when people started lining up at the gate at 2 A.M. on July 17, 1955. Soon traffic was backed up for seven miles. Some 30,000 people jammed into what had been 160 acres of orange groves outside Anaheim, California, for the theme park's debut.

The premiere was memorable, but not necessarily in the way that Disney had anticipated. Fantasyland developed a gas leak. When the southern California sun warmed up the pavement on Main Street, women in spike heels sank into the asphalt, which had been spread at dawn that morning. Rides broke down, long lines formed at every attraction

Disney signs autographs on Main Street.

(and at the bathrooms), and minor skirmishes erupted. To Disney's chagrin, the confusion was broadcast to the nation on live TV.

Once the initial chaos was brought under control, Disneyland won the hearts of its visitors. "I want [guests] to feel like they are in another world," said Disney. Patrons came from far and near to cruise the jungle rivers, take a nostalgic walk through Frontierland, visit London's historic landmarks, and enjoy dozens of other adventures. Because Mr. Toad's Wild Ride was considered a bit too frightening for children, it was toned down.

Disneyland quickly became a tourist mecca. By 1965 the Magic Kingdom had recorded more than 50 million visits. Then, as now, adults outnumbered children four to one.

Main Street, U.S.A., modeled in part on Disney's hometown of Marceline, Missouri, beckons visitors to experience life in a pretty-as-a-picture-postcard village at the turn of the century. In Sleeping Beauty Castle three-dimensional animated creatures bring Disney cartoons to life.

Before he died in 1966, Disney decreed that Disneyland should never be finished, and recent additions include the Indiana Jones Adventure. As visitors wend their way across a fragile bridge, they find themselves suspended over the Cavern of Bubbling Death, where lava shoots out of a skull. Walt Disney would be proud.

1956

It took a military leader to persuade Congress to provide for the nation's first interconnected highway system.

In October 1940 eager drivers lined up to travel the first leg of the interstate highway system, the Pennsylvania Turnpike, also known as I-76. (Interstates that run east-west bear even numbers; north-south arteries are odd-numbered.) Then money ran out, and interstate highway construction ground to a halt.

It resumed after World War II, when Congress began setting aside funds for road-building: $50 million in 1952, and $350 million more in 1954.

The man who caused it to happen was World War II hero Dwight D. Eisenhower, who was elected president in 1952. Finding the proposed road network in a state of suspension, he seized upon it as a way to boost the economy. The easier automobile travel

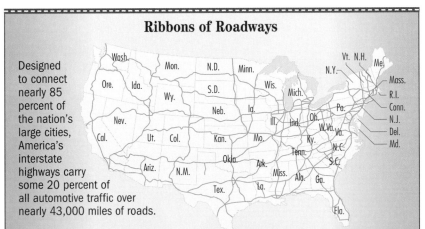
The turnpike halved the travel time between Pittsburgh and Philadelphia.

became, he reasoned, the healthier it would be for the nation's standard of living.

The president also recognized the national-security benefits of an efficient, well-functioning interstate highway system. In case of a nuclear attack, Americans would need to evacuate the cities, the most likely targets. And Eisenhower had never forgotten an exercise that he participated in as a young army officer, an effort designed to test the military preparedness of the nation's highways. The results had been sobering. Transporting 79 vehicles from Washington, D.C., to San Francisco, he recalled, had taken nearly two months.

In 1956, at Eisenhower's urging, Congress approved funding for 41,000 miles of interstate highways, which were to be completed no later than 1971. Construction actually continued into the 1990's.

The roadways spanned 42,795 miles, and they constituted a massive public-works undertaking. The amount of concrete poured in construction was enough to cover the entire state of West Virginia; the land claimed in rights-of-way could have blanketed the state of Delaware.

Ribbons of Roadways

Designed to connect nearly 85 percent of the nation's large cities, America's interstate highways carry some 20 percent of all automotive traffic over nearly 43,000 miles of roads.

W *1956*
hen a Swedish liner plowed into the *Andrea Doria*, a luxury cruise turned into a nightmare.

In the ballroom of the sleek *Andrea Doria*, the flagship of the Italian Line, an orchestra was serenading passengers en route from Genoa to New York with the song "Arrivederci, Roma." Downstairs in tourist class, 100 vacationers were watching the movie *Away All Boats*. It was July 25, 1956, the last night of the voyage.

Meanwhile, in the ship's control room, the mood was grim. Visibility stood at zero in a dense fog, and the crew watched for 40 minutes as a blip on the radar screen got closer and closer.

Capt. Piero Calamai had blown the foghorn every 100 seconds but to no avail. At 11:20 P.M. he sounded the ship's whistles and ordered a hard turn to the right. Just then, a blinding light appeared to the starboard side, and the bow of the liner *Stockholm* tore 30 feet into the *Andrea Doria*, slicing it open from top to bottom.

Stunned passengers — those who had escaped death or serious injury — clambered onto the deck of the wounded ship

Badly damaged in a collision, the Andrea Doria *sinks to the bottom of the Atlantic Ocean off the coast of Massachusetts.*

IN THEIR OWN WORDS

" We were asleep in our cabin . . . the collision served to knock us out of bed. There was a lot of smoke as well. I threw on my trousers, shirt and coat. My wife put on her skirt and coat.

We found we had to crawl through the passageways. It was a slow process. The linoleum floors were like a skating rink. It was a list of thirty to forty degrees.

We were on the top side about two hours. Then the crew advised us to get the women and children to the lower side to board the lifeboats. A lot of women and children were banged up getting there. My wife got a very bad black eye and banged up her knees and arms.

They took off the women and children first. It was a terrific problem. Half the passengers were over 45 years of age. The passengers were calm. There was no disorder, no panic. The crew was just wonderful. "

Philadelphia mayor Richardson Dilworth recalls the collision of the Andrea Doria *and the* Stockholm.

and slid to the sinking starboard side to wait for lifeboats. A small group of nuns huddled together clutching their beads.

Rescue vessels began to arrive within an hour, and the survivors were carried off. When the *Andrea Doria* went down at 10:09 the next morning, 45 miles off the coast of Massachusetts, some 20 people were believed dead and many were missing. Then one of those feared lost, a 14-year-old girl, miraculously reappeared. The impact of the crash had sent her flying from her bed onto the bow of the *Stockholm*, where she was found unconscious.

A *1956*
merica's first enclosed suburban shopping mall was designed to help Minnesota shoppers escape from some of the country's worst weather.

Southdale Center in suburban Edina, Minnesota, offered shoppers something they had never experienced before: a perfect climate every day of the year. Southdale's answer to southern Minnesota's frigid winters and often soggy weather (100 rainy days on average per year) was immediately popular.

When Southdale opened on October 8, 1956, shoppers could browse through 64 shops occupying 800,000 square feet of space on two levels of shopping "streets." And, for the first time, they could visit two large department stores in the same shopping center. The weary could rest on com-

Southdale: a new kind of shopping.

fortable benches in the spacious three-story, skylit Garden Court among full-size trees, flowers, fountains, sculptures, and birds. Kiddie rides kept the children entertained. The parking lot provided a generous allotment of spaces for thousands of cars.

If Southdale sounds familiar, it should. The basic design of the first modern regional mall has since been copied all over the United States. The gargantuan Mall of America, which comprises 4.2 million square feet of space in Bloomington, Minnesota, is an overgrown Southdale, with such added features as an indoor amusement park and restaurants with meals to suit virtually any diner. Putting "everything under one roof" has made the mall an everyday destination for millions of Americans.

S 1957

Sen. Joseph McCarthy died powerless and broken only a few years after his anti-Communist crusade had gained him national fame and unparalleled power.

In February 1950 Joseph McCarthy, the junior senator from Wisconsin, burst into the limelight, charging that the U.S. Department of State was riddled with "individuals who would appear to be either card-carrying members or certainly loyal to the Communist Party."

For five years McCarthy waged war on a variety of supposed enemies, both in and out of government. Thousands of government employees were forced to sign loyalty oaths. He reached as far as college campuses, where academics who refused to sign oaths were fired, and to Hollywood, where his scorching attacks caused numerous writers, actors, and playwrights to be blacklisted.

Neither President Harry S Truman nor President Dwight D. Eisenhower spoke out against McCarthy. Then in 1954, when the senator accused the U.S. Army itself of "coddling Communists," televised hearings finally revealed him as a brutal, lying demogogue.

McCarthy's colleagues decided that he had gone too far, and in December 1954 they voted 67 to 20 to censure him. By the last year of his term in the Senate, McCarthy had turned into a caricature of his former self. Ashen and stooped, he would limp into a committee meeting late, pursue an irrelevant line of questioning, then wander distractedly out of the room.

When he died at the age of 48 on May 2, 1957, the hospital where McCarthy had undergone treatment said simply that the cause of death was a liver ailment — a common side effect of excessive drinking. "His rise to fame," said one newspaper editorial writer, "had the sudden, spectacular violence of a rocket splitting the night sky with unhealthy brilliance. With equal speed the glare faded and the spent stick came racing downward. Now it has struck earth." ✈

Army counsel Joseph N. Walsh listens as McCarthy rails against Communists.

J 1957

Jimmy Hoffa, a high school dropout, muscled his way to the top of his profession, becoming president of the powerful International Brotherhood of Teamsters.

Quitting high school at 14, Jimmy Hoffa helped support his widowed mother by working as a stock boy in a grocery store in Detroit. He hated the way the workers were treated: the manager would fire a person simply on a whim. In 1930, at the age of 17, Hoffa organized the warehouse workers into a union, and he led them on a strike that succeeded in winning them job security.

By 1942, as vice president of the union, Hoffa had made alliances with several underworld crime figures, who helped him squeeze out the competition in exchange for posts as union officials. Hoffa used his considerable powers of persuasion, his mob connections, and his union's funds to consolidate his power.

When the union president, Dave Beck, was convicted of misusing union funds in 1957, Hoffa finally achieved his goal: on October 4, 1957, he was elected president. The International Brotherhood of Teamsters, which had 1.5 million members, was on its way to becoming the nation's biggest and wealthiest labor union.

Hoffa's greatest coup was yet to come. In 1964 he united America's 400,000 truckers and negotiated a single national contract for them. Teamster drivers were now able to transport everything from milk to cars, and, if they decided to strike, they could cripple the nation. Hoffa's goal of bringing other transport workers, such as those in the railway, airline, and shipping industries, into the Teamsters did not sit well with the government officials.

Hoffa fended off several prosecution attempts by the government. For a while he even eluded

Hoffa rides high as the Teamsters' new president.

Attorney General Robert F. Kennedy, who had set up a special "Hoffa unit" to investigate his underworld connections. Then in 1967, Hoffa was sent to a federal prison for jury tampering, fraud, and conspiracy.

After his release in 1971, Hoffa tried to maneuver himself back into power. On July 30, 1975, shortly after going to a Detroit restaurant to meet with underworld crime figures, Hoffa disappeared, an apparent murder victim. ✈

323

1957

The launch of Sputnik, Russia's first satellite to circle the earth, prompted dismay and gloomy predictions in the United States.

American scientists were stunned when they learned the news. For years it had been known that the Soviets were trying to put a spacecraft into orbit, but it had seemed impossible that they would do it first. Outside the scientific community, Americans were humiliated and scared. *Sputnik* (which means fellow traveler in Russian) was launched into space on October 4, 1957, and began circling the earth once every 95 minutes. It carried two radio transmitters that sent a signal allowing scientists to track its whereabouts.

Sputnik I: *a scientific feat and a public-relations coup.*

Soviet premier Nikita Khrushchev boasted that the Soviets would now produce long-range missiles by the dozen, "like sausages." Physicist Edward Teller, who had worked on the atomic bomb, announced that the United States had lost "a battle more important than Pearl Harbor."

Barely a month after *Sputnik I* took flight, *Sputnik II* was launched, carrying a small dog hooked up to monitors that would indicate what conditions human astronauts would have to tolerate. Then, on December 6, 1957, America's *Vanguard* missile had a disastrous test launch: it rose two feet off the ground, crashed, and exploded. The foreign press called it "Flopnik" and "Stay-putnik," but to most Americans the failure was not a laughing matter.

Despite a flurry of gloomy predictions, *Sputnik* posed no imminent threat to American security, and President Dwight D. Eisenhower remained calm. Aerial-reconnaissance reports had convinced him that the United States was way ahead of the Soviets in designing missiles that could launch thermonuclear warheads — an oddly comforting thought at the time.

Still, some Americans feared that the advantage wouldn't last, and the so-called missile and space gap became a national obsession. One of the outcomes was a revamping of the American educational system, with an emphasis on raising standards in science, mathematics, and foreign languages.

The first successful launch of an American satellite, the 31-pound *Explorer I,* came on January 31, 1958. It transmitted data that led to the discovery of two Van Allen radiation belts that encircle the earth. Later that year the National Aeronautics and Space Administration was formed, and soon the U.S. space program took off.

1959

When Alaska and Hawaii joined the United States, the geographic center of the country moved from Kansas to South Dakota.

Ever since the admission of Arizona and New Mexico to the union in 1912, the United States had been a country of 48 contiguous states. The boundaries were Canada, Mexico, and the Atlantic and Pacific oceans. The center of the country lay in the Midwest, near Lebanon, Kansas.

The admission of faraway Alaska, on Canada's northwest border, as the 49th state changed this simple picture. When the United States purchased the land from Russia in 1867, the vast territory (more than 500,000 square miles in area) had been widely considered a huge waste of money. By the end of the 19th century, however, Alaska's assets — fur, salmon, and gold — were well known. Military bases built during World War II caused a population boom that increased the number of Alaska resi-

dents by more than 75 percent by 1950. The discovery of rich oil reserves in 1957 spurred Congressional interest in making Alaska a state, and on January 3, 1959, it joined the union.

Hawaii became the 50th state on August 21, 1959. Located more than 2,000 miles southwest of San Francisco, it had once been an independent kingdom. In 1898 it became a U.S. territory, with pineapple and sugarcane as its major products.

The 1941 attack by the Japanese on Pearl Harbor transformed Hawaii into an important U.S. military center. After World War II ended and Hawaii added tourism to its powerful military and agricultural assets, the time was ripe for statehood — a status it had worked for since the 1920's.

From then on, maps of the United States would include Alaska and Hawaii in boxes near the margin. And the geographic center of the nation moved from Kansas to the vicinity of Castle Rock, South Dakota.

A newsboy in Honolulu and commemorative stamps.

B *1959*
arbie dolls, which sell worldwide at the rate of two per second, got a lukewarm reception from toy buyers when the dolls debuted.

In 1945 Ruth Handler, who, with her husband, Elliot, owned the Mattel toy company, watched as her four-year-old daughter, Barbara, played with paper dolls. When the Handlers began working on a teenage fashion doll so that their toddler would have a new plaything, they named her Barbie, after their daughter.

Almost a foot tall, Barbie was billed as the "only anatomically perfect doll." Her shapely plastic body was modeled

Barbie wears her "commuter set."

after a German doll named Lilli, who — unbeknownst to the Handlers — was based on a prostitute in a popular German comic strip.

In March 1959, when Barbie made her debut at the New York Toy Fair, many male toy buyers scorned her. "Mothers aren't going to buy a doll with breasts," one of them remarked, and Sears, Roebuck, deeming the doll "too sexy," declined to stock her.

But little girls loved Barbie, shapely curves and all, from her zebra-striped bathing suit and hoop earrings right down to her high heels. With Barbie's large collection of stylish out-

fits, girls enjoyed experimenting with the latest fashions and fantasizing about what it was like to be a grown-up.

By the end of her first year, all 351,000 Barbies had been sold (at $3 each). In 1961 the Handlers created Ken, Barbie's handsome companion, and together the dolls changed with the times.

Ken grew sideburns and sported a Nehru outfit in the 1960's, while Barbie went mod with mini skirts and go-go boots. The year 1976 saw the arrival of the Barbie Fashion Plaza, a toy mall with fashion boutiques, a snack patio, a bridal shop, and even a working elevator. Barbie's popularity continues to this day, with two dolls being sold every second somewhere in the world.

T *1959*
he St. Lawrence Seaway, America's fourth coastline, was an engineering marvel that was four centuries in the making.

The idea of developing a waterway extending from the landlocked Great Lakes region to the Atlantic coast may have originated with Jacques Cartier, a French explorer who, in 1535, was the first European to sight the St. Lawrence River. At the time Cartier thought that he had discovered a transcontinental passage that would allow trade between Europe and India.

In 1933 the United States and Canada negotiated a treaty to start the project, but it stalled. Seaports on the Atlantic coasts, as well as some railroads and utilities, opposed the waterway, fearing the competition would cause them to lose business. Impatient with the delays, Canada threatened to forge ahead on its own. In 1954 the United States finally agreed to split the costs.

One of the world's largest engineering feats was set in motion. The seaway system runs 2,700 nautical miles from the mouth of the St. Lawrence River to Duluth, Minnesota — far longer than the canals of Suez (101 miles) or Panama (50 miles).

More than 210 million cubic yards of earth and rock were excavated. A total of 6.1 million cubic yards of concrete (enough to build a four-lane highway between London and Rome) was poured for the 13 locks that raised and lowered ships in the stretch between Lake Erie and Montreal. To construct the needed canals, roads, and bridges, 47 miles of highways and 40 miles of railways had to be moved. What's more, thousands of people had to be relocated: construction required the flooding of 38,000 acres of land.

After five years and $1 billion, President Dwight D. Eisenhower and Britain's Queen Elizabeth officially dedicated the seaway near Montreal on June 26, 1959. During the first year of operation, about 200 million tons of freight were shipped along the waterway, and the cities of Chicago, Detroit, and Cleveland became world ports.

Foreign ships from distant ports celebrated the seaway's opening.

Dredging Out a Coastline

To create the St. Lawrence Seaway, 189 miles of the St. Lawrence River had to be expanded or excavated, including a 27-foot-deep channel between Montreal and Lake Ontario. Westbound ships that pass through the locks at Lake Superior are raised 602 feet above sea level.

Duluth

Lake Superior

CANADA

Montreal

Lake Huron

Lake Michigan

Detroit

Lake Ontario

Buffalo

Atlantic Ocean

Chicago

Toledo

Lake Erie

UNITED STATES

······ Seaway

A jovial Nikita Khrushchev holds a turkey during his tour of Iowa farms.

1959
Soviet premier Nikita Khrushchev threw a tantrum when he couldn't get into Disneyland.

On September 15, 1959, during the Cold War between the United States and the Soviet Union, Nikita Khrushchev, the Soviet premier, arrived at Andrews Air Force Base in Maryland for his first American visit. Accompanying him were his wife, son, two daughters, and 63 Soviet officials. A smiling President Dwight D. Eisenhower greeted him as he stepped off the plane.

Khrushchev mischievously presented Eisenhower with a small model of a moon probe Russia had recently launched, just two years after his nation's *Sputnik* became the first satellite to circle the earth. Eisenhower, refusing to show concern that the United States still lagged in the space race, thanked him politely.

Khrushchev then began a two-week tour, visiting mostly farms, factories, and stores. In Los Angeles he went to see the filming of *Can-Can.* When the female dancers lifted their skirts and revealed their backsides, he was shocked and called the movie pornographic.

The Soviet leader was alternately bad-tempered and funny, rude and charming. He spoke about "peaceful coexistence" and then, in almost the same breath, warned of the continuing arms race. He predicted that his country would one day surpass the United States economically. Overall the trip seemed to be going well. Then the premier tried to visit Disneyland.

Local officials refused to allow him in. They worried about the safety of the premier and his family during the 30-mile trip between Los Angeles and Anaheim, California, site of the theme park, as well as their security within the park premises. When Khrushchev heard that he would be denied entry, his face grew dark and he sputtered: "Is there an epidemic of cholera there or something? Or have gangsters taken hold of the place? . . . this situation is inconceivable."

Khrushchev later apologized for his outburst. Before leaving, he gave a televised speech in which he thanked Americans for their hospitality. "Goodbye," he said in English, "good luck, friends."

1959
Television's first major scandal erupted when the celebrated Charles Van Doren confessed to cheating on a game show.

Quiz shows became the nation's favorite weekly entertainment in the mid-1950's. *The $64,000 Question* was the first such program to lure huge television audiences. Virtually every week it managed to find a new contestant to capture the nation's heart. Among the more memorable: an Italian cobbler and opera buff who won $32,000, and a U.S. Marine captain (the first person to win $64,000) whose specialty was French cuisine.

The most popular quiz-show contestant appeared on a rival program, *Twenty-One.* He was Charles Van Doren, a Columbia University English instructor and an unlikely game-show star.

Van Doren's ride to fame began when the show's producers ordered a less telegenic contestant, Herbert Stempel, to lose to him. The Ivy League prof increased the drama by wiping his brow, biting his lip, and pretending to rack his brain.

All the while, no one in the studio audience or at home knew that the program was fixed — that favored contestants were given the answers in advance.

Van Doren won a record $129,000 and received thousands of letters from parents and teachers praising him as a fine role model for youngsters. The show's sponsors saw their sales explode. Meanwhile, Stempel, bitter about having been coerced to answer incorrectly, began talking to newspaper reporters.

Finally a Congressional subcommittee looked into Stempel's charges that the show was rigged — charges Van Doren steadfastly denied. Subpoenaed to appear before the subcommittee on November 2, 1959, Van Doren belatedly confessed to the hoax. "I have deceived my friends," he said, "and I had millions of them."

TV Posers for the Professor

Charles Van Doren had no trouble answering these questions on *Twenty-One:*

1. What are the common names for caries, myopia, and missing patellar reflex?

2. Name the three players in the history of baseball (up to 1957) who amassed more than 3,500 hits in their major-league careers.

3. In what church and in what city is Leonardo da Vinci's fresco "The Last Supper"?

ANSWERS 1. Cavities, nearsightedness, and lack of knee reflex. 2. Ty Cobb, Cap Anson, and Tris Speaker. 3. Santa Maria delle Grazie in Milan.

1959

Berry Gordy's magic formula for making hit records helped his Motown stars dominate the pop charts in the 1960's — but not without a price.

In the 1950's black musicians and singers often fared badly in the entertainment arena. They were heard almost exclusively in clubs for black patrons and on radio stations with black audiences. Only when white singers recorded their songs could black composers hear their music on radio stations with white audiences.

Berry Gordy helped change all that. In 1957 Gordy met singer/songwriter Smokey Robinson, who convinced him to start his own music company. With $800 that he borrowed from his family, the former record-store owner and part-time songwriter founded Motown Records in 1959. He quickly signed Robinson's group, the Miracles, and in 1961 their recording of "Shop Around" became Motown's first gold record (one that sells 500,000 copies).

Soon Motown artists — the Temptations, the Supremes, the Four

Among Gordy's "girl groups," the Supremes were the most successful.

Tops, the Jackson 5, among others — dominated the pop and rhythm-and-blues charts. Between 1961 and 1971, 110 Motown singles captured a slot on the Top Ten music charts. The Supremes alone had twelve No. 1 hits.

Motown put black music squarely into the pop-music mainstream. A thumping backbeat, clapping hands, jangling tambourines, and background vocals made recordings by Motown's artists easily recognizable and irresistibly danceable. The powerful formula concentrated on upbeat songs and gospel-tinged melodies with simple lyrics, mostly about love.

Gordy provided not only musical training for his singers, but dance teachers for their choreography, designers for their wardrobes, as well as lessons in the social graces for their offstage lives. After a time some singers felt boxed in by his tightly controlled system. By the end of the 1960's, many stars had left to manage their own careers, and Motown's reputation as Hitsville, USA, began to fade. But its legacy of music magic lives on still. ✈

1960

The downing of a U-2 spy plane ruined the chances for an American–Soviet nuclear test ban treaty and turned the Cold War into an even chillier standoff.

American U-2 reconnaissance planes had penetrated Russian air space for years, gathering information on Soviet missile development. Even so, as the May 16, 1960, date for a major summit meeting approached, President Dwight D. Eisenhower took the precaution of suspending the spy missions. The president did not want anything to jeopardize the conference, where he hoped to negotiate a nuclear test ban treaty that could be enforced by teams of inspectors inside the Soviet Union. If by some extraordinary chance a spy plane were shot down, Moscow might then accuse the West of being insincere.

On May 1, 1960, Eisenhower's worst fears came true: a U-2 was shot down over Sverdlovsk, some 1,300 miles inside the Soviet Union. The Central Intelligence Agency assured the president that the pilot, Francis Gary Powers, had not survived. When the crash was reported in the news

media, the U.S. government initially claimed that the Russians had downed a weather plane that had strayed off course. Then on May 7 Soviet premier Nikita Khrushchev announced that the Soviets had captured Powers, obtained a confession, and salvaged his reconnaissance photographs.

For several days the U.S. government issued denials. But on May 11, Eisenhower told the American people the truth. He admitted that he had authorized spying missions over the Soviet Union for the last four years as a security measure. He also said that the Soviets had long known about the planes and were engaged in similar espionage activities. He expected that the incident would not hinder the summit talks.

Unfortunately, as one columnist wrote, Eisenhower had "handed Mr. Khrushchev his propaganda triumph on a plate." Some in the West suspected that Khrushchev, under pressure from hard-liners in his country, had been looking for an excuse to pull out of the talks.

When Eisenhower arrived in Paris, two days before the summit was set to begin, he

A political cartoon dramatizes how the U-2 incident doomed the upcoming summit.

encountered a furious Khrushchev. The Soviet leader canceled the negotiations and withdrew an invitation he had extended for Eisenhower to visit Russia. Disheartened and embarrassed, Eisenhower returned to the United States. ✈

A¹⁹⁶⁰

After overcoming childhood paralysis, Wilma Rudolph became the first American woman to win three gold medals in track in a single Olympics.

Wilma Rudolph started defying the odds early. She weighed only 4½ pounds at birth but somehow managed to pull through. Then, at the age of 4, she was struck by double pneumonia, scarlet fever, and polio, and her left leg was paralyzed. The family had little money — her mother was a maid, her father a retired porter with 22 children from his two marriages — but they did everything they could to help Wilma.

Each week Mrs. Rudolph would take her daughter on a 45-minute bus ride from Clarksville, Tennessee, to a clinic in Nashville for physical therapy. Back home, a family member would spend hours massaging Wilma's leg. By the age of 8, she had exchanged her leg braces for an orthopedic shoe, but schoolmates still ostracized her, especially when it came to playing sports.

"One day I'm going to be somebody very special," the little girl would reassure herself. When one of her brothers put a basketball hoop in the yard, Wilma spent hours shooting and dribbling, clomping around in her orthopedic shoe.

At the age of 11, Wilma suddenly discovered that her leg was healed and she no longer needed the shoe. By high school she had become an accomplished basketball player. It was not her dunking technique, however, but her running that caught the eye of a well-known track coach, who offered to train her.

By then Rudolph was a svelte, 5-foot 11-inch young woman whose speed made her feel "like a butterfly." When she was 16, Rudolph ran with the U.S. track relay team in the Melbourne Olympics, where she earned a bronze medal. She continued to run while attending Tennessee State University and, at the age of 20, competed at the 1960 Olympics in Rome. There she won the 100-meter and 200-meter dashes and anchored the victorious 400-meter relay team. The Italians called her *Gazzella Nera*, or "the black gazelle."

Rudolph dashes to victory in the 100-meter finals during the 1960 Olympics.

T¹⁹⁶⁰

There were four debates between presidential contenders John Kennedy and Richard Nixon, but only one really mattered.

According to a 1960 Gallup Poll, America's choice for president in the upcoming election was Vice President Richard M. Nixon. He had served under the hugely popular President Dwight Eisenhower for two terms, and he had proven himself a strong anti-Communist who could hold his own against Soviet premier Nikita Khrushchev at their 1959 "kitchen debate" in Moscow. Nixon's lead was strong.

The front-runner was confident that he would beat the Democratic nominee, Massachusetts Senator John F. Kennedy. After seeing Kennedy deliver a rushed acceptance speech at the Democratic convention, Nixon — ignoring his advisers — agreed to a series of presidential debates. They would be the first such debates to be broadcast on television.

Someone who merely listened to the verbal punches at the first debate, on September 26, 1960, would have judged the match a

His youth and charisma aided Kennedy in the debates with Nixon.

draw. But to television viewers, it was a different story. Recovering from an infection, Nixon looked haggard. He perspired profusely, and the stage makeup that was meant to cover his five o'clock shadow only made him paler. Kennedy, with a healthy tan and clothing that softened his appearance under harsh studio lights, came across as calm and youthful.

Three more debates followed, but the viewing audience dropped from 70 million to 50 million after the first one. On election eve the race was a dead heat. A near-record turnout of voters produced the closest popular vote in history. By slightly more than 100,000 votes, or less than 1 percent of the 69 million votes cast, Kennedy was elected president.

An accurate measure of the impact of the Kennedy-Nixon debates on the election outcome will never be known, but its impact on future presidential contests was unquestioned. Said one journalist, the American electorate had become a group that "looked more than listened."

1960

Caroline Kennedy was a toddler and John Kennedy, Jr., was not yet born when their father was elected president of the United States.

On November 9, 1960, the day after his election as president, John F. Kennedy concluded his first press briefing with the words, "So now my wife and I prepare for a new administration and for a new baby." Two weeks later, John F. Kennedy, Jr. (John-John), was born, and in January 1961 the infant and his three-year-old sister, Caroline, moved with their parents into the White House.

For three years John-John and Caroline Kennedy enjoyed a fairly normal childhood, thanks largely to the devotion of their mother, Jacqueline. The South Lawn began to resemble a suburban backyard with a treehouse and a playground. There was also a dog, a canary, a cat, and Caroline's pony, Macaroni.

The children would periodically wander into the Cabinet Room. John-John was especially fond of hiding under the president's desk. Despite Jackie's attempts to keep them out of the limelight, the children were the subjects of frequent news stories: John-John's first haircut received widespread media attention, and Caroline appeared on the cover of *Newsweek*. The children were the living embodiment of the energy, youth, and vitality that President and Mrs. Kennedy so strikingly conveyed.

On November 22, 1963, Kennedy fell to an assassin's bullet. In the Capitol rotunda, Caroline and her mother prayed beside his casket. Three days later — it was John-John's third birthday — the casket was placed on a caisson bound for Arlington National Cemetery. The toddler raised his hand in a memorable salute.

IN THEIR OWN WORDS

> ❝ Summoning artists to participate in the august occasions of the state Seems something for us all to celebrate.
>
> This day is for my cause a day of days,
> And his be poetry's old-fashioned praise
> Who was the first to think of such a thing.
> This tribute verse to be his own I bring
> Is about the new order of the ages
> That in the Latin of the founding sages
> God nodded his approval of as good.
> So much those sages knew and understood. ❞

An excerpt from Robert Frost's "The Preface," specially written for John F. Kennedy's 1961 inauguration.

1961

Wintry winds and glare from the sun prevented 86-year-old poet Robert Frost from reading the poem he had written for the inauguration of a president who was half his age.

A few weeks after his election as president, John F. Kennedy invited fellow New Englander Robert Frost to read one of his poems at the inaugural ceremony on January 20, 1961. "If you can bear at your age the honor of being made President of the United States," Frost wired by way of acceptance, "I ought to be able at my age to bear the honor of taking some part in your inauguration." At the age of 43, Kennedy was the youngest president ever elected.

The poem Frost had selected for the occasion was "The Gift Outright," a paean to the American people's love of their land. On the morning of the inauguration, however, Frost announced that he would also read a dedication to the new president that he had written a few days before.

When Frost stepped up to the podium, a cold wind riffled the pages of his manuscript, and the glare of sun off the new-fallen snow made it impossible for him to read more than the first few lines of his dedication. Seeing the difficulty Frost was having, Vice President Lyndon B. Johnson approached the podium and took off his top hat to try to shade the stand.

Frost jauntily waved Johnson aside and, squaring his shoulders, recited the familiar poem from memory. As he finished, the audience broke into a warm round of applause. Later a friend ribbed Frost about the "cosmic joke" that had been played on him: "You've written all these years about the snow and sun and wind, and there you were, standing exposed where the elements could say, 'The old man's overreaching himself, let's put him in his place.' "

1961
Just six months after the founding of the Peace Corps, 52 volunteers were on their way to work in a developing country.

On March 1, 1961, only a few weeks after his inauguration, President John F. Kennedy signed an order creating the Peace Corps. Three days later he named his brother-in-law Sargent Shriver, a businessman, to head the new agency.

The idea of a volunteer corps to help economically strapped nations did not originate with Kennedy, but he had made it a last-minute campaign issue before his election in 1960. America wasn't rich enough to relieve misery around the world, he declared in a speech, "But there is enough know-how and enough knowledgeable people to help those nations help themselves."

By July 1961 the first 52 Peace Corps volunteers were being trained at the University of California at Berkeley for two-year assignments in Ghana. Two months later they arrived in that newly independent African nation, the vanguard of the more than 140,000 Americans sent to 96 countries

over the next three decades.

Although the Peace Corps received bipartisan support in subsequent administrations, it was also criticized for its recruiting and training. Volunteers tended to be liberal-arts college graduates who couldn't do plumbing, install electrical lines, or run a business — the skills most needed in many of the host countries. But by general consensus the corps did wonders to promote an appreciation of other cultures. Said one Peace Corps alumnus, "It was the most profound experience of my life. I got more out of it than I was able to give."

A Peace Corps volunteer in North Borneo, Malaysia.

IN THEIR OWN WORDS

"I didn't go to a lot of speeches in college but I went to hear Kennedy because someone told me he was probably going to run for President. This was in 1959. . . . I followed his campaign and when he announced the Peace Corps idea, I wrote him a letter saying, 'If you will do it, I will volunteer.'

I grew up in rural Michigan and I'd never been overseas before. I was at my mother's house when the telegram came inviting me to train for Nigeria. I remember my hands were shaking as I opened it. I had never heard of Nigeria but I definitely felt I was participating in history. This was a new era of American participation in the world."

Volunteer Roger Landrum recalls his introduction to the Peace Corps.

Kennedy consults Eisenhower at Camp David after the failed invasion.

1961
Despite assurances of victory by the top military brass, a CIA-trained invasion force turned an attempt to overthrow Cuba's Fidel Castro into one of the worst U.S. foreign-policy fiascos.

In one of his last acts as president, Dwight D. Eisenhower severed relations with Cuba. His move capped two years of growing tensions between the United States and Fidel Castro, the rebel leader who had seized power in January 1959. Castro had confiscated private property in Cuba (much of it owned by Americans) and reached out to Communist countries in Europe for support.

When he succeeded Eisenhower in the Oval Office in January, 1961, President John F. Kennedy reluctantly endorsed a Central Intelligence Agency plan to land an expeditionary force on the island nation, just 90 miles south of Florida, to oust Castro. The site that had been chosen was Bahía de Cochinos, the Bay of Pigs, on Cuba's southwestern coast. Castro's support would melt away, the president was told. All that the invaders would have to do was "turn left, and go straight into Havana."

Of the 1,500 members of the brigade of exiled Cuban dissidents, only 300 had been trained in guerrilla warfare and only 135 were soldiers. From the very beginning, anything that could go wrong with the landing went wrong in the very worst way.

The invaders boarded five leaky World War II transports in Nicaragua. In the early hours of April 17, 1961, open launches with outboard motors took them ashore to what was supposed to be a deserted beach. Instead it was a busy construction site in an area where 20,000 of Castro's troops were waiting. The element of surprise had been lost.

Within 72 hours 114 invaders were dead, more than 1,000 had been captured, and the rest had fled into the countryside. Desperately sought help from the United States never came: Kennedy had said from the outset that no American troops would be involved, nor would he provide direct air support. The president later lamented, "Victory has many fathers, but defeat is an orphan."

1961

The rocket that lifted Alan Shepard from a launch pad at Cape Canaveral did more than send the first American into space — it launched the nation on a trip to the moon.

After waiting more than three hours in his tiny capsule atop a Redstone rocket at Cape Canaveral, Florida, Navy Commander Alan B. Shepard, Jr., grew impatient. Technical problems and the weather were delaying him. "Why don't you fix your little problem and light this candle?" he asked.

At 9:34 A.M. on May 5, 1961, Shepard's 6- by 9-foot *Mercury 3* capsule, which he had named *Freedom 7* but was dubbed "the garbage can" by his fellow astronauts, achieved liftoff in a blast of fire. Reaching an altitude of 116 miles and a speed of 5,180 miles per hour, *Freedom 7* splashed down near Bermuda in the Atlantic Ocean 15 minutes later. "Boy, what a ride!" Shepard exclaimed after he was taken aboard a Marine Corps helicopter to a waiting aircraft carrier. A television audience of 45 million in schools, offices, and homes across the country shared his excitement.

Shepard was the second man in space. His Russian predecessor, Yuri Gagarin, had beat him by 23 days. Unlike Gagarin, however, Shepard had actually manipulated his craft in space. By firing hydrogen peroxide thrusters he was able to control the capsule's roll, pitch, and yaw. The experiment proved that weightlessness would not prevent astronauts from carrying out various maneuvers in space.

Shepard's achievement gave a boost to what had been a lagging American space program. Three weeks after Shepard's flight, President John F. Kennedy went before Congress to ask that the nation commit itself "to achieving the goal, before this decade is out, of landing a man on the moon and returning him safely to earth." In 1961 Shepard was awarded a Distinguished Service Medal by the National Aeronautics and Space Administration. ✈

Shepard helped pave the way for the 1969 lunar landing by Neil Armstrong.

1961

Boarding buses in the nation's capital, a biracial group set out to test enforcement of a Supreme Court desegregation ruling in the South.

Back in 1960, the Supreme Court extended the ban on racial segregation in interstate travel to include waiting rooms, restaurants, restrooms, and other facilities at bus terminals. But the federal government made no moves to enforce the ruling. In the spring of 1961, James Farmer, the director of the Congress of Racial Equality (CORE), a pacifist civil rights organization, decided to take matters into his own hands.

Joined by six whites and six other African-Americans, Farmer boarded one of two buses in Washington, D.C. After a minor incident in South Carolina, the bus riders reached Atlanta on May 13, 1961. Farmer left the group to attend his father's funeral, but the next day an angry mob met the remaining 12 riders at Anniston, Alabama. The marauders firebombed one bus and pulled passengers off both buses, then beat them up.

The Freedom Riders (as they were soon known) continued in the second bus to Birmingham, where they encountered another mob. Asked why his force did not protect the riders — who never fought back — Police Chief Eugene "Bull" Connor said that most of his men had been off duty, visiting their mothers on Mother's Day.

Within days, another group of Freedom Riders left Nashville, Tennessee; when they reached Montgomery, Alabama, on May 20, they too were savagely beaten. Alabama governor John Patterson announced he couldn't guarantee protection "for this bunch of rabble-rousers." In response

Under pressure, the governor of Alabama ordered the National Guard to escort the Freedom Riders safely to the Mississippi state line, averting further attacks on the buses and their riders.

Attorney General Robert F. Kennedy sent some 500 federal marshals to restore order.

The ride ended with arrests for violation of segregation laws in Jackson, Mississippi. More Freedom Riders joined the crusade; by summer's end 360 of them had been arrested. Then in September, under orders from Kennedy, the Interstate Commerce Commission began to enforce the ban on segregated travel facilities, and the "For Whites Only" signs came down across the South. ✈

1962

Folk singer and composer Bob Dylan became the voice of the 1960's protest generation.

A 20-year-old Bob Dylan stood in a Greenwich Village coffee-house and brayed out a song, punctuating it with mournful blasts on his harmonica. He wouldn't collect much money for his performance, but it was what he wanted to do. In the months since Dylan had left his hometown of Hibbing, Minnesota, in the spring of 1961, he had haunted coffee houses all over lower Manhattan, plying his unique brand of country blues. He might have gone right on working for pocket change if a Columbia Records executive had not been impressed enough by Dylan's distinctive style to sign him to a contract.

Sheer enthusiasm, however, was not enough to make the scruffy guitarist a star. His first album, released in February 1962 and titled simply *Bob Dylan,* sold only 5,000 copies — a flop by record industry standards. But the next year came "Blowin' in the Wind," written by Dylan and recorded by the folk group Peter, Paul, and Mary. It sold 300,000 copies in two weeks. After this success, Dylan paid homage to his musical hero,

Bob Dylan strikes a pose on a table in Paris. His voice was once described as sounding "like a dog with its foot caught in barbed wire."

folk singer Woody Guthrie, with a procession of protest ballads. Nuclear war, civil rights, the generation gap — nothing escaped Dylan's angry scrutiny. He became a spokesman for disaffected youth. "He's all the things we always felt but could never eloquently express," said one enraptured teenage fan in *Time* magazine. Dylan himself was skeptical of his role: "I just have thoughts in my head and I write them," he said. "I'm not trying to lead any causes for anyone else."

By the time he appeared at the Newport Folk Festival in 1965, Dylan had recorded four albums and a Top Ten single, and had won the praise of fellow folk singers Pete Seeger and Joan Baez. Yet when he stepped onto the stage, his fans were shocked.

Gone was the old Dylan, replaced by a man clad in tight black jeans and wielding an electric guitar. When he played his songs with a rock beat, he was booed off the stage.

And so folk rock, a genre inspired by such Dylan classics as "Subterranean Homesick Blues" and "Like a Rolling Stone" had its tempestuous birth. Dylan, as one critic observed, "helped shape the probability that contemporary music [would] become the literature of our time." ✈

Every bit the royal consort, Princess Grace accompanies her husband Prince Rainier of Monaco to a gala reception.

1962

Only six years after her much-publicized wedding to Prince Rainier of Monaco, the former Grace Kelly announced that she was returning to films.

The brief bulletin released from Monaco's palace on March 18, 1962, stunned the cinema world. Beginning late in the summer, Princess Grace would make a movie in the United States. Alfred Hitchcock had directed the princess, then known as Grace Kelly, in several of her greatest successes. Then her six-year career ended abruptly with a fairy-tale wedding — replete with couture dresses, celebrities, cheering throngs, and eager reporters — to Prince Rainier of Monaco in 1956. Now, after six years of domesticity, she was accepting the title role as a repressed kleptomaniac in the movie *Marnie.*

What had happened? Why had Princess Grace — apparently happy with official duties such as heading Monaco's Red Cross, sponsoring art events, and caring for her children — decided to resume her career? She had been turning down movie offers for several years as a matter of course. Even a $1 million bid to play the Virgin Mary in *The Greatest Story Ever Told* had not tempted her. When the press speculated that Rainier's one-square-mile principality in the south of France was in financial straits, the palace quickly announced that the princess's fee would go to charity. Columnist Sheilah Graham went so far as to suggest that "something in some way has gone wrong with their marriage."

After the citizens of Monaco expressed public outrage at the possibility of her royal highness kissing a Hollywood movie star (Sean Connery), Princess Grace called off the film deal early in June and wrote to Hitchcock that she was heartbroken. He wrote back, saying that she had reached the best decision. "After all, it was only a movie," said the famed director. ✈

R *1962*

achel Carson's *Silent Spring* awakened the public to the hazards of indiscriminate use of toxic chemicals in agriculture and industry.

In increasingly large areas of the United States, Rachel Carson wrote in her book *Silent Spring* — a 1962 bestseller — spring arrived unheralded by birds, and early mornings once filled with the beauty of their songs were now "strangely silent." Carson, a marine biologist with a flair for poetic prose, argued that the eerie situation was due to the aggressive promotion by manufacturers and government agencies of chemical pesticides such as dichloro-diphenyl-trichloro-ethane (DDT). Although the chemicals were sprayed on weeds and insects, they eventually made their way into the bodies of vast numbers of animals, plants, and human beings — even mother's milk, and quite possibly the tissues of unborn babies.

The chemical industry rushed to attack Carson's thesis, but in May 1963 President John F. Kennedy's Science Advisory Committee endorsed it. The uncontrolled use of chemicals, especially pesticides, the committee chairman declared, was "potentially a much greater hazard than radioactive fallout." The furor caused by Carson's book ultimately led to passage of clean air and water acts, the banning of some 30 pesticides including DDT, and creation of the Environmental Protection Agency (EPA). "A few thousand words from her," a newspaper editor wrote of Carson's clarion call, "and the world took a new direction."

IN THEIR OWN WORDS

" Some evil spell had settled on the community: mysterious maladies swept the flocks of chickens. . . . There had been several sudden and unexplained deaths, not only among adults but even among children, who would be stricken suddenly while at play and die within a few hours.

There was a strange stillness. The birds, for example — where had they gone? . . . . It was a spring without voices. . . .

Even the streams were now lifeless. Anglers no longer visited them, for all the fish had died. . . .

No witchcraft, no enemy action had silenced the rebirth of new life in this stricken world. The people had done it themselves. **"**

In Silent Spring, *Rachel Carson describes the fate of a hypothetical town stricken with insecticide poisoning.*

E *1962*

vidence that the Soviet Union was equipping Communist Cuba with nuclear weapons led to the single most dangerous confrontation of the Cold War.

As the United States increased its economic blockade of Cuba in the wake of the Bay of Pigs fiasco, Fidel Castro was driven further into the Soviet camp. By the summer of 1962, the Soviet Union was sending oil and machinery to the Caribbean nation at a rate of 1 million dollars worth per day. Late in August, American intelligence began receiving reports that Soviet technicians and troops were arriving in Cuba. They were accompanied by fighter planes, antiaircraft weapons, and mysterious cylindrical objects that were being moved along Cuban highways at night. U.S. aerial-reconnaissance photographs taken on October 14 confirmed that, within two weeks, the Soviet Union would have in place missiles with the capability of destroying nearly any American city on the Eastern seaboard.

The Kennedy administration swung into action, putting troops on the alert in the United States and Germany, targeting nuclear missiles at the Soviet Union, and deploying vessels to the Caribbean to establish a quarantine of Cuba. On October 22, President John F. Kennedy told the nation that the "deliberately provocative and unjustified" move by the U.S.S.R. could not be accepted by the United States. Kennedy had feared that if he backed down, the Soviets would try to invade new territories. (They had already broken an agreement to maintain free access in Berlin by building a wall between the Eastern and Western zones.) Four days later Soviet leader Nikita Khrushchev sent Kennedy a personal note offering to remove the missiles in exchange for a U.S. promise not to invade Cuba. The two superpowers had come "eyeball to eyeball" in a confrontation that could have led to a nuclear Armageddon.

An October 23, 1962, aerial reconnaissance photo reveals a missile construction site in San Cristobal, Cuba.

1963

The Reverend Dr. Martin Luther King, Jr., preached to a crowd of 250,000 who had marched on Washington in a peaceful protest against racial injustice.

At the age of 34, the Reverend Dr. Martin Luther King, Jr., was already a veteran of the civil rights movement in the United States. He had organized a bus boycott to protest segregated seating in Montgomery, Alabama, and had helped found the Southern Christian Leadership Conference, of which he was president. For his efforts he had seen his home firebombed, and he had been arrested and convicted several times on various charges of civil disobedience. Undaunted, King

The Reverend Martin Luther King, Jr., stands to deliver his famous speech at the Lincoln Memorial.

decided to join a coalition of black and white leaders who were organizing a March on Washington. The expected turnout was about 100,000 people.

Shortly after noon on August 28, 1963, an estimated 250,000 black and white marchers assembled along the reflecting pool that stretches from the Washington Monument to the Lincoln Memorial. After a number of speeches and songs, King rose to speak. Standing in front of the brooding statue of Abraham Lincoln, he reminded his audience that, 100 years after the Emancipation Proclamation, black people were still not free. In his resonant voice he spoke of his hopes for America: "I have a dream," he intoned to an enraptured crowd, "that one day this nation will rise up and live out the true meaning of its creed: 'We hold these truths to be self-evident; that all men are created equal.' " King spoke repeatedly of his dream, and called for all Americans to "let freedom ring." Then, in a voice alive with emotion, he concluded: "When we let freedom ring . . . all of God's children . . . will be able to join hands and sing in the words of the old Negro spiritual, 'Free at last! Free at Last! Thank God Almighty, we are free at last!' "

After the rally King and other leaders met with President John F. Kennedy, who praised the marchers for their "deep fervor and their quiet dignity." Historians would credit the March on Washington with pushing Congress to pass the Civil Rights Act of 1964 and the Voting Rights Act of 1965. And, in December 1964, King became the youngest laureate ever to receive the Nobel Peace Prize.

1963

More than three decades after the assassination of John F. Kennedy, doubts persist as to whether Lee Harvey Oswald acted alone.

For days after the assassination of President John F. Kennedy on November 22, 1963, millions across the land watched in horrified fascination as the tragedy was played out in the press and on television: Lyndon B. Johnson taking the presidential oath of office aboard *Air Force One;* Jacqueline Kennedy still wearing her blood-spattered pink suit; the arrest of Oswald after he killed a Dallas police officer; restaurant owner Jack Ruby fatally shooting Oswald; the heartbreaking funeral.

Soon after taking office, President Johnson appointed a panel headed by Chief Justice Earl Warren to investigate the assassination. On September 24, 1964, after collecting 26 volumes of testimony from 552 witnesses, the Warren Commission submitted its report. It concluded that Oswald had acted on his own, although it was unable to determine his motive.

The Warren Report failed to silence theorists who turned out a small library of assassination books that pointed the finger at practically everyone, including the Soviet Union's KGB, both anti- and pro-Castro Cubans, the Mafia, the CIA, the FBI, even Lyndon Johnson. In July 1979, after a 2½-year investigation, a select committee of the House of Representatives issued its own

report: Kennedy was probably the victim of a conspiracy.

A poll taken in October 1983, as the 20th anniversary of Kennedy's death neared, revealed that 74 percent of all Americans believed that Oswald had not acted alone. Oliver Stone's 1991 movie *JFK*, based on the conspiracy theory of former New Orleans district attorney Jim Garrison, raised the issue again. But Louisiana businessman Clay Shaw, following his acquittal on Garrison's conspiracy charge, had an explanation for the doubts: "It's hard to accept that this handsome young man [Kennedy], this great leader of the world, was struck down by a sorry little loser crouched behind a stack of cardboard boxes."

Jack Ruby, gun in hand, seconds before he shot Lee Harvey Oswald (center).

Betty Friedan at home in 1963.

The Struggle for Equality

Over the last few decades, the women's movement has been marked by a number of significant events, as well as some female firsts.

1961 President John F. Kennedy forms the Commission on the Status of Women.

1963 President Kennedy signs the Equal Pay Act, banning salary discrimination based on sex or race.

1964 The Civil Rights Act of 1964 prohibits discrimination on the basis of sex.

1966 The National Organization for Women (NOW) is formed; Betty Friedan is its first president.

1972 Congress approves the Equal Rights Amendment. A decade later, lacking the minimum support of 38 states, the amendment is defeated.

Ms. magazine publishes its first issue.

1973 In *Roe* vs. *Wade*, the U. S. Supreme Court overturns laws prohibiting abortions during the first trimester.

1984 Democrat Geraldine Ferraro becomes the only woman to win a major party nomination for the vice presidency.

1963

The *Feminine Mystique* inspired millions of American women to seek equality and fulfillment outside their roles as wives and mothers.

In 1957 Betty Friedan, a housewife and mother of three who also worked as a freelance magazine writer, sent a questionnaire to her former Smith College classmates about the impact of college education on their lives. When she received their replies, she was taken aback; many of the women, now wives and mothers, said they were deeply discontented.

Based on further questionnaires and interviews with psychologists and other behavioral scientists, Friedan wrote the 1963 bestseller *The Feminine Mystique.* In it she stated that women lived in a society that encouraged them to find fulfillment only by living vicariously through their husbands and children. If a woman chose not to accept her traditional domestic role, she was deemed abnormal and made to feel guilty.

Through lectures and radio and television appearances around the country, Friedan elaborated on her book, describing the pressures a woman commonly experiences by trying to live the way society wants her to live, but "never as a person defining herself by her own actions in society."

Joined by other feminists, Friedan founded the National Organization for Women (NOW) in 1966. Among its goals were equal opportunity for women in the workplace, legalized abortion, and adoption of the Equal Rights Amendment (ERA). Although the ERA died in 1982 when it fell short of the 38 states needed for ratification, the Supreme Court had already struck down most of the laws the amendment would have changed.

Looking back on her work years later, Friedan has said that not even she could have predicted the "irreversible changes in women's lives" that were to come.

1964

Americans fell head over heels for four mop-haired lads from Liverpool, England.

"They've got everything over there, what do they want us for?" asked Paul McCartney as he and the other three Beatles flew to the United States for their first American tour. McCartney's question was answered on February 9, 1964, when the "Fab Four" from Liverpool, England, made their American debut on the *Ed Sullivan Show.* Seventy million viewers could barely hear the music for the screams of enraptured young women in the audience.

Not everyone was beguiled by the group's wise-cracking innocence. The *Washington Post* described the four lads as "asexual and homely," while *The New York Times* dismissed the group's performance as "a fine mass placebo."

Such criticisms flew in the face of a cultural phenomenon. Released just in time for their

Paul McCartney, George Harrison, John Lennon, with Ringo Starr on drums.

American arrival, the group's first stateside LP, *Meet the Beatles,* sold in record numbers, and by April no fewer than five Beatles' singles topped the charts. While many of the older generation shook their heads in disbelief, Beatlemania took hold. Fans mobbed theaters to see the first Beatles' movie, *A Hard Day's Night,* and horrified adults by growing their own versions of the group's signature shag haircut.

Behind the smiles and mop-tops was the continuing creative tension of Paul McCartney's romanticism and John Lennon's biting satire, George Harrison's guitar virtuosity and Ringo Starr's steady beat. This was a band that had paid its dues in small clubs throughout Europe, where they learned to fuse the beat and energy of 1950's American rockers like Little Richard and Carl Perkins with a style that helped turn rock and roll into the international language of youth.

335

A 1964
fter a bitter Congressional fight, the Civil Rights Act of 1964 finally provided equal protection for millions.

"We are confronted primarily by a moral issue," President John F. Kennedy declared in June 1963. "It is as old as the Scriptures and is as clear as the American Constitution. The heart of the question is whether all Americans are to be afforded equal rights and equal opportunities, whether we are going to treat our fellow Americans as we want to be treated."

First proposed by Kennedy, and taken up by his successor, Lyndon B. Johnson, the Civil Rights Act would be the most sweeping piece of civil rights legislation since the Civil War. It barred discrimination in all public facilities, banned racial bias in employment and union membership, authorized federal intervention to end school seg-

Having just signed the Civil Rights Act, President Johnson passes a pen to Dr. Martin Luther King, Jr.

regation, and guaranteed equal voting rights to African-Americans.

Although the need was clear, the passage of the Civil Rights Act was not easy. It faced a grueling ride through the Senate, where 11 civil rights bills had died since 1937. Finally, on June 19, 1964, after 81 days of hearings, 9 days of House debate, and an 83-day filibuster in the Senate, the Civil Rights Act passed by a vote of 73 to 27.

Two weeks later, on July 2, a nationwide television audience watched President Johnson sign the bill into law. "There is an inexorable moral force that moves us forward," declared Republican senator Everett Dirksen of Illinois. "No matter what the resistance of people who do not fully understand, it will not be denied." The fight for equality was far from over, to be sure. There would be strong resistance to the new laws, often marked by violence. But civil rights leaders could now carry the struggle forward with the full force of the federal government behind them. 🕊

I 1965
n the Watts section of Los Angeles, an apparently routine traffic stop by a policeman ignited a powder keg of seething rage.

On the sultry night of August 11, 1965, a white police officer stopped a weaving car in the predominantly black Watts section of Los Angeles. No one knows for certain what happened next. A crowd gathered, and witnesses reported that the arresting officer used excessive force. More policemen arrived and were met by an angry mob armed with stones and bottles. The Watts riots had begun.

For six days the police and National Guardsmen fought with the rioters. When it was all over, 34 people — 28 of them African-Americans — had been killed and more than 1,000 injured. Countless buildings and stores were damaged or destroyed. In one of the poorest areas of Los Angeles, property losses amounted to $40 million.

More violence was to come. During the long hot summers of 1966 and 1967, Cleveland, Chicago, Detroit, and Newark suffered more

A National Guardsman surveys the devastation caused by six days of rioting in Watts.

rioting, and when Martin Luther King was assassinated in the spring of 1968, more than 100 cities erupted in violence.

Despite the successes of the civil rights movement, America remained a profoundly polarized society. Resentment continued to seethe in the black neighborhoods of Los Angeles, and the violence of the Watts riots was eerily replayed 16 years later, in 1991. Another black motorist, Rodney King, was beaten by white police officers, this time in full view of a video camera. The incident seemed a clear-cut case of police brutality, but the mostly white jury acquitted the four officers. Once again Los Angeles exploded in rage.

The tallies: 38 dead, 4,000 people arrested, 3,700 buildings burned, and more than $500 million in damage. Two of the officers were later convicted on federal civil rights charges, but to many African-Americans, the name Rodney King reminded them of how slow things were to change, even after two decades. 🕊

1965
Lady Bird Johnson led the fight for the passage of the Highway Beautification Act.

Traveling by car out of Washington, D.C., Claudia (Lady Bird) Johnson was troubled by the cluttered highways along the way. To her they were a "tunnel of filling stations, billboards, neon signs, and dilapidated little buildings." In keeping with her belief in nature's powers to improve the quality of life, the woman nicknamed for being "purty as a lady bird" made the beautification of America her primary cause as first lady.

One of Mrs. Johnson's first moves was to urge conservationists, architects, and planners to speak out on the need to preserve the country's natural splendor. Responsible for the planting of some 300,000 flowers, trees, and shrubs, she traveled the country giving speeches about the close relationship between ugly surroundings and crime, dedicating new parks and gardens, and attending tree- and flower-planting ceremonies. With the help of her husband, President Lyndon B. Johnson, she lobbied for passage of the Highway Beautification Act, which became law in October 1965. Aimed at encouraging better federal highway planning, its provisions included the limiting of billboards and junkyards along these roads.

However active her role in conservation, Mrs. Johnson always remained humble about her efforts, which have since included the founding of the National Wildflower Research Center near Austin, Texas, in 1982. "I'm not interested in any legacy," she once said. "If we can get people to see the beauty of the native flora of their own corner of the world with caring eyes, then I'll be real happy."

Manhattan stands in uncustomary darkness after a massive power failure cut off the city's electricity.

Television star Lassie helps Lady Bird Johnson to beautify America.

1965
The largest power failure of modern times darkened nine Eastern states and parts of Canada — and may have caused a mini baby boom.

The trouble began on November 9, 1965, with a faulty relay at a Canadian hydroelectric generating plant near Niagara Falls. Overloaded, the circuit shut down; 1.6 million kilowatts of energy destined for Toronto surged like lightning down the line into New York State, knocking out generating plants from Buffalo to Boston. Each utility in turn tried to draw reserve juice from the Consolidated Edison Company in New York, which strained under the load. In less than 30 minutes the great Northeastern power grid — covering an area of some 80,000 square miles from Canada to New York and Lake Huron to Boston — went out like a candle and left a population of 30 million in darkness.

Amazingly, few people panicked. Even in New York, the largest of the cities affected, people cheerfully improvised their way through the crisis, and civil disorder was practically nil. Trapped in elevators, subways, high-rise offices, and traffic jams, people joked and sang the time away. Restaurants stayed open to feed stranded commuters, who savored their food by candlelight; department store clerks led marooned shoppers to the furniture department to bed down for the night, while others sought the comfort of a carpeted hotel lobby or a barber chair.

Under the light of a full moon, many city dwellers found that, despite the inconvenience, a vacation from modern technology was just what the doctor ordered. And, with nowhere to go and nothing to do, not a few couples found a productive way to pass the time: exactly nine months after the lights went out, hospitals in the New York City area reported a rise in the number of births.

A¹⁹⁶⁷**lthough viewers have since made it the most popular sporting event in America, the first Super Bowl was no sellout.**

The National and American football leagues were locked in a bitter rivalry for six years, vying for players, fans, and network television dollars. By 1966 spiraling contract offers for established stars finally led to an idea: the two leagues would merge. In four years the teams would all come under the National Football League (NFL) rubric, with separate American and National conferences. A game played by the best teams from each league was planned to celebrate the union.

A Kansas City Chief runs for the end zone in an attempt for the first Super Bowl trophy (left).

But the first Super Bowl, held on January 15, 1967, was hardly a financial success. After a closely played first half, coach Vince Lombardi's NFL champion

Green Bay Packers crushed Hank Stram's AFL winners, the Kansas City Chiefs, 35–10. Despite a media blitz that included endless sports commentaries and interviews, more than 30,000 seats — a third of the giant Los Angeles Memorial Coliseum — were empty.

These would be the last empty seats at any Super Bowl. By the time the two leagues merged in 1970, "The Game" had become one of the most popular sporting events in the world. Advertising space on network television would be sold for hundreds of thousands of dollars a minute, and fans would pay hundreds of dollars for tickets. The Super Bowl had become a bona fide national obsession, with an estimated one-third of all Americans — and a billion people around the globe — tuning in. ✈

M¹⁹⁶⁸**illions of TV viewers watched in dismay as the police clubbed and teargassed demonstrators on the streets of Chicago during the Democratic National Convention.**

With President Lyndon B. Johnson now out of the race, and Robert F. Kennedy having been felled by an assassin's bullet, Vice President Hubert H.

Humphrey seemed guaranteed to receive his party's nomination at the Democratic National Convention in August 1968. The party was badly divided over Vietnam; the most bitterly contested plank in the party platform was an anti-war statement that the followers of peace-movement candidate Eugene McCarthy and the late Robert

Kennedy supported. At times the debate over the statement became contentious, and when the motion to make it part of the platform failed, antiwar delegates donned black armbands and sang the civil rights anthem "We Shall Overcome."

Outside the convention hall the situation was explosive. Heeding a call from the National Mobilization to End the War in Vietnam, thousands of antiwar demonstrators had converged on Chicago. But Mayor Richard Daley would have none of the protests. The iron-fisted politico called out the National Guard and put all 12,000 of the city's uniformed officers on 12-hour shifts; skirmishes between the protesters and the police kept the city on edge. Nothing, however, could have prepared Chicago — or the nation — for the events of "Bloody Wednesday." In what was later called an all-out police riot, officers and guardsmen outside the convention hall charged a group of

demonstrators, indiscriminately teargassing and beating everyone in their path, including reporters and passersby.

When images of the bloody clash were shown on screens inside the convention amphitheater, bedlam ensued as the party deliberated how to proceed. Tempers flared. "Gestapo tactics in the streets of Chicago!" cried Connecticut senator Abraham Ribicoff from the podium, to which Mayor Daley replied with all manner of invective. In millions of homes across the nation, Americans watched with horror and disgust. Some people blamed the police for the violence, many others the protesters.

The next night, while accepting his party's nomination for president, Humphrey decried the violence, while at the same time calling for law and order. At what should have been the apex of his career, he found himself leading a party that seemed hopelessly divided. ✈

Faced with a wall of rifles, a protester taunts National Guardsmen outside the Democratic National Convention headquarters in August 1968.

A 1969 major oil spill off the coast of Santa Barbara, California, alerted the nation to the dangers of offshore drilling.

On January 28, 1969, environmentalists' worst fears were realized when a drill pipe at the Union Oil Company's "Platform A" struck a high-pressure deposit. Oil was forced into fissures below the drill pipe, then up through the ocean floor. Seeping from five "boil points," the sticky muck formed a 200-square-mile slick; by the time the offshore gusher had been plugged with concrete, estimates of the total number of gallons that had leaked into the ocean ranged from 230,000 to 10 times that much.

As the oil began to wash ashore, it fouled beaches and destroyed wildlife up and down the southern California coast. Bystanders watched, appalled, as crippled birds, crying out plaintively, floundered on the beach. Many birds, drenched in heavy black crude, were picked up by concerned citizens and dipped in a solution that would clean their

A once-clean beach between Santa Barbara and Ventura, California, is coated with sticky oil.

feathers. Dolphins were found suffocated after oil clogged their breathing holes.

Conservationists clamored that the long-term effects of the oil slick would be severely detrimental to the environment. Interior Secretary Walter J. Hickel announced a suspension of oil-drilling activities in the area, claiming that the damage

was "as much the fault of the government as anyone," since federal officials had not established stricter regulations against pollution. This was soon to change. With the creation of the Environmental Protection Agency the next year and the passage of tougher laws, the oil industry would now be under heavy scrutiny.

T 1969 he first manned lunar landing was nearly a disaster.

When Apollo 11 mission commander Neil Armstrong looked down at the lunar surface 700 feet below, he wasn't happy with what he saw. It was July 20, 1969, and the automatic landing sequence was heading the lunar module *Eagle* straight for a field of boulders. Armstrong switched over to the manual controls and began to search for a smooth place to touch down. If he did not find one, the descent would have to be aborted. With just 20 seconds of fuel remaining in the lunar module's descent tank, Armstrong beeped Mission Control. "Houston, Tranquillity Base here," he said. "The *Eagle* has landed."

"Roger, Tranquillity," Houston replied, "we copy you on the ground. You've got a bunch of guys about to turn blue. We're breathing again. Thanks a lot."

Astronaut Edwin (Buzz) Aldrin, Jr., walks on the moon near the lunar module Eagle.

Although the astronauts were supposed to rest before venturing out, neither one wanted to wait. Armstrong and Edwin (Buzz) Aldrin ate a meal, readied the spacecraft for their return, and helped each other climb into bulky spacesuits. Six-and-a-half hours after touchdown — and five months ahead of the late president John F. Kennedy's deadline — Armstrong bounded down the ladder and left mankind's first footprints on the dusty lunar surface. A television camera attached to the lunar module's base strut beamed the image back to millions around the world, and with it Armstrong's immortal words: "That's one small step for a man, one giant leap for mankind." A giant leap perhaps, but it all looked easy somehow, and most Americans never knew how close the mission had come to being aborted — or worse, ending in catastrophe.

Farmland in New York State is transformed into a sea of people as music fans from as far away as California turn their attention toward the distant stage.

1969
Thousands of young people from across America converged on the small town of Bethel, New York, for a music festival.
More than just a rock concert, the Woodstock Music and Art Fair, held August 15–17, 1969, on a dairy farm in Bethel, New York, turned out to be the baby boom generation's defining moment. The concert's planners expected just 50,000 people; some 400,000 showed up, creating a counterculture army almost as large as the U.S. military force in Vietnam. The result was a celebration of music, free love, and psychedelic good feeling unlike any in history.

The event wasn't entirely trouble free. Yet despite food shortages, drenching rains, monster traffic jams, and some bad LSD that someone passed around, not a single violent incident was reported. Just in case, 50 doctors were flown in from New York City to treat possible injuries. Three deaths did occur, at least one from a drug overdose; but at the same time two new citizens were born to women attending the concert.

The main attraction was the music, of course, and to pull in the hippies, Yippies, campus radicals, and other assorted members of the under-30 generation, the concert promoters delivered a pantheon of performers whose songs became the common anthem of the times. Among the many who took the stage were the Grateful Dead, Joan Baez, Janis Joplin, Carlos Santana, and Jimi Hendrix, whose electrified deconstruction of "The Star-Spangled Banner" — one part parody, one part tribute — eloquently captured the youthful spirit of the moment. But there was something else. For during that one weekend at Woodstock, the Age of Aquarius — an era marked by harmony and goodwill — did not seem so far off after all.

1970
On the nation's first Earth Day, 20 million Americans participated in programs to clean up the environment.
In an era of mass demonstrations, the largest — and surely the most buoyantly high-spirited — was held on April 22, 1970, when the nation devoted an entire day to celebrating the environment. Some 20 million Americans across the country participated in the day's events — attending lectures, rallies, and workshops, and picking up trash. In New York City, Fifth Avenue was closed to traffic, and in the nation's capital huge crowds gathered at the Washington Monument to share the ecological gospel. Congress declared a recess so that members could participate in panel discussions and give speeches on environmental concerns.

The mood of the day was mainly upbeat, but behind it lay an increasing public anxiety. Decades of neglect had caused stress on the environment, and

New York City children celebrate the first Earth Day.

Americans could see, smell, and taste the damage. Scientists, bemoaning the dwindling resources of the nation's air, water, and wildlife, issued dire warnings about a planet poisoned by pesticides and exhaust fumes. Even the bald eagle, the beloved national symbol, was threatened with extinction.

The very day of the rallies, lawmakers got to work. A House subcommittee unanimously approved a bill setting national auto emission standards aimed at reducing air pollution. Within months the Environmental Protection Agency (EPA) was formed. Throughout the decade some 35 new environmental laws went into effect, and Americans slowly began to change their living habits. They bought fuel-efficient cars, sorted trash for recycling, chose environment-friendly products, and assumed greater personal responsibility for the natural systems all around them.

D *1970*
Dissension led to tragedy at Kent State University when National Guardsmen fired on student demonstrators.

"Those are real bullets!" the young professor yelled. "Take cover!" But for four students at Kent State University in Ohio, the warning came too late: they lay dead where they had fallen, struck down in a 15-second spatter of gunfire. Nine others were wounded; one, shot in the spine, would never walk again.

Trouble had been brewing at Kent State for four days, ever since President Richard M. Nixon announced on April 30, 1970, that American ground troops had invaded Cambodia. In response to this escalation of the war in Southeast Asia, protests had broken out on many campuses across America. When students burned down the ROTC building at Kent State, Ohio Governor James Rhodes quickly called up 900 National Guardsmen to restore calm. On May 4, guardsmen ordered a gathering of student protesters to disperse; when they refused, the guardsmen lobbed tear-gas canisters into the group. Some protesters began to throw rocks, but few if any hit their mark; many of the students were laughing, and a crowd of onlookers formed, flanking the soldiers, who retreated to a nearby hill. Some of the students approached them, jeering. The guardsmen aimed their weapons and fired.

Three of the four students killed weren't even protesters: two were spectators, and one, Sandra Lee Scheuer, was walking to class when she stepped into the line of fire. As for the guardsmen, most were young people from Ohio — very much like the students themselves. It has never been established whether or not an order had been given to fire. While several guardsmen later told the FBI that they had not been in danger, others said they had feared for their lives. A special investigatory commission concluded that the shootings were "unnecessary, unwarranted, and inexcusable," but claims against the Guard were eventually settled out of court. And for many Americans, the incident at Kent State would be remembered as one of the darkest moments of a deeply troubled era. ✈

The Ohio National Guard moves across the Kent State campus to confront protesting students.

E *1970*
Eighteen-year-olds won the right to vote — but would they use it?

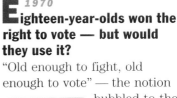
A 19-year-old votes in 1972.

"Old enough to fight, old enough to vote" — the notion bubbled to the surface every time the United States went to war. President Dwight D. Eisenhower had endorsed it back in 1954, after the end of the Korean conflict. So too, in the mid 1960's, did President Lyndon Johnson, who hoped to lure anti–Vietnam War student protesters from the barricades to the ballot box. And now the time had come. On June 17, 1970, Congress passed a law that lowered the voting age from 21 to 18.

Formidable barriers remained before the law took effect, however. Voting age standards had always been set by the individual states, and some state legislatures wanted to keep it that way. Several filed suits with the Supreme Court.

A constitutional amendment finally resolved the issue. In March 1971 Congress approved the 26th Amendment, and within three months it became the law of the land.

The majority of young people seemed barely to notice. Some 11 million citizens between ages 18 and 21 had suddenly won the franchise. Only half of them registered to vote in the 1972 presidential elections — and of these only 35 percent showed up to cast their ballots. ✈

President and Mrs. Nixon visit the famed Great Wall of China.

P¹⁹⁷²
resident Nixon's history-making visit to main-land China ended two decades of Cold War silence — with a little help from Ping-Pong.

Since 1949 and the revolution that brought the Communist regime of Mao Tse-tung to power, American foreign policy had all but ignored main-land China, home to nearly a quarter of the world's people. Then little by little relations began to thaw. In the spring of 1971 U.S. officials began lifting a trade embargo and long-standing travel restrictions against China. Suddenly, to the world's astonishment, the U.S. table tennis team was jetting to Beijing at China's invitation to play Ping-Pong. There was more to come. National Security Adviser Henry Kissinger, on a trip to Pakistan, complained of feeling ill and disap-peared into his hotel room. In fact, he was making a secret flight to Beijing to arrange for a presiden-tial visit the following winter. Kissinger cabled back a one-word message to indicate that he had successfully secured an invitation: "Eureka."

On February 21, 1972, President Richard M. Nixon's plane *The Spirit of '76* arrived in China,

and the nation was treated to an amazing sight: an American presi-dent on Chinese soil, listening to a Chinese military band play "The Star-Spangled Banner" and shaking hands with Chinese leader Chou En-lai. In the frigid Asian winter, Nixon walked the Great Wall, toured the Forbidden City, spent hours in conversation with Premier Chou, and visited with an ailing Chairman Mao, the spiritual and political leader of 1 billion Chinese. Accompanying the president and his wife were a planeload of aides, members of the press, and two musk oxen — gifts from the Amer-ican people to the Beijing Zoo. (In return, first lady Patricia Nixon was given two giant pandas for the National Zoo.) For a week Ameri-cans sat spellbound in front of their television screens, watching images beamed from a mysterious land halfway around the world.

Tensions would remain between the two superpowers, but some-thing momentous had happened, and at the end of the visit, both nations issued a statement pledging normalization of relations. "This was the week that changed the world," Nixon said, and he was right. China would stand as the greatest tri-umph of his presidency.

Culinary Détente

One of the highlights of President Richard M. Nixon's visit to China was a three-hour banquet in the Great Hall of the People. Attended by nearly 700 American and Chinese guests, the sumptuous eight-course meal included:

- Aged eggs
- Bacon and small carp in vinegar sauce
- Spongy bamboo shoots and egg-white consommé
- Shark's fin in three shreds
- Fried and stewed prawns
- Mushrooms and mustard greens
- Steamed chicken with coconut
- Almond junket
- North China tangerines

L¹⁹⁷²
ittle-known writer Clifford Irving nearly got away with one of the publishing indus-try's greatest hoaxes — the "authorized autobiography" of famous recluse Howard Hughes.

When Clifford Irving approach-ed editors at McGraw-Hill with what he claimed was a ghost-written autobiography of Amer-ica's most famous billionaire hermit, they jumped at the chance to publish it. What they

Clifford and Edith Irving plead guilty in a Manhattan criminal court.

didn't know was that every word of Irving's manuscript was phony — some of it taken from an unpublished biography writ-ten by one of Hughes's employ-ees, some gleaned from conversations with associates of the multimillionaire, and the rest dreamed up by Irving and his researcher and co-conspira-tor, Richard Suskind.

Publication of the Hughes memoir was scheduled for March 27, 1972; McGraw-Hill announced in a press release that the book was the result of

100 taped interviews with Hughes, mostly conducted in parked cars. *Life* magazine was set to print three installments from the book, as well as an article by Irving about his meetings with the reclusive Hughes. In all, Irving received an advance of some $750,000 — $100,000 for himself, the rest in checks reportedly made out to Howard Hughes.

But as the day of publication neared, Irving's plan began to unravel. Authorities in Switzerland discovered that a bank account in the name of H. R. Hughes, and into which the checks for Howard Hughes had been deposited, actually belonged to Helga R. Hughes — an alias for Irving's Swiss wife, Edith. Even more damaging was a telephone call from Howard Hughes himself, who announced that he had never met anyone named Clifford Irving. Worse, Irving's publishers had already learned that Hughes had signed a contract with another writer, Robert Eaton, to write his autobiography. Irving finally admitted to the hoax, and on March 9 he was indicted on federal conspiracy charges. Three months later he was sentenced to 2½ years in prison and fined $10,000. He later wrote a book about the experience. ✈

S ¹⁹⁷³ ome of the American POW's endured captivity in North Vietnam for more than eight years.

When the first plane of freed American prisoners arrived at Clark Air Base in the Philippines on February 12, 1973, naval aviator Lieut. Comdr. Everett Alvarez, Jr., was among its passengers. Alvarez held the unhappy distinction of having been the first pilot shot down and captured during the Vietnam War. A cease-fire agreement, signed in Paris a month earlier, had put an end to nine years of suffering. As he and other former captives emerged from the plane to a red-carpet welcome, 1,000 base residents looked on, many with tears in their eyes. For some of the POW's, nearly a decade had passed since they had set foot on American soil. Most walked, others ran, a few were carried on stretchers. All were overjoyed to be home.

The return of American POW's was made even more poignant by the fact that so little had been known about their condition. Because there was no declaration of war between the United States and North Vietnam, Hanoi had refused to allow prisoners their rights under the Geneva Convention, among them the right to send and receive mail. More than 700 Americans, most of them airmen, had been taken prisoner. Of the 591 who survived, most had suffered under the most horrendous conditions.

Whether housed in one of North Vietnam's half-dozen prisons (such as the infamous "Hanoi Hilton") or in remote jungle camps, prisoners endured prolonged torture — both physical and psychological. Some were paraded through the streets to jeering crowds. Many were forced to sign statements and make video-taped confessions condemning the war and acknowledging their "crimes." One of the biggest hardships was the isolation. To pass the time and stave off madness, prisoners communicated with one another with hand signals or messages tapped out on cell walls — everything from plans to resist their captors to the plots of novels and movies. Despite the hardship, the will to survive ran high. As one man later said, "Dying in a prison camp wouldn't achieve anything." ✈

American POW's at the notorious "Hanoi Hilton."

Spiro Agnew speaks to the nation after his resignation.

S ¹⁹⁷³ piro Agnew was forced to resign the vice presidency because he failed to pay federal income taxes while he was governor of Maryland.

One of the most controversial politicians to run on a presidential ticket, Spiro Agnew was so disliked by liberals that many jokingly called him Richard Nixon's insurance policy against impeachment. Unluckily for his boss, Agnew fell into hot water in August 1973, when evidence came to light that the onetime Maryland governor had been taking kickbacks from contractors for more than a decade, and that he had not paid federal income taxes. Agnew's fall from grace was swift; on October 10 he pleaded no contest to the lesser charge of tax evasion and resigned from office.

Agnew was not the first vice president to step down — John C. Calhoun resigned in 1832 over political differences with President Andrew Jackson — but he was the first to leave the office in disgrace. And with Agnew removed from the line of succession (replaced by House Minority Leader Gerald Ford), Nixon's opponents began to call in earnest for the president's impeachment. ✈

1973
The Arab oil embargo sent fuel prices sky-rocketing and created a national panic.
Until the autumn of 1973, most Americans didn't even know that the United States imported 35 percent of its oil, much less where the oil came from. Oil was cheap and abundant, and since the end of World War II Americans had used increasing amounts of it each year to fuel their cars, light their homes, and run their appliances. Between 1950 and 1970, America's consumption per household more than doubled. Oil — and plenty of it — was a resource that everyone took for granted.

The illusion of an endless fuel supply vanished on October 17, 1973. Responding to America's support for Israel in the Yom Kippur War, OPEC (an acronym for Organization of Petroleum Exporting Countries, many of them Arab states that opposed Israel) announced a temporary halt to exports. From now on the OPEC cartel intended to set prices unilaterally, rather than bargain, country by country with individual oil companies. When the exports resumed, the cost of a barrel of oil soared from $2.90 to more than $11.00. Pessimists began to forecast a time when the OPEC ministers would demand $100 a barrel.

That day never came, but in the meantime America found itself in the throes of a bona fide energy panic. Although the United States held oil reserves of more than a billion barrels, enough to make up the export shortfall for nearly two years, Americans prepared for the worst. They soon discovered that the nation's system of fuel distribution was woefully inadequate. "NO GAS" signs appeared at thousands of service stations, and motorists formed long lines at gas pumps that still had fuel. Some states adopted rationing systems to discourage hoarding, and across the country the maximum speed limit was reduced to 55 miles an hour in order to conserve fuel.

The immediate crisis was over in a matter of months; but the era of limitless, low-cost energy was gone forever.

1973
A denim design contest put on by Levi Strauss & Co. celebrated the evolution of blue jeans from work clothes to fashion statement.
Levi Strauss, the Bavarian-born immigrant who invented the best-known pants in the world, never called them jeans. In his day they were called waist-high overalls.

But it was as jeans that Strauss's creation — originally sewn for California miners who needed durable garb — won fame. In 1873 Levi Strauss & Co. started making copper-riveted, waist-high overalls out of denim, a sturdy cotton fabric that originated in France in the Middle Ages. In no time cowboys made the trousers a part of their everyday working attire. Fashionable men and women vacationing at dude ranches during the 1930's adopted the pants, and in the following decade bobby-soxers wore jeans rolled up at the bottom and marked with fanciful designs. It was the teenagers of the 1960's, however, who made jeans their own, adorning them with peace symbols, antiwar slogans, and other personal touches. Paints and dyes were used to create unique psychedelic landscapes, and colored beads and rhinestones decorated seams and cuffs.

By the early 1970's expensive boutiques began selling denim trousers and jackets with elaborate designs. Interest in decorated jeans was so great that in 1973 Levi Strauss & Co. sponsored a denim design contest that drew 3,000 entries. The 50 winning entries were exhibited at the New York Museum of Contemporary Crafts and then toured museums around the globe.

Prize-winning jeans from the Denim Art Contest.

As his wife, Pat, looks on, President Nixon bids a tearful farewell to his staff and cabinet.

1974
Under threat of impeachment, Richard Nixon became the first president to resign.
On August 8, 1974, Richard Nixon faced a television camera and spoke the words that no American president had ever before uttered. To spare the country from a prolonged distraction from more vitally pressing issues, he said, "I shall resign the presidency effective at noon tomorrow." In less than two years Nixon had spiraled from a landslide election victory over George McGovern to abysmal disgrace.

Nixon's descent into infamy began on June 17, 1972, when a group of burglars were caught tapping phones and stealing documents from the Democratic National Committee's Watergate Hotel headquarters in Washington, D.C. Two *Washington Post* reporters discovered that the burglars were all connected with Nixon's Committee to Re-

Elect the President (CREEP), and wrote an article for their newspaper. Secretly recorded White House conversations during the months following the break-in showed that Nixon had participated in a cover-up.

The president refused to release the secret tapes to Watergate special prosecutor Archibald Cox. Even after he fired Cox, he held the tapes back from the replacement prosecutor, Leon Jaworski. Nixon relinquished them only after the U.S. Supreme Court unanimously ruled in July 1974 that he must. That same month the House Judiciary Committee adopted three articles of impeachment against Nixon for obstruction of justice, the misuse of federal agencies to violate citizens' rights, and flouting the authority of Congress.

In early August, Nixon spent three days agonizing over his next move. His chief of staff, Alexander Haig, fearing for the president's well-being, ordered all medications kept away from the president during this time. Finally, Nixon made up his mind and went before the American people to resign, the first president ever to do so. 🦋

With the fall of Saigon imminent, some of the last to leave the city board a helicopter inside the U.S. Embassy compound.

1975
Both Americans and Vietnamese made desperate attempts to evacuate as Saigon fell.

America's 1973 cease-fire with North Vietnam did not end the fighting between the North and South. After two years of struggle, the North began aggressively attacking Vietnam's Central Highlands, forcing thousands of South Vietnamese to flee. As people with money or political clout left the country, Saigon filled with refugees. In April, South Vietnamese president Nguyen Van Thieu resigned and joined the escapees.

On April 27, 1975, 14 North Vietnamese army divisions with some 200,000 troops surrounded Saigon. Two days later the United States launched a final effort to evacuate all remaining Americans, plus any Vietnamese civilians who had worked for the U.S. military or government. A fleet of 81 helicopters carried thousands of people from Tan Son Nhut airport to U.S. ships anchored offshore. The war's last American fatalities were two U.S. Marines felled by North Vietnamese rocket fire not far from the airport.

The evening of April 29 saw the frantic evacuation of the U.S. Embassy in Saigon. Thousands of people, mostly South Vietnamese, gathered around the compound, some trying to scale the 10-foot walls, in the hope of finding a place aboard an American helicopter. Early the next morning a frenzied crowd pushed its way through the gate and up to the embassy's roof, where Marines sprayed tear gas in order to protect the final groups of U.S. evacuees. At 7:52 A.M., the last American jumped on board the last outbound helicopter. More than 7,000 people were flown out of South Vietnam in 19 hours — a desperate final exit from America's longest war. 🦋

The Longest Conflict (1954–1975)

American involvement in Vietnam began in 1950 when economic aid and military advisers were sent to help fight Communist aggression in Southeast Asia. It continued for 25 years, cost the lives of 57,605 Americans, and sparked a crisis of national conscience within the United States.

1955 U.S.-supported Ngo Dinh Diem becomes president of the newly created Republic of South Vietnam.

1963 Dissident generals overthrow the South Vietnamese government and assassinate President Diem.

1964 North Vietnamese torpedo boats attack U.S. destroyers in the Gulf of Tonkin. Congress passes a resolution authorizing the use of military force in Southeast Asia.

1965 U.S. bombers strike North Vietnam; the first American combat troops arrive.

1968 North Vietnam launches a surprise offensive during Tet, the Vietnamese lunar new year, and is driven back with heavy losses.

1969 President Nixon begins the gradual withdrawal of U.S. troops.

1970 U.S. and South Vietnamese forces stage devastating attacks on North Vietnamese bases in Cambodia.

1972 The North Vietnamese thrust across the 17th parallel, the geographic line that divides North and South Vietnam, and are turned back.

1973 After heavy U.S. air attacks, North Vietnam signs a cease-fire agreement in Paris on January 27. The last U.S. troops leave Vietnam two months later.

1975 North Vietnamese troops overwhelm Saigon, capital of South Vietnam, forcing the surrender of the South Vietnamese government.

New York City celebrated the Bicentennial with fantastic fireworks.

1976
For one festive year, Americans joined together to celebrate a shining event: their nation's bicentennial.

Skeptics insisted that it would be a disaster: Americans, embittered by the Vietnam War and Watergate, were in no mood to celebrate their country's 200th birthday. But by the end of 1976, the American people proved the cynics dead wrong. More than 27,000 Bicentennial-related events and projects in some 12,000 communities had taken place, including the restoration of St. Louis Cathedral in New Orleans, the baking of a 60-square-foot cherry pie in George, Washington, and the swearing-in of 1,776 new citizens in Chicago.

In a show of international goodwill, royalty and heads of state came to pay tribute, among them Israeli prime minister Yitzhak Rabin, King Juan Carlos I of Spain, and Queen Elizabeth II of Great Britain — who became an honorary citizen of New York City during her stay. In addition, various countries sent gifts to the United States. Japan presented a collection of bonsai plants, Italy an 18th-century miniature portrait of Thomas Jefferson. Great Britain even loaned a copy of the Magna Carta.

On the big birthday itself, July 4, 1976, celebrants at Mars Hill in Maine greeted the dawn by raising the Bicentennial flag. Philadelphians rang the Centennial Bell 13 times, and bells across the nation pealed in answer. Time capsules, to be opened in 2076, were buried in all 50 states. In New York Harbor, 225 ships glided up the Hudson as 6 million people watched, and a crowd of 400,000 in Boston saw Arthur Fiedler conduct Tchaikovsky's *1812 Overture*. What President Gerald Ford called the "spirit of unity and togetherness deep within the American soul" truly lived. ✈

1977
Two computer pioneers built a small, affordable desktop computer and launched a giant industry.

Working in a Cupertino, California, garage, whiz kids Steven Jobs and Stephen Wozniak — neither of whom ever finished college — put together their first microprocessor computer board. Unlike other microprocessors, their device was relatively cheap and uncomplicated, and it was hooked up directly to a video monitor.

In 1976 Jobs and Wozniak formed the Apple Computer Company. They had a product and a company, but no cash to get started. Jobs sold his van and Wozniak parted with his programmable calculator, and with a loan of $5,000 from a friend and a 30-day line of credit at an electronics company, they hired two firms to make the boards. They ended up selling about 175 Apple I microprocessors.

Sparked by their modest success, Wozniak designed a more sophisti-cated version of their computer, the Apple II. By April 1977 it was on the market. Although primitive by today's standards (it used audiotapes for data storage and an ordinary television set for a screen), Wozniak's machine was an instant hit. In the next three years the pair sold 130,000 Apple II's at a price of just $1,298 — a mere fraction of the cost of a bulky mainframe computer.

Four years later, computer giant IBM introduced its first desktop computer, the IBM PC, and by the end of the decade, microcomputers had become an everyday part of life in businesses, schools, and homes across America. So momentous was the personal computer revolution that in 1983 *Time* magazine named the computer the "Man of the Year." ✈

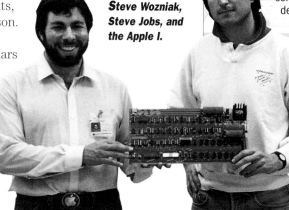

Steve Wozniak, Steve Jobs, and the Apple I.

Tech Talk

Computers have revolutionized our lives in countless ways, even influencing our language. Many familiar words have taken on additional meanings. The following are just a few examples.

Bit–A single binary digit (either 1 or 0): the smallest unit of electronic information.

Bug–A glitch in the design of software that can cause crashes or other problems.

Crash–An error in the operation of a computer that can shut it down, possibly destroying data.

Gig–Short for gigabyte, a measure of computer memory roughly equal to 179 million words.

Hack–Originally a term for the act of programming computers, it now also refers to the act of electronically breaking into them.

Virus–An intentionally disruptive program that can alter or destroy data. Like its biological counterpart, a computer virus "infects" other programs or terminals by passing along copies of itself.

If a technician at Three Mile Island had read the control-room information correctly, the accident might never have happened.

In the spring of 1979 Americans were still feeling the effects of an energy crisis that had begun six years earlier, when the Organization of Petroleum Exporting Countries (OPEC) had created oil shortages in America. As an alternative to oil and gas, nuclear power appeared highly promising.

An open valve in a reactor at the Three Mile Island (TMI) facility near Harrisburg, Pennsylvania, changed that viewpoint entirely. On March 28, 1979, the valve in the second reactor (Unit 2) at TMI caused coolant for the hot nuclear cores to escape. The emergency system began to replace the liquid, but control-room workers misinterpreted the system's readings and deactivated the backup system. Because the nuclear core failed to receive protective coolant, approximately one-half of the core melted, releasing fission-related gases into adjoining buildings and, ultimately, into the environment.

The vessel containing the reactor retained its structural integrity, and authorities announced that most of the leakage took the form of inert gases that do not harm the human body. But later studies showed that the damage to Unit 2 was much greater than reported: the vessel had almost reached the point of meltdown. Especially worrisome since the accident, cancer death and infant-mortality rates within the Three Mile Island area increased sharply.

Public reaction to the Three Mile Island accident was vehement. The popularity of nuclear energy took a nosedive, and tough safety regulations slowed the industry. By the 1990's, no new nuclear power plants had been shut down, and no new plants were under construction.

The Three Mile Island cooling towers.

An attempted commando raid to free American hostages in Iran ended in a fiery crash in the desert.

On November 4, 1979, Iranian students stormed the U.S. embassy in Tehran, Iran, and captured 66 of its personnel. Supported by an Islamic fundamentalist spiritual leader, the Ayatollah Ruhollah Khomeini, the students demanded the return and trial of the deposed Mohammad Reza Shah Pahlavi, who had been admitted to the United States for cancer treatment. Fifteen days later, claiming respect for women and sympathy toward blacks, the Ayatollah released 13 African–American and female hostages; for the others, the crisis dragged on. Then, in April 1980, President Jimmy Carter authorized a secret commando raid to free the hostages.

Months in the planning, the raid on April 24 was an unmitigated disaster. Six cargo planes landed at night in the desert 270 miles from Teheran and were caught in a violent sandstorm. Three of the mission's eight helicopters developed mechanical problems, including an overheated gyroscope, a faulty rotor blade, and a failed hydraulic pump. The mission had to be aborted before it was ever fully launched. The worst mishap occurred during the attempted retreat: a fourth helicopter accidentally crashed into a cargo plane, igniting ammunition on board. The collision killed eight soldiers, severely burned five, and destroyed seven aircraft.

By projecting an image of bumbling incompetence, the failed raid was a propaganda coup for Khomeini. By the same token, it spelled doom for Carter's reelection efforts. And it drove the two nations still further apart, making an end to the crisis even more unlikely. Not until January 20, 1981, moments after Ronald Reagan's inauguration, were the hostages freed. They had been in captivity for 444 days.

Iran's Ayatollah Sadegh Khalkhali surveys the damage after the failed U.S. commando raid to rescue the American hostages.

Mt. St. Helens blows its top, belching forth gases and hot ash.

1980
The eruption of Mt. St. Helens in the Cascade Range caused the largest landslide in recorded history.

On the bright morning of May 18, 1980, 30-year-old volcanologist David A. Johnston was keeping close tabs on Mt. St. Helens in Washington's Cascade Range. For weeks scientists had known something was up. Beginning on March 20, a series of earthquakes had shaken the slumbering volcanic giant, and ominous noises issued from fresh cracks in the mountain's face. Alone at his observation post, some five miles from the mountain's summit, Johnston had his binoculars trained on a curious bulge, when suddenly the whole mountain seemed to shudder. He reached for his radio to call the U.S. Geological Survey Center in Vancouver, Washington. "Vancouver, Vancouver, this is it!" the young scientist cried.

It was Johnston's last transmission. Moments later, the mountain's north face collapsed into Spirit Lake, which lay at its base. Like pressure released from a champagne bottle, hot gases and rock fragments shot out of the mountain at speeds of up to 250 miles an hour, leveling 230 square miles of pristine evergreen forest and turning the denuded area into a steaming wasteland of boiling mud. A second explosion knocked 1,300 feet off the mountaintop and hurled a plume of ash and smoke 13 miles into the air. Ash fell like dirty snow across the Northwest, draping the region in a dust-filled darkness as black as a moonless midnight.

Fifty-seven people were killed or missing. Among the dead were Johnston and Harry Truman, an 84-year-old resident of Spirit Lake who had refused to leave.

Once the dust cleared, scientists were astonished at the speed with which the forest recovered. Within weeks hearty plants began to poke through the ashfall, and three years later 90 percent of the area's original plant species had rebloomed. ✈

1981
The Centers for Disease Control reported on a deadly immune system condition that was later named AIDS.

In April 1981 many doctors in Atlanta, Los Angeles, and New York were baffled. A large number of young, otherwise healthy homosexual men were turning up at their offices with severe cases of two rare diseases: pneumocystis carinii pneumonia (PCP) and a skin cancer called Kaposi's sarcoma (KS). Even more astonishing was the rapid deterioration of the afflicted men, who were often plagued with swollen glands, high fevers, weight loss, and severe intestinal disorders. Within months many of the patients died, usually after terrible suffering.

In a report that year in the Centers for Disease Control newsletter, *Morbidity and Mortality Weekly Report,* doctors discussed the surprising prevalence of the two diseases. But they could not answer their own nagging questions. Were the two conditions linked? Why did they seem to strike only homosexual men? Were they infectious?

By the summer of 1982, there were disturbing answers. Medical research compiled by the Centers for Disease Control showed that the men had a disorder that attacked the immune system, leaving it vulnerable and unable to protect the body from disease. The pneumonia and cancer, along with a host of other ailments, were opportunistic diseases that thrived in the compromised immune system.

Contrary to what was first believed, the illness struck not only homosexual men but also heterosexual men, women, and children. Perhaps the most chilling news was that it was infectious — transmitted from person to person through bodily fluids such as blood and semen. People who were sexually promiscuous, as well as intravenous drug users and hemophiliacs, were seen to be at high risk. Beyond trying to alleviate the patient's suffering, the doctors could do nothing to help. No cure existed for this seemingly fatal disease. But medical researchers were able, after much debate, to give it a name — Acquired Immune Deficiency Syndrome, or AIDS.

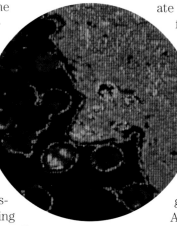

The AIDS virus (shown in red) attacks a white blood cell.

In 1984 scientists in the United States and France announced that they had found the probable cause of AIDS — a microbe commonly known as HIV, for human immunodeficiency virus. Pharmaceutical companies developed drugs that appeared to slow the onslaught of HIV. The relief, however, was only temporary. To this day, there is still no effective vaccine or permanent cure. ✈

S 1981

Sandra Day O'Connor became the nation's first female Supreme Court justice — even though, back when she was fresh out of law school, almost no one wanted to hire her.

It didn't matter that 22-year-old Sandra Day O'Connor had graduated third in her class from the prestigious Stanford Law School. (A young man named William Rehnquist, who would go on to become chief justice of the Supreme Court, graduated first.) Back in 1952 none of the firms where she applied for work was interested in hiring a female lawyer. Only one law office offered her a position — as a legal secretary. She promptly turned it down.

Undeterred, she found a job as a deputy county attorney in San Mateo, California, and later went into private practice with a partner near Phoenix, Arizona. After a five-year sabbatical to raise her three sons, she returned to

Sandra Day O'Connor poses with fellow Supreme Court justices in 1981.

the public sector as an assistant attorney general and then ran successfully for the state senate. In 1975 O'Connor won her first judicial position as a superior court judge in Maricopa County; four years later she was appointed to the Arizona Court of Appeals.

Known as a judicial conservative in most matters (save women's rights), O'Connor soon caught the attention of Washington's Republican leadership. In 1981 President Reagan, fulfilling a campaign pledge to appoint a woman to the bench, nominated her to be the 102nd justice of the Supreme Court. He described her as "a person for all seasons," possessing "unique qualities of temperament, fairness, [and] intellectual capacity." The Senate was quick to agree; it confirmed O'Connor's nomination by a vote of 99 to 0. On September 25, 1981, the nation's first female Supreme Court justice was sworn in, ending 191 years of male dominance.

A 1984

Americans reelected Ronald Reagan — at age 73, the nation's oldest president — by the largest majority for a Republican in history.

"The Great Communicator" Ronald Reagan had little trouble getting his point across to the American people in 1984. Not even criticism of Reagan's long-standing economic plan — "Waiting for supply-side economics to work," carped one observer, "is like leaving the landing lights on for Amelia Earhart" — seemed to stick. The economy seemed to be improving, in fact, and the chief executive found himself riding a crest of popularity that was unprecedented in modern history. Astute campaign salesmanship didn't hurt him, either. Stressing themes of patriotism, hard work, and traditional American values, television commericals featured Reagan tearfully embracing veterans, congratulating Olympic champions, and aiming a defiant gaze across the South Korean border into Communist North Korea. He also had devised a winning slogan, "America Is Coming Back."

By contrast, Democratic nominee Walter Mondale seemed a hapless naysayer. Although he briefly excited the electorate by choosing New York congresswoman Geraldine Ferraro to share the ticket, his message of sacrifice — and higher taxes — could scarcely compete. In November, Americans couldn't wait to reelect 73-year-old Ronald Reagan. Taking 49 states, the Ronald Reagan–George Bush ticket rode back into office in the greatest Republican landslide in history, losing only the District of Columbia and Mondale's native Minnesota — the latter by just 3,800 votes.

President and Mrs. Reagan in 1985.

Pre-Presidential Occupations

Not every president was a former lawyer, teacher, or army officer. Some held surprising jobs on their path to the presidency:

George Washington	Farmer	John F. Kennedy	Journalist
Grover Cleveland	Sheriff	Jimmy Carter	Peanut farmer
Warren G. Harding	Insurance salesman	Ronald Reagan	Actor, radio announcer
Herbert Hoover	Mining engineer	George Bush	Oil company entrepreneur
Harry S Truman	Bank clerk, farmer, haberdasher		

Just seconds after takeoff, the Challenger space shuttle exploded into flames in midair.

1986
The worst space disaster in American history was caused by the malfunction of a simple gasket.

America's space program suffered a heartbreaking setback on January 28, 1986, when the space shuttle *Challenger* disintegrated in a fireball 73 seconds after liftoff. On board was a crew of seven, including civilian Christa McAuliffe, a New Hampshire high school teacher who had been chosen in a nationwide search.

It was America's worst space disaster ever. Although three astronauts had burned to death during a simulation in 1967, none had ever died on an actual space flight, and the entire country was plunged into mourning. In one of the most eloquent addresses of his presidency, Ronald Reagan comforted the nation. The seven *Challenger* astronauts, he said, had "slipped the surly bonds of Earth to touch the face of God."

A special commission later traced the explosion to the spacecraft's right rocket booster and a simple O-ring gasket. Design errors and atypically low temperatures on the morning of the launch had combined to weaken the seal. As the *Challenger* ascended, flames had leaked from the booster, burning into the shuttle's main fuel tank like a match held to dynamite. The tank had exploded, pulling the *Challenger* apart.

Unfortunately, the disaster might have been prevented. For seven successive launches, engineers had known about the gasket problem, only to have the information lost somewhere in NASA's chain of command.

"There was a serious flaw in the decision-making process," the commission concluded. The result wasn't just an overhaul of the space shuttle, but of NASA itself. And American astronauts would not return to space for nearly three years.

1987
On "Black Monday," plunging stock prices rocked Wall Street, but "Terrible Tuesday" ended with stocks heading up.

It was not a good day on the New York Stock Exchange. When the closing bell rang at 4 P.M. on Monday, October 19, 1987, a record 604 million shares had been traded, nearly all at a loss.

The panic had been aggravated by something called pro-

gram trading — huge blocks of stocks bought and sold by computers as the market fell. After months of scoring one new high after another, the Dow Jones Industrial Average was hit by a loss of 508 points, the largest one-day decline in its history.

Not since the crash of 1929, which kicked off the Great Depression, did the future seem so bleak. In just seven hours, on what would become known as Black Monday, stock prices had plunged a sickening 22.6 percent. Stock Exchange chairman John Phelan called it "the nearest thing to a financial meltdown I ever want to see."

Tuesday started out even worse. So many sell orders flooded the exchange that trading in some securities came to a halt. Nobody wanted to buy. Banks refused to extend short-term credit, thus drying up potential funds.

Relief came from the Federal Reserve Board in Washington, D.C., which acted to flood the market with sorely needed dollars. Corporations began to buy back their own stocks. By the end of that "Terrible Tuesday," the Dow index had risen more than 100 points. Wednesday's rally was even more robust — a record gain of 187 points.

As the market recovered, there was a collective sigh of relief. The panic had sent a clear message that ballooning federal and trade deficits had put the nation's economy on shaky ground, but by week's end Wall Street had returned to business as usual.

The stock market hadn't taken such a beating since the crash of 1929.

Oil-field fires blaze behind an American soldier in the Kuwaiti desert.

A 1991
Americans remained glued to their television screens as Operation Desert Storm was broadcast live into their homes.

Operation Desert Storm began on the evening of January 16, 1991, with a massive aerial bombardment of Baghdad and Iraqi positions inside occupied Kuwait. It would be the first real test of America's new arsenal of computer-aided weaponry. Over the next month living rooms across the United States glowed with taped news footage interspersed with live broadcasts of the actual war. Americans watched in awe as radar-dodging stealth aircraft delivered payloads of laser-guided bombs and Patriot missiles snatched Iraqi scuds right out of the air.

When the ground offensive began on February 24, it seemed almost anticlimactic. Iraqi leader Saddam Hussein's pledge to fight "the mother of all battles" failed to materialize. The Iraqi threat to use chemical weapons proved just that — a threat — and coalition forces met only minimal resistance as they advanced to Kuwait City. On February 26, Hussein announced a "victorious" retreat, but he was too late; weighted down with booty, Iraqi forces had begun to flee Kuwait City the day before, only to be caught in a merciless air attack on the road to the border.

In just 100 hours the ground conflict was over. On Feburary 28, declaring that the 28-nation coalition had achieved the liberation of Kuwait, President George Bush announced an end to the offensive. By the time Iraq formally accepted the terms of a U.N. cease-fire on April 6, some 200,000 American troops were on their way home. In all, the coalition forces had suffered just 343 combat deaths, 146 of them American. As many as 100,000 Iraqis had lost their lives. Saddam Hussein remained in power, but for taking a stand against him, George Bush saw his approval rating soar to 83 percent — making him, for a brief moment, the most popular president of modern times.

B 1993
Basketball superstar Michael Jordan led the Chicago Bulls to their fourth NBA championship.

When more than 100,000 fans turned out to cheer the Chicago Bulls' historic third straight National Basketball Association championship, they saw only glory in the years ahead. Their signs and banners demanded: "Four-peat!" and "Four-ever!" A fourth win for the championship Bulls was not far-fetched: with showstopping guard Michael Jordan on the team, almost anything was possible.

The championship sweep got rolling when the Bulls beat the Los Angeles Lakers in 1991, then triumphed over the Portland Trail Blazers a year later. The Chicago team made it three in a row when they squeezed by the Phoenix Suns for a 99–98 victory in the sixth game of the 1993 NBA Finals.

Much of this was due to Jordan. A superbly well-rounded player, he showed an almost uncanny ability to score. In the 1993 finals he averaged 41 points a game, the highest in NBA finals history. In regular season play, Jordan's 32.6-point average earned him his seventh straight NBA scoring title.

Jordan's ability to win victories and attract crowds made him one of the most sensational players ever to slam-dunk a basketball. Then, to everyone's surprise, he quit to pursue a career in baseball. The Chicago Bulls lost the next NBA championship to the Houston Rockets.

Jordan after a job well done.

After a 17-month hiatus, Jordan returned to basketball in 1995. The Bulls made it to the finals against the Seattle Supersonics, and after winning the first three of seven games, a fourth NBA title seemed certain. Then the Bulls lost two in a row. The sixth game was set to be played in Chicago on Father's Day. The pressure was on; Jordan had dedicated the game to his own father, who had earlier been shot to death by a pair of teenage muggers. Nothing then, could match the unbridled joy of Jordan and his teammates when the Bulls beat the Supersonics 87–75. (The Bulls continued their winning streak in 1997 and 1998.)

> ## IN THEIR OWN WORDS
> **From a distance they appeared to be nothing more than a clutch of soldiers. . . . Someone said hopefully, 'Syrians?' But it was clear . . . that they were Iraqis — and for a moment we felt the closeness of our own capture or death. And then two of them lifted over their heads . . . leaflets that bore instruction in the art of surrender. . . . Although the men looked healthy, it was clear that they had been through a kind of hell. . . . But nothing showed their condition more clearly than their blank, accepting faces . . . . They were putting themselves at our mercy.**
>
> *Reporter Edward Barnes describes how four defectors from the Iraqi Army surrendered to him and three other journalists in February 1991.*

E 1994
x-president Jimmy Carter, trounced at the polls, returned to the spotlight as a roving global peacemaker.

Jimmy Carter would have preferred to defeat Ronald Reagan in the 1980 election and serve a second term as president of the United States. Instead, he lost by a landslide. Returning home to Plains, Georgia, he busied himself with writing his memoirs, relaxing, and making fine wooden furniture in his carpentry shop.

But the former president was possessed by a lifelong ambition to do good, and in 1982 he founded the Carter Center at Emory University. Its program: to support human rights, to help prevent war, and to improve the lives of people around the world through education and better health care. And so, relying on his contacts with politicians and statesmen, he embarked

Jimmy and Rosalynn Carter with Israel's Shimon Peres.

on a second career as a private ambassador in the cause of international peace.

He had brokered his first peace agreement back in 1978, while he was still president. Using his warm personal friendship with both Menachem Begin of Israel and Anwar Sadat of Egypt, he brought the two men together to hammer out the Camp David Accords, ending 30 years of hostility between their two countries.

Now, as a private citizen, Carter began traveling to the world's hot spots, trying to resolve disputes. His best year was 1994, when he successfully intervened in three major global concerns: ending a nuclear arms buildup in North Korea; preventing bloodshed when U.S. troops landed in Haiti to restore that country's president, and helping bring about a temporary cease-fire in war-torn Bosnia. 🛩

A 1997
t the end of the millennium, scientists began using new technology to probe the depths of the ocean.

Long after mankind had conquered the Poles, scaled Mt. Everest, and hurled rockets into space, vast sections of the ocean floor were still unknown territory. Scientists had caught their first glimpse of the ocean's lower depths in 1939, when a remotely operated camera snapped the first gray, murky photograph of a small section of the sea floor. For years, there was not much else.

Gradually the picture began to change. Naval engineers in the 1950's devised techniques for overcoming the hazards — extreme pressures, low temperatures, and inky darkness — that had thwarted earlier deep-sea exploration. In 1960 the submersible research vehicle *Trieste* carried two men to the bottom of the Pacific's Marianas

Trench, some 35,800 feet down. Four years later the manned submarine *Alvin* began the first of many trips into the deep.

As the technology improved, remotely operated vehicles (ROV's) made their debut. These robot-like craft allowed scientists to take videotapes, collect geological samples, and bring up specimens of plant and animal life. Researchers, embarking on a systematic study of the ocean floor, discovered a topographical wonderland of deep canyons and vast mountain ranges.

A new generation of more efficient submersibles began to probe the ocean's depths in the century's final decade. Using sophisticated robotics, computer-aided guidance, and fiber-optic communications, ROV's such as *Sea Cliff*, *Turtle*, and *Tiburon* (fully operational in 1997) provided scientists with a

laser-sharp view of the mysterious world beneath the sea — all from the comfort and safety of a research vessel bobbing in the waves above. The retrieved data began to give up the secrets of the almost 336 million cubic miles of ocean that cover the earth's surface. 🛩

Alvin lands on the wreck of the Titanic (below) to take photos such as this one of the ship's prow (right).

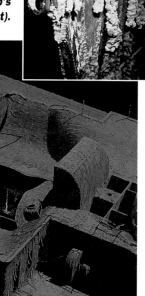

W 1999

William Jefferson Clinton becomes only the second president in the history of the United States to face impeachment.

Just after noon on February 22, 100 United States Senators stood poised to vote on whether to remove him from office. The question was posed by Chief Justice William H. Renquist, who had presided over the 37-day trial in the Senate.

Clinton, the forty-second president and a Democrat, faced two impeachment counts resulting from his efforts to hide his affair with a young White House intern, Monica S. Lewinsky. The first count, perjury, was rejected by a vote of 55 to 45. (Ten Republicans broke ranks to join a solid block of Democrats to support Clinton.) The second count, obstruction of justice, split the Senate 50 to 50 (only five Republicans broke ranks) and left Clinton in office. The Constitution requires a two-thirds majority of the Senate (67 votes) to remove the Chief Executive.

In the celebrity-happy 1990's, the private lives of public figures were no longer out of bounds for the press or political dirty tricksters. Scandalmongering was the decade's national sport, spurred on by an aggressive press and publicity-seeking entertainers.

The Clinton trial sobered the President, tainted his considerable accomplishments, and left the public exhausted. The sordid 18-month-long story of the President's extramarital sex life had paralyzed official Washington, stymied the work of Congress, and made American voters more cynical than ever about politicians.

T 1999-2000

he optimists were right. As the world greeted a new millennium, key computers effortlessly flipped their digital dates from 1999 to 2000 at midnight without a glitch from time zone to time zone.

Pessimistic Y2K (year 2000) fears that the turnover would create havoc in our computer-dependent society were quickly laid to rest. Some 72 percent of Americans stayed home that night—out of fear or simply to share a momentous event quietly with family and close friends. Twenty-four or more continuous hours of satellite television coverage of the world-wide happening assured the stay-at-homes that all was well. Trains kept their schedules and airplanes took off and landed without mishap. ATM machines gave out money and electricity lit up the night.

As the new millennium rolled in, starting at the international date line and moving west, joyous celebrations from Kiribati's Millennium Island and New Zealand's Chatham Islands began an all-night party that was telecast all over the world. The global festivities continued from time zone to time zone, showing off spectacular light displays at Red Square in Moscow, the Acropolis in Athens, the Pyramids in Egypt, the Eiffel Tower in Paris, and the new Millennium Dome in London, built for the occasion.

New year's celebration 2000

In New York City, nearly two million adventurous revelers saw the ball drop at midnight on the top of One Times Square, signaling riotous displays of fireworks over the center of Manhattan. For 12 hours, giant television screens allowed the cheerful throng to watch peoples all over the globe greet the new year and the new millennium with cheers, dances, music, grins, and almost endless pyrotechnics. Similar all-night parties with huge outdoor television monitors took place in big cities all across the United States.

In many a suburban setting, sheepish American families who had stocked up on cash, water, and canned goods for the projected period of chaos after computer meltdown asked to join the parties of their more optimistic neighbors. Few were refused.

At the Center for Year 2000 Strategic Stability at Colorado's Peterson Air Force Base, U.S. and Russian military officers kept a joint watch over computer-controlled nuclear missiles, still viable weapons from the cold war. Applause broke out in the control room when the new year arrived in Moscow without a hitch. The Russians had spent the equivalent of $4 million on Y2K military preparations; the U.S. had spent almost a thousand times that amount.

A TREASURY OF FACTS AND DOCUMENTS

The foundations of democracy in America rest upon the memorable words of its leading political thinkers and doers — the Pilgrims who sailed on the Mayflower, *the Patriots of the Revolutionary War period, the Founding Fathers, and the great national leaders who came after them. Herewith is an archive of important documents and speeches, along with a selection of basic facts about the nation, the presidents, and the individual states.*

THE MAYFLOWER COMPACT

NOVEMBER 11, 1620

In The Name of God, Amen. We, whose names are underwritten, the Loyal Subjects of our dread Sovereign Lord King *James*, by the Grace of God, of *Great Britain, France,* and *Ireland*, King, *Defender of the Faith*, &c. Having undertaken for the Glory of God, and Advancement of the Christian Faith, and the Honour of our King and Country, a Voyage to plant the first colony in the northern Parts of Virginia; Do by these Presents, solemnly and mutually in the Presence of God and one another, covenant and combine ourselves together into a civil Body Politick, for our better Ordering and Preservation, and Furtherance of the Ends aforesaid; And by Virtue hereof do enact, constitute, and frame, such just and equal Laws, Ordinances, Acts, Constitutions, and Offices, from time to time, as shall be thought most meet and convenient for the general Good of the Colony; unto which we promise all due Submission and Obedience. In WITNESS whereof we have hereunto subscribed our names at *Cape Cod* the eleventh of *November*, in the Reign of our Sovereign Lord King *James* of *England, France,* and *Ireland*, the eighteenth and of *Scotland,* the fifty-fourth. *Anno Domini*, 1620.

TO THE SECOND VIRGINIA CONVENTION

PATRICK HENRY 1775

. . . It is natural for man to indulge in the illusions of hope. We are apt to shut our eyes against a painful truth, and listen to the song of that siren, till she transforms us into beasts. Is this the part of wise men, engaged in a great and arduous struggle for liberty? . . .

I have but one lamp by which my feet are guided; and that is the lamp of experience. I know of no way of judging of the future but by the past. And judging by the past, I wish to know what there has been in the conduct of the British ministry for the last ten years to justify those hopes with which gentlemen have been pleased to solace themselves and the House? Is it that insidious smile with which our petition has been lately received? Trust it not, sir; it will prove a snare to your feet. Suffer not yourselves to be betrayed with a kiss. . . . Are fleets and armies necessary to a work of love and reconciliation? . . . Let us not deceive ourselves, sir. These are the implements of war and subjugation; the last arguments to which kings resort. . . .

It is in vain, sir, to extenuate the matter. Gentlemen may cry peace, peace — but there is no peace. The war is actually begun! The next gale that sweeps from the North will bring to our ears the clash of resounding arms! Our brethren are already in the field! Why stand we here idle? What is it that gentlemen wish? What would they have? Is life so dear, or peace so sweet, as to be purchased at the price of chains and slavery? Forbid it, Almighty God! I know not what course others may take; but as for me, give me liberty, or give me death!

COMMON SENSE
THOMAS PAINE 1776

Volumes have been written on the subject of the struggle between England and America. Men of all ranks have embarked in the controversy, from different motives, and with various designs: but all have been ineffectual, and the period of debate is closed. . . .

I have heard it asserted by some, that as America hath flourished under her former connection with Great Britain, the same connection is necessary towards her future happiness, and will always have the same effect. Nothing can be more fallacious than this kind of argument. We may as well assert that because a child has thriven upon milk, that it is never to have meat, or that the first twenty years of our lives is to become a precedent for the next twenty. . . . I answer roundly, that America would have flourished as much, and probably much more, had no European power taken any notice of her. . . .

. . . As to government matters, it is not in the power of Britain to do this continent justice: the business of it will soon be too weighty and intricate to be managed with any tolerable degree of convenience, by a power so distant from us, and so very ignorant of us; for if they cannot conquer us, they cannot govern us. . . . There was a time when it was proper, and there is a proper time for it to cease.

Small islands not capable of protecting themselves are the proper objects for kingdoms to take under their care; but there is something very absurd in supposing a continent to be perpetually governed by an island. In no instance hath nature made the satellite larger than its primary planet; and as England and America, with respect to each other, reverse the common order of nature, it is evident that they belong to different systems. England to Europe: America to itself. . . .

COMMON SENSE;

ADDRESSED TO THE

INHABITANTS

OF

AMERICA,

On the following interesting

SUBJECTS.

I. Of the Origin and Design of Government in general, with concise Remarks on the English Constitution.

II. Of Monarchy and Hereditary Succession.

III. Thoughts on the present State of American Affairs.

IV. Of the present Ability of America, with some miscellaneous Reflections.

Man knows no Master save creating HEAVEN,
Or those whom choice and common good ordain.
THOMSON.

PHILADELPHIA;
Printed, and Sold, by R. BELL, in Third-Street.
MDCCLXXVI.

THE AMERICAN CRISIS
THOMAS PAINE 1776

These are the times that try men's souls. The summer soldier and the sunshine patriot will, in this crisis, shrink from the service of his country; but he that stands it NOW, deserves the love and thanks of man and woman. Tyranny, like hell, is not easily conquered; yet we have this consolation with us, that the harder the conflict, the more glorious the triumph. What we obtain too cheap, we esteem too lightly; 'tis dearness only that gives every thing its value. Heaven knows how to put a proper price upon its goods; and it would be strange indeed, if so celestial an article as FREEDOM should not be highly rated. Britain, with an army to enforce her tyranny, has declared that she has a right (*not only* to TAX) but "to BIND *us in* ALL CASES WHATSOEVER," and if being *bound in that manner,* is not slavery, then is there no such a thing as slavery upon earth. Even the expression is impious, for so unlimited a power can belong only to God. . . .

I have as little superstition in me as any man living, but my secret opinion has ever been, and still is, that God Almighty will not give up a people to military destruction, or leave them unsupportedly to perish, who have so earnestly and so repeatedly sought to avoid the calamities of war, by every decent method which wisdom could invent. Neither have I so much of the infidel in me, as to suppose that He has relinquished the government of the world, and given us up to the care of devils; and as I do not, I cannot see on what grounds the king of Britain can look up to Heaven for help against us: a common murderer, a highwayman, or a housebreaker, has as good a pretence as he. . . .

I call not upon a few, but upon all: not on *this* state or *that* state, but on *every* state; up and help us; lay your shoulders to the wheel; better have too much force than too little, when so great an object is at stake. Let it be told to the future world, that in the depth of winter, when nothing but hope and virtue could survive, that the city and the country, alarmed at one common danger, came forth to meet and to repulse. . . . Throw not the burden of the day upon Providence, but "*show your faith by your works,*" that God may bless you. . . . The heart that feels not now is dead: . . . 'Tis the business of little minds to shrink; but he whose heart is firm, and whose conscience approves his conduct, will pursue his principles unto death. . . .

THE DECLARATION OF INDEPENDENCE

1776

WHEN IN THE COURSE of human events, it becomes necessary for one people to dissolve the political bands which have connected them with another, and to assume among the powers of the earth, the separate and equal station to which the Laws of Nature and of Nature's God entitle them, a decent respect to the opinions of mankind requires that they should declare the causes which impel them to the separation.

We hold these truths to be self-evident, that all men are created equal, that they are endowed by their Creator with certain unalienable Rights, that among these are Life, Liberty and the pursuit of Happiness. —— That to secure these rights, Governments are instituted among Men, deriving their just powers from the consent of the governed. —— That whenever any Form of Government becomes destructive of these ends, it is the Right of the People to alter or to abolish it, and to institute new Government, laying its foundation on such principles and organizing its powers in such form, as to them shall seem most likely to effect their Safety and Happiness.

Prudence, indeed, will dictate that Governments long established should not be changed for light and transient causes; and accordingly all experience hath shewn, that mankind are more disposed to suffer, while evils are sufferable, than to right themselves by abolishing the forms to which they are accustomed. But when a long train of abuses and usurpations, pursuing invariably the same Object evinces a design to reduce them under absolute Despotism, it is their right, it is their duty, to throw off such Government, and to provide new Guards for their future security.

Such has been the patient sufferance of these Colonies; and such is now the necessity which constrains them to alter their former Systems of Government. The history of the present King of Great Britain is a history of repeated injuries and usurpations, all having in direct object the establishment of an absolute Tyranny over these States. To prove this, let Facts be submitted to a candid world. —— He has refused his Assent to Laws, the most wholesome and necessary for the public good. —— He has forbidden his Governors to pass Laws of immediate and pressing importance, unless suspended in their operation till his Assent should be obtained; and when so suspended, he has utterly neglected to attend to them. —— He has refused to pass other Laws for the accommodation of large districts of people, unless those people would relinquish the right of Representation in the Legislature, a right inestimable to them and formidable to tyrants only. —— He has called together legislative bodies at places unusual, uncomfortable, and distant from the depository of their public Records, for the sole purpose of fatiguing them into compliance with his measures. —— He has dissolved Representative Houses repeatedly, for opposing with manly firmness his invasions on the rights of the people. —— He has refused for a long time, after such dissolutions, to cause others to be elected; whereby the Legislative powers, incapable of Annihilation, have returned to the People at large for their exercise; the State remaining in the meantime exposed to all the dangers of invasion from without, and convulsions within. —— He has endeavoured to prevent the population of these States; for that purpose obstructing the Laws for Naturalization of Foreigners; refusing to pass others to encourage their migration hither, and raising the condition of new Appropriations of Lands. —— He has obstructed the Administration of Justice, by refusing his Assent to Laws for establishing Judiciary powers. —— He has made Judges dependent on his Will alone, for the tenure of their offices, and the amount and payment of their salaries. —— He has erected a multitude of New Offices, and sent hither swarms of Officers to harass our people, and eat out their substance. He has kept among us, in times of peace, Standing Armies without the Consent of our legislatures. —— He has affected to render the Military independent of and superior to the Civil power.

He has combined with others to subject us to a jurisdiction foreign to our constitution, and unacknowledged by our laws; giving his Assent to their Acts of pretended Legislation: —— For quartering large bodies of armed troops among us: —— For protecting them, by a mock Trial, from punishment for any Murders which they should commit on the Inhabitants of these States: —— For cutting off our

Trade with all parts of the world: —— For imposing Taxes on us without our Consent: —— For depriving us in many cases, of the benefits of Trial by Jury: —— For transporting us beyond Seas to be tried for pretended offences: —— For abolishing the free System of English Laws in a neighbouring Province, establishing therein an Arbitrary government, and enlarging its Boundaries so as to render it at once an example and fit instrument for introducing the same absolute rule into these Colonies: —— For taking away our Charters, abolishing our most valuable Laws, and altering fundamentally the Forms of our Governments: —— For suspending our own Legislatures, and declaring themselves invested with Power to legislate for us in all cases whatsoever. —— He has abdicated Government here, by declaring us out of his Protection and waging War against us.

He has plundered our seas, ravaged our Coasts, burnt our towns, and destroyed the lives of our people. —— He is at this time transporting large Armies of foreign Mercenaries to compleat the works of death, desolation and tyranny, already begun with circumstances of Cruelty & perfidy scarcely paralleled in the most barbarous ages, and totally unworthy the Head of a civilized nation. —— He has constrained our fellow Citizens taken Captive on the high Seas to bear Arms against their Country, to become the executioners of their friends and Brethren, or to fall themselves by their Hands. —— He has excited domestic insurrections amongst us, and has endeavoured to bring on the inhabitants of our frontiers, the merciless Indian Savages, whose known rule of warfare, is an undistinguished destruction of all ages, sexes and conditions.

In every stage of these Oppressions We have Petitioned for Redress in the most humble terms: Our repeated Petitions have been answered only by repeated injury. A Prince, whose character is thus marked by every act which may define a Tyrant, is unfit to be the ruler of a free People. —— Nor have We been wanting in attentions to our British brethren. We have warned them from time to time of attempts by their legislature to extend an unwarrantable jurisdiction over us. We have reminded them of the circumstances of our emigration and settlement here. We have appealed to their native justice and magnanimity, and we have conjured them by the ties of our common kindred to disavow these usurpations, which would inevitably interrupt our connections and correspondence. They too have been deaf to the voice of justice and of consanguinity. We must, therefore, acquiesce in the necessity, which denounces our Separation, and hold them, as we hold the rest of mankind, Enemies in War, in Peace Friends.

WE, THEREFORE, the Representatives of the UNITED STATES OF AMERICA, in General Congress, Assembled, appealing to the Supreme Judge of the world for the rectitude of our intentions, do, in the Name, and by Authority of the good People of these Colonies, solemnly publish and declare, That these United Colonies are, and of Right ought to be FREE AND INDEPENDENT STATES; that they are Absolved from all Allegiance to the British Crown, and that all political connection between them and the State of Great Britain, is and ought to be totally dissolved; and that as Free and Independent States, they have full Power to levy War, conclude Peace, contract Alliances, establish Commerce, and to do all other Acts and Things which Independent States may of right do. —— And for the support of this Declaration, with a firm reliance on the Protection of divine Providence, we mutually pledge to each other our Lives, our Fortunes and our sacred Honor.

We the People

of the United States, in order to form a more perfect Union, establish Justice, insure domestic Tranquility, provide for the common defence, promote the general Welfare, and secure the Blessings of Liberty to ourselves and our Posterity, do ordain and establish this Constitution for the United States of America.

Article. I.

Section. 1. All legislative Powers herein granted shall be vested in a Congress of the United States, which shall consist of a Senate and House of Representatives.

Section. 2. The House of Representatives shall be composed of Members chosen every second Year by the People of the several States, and the Electors in each State shall have the Qualifications requisite for Electors of the most numerous Branch of the State Legislature.

No Person shall be a Representative who shall not have attained to the Age of twenty five Years, and been seven Years a Citizen of the United States, and who shall not, when elected, be an Inhabitant of that State in which he shall be chosen.

Representatives and direct Taxes shall be apportioned among the several States which may be included within this Union, according to their respective Numbers, which shall be determined by adding to the whole Number of free Persons, including those bound to Service for a Term of Years, and excluding Indians not taxed, three fifths of all other Persons. The actual Enumeration shall be made within three Years after the first Meeting of the Congress of the United States, and within every subsequent Term of ten Years, in such Manner as they shall by Law direct. The Number of Representatives shall not exceed one for every thirty Thousand, but each State shall have at Least one Representative; and until such enumeration shall be made, the State of New Hampshire shall be entitled to chuse three, Massachusetts eight, Rhode Island and Providence Plantations one, Connecticut five, New York six, New Jersey four, Pennsylvania eight, Delaware one, Maryland six, Virginia ten, North Carolina five, South Carolina five, and Georgia three.

When vacancies happen in the Representation from any State, the Executive Authority thereof shall issue Writs of Election to fill such Vacancies.

The House of Representatives shall chuse their Speaker and other Officers; and shall have the sole Power of Impeachment.

Section. 3. The Senate of the United States shall be composed of two Senators from each State, chosen by the Legislature thereof, for six Years; and each Senator shall have one Vote.

Immediately after they shall be assembled in Consequence of the first Election, they shall be divided as equally as may be into three Classes. The Seats of the Senators of the first Class shall be vacated at the Expiration of the second Year, of the second Class at the Expiration of the fourth Year, and of the third Class at the Expiration of the sixth Year, so that one third may be chosen every second Year; and if Vacancies happen by Resignation, or otherwise, during the Recess of the Legislature of any State, the Executive thereof may make temporary Appointments until the next Meeting of the Legislature, which shall then fill such Vacancies.

No Person shall be a Senator who shall not have attained to the Age of thirty Years, and been nine Years a Citizen of the United States, and who shall not, when elected, be an Inhabitant of that State for which he shall be chosen.

The Vice President of the United States shall be President of the Senate, but shall have no Vote, unless they be equally divided.

The Senate shall chuse their other Officers, and also a President pro tempore, in the Absence of the Vice President, or when he shall exercise the Office of President of the United States.

The Senate shall have the sole Power to try all Impeachments. When sitting for that Purpose, they shall be on Oath or Affirmation. When the President of the United States is tried, the Chief Justice shall preside: And no Person shall be convicted without the Concurrence of two thirds of the Members present.

Judgment in Cases of Impeachment shall not extend further than to removal from Office, and disqualification to hold and enjoy any Office of honor, Trust or Profit under the United States: but the Party convicted shall nevertheless be liable and subject to Indictment, Trial, Judgment and Punishment, according to Law.

Section. 4. The Times, Places and Manner of holding Elections for Senators and Representatives, shall be prescribed in each State by the Legislature thereof; but the Congress may at any time by Law make or alter such Regulations, except as to the Places of chusing Senators.

The Congress shall assemble at least once in every Year, and such Meeting shall be on the first Monday in December, unless they shall by Law appoint a different Day.

Section. 5. Each House shall be the Judge of the Elections, Returns and Qualifications of its own Members, and a Majority of each shall constitute a Quorum to do Business; but a smaller Number may adjourn from day to day, and may be authorized to compel the Attendance of absent Members, in such Manner, and under such Penalties as each House may provide.

Each House may determine the Rules of its Proceedings, punish its Members for disorderly Behaviour, and, with the Concurrence of two thirds, expel a Member.

Each House shall keep a Journal of its Proceedings, and from time to time publish the same, excepting such Parts as may in their Judgment require Secrecy; and the Yeas and Nays of the Members of either House on any question shall, at the Desire of one fifth of those Present, be entered on the Journal.

Neither House, during the Session of Congress, shall, without the Consent of the other, adjourn for more than three days, nor to any other Place than that in which the two Houses shall be sitting.

Section. 6. The Senators and Representatives shall receive a Compensation for their Services, to be ascertained by Law, and paid out of the Treasury of the United States. They shall in all Cases, except Treason, Felony and Breach of the Peace, be privileged from Arrest during their Attendance at the Session of their respective Houses, and in going to and returning from the same; and for any Speech or Debate in either House, they shall not be questioned in any other Place.

No Senator or Representative shall, during the Time for which he was elected, be appointed to any civil Office under the Authority of the United States, which shall have been created, or the Emoluments whereof shall have been encreased during such time; and no Person holding any Office under the United States, shall be a Member of either House during his Continuance in Office.

Section. 7. All Bills for raising Revenue shall originate in the House of Representatives; but the Senate may propose or concur with Amendments as on other Bills.

Every Bill which shall have passed the House of Representatives and the Senate, shall, before it become a Law, be presented to the President of the

Constitution of the United States of America

ADOPTED BY CONGRESS: 17 SEPTEMBER 1787

ARTICLE I *describes the structure, composition, and operation of the legislative branches (Congress) as well as the powers invested therein. It outlines the procedures by which a bill is made into law, and it lists various restrictions on the powers of the states.*

ARTICLE II *describes the structure and operation of the executive branch (the President and Vice President); and it delineates the extent of presidential power. This section lays down the procedures for presidential elections, and it spells out the president's Oath of Office. It also states that a president can be removed for high crimes and misdemeanors.*

ARTICLE III *gives the structure, composition, and operation of the judicial branch (Supreme Court), along with a description of federal judicial powers. Outlined in this section is the definition of treason and the conditions under which a person may be charged and brought to trial.*

ARTICLE IV *describes the relationship between the states, and between the states and the federal government. Included is a guarantee of a republican form of government for all states.*

ARTICLE V *describes the procedure by which the Constitution may be amended.*

ARTICLE VI *states that a national law will always supersede a state law, provided the national law is constitutional.*

ARTICLE VII *outlines the requirements necessary for the ratification of the Constitution.*

The Bill of Rights
1791

AMENDMENT I – Congress shall make no law respecting an establishment of religion, or prohibiting the free exercise thereof, or abridging the freedom of speech, or of the press, or the right of the people peaceably to assemble and to petition the Government for a redress of grievances.

AMENDMENT II – A well-regulated Militia, being necessary to the security of a free State, the right of the people to keep and bear Arms, shall not be infringed.

AMENDMENT III – No Soldier shall, in time of peace, be quartered in any house, without the consent of the Owner, nor in time of war, but in a manner to be prescribed by law.

AMENDMENT IV – The right of the people to be secure in their persons, houses, papers, and effects, against unreasonable searches and seizures, shall not be violated. . . .

AMENDMENT V – No person shall be held to answer for a capital, or otherwise infamous crime, unless on a presentment or indictment of a Grand Jury, except in cases arising in the land or naval forces, or in the Militia, when in actual service in time of War or public danger; nor shall any person be subject for the same offence to be twice put in jeopardy of life or limb; nor shall be compelled in any criminal case to be a witness against himself, nor be deprived of life, liberty, or property, without due process of law; nor shall private property be taken for public use, without just compensation.

AMENDMENT VI – In all criminal prosecutions, the accused shall enjoy the right to a speedy and public trial, by an impartial jury of the State and district wherein the crime shall have been committed . . . and to be informed of the nature and cause of the accusation; to be confronted with the witnesses against him . . . and to have the Assistance of Counsel for his defence.

AMENDMENT VII – In suits at common law, where the value in controversy shall exceed twenty dollars, the right of trial by jury shall be preserved. . . .

AMENDMENT VIII – Excessive bail shall not be required, nor excessive fines imposed, nor cruel and unusual punishments inflicted.

AMENDMENT IX – The enumeration in the Constitution, of certain rights, shall not be construed to deny or disparage others retained by the people.

AMENDMENT X – The powers not delegated to the United States by the Constitution, nor prohibited by it to the States, are reserved to the States respectively, or to the people.

PRESIDENTIAL ADDRESSES

GEORGE WASHINGTON'S
INAUGURAL ADDRESS 1789

Fellow-Citizens of the Senate and of the House of Representatives: Among the vicissitudes incident to life no event could have filled me with greater anxieties than that of which the notification was transmitted by your order. . . .

I have . . . repaired to the present station, [and] it would be peculiarly improper to omit in this first official act my fervent supplications to that . . . Almighty Being . . . that His benediction may consecrate to the liberties and happiness of the people of the United States a Government instituted by themselves for these essential purposes. . . .

By the article establishing the executive department it is made the duty of the President "to recommend to your consideration such measures as he shall judge necessary and expedient." . . . It will be far more congenial . . . to substitute . . . the tribute that is due to the talents, the rectitude, and the patriotism which adorn the characters selected to devise and adopt them. In these honorable qualifications I behold the surest pledges that . . . the foundation of our national policy will be laid in the pure and immutable principles of private morality. . . . We ought to be no less persuaded that . . . the preservation of the sacred fire of liberty and the destiny of the republican model of government are justly considered perhaps, as *deeply*, as *finally*, staked on the experiment intrusted to the hands of the American people. . . .

THOMAS JEFFERSON'S
INAUGURAL ADDRESS 1801

Friends and Fellow-Citizens: Called upon to undertake the duties of the first executive office of our country, I avail myself of the presence of that portion of my fellow-citizens which is here assembled to express my grateful thanks for the favor with which they have been pleased to look toward me, to declare a sincere consciousness that the task is above my talents, and that I approach it with those anxious and awful presentiments which the greatness of the charge and the weakness of my powers so justly inspire. A rising nation, spread over a wide and fruitful land, traversing all the seas with the rich productions of their industry, engaged in commerce with nations who feel power and forget right, advancing rapidly to destinies beyond the reach of mortal eye — when I contemplate these transcendent objects, and see the honor, the happiness, and the hopes of this beloved country committed to the issue and the auspices of this day, I shrink from the contemplation, and humble myself before the magnitude of the undertaking. Utterly, indeed, should I despair did not the presence of many whom I here see remind me that in the other high authorities provided by our Constitution I shall find resources of wisdom, of virtue, and of zeal on which to rely under all difficulties. To you, then, gentlemen, who are charged with the sovereign functions of legislation, and to those associated with you, I look with encouragement for that guidance and support which may enable us to steer with safety the vessel in which we are all embarked amidst the conflicting elements of a troubled world. . . .

ABRAHAM LINCOLN'S
HOUSE DIVIDED SPEECH 1858

Mr. President and Gentlemen of the Convention: If we could first know where we are, and whither we are tending, we could better judge what to do, and how to do it. We are now far into the fifth year since a policy was initiated with the avowed object and confident promise of putting an end to slavery agitation. Under the operation of that policy, that agitation has not only not ceased, but has constantly augmented. In my opinion, it will not cease until a crisis shall have been reached and passed. "A house divided against itself cannot stand." I believe this government cannot endure permanently half slave and half free. I do not expect the Union to be dissolved; I do not expect the house to fall; but I do expect it will cease to be divided. It will become all one thing, or all the other. Either the opponents of slavery will arrest the further spread of it, and place it where the public mind shall rest in the belief that it is in the course of ultimate extinction, or its advocates will push it forward till it shall become alike lawful in all the States, old as well as new, North as well as South.

THEODORE ROOSEVELT
ON WORLD WAR I 1914

One of the main lessons to learn from this war is embodied in the homely proverb, "Speak softly and carry a big stick." . . . [It] is necessary to be respectful toward all people and scrupulously to refrain from wronging them, while at the same time keeping ourselves in condition to prevent wrong being done to us. If a nation does not in this sense speak softly, then sooner or later the policy of the big stick is certain to result in war. . . .

America should have a coherent policy of action toward foreign powers, and this should primarily be based on the determination never to give offense when it can be avoided, always to treat other nations justly and courteously, and, as long as present conditions exist, to be prepared to defend our own rights ourselves. No other nation will defend them for us. . . .

Above all, let us avoid the policy of peace with insult, the policy of unpreparedness to defend our rights, with inability to restrain our representatives from doing wrong to or publicly speaking ill of others. The worst policy for the United States is to combine the unbridled tongue with the unready hand. . . .

From the beginning we have recognized what is taught in the words of Washington, and again in the great crisis of our national life

Four score and seven years ago our fathers brought forth on this continent, a new nation, conceived in Liberty, and dedicated to the proposition that all men are created equal.

Now we are engaged in a great civil war, testing whether that nation, or any nation so conceived and so dedicated, can long endure. We are met on a great battle field of that war. We have come to dedicate a portion of that field, as a final resting place for those who here gave their lives, that that nation might live. It is altogether fitting and proper that we should do this.

But, in a larger sense, we can not dedicate— we can not consecrate— we can not hallow— this ground. The brave men, living and dead, who struggled here, have consecrated it, far above our poor power to add or detract. The world will little note, nor long remember what we say here, but it can never forget what they did here. It is for us the living, rather, to be dedicated here to the unfinished work which they who fought here have thus far so nobly advanced. It is rather for us to be here dedicated to the great task remaining before us— that from these honored dead we take increased devotion to that cause for which they gave the last full measure of devotion— that we here highly resolve that these dead shall not have died in vain— that this nation, under God, shall have a new birth of freedom— and that government of the people, by the people, for the people, shall not perish from the earth.

Abraham Lincoln

November 19. 1863

361

in the words of Lincoln. . . . Washington and Lincoln believed that ours was a strong people, and therefore fit for a strong government. They believed that it was only weak peoples that had to fear strong governments, and that to us it was given to combine freedom and efficiency. . . .

At present each nation must in the last resort trust to its own strength if it is to preserve all that makes life worth having. At present this is imperative. This state of things can be abolished only when we put force, when we put the collective armed power of civilization, behind some body which shall with reasonable justice and equity represent the collective determination of civilization to do what is right.

WOODROW WILSON'S
FOURTEEN POINTS 1918

. . . We entered this war because violations of right had occurred which . . . made the life of our own people impossible unless they were corrected and the world secured once for all against their recurrence. What we demand in this war, therefore . . . is that the world be made fit and safe to live in. . . . All the peoples of the world are in effect partners in this interest, and for our own part we see very clearly that unless justice be done to others it will not be done to us. . . .

Here follows a summary of Wilson's Fourteen Points:

I. Covenants of peace openly arrived at, with no secret agreements made between any nations.

II. Absolute freedom to navigate the seas, restricted only when international treaties must be enforced.

III. The removal of economic barriers and the establishment of equal trade between nations.

IV. The reduction of national armaments.

V. A fair adjustment of all colonial claims.

VI. The evacuation of all Russian territory, and a chance for Russia to decide its own national policy.

VII. The evacuation and restoration of Belgium.

VIII. The restoration of French territory, and the return of Alsace-Lorraine to France.

IX. A readjustment of Italian borders, taking into account clearly recognizable lines of nationality.

X. Self-government for Austria-Hungary.

XI. The evacuation of Romania, Serbia, and Montenegro, and independence for the Balkan nations.

XII. Independence for Turkey; an opportunity for self-rule for other nations under Turkey; the opening of the Dardanelles for free passage to all ships.

XIII. Independence for Poland.

XIV. An alliance of nations to safeguard the political independence and territorial integrity of all countries.

FRANKLIN DELANO ROOSEVELT'S
INAUGURAL ADDRESS 1933

I am certain that my fellow Americans expect that on my induction into the presidency I will address them with a candor and a decision which the present situation of our Nation impels. This is preeminently the time to speak the truth, the whole truth, frankly and boldly. Nor need we shrink from honestly facing conditions in our country today. This great nation will endure as it has endured, will revive and will prosper.

So, first of all, let me assert my firm belief that the only thing we have to fear is fear itself — nameless, unreasoning, unjustified terror which paralyzes needed efforts to convert retreat into advance. In every dark hour of our national life a leadership of frankness and vigor has met with that understanding and support of the people themselves which is essential to victory. . . .

If I read the temper of our people correctly, we now realize as we have never realized before, our interdependence on each other; that we cannot merely take but we must give as well; that if we are to go forward, we must move as a trained and loyal army willing to sacrifice for the good of a common discipline. . . .

With this pledge taken, I

assume unhesitatingly the leadership of this great army of our people, dedicated to a disciplined attack upon our common problems. . . .

For the trust reposed in me I will return the courage and the devotion that befit the time. I can do no less. . . .

DWIGHT D. EISENHOWER'S
FAREWELL ADDRESS 1961

. . . We now stand ten years past the midpoint of a century that has witnessed four major wars among great nations. . . . Despite these holocausts America is today the strongest, the most influential, and most productive nation in the world. . . .

Our basic purposes have been to keep the peace; to foster progress in human achievement, and to enhance liberty, dignity and integrity among people and among nations. To strive for less would be unworthy of a free and religious people. . . . We face a hostile ideology — global in scope, atheistic in character, ruthless in purpose, and insidious in method. . . . To meet it successfully, there [are] called for [sacrifices]. . . which enable us to carry forward steadily, surely, and without complaint the burdens of a prolonged and complex struggle — with liberty the stake. . . .

A vital element in keeping the peace is our military establishment. Our arms must be mighty, ready for instant action, so that no potential aggressor may be tempted to risk his own destruction. . . .

This conjunction of an immense military establishment and a large arms industry is new in the American experience. . . . we must guard against the acquisition of unwarranted influence, whether sought or unsought, by the military-industrial complex. The potential for the disastrous rise of misplaced power exists and will persist. . . .

JOHN F. KENNEDY'S
INAUGURAL ADDRESS 1961

We observe today not a victory of party but a celebration of freedom — symbolizing an end as well as a beginning — signifying renewal as well as change.

. . . In your hands, my fellow citizens, more than mine, will rest the final success or failure of our course. Since this country was founded, each generation of Americans has

been summoned to give testimony to its national loyalty. The graves of young Americans who answered the call to service surround the globe.

Now the trumpet summons us again — not as a call to bear arms, though arms we need — not as a call to battle, though embattled we are — but a call to bear the burden of a long twilight struggle, year in and year out, "rejoicing in hope, patient in tribulation" — a struggle against the common enemies of man: tyranny, poverty, disease, and war itself.

Can we forge against the enemies a grand and global alliance, North and South, East and West, that can assure a more fruitful life for all mankind? Will you join in that historic effort? . . .

The energy, the faith, the devotion which we bring to this endeavor will light our country and all who serve it — and the glow from that fire can truly light the world.

And so, my fellow Americans: ask not what your country can do for you—ask what you can do for your country.

My fellow citizens of the world: ask not what America will do for you, but what together we can do for the freedom of man.

Finally, whether you are citizens of America or citizens of the world, ask of us here the same high standards of strength and sacrifice which we ask of you. With a good conscience our only sure reward, with history the final judge of our deeds, let us go forth to lead the land we love, asking His blessing and His help, but knowing that here on earth God's work must truly be our own.

PRESIDENTIAL FACTS

1. GEORGE WASHINGTON
LIVED: 1732–99
YEARS IN OFFICE: 1789–97
POLITICAL PARTY: Federalist
HOME STATE: Virginia
OPPOSING CANDIDATE: None
VICE PRESIDENT: John Adams
FIRST LADY: Martha Dandridge Custis
FACT: The only president who did not live in Washington, D.C., he was also the first and only president to be unanimously elected.

2. JOHN ADAMS
LIVED: 1735–1826
YEARS IN OFFICE: 1797–1801
POLITICAL PARTY: Federalist
HOME STATE: Massachusetts
OPPOSING CANDIDATE: Thomas Jefferson (1796)
VICE PRESIDENT: Thomas Jefferson
FIRST LADY: Abigail Smith
FACT: Adams lived the longest of any president to date. He died at the age of 90 on the same day as his successor, Thomas Jefferson — July 4, 1826.

3. THOMAS JEFFERSON
LIVED: 1743–1826
YEARS IN OFFICE: 1801–9
POLITICAL PARTY: Democratic-Republican
HOME STATE: Virginia
OPPOSING CANDIDATES: Aaron Burr (1800); Charles Pinckney (1804)
VICE PRESIDENTS: Aaron Burr, George Clinton
MARRIED: Martha Wayles Skelton (died 1782)
FACT: Jefferson was an architect as well as a president. He used his talent to design the University of Virginia, a school that he also founded.

4. JAMES MADISON
LIVED: 1751–1836
YEARS IN OFFICE: 1809–17
POLITICAL PARTY: Republican
HOME STATE: Virginia
OPPOSING CANDIDATES: Charles Pinckney (1808); DeWitt Clinton (1812)
VICE PRESIDENTS: George Clinton, Elbridge Gerry
FIRST LADY: Dolley Dandridge Payne Todd
FACT: The first president to involve the nation in war (1812), he was the last surviving signer of the Constitution.

5. JAMES MONROE
LIVED: 1758–1831
YEARS IN OFFICE: 1817–25
POLITICAL PARTY: Republican
HOME STATE: Virginia
OPPOSING CANDIDATES: Rufus King (1816); John Quincy Adams (1820)
VICE PRESIDENT: Daniel D. Tompkins
FIRST LADY: Elizabeth Kortright
FACT: He was the first president to have a daughter marry in the White House.

6. JOHN QUINCY ADAMS
LIVED: 1767–1848
YEARS IN OFFICE: 1825–9
POLITICAL PARTY: Democratic-Republican
HOME STATE: Massachusetts
OPPOSING CANDIDATES: Andrew Jackson, Henry Clay, William H. Crawford (1824)
VICE PRESIDENT: John C. Calhoun
FIRST LADY: Louisa Catherine Johnson
FACT: He was the only president whose father — John Adams — was also a president.

7. ANDREW JACKSON
LIVED: 1767–1845
YEARS IN OFFICE: 1829–37
POLITICAL PARTY: Democratic
HOME STATE: Tennessee
OPPOSING CANDIDATES: John Quincy Adams (1828); Henry Clay (1832)
VICE PRESIDENTS: John C. Calhoun, Martin Van Buren
MARRIED: Rachel Donelson (died 1828)
FACT: In his first run for president, in 1824, Jackson captured the most votes but lost the election; because he did not win a clear majority, the House of Representatives chose John Quincy Adams.

8. MARTIN VAN BUREN
LIVED: 1782–1862
YEARS IN OFFICE: 1837–41
POLITICAL PARTY: Democratic
HOME STATE: New York
OPPOSING CANDIDATE: William H. Harrison (1836)
VICE PRESIDENT: Richard M. Johnson
MARRIED: Hannah Hoes (died 1819)
FACT: Van Buren was the first president not born under British colonial rule.

9. WILLIAM HENRY HARRISON
LIVED: 1773–1841
YEARS IN OFFICE: 1841
POLITICAL PARTY: Whig
HOME STATE: Ohio
OPPOSING CANDIDATE: Martin Van Buren (1840)
VICE PRESIDENT: John Tyler
FIRST LADY: Anna Tuthill Symmes
FACT: The first president to die in office, he gave the longest presidential address (one hour, forty minutes), but served the shortest term as president (one month).

10. JOHN TYLER
LIVED: 1790–1862
YEARS IN OFFICE: 1841–5
POLITICAL PARTY: Whig
HOME STATE: Virginia
OPPOSING CANDIDATE: None
VICE PRESIDENT: None
FIRST LADIES: Letitia Christian (died 1842), Julia Gardiner
FACT: The first vice president to become president because of the death of a chief executive, he was also the first president to be married while in office.

11. JAMES K. POLK
LIVED: 1795–1849
YEARS IN OFFICE: 1845–9
POLITICAL PARTY: Democratic
HOME STATE: Tennessee
OPPOSING CANDIDATE: Henry Clay (1844)
VICE PRESIDENT: George M. Dallas
FIRST LADY: Sarah Childress
FACT: Staunch moralists, President and Mrs. Polk banned card playing, alcohol

drinking, and dancing in the White House.

12. ZACHARY TAYLOR

LIVED: 1784–1850
YEARS IN OFFICE: 1849–50
POLITICAL PARTY: Whig
HOME STATE: Louisiana
OPPOSING CANDIDATES: Lewis Cass, Martin Van Buren (1848)
VICE PRESIDENT: Millard Fillmore
FIRST LADY: Margaret Mackall Smith
FACT: A career officer, he was the first president with no prior political experience. Taylor never qualified as a resident voter until he was 62 years old — only two years before he became president.

13. MILLARD FILLMORE

LIVED: 1800–74
YEARS IN OFFICE: 1850–3
POLITICAL PARTY: Whig
HOME STATE: New York
OPPOSING CANDIDATE: None
VICE PRESIDENT: None
FIRST LADY: Abigail Powers
FACT: Using a congressional allowance of $250, Fillmore created the first White House library.

14. FRANKLIN PIERCE

LIVED: 1804–69
YEARS IN OFFICE: 1853–7
POLITICAL PARTY: Democratic
HOME STATE: New Hampshire
OPPOSING CANDIDATE: Winfield Scott (1852)
VICE PRESIDENT: William R. King
FIRST LADY: Jane Means Appleton

FACT: Pierce delivered his inaugural address from memory. He was the only president to seek renomination but be rejected by his party for a second term.

15. JAMES BUCHANAN

LIVED: 1791–1868
YEARS IN OFFICE: 1857–61
POLITICAL PARTY: Democratic
HOME STATE: Pennsylvania
OPPOSING CANDIDATES: John C. Fremont, Millard Fillmore (1856)
VICE PRESIDENT: John C. Breckinridge
FIRST LADY: None
FACT: He was the first president who never married.

16. ABRAHAM LINCOLN

LIVED: 1809–65
YEARS IN OFFICE: 1861–5
POLITICAL PARTY: Republican
HOME STATE: Illinois
OPPOSING CANDIDATES: Stephen A. Douglas, John C. Breckinridge, John Bell (1860); George McClellan (1864)

VICE PRESIDENTS: Hannibal Hamlin, Andrew Johnson
FIRST LADY: Mary Todd
FACT: The first president born outside of the original 13 states, he was also the first president to be assassinated.

17. ANDREW JOHNSON

LIVED: 1808–75
YEARS IN OFFICE: 1865–9
POLITICAL PARTY: Democratic
HOME STATE: Tennessee

OPPOSING CANDIDATE: None
VICE PRESIDENT: None
FIRST LADY: Eliza McCardle
FACT: The first president who did not have legal or military experience, he was also the only president to be impeached. (He was acquitted.)

18. ULYSSES S. GRANT

LIVED: 1822–85
YEARS IN OFFICE: 1869–77
POLITICAL PARTY: Republican
HOME STATE: Illinois
OPPOSING CANDIDATES: Horatio Seymour (1868); Horace Greeley (1872)
VICE PRESIDENTS: Schuyler Colfax, Henry Wilson
FIRST LADY: Julia Boggs Dent
FACT: Grant was the first president whose administration was involved in major financial scandal.

19. RUTHERFORD B. HAYES

LIVED: 1822–93
YEARS IN OFFICE: 1877–81
POLITICAL PARTY: Republican
HOME STATE: Ohio
OPPOSING CANDIDATE: Samuel J. Tilden (1876)
VICE PRESIDENT: William A. Wheeler
FIRST LADY: Lucy Ware Webb
FACT: Hayes was the first president to have a telephone at the White House.

20. JAMES A. GARFIELD

LIVED: 1831–81
YEARS IN OFFICE: 1881
POLITICAL PARTY: Republican
HOME STATE: Ohio
OPPOSING CANDIDATE: Winfield S. Hancock (1880)
VICE PRESIDENT: Chester A. Arthur

FIRST LADY: Lucretia Rudolph
FACT: In 1880 Garfield was eligible for three federal posts at the same time. He was a congressman as well as a senator-elect and president-elect. He gave up his senatorial seat and resigned from the House before his inauguration as president.

21. CHESTER A. ARTHUR

LIVED: 1829–86
YEARS IN OFFICE: 1881–5
POLITICAL PARTY: Republican
HOME STATE: New York
OPPOSING CANDIDATE: None
VICE PRESIDENT: None
MARRIED: Ellen Lewis Herndon (died 1880)
FACT: Arthur was the last of four presidents who did not give an inaugural address (Tyler, Fillmore, and Andrew Johnson were the other three).

22. GROVER CLEVELAND

LIVED: 1837–1908
YEARS IN OFFICE: 1885–9
POLITICAL PARTY: Democratic
HOME STATE: New York
OPPOSING CANDIDATE: James G. Blaine (1884)
VICE PRESIDENT: Thomas A. Hendricks
FIRST LADY: Frances Folsom
FACT: Cleveland was the only president to get married in the White House.

23. BENJAMIN HARRISON

LIVED: 1833–1901
YEARS IN OFFICE: 1889–93
POLITICAL PARTY: Republican
HOME STATE: Indiana
OPPOSING CANDIDATE: Grover Cleveland (1888)
VICE PRESIDENT: Levi P. Morton
FIRST LADY: Caroline Lavinia Scott (died 1892)
FACT: He was the only grandson of a president (William Henry Harrison) to also become president.

24. GROVER CLEVELAND

(see # 22)
YEARS IN OFFICE: 1893–7
OPPOSING CANDIDATES: Benjamin Harrison, James Weaver (1892)
VICE PRESIDENT: Adlai E. Stevenson
FACT: The only president to serve two non-consecutive terms, Cleveland was also the first president to have a child born at the White House.

25. WILLIAM MCKINLEY

LIVED: 1843–1901
YEARS IN OFFICE: 1897–1901
POLITICAL PARTY: Republican
HOME STATE: Ohio
OPPOSING CANDIDATES: William J. Bryan (1896); William J. Bryan (1900)
VICE PRESIDENTS: Garret A. Hobart, Theodore Roosevelt
FIRST LADY: Ida Saxton

FACT: McKinley was the first president to use the telephone for presidential campaigning.

26. THEODORE ROOSEVELT

LIVED: 1858–1919
YEARS IN OFFICE: 1901–9
POLITICAL PARTY: Republican
HOME STATE: New York
OPPOSING CANDIDATE: Alton B. Parker (1904)
VICE PRESIDENT: Charles W. Fairbanks
FIRST LADY: Edith Kermit Carow
FACT: The youngest president to take office, he was the first president to win a Nobel Peace Prize, to travel in a submarine, and to visit a foreign country while in office.

27. WILLIAM H. TAFT

LIVED: 1857–1930
YEARS IN OFFICE: 1909–13
POLITICAL PARTY: Republican
HOME STATE: Ohio
OPPOSING CANDIDATE: William J. Bryan (1908)
VICE PRESIDENT: James S. Sherman
FIRST LADY: Helen Herron
FACT: Taft was the only president later to become chief justice of the U.S. Supreme Court.

28. WOODROW WILSON

LIVED: 1856–1924
YEARS IN OFFICE: 1913–21
POLITICAL PARTY: Democratic
HOME STATE: New Jersey
OPPOSING CANDIDATES: Theodore Roosevelt,

William H. Taft (1912); Charles E. Hughes (1916)
VICE PRESIDENT: Thomas R. Marshall
FIRST LADIES: Ellen Louise Axson (died 1914), Edith Bolling Galt
FACT: Within two and a half years, Wilson went from having never held public office to being president of the United States. He was also the first president to hold a press conference.

29. WARREN G. HARDING

LIVED: 1865–1923
YEARS IN OFFICE: 1921–23
POLITICAL PARTY: Republican
HOME STATE: Ohio
OPPOSING CANDIDATE: James M. Cox (1920)
VICE PRESIDENT: Calvin Coolidge
FIRST LADY: Florence Kling De Wolfe
FACT: Harding was the first president to make a speech over the radio.

30. CALVIN COOLIDGE

LIVED: 1872–1933
YEARS IN OFFICE: 1923–9
POLITICAL PARTY: Republican
HOME STATE: Massachusetts
OPPOSING CANDIDATES: John W. Davis, Robert M. La Follette (1924)
VICE PRESIDENT: Charles G. Dawes
FIRST LADY: Grace Anna Goodhue
FACT: The only president sworn in by his father (who was a justice of the peace), Coolidge was also the first president whose oath was administered by a former president (Chief Justice William Howard Taft).

31. HERBERT C. HOOVER

LIVED: 1874–1964
YEARS IN OFFICE: 1929–33
POLITICAL PARTY: Republican
HOME STATE: California
OPPOSING CANDIDATE: Alfred E. Smith (1928)
VICE PRESIDENT: Charles Curtis
FIRST LADY: Lou Henry
FACT: The first president born west of the Mississippi River, he held more than 75 honorary degrees from American and foreign universities and was awarded more than 150 medals, awards, and honors.

32. FRANKLIN D. ROOSEVELT

LIVED: 1882–1945
YEARS IN OFFICE: 1933–45
POLITICAL PARTY: Democratic
HOME STATE: New York
OPPOSING CANDIDATES: Herbert Hoover; Alfred Landon (1936); Wendell Willkie (1940); Thomas E. Dewey (1944)
VICE PRESIDENTS: John Nance Garner, Henry Wallace, Harry S Truman
FIRST LADY: (Anna) Eleanor Roosevelt
FACT: Related by blood or marriage to eleven former presidents, FDR was the only president elected to four terms.

33. HARRY S TRUMAN
LIVED: 1884–1972
YEARS IN OFFICE: 1945–53
POLITICAL PARTY: Democratic
HOME STATE: Missouri
OPPOSING CANDIDATES: Thomas E. Dewey, James Strom Thurmond, Henry A. Wallace (1948)
VICE PRESIDENT: Alben W. Barkley
FIRST LADY: Elizabeth (Bess) Virginia Wallace
FACT: Truman gave the first presidential address telecast from the White House.

34. DWIGHT D. EISENHOWER
LIVED: 1890–1969
YEARS IN OFFICE: 1953–61
POLITICAL PARTY: Republican
HOME STATE: New York
OPPOSING CANDIDATES: Adlai E. Stevenson (1952); Adlai E. Stevenson (1956)
VICE PRESIDENT: Richard M. Nixon
FIRST LADY: Marie (Mamie) Geneva Doud
FACT: Eisenhower held the first presidential news conference covered by newsreels and television.

35. JOHN F. KENNEDY
LIVED: 1917–63
YEARS IN OFFICE: 1961–3
POLITICAL PARTY: Democratic
HOME STATE: Massachusetts
OPPOSING CANDIDATE: Richard M. Nixon (1960)

VICE PRESIDENT: Lyndon B. Johnson
FIRST LADY: Jacqueline Lee Bouvier
FACT: The first president born in the 20th century, Kennedy was also the first Roman Catholic president.

36. LYNDON B. JOHNSON
LIVED: 1908 73
YEARS IN OFFICE: 1963–9
POLITICAL PARTY: Democratic
HOME STATE: Texas
OPPOSING CANDIDATE: Barry M. Goldwater (1964)
VICE PRESIDENT: Hubert H. Humphrey
FIRST LADY: Claudia Alta (Lady Bird) Taylor
FACT: Johnson was the first president sworn in by a woman (Judge Sarah Tilghman Hughes), and he was the second president named Johnson to become president after the death of the incumbent.

37. RICHARD M. NIXON
LIVED: 1913–94
YEARS IN OFFICE: 1969–74
POLITICAL PARTY: Republican
HOME STATE: California
OPPOSING CANDIDATES: Hubert H. Humphrey, George C. Wallace (1968); George S. McGovern (1972)
VICE PRESIDENTS: Spiro T. Agnew, Gerald Ford
FIRST LADY: Thelma Catherine (Pat) Ryan
FACT: The first president to choose a vice presidential running mate under the 25th Amendment, the first president to travel to China while in office, and the first president to resign.

38. GERALD R. FORD
LIVED: 1913–
YEARS IN OFFICE: 1974–7
POLITICAL PARTY: Republican
HOME STATE: Michigan
OPPOSING CANDIDATE: None
VICE PRESIDENT: Nelson A. Rockefeller
FIRST LADY: Elizabeth (Betty) Anne Bloomer Warren
FACT: Ford became vice president, and then president, without having been elected to either office; he was also the first president to pardon a former president.

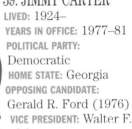

39. JIMMY CARTER
LIVED: 1924–
YEARS IN OFFICE: 1977–81
POLITICAL PARTY: Democratic
HOME STATE: Georgia
OPPOSING CANDIDATE: Gerald R. Ford (1976)
VICE PRESIDENT: Walter F. Mondale
FIRST LADY: Rosalynn Smith
FACT: Carter was the first president sworn in using his nickname, the first to walk to the White House from the Capitol after his inauguration, and the first to assign three women to cabinet posts.

40. RONALD REAGAN
LIVED: 1911–
YEARS IN OFFICE: 1981–89
POLITICAL PARTY: Republican
HOME STATE: California
OPPOSING CANDIDATES: Jimmy Carter, John B. Anderson (1980); Walter F. Mondale (1984)
VICE PRESIDENT: George Bush
FIRST LADY: Nancy Davis (Anne Francis Robbins)

FACT: The first divorced president, he was also the first to appoint a woman Supreme Court justice (Sandra Day O'Connor) and the oldest president to take office.

41. GEORGE BUSH
LIVED: 1924–
YEARS IN OFFICE: 1989–93
POLITICAL PARTY: Republican
HOME STATE: Texas
OPPOSING CANDIDATE: Michael S. Dukakis
VICE PRESIDENT: J. Danforth Quayle
FIRST LADY: Barbara Pierce
FACT: Bush was the first president who had earlier served as Ambassador to the United Nations, as well as head of the Central Intelligence Agency (CIA).

42. WILLIAM J. CLINTON
LIVED: 1946–
YEARS IN OFFICE: 1993–
POLITICAL PARTY: Democratic
HOME STATE: Arkansas
OPPOSING CANDIDATES: George Bush, H. Ross Perot (1992)
VICE PRESIDENT: Albert Gore, Jr.
FIRST LADY: Hillary Rodham
FACT: The first president born after World War II, Clinton was also the first president to have been a Rhodes scholar. Elected at age 46, along with 44-year-old Al Gore, he headed the youngest president-vice president ticket ever. Reelected for a second term on November 5, 1996 with 375 electoral votes and 49% of the popular vote.

STATE FACTS

ALABAMA
NICKNAMES: Heart of Dixie, Camellia State
CAPITAL: Montgomery
ADMISSION TO THE UNION: Dec. 14, 1819
TOTAL AREA: 51,705 sq. mi.
RANK IN SIZE: 29
FLOWER: Camellia
TREE: Southern pine
BIRD: Yellowhammer
FAMOUS SONS AND DAUGHTERS: Tallulah Bankhead, Nat (King) Cole, Helen Keller, Willie Mays, Rosa Parks

ALASKA
NICKNAME: Land of the Midnight Sun
CAPITAL: Juneau
ADMISSION TO THE UNION: Jan. 3, 1959
TOTAL AREA: 591,004 sq. mi.
RANK IN SIZE: 1
FLOWER: Forget-me-not
TREE: Sitka spruce
BIRD: Willow ptarmigan
FAMOUS SONS: Joe Juneau, Chief Katlian

ARIZONA
NICKNAME: Grand Canyon State
CAPITAL: Phoenix
ADMISSION TO THE UNION: Feb. 14, 1912
TOTAL AREA: 114,000 sq. mi.
RANK IN SIZE: 6
FLOWER: Saguaro
TREE: Paloverde
BIRD: Cactus wren
FAMOUS SONS AND DAUGHTERS: Cochise, Geronimo, Barry Goldwater, Sandra Day O'Connor

ARKANSAS
NICKNAME: Land of Opportunity
CAPITAL: Little Rock
ADMISSION TO THE UNION: June 15, 1836
TOTAL AREA: 53,187 sq. mi.
RANK IN SIZE: 27
FLOWER: Apple blossom
TREE: Pine
BIRD: Mockingbird
FAMOUS SONS: Johnny Cash, J. William Fulbright, Douglas MacArthur, Edward Durell Stone

CALIFORNIA
NICKNAME: Golden State
CAPITAL: Sacramento
ADMISSION TO THE UNION: Sept. 9, 1850
TOTAL AREA: 158,706 sq. mi.
RANK IN SIZE: 3
FLOWER: Golden poppy
TREE: California redwood
BIRD: California valley quail
FAMOUS SONS AND DAUGHTERS: Joe DiMaggio, Isadora Duncan, William Randolph Hearst, Jack London, George S. Patton, Jr., John Steinbeck

COLORADO
NICKNAMES: Centennial State, Rocky Mountain State
CAPITAL: Denver
ADMISSION TO THE UNION: Aug.1,1876
TOTAL AREA: 104,091 sq. mi.
RANK IN SIZE: 8
FLOWER: Rocky Mountain columbine
TREE: Colorado blue spruce
BIRD: Lark bunting
FAMOUS SONS AND DAUGHTERS: Molly Brown, M. Scott Carpenter, Jack Dempsey

CONNECTICUT
NICKNAMES: Constitution State, Nutmeg State
CAPITAL: Hartford
ADMISSION TO THE UNION: Jan. 9, 1788
TOTAL AREA: 5,018 sq. mi.
RANK IN SIZE: 48
FLOWER: Mountain laurel
TREE: White oak
BIRD: American robin
FAMOUS SONS AND DAUGHTERS: Katharine Hepburn, Harriet Beecher Stowe, Noah Webster

DELAWARE
NICKNAMES: First State, Diamond State
CAPITAL: Dover
ADMISSION TO THE UNION: Dec. 7, 1787
TOTAL AREA: 2,045 sq. mi.
RANK IN SIZE: 49
FLOWER: Peach blossom
TREE: American holly
BIRD: Blue hen chicken
FAMOUS SONS AND DAUGHTERS: Thomas Francis Bayard, Annie Jump Cannon, E. I. Du Pont

FLORIDA
NICKNAME: Sunshine State
CAPITAL: Tallahassee
ADMISSION TO THE UNION: Mar. 3, 1845
TOTAL AREA: 58,664 sq. mi.
RANK IN SIZE: 22
FLOWER: Orange blossom
TREE: Sabal palm
BIRD: Mockingbird
FAMOUS SONS AND DAUGHTERS: Marjorie Kinnan Rawlings, Janet Reno, Joseph W. Stilwell

GEORGIA
NICKNAMES: Empire State of the South, Peach State
CAPITAL: Atlanta
ADMISSION TO THE UNION: Jan. 2, 1788
TOTAL AREA: 58,876 sq. mi.
RANK IN SIZE: 21
FLOWER: Cherokee rose
TREE: Live oak
BIRD: Brown thrasher
FAMOUS SONS AND DAUGHTERS: Martin Luther King, Jr., Margaret Mitchell, Flannery O'Connor, Jackie Robinson

HAWAII
NICKNAME: Aloha State
CAPITAL: Honolulu
ADMISSION TO THE UNION: Aug. 21, 1959
TOTAL AREA: 6,471 sq. mi.
RANK IN SIZE: 47
FLOWER: Hibiscus
TREE: Candlenut
BIRD: Hawaiian goose (nene)
FAMOUS SONS AND DAUGHTERS: Sanford B. Dole, Daniel K. Inouye, Kamehameha I, Queen Liliuokalani

IDAHO
NICKNAME: Gem State
CAPITAL: Boise
ADMISSION TO THE UNION: July 3, 1890
TOTAL AREA: 83,564 sq. mi.
RANK IN SIZE: 13
FLOWER: Syringa
TREE: Western white pine
BIRD: Mountain bluebird
FAMOUS SONS AND DAUGHTERS: Gutzon Borglum, Ezra Pound, Sacagawea

ILLINOIS

NICKNAME: Prairie State
CAPITAL: Springfield
ADMISSION TO THE UNION:
Dec. 3, 1818
TOTAL AREA: 56,345 sq. mi.
RANK IN SIZE: 24
FLOWER: Native violet
TREE: White oak
BIRD: Cardinal
FAMOUS SONS AND DAUGHTERS:
Jane Addams, Jack Benny,
Walt Disney, Benny Goodman,
Ernest Hemingway,
Carl Sandburg

INDIANA

NICKNAME: Hoosier State
CAPITAL: Indianapolis
ADMISSION TO THE UNION:
Dec. 11, 1816
TOTAL AREA: 36,185 sq. mi.
RANK IN SIZE: 38
FLOWER: Peony
TREE: Tulip poplar
BIRD: Cardinal
FAMOUS SONS:
James Dean, Theodore
Dreiser, Cole Porter, Ernie
Pyle, Knute Rockne, Red
Skelton, Kurt Vonnegut, Jr.

IOWA

NICKNAME: Hawkeye State
CAPITAL: Des Moines
ADMISSION TO THE UNION:
Dec. 28, 1846
TOTAL AREA: 56,275 sq. mi.
RANK IN SIZE: 25
FLOWER: Wild rose
TREE: Oak
BIRD: Eastern goldfinch
FAMOUS SONS AND DAUGHTERS: Bix
Beiderbecke, Buffalo Bill
Cody, Glenn Miller, Lillian
Russell, John Wayne,
Grant Wood

KANSAS

NICKNAME:
Sunflower State
CAPITAL: Topeka
ADMISSION TO THE UNION:
Jan. 29, 1861
TOTAL AREA: 81,781 sq. mi.
RANK IN SIZE: 14
FLOWER: Sunflower
TREE: Cottonwood
BIRD: Western meadowlark
FAMOUS SONS AND DAUGHTERS:
Amelia Earhart, Buster
Keaton, Edgar Lee Masters,
Charlie Parker, Damon
Runyon

KENTUCKY

NICKNAME: Bluegrass State
CAPITAL: Frankfort
ADMISSION TO THE UNION:
June 1, 1792
TOTAL AREA: 40,409 sq. mi.
RANK IN SIZE: 37
FLOWER: Goldenrod
TREE: Kentucky coffee tree
BIRD: Cardinal
FAMOUS SONS AND DAUGHTERS:
Muhammad Ali, D. W. Griffith,
Loretta Lynn, Carrie Nation

LOUISIANA

NICKNAME: Pelican State
CAPITAL: Baton Rouge
ADMISSION TO THE UNION:
April 30, 1812
TOTAL AREA: 47,752 sq. mi.
RANK IN SIZE: 31
FLOWER: Magnolia
TREE: Bald cypress
BIRD: Brown pelican
FAMOUS SONS AND DAUGHTERS: Louis
Armstrong, Truman Capote,
Lillian Hellman, "Jelly Roll"
Morton

MAINE

NICKNAME: Pine
Tree State
CAPITAL: Augusta
ADMISSION TO THE UNION:
Mar. 14, 1820
TOTAL AREA: 33,265 sq. mi.
RANK IN SIZE: 39
FLOWER: White pine cone
and tassel
TREE: White pine
BIRD: Chickadee
FAMOUS SONS AND DAUGHTERS:
Dorothea Dix, Henry
Wadsworth Longfellow, Edna
St. Vincent Millay

MARYLAND

NICKNAMES: Old Line State,
Free State
CAPITAL: Annapolis
ADMISSION TO THE UNION:
April 28, 1788
TOTAL AREA: 10,460 sq. mi.
RANK IN SIZE: 42
FLOWER: Black-eyed Susan
TREE: White oak
BIRD: Baltimore oriole
FAMOUS SONS AND DAUGHTERS:
Benjamin Banneker, William
Halsted, Billie Holliday, Babe
Ruth, Harriet Tubman

MASSACHUSETTS

NICKNAMES: Bay State,
Old Colony State
CAPITAL: Boston
ADMISSION TO THE UNION:
Feb. 6, 1788
TOTAL AREA: 8,284 sq. mi.
RANK IN SIZE: 45
FLOWER: Mayflower
TREE: American elm
BIRD: Chickadee
FAMOUS SONS AND DAUGHTERS:
Susan B. Anthony, Clara
Barton, W.E.B. Dubois, Emily
Dickinson, Robert Goddard,
Nathaniel Hawthorne

MICHIGAN

NICKNAMES: Great Lakes
State, Wolverine State
CAPITAL: Lansing
ADMISSION TO THE UNION:
Jan. 26, 1837
TOTAL AREA: 96,705 sq. mi.
RANK IN SIZE: 11
FLOWER: Apple blossom
TREE: White pine
BIRD: Robin
FAMOUS SONS AND DAUGHTERS:
Ralph Bunche, Edna Ferber,
Henry Ford, Joe Louis, Diana
Ross, Stevie Wonder

MINNESOTA

NICKNAMES: North Star
State, Gopher State
CAPITAL: St. Paul
ADMISSION TO THE UNION:
May 11, 1858
TOTAL AREA: 84,402 sq. mi.
RANK IN SIZE: 12
FLOWER: Pink and white lady's
slipper
TREE: Norway pine
BIRD: Common loon
FAMOUS SONS AND DAUGHTERS:
Warren E. Burger, William O.
Douglas, F. Scott Fitzgerald,
Judy Garland, Sinclair Lewis

MISSISSIPPI

NICKNAME:
Magnolia State
CAPITAL: Jackson
ADMISSION TO THE UNION:
Dec. 10, 1817
TOTAL AREA: 47,716 sq. mi.
RANK IN SIZE: 32
FLOWER: Magnolia
TREE: Magnolia
BIRD: Mockingbird
FAMOUS SONS AND DAUGHTERS:
William Faulkner, Elvis
Presley, Leontyne Price,
Tennessee Williams

MISSOURI

NICKNAME: Show Me State
CAPITAL: Jefferson City
ADMISSION TO THE UNION:
Aug. 10, 1821
TOTAL AREA: 69,697 sq. mi.
RANK IN SIZE: 19
FLOWER: Hawthorn
TREE: Dogwood
BIRD: Bluebird
FAMOUS SONS AND DAUGHTERS: Maya Angelou, Josephine Baker, George Washington Carver, Walter Cronkite, Langston Hughes, Mark Twain

MONTANA
NICKNAME: Treasure State
CAPITAL: Helena
ADMISSION TO THE UNION:
Nov. 8, 1889
TOTAL AREA: 147,046 sq. mi.
RANK IN SIZE: 4
FLOWER: Bitterroot
TREE: Ponderosa pine
BIRD: Western meadowlark
FAMOUS SONS AND DAUGHTERS: Gary Cooper, Chet Huntley, Myrna Loy, Jeannette Rankin

NEBRASKA

NICKNAME: Cornhusker State
CAPITAL: Lincoln
ADMISSION TO THE UNION:
Mar. 1, 1867
TOTAL AREA: 77,227 sq. mi.
RANK IN SIZE: 15
FLOWER: Goldenrod
TREE: Cottonwood
BIRD: Western meadowlark
FAMOUS SONS AND DAUGHTERS:
Marlon Brando, Johnny Carson, Willa Cather, Henry Fonda, Malcolm X

NEVADA
NICKNAMES: Sagebrush State, Battle Born State, Silver State
CAPITAL: Carson City
ADMISSION TO THE UNION:
Oct. 31, 1864
TOTAL AREA: 110,561 sq. mi.
RANK IN SIZE: 7
FLOWER: Sagebrush
TREE: Single-leaf piñon
BIRD: Mountain bluebird
FAMOUS SONS AND DAUGHTERS: Sarah Winnemucca, Wovoka

NEW HAMPSHIRE
NICKNAME: Granite State
CAPITAL: Concord
ADMISSION TO THE UNION:
June 21, 1788
TOTAL AREA: 9,279 sq. mi.
RANK IN SIZE: 44
FLOWER: Purple lilac
TREE: White birch
BIRD: Purple finch
FAMOUS SONS: Robert Frost, Alan B. Shepard, Jr., Daniel Webster

NEW JERSEY
NICKNAME: Garden State
CAPITAL: Trenton
ADMISSION TO THE UNION:
Dec. 18, 1787
TOTAL AREA: 7,787 sq. mi.
RANK IN SIZE: 46
FLOWER: Purple violet
TREE: Red oak
BIRD: Eastern goldfinch
FAMOUS SONS AND DAUGHTERS:
William (Count) Basie, Dorothea Lange, Paul Robeson, Frank Sinatra

NEW MEXICO
NICKNAME: Land of Enchantment
CAPITAL: Santa Fe
ADMISSION TO THE UNION: Jan. 6, 1912

TOTAL AREA: 121,593 sq. mi.
RANK IN SIZE: 5
FLOWER: Yucca
TREE: Piñon
BIRD: Roadrunner
FAMOUS SONS AND DAUGHTERS: Billy the Kid, Kit Carson, Bill Mauldin, Georgia O'Keeffe

NEW YORK

NICKNAME: Empire State
CAPITAL: Albany
ADMISSION TO THE UNION:
July 26, 1788
TOTAL AREA: 49,108 sq. mi.
RANK IN SIZE: 30
FLOWER: Rose
TREE: Sugar maple
BIRD: Bluebird
FAMOUS SONS AND DAUGHTERS:
Lucille Ball, Maria Callas, George Gershwin, J. Robert Oppenheimer, Jr., Jonas Salk

NORTH CAROLINA
NICKNAMES: Tarheel State, Old North State
CAPITAL: Raleigh
ADMISSION TO THE UNION:
Nov. 21, 1789
TOTAL AREA: 52,669 sq. mi.
RANK IN SIZE: 28
FLOWER: Flowering dogwood
TREE: Pine
BIRD: Cardinal
FAMOUS SONS: Billy Graham, O. Henry, Charles Kuralt, Edward R. Murrow

NORTH DAKOTA
NICKNAME: Peace Garden State
CAPITAL: Bismarck
ADMISSION TO THE UNION:
Nov. 2, 1889
TOTAL AREA: 70,702 sq. mi.
RANK IN SIZE: 17
FLOWER: Wild prairie rose
TREE: American elm

BIRD: Western meadowlark
FAMOUS SONS AND DAUGHTERS:
Louis L'Amour, Peggy Lee, Eric Sevareid

OHIO
NICKNAME: Buckeye State
CAPITAL: Columbus
ADMISSION TO THE UNION:
Mar. 1, 1803
TOTAL AREA: 41,330 sq. mi.
RANK IN SIZE: 35
FLOWER: Scarlet carnation
TREE: Buckeye
BIRD: Cardinal
FAMOUS SONS AND DAUGHTERS: Neil Armstrong, Thomas Edison, Clark Gable, John Glenn, Annie Oakley, James Thurber

OKLAHOMA
NICKNAME: Sooner State
CAPITAL: Oklahoma City
ADMISSION TO THE UNION:
Nov. 16, 1907
TOTAL AREA: 69,919 sq. mi.
RANK IN SIZE: 18
FLOWER: Mistletoe
TREE: Redbud
BIRD: Scissor-tailed flycatcher
FAMOUS SONS AND DAUGHTERS:
Woody Guthrie, Will Rogers, Maria Tallchief, Jim Thorpe

OREGON
NICKNAME: Beaver State
CAPITAL: Salem
ADMISSION TO THE UNION:
Feb. 14, 1859
TOTAL AREA: 97,073 sq. mi.
RANK IN SIZE: 10
FLOWER: Oregon grape
TREE: Douglas fir
BIRD: Western meadowlark
FAMOUS SONS:
Chief Joseph, Linus Pauling, John Reed

PENNSYLVANIA
NICKNAME: Keystone State
CAPITAL: Harrisburg
ADMISSION TO THE UNION:
Dec. 12, 1787
TOTAL AREA: 45,308 sq. mi.
RANK IN SIZE: 33
FLOWER: Mountain laurel
TREE: Hemlock
BIRD: Ruffed grouse
FAMOUS SONS AND DAUGHTERS:
Marian Anderson, Andrew
Carnegie, Mary Cassatt, Gene
Kelly, Margaret Mead, Jimmy
Stewart, Andy Warhol

RHODE ISLAND
NICKNAMES: Little Rhody,
Ocean State
CAPITAL: Providence
ADMISSION TO THE UNION:
May 29, 1790
TOTAL AREA: 1,210 sq. mi.
RANK IN SIZE: 50
FLOWER: Violet
TREE: Red maple
BIRD: Rhode Island red hen
FAMOUS SONS: George M. Cohan,
H. P. Lovecraft, Massasoit

SOUTH CAROLINA
NICKNAME: Palmetto State
CAPITAL: Columbia
ADMISSION TO THE UNION:
May 23, 1788
TOTAL AREA: 31,113 sq. mi.
RANK IN SIZE: 40
FLOWER: Yellow jessamine
TREE: Palmetto
BIRD: Carolina wren
FAMOUS SONS AND DAUGHTERS:
Bernard Baruch, John C.
Calhoun, Althea Gibson

SOUTH DAKOTA

NICKNAMES: Coyote State,
Mount Rushmore State
CAPITAL: Pierre
ADMISSION TO THE UNION:
Nov. 2, 1889
TOTAL AREA: 77,116 sq. mi.
RANK IN SIZE: 16
FLOWER: Pasqueflower
TREE: Black Hills spruce
BIRD: Ring-necked pheasant
FAMOUS SONS: Tom Brokaw
Crazy Horse, George
McGovern, Sitting Bull

TENNESSEE
NICKNAME: Volunteer State
CAPITAL: Nashville
ADMISSION TO THE UNION:
June 1, 1796
TOTAL AREA: 42,144 sq. mi.
RANK IN SIZE: 34
FLOWER: Iris
TREE: Tulip poplar
BIRD: Mockingbird
FAMOUS SONS AND DAUGHTERS:
Davy Crockett, Sequoya,
Bessie Smith

TEXAS
NICKNAME: Lone Star State
CAPITAL: Austin
ADMISSION TO THE UNION:
Dec. 29, 1845
TOTAL AREA: 266,807 sq. mi.
RANK IN SIZE: 2
FLOWER: Bluebonnet
TREE: Pecan
BIRD: Mockingbird
FAMOUS SONS AND DAUGHTERS: Carol
Burnett, Babe Didrikson,
Howard Hughes, Mary Martin

UTAH

NICKNAME: Beehive State
CAPITAL: Salt Lake City
ADMISSION TO THE UNION:
Jan. 4, 1896
TOTAL AREA: 84,899 sq. mi.
RANK IN SIZE: 11

FLOWER: Sego lily
TREE: Blue spruce
BIRD: Seagull
FAMOUS SONS AND DAUGHTERS:
Maude Adams, Philo T.
Farnsworth, John Held, Jr.,
Brigham Young

VERMONT
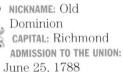
NICKNAME: Green
Mountain State
CAPITAL: Montpelier
ADMISSION TO THE UNION:
Mar. 4, 1791
TOTAL AREA: 9,609 sq. mi.
RANK IN SIZE: 43
FLOWER: Red clover
TREE: Sugar maple
BIRD: Hermit thrush
FAMOUS SONS:
John Deere, Thaddeus
Stevens, Rudy Vallee

VIRGINIA
NICKNAME: Old
Dominion
CAPITAL: Richmond
ADMISSION TO THE UNION:
June 25, 1788
TOTAL AREA: 40,767 sq. mi.
RANK IN SIZE: 36
FLOWER: Flowering dogwood
TREE: Flowering dogwood
BIRD: Cardinal
FAMOUS SONS AND DAUGHTERS: Ella
Fitzgerald, Pocahontas,
Walter Reed, Booker T.
Washington

WASHINGTON
NICKNAME: Evergreen
State
CAPITAL: Olympia
ADMISSION TO THE UNION:
Nov. 11, 1889
TOTAL AREA: 68,139 sq. mi.
RANK IN SIZE: 20
FLOWER: Rhododendron
TREE: Western hemlock
BIRD: Willow goldfinch

FAMOUS SONS AND DAUGHTERS: Bing
Crosby, Bill Gates, Mary
McCarthy, Seattle, James
Whittaker

WEST VIRGINIA
NICKNAME: Mountain
State
CAPITAL: Charleston
ADMISSION TO THE UNION:
June 20, 1863
TOTAL AREA: 24,231 sq. mi.
RANK IN SIZE: 41
FLOWER: Big rhododendron
TREE: Sugar maple
BIRD: Cardinal
FAMOUS SONS AND DAUGHTERS:
Pearl S. Buck, Thomas J.
"Stonewall" Jackson, Charles
E. "Chuck" Yeager

WISCONSIN
NICKNAME: Badger State
CAPITAL: Madison
ADMISSION TO THE UNION:
May 29, 1848
TOTAL AREA: 56,153 sq. mi.
RANK IN SIZE: 26
FLOWER: Wood violet
TREE: Sugar maple
BIRD: Robin
FAMOUS SONS: Spencer Tracy,
Orson Welles, Frank Lloyd
Wright

WYOMING
NICKNAME: Equality State
CAPITAL: Cheyenne
ADMISSION TO THE UNION:
July 10, 1890
TOTAL AREA: 97,809 sq. mi.
RANK IN SIZE: 9
FLOWER: Indian paintbrush
TREE: Cottonwood
BIRD: Meadowlark
FAMOUS SONS AND DAUGHTERS:
Jackson Pollock, Nellie
Tayloe Ross

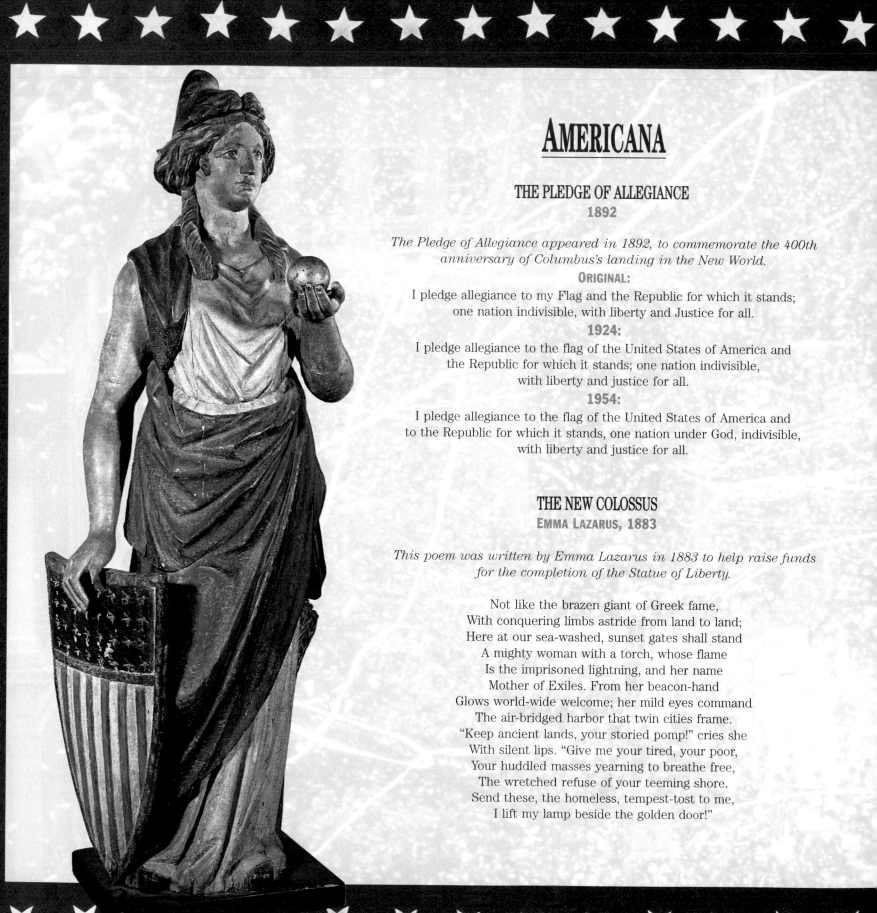

AMERICANA

THE PLEDGE OF ALLEGIANCE
1892

The Pledge of Allegiance appeared in 1892, to commemorate the 400th anniversary of Columbus's landing in the New World.

ORIGINAL:

I pledge allegiance to my Flag and the Republic for which it stands;
one nation indivisible, with liberty and Justice for all.

1924:

I pledge allegiance to the flag of the United States of America and
the Republic for which it stands; one nation indivisible,
with liberty and justice for all.

1954:

I pledge allegiance to the flag of the United States of America and
to the Republic for which it stands, one nation under God, indivisible,
with liberty and justice for all.

THE NEW COLOSSUS
EMMA LAZARUS, 1883

*This poem was written by Emma Lazarus in 1883 to help raise funds
for the completion of the Statue of Liberty.*

Not like the brazen giant of Greek fame,
With conquering limbs astride from land to land;
Here at our sea-washed, sunset gates shall stand
A mighty woman with a torch, whose flame
Is the imprisoned lightning, and her name
Mother of Exiles. From her beacon-hand
Glows world-wide welcome; her mild eyes command
The air-bridged harbor that twin cities frame.
"Keep ancient lands, your storied pomp!" cries she
With silent lips. "Give me your tired, your poor,
Your huddled masses yearning to breathe free,
The wretched refuse of your teeming shore.
Send these, the homeless, tempest-tost to me,
I lift my lamp beside the golden door!"

THE STAR-SPANGLED BANNER
FRANCIS SCOTT KEY, 1814

Designated the National Anthem by Congress in 1931.

Oh say can you see by the dawn's early light
What so proudly we hail'd at the twilight's last gleaming,
Whose broad stripes & bright stars through the perilous fight
O'er the ramparts we watch'd, were so gallantly streaming?
And the rocket's red glare, the bombs bursting in air,
Gave proof through the night that our flag was still there,
O say does that star-spangled banner yet wave
O'er the land of the free & the home of the brave? . . .

O thus be it ever when freemen shall stand
Between their lov'd home & the war's desolation!
Blest with vict'ry & peace may the heav'n rescued land
Praise the power that hath made & preserv'd us a nation!
Then conquer we must, when our cause it is just,
And this be our motto — "In God is our Trust."
And the star-spangled banner in triumph shall wave
O'er the land of the free & the home of the brave.

AMERICA THE BEAUTIFUL
KATHERINE LEE BATES, 1893

O beautiful for spacious skies,
For amber waves of grain,
For purple mountain majesties
Above the fruited plain!
America! America!
God shed His grace on thee
And crown thy good with brotherhood
From sea to shining sea!

O beautiful for pilgrim feet,
Whose stern, impassioned stress
A thoroughfare for freedom beat
Across the wilderness!
America! America!
God mend thine every flaw,
Confirm thy soul in self-control,
Thy liberty in law!

THE BATTLE HYMN OF THE REPUBLIC
JULIA WARD HOWE, 1861

*Julia Ward Howe wrote the lyrics for "The Battle Hymn
of the Republic," set to the melody of the popular
marching song "John Brown's Body,"
on November 18, 1861.*

Mine eyes have seen the glory of the coming
of the Lord;
He is trampling out the vintage where the
grapes of wrath are stored;
He hath loosed the fateful lightning of His
terrible swift sword:
His truth is marching on.

I have seen Him in the watch-fires of a hundred
circling camps;
They have builded Him an altar in the evening
dews and damps;
I can read His righteous sentence by the dim
and flaring lamps:
His day is marching on....

CREDITS & ACKNOWLEDGMENTS

Well Museum. **167** *clockwise from left* Gift of Elwin M. Eldredge, Museum of the City of New York (detail); Courtesy Gilcrease Museum, Tulsa; Courtesy Colorado Historical Society. **172** *top* National Portrait Gallery, Smithsonian Institution/Art Resource, NY, On loan from Serena Williams Miles Van Rensselaer; *bottom* M. and M. Karolik Collection, Courtesy Museum of Fine Arts, Boston. **172-173** *bottom center* Philadelphia Museum of Art, The John G. Johnson Collection. **173** *top* Chicago Historical Society, neg. no. 1980.227. **174** *top left* State Archives of Michigan; *top right* West Virginia Division of Culture and History. **175** *top* Facsimile Courtesy California State Railroad Museum; *bottom* LOC. **176** *left* National Portrait Gallery, Smithsonian Institution/Art Resource, NY; *top right* Eleanor S. Brockenbrough Library, The Museum of the Confederacy, Richmond, VA, copy photography by Katherine Wetzel *(left)*; LOC *(right)*. **177** *top left* LOC; *right* Courtesy Stamatelos Brothers Collection, Cambridge, MA, photograph by Larry Sherer/High Impact Photography, from "Echoes of Glory: Arms and Equipment of the Union," ©1991 Time-Life Books. **178** *top left* Lester S. Levy Collections of Sheet Music, Special Collections, Milton S. Eisenhower Library, The Johns Hopkins University; *top right* Anne S. K. Brown Military Collection, Brown University Library. **178-179** *bottom center* The Art Collection of the Union League of Philadelphia. **179** *all* LOC. **180** *left* Culver Pictures; *right* State Historical Society of Iowa, Iowa City. **181** *top* Antietam National Battlefield, Sharpsburg, MD, photograph by Larry Sherer/High Impact Photography; *bottom* LOC. **182** *left* Courtesy, Peabody Essex Museum, Salem, MA, photograph by Mark Sexton; *right* LOC. **183** *top* Courtesy State of New York, Division of Military and Naval Affairs, photograph by Henry Groskinsky; *bottom* Chicago Historical Society, ICHi-22095. **184** *top* Rinhart Galleries, courtesy "Civil War Times Illustrated;" *bottom* U. S. Army Military History Institute. **185** *top right* National Postal Museum, Smithsonian Institution; *bottom* West Point Museum Collections, U. S. Military Academy, West Point, NY. **186** *top* Culver Pictures; *bottom left* By permission of the Houghton Library, Harvard University. **187** *left* Wadsworth Atheneum, Hartford, Gift of the Citizens of Hartford by Subscription (detail); *right* National Portrait Gallery, Smithsonian Institution/Art Resource, NY. **188** *top* Anne S. K. Brown Military Collection, Brown University Library; *bottom* Courtesy Colorado Historical Society. **189** *top left* Corbis Bettmann *(both)*. **190** *top and bottom left* GRANGER. **191** *left* Courtesy U. S. Naval Academy Museum; *right* Archives and Manuscripts Division of the Oklahoma Historical Society. **192** *left* GRANGER; *right* Nawrocki Stock Photo. **193** *top* National Archives, photograph courtesy of the Eleanor S. Brockenbrough Library, The Museum of the Confederacy, Richmond, VA. **194** *top* Culver Pictures; *bottom right* Museum of History and Industry, Seattle. **195** *top* GRANGER; *bottom* Culver Pictures. **196** *top* Culver Pictures; *bottom* LOC. **197** *left* LOC; *right* Courtesy of the Seward Museum, Auburn, NY, photograph by E. Bruce Walter. **198** *left* Smithsonian Institution. **198-199** *bottom* Buffalo Bill Historical Center, Cody, WY (detail). **199** *center* GRANGER. **200** *clockwise from left* Collection of the Children's Museum of Indianapolis; GRANGER; Corbis Bettmann. **201** *top* GRANGER; *bottom* Courtesy King Ranch, Inc. **202** *top* Courtesy Adirondack Museum. **202-203** *bottom center* Union Pacific Museum Collection, photograph by Andrew J. Russell, image no. 1-23. **203** *top* GRANGER; *bottom* Culver Pictures. **204** *left* ©Peter Bussian/Omni-Photo Communications, Inc.; *right* GRANGER. **205** *top* National Portrait Gallery, Smithsonian Institution/Art Resource, NY; *bottom* Photograph by Berenice Abbott, Museum of the City of New York. **206** *all* LOC. **207** *left* Chicago Historical Society, G1984.0527.56. **208** *all* Culver Pictures. **209** *top* LOC; *bottom right* California State Railroad Museum. **210** *left* The Print and Picture Collection, Free Library of Philadelphia; *right* Nebraska State Historical Society. **211** *top* C. Marshall Beale & John Summerhayes Beale, Jr.; *bottom right* Kentucky Derby Museum. **212** *top* Culver Pictures; *bottom* GRANGER. **213** *clockwise from top* Museum of American Political Life, University of Hartford, photograph by Sally Andersen-Bruce; Culver Pictures; Ephymou/Corbis Sygma (hands only). **214** GRANGER; *bottom* Nicodemus Historical Society Collection, Kansas Collection, University of Kansas Libraries. **215** *top* The Print and Picture Collection, Free Library of Philadelphia; *bottom left* National Portrait Gallery, Smithsonian Institution/Art Resource, NY. **218** *top* From a doll at the Museum of American Political Life, University of Hartford. **220** *top left* The Institute of Texan Cultures, San Antonio, TX, Courtesy Mrs. Polk Shelton; *bottom center* Brown Brothers. **220-221** *top center* Arizona Historical Society, Tucson, photo Acc. #1447, #1442, # 1443 *(all)*. **221** *top right* The Biltmore Company; *bottom* The New-York Historical Society. **222** *top left* Museum of the City of New York; *right center* Nedjeljko Matura. **223** *top* National Museum of American History, Smithsonian Institution; *bottom* GRANGER. **224** *left (top to bottom)* Brown Brothers, Museum of the City of New York, Brown Brothers, Museum of the City of New York; *top right* The Mark Twain House, Hartford, CT; *bottom right* Culver Pictures. **225** *left* The Schmidt Museum of Coca-Cola Memorabilia. **226** *top* Smithsonian Institution; *bottom* Musée Bartholdi, Colmar, photograph by C. Kempf *(left)*, Courtesy of Andrew Spano *(right)*. **227** *top* Corbis Bettmann; *bottom* Kansas State Historical Society, Topeka. **228** *left* National Baseball Library and Archive, Cooperstown, NY; *top right* Permission of AT&T Archives. **228-229** Western History Collections, University of Oklahoma. **229** *top* Corbis Bettmann. **230** *left* LOC; *right* GRANGER. **231** *top and bottom left* LOC. **232** *left* Photograph by Matthew Girard/ Concept by Damon Torres; *right* "The Courier Journal" *(both)*. **233** *top* LOC; *bottom left* Courtesy Peabody Essex Museum, Salem, MA. **234** *left* Courtesy The Gillette Company; *right* Brown Brothers. **235** *top and bottom right* GRANGER. **236** *top* Corbis Bettmann; *bottom left and right* Courtesy Sears, Roebuck and Co. **237** *top* LOC; *bottom* GRANGER. **238** *left* UPI/Corbis Bettman; *right* The National Cowboy Hall of Fame and Western Heritage Center, Oklahoma City, OK. **239** *top* Division of Rare and Manuscript Collections, Cornell University; *bottom left* The Huntington Library, San Marino, CA. **240** *top* Brown Brothers; *bottom left* Niagara Falls Public Library, Local History Department, Niagara Falls, NY. **240-241** Clyde H. Smith. **241** *top* LOC; *bottom right* Courtesy Department of Library Services, American Museum of Natural History. **242** *top* Henry W. and Albert A. Berg Collection, NYPL; *bottom* National Baseball Library and Archive, Cooperstown, NY. **243** *counterclockwise from top* LOC; GRANGER; Culver Pictures. **244** *top* Buick Motor Division; *bottom left* Auburn Cord Duesenberg Museum. **244-245** Corbis Bettmann. **245** *right* Popperfoto/Archive. **246** *left* Brown Brothers; *right* Culver Pictures. **247** *clockwise from top left* Corbis Bettmann; Photoplay Productions, London; Superstock. **248** *counterclockwise from right* Federal Bureau of Investigation; GRANGER; The Schomburg Center for Research in Black Culture, NYPL. **249** *top* California Department of Parks and Recreation. **250** *top* Reprinted with permission from Kalmbach Publishing Co., "Trains" Magazine collection; *bottom* Girl Scouts of America. **251** *top* Brown Brothers; *bottom* Henri Matisse, "The Red Studio," Issey-les-Moulineaux (1911), oil on canvas, 71 1/4 x 86 1/4 in (181 x 219.1 cm). The Museum of Modern Art, New York, Mrs. Simon Guggenheim Fund, photograph ©The Museum of Modern Art, New York. ©1995 Succession H. Matisse, Paris/Artist Rights Society (ARS), New York. **252** *left* The Archives of The University of Notre Dame; *right* Courtesy "Vogue," ©1935 (renewed 1963) by The Condé Nast Publications Inc. **253** *top left* Brown Brothers; *bottom left* The New-York Historical Society. **254** *left* Ford Motor Co.; *top right* LOC. **255** *top* UPI/Corbis Bettman; *bottom* Boys Town Hall of History Photograph Collection. **256** *all* Culver Pictures. **257** *clockwise from top left* John T. McCoy, Jr.; UPI/Corbis Bettman; GRANGER. **262** *left* UPI/Corbis Bettman; *right* GRANGER. **263** *counterclockwise from top left* UPI/Corbis Bettman *(two)*; The New York Yankees. **264** *top* UPI/Corbis Bettman; *bottom* Brown Brothers. **265** *left* Culver Pictures; *right* Photograph by Underwood & Underwood, Washington, DC, Courtesy Vermont Historical Society. **266** *left* National Portrait Gallery, Smithsonian Institution/Art Resource, NY; *right* Brown Brothers. **267** *clockwise from top* Tribune Media Services Inc., All Rights Reserved, reprinted with permission; Brown Brothers; Culver Pictures. **268** *top* Courtesy Carrier Corporation; *bottom* Brown Brothers. **269** *clockwise from top* Grand Ole Opry; Culver Pictures; Florida State Archives. **270** *top* Swann Galleries, Inc.; *bottom* Goddard Collection/Clark University. **271** *counterclockwise from top right* Brown Brothers; Culver Pictures; Nicolas Russell/The Image Bank (lasso only). **272** *top* San Diego Aero-Space Museum; *bottom* Corbis Bettmann. **272-273** *bottom center* UPI/Corbis Bettman. **273** *top center* ©The Walt Disney Company; *right* Stephen Marks/The Image Bank. **274** *top* Corbis Bettmann; *bottom* UPI/Corbis Bettman. **275** *left* GRANGER; *right* National Geographic Society. **276** *top* UPI/Corbis Bettman; *bottom left* Culver Pictures. **276-277** *bottom center* Brown Brothers. **277** *right* Brown Brothers. **278** *top* Courtesy The Minneapolis Institute of Arts, the John De Laittre Fund; *bottom* Culver Pictures. **279** *top* From the Collection of the Louisiana State Museum; *bottom* National Baseball Library and Archive, Cooperstown, NY. **280** *all* UPI/Corbis Bettman. **281** *center* UPI/Corbis Bettman. **282** *left* Margaret Bourke-White/LIFE Magazine, ©Time Inc.; *right* UPI/ Corbis Bettman. **283** *top* Culver Pictures; *bottom* GRANGER. **284** *left* Brown Brothers; *bottom right* UPI/Corbis Bettman. **285** *top* Lawrence Marx Collection, Carnegie Hall Archives; *bottom* Corbis Bettmann. **286** *top* UPI/Corbis Bettman; *bottom* Photograph by Steven Mays. **287** *left* UPI/Corbis Bettman; *right* Culver Pictures. **288** *left* Brown Brothers; *right* Corbis Bettmann. **289** *right* Photograph by Steven Mays. **290** *top* Culver Pictures; *bottom* Social Security Administration. **291** *bottom left* Courtesy Hagley Museum and Library; *right* National Portrait Gallery, Smithsonian Institution/Art Resource, NY. **292** *top* Brown Brothers; *bottom* Franklin D. Roosevelt Library. **292-293** *bottom center* UPI/Corbis Bettman. **293** *top right* Chicago Historical Society. **294** *bottom* Imperial War Museum. **295** *left* GRANGER; *right* Brown Brothers. **296** *top* U.S. Army; *bottom* Iowa State University Library, University Archives. **296-297** *top center* Naval Historical Foundation. **297** *right* UPI/Corbis Bettman. **298** *right* Culver Pictures. **299** *top* UPI/Corbis Bettman; *bottom* National Archives. **300** *left* Northern Indiana Historical Society; *right* U.S. Army. **301** *counterclockwise from top* Magnum Photos Inc., ©1944 Robert Capa; UPI/Corbis Bettman; Manfred Danegger/ OKAPIA/Photo Researchers. **302** *top center* U.S. Army *(top)*; Smithsonian Institution *(bottom)*. **302-303** *bottom center* Hulton Deutsch Collection Ltd. **303** *top center* GRANGER. **304** *all* AP/Wide World Photos. **305** *center* ©1945 by The New York Times Co., reprinted by permission. **310** *left* Reprinted with the permission of Pocket Books, a Division of Simon & Schuster from "Baby and Child Care" by Dr. Benjamin Spock. ©1946, copyright renewed 1974 by Benjamin Spock, M.D.; *right* Winston Churchill Memorial and Library, Westminster College, Fulton, MO. **311** *top* AP/Wide World Photos; *bottom* Archive Photos. **312** *top* Sketch by René Gruau, Courtesy Christian Dior; *bottom* UPI/Corbis Bettman. **313** *top* Mary Evans Picture Library; *bottom* UPI/Corbis Bettman. **314** *top* National Air and Space Museum, Smithsonian Institution; *bottom* UPI/Corbis Bettman. **315** *bottom* UPI/Corbis Bettman. **316** *top* Citicorp Diners Club; *bottom* Alfred Eisenstaedt/LIFE Magazine, ©Time Inc. **317** *top* UPI/Corbis Bettman; *bottom* Photograph by Steven Mays. **318** *top* Unysis Corporation; *bottom* UPI/Corbis Bettman. **319** *top left* Werner Wolff/ Black Star; *top right* UPI/Corbis Bettman. **320** *top* Printed by permission of the Norman Rockwell Family Trust, ©1964 The Norman Rockwell Family Trust, Photograph Courtesy Norman Rockwell Museum at Stockbridge; *bottom* UPI/Corbis Bettman. **321** *top left* Thomas Nebbia/National Geographic Society; *top right* Collection of Peggy Stapleton. **322** *top* UPI/Corbis Bettman; *bottom* Southdale Shopping Center. **323** *left* UPI/Corbis Bettman; *right* AP/Wide World Photos. **324** *clockwise from top left* Sovfoto/Eastfoto; Courtesy Edmund H. Harvey, Jr., photograph by Richard Levy; AP/Wide World Photos. **325** *top left* "Barbie Bazaar" Magazine; *center right* Northeast Minnesota Historical Center. **326** *left* Bill Ray; *center right* Archive Photos. **327** *top* Tony Spina/"Detroit Free Press"; *bottom* "The Courier-Journal." **328** *top* Globe Photos; *bottom* UPI/Corbis Bettman. **329** *left* John Fitzgerald Kennedy Library; *right* UPI/Corbis Bettman. **330** *clockwise from center left* Tor Eigeland/Black Star; Ed Clark/LIFE Magazine, ©Time Inc.; Courtesy The Peace Corps. **331** *top* NASA; *bottom* Bruce Davidson/Magnum Photos, Inc. **332** *all* Archive Photos. **333** *left* Alfred Eisenstaedt/LIFE Magazine, ©Time Inc.; *right* UPI/Corbis Bettman. **334** *left* AP/Wide World Photos; *right* "The Dallas Morning News"/AP/Wide World Photos. **335** *top left* Steve Shapiro/Black Star; *center right* Popperfoto/Archive Photos. **336** *all* UPI/Corbis Bettman. **337** *bottom left* Archive Photos; *top right* Bob Gomel/LIFE Magazine, ©1965 Time Inc. **338** *top* Vernon J. Biever *(both)*; *bottom* AP/Wide World Photos. **339** *top* Shelly Grossman/Woodfin Camp; *bottom* NASA/Black Star. **340** *top* John Dominis/LIFE Magazine, ©Time, Inc.; *bottom* Werner Wolff/Black Star. **341** *left* AP/Wide World Photo; *right* UPI/Corbis Bettman. **342** *top left* Dirck Halstead/ Gamma Liaison; *top right* UPI/Corbis Bettman. **343** *left* Leclerc/Gamma Liaison; *right* Dennis Brack/Black Star. **344** *left* Courtesy American Craft Council, American Craft Museum, New York; *right* J. P. Laffont/Corbis Sygma. **345** *top* Nik Wheeler/Black Star. **346** *top left* J. P. Laffont/Corbis Sygma; *bottom right* Apple Computer, Inc. **347** *top* Dirck Halstead/Gamma Liaison; *bottom* Manoocher/Sipa Press. **348** *left* James Mason/Black Star; *right* David A. Wagner/ Phototake, New York City. **349** *clockwise from top* Sygma; Dennis Brack/Black Star; Museum of American Politcal Life, University of Hartford, photograph by Sally Andersen-Bruce. **350** *top* David Welcher/Corbis Sygma; *bottom* Tom Sobolik/Black Star. **351** *left* Peter Turnley/Black Star; *right* AP/Wide World Photos. **352** *top* AP/Wide World Photos; *center* Woods Hole Oceanographic Institution; By Ken Marschall from the book "The Discovery of the Titanic" by Dr. Robert Ballard. **353** Photodisc. **354-355** *background* Culver Pictures. **355** GRANGER. **357** GRANGER. **358** GRANGER. **360** *left* National Portrait Gallery, Smithsonian Institution/Art Resource, NY; *right* The New-York Historical Society. **361** *top center* National Portrait Gallery, Smithsonian Institution/Art Resource, NY; *bottom left* ©White House Historical Association, photograph by the National Geographic Society. **362** *all* ©White House Historical Association, photograph by the National Geographic Society. **363** *left* National Portrait Gallery, Smithsonian Institution/Art Resource, NY; *right* ©1967 James Wyeth, photograph courtesy of the artist. **364** *clockwise from top left* LOC; Museum of American Political Life, University of Hartford, photograph by Stephen Laschever; "Fireman's Bucket," Index of American Design, ©1995 Board of Trustees, National Gallery of Art, Washington, DC. **365** *counterclockwise from top left* Collection of Stanley King; The New-York Historical Society; GRANGER. **366-367** *all* Museum of American Political Life, University of Hartford, photographs by Sally Andersen-Bruce. **372** *left* New York State Historical Association, Cooperstown. **372-373** *background* S. Compoint/Corbis Sygma. **373** *bottom right* R. Maiman/Corbis Sygma.

Text

Permission to excerpt or adapt material from the following works is gratefully acknowledged: **289** *The Atomic Age*, by Morton Grodzins and Eugene Rabinowitch, Copyright © 1964 by Basic Books, Inc. Reprinted by permission of HarperCollins Publishers, Inc. **293** *The Attack on Pearl Harbor*, Copyright © 1991 by Larry Kimmett and Margaret Regis. Reprinted by permission of Navigator Publishing. **265** *Etiquette in Society, in Business, in Politics and at Home* by Emily Post, Replica Edition, Copyright © 1922 by Funk & Wagnalls Company. Copyright © 1969 by the Emily Post Institute. Reprinted by permission of HarperCollins Publishers, Inc. **277** *Hard Times*, by Studs Terkel, Copyright © 1970 by Studs Terkel. Reprinted by permission of Random House, Inc. **283** *How to Win Friends and Influence People*, by Dale Carnegie, Copyright © 1936 by Dale Carnegie, Copyright renewed 1964 by Donna Dale Carnegie and Dorothy Carnegie. Reprinted by permission of Simon &. Schuster. **229** *The Johnstown Flood*, by David McCullough, Copyright © 1968 by David McCullough. Reprinted by permission of Simon & Schuster. **281** "The Life and Death of 470 Acres" by Robert D. Lusk, Copyright © 1938 by *The Saturday Evening Post*. Reprinted by permission of *The Saturday Evening Post*. **329** "The Preface" by Robert Frost, Copyright © 1961 by Robert Lee Frost. Reprinted by permission of the Estate of Robert Lee Frost. **297** *Rickenbacker*, by Booton Herndon, Copyright © 1967 by Edward V. Rickenbacker. Reprinted by permission of Simon & Schuster. **333** *Silent Spring*, by Rachel Carson, Copyright © 1962 by Rachel L. Carson, renewed 1990 by Roger Christie. Reprinted by permission of Houghton Mifflin Company.

INDEX

Page numbers in **bold type** refer to illustrations and tables.

A

Aaron, Hank, **263**
Abenaki Indians, 27, 34, **34**
Abolition movement, 91, 125-126, 129, 130, 139, 146, 152, 160
  Civil War and, 169, 170, 183
Abortion issue, **335**
Academy Awards (Oscars), 273, 274, **274**
Academy of Motion Picture Arts and Sciences, **273**, 274
Acquired Immune Deficiency Syndrome (AIDS), 348
Adams, Abigail, 58, 84, 99
Adams, Charles Francis, 173
Adams, Henry, 173, 240
Adams, John, 42, **47**, 49, **51**, 104, 173, 364
  American Revolution and, 51, 54-55, 58, **63**
  peace negotiations and, 77, **77**
  as president, 84, 87, 99, 100
  in presidential elections, 89, 98, 100, 101
  as vice president, 84, **84**, 85
Adams, John Quincy, 116, 129, **129**, 173, 364
Adams, Samuel, 38, 42, 46, **46**, 49, 50, 54-55, 64, 79, 104
Adams, Thomas, 154
Addams, Jane, 218, 248
Adultery, 32
Adventures in the Wilderness (Murray), 202
Adventures of Huckleberry Finn, The (Twain), 224
African-Americans, 259-260, 307, 308
  in American Revolution, 56, **56**
  blood banks and, 291
  in colonial era, **27**, 60
  as Exodusters, 214, **214**
  in later nineteenth century, 170, 192, 197
  music of, 248, 327
  in Union military, 183, 184
  voting rights for, 197, 219, 336
  See also Abolition movement; Segregation; Slavery; Slaves.
Agriculture:
  in colonial era, 21, 23, 48
  in early twentieth century, 217, 259, 260
  in late eighteenth century, 95
  in nineteenth century, 114, 124, 125, 131, 137, 170-171, 206, 210, 217
  technology of, 90, 95, 125, 131, 137
AIDS (Acquired Immune Deficiency Syndrome), 348
Air conditioning, 268
Airplanes, 216, 243, 272, 275, 314
Airships, 284

Alabama, **80**, 368
  in Civil War, 169, **177**, 187
Alamo, Battle of, 136, **136**
Alaska, 97, **97**, 146, 197, 324, 368
Alaska gold rush, 197
Albee, Edward Franklin, 193
Alcatraz prison, 284, **284**
Alcohol, 79
  Prohibition on, 259, 274, 276, **276**
Alcott, Louisa May, 186, **186**, 224
Aldrin, Edwin, Jr. (Buzz), **339**
Aleuts, 10, 111
Alexis Romanov, Grand Duke, 208, **208**
Algeria, 96
Alien and Sedition Acts (1798), 89
Allen, Ethan, 38, 49, **49, 57**, 65, 73
Allen, Gracie, **193**
All Quiet on the Western Front, 287
Alvin, 352, **352**
American Anti-Slavery Society, 125
American Crisis, The (Paine), 355
American Dictionary of the English Language, An (Webster), 78
American Federation of Labor (AFL), 217, 227, **227**, 282
American Fur Company, 133
American Historical Association, 231
American Language, The (Mencken), 267
American Medical Association, **155**
American Mercury, 267
American Party, 135
American Psychiatric Association, 155
American Railway Union, 233
American Red Cross, 180, **180**, 291, 295
American Revolution, 40, 43-45, 52-77
  documents of, 354-357
  events leading to, 13, 42-43, 46-51
  histories of, 104
  key events in, **53**
  peace negotiations after, 77
  prisoners of war in, 77, **77**
  spies in, 56, 59, 73, **73**
  women in, 58-59
American Society for the Prevention of Cruelty to Animals (ASPCA), 194
American Spelling Book, The (Webster), 78
American Temperance Society, 156-157
"America the Beautiful" (Bates), 373
Ames, Fisher, 83
Amsterdam Olympics of 1928, 266
Amundsen, Roald, 275
Anami, Korechika, 305
Anastasia, Albert, 140
Anderson, Marian, 287, **287**
André, John, **53**, 73, **73**, 115
Andrea Doria, 322, **322**
Andrews, James J., 184
Anesthesia, 143
Angel Island, 249
Animal cruelty, 194
Anschluss, 285
Antarctica, 275
Anthony, Susan B., 167, 209

Antietam, Battle of, **177**, 181, **181**, 183
Anti-Federalists, 45, 81, 82, 98
Anti-Masonic Party, 135
Apache Indians, 171, 211, 226
Apartment buildings, 205, **205**
Apollo 11, 270, 339
Apple Computer Company, 346
Appleseed, Johnny, 97, **97**
Apple sellers, 277, **277**
Apple trees, 97
Arab oil embargo (1973), 344
Arapaho Indians, 171, 189
Arbuthnot, Marriott, 72
Architecture, 103, 133, 232
Argentia conference (1941), 292
Arizona, 368
Arizona, 293, **293**
Arkansas, 368
  in Civil War, **177**
Arkwright, Sir Richard, 87
Arlington National Cemetery, 264, **264**
Armistead, James, **73**
Armory Show (1913), 251, **251**
Armstrong, Edwin H., 289
Armstrong, Louis, 258
Armstrong, Neil, **331**, 339
Army military academy, U.S., 252
Army Signal Service, U.S., 230
Arnold, Benedict, 49, 60, 65, 66, 72, 73, 73
Arnold, Kenneth, 313, **313**
Aroostook War, 140, **140**
Arthur, Chester A., **145**, 217, 222, 365
Arthur, Jean, 290, **290**
Arthur, Timothy Shay, 157
Articles of Confederation, 45
Ashburton, Lord, 140
Ashley, James, 201
Associated Press, 304
Astaire, Adele, **193**
Astaire, Fred, **193**
Astor, Caroline, 221
Astor, John Jacob, 90, 109, 133, 221
Astor, Vincent, 280
Astor, William, 221
Astronomy, 156
Atanasoff, John, 296
Atanasoff-Berry Computer (ABC), 296, **296**
Atlantic Charter (1941), 292, 301
Attucks, Crispus, **27**
Audubon, John James, 253, **253**
Austin, Stephen, 118, **118**, 136
Austria, 40, 261, 285
Austria-Hungary, 257, **257**
Automobiles, 216, 244, 254, 259
Ayokeh, 118
Aztec Indians, 10

B

Baby boomers, 310, **310**
Bacall, Lauren, 236
Baden-Powell, Sir Robert, 250
Baez, Joan, 332, 340

Baffin, William, 15
Bagnetto, A., **230**
Bahamas, 14
Bailey, James A., 208, **208**
Baird, John Logie, 288
Baker, W. H., **180**
Balloon framing, 133, **133**
Baltimore, Cecilius Calvert, Lord, 28, 29
Baltimore and Ohio Railroad, 135
Baltimore fire (1904), 207
Bancroft, George, 147
Bank of North America, 38
Bank of the United States, 88
Banks, John, 56
Baptists, 24, 101
Baranov, Alexander, 97, **97**
Barbados, 37
Barbary pirates, 96
Barbie dolls, 325, **325**
Barclay, Robert H., 112
Barkley, Alben, 290
Barnes, Edward, **351**
Barnett, Ferdinand Lee, 223
Barnum, P. T., 166, 208, **208**
Bartholdi, Auguste-Charlotte, 226, **226**
Bartholdi, Frédéric-Auguste, 226
Barton, Clara, 180, **180**, 229
Bartram, John, 35, **35**
Baseball, 147, **147**, 203, 228, 242, 263, 279, 288, 300, 312
Basie, Count, 285
Basketball, 351
Bates, America, **214**
Bates, Katherine Lee, 373
"Battle Hymn of the Republic, The" (Howe), 178, 373
Bay of Pigs invasion (1961), 308, 330, 333
Beanes, William, 113
Beatles, 335, **335**
Beaton, Cecil, **252**
Beaumont, Gustave de, 131, **131**
Beauregard, P.G.T., 175
Beck, Dave, 323
Becknell, William, 117
Beecher, Henry Ward, 125, **125**, 209
Beecher, Lyman, 157, 160
Begin, Menachem, 352
Belgium, 257, 261
Bell, Alexander Graham, 93, 212
Bell, Thomas, 37
Ben Hur, 274
Bennett, Floyd, 275
Benny, Jack, **193**
Benton, Thomas Hart, 146
Bergh, Henry, 194, **194**
Berlin blockade (1948-1949), 314, **314**
Berlin Wall, **310**
Bernays, Edward, 276, **276**
Bernhardt, Sarah, 166
Berry, Clifford, 296
Berryman, Clifford, **241**
Bicentennial, U.S., 346, **346**
Bierstadt, Albert, **142**
Bigler, Henry, 151
Bikini Atoll, 311, **311**

Bill of Rights, U.S., 45, 61, 81, 82, 85, 359
Bingham, Anne E., **211**
Bissel, Israel, 52
Blackbeard (Edward Teach), 34-35, **34, 35**
Black Codes, 170, 192
Black Crook, The, 196, **196**
Blackfeet Indians, 109
Black Friday (1869), 204
Black Kettle, Cheyenne chief, 189
Black Monday (1987), 350
Blacks. *See* African-Americans.
Black Tuesday (1929), 204, 260, 275
Blackwell, Elizabeth, 154, **154**
Blackwell, Emily, 154
Blalock, Alfred, 302
Blood banks, 291, **291**, 295
"Blue babies," 302
Bohr, Niels, 293
Bonaparte, Charles, 248
Bonus Army, 278-279, **278**
Boone, Daniel, 42, 51, 55, **55**
Booth, John Wilkes, 190, **190**
Borzage, Frank, 274
Bosnia, 352
Boston fire (1872), 207
Boston Massacre (1770), **27**, 43, 46, 49, 49, 52
Boston *Morning Post*, 141
Boston News-Letter, **35**, 38
Boston Pilgrims, 242
Boston Red Sox, 203, 263
Boston Tea Party (1773), 43, 46, 50, 50, 51
Botany, 35
Boudinot, Elias C., 228
Bounty jumpers, 188
Bourbon County, 79
Bourke-White, Margaret, 282
Bow, Clara, 269, **269, 273**
Bowie, Jim, 129, 136
Bowie knife, 129, **129**
Bowser, Sylvanus, 244
Boyd, Belle, **180**
Boys Town, 255
Boyton, Paul, 234
Braddock, Edward, **40, 41**
Bradford, William, 23
Bradish, Vashti, 25
Bradley, Caleb, 140
Bradley, Omar, 317
Bradstreet, Anne, 24, **24**
Brancusi, Constantin, 251
Brandywine, Battle of, 73
Braque, Georges, 251
Breckinridge, John C., 127
Brent, Margaret, 28-29
Brewer, David J., 235
Brezhnev, Leonid, **310**
Bridger, Jim, 150
Brier, John, 155
Brier, Juliet, 155
Briggs, Joseph, 185
Bright, William H., 204
Broadway Melody, **273**
Brooklyn Bridge, 222, **222**

Brooklyn Dodgers, 312
Brooks, Preston S., 163, **163**
Brown, John, 127
Brown, Michael S., **319**
Brown, Moses, 87
Brown, Noah, 112
Brown, Vernon, **285**
Brown v. *Board of Education*, 235, 307, 318, 320
Bryan, William Jennings, 218, 235, **235**
Buchanan, James, 365
Buffalo hunts, 208, **208,** 223
Buick, David, 244
Buick Motor Company, 244, **244**
Building techniques, 133, 224-225, 313
Bulgaria, 257, 306
Bulge, Battle of the, **303**
Bullitt, William, 288
Bull Moose Party, 251
Bull Run, First Battle of, 168, 175, **175**
Bull Run, Second Battle of, 180
Bunau-Varilla, Philippe, 243
Bunker Hill, Battle of, 54, **54, 56,** 57
Burgoyne, John, **58,** 69, 72, 75
Burma, 296, **305**
Burn, Febb Ensminger, 262
Burn, Harry Thomas, 262
Burnet, Bishop, 37
Burnett, John, 138
Burns, George, 193, **193**
Burr, Aaron, 86, 89, 98, **98,** 100, 104, **104,** 108
Burroughs, Edgar Rice, 236
Bush, George, 309, **310,** 349, 351, 367
Bushnell, David, 64
Butler, Andrew, 163, **163**
Butler, Pierce, 139
Butterfield, Daniel, 178
Byelorussia, **310**
Byrd, Richard E., 275, **275**
Byrd, Robert C., **247**

C

Cable cars, 209
Cabot, John, 11, 14, **14, 15,** 16
Calhoun, John C., 126
California, 111, 127, 146, 148, 155, 156, 368
California gold rush, 111, 151, 152, **152,** 153, **153**
Callaghan, Margaret, **300**
Calling cards, 224, **224**
Call of the Wild, The (London), 242
Calvert, Frederick, 46
Calvert, Leonard, 28
Cambodia, 341
Cambridge, Mass., 38
Camden, Battle of, 72, 73
Campbell, John A., 204
Camping, 202
Canada, 10, 13, **310,** 325
Canals, 115, 124
Canby, William J., 57
Candler, Asa, 225
Capa, Robert, 282, 301
Capital cities (U.S.), **85**
Capone, Al, 274, **274,** 276

Capra, Frank, 290
Caraway, Hattie, 279, **279**
Caraway, Thaddeus, 279
Carib Indians, 16
Carnegie, Andrew, 167, 216, **216, 221,** 241
Carnegie, Dale, 283, **283**
Carnegie Steel Company, 241
Carney, William, **184**
Carpetbaggers, 200, **200**
Carrel, Alexis, **319**
Carrier, Willis, 268
Carson, Kit, 189
Carson, Rachel, 333, **333**
Carter, Jimmy, 347, 352, **352,** 367
Carter, Rosalynn, **352**
Cartier, Jacques, 14, **15,** 18, 325
Cartoons, 273
Cartwright, Alexander J., 147
Caruso, Enrico, 276
"Casey at the Bat" (Thayer), 228
Cass, Lewis, 145
Castell, Robert, 36
Castro, Fidel, 330, 333
Catcher in Rye (Salinger), 317
Cathedral of St. John the Divine, 232, **232**
Catlin, George, **31,** 140, 161, **161,** 223
Cattle industry, 162, 171, 198-199, 200, 201, 220
CBS, 285, 318
Censorship:
   in Civil War, 184
   in colonial era, 37
Census, 93
Centennial Exhibition (1876), 212, **212**
Centers for Disease Control, 348
Central Intelligence Agency (CIA), 327, 330
Cermak, Anton, 280, **280**
Cézanne, Paul, 251
Challenger, 350, **350**
Chancellorsville, Battle of, 168
Chaplin, Charlie, 274
Chapman, John, 97, **97**
Charles II, King of England, 26, 31
Charleston, S.C., capture of (1780), 71, 72, **72**
Charter of Privileges (1701), 63
Cherokee Indians, 51, 118, 124, 132, 138, **138,** 191
Cherokee Phoenix, 118
Chesnut, James, Jr., 172
Chesnut, Mary Boykin, 172, **172**
Chevalier, Michel, **133**
Chewing gum, 154, **154**
Chewing tobacco, 120, **120**
Cheyenne Indians, 171, 189
Chicago, Ill.:
   cattle industry and, 200
   Democratic Convention in (1968), 338, **338**
   fire in (1871), 207, **207,** 224-225
   founding of, 70
   railroads and, 159
Chicago Bulls, 351
Chicago *Daily Democratic Press,* 159
Chickasaw Indians, 102, 124
China:

in Korean War, 306, **315,** 317
   U.S. trade with, 94, 161
   in World War II, 296, 305
Chinese-Americans, 202-203, 249
Chinese Exclusion Act (1882), 249
Chivington, John M., 189
Choctaw Indians, 102, 121, 124, 191
Cholera, 132
Christmas trees, 265
Christy, Edwin, 158
Church, Benjamin, **73**
Churchill, Winston, 256, 265, 292, **292,** 301, **303,** 310, **310**
Church of England, 11, 24
Cincinnati Red Stockings, 147, 203
Circus, The, 274
Circuses, 95, 208
Civil rights, 223, 334. *See also* Segregation; Voting rights.
Civil Rights Act (1964), 334, **335, 336, 336**
Civil Service Commission, 217
Civil service reform, 217
Civil War, U.S., 168-191
   Balloon Corps in, 182
   blockading in, 182
   as brothers' war, 176
   casualties in, 177
   draft in, 179, 188
   emigration after, 193
   immigrants in, 183
   spies in, 180, **180,** 181
   summary of, **186**
   uniforms in, 177
   women in, 172, 174, 180
Clanton, Ike, 221
Clark, Edward, 164
Clark, George Rogers, 44, 69, **69**
Clark, M. Lewis, 211
Clark, William, 90, 102, 105, 109, **301**
Clay, Henry, 116, 126, **126,** 129, 145, 156, **156,** 161, 234
Clermont, 107, **107**
Cleveland, Grover, 135, 217, 238, **349,** 365, 366
Clinton, William Jefferson (Bill), **185,** 309, 353, 367
Clinton, DeWitt, 115, 116
Clinton, Sir Henry, 54, 72
Clothing, 177, 291, 312, 344
Cloyce, Sarah, **33**
Coca-Cola, 225, **225,** 309
Cocoanut Grove nightclub, 299, **299**
Cody, William F. (Buffalo Bill), 199, **199,** 208, **208**
Coeur d'Alene fires (1910), 249
Coeur d'Alene Indians, 139
Cohan, George M., **193**
Colbert, Claudette, 290
Cold War, 306, 309, 310, 314, 315, 326, 327, 333, 353
Cole, Theodore, 284
College of William and Mary, 25
Collier's, **245**
Collinson, Peter, 35
Colombia, 242-243
Colonial era, 10-50
   economic conditions in, 12, 14, 18,

21, 27, 29, 41
   religion in, 11-12, 23, 24, 25, 26, **28**
Colonna, Jerry, 298
Colorado, 368
Colter, John, 107
Columbus, Christopher, 10, **10,** 14, **14, 15**
Comanche Indians, 132, 171
Comic strips, 267
Coming and Going of the Pony Express, The (Remington), **167**
Commerce. *See* Economic and business conditions.
Commission on the Status of Women, **335**
Committees of Correspondence, 42, 50, 51
Committee to Re-Elect the President (CREEP), 344-345
Common Sense (Paine), 62, 355
Communism, 158, 262, 323
   and Red Scare of 1919-1920, 258, 262
Compromise of 1850, 127, 156
Compromise of 1877, 213
Computers, 296, **296,** 318, 346
Comstock Lode, 166, **166**
Concord, Battle of, 49, 51, 52, 53, 56
Coney Island, 234, **234, 235**
Congressional Medal of Honor, 184
Congress of Industrial Organizations (CIO), 282
Congress of Racial Equality (CORE), 331
Congress of the Confederation, 80
Connecticut, 38, **80,** 85, 368
Connecticut colony, 12, **24**
Connor, Eugene (Bull), 331
Conrad, Thomas Nelson, 180
Conservationism, environmentalism, 218, 246, 333, 337, 339, 340
Constitution, 111, **111**
Constitution, U.S., 45, 61, 81, 82, 90, 100
   ratification of, 81, **81**
   summary of, 359
Constitutional amendments, 130, 170, 183, 253, 259, 262, **262,** 276, **276**
   Bill of Rights, 45, 61, 81, 82, 85, 359
Constitutional Convention (1787), 80, 81
Continental Congress, 44, 51, **53,** 60, 62, 63, 64, 66, 67, 69, 70, 73, 75, 77
Continental Congress, First (1774), 43, 46, 49, 81, 85
Cook, Jesse, 245
Coolidge, Calvin, 99, **145, 258,** 259, 265, **265,** 267, 271, 290, 366
Cooper, Gary, 269, **273**
Cooper, James Fenimore, 91, 117, **117**
Cooper, Peter, 167, **167**
Cooper Union, 167, **167**
Copley, John Singleton, 115
Corbin, Abel R., 204
Corey, Laura, 245
Corey, William, 245
Cornell University, 239
Cornwallis, Charles, **53,** 66, 72, **73,** 74, 75
Coronado, Francisco Vásquez de, **15,**

120
Corporal punishment, 145
Cosby, William, 37
Costello, Frank, 316, **316**
Cotton, 90, 124, 168, 173
Cotton, John, 25, **28**
Cotton gin, 95
Cowboys, 198-199, **198**
Cox, Archibald, 345
Cox, James M., 262
Craft, Ellen, 153, **153**
Craft, William, 153
Craig, Elijah, 79
Crawford, Jane, 109
Credit cards, 316
Creek Indians, 94, 121, 124, 132, 191, 228
Crick, Francis H., **319**
Crime:
   in colonial era, 34-35, 37
   in nineteenth century, 196, 230
   in twentieth century, 259, 263, 284, 316, 323
Crime in America (Kefauver), 316
Crisis, The (Paine), **65**
Crittenden, George, **176**
Crittenden, Thomas, **176**
Croatan Indians, 19
Crocker, Charles, 175
Crockett, Davy, 136, **136**
Cromwell, Oliver, 56
Crook, George, 226
Crow Indians, 107, 215
Crump, Edward, 248
Crystal Palace Exhibition (1853), 162, **162**
Cuba, 146, 219, 237
Cuban missile crisis (1962), 308, **310, 333, 333**
Cugat, Xavier, 285, 311
Cummings, E. E., 270
Currency:
   in colonial era, 29
   in early republic, 88
   in nineteenth century, 134, 192, 218, 235
Curtis, John B., 154
Curtiss, Glenn, **243**
Cushman, Pauline, **180**
Custer, George Armstrong, 199, 208
Czechoslovakia, 276, 306
Czolgosz, Leon, **190,** 239

D

Dalai Lama, 232
Daley, Richard, 338
Dal Verme, Francesco, **78**
D'Amato, Alphonse, **247**
Dana, Charles, 158
Dare, Virginia, 19
Dark Angel, The, 287
Darwin, Charles, 258
Daughters of Liberty, 58
Daughters of the American Revolution (DAR), 287
Davenport, John, 38
Davie, William Richardson, 87
Davis, Bette, 298

Davis, Jefferson, 168, 172, 176, 179, **180**, 190, **190**
Davis, John, 15
Davis, Varina, 176, 190
Dawes, William, 52
Day of Doom, The (Wigglesworth), 30
D-Day, 300, 301, **303**
Deane, Silas, 61, 68, 69
DeBernardi, Peter, **241**
Debs, Eugene V., 217, 233
Declaration des droits de l'homme et du citoyen (1789), 61
Declaration of Independence (1776), 44, 61, 62, 63, **63**, 356-357
"Declaration of Independence, The" (Trumbull), **63**
Declaration of Sentiments and Resolutions (1848), 152
Deere, John, 125, 137, **137**
Delaware, 62, 69, 81, 368
  in Civil War, 168
Delaware colony, 12
Delaware Indians, 41, 98
De Mille, Cecil B., 287
Democracy in America (Tocqueville), 131, **131**
Democratic National Convention (1968), 338, **338**
Democratic-Republicans, 88, 89
Democrats, 126, 127, 135, 170, 171, 217, 218, 260, 304, 353
Denmark, 261
Densmore, James, 198
Depression, Great, 260-261, 275, 277, **277**, 281
Description of New England, A (Smith), 22
Desert Storm, Operation, 351, **351**
De Smet, Pierre Jean, 139, **139**
De Soto, Hernando, 10, **15**, 17, 102
Deverich, Nat, **273**
Dewey, Thomas, 304
De Wolfe, Elsie, 252, **252**
Diary From Dixie (Chesnut), 172
Dickens, Charles, **120**, 142, **142, 143**
Dickerson, Susanna, 136
Dickinson, Emily, **141**
Diem, Ngo Dinh, **345**
Dietrich, Marlene, 298
DiMaggio, Joe, 279
Diners Club, 316, **316**
Dior, Christian, 312, **312**
Dirksen, Everett, 336
Discovery, Settlement, and Present State of Kentucky, The (Filson), 55
Disney, Walt, 273, 274, 321, **321**
Disneyland, 321, 326
Divorce, 245
Dix, Dorothea, 141, **141**, 218
Dixon, Jeremiah, 46
Dole, Sanford B., 238
Dolls, 325
Donner, George, 150
Donner, Jacob, 150
Donner party, 150, **150**
Dorais, Charles (Gus), 252
Dorr, Thomas, 143, **143**
Douglas, Stephen A., 127, 131, 165, **165**
Douglass, Frederick, 125, 146, **146**

Dow, Neal, 156
Drake, Edwin, 166, **166**
Drake, Sir Francis, 14-15, **15**
Dred Scott v. Sandford, 127, 165
Dreiser, Theodore, 259
Drew, Charles Richard, 291, **291**
Dring, Thomas, **77**
Duchamp, Marcel, 251
Dulles, John Foster, 307
Dunant, Jean-Henri, 180
Du Pont Company, 291
Durant, William Crapo, 244
Durante, Jimmy, 311
Du Sable, Jean Baptiste Pointe, 70, **70**
Dust Bowl, 281, **281**
Dustin, Hannah, 27
Dutch West Indies Company, 26
Dylan, Bob, 332, **332**

E

Earp, Morgan, **220,** 221
Earp, Virgil, 220, **221**
Earp, Wyatt, 220-221, **220**
Earth Day (1970), 340, **340**
Earthquakes, 110, 207, 209, 245
Easty, Mary, 33, **33**
Eaton, Nathaniel, 25
Economic and business conditions:
  in colonial era, 12, 14, 18, 21, 27, 29, 38, 41
  in early twentieth century, 204, 216-217, 241, 250, 251, 254, 259, 260, 275
  Great Depression and, 260-261, 275, 277, **277**, 281
  in late eighteenth century, 87, 88, 90, 94, 97
  in nineteenth century, 90-91, 107, 109, 117, 124, 149, 161, 171, 182, 184, 204, 215, 216-217, 218, 220, 236
  in post-World War II era, 307, 309, 316, 349, 350
  See also specific industries.
Eden, Charles, 34
Edison, Thomas, 93, 138, 205, **205,** 272, 276
Edmonds, Sarah Emma, 174
Ed Sullivan Show, 335
Education, 87, 91, 125, 154, 167, 258
  in colonial era, 25
  corporal punishment in, 145
  segregation in, 320, **320**
  women and, 116, 137, 206, 232, 239
Einstein, Albert, **253, 289**
Eisenhower, Dwight D., 276, 278, 279, **330**
  farewell address of, 363
  as president, 102, 307, 308, 315, 318, **318**, 321, 323, 324, 325, 330, 341
  in World War II, 300, **300, 303**
Eisenstaedt, Alfred, 282
Elcano, Juan de, **15**
Electricity, 39, 216
Electric lights, 205
Electronic numerical integrator and

computer (ENIAC), 296
Elevators, 216
Elizabeth, Queen of Belgium, 310
Elizabeth I, Queen of England, 11, 19
Elizabeth II, Queen of England, 325, 346
Ellington, Duke, 258
Elliot, Jesse Duncan, 112
Ellis Island, 231, **231**
Ellsworth, Elmer, 173, **173**
Ely, Ben-Ezra Stiles, **149**
Emancipation Proclamation (1863), 129, 169, 183, **183**
Emergency Banking Relief Act (1933), 281
Emerson, Ralph Waldo, 125, 163
Emma, Queen of Hawaii, 195, **195**
Emmet, Dan, 178
Enders, John F., **319**
Engels, Friedrich, 158
England, 11, 14-15, 18, 19-40
  See also Great Britain.
ENIAC (electronic numerical integrator and computer), 296
Enlightenment, 42
Environmentalism, conservationism, 218, 246, 333, 337, 339, 340
Environmental Protection Agency (EPA), 333, 339, 340
Epitaphs, 141
Equal Pay Act (1963), **335**
Equal Rights Amendment (ERA), 335, **335**
E. Remington & Sons, 198
Erie Canal, 115, **115**
Eskimos, 10
Esteban (slave), 17, **27**
Ether, 143, **160**
Etiquette (Post), 265, **265**
Evans, John, 189
Everett, Edward, **185**
Evolution, 258
Exodusters, 214, **214**
Experiments and Observations on Electricity (Franklin), 39
Exploration, 10-11, 14-17, **15**, 30, 31, 94, 105, 106, 109, 148, 203, 275
Explorer I, 324

F

Fairbanks, Douglas, **141**, 245, **245, 274**
Fair Deal, 306
Fair Labor Standards Act (1938), 251
Fair Oaks, Battle of, 182
Fala (dog), 301
Faneuil, Peter, 38
Faneuil Hall, 38, **38**
Farmer, James, 331
Farmers' Alliance, 217
Farnsworth, Philo, 288
Farragut, David, 169, 187, **187**
Fashion, 312, 344
Faulkner, William, 278
Faut, Jean, 300
Federal Bureau of Investigation (FBI), 248, **248**
"Federal City," 93

Federal Communications Commission (FCC), 289
Federalist, The (Madison, Hamilton, and Jay), 81
Federalists, 45, 82, 88, 89, 98, 100, 101, 103, 104, 110
Female Anti-Slavery Society, 152
Feminine Mystique (Friedan), 335
Feminism, 335. *See also* Women; Women's rights.
Ferdinand II, King of Aragon, 14
Ferguson, Patrick, 66
Fermi, Enrico, 93, **289,** 293
Ferraro, Geraldine, **335,** 349
Fiedler, Arthur, 346
Field, Cyrus, 195
Field, Marshall, 215
Fields, W. C., **193**
Filibusters, 247, **247**
Filling stations, 244
Fillmore, Millard, 135, 161, 365
Film industry, 247, **247**, 268, 269, 271, 272, 274, 287, 290, **291**
Filson, John, 55
Finland, 256
Finney, Charles G., 128, **128, 129**
Fires, 199, 207, 209, 224-225, 249, 299
Fishing, 14
Fisk, James, 204
Fitzgerald, F. Scott, 259, 269, 270, **270**
Fitzgerald, Zelda Sayre, 270
Fitzpatrick, Thomas, 142
Flags, 57, **57**
Flamingo Hotel, 311, **311**
Flanagan, Edward J., 255
Flanner, Janet, 270
Flathead Indians, 139
Floods, 229
Florida, 10, 13, 16, 18, 368
  in Civil War, **177**
Florida land boom, 268, **268, 269**
Flying saucers, 313, **313**
FM radio, 289
Folk music, 332
Food and nutrition, 16, 138
Food-processing industry, 246
Football, 252, 338
Ford, Antonia, **180**
Ford, Gerald R., 299, 346, 367
Ford, Henry, 93, 216, 254, 267
Ford Motor Company, 254
Forster, E. M., 273
Fort Mifflin, Battle of, 73
Fort Ticonderoga, Battle of (1775), 49, **49,** 73
Fort Ticonderoga, Battle of (1777), 67, 75
Fort William and Mary, capture of (1774), 51
Foster, Bill, **273**
Foster, Stephen, 158, **158**
Fourteen Points, 362
Four Tops, 327
Fox, William, 272
France, 86, 88, 96, 119, 348
  American Revolution and, 61, 66, 69, 74, 75, 77
  in Cold War, 314
  exploration and colonization by, 10, 12, 16, 18, 22, 30, 31, 34

in French and Indian War, 40, **41**
  Louisiana Purchase from, 89-90, 103
  in World War I, 254, 257, **257**
  in World War II, 261, 288, 289, 300, 301, **303**
Francis I, King of France, 16
Franciscan missionaries, 48
Francisco, Peter, 73, **73**
Francis Ferdinand, Archduke of Austria, **257**
Franklin, Benjamin, 35, 39, **39**, 42, 62, 63, **63**, 68, 69, **69**, 77, **77**, 78, **80**, 84, **253**
Franklin, state of, 78, **78**
Fraunces, Samuel, **27**
Frazee, H. Harrison, 263
Fredericksburg, Battle of, 168, 182, 183
Freedom Riders, 331, **331**
Free-Soil Party, 127, 135
Frémont, John Charles, 148
French and Indian War, 13, 40, **40, 41**, 42, 55
French Revolution, 95
Frick, Henry Clay, 204
Friedan, Betty, 335, **335**
Frobisher, Sir Martin, 15, **15**
Frontier, westward expansion, 55, 80, 89-90, 142, **146**, 148, 150, 155, 194, 198-199, 206, 211, 219, 220-221, 231
Frost, Robert, **141**, 329, **329**
Fuchida, Mitsuo, 292, 293
Fugitive Slave Law (1850), 127, 156, 160
Fuller, Ida Mae, 290, **290**
Fulton, Robert, **90,** 107
Funk, Casimir, **319**
Fur trade, **12**, 18, 40, 41, 70, 90, 97, 109, 133, **133**

G

Gable, Clark, 290, 298
Gadsden Purchase, 126
Gagarin, Yuri, 331
Gage, Thomas, 51, 64
Gallo, Joey, 140
Gallup, George Horace, 289
Gálvez, Bernardo de, 74, **74**
Gambling, 134, **134,** 311
Game shows, 326
Gandhi, Mohandas K., 282
Gardening, 35
Gardner, Isabella Stewart, **221**
Garfield, James A., **190**, 217, 365
Garland, Judy, 193
Garrard, James, 79
Garrison, Jim, 334
Garrison, William Lloyd, 125, 130, **130**
Gaspée, 43, 50, **50**
Gates, Horatio, **58**, 72, **72,** 76
Gaynor, Janet, 274, **274**
Gehrig, Lou, 288, **288**
General Electric, 289
General Motors Corporation, 244
Genêt, Edmond Charles, 95, **95**
Geological Survey, U.S., 203
George II, King of England, 36

George III, King of England, 13, 35, 41, 43, **43**, 44, 50, 60, 62, **62**, 63, 66, 100
Georgia, **80**, 85, 94, 368
  in Civil War, 169, **177**, 187
Georgia colony, 12, 36, 43
German-Americans, 12, 125, 183
Germantown, Battle of, 73
Germany:
  in World War I, 219, 254, 256, 257, **257**, 258, 310
  in World War II, 261, 270, 285, 288, 292, 294, 298, 300, **303**
  between the world wars, 258
Germany, East, 306, **310**, 314
Germany, West, 314, 333
Geronimo, Apache chief, 226, **226**
Gershwin, George, 258, 266, **266**
Gershwin, Ira, 266
Gettysburg, Battle of, 169, 184-185, **185**
Gettysburg Address (1863), **185**, 361
Ghent, Treaty of (1814), 110, **111**, 114
Gibbon, John, 215
Gibson, Charles Dana, 282
Gift-giving, 102
Gilbert, Deborah Champion, 52
Gillette, King Camp, 234
Girl Scouts, 250, **250**
Glenn Miller Story, The, 302
Glorious Revolution, 32
Goddard, Robert H., 270, **270**
Godey, Louis, 128
Godey's Lady's Book, 128, **128**, 186
Golden Gate International Exposition (1939), 286
Gold market, 204
Gold mining, 166
Gold rushes:
  Alaska, 197
  California, 111, 151, 152, **152**, 153, **153**
Gold standard, 235
Goldstein, Joseph L., **319**
Goldwyn, Sam, 287, **287**
Goldwyn Pictures, 287
Golf, 277
Gompers, Samuel, 217, 227, **227**
Gone With the Wind (Mitchell), 182
Goodman, Benny, 258-259, 285, **285**
Goodyear, Charles, 93
Gordy, Berry, 327, **327**
Gore, Thomas, 247
Gorman, Margaret, 264
Gorrie, John, 159, **159**
Gould, Jay, 204, 216
Grable, Betty, 295, **295**, 298
Graham, Sheilah, 332
Graham, Sylvester, 138, **138**
Grammatical Institute of the English Language, A (Webster), 78
Grand Canyon, 203
Grand Ole Opry, 269, **269**
Grange (Patrons of Husbandry), 206, **206**, 217
Grant, Cary, **193**
Grant, Ulysses S., **145**, 198, 201, 365
  in Civil War, 169-170, 184, 189, **189**
  as president, 99, 102, 171, 176, 204,

212, 230
Grasse, Francois Joseph Paul de, 74, **74**, 75
Grasshopper plague (1874), 210, **210**, **211**
Grassland fires, 199
Grateful Dead, 340
Graves, Thomas, 74
Gray, Harold, 267
Gray, Robert, 94, **94**
Great American Desert, 120, **120**
Great Awakening, Second, 101
Great Britain, 86, 88, 95, 96, 125
  Civil War and, 168, 173
  in Cold War, 314
  in French and Indian War, 40, 41, **41**
  territorial disputes with, 94, 126, 140
  in War of 1812, 91, 110-114, 121
  in World War I, 219, 254, 256, 257
  in World War II, 261, 288, 289, 294, **294, 303**, 305
  See also American Revolution; England.
Great Depression, 260-261, 275, 277, **277**, 281
Great Eastern, 185, **195**
Great Gatsby, The (Fitzgerald), 270, **270**
Great Seal of the United States, 75, **75**
Great Society, 308
Great Train Robbery, The, **273**
Greek Revival architecture, 103
Greeley, Horace, 138, 140, 158, 162, 190
Green Bay Packers, 338
Greene, Catherine, 95
Greenhow, Rose O'Neal, **180**
Greenland, 10
Green Mountain Boys, 49
Greenwood, John, 83
Green-Wood Cemetery, 140, **140**
Griffith, D. W., 247
Griggs, William, 33
Guadalcanal, **305**
Guam, 219, 237, **305**
Guerrière, 111, **111**
Guilford Courthouse, Battle of, **53**, 73
Guinan, Texas, 276
Guiteau, Charles, **190**
Guthrie, Woody, 332
Gwin, William M., 155

Haig, Alexander, 345
Haiti, 352
Hale, Nathan, **57, 73**
Hale, Sarah Josepha, 128, 186
Hallidie, Andrew Smith, 209
Halsted, William Stewart, **155**
Hamilton, Alexander, 45, 81, 85, 86, 88, 93, 96, 98, 100, 104, **104**
Hamilton, Andrew, 37, **37**
Hamilton, Henry, 69
Hamilton, Philip, 104
Hanaway, Frank, **273**
Hancock, Dorothy Quincy, **64**

Hancock, John, 44, 54, 60, 63, **63**, 64, **64**
Handler, Elliot, 325
Handler, Ruth, 325
Handy, William Christopher, 248, **248**
Hanna, Marcus Alonzo, 236, **236**, 240
"Happy Birthday to You" (Hill and Hill), 232
Hard Day's Night, A, 335
Harding, Warren G., 99, **190, 258,** 259, 262, 264, **349**, 366
Harlan, John Marshall, 235, **235**
Harlow, Jean, **260**
Harper's, 234
Harper's Ferry, Va., 127
Harper's New Monthly Magazine, 162, **162**
Harper's Weekly, 213
Harrison, Benjamin, 99, 230, 366
Harrison, George, 335, **335**
Harrison, William Henry, 112, 126, **126, 145,** 176, **190,** 364
Hart, Nancy, 59
Harvard, John, 25
Harvard University, 25, **25**, 37, 93
Hastings, Lansford, 150
Havel, Vaclav, 232
Hawaii, 97, 195, 219, 238, **238**, 324, **324,** 368
Hawley-Smoot Act (1930), 260
Hawthorne, Nathaniel, 32, 91, 125
Hay, George, 269, **269**
Hay, John, 237
Hayes, Rutherford B., **145**, 171, 213, **213,** 214, 365
Haymarket Square incident (1886), 217, **217**
Hays, Mary Ludwig, 59, **59**
Health and medicine:
  in American Revolution, 65, 77
  in Civil War, 180
  in nineteenth century, 109, 132, 143, 154, **155,** 159, 160
  in twentieth century, 291, 302, 315, 319, **319,** 348
Hearst, William Randolph, **221,** 228, 237
Heifetz, Jascha, 266
Hemingway, Ernest, 259, 270, 278, **307**
Henderson, Fletcher, 285
Henderson, Richard, 51
Hendrix, Jimi, 340
Henke, Milburn H., 294, **294**
Hennessy, David, 230
Henry, Joseph, 92
Henry, Patrick, 42, 47, **57,** 61, 69, 82, **82, 141,** 354-355
Henry VII, King of England, 14
Herbert, Victor, **266**
Hershfield, Leo, 301
Heth, Joice, 208
Highway Beautification Act (1965), 337
Highways, roads, 90, 102, 105, 283, 321, **321**
Hill, Mildred, 232, **232**
Hill, Patty Smith, 232, **232**

Hill, Virginia, 311, 316
Hill, William, Jr. (Red), **240**
Hindenburg, 284, **284**
Hippocrates, 232
Hirohito, Emperor of Japan, 305
Hiroshima, atomic bombing of (1945), 261, 293, 304, **305**
History of the Rise, Progress, and Termination of the American Revolution (Warren), 104
Hitchcock, Alfred, 332
Hitler, Adolf, 261, 285, 288
Hoar, Edward, 148
Hoban, James, 99
Hoffa, Jimmy, 323, **323**
Hoffman, Matilda, 108
Holland, Clifford, 272-273
Holland Tunnel, 272-273, **272**
Holliday, John (Doc), 220, 221
Holmes, Oliver Wendell, Jr., **253**
Holmes, Oliver Wendell, Sr., 24
"Home! Sweet Home!," 178
Homestead Act (1862), 171, 179, 206
Hong Kong, **305**
Hoover, Herbert, 99, 259, 260, 275, 276, 277, 278, 280, **349**, 366
Hoover, J. Edgar, 248
Hoover, Lou, 280
Hope, Bob, 298, **298**
Hopkins, Mark, 175
Hopkins, Samuel, 92
Hopkins, Stephen, 63
Hopkinson, Francis, 57
Hopper, William DeWolf, 228
Horse racing, 211
Hosford, Mary, 137, **137**
Houdini, Harry, **193**
House of the Seven Gables, The (Hawthorne), 32
Houston, Sam, 118, 132, **132,** 136
Howard, Otis, 214, **215**
Howe, Elias, 164
Howe, Frederic C., 218
Howe, Julia Ward, 178, 373
Howe, Richard, 64
How to Win Friends and Influence People (Carnegie), 283, **283**
Hudson, Henry, 16, 20-21, **20**
Hudson River "watch chain," 68
Hudson's Bay Company, 18, 111
Hull, Isaac, 111
Humphrey, Hubert H., 338
Hungary, 306
Hunt, Wilson Price, 109
Hunting, 208
Huntington, Collis P., 175
Huron Indians, 11
Hurricanes, 286, **286**
Hurst, M. T., **293**
Huss, Pierre, 285
Hussein, Saddam, 351
Hussey, Christopher, 38
Hutchinson, Anne, 12, 25
Hutchinson, Thomas, 46, 49
Hutchinson, William, 25

I

IBM, 346
Ice making, 159, **159**
Ickes, Harold L., 287, **287**
Idaho, 368
Idaho fires (1910), 249, **249**
Illinois, 80, **80**, 369
I Love Lucy, 307
Immigration, 12, 125, 183, 231, **231**, 249
Impressment, 106
Inca Indians, 10
Indentured servants, 13
Independence Hall, 37, **60**
India, 296
Indiana, 80, **80**, 369
Indian Removal Act (1830), 138
Indians, American, 97, 102, 105, 120, 161, 167, 203, 259
  American Revolution and, 41
  and European exploration and colonization, 10, 11, 12, 16, 17, 18, 19, **19,** 20, **20,** 21-22, **21, 22,** 23, 24, 25, 27, **27, 30,** 34
  in French and Indian War, 40, 41, **41**
  missionaries to, 48, 139
  Oklahoma lands ceded by, 228
  U.S. expansion and, 51, 78, 80, 90, 112, 117, 124, 142, 152, 171
  U.S. removal of, 121, 124, 138
  U.S. treaties with, 94, 121
  U.S. wars with, 112, 171, 189, 211, 214-215, 219, 226
  in War of 1812, 121
  See also specific tribes.
Indigo, 38, 39, **39**
Industrialization, 87, 90-91, 124, 171
Influenza pandemic (1918-1919), 256
Institute of Radio Engineers, 289
Interior decorating, 252
International Brotherhood of Teamsters, 323, **323**
International Exhibition of Modern Art (1913), 251, **251**
Interstate Commerce Commission, 217, 250, 331
Intolerable Acts (Great Britain; 1774), 43
Inventions, 90, 205
Iowa, 369
Iran hostage crisis, 347, **347**
Iraq, 351, **351**
Iredell, James, 92
Irish-Americans, 12, 125, 183, 202
"Iron curtain," 310
Iroquois Indians, **27,** 41
Irving, Washington, 91, 108, **108**
Isabella I, Queen of Castille, 14
Italian-Americans, 230
Italy, 10, 257, 261, **303**
It Happened One Night, 290
Iwo Jima, 304, **304, 305**

J

Jackson, Andrew, 26, 99, 132, 145, **145** 364
  inauguration of, 123, **123**
  as president, 38, 102, 109, 125, 126, 132, 134, 135
  in presidential elections, 91, 129
  in War of 1812, 91, **102**, 114, **114,** 121
Jackson, Charles, 143
Jackson, Thomas J. (Stonewall), 175, **180**
Jackson 5, 327
Jacobs, Joseph, 225
James, Frank, 196
James, Harry, 285
James, Jesse, **141,** 196
James I, King of England, 20, 21
James II, King of England, 32
Jamestown colony, 11, **11**, 19, 20, 21, **21,** 22
Jannings, Emil, 274
Japan, 144, 161, 346
  in World War II, 261, 292-293, 296-297, 302, 304, 305, **305**
Jaworski, Leon, 345
Jay, John, 77, **77,** 81
Jay Cooke & Company, 204, **204**
Jazz Singer, The, 272, **272, 273,** 274
Jefferson, Thomas, 42, 79, 82, 85, 91, 93, 99, 115, 116, 121, **301,** 346, 364
  American Revolution and, 52, 58
  and Declaration of Independence, 61, 62, **63**
  inaugural address of, 360
  on North vs. South, **86**
  as president, 89-90, 99, 101, 102, 103, 105, 106, 108
  in presidential elections, 98, 100, **100,** 101, **101**
  as secretary of state, 86, 88, 92
Jenney, William Le Baron, 224, **225**
Jerome, Chauncey, **114**
Jesuit missionaries, 30, 139
Jews, Sephardic, 24
JFK, 334
J. L. Hudson, 268
Jobs, Steven, 346, **346**
Jogues, Isaac, 26
Johnson, Andrew, 195, 197, 201, **201,** 365
Johnson, Anthony, **27**
Johnson, Claudia (Lady Bird), 337, **337**
Johnson, Eliza, 195
Johnson, Lyndon B., 308, 329, 334, 336, **336,** 337, 338, 341, 367
Johnson, Philip, **225**
Johnson, William, 41
Johnston, David A., 348
Johnstown flood, 229, **229**
Joliot, Frédéric, **289**
Jolliet, Louis, 30
Jolson, Al, **193, 272, 273**
Jones, Bobby, 277, **277**
Jones, John Paul, 44, **57,** 70, **70**
Joplin, Janis, 340
Jordan, Michael, 351, **351**

Joseph, Nez Percé chief, 214-215, **215**
Jouett, John, 52
Journal of a Residence on a Georgian Plantation (Kemble), 139
Joyce, James, 258
Juan Carlos I, King of Spain, 346
Judson, E.Z.C., 199
Judson, Whitcomb, 93
Jumonville, sieur de, 40
Jungle, The (Sinclair), 246

K

Kalispel Indians, 139
Kamehameha I, King of Hawaii, 97
Kamehameha IV, King of Hawaii, 195
Kamehameha V, King of Hawaii, 195
Kamenshek, Dorothy (Kammie), 300
Kandinsky, Wassily, 251
Kansas, 127, 163, 369
Kansas City Chiefs, 338, **338**
Kansas-Nebraska Act (1854), 127
Kapital, Das (Marx), 158
Kefauver, Estes, 316
Keith, Benjamin Franklin, 193
Kelley, Oliver Hudson, 206
Kellogg, Mary, 137
Kelly, Grace, 332, **332**
Kemble, Fanny, 139, **139**
Kendall, George, 151
Kendrick, John, 94
Kennedy, Caroline, 329, **329**
Kennedy, Jacqueline, 334
Kennedy, John F., **185, 190,** 231, 307, 308, 328, **328,** 329, **329, 330, 330,** 331, 333, 334, **335,** 336, 367
  inaugural address of, 363
Kennedy, John F., Jr., 329, **329**
Kennedy, Robert Cobb, 188
Kennedy, Robert F., 308, 323, 331, 338
Kent State University, 341, **341**
Kentucky, 51, **80,** 369
  in Civil War, 168, 169
Kentucky Derby, 211, **211**
Kerr, Robert, 26
Key, Francis Scott, 113, 373
Keystone Kops, 247
Khalkhali, Sadegh, **347**
Khomeini, Ruhollah, 347
Khrushchev, Nikita, 324, 326, **326,** 327, 328, 333
Kilroy, 305
Kilroy, Francis J., 305
Kilroy, James J., 305
Kimmel, Husband E., 292-293
King, Martin Luther, Jr., 307, 308, 334, **334, 336**
King, Richard, 201, **201**
King, Rodney, 336
King George's War, 12
King William's War, 12
Kissinger, Henry A., 308
Kiowa Indians, 171
Kit Carson, **273**
Knickerbocker's History of New York (Irving), 108
Knight, Tobias, 34

Knights of Labor, 217
Knox, Frank, 293
Knox, Henry, 55, **55,** 86
Knox, Thomas, 184
Kolleck, Teddy, 232
Korean War, 306, **310,** 315, **315,** 341
Kosciuszko, Tadeusz, 44, 67, **67**
Krupa, Gene, 285
Ku Klux Klan, 171, 258, 320
Kurys, Sophie, 300
Kuwait, 351, **351**

L

Labor conditions, 254, 261
Labor Department, U.S., 227
Labor legislation, 251
Labor movement, 125, 217, 227, 261, 282, **282,** 323
  strikes and, 214, 233, **233**
Laboulaye, Édouard de, 226
Lady Washington, 94
Lafayette, Marie Adrienne de, **66**
Lafayette, marquis de, 38, 44, 66, **66,** 71, 79, 121, **121,** 144
Laffite, Jean, 114
La Follette, Robert, Sr., 247, **247**
La Guardia, Fiorello, 24, 98, 297
Lamarr, Hedy, 295
Lancaster, Burt, 298
Landrum, Roger, **330**
Langford, Frances, 298, **298**
Langley, Samuel P., 243
La Salle, Robert Cavelier, sieur de, 31, **31**
Last Command, The, 274
Las Vegas, Nev., 311, **311**
Latrobe, Henry, 103, **103**
Laughing gas, 143
Lazarus, Emma, 372
Leach, Bobby, **240**
League of Nations, 258
Leaves of Grass (Whitman), 163
Lee, Arthur, 61, 69
Lee, Henry, 96
Lee, Richard Henry, 45, 62, 69
Lee, Robert E., 168, 169, 170, 176, 178, 179, 181, 184, 185, 189, **189,** 190, 191, **191,** 201, 271
Legal system:
  in colonial era, **24,** 28-29, 37
  See also Supreme Court, U.S.
Legal Tender Act (1862), 192
Leisler, Jacob, 32, **32**
Leland, John, 102
LeMayeur, Jean Pierre, 83
Le Moyne de Morgues, Jacques, **19**
Lend-Lease Act (1941), **303**
L'Enfant, Pierre Charles, 99
Lennon, John, 335, **335**
Leonardo da Vinci, **243**
Let's Dance, 285
Levi Strauss & Co., 344
Levitt, William, 313, **313**
Levittown, N.Y., 313
Lewinsky, Monica S., 353
Lewis, John L., 282, **282**
Lewis, Mercy, 33
Lewis, Meriwether, 90, 102, 105, 109,

301
Lewis, Oliver, 211, **211**
Lewis, Sinclair, 218, 259, 278, **278**
Lexington, Battle of, 49, 51, 52, 53, 56
Liberal Republican Party, 135
Liberator, 125, 130
Liberty Bell, 63
Life, 282, **282,** 286, 312
Life and Adventures of Martin Chuzzlewit, The (Dickens), 142, **143**
Life and Memorable Actions of George Washington, The (Weems), 98
Life on the Mississippi (Twain), 198
Lilienthal, Otto, 243
Liliuokalani, Queen of Hawaii, 238, **238**
Lillehei, Clarence W., **319**
Lincoln, Abraham, 26, 92, 102, 131, **145,** 169, 173, 175, 176, **181,** 182, **185,** 186, **189,** 232, **301,** 349
  arrival of, in Washington, 172, **172**
  assassination of, 190, **190**
  emancipation and, 168, 183, **183**
  Gettysburg Address of, **185,** 361
  "house divided" speech of, 360-361
  in presidential elections, 127, 165, **165,** 167, 170
Lincoln, Mary Todd, 176
Lincoln, Tad, 102
Lind, Jenny, 208
Lindbergh, Charles A., **243,** 272, **272**
Linnaeus, Carolus, 35
Literature:
  in nineteenth century, 91, 108, 117, 125, 148, 157, 186, 224
  in twentieth century, 242, 258, 259, 270, 278, 317
Little Orphan Annie, 267, **267**
Little Richard, 335
Little Women (Alcott), 186
Livingston, Robert, **63,** 83, 103, 107
Locke, John, 42
Loco Focos, 135, **135**
Lombardi, Vince, 338
London, Jack, 242, **242, 245**
London Company, 11
Long, Crawford W., 143, **155**
Long, Huey P., **247,** 279, **279**
Long, Stephen H., 120
Longfellow, Henry Wadsworth, 52
Long Island Express hurricane (1938), 286
Los Alamos, N. Mex., 293
Los Angeles, Calif.:
  1965 riots in, 336
  1991 riots in, 336
Lost Generation, 270
Louis XIV, King of France, 31
Louis XV, King of France, 22
Louis XVI, King of France, 66
Louisiana, 38, 369
  in Civil War, **177**
Louisiana Purchase, 89-90, 103, **103,** 105, 197
Lovejoy, Elijah, 125
Low, Juliette, 250, **250**
Low, Seth, 222
Low, William Mackay, 250
Lowe, Thaddeus, 182, **182**

Lowell, James Russell, 24
Lucas, Eliza, 38, 39
Lucas, George, 39
Luce, Henry, 282
Ludington, Sybil, 52, **52**
Lusk, R. D., **281**
Lussier, Jean, **240**
Luxembourg, 261

M

MacArthur, Douglas, 278-279, 297, 315, 317, **317**
Macheca, Joseph P., **230**
Machin, Thomas, 68
Maclay, William, 85, **85**
Macy, Rowland Ussey, 215
Macy's, 215
Madison, Dolley, 108, **108,** 113, **113**
Madison, James, 45, 80, 81, 85, 89, 91, 99, 108, **108,** 113, 121, 364
Madison, Payne, 108
Mafia, 230
Magazines, 128, 282
Magellan, Ferdinand, **15**
Maine, 116, 140, 156, 369
Maine, **219,** 237, **237**
Main Street (Lewis), 278
Malaya, **305**
Mall of America, 322
Mallory, Stephen, 178
Malone, Washington, 162
Manassas. *See* Bull Run, First Battle of; Bull Run, Second Battle of.
Mandela, Nelson, 232
Manet, Edouard, **173**
Manhattan, 38
Manhattan Project, 293
Manifest Destiny, 145, 146
Manjiro, 144, **144**
Mann, Horace, 145, **145**
Mann, Matthew D., 239
Mansions, **221**
Manteo, Croatan chief, 19
Map of Virginia, A (Smith), 21
Mardi Gras, 164
Marion, Francis, 71, **71**
Maris, Roger, **263**
Marnie, 332
Marquette, Jacques, 30
Marshall, George C., 293, 304, 306, 317
Marshall, James Wilson, 151, 152
Marshall, John, 63, 89, 100, **100,** 123
Marshall, Thurgood, 320
Marshall Field's, 215
Marshall Plan, 304, 306
Martin, Edward Sandford, 282
Martin, Joseph, **71**
Martin, Lori, **241**
Martin, Robert M., 188
Marx, Groucho, 193
Marx, Karl, 158
Marx Brothers, 193
Mary II, Queen of England, 32
Maryland, 93, 369
  in Civil War, 168, 181
Maryland colony, 21, **24,** 46

Masaryk, Tomás, 276
*M*A*S*H*, 315
Mason, Charles, 46
Mason, George, 61, **61,** 85
Mason, Richard B., 152
Mason, Samuel, 102
Mason Dixon Line, 46
Massachusetts, 79, **80,** 85, 125, 145, 299, 369
Massachusetts colony, 11-12, 23, **24,** 27, 29, 33, 38, 43
Massachusetts Magazine, 38
Massasoit, Wampanoag chief, **22**
Mather, Cotton, 33
Matisse, Henri, 251, **251**
Matranga, John, **230**
Mattel toy company, 325
Matthews, John, 140
Mauchly, John, 296
Mauldin, Bill, 305
Maurer, Katherine, 249
Maximilian, Emperor of Mexico, 193
Maya Indians, 10
Mayer, Louis B., 274
Mayflower Compact (1620), **11,** 23, 354
Maynard, Robert, 35, **35**
McAuliffe, Christa, 350
McCarthy, Eugene, 338
McCarthy, Joseph, 307, 323, **323**
McCartney, Paul, 335, **335**
McClellan, George B., 180, 181
McClernand, John, **181**
McCormick, Cyrus, 93, 125, 131, **131,** 162
McCoy, Joseph G., 198, 200
McCulloch v. *Maryland*, 89
McDowell, Ephraim, 109, **109**
McDowell, Irwin, 175
McDowell, Jane, 158
McGillivray, Alexander, 94
McGovern, George, 344
McGraw, John, 242
McGready, Jim, 101
McGregor, John, 136
McIntire, Rufus, 140
McKinley, William, 102, **190,** 218, 219, 235, 236, 238, 239, **239,** 240, 366
McNamara, Frank, 316
Meade, George, 184, 185
Meagher, Thomas, 183
Medicine. *See* Health and medicine.
Meet the Beatles, 335
Mellon, Andrew, 275
Melville, Herman, 125, 157, 234
Memphis *Free Speech*, 223
Mencken, H. L., 267, **267,** 271
Menéndez de Avilés, Pedro, 18
Mental institutions, 141, **141**
Mercer, Asa, 194
Merrimack, 178-179, **178-179**
Methodists, 101
Meuse-Argonne campaign, 257, **257**
Mexican-American War, 145, **151,** 189
Mexico, 10, 111, 117, 118, 126, 146, 148, 193
Michigan, 80, **80,** 369
Michtom, Morris, 241
Mickey Mouse, **273**
Midway, Battle of, 261, 296-297, **297,**

305
Miles, Nelson, 226
Milestone, Lewis, 274
Millennium, 353
Miller, Glenn, 302-303, **302**
Minimum wage, 251
Minnesota, 369
Minutemen, 53
Miranda v. *Arizona*, 318
Miss America pageant, 264, **264**
Missionaries, 10
    Franciscan, 48
    Jesuit, 30, 139
Mississippi, **80,** 192, 369
    in Civil War, **177**
Mississippi River, 30
Missouri, 91, 116, 370
    in Civil War, 168, 169
Missouri Compromise (1820), 91, 116, 127
Mr. Smith Goes to Washington, 290, **290**
Mistick Krewe of Comus, 164
Mitchell, Archie, 302
Mitchell, Elsye, 302
Mitchell, Margaret, 182
Mitchell, S. Weir, 210
Mobile Army Surgical Hospital (MASH) units, 315, **315**
Mobile Bay, Battle of, 187
Moby Dick (Melville), 157, **157**
Modoc Indians, 171
Mohammed Reza Shah Pahlavi, 347
Mohawk Indians, 41
Moley, Raymond, 281
Molly Pitcher, 59, **59**
Monastero, Pietro, **230**
Mondale, Walter, 349
Monitor, 178-179, **178-179**
Monmouth, Battle of, 59, 73
Monroe, James, 89, 99, 119, **119,** 121, 364
Monroe Doctrine, 119, 193
Montana, 255, 370
Montgomery, Ala., bus boycott in (1955), 334
Montgomery Ward & Co., 236
Moody, Dwight, 212, **212**
Moore, Annie, 231
Moran, George (Bugs), 274
Morgan, John Pierpont, **204,** 241, **241, 253,** 262
Mormons, 126, 150, **150,** 151, **151**
Morocco, 96, 102
Morris, Esther, 204
Morris, Gouverneur, 81, **81**
Morris, Lewis, 37
Morrison, Herbert, 284, **284**
Morristown, N.J., winter camps in, 71, **71**
Morse, Samuel F. B., 93, 144, **144,** 162
Morse, Wayne, **247**
Morton, James Parks, 232
Morton, William, 143
Moscoso, Luis de, 17
Moses, Robert, 283, **283**
Motown Records, 327
Mott, Lucretia, 152, **152,** 262
Mt. St. Helens, 348, **348**

Movie industry. *See* Film industry.
Mowrer, Edgar, 285
Ms., **335**
Muckrakers, 218
Mugwumps, 135
Muir, John, **246**
Mulhall, Lucille, 238, **238**
Mulhall, Zack, 238
Munday, John David, **241**
Mundus Novus (Vespucci), 15
Murphy, Frank, 282
Murray, William Henry Harrison, 202, **202**
Murrow, Edward R., 285, **285,** 318
Museums, 148
Musgrove, Mary, 36
Music:
    in American Revolution, 56-57
    in early twentieth century, 248, 258-259, 266, 269, 285, 287, 302-303
    in nineteenth century, 158, 178, **178**
    in post-World War II era, 320, 327, 332, 335, 340
Musket-making, 95
Mussolini, Benito, 261
My Day, 287

N

Nagasaki, atomic bombing of (1945), 261, 293, 304, **305**
Napoleon I, Emperor of France, 89-90, 103, 106, 107, 113
Napoleon III, Emperor of France, 193
Narragansett Indians, 12, 24, **30**
Narrative of the Life of Frederick Douglass (Douglass), 146
Nast, Thomas, 213
Natchez Indians, 102
Natchez Trace, 102
Nathan, George Jean, 267
Nation, Carry, **141**
National Aeronautics and Space Administration (NASA), 324, 331, 350
National Association for the Advancement of Colored People (NAACP), 320
National debt, 134
National Defense Act (1916), **257**
National Mobilization to End the War in Vietnam, 338
National Organization for Women (NOW), 335, **335**
National parks, 107, 246
National Reclamation Act (1902), 246
National Recovery Act (NRA) (1933), 261
National Road, 90, 105, **105**
National Weather Service, 230
National Wildflower Research Center, 337
Native Americans. *See* Indians, American.
Nautilus, 319, **319**
Naval Academy, U.S., 147, **147**
Navy, U.S., 96
NBC, 288

Nebraska, 127, 370
Nebraska City News, 199
Negri, Pola, 287
Netherlands, 88, 95, 261
    in colonial era, 12, 18, 26, 28-29
Neutrality Act (1939), 288-289
Nevada, 245, 311, 370
New Amsterdam colony, 12, **24,** 26, 28-29
"New Colossus, The" (Lazarus), 372
New Deal, 260-261, 290, 307, 308
New England, 22, 23, 110
New Hampshire, 65, 81, 370
New Hampshire colony, 12, 49, 51
New Harmony, Ind., 122, **122**
New Jersey, 85, 370
New Jersey colony, 12
New Madrid, Mo., earthquake (1811), 110
New Mexico, 127, 370
New Netherland, 28-29
New Orleans, La., 164, 230
    Battle of, 91, **91,** 114, **114**
New Orleans *Picayune*, 151
Newport, Christopher, 20
Newport Folk Festival (1965), 332
New Republic, **269**
Newspapers:
    in colonial era, 37
    in nineteenth century, 130, 151, 158, 166, 184, 237
Newsweek, 329
New York, N.Y., 98, 135, 140, 213
    in Civil War, 188
    in colonial era, 12, 26, **27,** 28-29, 32
    at millennium, 353
New York, Treaty of (1790), 94
New York City Board of Health, 132
New York colony, 12, 49
New York Commercial Advertiser, **101**
New York *Daily News*, 267
New Yorker, 270, **341**
New York Giants, 242
New York Herald, 253
New York Knickerbockers, 147
New York Museum of Contemporary Crafts, 344
New York State, 62, 65, **80,** 81, 370
New York Stock Exchange, 204, 260, 275, 350
New York Times, The, 140, **194,** 196, 213, 226, **227,** 251, **251,** 252, 266, 270, 285, 286, 289, 305, 318, 320, 335
New York Tribune, 158, 162, 212
New-York Weekly Journal, 37, **37**
New York *World*, 226
New York World's Fair (1939), 286, **286**
New York Yankees, 263, 288
Nez Percé Indians, 171, 214-215, **215**
Niagara Falls, 240, **240-241**
Nicholson, Francis, 32
Nicola, Lewis, **75**
Nijinsky, Vaslav, 276
Nimitz, Chester W., 297
Nipmuck Indians, 12
Nitrous oxide, 143
Nixon, Richard M., **185,** 248, 269, 308, **310,** 328, **328,** 341, 344-345,

344, 345, 367
Niza, Fray Marcos de, 17
Nobel Peace Prize, 334
Nobel Prize, 278, 308
Norse sailors, 10
North, South vs., **86**
North Atlantic Treaty Organization (NATO), 306, **310**
North Carolina, 78, **80,** 81, 370
    in Civil War, **177,** 187
    Constitution and, 45
North Carolina, University of, 87, **87**
North Carolina colony, 12, 21, 51
North Dakota, 370
North Korea, 306, 352
North Pole, 275
North Star, 146, **146**
North Vietnam, 308
Northwest Ordinance (1787), 80
Northwest Passage, 14, 16
Norway, 261, **303**
Notre Dame University, 252
Nuclear power, 319, 347
Nuclear weapons, 261, 293, **293,** 305
    testing of, 311, **311,** 327
    treaties on, **310**
    use of, 261, 293, 304, **305**
Nullification, 126
Nurse, Rebecca, **32**
Nutt, Emma, 228
Nylon, 291, **291**

O

O'Banion, Dion, 274
Oberlin College, 137
Oberon, Merle, **287**
Ocean exploration, 352
Ocean travel, 153, 322
O'Connor, John (Jumping Jack), 188
O'Connor, Sandra Day, 349, **349**
O'Connor, William, 230
Office of Price Administration, 295
Of Plimoth Plantation (Bradford), 23
Oglethorpe, James, 36, **36**
Ohio, 80, **80,** 370
Oil crisis, 309, 344
Oil industry, 166
Oil spills, 339, **339**
"OK," 141, **141**
Okinawa, **305**
Oklahoma, 370
Oklahoma Land Rush (1889), 228-229
Olive Branch Petition (1775), 60
Olympics, 266, 328, **328**
Oman, 102
O'Neill, Eugene, 259, 278
Oppenheimer, J. Robert, 293
Ordway, Lizzie, **194**
Oregon, 370
Oregon Territory, 94, 126, 145, 146
Oregon Trail, 109, 142
Oregon Trail (Bierstadt), **142**
Organization of Petroleum Exporting Countries (OPEC), 344, 347
Organized crime, 316, 323
Orphans, 255
Orteig, Raymond, 272
Osage Indians, 121

Oscars (Academy Awards), 273, 274, **274**
O'Sullivan, John L., 146
O'Sullivan, Maureen, 266
Oswald, Lee Harvey, 334, **334**
Otis, James, 38, **57,** 104
Ottawa Indians, 41
Ottumvo, Vincenzo, 230
Overacker, Robert, **241**
Owen, Robert, 122

P

Pacific Fur Company, 109
Paige, Leroy (Satchel), 279, **279**
Paine, Thomas, **57,** 62, **65,** 355
Painting, 115, 144, 161, 251
Pakenham, Edward, 114
Paley, William S., 285
Palmer, A. Mitchell, 258, 262, **262**
Palmer, Bertha Honoré, **221**
Panama Canal, 219, **219,** 242-243, **243,** 245
Pan-American Exposition (1901), 239
Panic of 1837, **134**
Panic of 1873, 204
Papanicolaou, George N., **319**
Paris, Treaty of (1763), 40, 41
Paris, Treaty of (1783), **53,** 75, 77
Paris Exposition (1889), **205**
Paris Olympics of 1924, 266
Parke, John, 229
Parkerson, William S., 230
Parnell, Harvey, 279
Passenger pigeons, 253, **253**
Pasteur, Louis, 232
Patent Office, U.S., 92, **92**
Patrons of Husbandry (Grange), 206, **206,** 217
Patterson, John, 331
Patterson, Joseph, 267
Paul I, Czar of Russia, 97
Peace Corps, 330, **330**
Peale, Charles Willson, 67, 115
Peale, Titian R., **120**
Pearl Harbor attack, 292-293, **292-293, 305**
Pearson, Richard, 70
Pederson, Ivan, 231
Pedro II, Emperor of Brazil, 212
Peebles, Thomas, **319**
Pemberton, John Styth, 225
Pendergast, Maurice, 251
Penn, Richard, 46
Penn, Thomas, 46
Penn, William, 12, 31, 37, 46, 63
Pennsylvania, 31, 62, 81, 371
  in Civil War, 184-185
Pennsylvania colony, 46
Pennsylvania Turnpike, 321
People's (Populist) Party, **135,** 217-218
Pequot Indians, 12
Peres, Shimon, **352**
Perkins, Carl, 335
Pernin, Peter, **207**
Perry, Matthew C., 161, **161**
Perry, Oliver Hazard, **111,** 112, **112**
Pershing, John, 257

Persian Gulf War, 351
Peshtigo fire (1871), 207, **207**
Petkovich, Jeffery, **241**
Phelan, John, 350
Philadelphia, Pa., 37
Philadelphia Zoo, 210, **210**
Philip II, King of Spain, 18
Philippines, 219, 237, **305**
Phillippe, Deacon, 242
Photography, 156
Photojournalism, 282, **282,** 301, **301,** 304
Piasaw, 30
Picasso, Pablo, 251
Pickerell, W. H., **229**
Pickersgill, Mary, 113
Pickett, George E., 185
Pickford, Mary, 245, **245**
Pierce, Franklin, 365
Pierrepont, Henry E., 140
Pike, Albert, 191
Pike, Zebulon, 90, 106, **106,** 120
Pilgrims, 11, 22, 23
Pinckney, Charles, 39
Pinkerton, Allan, 172, 181, **181,** 196
Pioneers, The, 273
Pipp, Wally, 300
Pirates, 34-35, 96, 233
Pitcairn, John, 53, **53**
Pitt, William, the Elder, 41
Pittsburgh Pirates, 242
Pius IX, Pope, 141
Plants, 35
Plastic Age, The, 269
"Pledge of Allegiance, The," 372
Plessy v. *Ferguson,* 219, 235
Plymouth Colony, 11, **22,** 23
Pocahontas, 20, **20**
Pocket Book of Baby and Child Care, The (Spock), 310
Poe, Edgar Allan, 130, **130, 141**
Poetry:
  in colonial era, 24, **27,** 30, 60
  in nineteenth century, 130, 163, 228
Poland, 288, 306
Polio, 319, **319**
Polk, James K., 102, 109, 126, 145, **145,** 152, 364
Polk, Sarah, **145**
Pompey (Revolutionary soldier), 56, **73**
Ponce de León, Juan, 10, **15,** 16, 18
Pontiac, Ottawa chief, 41
Ponting, Tom Candy, 162
Pony Express:
  eastern, 122, **122**
  western, 167, **167**
Ponzi, Charles, 263, **263**
Poor Richard's Almanack, 39
Pope, John, 180
Populist party, **135,** 217-218
Porter, Edwin S., **273**
Portugal, 10
Post, Emily, 265, **265**
Post, Wiley, **243**
Postal service, 122, 167, 185
Potawatomi Indians, 139
Potomac River, 93, **93**
Powell, John Wesley, 203, **203**
Power failure (1965), 337, **337**
Power of Love, 273

Powers, Francis Gary, 327
Powhatan, Chief, 20
Prall, Elizabeth, 137, **137**
Presbyterian Ministers Fund, 38
Presbyterians, 101
Prescott, Samuel, 52, 54, **57**
Presidents:
  deaths of, **190**
  facts on, 364-367
  gifts to, 102
  nicknames of, **145**
  pets of, 301
  previous occupations of, **349**
Presley, Elvis, 320, **320**
Preston, Thomas, 49
Pride of the Yankees, 288
Princeton, Battle of, **53**
Privateering, 15
Proclamation Act (Great Britain; 1763), 42
Proclamation Line, 41
Progressive Party, 251
Progressives, 218
Prohibition, 259, 274, 276, **276**
Proxmire, William, **247**
Prussia, 40
Public relations, 276
Public Works Administration (PWA), 260
Puerto Rico, 16, 219, 237
Pulitzer, Joseph, 226, 237
Pulitzer Prizes, 278
Pullman, George, 174
Pullman strike (1894), 233, **233**
Puritans, 11-12, 23, 24, 25, **28,** 32, 33
Pushmataha, Choctaw chief, 121
Putnam, Israel, 54, **57**
Pyle, Ernie, 292, **292,** 305

Q

Quakers (Society of Friends), 11, 12, 24, 31
Quartering Act (Great Britain; 1765), 42
Queen Anne's War, 12, 34

R

Rabin, Yitzhak, 346
Rachmaninoff, Sergei, 266
Radio, 269, **269,** 285, 289, 299
Radio Corporation of America (RCA), 288, 289
Railroads, 124-125, 135, 159, **159,** 174, 175, **175,** 179, 200, 201, 206, 216, 228, 250
  robbery on, 196
  segregation on, 223, 235
  strikes on, 214, **214,** 217
  time zones of, 222, **222**
  transcontinental, **174,** 175, 202-203, **202**
Rainier, Prince of Monaco, 332, **332**
Raleigh, Sir Walter, 11, 19, 21
Randolph, Edmund, 86, **86**
Rankin, Jeannette, 255, **255**
Rationing, 295

Rayburn, Sam, 304
Razor blades, 234, **234**
Reagan, Nancy, **349**
Reagan, Ronald, 309, 347, 349, **349,** 350, 367
Reconstruction, 170, 192, 197, 200
Red Scare (1919-1920), 258, 262
Reed, Esther, 58
Reed, James, **150**
Reed, Margaret, **150**
Reformation, 11
Reform movement, 217, 218
Rehnquist, William, 349
Religion:
  in colonial era, 11-12, 23, 24, 25, 26, **28**
  in nineteenth century, 101, 128, **129,** 212
  in twentieth century, 258
Religious freedom, 24
Remington, Frederic, **167**
Remotely operated vehicles (ROV's), 352
Reno, John, 196
Renquist, Chief Justice William H., 353
Republicans, 127, 170, 171, 258, 259, 260, 307
Republicans, Jeffersonian, 89, 98, 100, 101, 103
Republicans, radical, 201
Revere, Paul, 47, 49, 51, 52, **52, 53,** 76, **76**
Revolutionary War. *See* American Revolution.
Rezanov, Nicholas, 111
Rhapsody in Blue (Gershwin), 266
Rhode Island, 24, 81, 143, **143,** 371
  Constitution and, 85
Rhode Island colony, 37, 50
Rhodes, James, 341
Ribaut, Jean, 18
Ribicoff, Abraham, 338
Rice, Grantland, 211
Richmond, Va., 38
Rickenbacker, Eddie, 297, **297**
Ricketts, John Bill, 95, **95**
Rickey, Branch, 312
Rickover, Hyman, 319
Riedesel, Baroness Frederica von, 58, **58**
Riedesel, Friedrich von, 58
Riley, Bennett, 155
Ripken, Cal, 288
River transportation, 102, 107
  steamboats, 90, **90,** 134
Rivoli Theater, 268, **268**
Roads, highways, 90, 102, 105, 283, 321, **321**
Roanoke colony, 11, 19, **19**
Robinson, Frank, 225
Robinson, Jackie, 312, **312**
Robinson, Smokey, 327
Rock and roll music, 320, 335
Rockefeller, John D., 166, 216, 262
Rockets, 270
Rockne, Knute, 252, **252**
Rodgers, Calbraith, **243**
Rodney, Caesar, 62, **62,** 63
Roe, Ralph, 284
Roebling, John A., 222

Roebling, Washington, 222
Roebuck, Alvah, 236
Roe v. *Wade,* 335
Rogers, Will, 193, **193,** 238, **253,** 271, **271,** 287
Roland, Gilbert, 269
Rolfe, John, 20, 21, 38
Rome Olympics of 1960, 328, **328**
Roosevelt, Alice, 240
Roosevelt, Edith, 240
Roosevelt, Eleanor, 261, 276, 280, **280,** 287, 304
Roosevelt, Franklin Delano, 99, **190,** 248, 280, 301, 304, 366
  Great Depression and, 260-261, 277, 281
  inaugural address of, 362-363
  on television, 288, **288**
  World War II and, **185,** 265, 288, **289,** 292, **292, 293,** 303
Roosevelt, Theodore, 99, **145,** 218, **218,** 219, 226, 237, 238, 240, **240,** 241, 242, **243,** 246, **246,** 248, 251, **301,** 361-362, 366
Rosenthal, Joe, 304
Ross, Betsy, 57, **57**
Ross, Robert, 113
Rotch, Francis, 50
ROV's (remotely operated vehicles), 352
Rowlandson, Mary, **30**
Rubinstein, Helena, 300
Ruby, Jack, 334, **334**
Rudd, Caroline, 137, **137**
Rudolph, Wilma, 328, **328**
Running a Thousand Miles for Freedom (Craft and Craft), 153
Runyon, Damon, 211
Ruppert, Jacob, 263
Russell, Lillian, 166, 193
Russia, 18, 40, 67, 111
  Alaska and, 97, 197
  in World War I, 256, **256**
  See also Soviet Union.
Russian-American Company, 97, **97**
Russian Revolution (1917), 262
Ruth, George Herman (Babe), **141,** 263, **263**

S

Sabin, Alfred, 319
Sacagawea, 105
Sadat, Anwar, 352
St. Augustine colony, 10, 18, **18**
St. Lawrence Seaway, 325, **325**
Saint Louis, Mo., 31
"St. Louis Blues" (Handy), 248
St. Valentine's Day Massacre, 274, **274**
Salem, Peter, **56**
Salem witch trials (1692), 32, 33
Salinger, J. D., 317, **317**
Salk, Jonas, 319, **319**
Salter, Susanna (Dora), 227
Saltonstall, Dudley, 76
Samoset, 23
Sampson, Deborah, 59
Sand Creek Massacre (1864), 189, **189**

San Francisco earthquake and fire (1906), 207, 209, 245, **245**
San Jacinto, Battle of, 132, **132,** 136
San Juan Hill, Battle of, 237
Sankey, Ira, 212
Santa Anna, Antonio Lopez de, **132,** 136
Santa Barbara, Calif., oil spill (1969), 339, **339**
Santa Fe Trail, 117
Santana, Carlos, 340
Saratoga, Battle of, **53,** 67, 69, 72, 73, 75
Sargent, John G., 290
Sarnoff, David, 288, 289
Satellites, 324
Saturday Evening Post, **281**
Savannah, Ga., 36
Saxon, Eileen, 302
Saxony, 40
Scaffidi, Antonio, **230**
Scalawags, 200, **200**
Scalping, 27, **27**
Scarlet Letter, The (Hawthorne), 32
Scheuer, Sandra Lee, 341
Schneider, Ralph, 316
Schultz, "Dutch," 276
Schuyler, Philip, 72
Schwab, Charles W., 241
Schwellenbach, Lewis, 285
Science, 148-149
Scopes, John T., 258
Scott, Winfield, 189
Scottish-Americans, 12
Sea otters, 111
Sears, Richard, 236
Sears, Roebuck catalog, 236, **236**
Seattle Supersonics, 351
Secession, 126
Securities and Exchange Commission, 261
Sedgwick, Theodore, 162
Seeger, Pete, 332
Segregation, 219, 304, 334, 336
  in education, 320, **320**
  in sports, 312
  in transportation, 223, 235, 331
Self-help, 283
Selig, William, 247
Seminole Indians, 121, 124, 228
Seneca Falls, N.Y., conference (1848), 125, 152, 262
Seneca Indians, 166
Sennett, Mack, 247
Separatists, 11
Sequoia National Park, 118
Sequoyah, 118
Serbia, **256**
Serra, Junípero, 48, **48**
Seven Cities of Cíbola, 17, **17, 27**
Seven Days, Battle of, 168
Seventh Heaven, 274, **274**
Seven Years' War, 40. *See also* French and Indian War.
Sevier, John, 78, **78**
Seward, Frederick, 172
Seward, William, 172, **191,** 197, **197**
Sewing machines, 164, **164**
Shafter, William R., 237
Shah of Iran (Mohammed Reza Shah

Pahlavi), 347
Shakespeare, William, 190
Sharecropping, 170-171
Sharpe, George H., **180**
Shaw, Clay, 334
Shawnee Indians, 55, 69, 112
Shays, Daniel, 79, **79**
Shays's Rebellion, 79, **79**
Shelby, Joseph O., 193
Shelley, Mary, 108
Shepard, Alan B., Jr., 270, 331, **331**
Sheridan, Philip, 208
Sherman, Roger, **63**
Sherman, William Tecumseh, 169, 170, 184, 187, **187**
Shirer, William L., 285, **285**
Ships:
  in American Revolution: *Alliance,* 70; *Bonhomme Richard,* 70; *Dartmouth,* 50; *Eagle,* 64; *Gálveztown,* 74; *Jersey,* 77; *Liberty,* 64; *Pallas,* 70; *Serapis,* 70
  in Civil War: *Hartford,* 187; Harvey Birch, **182;** *Nashville,* **182;** *Tennessee,* 187
  in colonial era: *Desire,* 27; *Golden Hind,* 15; *Half Moon,* 21; *Mayflower,* 11, 23; *Niña,* 10, 14; *Pinta,* 10, 14; *San Pelayo,* 18; *San Salvador,* 18; *Santa María,* 10, 14
  in late eighteenth century: *Columbia,* 94; *Lady Washington,* 94
  in nineteenth century: *Intrepid,* **96;** *Chesapeake,* 106; *Lawrence,* 112; *Niagara,* 112; *Leopard,* 106; *Somers,* 147; *Tonquin,* 109
  in twentieth century: *Lusitania,* **257;** *Stockholm,* 322
Shivwit Indians, 203
Sholes, Christopher Latham, 198, **198**
Shopping malls, 322
Short, Luke, 220
Shriver, Sargent, 330
Siegel, Benjamin (Bugsy), 311, 316
"Significance of the Frontier in American History, The" (Turner), 231
Silent Spring (Carson), 333, **333**
Silver currency, 218, 235
Silver mining, 166
Sinclair, Upton, 246, **246**
Singer, Isaac, 164
Sioux Indians, 171, 208
Sitting Bull, Sioux chief, 139, 215
$64,000 Question, The, 326
Sketch Book, The (Irving), 108
Skyscrapers, 224, **225**
Slater, Samuel, 87
Slavery, 45, 90, 116, 127, 165
  debates on expansion of, 80, 91, 116, 127, 156, 163, 165
  See also Abolition movement.
Slaves, 95, 153
  in colonial era, 13, **27,** 48, 62
  revolts of, **27,** 119, 126
Slave trade, 127
  in colonial era, 27
Sloan, John, 251
Slocum, Joshua, 233, **233**

Sloughter, Henry, 32
Smallpox, 65, **65**
Smith, Al, 272
Smith, James, 113
Smith, Jedediah, 123, **123**
Smith, John, 11, 20, **21,** 22, **22**
Smith, W. Eugene, 282
Smithson, James, 148-149
Smithsonian Institution, 148-149, **149**
Socialism, 217
Socialist Party, 233
Social Security, 290
Society of Friends (Quakers), 11, 12, 24, 31
Sons of Liberty, 46
South, North vs., **86**
South Carolina, 62, **80,** 192, 371
  in Civil War, **177,** 187
South Carolina colony, 12, **27**
South Dakota, 371
South Korea, 306
South Vietnam, 308
Southdale Center, 322, **322**
Southern Christian Leadership Conference, 334
Southern Manifesto (1954), 320
South Pole, 275
Soviet Union, 258
  in Cold War, 306, 309, 310, **310,** 314, 315, 326, 327, 333
  space program of, 324
  in World War II, 288, **303,** 305
  See also Russia.
Spaatz, Carl (Tooey), 311
Space programs, 270, 324, 331, 339, 350
Spain, 40, 88, 95, 103, 106, 117, 119, 261
  in American Revolution, 74
  exploration and colonization by, 10, 11, 14, 16, 17, 18, 48
  missionaries from, 30
Spanish-American War, 219, **219,** 233, 237, 242-243
Spock, Benjamin, 310, **310**
Sporting News, 312
Sports. *See specific sports.*
Sports Illustrated, 266
Spray, 233, **233**
Sputnik, 324, **324**
Squanto, 23, **23**
Squaw Man, The, 287
Squibb, Edward R., 160
Stagg, J. M., 300
Stalin, Joseph, **303,** 314
Stamp Act (Great Britain; 1765), 42, **42,** 47, 64
Stamp Act Congress (1765), 42, 47
Standard Time Act (1918), 222
Stanford, Leland, 175
Stanky, Eddie, 312
Stanton, Edwin M., 184, 201
Stanton, Elizabeth Cady, 152, **152,** 262
Starr, Ringo, 335, **335**
"Star-Spangled Banner, The" (Key), 113, 373
State Department, U.S., 323
States' right, 126
Stathakis, George, **240**

Statue of Liberty, 226, **226, 227**
Steamboats, 90, **90,** 134
Steamboat Willie, 273, **273**
Steel industry, 216, 241
Steffens, Lincoln, 218
Steiff, Margaret, 241
Stein, Gertrude, 270
Steinbeck, John, 307
Stella Dallas, 287
Stempel, Herbert, 326
Stephens, Alexander, 170
Stephens, Annie, 194
Stephens, Charles, **240**
Stevens, Robert L., 174
Stevens, Thaddeus, 197, **197**
Stevenson, Adlai, 318
Stewart, James, 290, **290,** 298
Stilwell, Joseph (Vinegar Joe), 296, **296**
Stock market crash (1929), 204, 260, 275
Stock market crash (1987), 350
Stone, Harlan, **304**
Stone, Oliver, 334
Stone, William, 247
Stores, 215, 220
Story, Joseph, 92
Stowe, Harriet Beecher, 160
Stram, Hank, 338
Strategic Arms Limitation Treaty (SALT) (1972), 308, **310**
Strauss, Levi, 344
Stuart, Gilbert, 113, 115
Stuart, J.E.B., 180
Stuyvesant, Peter, 12, **24,** 28-29, **28**
Submarines, 64, 254, 294, **294**
Suburbs, 313, 322
Suckley, Margaret, 301
Sugar, 38
Sugar Act (Great Britain; 1764), 42, 46
Sullivan, Ed, 320, **320,** 335
Sullivan, John, 66
Summerhayes, John Wyer, 211
Summerhayes, Martha Dunham, 211
Sumner, Charles, 163, **163**
Super Bowl, 338, **338**
Supersonic airplanes, 314
Supreme Court, U.S., 89, 92, 100, **100,** 127, 165, 235, 261, 318, 320, 331, **335,** 345, 349, **349**
Supremes, 327, **327**
Sutter, John Augustus, 111, 151, 152
Suzuki, Kantaro, 305
Swanson, Gloria, 236
Sweden, 40
  immigrants from, 26
Swedenborg, Emanuel, 97
Swimming, 266
Szilard, L., 93, **289**

T

Taft, Robert, 315
Taft, William H., 99, **145,** 218, 366
Tamanend, Delaware chief, 98
Tamboro eruption (1815), 114
Tammany Hall, 98, 135
Taney, Roger, 165

Tarbell, Ida, 218
Tariff Act (1789), 88
Tariff of 1833, 134
Tariffs, 88, 91, 134, 218, 260
Tarleton, Banastre, 71
Tarzan, 266
Taussig, Helen, 302
Taverns, American Revolution and, 47
Taxes, 218
  in colonial era, 42-43, 46, 47
  income, 253, **253**
  rebellions against, 79, 88, 96
Taylor, Anna Edson, 240, **240**
Taylor, Zachary, 126, 189, **190,** 365
Tea Act (Great Britain; 1773), 43, 50
Teach, Edward (Blackbeard), 34-35, **34, 35**
Technology, 162, 164, 216
  agricultural, 90, 95, 125, 131, 137
Tecumseh, Shawnee chief, 112, 121
Telegraph, 144
Telephone, 212, 228
Television, 318, 326
  first news broadcast of, 288, **288**
Teller, Edward, 324
Temperance movement, 125, 156-157, 227
Temptations, 327
Tenements, 205
Tennessee, 78, **80,** 262, 371
  in Civil War, 168, 169, **177**
Tennessee Mountain Volunteers, 136
Ten Nights in a Barroom and What I Saw There (Arthur), 157, **157**
Tenskwatawa, 112
Tenure of Office Act (1867), 201
Terkel, Studs, **277**
Terrill, James, 176
Terrill, William Rufus, 176
Terry, Lucy, **27**
Terry, Peggy, **277**
Texas, 118, 126, 132, 136, 145, 146, 371
  in Civil War, **177**
Texas Rangers, 136, **136**
Textile industry, 87, **87, 89,** 90, 124
Thacher, James, **68**
Thailand, **305**
Thanksgiving, **22,** 23, **23,** 186, **186**
Thatcher, H. K., 195
Thayer, Ernest Lawrence, 228
Theater:
  musical, 196
  vaudeville, 193, **193**
Third parties, 135
Thomas, George H., 176
Thomas, Vivien, 302
Thompson, Benjamin, 56, **56**
Thompson, Franklin, 174
Thompson, Jimmy, 269
Thomson, Charles, 75, **75**
Thoreau, Henry David, 125, 145, 148, **148, 152**
Three Mile Island, 347, **347**
Thurmond, Strom, **247**
Tiffany, Louis Comfort, 140
Tilden, Samuel J., 213, **213**
Time, 282, 292, 301, 332
Time zones, 222, **222**
Tippecanoe, Battle of, 112